CULTURES of COPYRIGHT

COMMUNICATION LAW

Susan Drucker
General Editor

Vol. 4

The Communication Law series is part of the Peter Lang
Media and Communication list.
Every volume is peer reviewed and meets
the highest quality standards for content and production.

PETER LANG
New York • Bern • Frankfurt • Berlin
Brussels • Vienna • Oxford • Warsaw

CULTURES *of* COPYRIGHT

Dànielle Nicole DeVoss
Martine Courant Rife
editors

PETER LANG
New York • Bern • Frankfurt • Berlin
Brussels • Vienna • Oxford • Warsaw

Library of Congress Cataloging-in-Publication Data

Cultures of copyright / edited by Dànielle Nicole DeVoss, Martine Courant Rife.
pages cm. — (Communication law; vol. 4)
Includes bibliographical references and index.
1. Copyright—Social aspects—United States. 2. Culture and law—United States.
I. DeVoss, Dànielle Nicole, editor of compilation.
II. Rife, Martine Courant, editor of compilation.
KF2996.C85 346.7304'82—dc23 2014005850
ISBN 978-1-4331-2562-1 (hardcover)
ISBN 978-1-4331-2561-4 (paperback)
ISBN 978-1-4539-1347-5 (e-book)
ISSN 2153-1390

Bibliographic information published by **Die Deutsche Nationalbibliothek**.
Die Deutsche Nationalbibliothek lists this publication in the "Deutsche Nationalbibliografie"; detailed bibliographic data are available on the Internet at http://dnb.d-nb.de/.

The paper in this book meets the guidelines for permanence and durability of the Committee on Production Guidelines for Book Longevity of the Council of Library Resources.

29 Broadway, 18th floor, New York, NY 10006
www.peterlang.com

Printed in the United States of America

Contents

Part Two: Cultures of Production

Part Three: Cultures of Copyright

Part Four: Implications, Actions, and Pedagogical Work

• INTRODUCTION •

Cultures and/of/in Copyright

Dànielle Nicole DeVoss and Martine Courant Rife

All scholars have a role to play in analyzing, charting, and interrogating practices of intellectual property. We make knowledge, remediate information, remix theories, and produce a wide range of intellectual products. Issues orbiting around IP include appropriation, derivative work, invention practices, authority and authorship, trademarking, plagiarism, copyright, folklore and practices, storytelling, fair use, satire, parody, and more. All of the work we do, all of the work our students do, and all of the work at our institutions is, arguably, IP-implicated. Those of us who serve as faculty are, essentially, under work-for-hire contracts for our institutions. When creating texts, if we use the time and resources of our colleges and universities, these texts could possibly be considered the "property" of our institutions. Our ideas and our words go from our minds through our fingers on the keyboard, mesh with the computers' hard drives (university property) and become texts, texts that are then shared via email (often via institutional servers), and perhaps even printed on the departmental laser printer, using departmentally provided paper.

If we are research-active faculty, when we produce manuscripts and send them off, the outcome we hope for is a publication contract, which typically includes a copyright-release clause, where we acknowledge that we are assigning our rights to copy to the publisher and its representatives. We transfer these rights because, per the U.S. copyright revisions of 1976, the copyright to our work is born upon an original text's moment of creation and solidification as a "fixed" entity. That copyright, via the law, promises us control over subsequent iterations of the text, whether in the form of copies or reproductions, derivations, distributions, transfers of ownership, performances, public displays, and various sorts of licenses.

When we celebrate our publications by tweeting our good news, posting a status message on Facebook, or updating our LinkedIn profile, we're using proprietary systems that—due to the detailed terms-of-use statements we "consented" to when we created our accounts—could arguably own all of our posts, photos, and the other bits and bytes of our digital life as we live that life through those interfaces.

If we are teaching-oriented faculty, we may draw upon circulating cultural material to illuminate points we make in our lectures and discussions; we may engage students in composing work that requires that they draw upon these materials, mash them, and remix them. Students themselves typically hold the copyright to the work they produce in our classes, requiring us—if we are ethical and attentive scholars—to seek permission to share student work within and beyond our classrooms.

This is a long way of stating what isn't perhaps obvious to many of us, but what should be obvious to all of us, and a point Steve Westbrook (2006, 2009) has articulated quite well in his work: We are always already implicated in IP laws, guidelines, practices, and discussions. And in our classrooms, we are often implicating students in IP in the same way we ourselves are implicated. Often, however, the reach of IP on our lives is overlooked. Look around you, for example, for instances of the copyright symbol © or the registered trademark ® symbol. Sixty years ago in our society, these symbols were not often seen and only the most specialized of the specialized lawyers, specialized in copyright law. Now copyright law and all its related trajectories have become much more common knowledge. The copyright symbol © now shows up in the most unlikely places—in conference programs, in draft professional guidebooks, and in student texts. The symbols and signs of copyright law and related IP laws that we see on everyday texts have multiplied exponentially, especially over the last 15 years—in part due to the emergence of the web in the early 1990s and its explosion since then. Digital spaces have revolutionized access to content and also transformed the ways in which content is porous and malleable.

What "counts" as property must be understood as shifting terrain deeply influenced by historical, economic, cultural, religious, digital, etc. perspectives. In this collection, we focus specifically on copyright, and three arguments frame the chapters in this collection:

1. as the opening of this introduction evidences, we are always already implicated in intellectual property;
2. copyright cannot be truly engaged without situating it within its historical, technological, and cultural context; and
3. cultures make intellectual property, and intellectual property makes culture.

Below, we provide some further context for this collection, from three perspectives: a humanities vantage point, a digital vantage point, and a cultural vantage point. Although we present these as three perspectives, they are inseparably bound and connected, as the chapters in this collection reveal.

The Context: From Three Perspectives

Perspective 1: A Humanities Vantage Point

The two of us both teach writing courses, and both of us have witnessed an evolution in what "writing" means. We engage students in compositional acts that range from scripting podcasts to shooting digital video to creating web content, and more. Further, students produce in a context that has been labeled a "prosumer" space (Anderson, 2003) and a "remix culture" (Lessig, 2008). Historically, humanities pedagogy has asked that students deeply experience, analyze, and critique a range of media products. The connectivity of today's computers and digital spaces, however, requires that we also attend—equally, we would argue—to practices of creating, composing, and producing.

We work, today, in a context where a set of factors wrap together: Today's computers and robust networks allow composers access to a broad range of media, often unlocked from and unfettered by the technological constraints we faced years ago. Further, today's computers and robust networks allow composers to choreograph audio, video, still images, text, and more. Further still, composers may want to select among the circulating media to rethink it, revise it, mash it, or merely include it in a composition for particular rhetorical affect and effects. When these factors collide within a cultural, institutional, and economic context, we face issues of authorship, ownership, and property.

For humanists, attending to IP issues is a humanistic endeavor that connects directly with our history of both interrogating and protecting authorship, and with our history of developing, constructing, and delivering information—in print and digitally, including graphic and other visual arts, and via manuscripts, essays, plays, and much, much more (DeVoss & Porter, 2006; DeVoss & Webb, 2008a, 2008b; Heins & Beckles, 2005; Herrington, 2001, 2003, 2010; Lessig, 2004, 2008; Logie, 2006; Ray & Graeff, 2008; Reyman, 2010; Westbrook, 2006, 2009).

To deeply understand the dynamics of intellectual property, we—and our departure point, as both of us represent humanities-based disciplines is thus a humanistic one—require attention to legal issues and cases; to statutes, codes, and exemptions; and to official policies and governmental regulations. We also require deep attention to the cultural considerations surrounding the rhetorics of intellectual property. Cultural considerations, as we frame them for this collection, include (but are not limited to) global and international issues related to intellectual property, feminist research in intellectual property, issues of cultural cannibalism, and considerations of intellectual commons that span—and disrupt—time and/or cultures.

Perspective 2: A Digital Vantage Point

This may seem a trivial contextual anchor, but it is one that is emblematic of the ongoing culture wars regarding IP in digital spaces. In April 2013, the author–creators of two infamous Internet cat videos joined forces to protect their intellectual property. They filed suit with the U.S. District Court in California against Warner Bros. and 5th Cell. 5th Cell, the developers and maker of the Scribblenauts games, used images of both Keyboard Cat and Nyan Cat without authorization or any compensation to the original creators. The animated reproductions of the cats appear as "Easter eggs" (or hidden content, in this case requiring users to type out "nyan cat" or "keyboard cat," at least in the most recent version of the game) in the 2009 Scribblenauts game, and also in its 2010 sequel, the iOS "remix" version of the game, and the most recent production, 2011's Scribblenauts Unlimited.

Keyboard Cat was born when Charles Schmidt shot the original video in 1984, and digitized and uploaded it online in 2009. The video features a hefty orange tabby in a blue t-shirt plunking on a keyboard to an infectious beat. Nyan Cat was originally an animated GIF of Christopher Torres' cat Marty, uploaded to YouTube in 2011. Interestingly, Nyan Cat was a crowd-sourced production: According to its Wikipedia page, other users created and then added to the video. Schmidt also previously sued the online t-shirt company Threadless for an unauthorized use of Keyboard Cat in a "three Keyboard Cat moon" shirt (a play on the now-Internet-infamous three wolf mountain moon shirt). In that case, Schmidt was accompanied by Ben Lashes, an agent who secures and protects licensing deals primarily for Internet content. In an interview with *Upstart Business Journal*, Lash defended his clients by invoking one of the most notoriously fierce copyright protectionists, Disney; Lash said: "If it's not something you can do to Mickey Mouse then it's not something you can do to Keyboard Playing Cat, or Nyan, or anybody that I represent." In September 2013, the parties settled their dispute, with a resolution allowing Warner Bros. to continue to use the cats, and the creators receiving some compensation for that use.

We linger here on this case because it reflects the current context of content creation, copyright, and digital spaces. With a massive number of individuals creating and uploading content, the vast majority of circulating entertainment and information content is *not* produced by major media companies, as has been the case in the past. And, most interestingly perhaps, the ways in which individuals engage and use circulating content has altered the IP playing field. In the past, major media companies have fought to protect their IP through digital rights management, cease and desist orders, and through other actions. Currently, however, for a range of economic, cultural, and technical issues beyond the scope of this chapter, our traditional content producers are, to some extent and certainly where Keyboard Cat and Nyan Cat are concerned, trolling the Internet for created content to poach.

Perspective 3: A Cultural Vantage Point

Today's digital context brings content together in ways previous unimagined. The copyright troubles of the primarily analog 1980s are magnified in today's networked context. Although digital spaces provide us much more access to cultural objects, artifacts, and productions, digital spaces also provide us access to take, claim, remake, and appropriate these objects. Homi Bhabha (2004), a postcolonial/cultural studies theorist; Karen Fiss (2006), an arts studies researcher whose focus is globalization, postcolonialism, and design; and Guillermo Gómez-Peña, a performance artist and an interrogator of cultural hybridity each provide evidence and critiques of the complex hybridity that can emerge as cultures rub together in a globalized world. Too often, this cultural convergence results in one culture cannibalizing another—that is, one culture dominating and devouring aspects of the other culture. Intellectual property treaties and agreements can, in some instances, help protect against this sort of cannibalizing, but IP can also contribute to this practice.

Balancing the underprotection and overprotection of IP in contemporary digital spaces is critical; navigating public domain dynamics is essential. These considerations become all the more complex and compelling when addressing the intellectual property of cultures, communities, and collectives that have historically navigated outside of western hegemonic legal constructions. This collection contributes to ongoing discussions of intellectual property issues, with a particular focus on cultural considerations and consequences.

Our cultural context encompasses the disciplinary, scholarly, and digital dimensions discussed above, and this context is also anchored by attention to hybrid and global dynamics of information circulation, consumption, and production in the world today. By invoking the term *culture*, we are also explicitly, directly calling to and situating our work within a perspective that requires that we attend to the thick and layered complexities of the ways in which meaning is made in the world in different ways, in different spaces, and by different peoples.

Collection Overview

This collection is presented in four parts: an initial situating section, a section on cultures of production, a section on cultures of copyright, and a final section on implications and action.

Part One: Cultural Backdrops

In the opening chapter of this collection, Aaron Barlow explores questions related to the cultural limits of ownership in contemporary U.S. culture. To do so, Barlow provides some historical tracing that situates our current shifting context. Angela Daly and Ben Farrand, in the second chapter, provide an analysis of the *Scarlet v. SABAM* case and how it reveals aspects of the actions of—and against—current corporate copyright lobbies in Europe. Michelle Sidler and Chad Wickman discuss the dynamics of open-access practices, focusing on digital technologies to achieve large-scale, large-publication possibilities, along with the IP implications of sharing across digital spaces. The Obama "Hope" image is perhaps the most-iconic artifact of presidential elections past; in "Hindered Hope," Ben McCorkle provides the legal back-story of Shepard Fairey's digital–visual creation.

Next, Joan Francesc Fondevila Gascón and Raúl López García-Navas address the need for new production models appropriate for and adapted to digital cultures of production. The authors explore a range of IP possibilities and challenges related to doing so, and argue that copyright must make way for copyleft's philosophies. In the closing chapter of this section, Traci Zimmerman provides an analysis of *Golan v. Holder*, a U.S. Supreme Court case focused on whether the U.S. Congress may retroactively restore copyright to foreign works in the U.S. public domain. Zimmerman focuses on how public domain is defined and defended within the scope of this particular case.

Part Two: Cultures of Production

Steve Westbrook and James Ryan open the second section, focused on cultures of production, by providing a close look at the current culture of art publishing. They draw upon existing law to argue that some museums and galleries overprotect copyright and overassert their IP rights over work that, arguably, has entered the public domain. Next, Tim Amidon and Jessica Reyman discuss the implications of data-mining on authorship and ownership. They argue that new digital contexts create new dynamics for content creation, and that scholars and users need to be more aware of their IP within the terms-of-use of online spaces.

Nicole Nguyen addresses a YouTube practice of noting "No Copyright Intended"—text often employed by those engaging in remix practices and hoping to announce to viewers that their infringement is benign. Nguyen introduces *Cariou v. Prince* to discuss appropriation art and then turns her attention to the YouTube version of *Pulp Fiction*, which presents a revision to the original film, with its sequence in chronological order. In the next chapter, Liza Potts, Dean Holden, and Katie Dobruse interrogate rivalrous information and entertainment economies—both those that emerge and those that are manufactured to invent a seeming lack of resources, and thus, as they argue, digital platform loyalty.

In his second chapter—and the chapter that closes this section—in the collection, Aaron Barlow shares a personal tale related to finding his dissertation published online, in another country and in another language, as a book.

Part Three: Cultures of Copyright

Dave Jones explores the ways in which prosumers find, share, and generate new knowledge within specific participatory digital ecosystems. Collaborative knowledge work that rubs up against IP issues is the focus of his chapter.

In the chapter that follows, Gabriel Michael argues that although intellectual property as a social, political, and economic institution has received increasing attention from the social sciences and growing attention from the humanities, there is a dearth of scholarly religious and theological writing on the subject. To address this lack, Michael explores six ethical principles drawn from Jewish scripture and applies them to contemporary copyright law.

André Sirois moves the collection toward issues of authorship within DJ culture, arguing that DJ culture is an "open-source culture" within which certain DJs themselves have become, essentially, intellectual property. Sirois discusses the innovation that fuels DJ practices, and the implications of that innovation within and beyond DJ culture.

In another chapter that draws upon ecosystems and ecological constructs, Gabriela Ríos and Donnie Johnson Sackey consider the ways in which U.S. IP law fails to protect Indigenous artists and makers. They move quickly, however, to a focus on an additional concern: That the current IP system does not recognize relationships between land, knowledge, and ownership.

Jennifer Sano-Franchini, Robyn Tasaka, and Lehua Ledbetter extend and migrate the emphasis on land, identify, and IP in "Toward a Reflexive Approach to Remix—or—What Hawai'i Creole English and Corporate Tourism Can Teach Us about Copyright." Here, the authors turn our attention away from fixed artifacts and toward the shifting landscape of cultural processes and languages, which they argue are implicated in and by, yet not often enough considered within the scope of IP.

Angela Shetler considers authorship across continents, describing perspectives on copyright from a U.S. vantage point, Japanese views, and Australian law. Having lived and worked in each country, Shetler provides a wide-ranging discussion that explores cultural perspectives of authorship and copyright.

Jill Parrott considers "The Mutual Interests of Multicultural Studies and Some Rights Reserved Copyright," arguing that humanities scholars who focus their intellectual work on multicultural studies must more responsibly and deeply interrogate the relationships between multiculturalism and IP. Specifically, Parrott explores the ways in which multicultural authors have harnessed some-rights-reserved approaches to copyright.

Part Four: Implications, Actions, and Pedagogical Work

The collection's closing section, focused on implications, actions, and pedagogical work, begins with a chapter by Guiseppe Getto and Jessica Getto Rivait where the authors describe their experiences within a more sharing-oriented culture—nonprofits—and how these organizations approach and manage IP. Even in the face of accelerating copyright control, Getto and Getto Rivait find that small, community-anchored organizations often rely on an economy of sharing.

Clancy Ratliff moves the collection from the community to the classroom, focusing on K–12 curricula produced and distributed by two polarized IP groups: The Recording Industry Association of American (RIAA) and the Electronic Frontier Foundation (EFF). Both groups have addressed state and national technology standards that require students to engage in appropriate and ethical use of information technologies by producing lesson plans. Ratliff situates and analyzes the two curricula in a broader cultural context.

In the third chapter drawing upon an ecological model, Laural Lea Adams discusses the move toward open educational resources (OER) and copyright implications. She offers an ecofeminist approach for navigating the increasingly corporatized academic cultures in which OERs continue to grow.

Lisa Evans, a high school studio arts teacher, addresses the tangled issues that visual arts educators—across contexts from grade school to higher education—regularly traverse. Evans poses some complicated cases and discusses classroom (and beyond) implications. Ashley Hall, Jen Ware, and Sydney Stegall situate their chapter in the college classroom and address "Cultural Critique, First-year Composition, and Copyright." The authors specifically argue that practices of digital–visual parody are an important and protected facet of engaging students in cultural critique.

Cultures of Copyright concludes with a chapter by Nancy Schrock, who led a group that managed IP developments for a major chemical company in the U.S. Schrock connects a range of dots identified across the chapters, and across IP-implicated contexts. Specifically, she offers a set of practices that humanities scholars and higher education professionals can borrow from corporate practice to better protect and showcase our IP.

***

What we don't address in this collection is a comparative international approach. Given the scope of this text, our editorial vantage point, and the expertise of our authors, we focus here on the topics constellated above. Certainly, our authors represent a range of perspectives and internationally diverse institutions. However, we don't directly address, in a chapter-length manner, an international comparative approach (we refer readers to, e.g., Bently, Davis, & Ginsburg, 2010; Drucker & Gumpert, 2010; Goldstein & Hugenholtz, 2012; Hilty & Nérisson, 2012; Kono, 2012; Lucchi, 2006). That said, what we do offer here, across the chapters, are questions, concerns, and issues that must be addressed in future research and scholarship to address the ways in which copyright transcends specific geo-national space. There are a range of research directions we hope this collection will help to fuel—one of these would be the tracing of a work that falls under copyright protection in a particular country and culture and following that piece of work across national, global, and digital landscapes. Future research might trace cultural products closely in the global media environment as those products span and exceed geo-national, political, and legal boundaries; this is but one conversation and thread of future work we hope this collection inspires.

As editors, we have been privileged to work with this group of authors and believe that these chapters and this collection in its entirety will offer readers—scholars, researchers, practitioners, theorists, and others—key considerations to contemplate in terms of how we understand intellectual property's past and how we chart its futures.

• PART ONE •

Cultural Backdrops

• CHAPTER ONE •

The Limits of Ownership in the United States

Aaron Barlow

What are the cultural limits of intellectual property in the United States today? What are the cultural prerogatives of authorship? The former have expanded, while the latter, paradoxically, have shrunk. Thanks to digital technologies that may be changing, but the powers behind expanded IP ownership may prove stronger than digital possibilities for circumventing them. Authorship has been subsumed by ownership, and ownership is being subverted (for now) by the ease of digital copying and alteration—and audiences are now inclined to see themselves as owners, too. In this chapter, I trace the backgrounds to the questions above. Admittedly, changes in technologies of copying and in cultural attitudes toward created works are forcing North Americans to re-evaluate their assumptions about creators and their works, making complete answers, for now, impossible.

The Author as Troubled Owner

Authors have always been protective of their work. Chaucer, complaining to his scrivener, berated him for "to wryten newe" rather than to "wryte more trewe" (p. 650). By the time of Melville, the scrivener's profession was on the way to becoming antique. After all, "Bartleby, the Scrivener" was published in 1853; the direct ancestor of the twentieth-century typewriter, which put the nail in the profession's coffin, was introduced in 1868, just 15 years later. In many ways, part of the scrivener's function had already disappeared, superseded by moveable type in the fifteenth century—not so long after the time of Chaucer.

By the middle of the sixteenth century in England, the solitary task of individual copying had become an industry of mass production—an industry that actually threatened to steal prominence, prerogative, and profit from the author. Chaucer railed against his scrivener for errors in copying Boethius or Boccaccio, even having to "rubbe and scrape" to make corrections himself. Soon, such power over copying would be severely diminished as the new professions of printer and publisher and bookseller grew, taking a great deal of power away from authors by separating them further from the results of their work.

Eventually, authors would be moved an even greater distance away by the copyright laws initially enacted, supposedly, to protect them and fix their relationships to their work. By the twentieth century, authors would sometimes even be seen as nuisances by those in the industries of production, promotion, and distribution of art—industries once meant to further the reach of those very "nuisances."

Commerce in Words

At the same time that printing was allowing new and cheap distribution of the written word, other new ways of profiting from one's pen grew. There was Shakespeare, for example, who didn't need to publish to make money. In the words of Ben Jonson, "in his writing (whatsoever he penned) he never blotted out line" (Jonson & Gifford, 1879, p. 871). Although Jonson does famously complain, "would he had blotted a thousand," to Shakespeare, all was usable. He had to worry about actors, not scriveners and the value of his words was in performance, not in print. Only for future generations would scripts become sources of income.

Once they were published, plays would also fall under evolving concepts and laws of copyright and IP ownership. As technologies changed over even later centuries, sheet music, artwork, photography, and non-print products began to be added to copyright coverage. Things that no one, once, thought it was possible to monetize were now proving more and more valuable—their "ownership" now worth protecting.

Just as they have always been protective of their work, authors have also always worked for money. Chaucer grumbled to Henry IV of his light purse, which must "beth hevy ageyn, or ells moot I dye" (p. 656); Chaucer needed patronage to survive. For Shakespeare, his income was from paying attendance at his plays. Both Chaucer and Shakespeare were directly involved with the business aspect of their art. They had to be: No one mediated between them and their audiences, although that was beginning to change for the *written* word by the time of Shakespeare.

Given the realities of the sixteenth century, Shakespeare could have expected little money from any printed versions of his work. It's not likely, then, that he would have ever considered publication an important part of his business. At the time, after all, the English Company of Stationers had primary rights over printed material, rights that had grown through a century of printing before they were formalized by Royal Charter in 1557. The business went like this:

> There were scribes and scriveners who wrote them, limners and illuminators who illustrated and rubricated them, binders who bound them and retailers who sold them. There were also merchants who supplied the raw materials: paper and parchment for writing on, ink and pens for writing with, and skins for bindings. Since the early fifteenth century, the majority of those engaged in these trades in London had belonged to a trade guild which came to be called the Company of Stationers. (Fellowes, p. 23)

It was not the authors (who still relied on patronage or performance for their income) who were given responsibility for, or real profit from, works in print. This caused tension, especially as print sales continued becoming a dominant source of income. Although copyright laws and growing adulation of creative artists would seem to give artists the upper hand, by the twentieth century they would be eclipsed once more by the descendants of the Company of Stationers.

Even in Shakespeare's time, the relatively new possibility of cheap reproduction was beginning to create real wealth for printers, publishers and booksellers. For authors, who benefited as well, the mechanical process of print also served to divorce them from their products even though their names were often kept in close association with the printed page, making them as anxious about the state of the products as Chaucer had been before Gutenberg.

PUBLIC AUTHORITY AND CREATION

Nearly three centuries after Chaucer, colonial American author Anne Bradstreet (Bradstreet & Ellis, 1867), echoed Chaucer's frustration over errors in the copying or, now, in the printing of work. In "The Author To Her Book," she used a newer metaphor for the relationship between the author and the work, one that would become so prevalent that it came to be an important part of the contemporary American idea of "the author." Her book, she said, was an "ill-form'd offspring" (p. 389) due to typographical errors beyond her control. The sense of ownership inherent in this conceit would be picked up by Daniel Defoe almost half a century later in his 1704 *Essay on the Regulation of the Press*, where he argued that the connection between author and work needs to be forcefully protected:

> no Man has a Right to make any Abridgment of a Book, but the Proprietor of the Book; and I am sure no Man can be so well qualified for the doing it, as the Author, if alive, because no Man can be capable of knowing the true Sense of the Design, or of giving it a due Turn like him that compos'd it. (pp. 26–27)

In an era of publisher control, Defoe was trying to re-establish the primacy of the author in relation to the work. He was also reacting to what Adrian Johns

(2010), in *Piracy: The Intellectual Property Wars from Gutenberg to Gates*, called "the invention of piracy"' in the seventeenth century:

> A public sphere was coming into existence, based in the proliferation of print. Experimental philosophy was inaugurating what would become modern science, and a mercantile expansion was under way that would trigger the emergence of capitalist economies and commercial empires. (p. 18)

Johns continued: "when authorship took on a mantle of public authority, through the crafts of the printed book, its violation came to be seen as a paramount transgression—as an offense against the common good akin to the crime of the brigand, bandit, or pirate" (p. 19). The transgression was against the author and against the Company of Stationers both; a protective registry of books provided proof of ownership should the transgressor be brought before the law. Even so, authors, publishers, and booksellers were wary of each other—all three protective of their rights and none of them believing in the good faith of the others.

Walter Ong (1982) argued that "writing establishes what has been called 'context-free' language or 'autonomous' discourse which cannot be directly questioned or contested as oral speech can be because written discourse has been detached from its author" (p. 77). This is part of what led to Chaucer's concern about his scrivener and to the development of attitudes such as Defoe's, with his passionate defense of a connection between author and text that, outside of law and custom, no longer existed. After Gutenberg, the wedge that the physical act of writing (as opposed to composing) and, by extension printing, had inserted between the author and his or her work was providing an easy opening for that new constituency of printers and publishers and booksellers to step into.

Creating Authorial Rights and the Commons

Codified in the Statute of Anne of 1710, the rights of the author were seen as being as important in law as those of the printer, publisher, or bookseller. In fact, *two* new constituencies were now given rights: the author and (tacitly) the consumer through a new commons of uncopyrighted works. The Statute "was produced partly because of publishers' fights with booksellers; the authorial right grew as an afterthought" (Boyle, 2008, p. 8) and the commons by default. Rights over a work now reverted to the author after a period of 14 years, renewable once during the author's lifetime. These were not permanent property rights, but temporary grants. That copyright was a choice created the third constituency regarding the printed work: the commons.

Among the intents of the Statute of Anne, like those of the United States Constitution nearly a century later, were both protection of the author and publisher of works once they were in print and encouragement for those imagining profits from future enterprises (Gillespie, 2007). The same was true in Great Britain. To gain copyright protection under the Statute of Anne, an author or his or her agents had to comply with certain procedures, including registration and presentation of the work in question to specified libraries, and the rights were for a limited period of time. So there is, in the Statute, an implicit recognition of the existence and value of an unregulated commons in creative endeavors, one arising through the limitation of copyright prerogatives and the necessity of explicitly establishing them in each individual case. The concept was carried from there to America and into the Constitution. The result, intentional or not, was codification of the intellectual commons, a universe of "unowned" human creations available to all, but that has been eroding, along with the rights of the author, ever since.

At the time of the writing of the Constitution, the limitations on ownership of what we now call IP were still real and, obviously, considered necessary. Strangely, though:

> When delegates to the Constitutional Convention debated copyright and patent, [Benjamin] Franklin—the delegate most famous for his inventions—apparently remained silent... Nonetheless, his actions and his positions elsewhere make it clear that he would have understood the Constitutional language... as a balance between a short-term monopoly and a long-term grant to the public. That the clause might become ground for creating a perpetual property right for individuals and private corporations would have astounded him. (Hyde, 2010, p. 133)

Yet such changes had already begun by the time of the Constitutional Convention and can even be traced back at least to Defoe and his view of the bond between an author and his or her work, a vision not completely shared by either the Statute of Anne or the U.S. Constitution, but one that would later be used to change copyright laws both in the United States and in Great Britain.

Ownership of Words

Even though the phrase "intellectual property" was not yet in use, the conflicts concerning IP behind these laws was very much a part of Enlightenment thinking, stemming from recognition of conflicting rights and needs in terms of constituencies and of ideas and their expression. In a letter to Isaac McPherson in 1813, Thomas Jefferson put forth the real reason for establishing an intellectual commons while also protecting intellectual property:

> If nature has made any one thing less susceptible than all others of exclusive property, it is the action of the thinking power called an idea, which an individual may exclusively

> possess as long as he keeps it to himself; but the moment it is divulged, it forces itself into the possession of every one, and the receiver cannot dispossess himself of it. Its peculiar character, too, is that no one possesses the less, because every other possesses the whole of it... That ideas should freely spread from one to another over the globe... seems to have been peculiarly and benevolently designed by nature... Inventions then cannot, in nature, be a subject of property. Society may give an exclusive right to the profits arising from them... but this may or may not be done, according to the will and convenience of the society, without claim or complaint from anybody.

In both the Statute of Anne and the Constitution, the question of ownership became one of possession over a sequence of words for a period of time and not so much over the ideas contained. Both legal dictates were meant to limit competing needs for the ultimate good of all. That concept is disappearing today as patent and copyright laws expand to cover almost everything, using the concept of "originality" as developed in the eighteenth century as a justification for ownership of marketable property.

Reaction against limitations of ownership began early on, even by the 1740s, long before the Constitution or Jefferson's letter. The cleric and writer William Warburton (1811), in "A Letter from an Author, to a Member of Parliament; Concerning Literary Property," wrote "surely if there be *degrees of right*, that of *Authors* seemeth to have the advantage over most others; their property being, in the truest sense, their *own*, as acquired by a long and painful exercise of that very faculty which denominateth us MEN" (p. 405). This brooked no limitation and represented an imagined triumph over the publishers but, over the centuries, its ascendance would prove to be a pyrrhic victory, one leaving the writer, the commons, and even the bookseller disadvantaged in relation to the publisher and its corporate descendants.

In America, things were to change a little more slowly than in England, for America was, until after the Civil War, a net IP importer, making it loathe to close the door to easy copying of works from abroad. If China is seen as today's great pirate of IP, in the nineteenth it was the United States. Today, as then, "one nation's access to knowledge may be another's trade piracy" (Hyde, 2010, p. 123).

The Myth of the Author

The vision of the author as "original" continued to emerge, as Roland Barthes (1977) wrote, "from the Middle Ages with English empiricism, French rationalism and the personal faith of the reformation... [discovering] the prestige of the individual" (pp. 142–143). The modern image of the author arose also from political and economic motivations, from the attempt to wrest dominance over publications from printers and publishers and booksellers. The power of these industries grew not only from technologies of reproduction but from the mercantilism of the age. During the seventeenth century, according to Jürgen Habermas (1989):

> the press… developed a unique explosive power… It is questionable whether the interests of those who made a living by writing news pamphlets would have provided sufficiently strong impetus; still they *did* have an interest in publication… For the traffic in news developed not only in connection with the needs of commerce; the news itself became a commodity. (pp. 20–21)

The same was true of all printed work, which is why, of course, that authors, who are rarely good at commerce, often found themselves shunted aside when it came to real profits.

It is only in recent centuries that the primacy of the author was established. As Martha Woodmansee and Peter Jaszi (1994) wrote, "the modern regime of authorship, far from being timeless and universal, is a relatively recent formation—the result of a quite radical reconceptualization of the creative process that culminated less than 200 years ago in the heroic self-presentation of Romantic poets" (pp. 2–3). Perhaps the most impassioned defense of this new vision is that of William Wordsworth (Grosart, 2012) in his Preface to *Lyrical Ballads*. It's the best early explanation of why the artist is "better" than others, a view not universal even today, but one with great cultural impact. To Wordsworth, the poet is exactly this: "a man who, being possessed of more than usual organic sensibility, had also thought long and deeply" (p. 193). So much so "that the understanding of the Reader must necessarily be in some degree enlightened, and his affections strengthened and purified." He claimed the poet is:

> the rock of defence for human nature; an upholder and preserver, carrying everywhere with him relationship and love. In spite of difference of soil and climate, of language and manners, of laws and customs: in spite of things silently gone out of mind, and things violently destroyed; the Poet binds together by passion and knowledge the vast empire of human society. (pp. 197–198).

This may have appealed to authors and maybe even the public, but it also would be something the publishing business would turn to its own advantage, first through pirated editions of celebrity works and, later, by taking control of the machinery of celebrity, including control of copyright.

With the increasing public popularity of the author, and not simply of the author's texts, a popularity that peaked with the adulation of Byron and then Dickens and a host of others through Wilde and into the electronic age, the connection between artist and work took on new meaning. It found new room for profit and power vis-à-vis publisher and bookseller. As marketable personalities themselves, authors found themselves in a strong position—and wanted to protect that. This dovetailed quite well with the interests of their publishers—who knew that their own business acumen would outdo that of their authors.

The Growth of Ownership

In 1826 Noah Webster wrote to his cousin, the politician Daniel Webster, on the issue of copyright, putting forth a claim that both Defoe and Wordsworth would have probably found fair: "Among all the modes of acquiring property, or exclusive ownership, the act or operation of *creating* or *making* seems to have the first claim. If anything can justly give a man an exclusive right to the occupancy & enjoyment of a thing, it must be the fact that he has *made* it." This is an interesting argument for the lexicographer to have put forth. After all, his stock-in-trade was presentation of the creations of others. But Webster was writing in a milieu influenced by both Wordsworth and the economic and cultural realities of the Industrial Revolution.

Evidently, Webster assumed words to be part of the commons; it was their combined structure that signaled creativity. Words were not created but used *in creation*, the ontology of authorship stopping at the level of the sentence and the locus of creativity found in their compiler, in the author. Webster's real concern was with the business of authorship—he wanted more money for himself and for his family.

Webster was instrumental in sparking a process of change in American copyright law, one that continues today, moving IP ownership from the limited right granted in the Constitution "to promote the Progress of Science and useful Arts" (Article 1, Section 8) to nearly absolute and perpetual ownership for authors and their estates that also has been expanded to include corporate ownership of copyright, an ownership now much more powerful than that of the individual.

By the time of Emerson's "Self Reliance" in 1841, the idea of original genius had taken hold. Emerson listed a number of creative minds, asking "where is the master who could have instructed Franklin?" (p. 19). To Franklin, however, had he lived so long, the "master" would be the books he had read, the people he had talked to, and the work he had observed. The very question shows the cultural shifts from Franklin's time to Emerson's. As Lewis Hyde (2010) told it, Emerson's question would have been no less "bizarre" to Franklin than it is to Hyde himself:

> What Franklin's ranging intelligence contained, first and foremost, was a great store of other people's work. The Philadelphia electrical theory was additive, transformative, associative, cumulative... It built on what came before. Franklin saw further, true, but he did so by standing on the shoulders of those who came before. His is not the genius of the untutored "unique" but of the commoner who seeks and absorbs the wisdom of many masters. (p. 119)

Hyde's point is that we've taken ideas of genius and IP too far. What was once a rational compromise between needs of creators and commons had, by Emerson's time, been subverted—and would soon be perverted by corporate search for profit.

If "creativity," by 1800, had taken on new meanings anchored within the artist, it was over the next century that today's assumptions about IP ownership grew. The strange thing is that, while "creativity," in this view, is completely tied to the individual, the new vision of "ownership" is not: It centers on a commodity that can be traded. This may seem an odd development, but the nineteenth century represented a triumph of capitalism with its almost universal commodification. The genius was now seen as marketable, the genius's product no different from any other.

Copyright Constriction

The commodification of creativity, which actually began long before the nineteenth century (the English Statute of Monopolies established patents in 1624), had become, by the late twentieth century, a force, paradoxically, constricting creativity and scholarship. Creators now constantly look over their shoulders, wondering if what they are doing will fall afoul of patent or copyright laws. George Harrison's "My Sweet Lord" turned out to have an almost identical musical base as Ronnie Mack's song for The Chiffons, "He's So Fine." Likely, Harrison's was not conscious plagiarism, but it took years for the cases to be settled. Today, there are even "copyright trolls" looking for even unconscious infringement as a means of creating income.

Though copyright law saw constant extension through the nineteenth and much of the twentieth centuries, at first the growth was in size and not kind. Terms were extended, but the original intents and even renewal remained important. However, that has changed:

> The United States abandoned this sensible system in 1976. For all works created after 1978, there was only one copyright term—the maximum term.... Then, in 1992, Congress abandoned the renewal requirement for all works created before 1978. All works still under copyright would be accorded the maximum term then available. After the Sonny Bono Act [the Digital Millennium Copyright Act or DMCA], the term was ninety-five years. (Lessig, 2002a, p. 135)

The DMCA of 1998 is the most aggressive of the major encroachments on the intellectual commons in American law. Kembrew McLeod (2007) explained why:

> In the old days, for instance, we could purchase a book and take it home, read it, mark it up, store it for years on our bookshelves, photocopy a chapter, loan it to a friend, or

> whatever. Such uses are protected by what lawyers call the "first sale doctrine"... Unfortunately, this doctrine is quickly evaporating in the digital world. Under the DMCA, content providers can now regulate who can see its product, how long it can be viewed, whether or not it can be copied, and what can be done with it. This significantly rewrites rules that had been in place for years and struck a balance between copyright holders and the public. (pp. 271–272)

Over the last century, corporations have assumed the rights of the author and they fight to have those rights expanded at every possible opportunity. Digital possibilities have led to new ways for circumventing copyright, but they have also presented new means for control. This is generally corporate control; rarely have the artists benefitted. The publishers, controlling distribution, have assumed the profits and have pushed aside the authors. Musician Richard Berry sold the rights to "Louie, Louie" for less than a thousand dollars. The song made millions, but Berry saw nothing more. The long-gone authorial right of renewal would once have helped him. No more.

Derivative Ownership

Like any work of art, Berry's was itself derivative. This is the lie of the Romantic vision of the artist: "original genius" has never existed. Barthes (1977), in "The Death of the Author," asserted that "a text is made of multiple writings, drawn from many cultures and entering into mutual relations of dialogue, parody, contestation, but there is one place where this multiplicity is focused and that place is the reader, not, as was hitherto said, the author" (p. 148). That is, that the real home of creativity is found within the reader, not the author—the antithesis of the Romantic belief.

The expanding rights of author have been taken over, in large part, by publishers—now, generally vast corporations with a great deal of clout when it comes to the creation of laws. Because "ownership" has replaced "authorship" in the legislative conception of copyright—perhaps because of the introduction of phrases such as "Intellectual Property"—the place of the author has been diminished in terms of power over the work. Though the Romantic vision might once have seemed a way to provide a firmer connection between creator and creation, it ultimately served to move IP into the arena of everyday commerce and away from its special status under the Statute of Anne and its descendants and the U.S. Constitution and subsequent American laws.

Were Andy Warhol to exhibit his "32 Campbell's Soup Cans" for the first time today, he probably would hear from Campbell's, ordering him to remove them or face litigation. Instead of a generally cordial relationship that ended up benefitting both parties, the works of art would be suppressed—unless Warhol could pay Campbell's for rights.

Fighting for Control

Artists are learning how to fight back. For a long time the fame and glory they gathered from their work was incentive enough for them to cede control to those who said they could provide these, and other rewards. After all, one did not become a bestselling author or a successful actor or musician without media support. Corporations were often able to take advantage of naïve considerations of fame by artists whose work they distributed through electronic media.

Until the Digital Age, corporate control of production, promotion, and distribution created a bottleneck few artists could get around. Some successful musicians found that they could make more money through concerts than through royalties, but actors and authors have had few similar recourses. Musicians and authors, in particular, but even most actors lived on the success of their last projects and negotiated with knowledge of the uncertainty of the next. They were always dependent on a publishing and publicity machine that maintained a façade of skepticism towards them: there were always other artists waiting in the wings to take their places.

Few creative artists have ever really believed in themselves as creative geniuses in the Romantic mold. They know just how much luck has played in their successes and understand that others just as talented languish without industry outlets. In addition:

> Far from encouraging innovations that create... demand, the copyright industries... claim that the innovator's success is caused solely by the value provided by the copyright industries. The innovator is described metaphorically as a parasite, fattening itself off of copyright owners. Working themselves up into righteous indignation, copyright owners then insist that the innovator must disgorge a healthy share of its profits to them, even though if the copyright industries were left to their own devices, they would have starved to death decades ago. (Patry, 2009, p. 21)

The roles have switched: The copyright industries no longer saw themselves as "service" for the creators. The artist, they believe, doesn't do the real work, but simply provides raw material and serves as the public face for a complex production of which the artists are only a minor part. The beauty of this lies in the distinction between the popular conception of the creator and what the businesses behind them actually do—and how much they actually profit. Music mogul David Geffen is worth an estimated $5.5 billion ("David Geffen," 2012), many times what any creative artist he has been associated with can boast.

Because they have a natural publicity venue that twenty-first-century authors generally can't match, musicians, over the past few years, have been ahead of authors developing means of reaching audiences that avoid corporate copyright control. Venues like YouTube allow musicians to offer free music downloads, to entice listeners to buy more through digital channels or to purchase concert tickets. There are other ways distributing music cheaply online, ways that musicians are grabbing onto gladly, seeing that money can be made once they establish a fan base. To McLeod (2007), this is a shift to a "musician's business" from a "music business" model. In it:

> the money generated by music-related sales can be more fairly distributed among those who actually work to make art. There will be less need to deal with and pay for the layers of accountants, lawyers, executives, and others who have populated the music industry for years. Previously, musicians' labor subsidized the salaries of those who made far more annually than the vast majority of the musicians. (p. 319)

Although there is a reasserting of Romantic prerogatives of the artist in this—a feeling that it is the creator who is important, not the industry—there is also an element not so possessive as earlier attitudes of the artists towards their work. These new artists are willing to give work away, to add their own contribution to the commons, so to speak, recognizing that the commons, though benefitting all, could also end up rewarding creators a paying audience. Only recently has this sort of model, pioneered by musicians, been approximated by authors, who are now facilitated by print-on-demand options, with a model that leaves the author in control of copyright. This is only beginning to affect the traditional publishing business (which may one day become an "authors' business"), but the impact will grow.

Conclusion

It is too early to tell if these new business models will lead to a change in public perceptions of artists or the perceived place of artists' products within conceptions of ownership. Perhaps, as more work is given away, the "property" aspect will weaken, especially when use of extant works in new ones are increasingly obvious, as with sampling in music and with the much older art of collage or pastiche. Marcel Duchamp's 1919 "L.H.O.O.Q." is dependent upon a postcard of da Vinci's "Mona Lisa," something that would be seen as copyright violation by the postcard manufacturer (to say nothing of da Vinci) today. However, we will likely see a resurgence of this sort of work, even if merely for private distribution—in fact, we have. Fan Art, completely derivative, has had a strong presence on the Internet for years. People will accept that authorial rights need to be weakened, especially as more and more involve themselves in creative activities that demand collaboration and cooperation, and not possession.

The older American concepts of authorship and IP, while they may have had some limited utility in a "literacy" (borrowing the term from Walter Ong) culture, clearly are not sufficient to the developing "digital" culture and what will soon prove to be an increasingly demanding commons. The incredible expansion and strengthening of copyright over the past generation is a doomed exercise, for it is based on concepts of authority and subsequent ownership that cannot be sustained in a digital environment. Like "copy" itself and associated rights of copying, "creation" and "creating" no longer mean what once they did; they no longer aid the culture and its progress as once they could. A new model, one reflecting the realities of the new age yet also reflecting the Constitutional demand that both the commons and the creator (be it author or reader or both) be protected, needs continued development—and this needs to be developed soon or we will end up with copyright chaos, with laws increasingly meaningless as newer and stronger ways of circumventing them appear—and possibility of enforcement diminishes.

The limits of ownership of all sorts are determined by society and its needs, not by any natural right. So are all of the prerogatives granted to artists even concerning the work that they create—once the work is shared. Art cannot exist in a vacuum, and art is as dependent for creation and survival on whatever provides its "air" as any living being. When copyright laws are allowed to constrict that air, making it available only to a select few who can afford it, the artists (and the consumers of art—who are, in many ways, the real artists) will rise up and seize the sources of their sustenance.

• CHAPTER TWO •

Scarlet v. SABAM: An Emerging Backlash against Corporate Copyright Lobbies in Europe?

Angela Daly and Benjamin Farrand

The recent decision of the Court of Justice of the European Union (CJEU) in *Scarlet v. SABAM* is of high importance, especially for the ongoing debate around copyright enforcement online. The judges of the court decided that wide-ranging measures involving the monitoring of Internet users' activity and the blocking of peer-to-peer sites for an unlimited time where copyrighted material may be accessed illegally was a disproportionate measure, and emphasized the fact that intellectual property rights were not absolute rights but had to be balanced against other rights such as free expression and privacy. This chapter will present an in-depth analysis of *Scarlet v. SABAM*, and the background against which it was decided, in order to assess whether it represents an instance of a "fight back" against copyright lobbies in Europe. Over the last few years, Europe has followed the United States in enacting measures to extend copyright terms, and at the national level legislation has also been enacted specifically to target users allegedly infringing on copyright protections by downloading illicitly copyrighted material, especially from peer-to-peer file-sharing spaces (e.g., the Digital Economy Act in the United Kingdom) in the midst of heavy lobbying from corporate copyright holders for ever stricter measures.

However, *Scarlet v. SABAM* may also encompass the ascendancy in the copyright debate of another powerful lobby with its own interests, namely that of the telecommunications companies that provide Internet access to users, and for which monitoring user data to detect copyright violations represents a cost lacking a (profit-based) benefit. In the past, telecom companies have claimed that they are unable to monitor content; this, however, is not accurate at present given the availability of deep packet inspection (DPI) technologies used by these companies in a way that provides new means of exploitation and sources of profit by prioritizing and/or blocking certain types of Internet traffic.

The chapter will consider these issues through the adoption of an actor-based approach to analyze the case in light of the competing discourses presented by the creative and telecommunications industries, in addition to the views of consumer advocate groups. In doing so, *Scarlet v. SABAM* will be assessed in the context of the ongoing copyright-limits debate.

The Case of *Scarlet v. SABAM*

The Court of Justice of the European Union (CJEU) gave its decision on *Scarlet v. SABAM* in late 2011. A Belgian national court requested a preliminary ruling to determine whether an Internet Service Provider (ISP) could be obliged by a national court order to introduce a filtering system to monitor the communications of all of its customers as a measure to prevent copyright infringement, at the ISP's own cost and for an unlimited time.

The CJEU's decision is comprised of various parts. First, it held that the requirement for the ISP to implement this filtering system is prohibited by the European Union's E-Commerce Directive.[1] Second, the CJEU considered whether the requirement for the ISP to monitor communications in this way was incompatible with the EU's fundamental rights: It recognised that the protection of intellectual property was a fundamental right, but that it was not inviolable nor subject to absolute protection, and must be balanced against other rights. In this case, the relevant "other" rights were the freedom for the ISP to conduct a business, as well as the rights of the ISP's customers—such as their right to the protection of personal data and their freedom to receive and impart information. The CJEU decided that the mandatory filtering scheme would be a "serious infringement" of the ISP's freedom to conduct business, because the ISP would be forced to install "a complicated, costly, permanent computer system at its own expense"[2] to conduct a "systematic analysis" of information including users' IP addresses (protected personal data). Further, the analysis would not adequately distinguish between lawful and unlawful content passing through the ISP's network and could thus result in the blocking of lawful communications. The CJEU considered that a fair balance had not been struck between these rights, and so the Belgian court's order to force Scarlet to implement this filtering scheme could not be upheld.

The CJEU followed the (non-binding) opinion of Advocate General Cruz Villalón delivered earlier in 2011. The Advocate General considered the filtering system to be a restriction on the rights to privacy of communications, protection of personal data, and freedom of information. However, he went further than the CJEU's decision in positing that this kind of restriction would only be permissible if it was adopted on a national, accessible, clear, and predictable legal basis. This had not happened here, because the obligation for ISPs to install such a filtering and blocking system was not expressed in clear, precise, and predictable terms in the Belgian legal provision at issue.

The decision in this case is important for various reasons: It seems to represent a turning of the tide on the absolutism of copyright protection and enforcement and it brings user concerns and rights into the limelight. However, the decision is not an outright ban on this kind of monitoring system being used to detect copyright violations—indeed, it seems that other monitoring systems can be put into place so long as they adhere to the requirements in the CJEU's decision and maybe also those in the Advocate General's opinion. These requirements would seem to better balance the rights of all actors involved, offer more legal transparency, and perhaps hold copyright holders to bear costs, or at least share the costs of implementing and running such a system with ISPs.

Neoliberal Economics, Propertisation, and Intellectual Property: The Commodification of Creativity

The *Scarlet v.* SABAM case occurs during an interesting time for copyright law and policy in the European Union. The last 16 years have seen "a remarkable string of contentious mobilisations... [emerging] to challenge the normative and institutional frameworks that regulate how knowledge is produced, appropriated, and used" (Haunss, 2011, p. 129). A wide variety of groups critical of copyright law and policy are converging, and "more and more diverse actors are getting involved in IP issues... industry, legal specialists, national administrations, patent and trademark offices, and specialist courts are being joined by academics, farmers, indigenous people, consumers, political activists, and NGOs" (Robertson, 2008, pp. 217–218). The increased media and activist attention on copyright policy from non-specialists may perhaps be explained by developments in copyright law and policy in the U.S. and the EU. As Haunss stated, "the enormous expansion of intellectual property rights, in terms of protected subject matter, protection length and geographical coverage" (p. 131) not only indicates a reason for both greater focus upon, and greater contention regarding, intellectual property rights, but is also reflective of the approach of actors in favor of increased intellectual property protection.

Contemporary copyright policy has significant roots in neoliberal economics. As summarised by Robertson (2008), neoliberalism represents a return to "classical liberal ideas of limited government, unregulated free markets and the sanctity of private property... [in which] neoliberalism valorised property which was used in the production of goods and services for sale in the market" (p.

218). For copyright policy, the increased commodification of creativity therefore represents both the best way of ensuring further creativity and wealth production, and of distributing that product to the paying public. According to Robertson, this subsequently led to "more areas of life [becoming] subject to the rights of private property owners to exclude access unless it was paid for through a market transaction" (p. 218).

To quote Harvey (2011), in such a system, "the role of the State is to create and preserve an institutional framework appropriate to such practices" (p. 22). This entails the creation of markets in areas previously characterised by the absence of markets, such as healthcare or law enforcement. Combined with the dominance of neoliberal thought, Harvey argued that this has led to private property rhetoric "becoming hegemonic... incorporated into the common sense way we interpret, live in, and understand the world" (p. 23). David Tyfield (2010) stated that with the crisis in industrial profitability of the 1970s, capital started finding new areas in which to invest, in particular finance and services, resulting in a push into cultural creation and the creation of "cultural industries." Creativity as commodity identifies the very nature of creativity under a neoliberal economic system—a form of industrial output that must be traded in a manner accordant with profit maximisation.

Subsequently, intellectual property has developed its own internal property logic. According to Alexander Peukert (2011), rather than copyright protection being granted to facilitate greater creativity, protection appears to be granted as an end in itself. Peukert used the example of the Information Society Directive, implemented in 2001, as an indication of this mind-set. The Information Society Directive was intended to implement aspects of the Trade-Related Aspects of Intellectual Property Rights (TRIPS) Agreement into EU law, in addition to preparing the EU for the wide-scale use of the Internet by its citizens. The preamble to the Directive is particularly interesting in demonstrating the property as commodity viewpoint held with regard to copyright. Preamble paragraph 4 states that a harmonised legal framework for copyright in the EU:

> while providing for a high level of protection of intellectual property, will foster substantial investment in creativity and innovation, including network infrastructure, and lead in turn to growth and increased competitiveness of European industry.

The preamble states that a "high level of protection" is required; on this basis, intellectual property should be recognized as forming an integral part of property. Nowhere, Peukert contended, are the potential negatives of increasing intellectual property protection mentioned. The provision contains no limitation, nor balancing with other competing rights, but states the right as an absolute; as Christophe Geiger (2003) stated, "intellectual property stands as an end in itself" (p. 376).

Part of the success in promoting the neoliberal approach toward copyright is the promotion of it as property under a liberal conception. Helena Howe (2011) stated that one of the most significant developments in perceptions of copyright relates to the view of it as constituting a form of property analogous to property in land. Such an approach results in the acceptance of an absolute ownership of a copyrighted work. In this way, copyright becomes "influenced by one particular, traditional, model of property in land—the 'liberal' model—when this model is neither the only possible understanding of the nature of property in land nor even necessarily the most current understanding of property in land law" (Howe, p. 183). Thus, copyright becomes an absolute, sole possession of its owner. Obligations placed upon this ownership by the public, or even the creator of a copyrighted work where the right has been assigned, become impositions and exceptions to absolute possession.

Liberal Property Rhetoric in Copyright Law and Policy

Ideas of an exclusionary, self-referential view of intellectual property as an industrial commodity are not spontaneously generated in a vacuum; such ideas are developed, fostered, and then exchanged between different actors. David Miller (2010) argued that part of the success in the development of neoliberal policy approaches have depended upon "corporate lobbying organisations being at the forefront of organising and pursuing capitalist class interests through the promotion of neoliberal agendas and the planning of neoliberal projects" (p. 23). Policy aims can be achieved through participation in policy-forming organisations, such as think tanks or involvement in political bodies such as Parliamentary Groups, in addition to the application of pressure through lobbying organisations.

Influence on the Scope of Copyright

As stated in the preceding section, the Information Society Directive was ostensibly passed to implement the TRIPS Agreement. TRIPS was signed by 124 nations on April 15, 1994, with entry into force on January 1, 1995, and has been described as "the first comprehensive intellectual property agreement ever executed by most of the world's trading nations which establishes minimum standards of protection (and enforcement) for practically all categories of IP rights" (Moncayo von Hase, 1998, p. 83). It has also been referred to as being the outcome of collusion between key actors in the creative and innovation industries eager to ensure U.S. standards of intellectual property protection and propertization, with TRIPS emerging "primarily as the result of transnational corporations consensus and the coincidence of the perceived interests of that group with key governments such as the U.S." (Nicola, 2006, p. 25). According to Peter Drahos and John Braithwaite (2002), TRIPS was primarily written by corporate giants such as IBM and Pfizer as a means of effectively tying intellectual property protection to trade, reflecting the perception of creative/innovative works as commodities to be bought and sold.

Yet if the TRIPS Agreement was reflective of the effectiveness of the creative industries to embed certain property rhetoric in international legislation and enhance the perception of intellectual property as being a form of exclusive property right, then the EU's Information Society Directive was even more so, implementing "draconian" changes to intellectual property policy (Kretschmer, 2003). The directive resulted in the creation of new classes of right, such as the reproduction right under Article 2 (i.e., the exclusive right of a copyright holder to "authorise or prohibit direct or indirect, temporary or permanent reproduction by any means and in any form, in whole or in part" of a copyrighted work). Furthermore, the directive creates a closed, exhaustive list of exceptions to copyright. Where exceptions and limitations to copyright law are permitted, the preamble states that they "may not be applied in a way which prejudices the legitimate interests of the rightholder or which conflicts with the normal exploitation of his work or other subject-matter."

In addition, even where such exceptions or limitations may be permitted under such a narrow test, nothing should "prevent the definition of contractual relations designed to ensure fair compensation for the rightholders" (Directive 2001/29/EC). In other words, even where such an exception exists, it should be allowed to be contracted away. Again, this is reflective of a neoliberal perception of property; the directive presents "exceptions as being primarily interferences with the owner's ability to extract value from the work... for limitations to be drafted and interpreted narrowly" (Howe, 2011, pp. 195–196). Even where exceptions and limitations do exist, and where perhaps contractual relations would not be able to render such obsolete, the Directive also allows for the creation of digital fences through the use of technical-prevention measures such as Digital Rights Management (DRM) technology. Tampering with these fences, even to allow an otherwise legal use of a work, constitutes illegality.

P. Bernt Hugenholtz (2000) attributed the restrictive nature of the directive to the unprecedented level of corporate lobbying involved in its passage, a view that Martin Kretschmer (2003) agreed with, stating that the legislative proposals of the digital copyright agenda focus on "the industry's right to say NO in the on-line environment" (p. 334). Criticism of the ever-expanding scope of copyright does not come only from academics, but also from other institutions, such as in reviews ordered by governments (e.g., the 2006 Gowers Review undertaken on behalf of the British government).

Influence on the Duration of Copyright

Following the move in the U.S. to expand the duration of copyright protection to life plus 70 years in the case of an individual author, and up to 120 years for a work of corporate authorship with the Copyright Term Extension Act, a similar move was made in the EU, with the attempt to extend the duration of protection for sound recordings from 50 years to 95 years. The original attempt to extend the duration of protection was made in the UK. Following petitions by, in particular, the British Phonographic Industry (BPI), to increase the duration of copyright protection, the government commissioned Gowers to hold an inquiry into the benefits of changes to the intellectual property system. With regard to the duration of copyright, the Gowers Review (2006) ultimately concluded that an extension in the term of protection was not justified and recommended that the "European Commission should retain the length of protection on sound recordings and performers' rights at 50 years." Nevertheless, the BPI remained intent on ensuring an extension of protection (Hogge, 2006). In 2008, former Commissioner for the Internal Market, Charlie McCreevy, introduced a proposal for extending the duration of copyright protection over sound recordings. The impetus for legislative change was made emotively in the draft directive, where it was stated that more than 7,000 of Europe's musicians would lose all their royalties derived from the selling of sound recordings, a particularly devastating development given many of those performers were retired.

What is particularly interesting about this document is the references to the public domain: One passage states that "if after one year subsequent to the term extension, neither the phonogram producer nor the performer made the phonogram available to the public, the rights in the phonogram and the rights in the fixation of the performance shall expire" (Directive 2011/77/EU). In other words, if no financial value can be found in the work, it may then be allowed to enter the public domain. Despite the criticisms of the proposal, however, the Gowers Directive was ultimately passed in September 2011, albeit on slightly better terms (with the duration of protection being reduced from 95 years to 70) and became known as the Term Extension Directive (Standefort, 2011). Criticism came from both academics and others based on perceptions of the undue influence of lobbyists in addition to concerns about the negative impact of overlong terms of protection. For example, the Director General of the European Consumers' Organisation said that the Directive "further fossilises European copyright law" (Rohter, 2011). Kretschmer (2003) was more blunt, stating that the actions taken by policy makers in the field of copyright law were helping to "entrench a cynical attitude toward copyright law and brings it into further disrepute." Hugenholtz (2011) was also critical, stating that "many arguments against term extension are well rehearsed and almost universally endorsed by copyright scholars and economists across Europe." Interestingly, representatives of EU member states including Sweden and Belgium also raised concerns. In addendum documents, Sweden stated its reservations about protection extension. Belgium reiterated this position, stating that "a term extension is not an appropriate measure to improve the situation of the performing artists... we believe that the negative consequences the proposal entails outweigh the advantages it brings." However, the Term Extension Directive passed at a time when more attention is being paid to copyright issues by civil groups, NGOs, and individuals, which might partly be explained by increased media exposure, such as in the case of the Hargreaves Review (2011), a follow-up to the Gowers Review. Hargreaves mentioned that copyright law in particular appeared to be falling into disrepute with consumers, leading to an increase in levels of disregard for its restrictions.

Influence on the Enforcement of Copyright

Similar conclusions have been drawn concerning the Enforcement Directive (Directive 2004/28/EC) implemented to harmonise measures, procedures, and remedies both appropriate and relevant to proceedings relating to intellectual property infringement. The Enforcement Directive is again representative of the "absolute" notion of property, with the directive stating that "the protection of intellectual property is important not only for promoting innovation and creativity, but developing employment and improving competitiveness" and that the scope of the directive be enacted to encompass all intellectual property rights of all member states. Although initially the directive was only intended to deal with mass-scale commercial infringement, this appeared to have changed during the course of its implementation. The directive states at Article 2(1) that it applies to "any infringement of intellectual property rights," greatly expanding the scope of the initial proposal. As such, the directive does not appear to "distinguish between large-scale commercial infringement and counterfeiting enterprises from unintentional, non-commercial infringement of individuals." Josef Drexl, R. Hilty, and A. Kir (2003) stated that the directive suffers from

> considerable problems concerning the principles of subsidiarity and proportionality... the data on which [the justifications for the Directive were] founded were mostly compiled by interest groups and professional organisations from branches with a strong interest in enhancing the sanctions and measures presently existing for the protection of intellectual property. (p. 530)

The directive has also been criticised for being somewhat undemocratic in the manner of its passing. Despite disagreements by member states on some of its provisions, the directive was fast-tracked and not subject to a second reading, but passed quickly after the first. Such measures would be consistent with a neoliberal reading of intellectual property protection; given the nature of the right as being absolute, measures would be taken to ensure that the level of protection would be as high as possible. This may well include the freezing out of parties to a debate that may not be as amenable to high levels of protection.

However, the creative industries were not satisfied with the directive, and soon the European Commission enacted a proposal for a Criminal Enforcement Directive with specific penal sanctions for commercial-scale infringement. This was necessary, argued the Commission, on the grounds that "counterfeiting and piracy, and infringements of intellectual property in general, are a constantly growing phenomenon which nowadays has an international dimension, since they are a serious threat to national economies and governments" (Drexl et al., 2003, p. 489). A draft directive was introduced, which stated that the Commission intended that the EU take "criminal-law measures that are necessary to guarantee the full effectiveness of the rules it lays down on the protection of intellectual property" (Law Society of the UK, 2006). This appears to be the logical extreme of a liberal rhetoric on property—the protection of commodity through the use of criminal sanctions for non-compliance. Ultimately, a significant amount of resistance to the passing of the directive from countries such as the UK and the Netherlands halted this development, albeit on grounds other than concerns concerning the proportionality of criminal sanctions.

In 2008, however, then-Commissioner McCreevy announced his intention to reinitiate the Criminal Enforcement Directive program, stating: "I would like to begin by dealing with piracy. I have always had a problem with this term—it is too soft for what it defines... but as all of you here today know, there is nothing romantic about the theft of material illegally downloaded from the internet." Once again, the strong liberal approach is demonstrated, with McCreevy referring to infringement as "theft," reinforcing the view of intellectual property as a form of "real" property that must be protected. Civil society group La Quadrature du Net (LQdN, 2011) criticized the IPRED revision as being "too much in line with the copyright industry to break away from outdated policies," especially due to its determination to repress non-commercial sharing of copyrighted material. LQdN was specifically critical of the lack of empirical evidence from the Commission that the measures provided in the directive were inadequate to deal with serious online infringements and speculated that, in the absence of proper evidence, it seemed that the Commission had relied on the claims of the copyright industry, whose evidence that file-sharing had terrible economic consequences was "bogus."

One supposed aspect of the Criminal Enforcement Directive that may already be seen in domestic legislation in the EU is the notion of intermediaries performing the role of private policing of the Internet, ensuring the compliance of individuals with intellectual property rights online. One particular example currently implemented and enacted is the Digital Economy Act in the UK. The act is a highly controversial piece of legislation enacted in the final moments of Gordon Brown's Labour government in 2010 (see Cusack, 2011; Farrand, 2010). Its provisions include the creation of a mandate for ISPs to act not only as service providers for their customers, but also as enforcers of intellectual property rights. Section 3 of the act states that ISPs have an obligation to inform subscribers of infringements reported by content owners. Section 4 states that ISPs have the obligation to provide infringement lists to content owners, if so requested, but that these lists shall not allow a subscriber to be identified. Under a system referred to as "graduated response," Section 10 of the act allows for OFCOM (the British communications regulator) to create a code of obligations which can include the ability to limit Internet access if OFCOM determines that such limitation is necessary on the basis of a report or "any other matter that appears by the Secretary of State to be relevant." According to Section 9 of the Act, these technical measures include: limiting Internet access or bandwidth; preventing access to certain web sites, materials, or services; suspending service; or engaging in "any other appropriate measures." This may indicate that it was the intent of Parliament to change the role of an ISP from being a mere conduit, or solely a means of transferring communications data, into a gatekeeper charged with dictating the terms of entry and restricting entry to those unwilling to abide by the IP rules dictated.

Criticisms regarding the odd implementation of the Act ranged from those concerning the allegations of a meeting between David Geffen, an influential recording industry executive, and Peter Mandelson, then Business Secretary, for a private dinner in Corfu days before the announcement of a new bill to tackle online piracy (Illegal Downloaders, 2009), indicating the influence of corporate lobbyists on government policy, to the passing of the act during the "wash-up" period of Parliament, during which usually only non-controversial pieces of legislation are passed in order to clear the way for elections and the new sitting of Parliament, indicating a desire to rush the bill through the House of Commons with a minimum of scrutiny (Judge, 2010).

The first indication before *Scarlet v. SABAM* that EU institutions may be skeptical of the role of ISPs as regulators of intellectual property rights online can be found in the *Promusicae* case. The case dealt with a request by Promusicae, an organisation representing producers and publishers of musical and audiovisual recordings to demand the personal details of suspected infringers of copyright from Telefonica de Espana, in order to proceed with civil actions against them on the basis of the Enforcement Directive. The question as to whether this was permitted was referred to the CJEU for a preliminary reference. Interestingly, the Court, although recognising a fundamental right to property under the Charter, recognised a fundamental and equally important right to privacy and the protection of personal data under the same charter.

While not providing a clear and unequivocal answer as to whether an ISP was obliged to hand over personal data to be used in civil proceedings for copyright infringement, the Court appears to demonstrate at least some concern with the absolutist view of copyright protection. In particular, the Court stated that member states must interpret the directives in such a way as to ensure both proportionality and a fair balance between the various fundamental rights protected by community law. Furthermore, statements by Neelie Kroes (2011), Commissioner for the Digital Agenda, appear to indicate concern with an overarching and absolute view of intellectual property. In a statement made in November 2011, just days before the CJEU came to its decision in *Scarlet v. SABAM*, Kroes stated that there is more to creativity than just the enforcement of copyright, and noted that "citizens increasingly hear the word copyright and hate what is behind it. Sadly, many see the current system as a tool to punish and withhold, not a tool to recognise and reward." This is perhaps the strongest criticism made by an EU Commissioner on copyright law and policy. Combined with an increasingly hostile view of copyright enforcement taken by Internet intermediaries, academic criticism, and a loss of faith on the part of the European populace, could this change in rhetoric be a blow to the neoliberal perception of copyright being an absolute form of property?

Ascendancy of Telcos in the Copyright Debate

With development and use of techniques such as deep-packet inspection (DPI), ISPs now have the capacity to monitor traffic passing through their networks in real time and act accordingly on it (e.g., slowing down certain kinds of data, speeding up other kinds of data, and even blocking some data entirely). In the context of the worldwide net neutrality debate, the interest of ISPs is to use this capability to increase revenue by, for example, speeding up the content of a content provider that has paid a premium for its content to be provided to the ISP's users.

ISPs have become increasingly important in the copyright debate given this technological development. Previously, ISPs have enjoyed safe harbour provisions, which absolve them of responsibility for *inter alia* copyright infringements committed by their users if they do not have actual knowledge of their users' illegal activity, such as Section 512(b) of Title II of the Digital Millennium Copy-right Act in the U.S. and Article 14 of the E-Commerce Directive in the EU. The use of DPI technology certainly seems to have changed the situation regarding whether ISPs have actual knowledge of infringing activities both legally in terms of these safe harbours possibly no longer applying to ISPs with regard to material and activity that infringes copyright passing through their networks, and practically in terms of ISPs being able to know easily in practice whether this kind of activity is occurring.

Aside from the legal picture, absent some kind of additional incentive such as an ISP having a subsidiary content provider and wanting to protect that copyrighted material, ISPs do not *ipso facto* have an interest in monitoring traffic that may contain material that violates the copyrights of other entities, and indeed schemes such as the one in operation in *Scarlet v. SABAM* was a burden on the ISP with no benefit, which appears to be one factor the CJEU took into account when deciding that the screening scheme was invalid. Certainly this can be seen as a contest between different property owners: the IP holders and the ISPs that own the tangible property of their network infrastructures. ISPs want to be able to control their property in the way they want and not monitor traffic for copyright violations, which offers them only costs and no benefits. Although in practice, ISP hostility to monitoring traffic may be of benefit to Internet users as well, this is merely coincidental—the ISPs' primary concern is that of their own profits, and it is only because monitoring schemes may damage their profits that ISPs oppose them.

Despite this, however, ISPs may have their own interest in detection schemes, voluntarily blocking or otherwise affecting access to web sites thought to be facilitating copyright infringement in order to avoid direct litigation from rights holders. It may well be advantageous for rights holders to pursue ISPs rather than individual users violating copyright (who might be difficult to identify, may not have large financial resources, and whose pursuit may attract criticism from the general public, which may harm the rights holders' brand and/or public image) and entities such as the peer-to-peer filesharers themselves, who may be difficult to identify and located in other jurisdictions.

Furthermore, ISPs may also have a self-interest in blocking traffic from peer-to-peer filesharers, because they allegedly use a lot of bandwidth, which can create network congestion, creating another incentive for ISPs to disfavour them because their use may interfere with accessing other web sites, and so users may experience less-than-optimal service. This may allow ISPs to start charging users who want access to peer-to-peer services more for their Internet connection. Otherwise, these users will have to put up with the peer-to-peer services being blocked or running sub-optimally. Indeed, according to data from the Body of European Regulators for Electronic Communications (BEREC, 2012), even absent copyright monitoring systems and court orders, ISPs in various European countries are commonly using traffic-management practices to block or slow down peer-to-peer traffic on their networks.

It seems that the very problem with the scheme in *Scarlet v. SABAM* was that it was mandatory for ISPs. However, a voluntary scheme may not have been cause for concern, and indeed the increasing confluence between ISP and copyright holders' interests seems to have resulted in such an initiative between ISPs and major corporate copyright holders in the U.S., which was agreed to in 2011, and was eventually implemented in 2013. The agreement has been strongly criticised for not including any representation from consumer groups/civil society in the negotiations (McSherry & Goldman, 2011), as well as for the scheme itself constituting a private system of copyright enforcement agreed upon among entities which are otherwise horizontal and vertical competitors, thereby potentially causing a violation of U.S. antitrust law (Flaim, 2011). Ironically, U.S. ISPs were strongly against the proposed Stop Online Privacy Act (SOPA), which included the possibility of court orders being obtained so that ISPs would be forced to block access to sites which infringed intellectual property rights.

For detecting and dealing with copyright infringement, the UK has a "mixed" filtering system in operation, inasmuch as ISPs were told by the British government that if they did not implement this system voluntarily, then legislation would be enacted to force them to do so. The scope of the Cleanfeed system has been widened with the court decision won by the Motion Picture Association in 2011, which managed to obtain an order forcing BT to use Cleanfeed to block access to the Newzbin 2 site, which provides links to copyrighted content (Creative Industry, 2012). Furthermore, in April 2012, the High Court ordered British ISPs to block access to Swedish filesharing site Pirate Bay, following a decision from February of that year stating that Pirate Bay was jointly liable for copyright infringement committed by its users because it profited from these activities (Film-makers, 2011). Copyright holders can find it more effective to pursue ISPs from the same country through the courts rather than the site or platform that facilitates infringement, especially when the site or platform and its assets are located legally/geographically in another jurisdiction (e.g., Pirate Bay is located in Sweden). Even after the *Scarlet v. SABAM* judgment, this kind of measure may well be acceptable to the CJEU given its more "proportional" character (i.e., the blocking of certain sites/platforms known to be infringing copyright), rather than a blanket monitoring scheme of all Internet communications.

The British ISPs seem to have dragged their feet more on copyright enforcement than their U.S. counterparts, inasmuch as they wanted court decisions to clarify their position *vis-a-vis* copyright infringement taking place on their networks, as well as the fact two of them (BT and TalkTalk) were accused of engaging in "delaying tactics" regarding the implementation of the controversial Digital Economy Act provisions that involve letters being sent to Internet users who are suspected of infringing copyrights. The ISPs applied to the British High Court for clarification on the legality of this provision via European laws, as well as contesting the fact that, according to the legislation, they were to contribute financially to the setting up and running of the scheme. The High Court confirmed that the provisions were legal, and that they did have to pay 25% of the fees charged by the body that will hear appeals from users. The Court of Appeal subsequently upheld the finding of legality of the act, but ruled that ISPs could not be forced to pay this proportion of the appeals body's case fees, but a lesser amount. Nevertheless, at the time of writing, no letters have been sent to users suspected of piracy, and the likely date of implementation is now 2015.

From this picture, ISPs emerge as important players in the copyright debate, but ultimately they can be persuaded of the benefits of siding with rights holders, whether they themselves realize that there are also benefits for them in participating in copyright enforcement schemes (such as the avoidance of litigation and the protection of their own interests), or whether they are threatened with legislation and court orders into becoming a private copyright police force. In general, ISPs are somewhat reluctant to pursue their customers, but they certainly cannot be thought of as advancing anyone's interests but their own, which occasionally coincide with those of users in terms of retaining their free expression, data protection, and privacy. However, the examples above show the occasions in which the interests of ISPs and users regarding copyright diverge. Users certainly cannot rely on the telecommunications industry to uphold their online rights and freedoms vis-a-vis aggressive copyright enforcement online.

Future

From the discussion above, although copyright absolutism may have been disowned by the CJEU, and ISPs and users may see some respite from aggressive intellectual property enforcement, ISPs cannot be relied upon to advance user interests; they are as much a part of the neoliberal hegemony as corporate rightholders, in wanting to use their property as they see fit and not to have to face regulatory encroachments into this right. However, in the wake of actual protests over ACTA in Europe and SOPA/PIPA in the U.S., intellectual property reform can no longer be thought of as a "quiet politics" issue, and some kind of counter-hegemonic anti-copyright absolutism movement may well be afoot.

Nevertheless, the hegemony itself still remains of corporate rightholders that have managed to lobby governments and politicians successfully and in the process get ISPs on board. Yet the increased public consciousness of individual rights and freedoms, and of the production and dissemination of culture, puts legislative copyright absolutism to much more scrutiny by a wider section of the general public and civil society. With citizens becoming increasingly reliant on digitized methods to create, access, and enjoy culture, the effects of overly restrictive copyright laws and policies that benefit only large corporations are felt by more people, and their unfairness and injustice exposed.

Notes

1 Directive 2000/31 on certain legal aspects of information society services, in particular electronic commerce, in the Internal Market (Directive on Electronic Commerce). Article 15(1) forbids member states from forcing providers to monitor generally the information they process or store.

2 According to the CJEU, this would also be contrary to Article 3(1) of Directive 2004/48 on the enforcement of intellectual property rights, which provides that measures to enforce intellectual property rights should not be "unnecessarily complicated or costly, or entail unreasonable time-limits or unwarranted delays."

• CHAPTER THREE •

Discovery and Ownership in an Age of Networked Science

Michelle Sidler and Chad Wickman

It has been almost 70 years since C.P. Snow (1961) published his essay "The Two Cultures" wherein he argued that the sciences and the humanities existed in different, perhaps incommensurable, epistemic worlds. While much has changed in the intervening decades, Snow's argument continues to offer a relevant framework for discussing the relationship between the humanities and sciences in the twenty-first century. On the one hand, increasing specialization has contributed to a widening gap between scientific and humanities-based research cultures; on the other hand, there is still a need to identify where these cultures share common interests. Nowhere is this more apparent, perhaps, than with the topic of open access and its implications for authorship, copyright, and fair use in a digital age (see DeVoss & Porter, 2006; Johnson-Eilola, 1998; Reyman, 2010; Rife, Slattery, & DeVoss, 2010).

The aim of this chapter is to explore what scholars in the humanities might be able to learn from the sciences about issues related to open-access publishing and intellectual property. We do this in four related ways: First, we examine how early developments in scientific publishing contributed to the emergence of research genres and, more broadly, a cohesive scientific research culture; second, we discuss how journal indexing in the sciences has begun to shape the ways in which scientists communicate and manage information through citation networks; third, we discuss the open data movement and its ongoing impact on scientific research and communication; finally, we conclude by discussing the implications of our work for humanities scholarship and suggest some possible directions for developing cyber-infrastructures that do not simply replicate those in the sciences but rather strategize and adopt technologies appropriate to humanities-based inquiry.

Open-access Science

Scientists are increasingly embracing open-access principles and practices to communicate, collaborate, and share data. Indeed, some of the most-often cited examples of information commons come from the sciences (Borgman, 2007, 2009; Kranich, 2004; Tapscott & Williams, 2010). Many scientists are adapting their research and communication practices to what Willinsky (2006) referred to as the *access principle*, which is concerned with "increasing and improving access, impact, participation, and circulation" of information (p. 29). Often dubbed Science 2.0 or Open Science, open-access science leverages web 2.0 capabilities—for example, blogs, wikis, and robust search tools—to write text, upload data, and aggregate published research at little or no cost to the public. Peter Suber (2010), author of *Open Access News* and Director of the Harvard Open Access Project, summed up the philosophy thus: "Putting peer-reviewed scientific and scholarly literature on the internet. Making it available free of charge and free of most copyright and licensing restrictions. Removing the barriers to serious research." Some scientists have embraced this approach because they believe that the more information that gets shared—from data to research articles—the better equipped scientists are to make significant discoveries.

Advocates argue that the move toward open access facilitates processes of discovery by allowing members of the scientific community to collaborate more quickly and by making information available to a larger pool of researchers. However, opponents fear that open access will diminish individual scientists' claims on their research. As the history of the first scientific journal written in English—*Philosophical Transactions of the Royal Society*—reveals, scientists have always negotiated a tension between two overarching values: 1) community knowledge sharing, and 2) the recognition that comes from individual discovery. Michael Nielsen (2012) argued that much of this tension is located squarely in the politics of scientific publishing. Over the last 300 years, scientific journal articles have provided both a recognizable form of communication and community building among scientists and a mechanism for attributing recognition to individuals or groups of scientists. The flexibility of the genre has served the scientific community well, but the Open Science movement is beginning to transform the ways in which journal articles function for scientists and their constituencies. These changes are not without their problems: Some scientists are concerned about making their research available to others before they have a chance to publish or patent it; they do not want to be "scooped." Quality is also a concern. If open-access science opens up more publishing streams, will the quality of published work diminish? Even more vocal than scientists are journal publishers who argue that current publishing practices already offer enough access to scholarly information. Some fear, for instance, that a new publishing model will usurp their dominance (and, in some cases, profits) and question the long-term viability of the open-access publishing model. All of these questions and objections indicate that open-access is certainly not dominant in the sciences—at least not yet—but that the movement has gathered enough steam to warrant serious consideration by members of the community.

Discovery and Ownership in the Sciences

The relationship between discovery and ownership has always been a complex question for scientists. Watson and Crick's "discovery" of the structure of DNA offers a useful example for illustrating these complexities. The story is well-known: American scientist James Watson and British scientist Francis Crick were racing with Linus Pauling to confirm the structure of DNA, make their findings available to the scientific community through publication, and thus take credit for the discovery. The historical record attributes Watson and Crick with the "win" because they published a commentary on their work in 1953 in the journal *Nature* under the title "Molecular Structure of Nucleic Acids: A Structure for Deoxyribose Nucleic Acid." However, many scientists, including Pauling, Maurice Wilkins, and Rosalind Franklin all contributed to the discovery. The historical record, of course, is not always explicit in revealing the processes by which such knowledge was made public and the powerful rhetorical strategies scientists used to establish ownership over it within the scientific community (see Halloran, 1984; Miller, 1994).

We mention this episode from the history of science to suggest that questions related to intellectual property, copyright, and ownership have always been complex and will only become more so as digital technologies continue to transform the cultures in which scientists undertake and communicate about their work. The concept of ownership itself is complicated by the fact that scientists are often funded by federal agencies like the National Science Foundation (NSF) and National Institutes of Health (NIH). Researchers are thus accountable to these organizations and, in a broader sense, to American taxpayers who fund them. This relationship has been an ongoing source of deliberation ever since the NIH implemented the NIH Public Access Policy in 2008. Under this Policy, all NIH-funded researchers are required to submit article manuscripts to PubMed Central, a free, online database run by the National Library of Medicine.[1] The impact of the Public Access Policy reverberated throughout the scientific community and, especially, among science publishers who consistently lobbied Congress to roll back the policy.[2] These developments illustrate just some of the stakeholders involved in scientific research; in this case, the very same government policies that improve access for citizens potentially cut into profits for publishers, who in turn appeal to other government agencies for redress. Open-access policies have not wholly changed the relationship between taxpayers and funding agencies; but, they have begun to transform the scope of scientific inquiry. Primary scientific research is no longer an exclusive conversation among a closed community of scholars—it now potentially reaches all citizens.

We are not alone in pursing this line of inquiry. Borgman (2009), for instance, has suggested that the humanities could learn from the sciences when it comes to integrating digital technologies in research and publication. According to her, "a number of developments in cyberinfrastructure, eScience, and eResearch offer guidance to the digital humanities community in the quest to become a more established field with a broader base of infrastructure. One is in the area of publication practices" (p. 19). Borgman is attuned to the need for sharing data and developing infrastructures that facilitate collaboration within and between academic fields and believes that those who hold steadfast to a print-based model of scholarship are destined to become increasingly isolated if not wholly irrelevant to the world outside the academy. Borgman's call to action is well-taken but is not without its complications. Indeed, the cultures of the humanities and sciences differ in many ways: from objects of study to methodological and epistemological commitments to basic values. Looking to science as *the* model for research and communication is therefore not the answer to questions related to intellectual property and authorship so much as it is a generative strategy—something like a heuristic—for coming to grips with a digital humanities culture. The following sections attempt to lay the groundwork for envisioning humanities research and publishing in the twenty-first century.

Emerging Contexts in Scientific Communication

Thomas Huxley (1870), in his essay "On the Adviseableness of Improving Natural Knowledge," famously wrote that "if all the books in the world, except the *Philosophical Transactions*, were destroyed, it is safe to say that the foundations of physical science would remain unshaken." Currently appearing on the Royal Society's web site, Huxley's statement stands as a testament to the power of scientific publications to help develop a vast store of knowledge and thus assist in the growth of a scientific research culture. That tradition continues today. According to the organization's web site, "the Royal Society is committed to the widest possible dissemination of research outputs. Consequently, our own publishing operation is one of the most open access of all science publishers." The Royal Society is rooted in a longstanding tradition of print-based scholarly publishing but has begun to adapt its mission to a changing technological landscape and the needs of non-scientific audiences. These are recent developments but are also connected to a storied history that was in large part defined by the emergence of the *Philosophical Transactions* and the genre of the experimental report.

The Royal Society's first and most long-standing publication, *Philosophical Transactions* (hereafter *Transactions*) was first published in 1665, just 5 years after the founding of the society itself. According to the title page of the first volume, its aim was to give "some accompt [*sic*] of the present undertakings, studies, and labours of the ingenious in many considerable parts of the world." The journal's mission was thus to facilitate the sharing of information among independent practitioners worldwide by providing a forum in which to communicate about their scholarly investigations. Early letters submitted to the *Transactions* were originally directed toward its founding editor and publisher, Henry Oldenburg, and then, over time, developed into a genre of reporting directed toward the broader community of practitioners who had access to the journal.[3] Scholarly communication practices—from the process of peer review to the rhetorical structure and language deployed in experimental reports—were not simply implemented from the top down by Oldenburg but, rather, were developed in relation to printing technologies, experimental practices, and the style of discourse that the *Transactions* as a publication helped to reinforce.

Scholars have investigated how technologies of production and dissemination facilitated the emergence of a distinctive scientific community. Eisenstein's (1983) well-known research on the printing press as an agent of change, for example, examines the relationship between the Royal Society, the *Transactions*, and the power structures instantiated through publication practices oriented toward specialized audiences. She specifically draws out the connection between the printing press and the development of a systematized body of research that could be demarcated from other types of "non-scientific" knowledge (e.g., myth and religion). The audience for this work was not necessarily composed of every-day citizens but, instead, was designed "to make possible consensual validation by trained observers, experimenters and mathematicians [and] entailed a different use of the press than efforts to spread glad tidings to all men. Eventually, access to scientific journals and societies was shut to all save a professional trained elite" (Eisenstein, p. 695). Based on this account, the early formation of the journal was exclusionary in the sense that it aimed toward specialization and thus provided a means by which the emerging scientific community could discount knowledge that did not fall within its normative structure. Much has changed over the past 300 years in terms of conceptualizing the relationship between science and society; and the open-access movement promises only to complicate this relationship even further. What remains similar, however, is that scientific genres and publishing practices continue to offer coherence to a diffuse body of research and scholarly work.

Scholarship in the field of writing and rhetoric studies has been instrumental in showing how discourse practices contributed to the formation of scientific disciplines and fields. Bazerman (1988), for instance, examined the history of the experimental report and the dynamic relationship between genre conventions and the emergent social structure of a scientific research culture. According to him, one defining feature of scientific discourse is that it must be held accountable to the constraints of empirical research. Bazerman suggested that the experimental report emerged in response to this exigence—the need for accountability—and began to reinforce distinctly "scientific" forms of social and rhetorical action. He added that, over time, these reports replaced the act of public demonstration and began to offer a "virtual witnessing" of the experiments in question (see Shapin & Shaffer, 1985). The genre thus became a vehicle not simply for reporting information but also for reinforcing a type of communal *ethos* related to the conduct of experimental inquiry; likewise, writing for publication became a means for publicly signifying one's commitment to the methods and epistemology of the scientific enterprise. Scholars have continued to show how the genre developed over historical time as it was used to respond to new problems in scientific research and communication throughout the twentieth century (see Atkinson, 1999; Berkenkotter & Huckin, 1995). It stands to reason that the journal article will continue to evolve as scientists use it to respond to problems that arise in twenty-first century technological and cultural environments.

The early formation of the *Transactions*, the genre of the experimental report, and the development of a cohesive discourse community all provided a means for scientists to share information but, just as important, to discipline the ways in which individuals could effectively and persuasively communicate about their work. According to Valle (2006), these types of practices, and in particular the editorial influence of Henry Oldenburg, contributed to a "textual representation of the scientific debate—an instrument for the construction of a 'collective intelligence'" (pp. 88–89; see Gross, Harmon, & Reidy, 2002). We believe that the concept of a "collective" is a fitting way to describe the *Transactions* as a type of socio-cultural and textual infrastructure; and we would argue that it further invites comparison to twenty-first century network culture and recent developments in open-access publishing. In particular, online communities and cyber-infrastructures are developing around the needs of researchers who produce increasingly voluminous amounts of data and the needs of users who might benefit from its innovative application. Nielsen (2012) suggested that these collectives constitute a form of "shared praxis" that in turn allows for collective intelligence to develop between diverse audiences. Journals like the *Transactions* and genres like the experimental report have historically facilitated this type of activity; likewise, current trends in scientific publishing are starting to address a similar need.

Henry Oldenburg's editorial vision shaped the early development of the *Transactions* and, over time, the development of a research culture. Modern day editors in the sciences often take on a similar role. The challenge for them, however, is to disseminate information widely but to do so in a way that is economically viable for the stakeholders involved. Open-access journals attempt to disseminate scientific research to readers through funding methods that do not involve subscription fees, but this approach is complex and somewhat risky. Regardless, open-access journals are on the rise. According to the Directory for Open Access Journals (DOAJ), the number of open-access journals has risen from 19 in the year 2002 to 1,360 in the year 2012. And that is just the United States alone. Worldwide, the numbers reach approximately 7,600 and will likely continue to grow as scientists and other stakeholder groups continue to adapt their research and institutional practices to emergent technologies (see Björk et al., 2010). It would not be possible to discuss even a fraction of these journals within the scope of a single book chapter. We can, however, mention a widely recognized model: The Public Library of Science (PLoS). Founded in 2000, PLoS operates under a Creative Commons License that allows anyone to "share" or "remix" information as long as it gets attributed to the original source. The organization represents its *ethos* in a set of core principles—the foremost of which is open access—and a mission to provide "free immediate access to, and unrestricted reuse of, original works of all types." Yet providing "free" information still requires funding. Similar to the Royal Society, PLoS makes up for some of its publishing costs—from peer review to issue production to archiving—by charging authors or their "research sponsors" a fee; it also provides a waiver for authors who cannot actually afford the cost themselves. So, while journals like PLoS appear to be fully committed to principles of open access, scientists and publishers are still finding ways to make their efforts feasible in large-scale practice.

Citation Indexing as an Evolving Research Practice

Journal indexing is another technology that both aided and influenced scientific communications. By the mid-twentieth century and due in large part to the rise of government funding for scientific research, many scientists were experiencing information overload and needed efficient and effective ways to access and organize research publications. This "crisis" of information was an obsession of Eugene Garfield, who recognized the need to scale up science indexing practices as a way to help scientists filter published research. So, in 1960, Garfield created the Science Citation Index (SCI), or what is now called the ISI Web of Knowledge (ISI). The ISI leverages pre-existing information available in each journal article—in particular, the list of references—coding each citation and then compiling that information to create genealogies of cited works. Garfield stored and aggregated this data using mainframe computers (leading edge technology in 1960) and punch cards. The ISI has been maintained and updated constantly since its establishment, first by Garfield's initial company, then by the Institute for Scientific Information, and now by its parent company, Thomson Reuters. In essence, it has created a clearinghouse of information about science publishing that still continues to accumulate and aggregate data.

In 1955, Garfield introduced his plan in the journal *Science*, describing what he called "an association-of-ideas index" (p. 108). He maintained that the SCI would be based on scientists' own cognitive associations, as evidenced by their list of references. Scientists have a tacit understanding of the resources on which they draw, and their research requirements often supersede the disciplinary limitations of subject indexing. Even now, the ISI depends on a rudimentary crowd-sourcing approach to indexing, drawing on the collective wisdom of scientists to make visible the lineage of scientific discovery—that is, how scientific progress builds on the work of previous science—and to reveal the credibility and usefulness of previous research.

Interestingly, although Garfield leveraged the work of scientists themselves to compile the ISI, he did not make it freely available to them. In fact, over the years, ISI has become a monolith of science indexing, creating a near-monopoly for overall coverage in the sciences that charges a substantial (some would say exorbitant) fee for subscription.[4] Another limitation of ISI is its selectivity: As of 2012, the database covers only about 12,000 journals (from the physical sciences, social sciences, and humanities), and the editors are highly selective when reviewing new journals to include. Annually, they review about 2,000 journals for inclusion, but only add 10–12% of those to the database. The editors maintain that research shows only a small number of journals make up the bulk of cited research in any given field. (Thomson Reuters, 2012).[5] In other words, Garfield and his team have chosen selectivity over inclusion, creating a barrier both for emerging journals that wish to be added to the database and for readers who wish to view a wide spectrum of works on a given topic.

The ISI has become successful in part because of Garfield's intrinsic knowledge of the science community's broad values and needs. He recognized that scientific disciplines were at a particularly challenging juncture in the mid-twentieth century: The influx of so much government funding led to the rise of more and more published research. This infusion, in turn, led to an escalating publish-or-perish model in the sciences (and across higher education more broadly), which also led to more publications. The growing volume of published research needed to be aggregated and managed into a systematic, quantifiable format that would provide scientists with information about the quality of publications. In addition, universities needed a way to quantify the productivity and impact of scientists' research. Citation indexing fit the epistemological bill on both accounts.

The ISI was a kairotic technology in the 1960s, riding the wave of several socio-economic factors, including increased government funding, American dominance in the sciences, and a relatively stable system of print publishing. However, the ISI's rather conservative model of citation technology is now groaning under the weight of a twenty-first century scientific landscape in which all three of these conditions can no longer be taken for granted. More American researchers than ever are seeking publication, leading to more articles and more journals. The rise of international scientific research, particularly in Asian countries, is also adding to the number of science publications. Moreover, many of these markets cannot afford the high cost of the ISI (and journal subscriptions generally), so they are turning to open-access models, which may potentially threaten fee-based services like the ISI. Finally and most obviously, the rise of digital publishing and Internet connectivity affords new avenues for publishing research and destabilizes the conventional print model.

This destabilization can be seen in the emergence of at least two open-access citation databases: CiteSeerX and Citebase (Willinsky, 2006). CiteSeerX specifically targets full-text articles that are publicly available on the web, offering an alternative to the ISI that is both free and open to a wider array of online article publications. Because CiteSeerX is an automated process, it has the potential to be more expeditious, retrieving entries when they are immediately available online. And because CiteSeerX also has the potential to include more citations than ISI, it can potentially offer a more precise estimate of the article's impact on the field (Giles, Bollacker, & Lawrence, 1998). The open-access indexing system, Citebase, is more focused than CiteSeerX. Specifically, it scans for full-text documents, targeting databases of digital preprints (also known as eprints) made available for free online.[6] Overall, though, both CiteSeerX and Citebase circumvent costly subscription fees while providing access to manuscripts faster than most traditional publishers and indexes.

Citebase is a well-known example of the ways in which technologies can support particular values and needs in the sciences, just as Garfield did in the mid-twentieth century. Preprints are a much more vital component of scientific communication (physics in particular) than they are in the humanities. As a result, scientists have a long history of preprint swapping and are comfortable sharing research before final publication. Because of the need for immediate reporting of results in the sciences, preprint repositories developed soon after the establishment of the web. Such sites offer researchers the opportunity to distribute their manuscripts before the document undergoes peer review. The most well-known of these repositories is ArXiv. Manuscripts submitted to ArXiv are usually made public within one day of submission—weeks or months before they would be made available through traditional journal publisher web sites (Glazer, 2008).

Surprisingly, proprietary journal publishers tolerate the ArXiv repository and even publish many of the manuscripts that are first circulated there; arguably, then, ArXiv is one of the most successful combinations of open access and print publishing. This success can be largely attributed to the culture of physics and its affiliated disciplines, which have a long history of sharing preprints. Print journals are often viewed as places where scientists can take ownership of their discoveries; they are not places where scientists introduce those discoveries for the first time. In other words, like the ISI's citation infrastructure developed by Garfield, the cyber-infrastructure of open-access databases and preprint repositories emerged in response to the values and needs of working scientists.

Conclusions and Directions

The Open Data Movement

We have used the term "open-access science" throughout this chapter to refer primarily to journal publications and the aggregate technologies through which they are organized and distributed. Beyond the research article genre, however, we see the open-access movement developing in other, equally interesting directions. The open-data movement is one prominent example. Proponents of open data tend to advocate for the free and unrestrained distribution of raw scientific data, arguing that by making such information available, scientific progress will be hastened and improved. Unlike journal articles that report on the more-or-less cleaned up results of experimental inquiry (sometimes after a lengthy delay), open-data infrastructures allow scientists to scrutinize data sets before they get shaped into a particular form or argument. These data often get displayed in different formats, from spreadsheets or similar programs that allow for direct manipulation by other scientists to cyber-infrastructures that involve at least some attempt at interpretation and visual display.

Scientific publication is shifting from a print-oriented model of documentation and dissemination to a digital model where scientists can share their research openly and as it happens. We have shown how the research article is implicated in these changes, but other genres offer equally useful insights into open access in general and the open-data movement in particular. The practice of "open-notebook science" in particular embodies a range of possibilities for sharing information and tapping into the type of collective intelligence that open-access communities help to facilitate (see Bradley, 2008). What strikes us as useful about this practice is that, similar to the journal article, the notebook genre is beginning to evolve as scientists use it to respond to a changing media environment. It is not simply a top-down attempt to modify the ways in which scientists communicate their work; it is an attempt to adapt scientific communication to emerging technologies in a meaningful way. We see the open notebook itself as providing a useful analogy to a traditionally print-oriented genre: i.e., open-notebook science involves literally and figuratively opening up the most mundane details of one's intellectual work for public view and, potentially, public scrutiny. It is not only the sciences that can benefit from this type of open sharing. Indeed, scholars in the humanities stand to gain from making the most intimate details of their research available to academic and even public audiences. It is possible to imagine, for instance, that archival material gathered through painstaking research would be useful to others who investigate, or are simply curious about, similar subjects. Yet to value the research process itself—the art, the time, the effort, the funding—demands that we think more broadly about scholarship and what counts as viable intellectual work.

Open Access in the Humanities: Looking Forward

This chapter has focused primarily on the history of scientific communication and open-access publishing in the sciences. The concept of open access, however, is not necessarily new to researchers in the humanities. For instance, journals like *Postmodern Culture* (started in 1990) and *Kairos* (started in 1996) have been on the forefront of innovations that push the boundaries of academic publishing. Despite these promising developments, humanities disciplines have yet to experience an all-encompassing sea change with respect to scholarly publication. We would therefore like to close with some suggestions for how humanities scholars might begin to integrate principles of open access into their research and communication.

We believe that disciplines in the humanities can learn from the sciences—both in terms of successes and failures—but also develop their own approaches for dealing with open access in light of field-specific problems and concerns. Peter Suber (2004) discussed nine key differences between the sciences and humanities with respect to open-access publishing. These differences offer a basis for thinking about the current state of open access in the sciences and how some of these principles might benefit research and publication in the humanities. We believe four primary differences between science and humanities emerge from Suber's comparisons. These include the following: 1) Scientific research is better funded than work in the humanities, and more of it comes from federal agencies; 2) Acceptance rates for journal publications in the sciences are significantly higher than in the humanities; 3) Research in the sciences tends to be more time-sensitive than research in the humanities; and 4) Journal articles are the primary communication currency in the sciences, whereas humanities publications are a mixture of books and journal articles. These differences will impact how we in the humanities envision our scholarship based on open-access models of publishing.

With a larger pool of public funds, scientists have both the opportunity and the obligation to make their work more openly accessible to the public. In contrast, work in the humanities is often funded privately or by scholars' home institutions, making it more susceptible to proprietary practices. Any open-access approach must take into account these types of infrastructural restraints. More public funds have also led to an increasing number of journals in the sciences, which in turn has resulted in higher acceptance rates for those fields. The reverse is true in the humanities, where fewer publishing outlets exist. Academic presses that do exist are suffering from budget cuts, unlike large, profit-driven science publishers such as Elsevier and Wiley. Moving to online formats can potentially address some of these financial constraints. We have shown how publishing in open-access formats has benefited scientists who desire to share their publicly funded work without the lengthy delay that often attends print-based journal publishing. While humanities disciplines may have less of an imperative to publish their work in near-real time, they can nonetheless benefit from a more efficient process where their research gets disseminated to interested audiences. Finally, the research article genre has historically shaped scientific research and communication practices and will continue to do so. Humanities-based scholarship is less tied to this particular genre but will still face the challenge of adapting other genres, like the scholarly monograph, to digital formats.

The sciences have established an impressive record of adapting to and taking advantage of new technologies and open-access practices. The humanities have not been so quick to adapt to technological change due in part to the fact that a predominantly print-based intellectual tradition has not required radical shifts in the way it conceptualizes research and communication. We contend, however, that the diminished dominance of print texts, combined with ongoing developments in digital communication, is challenging traditional humanities approaches and thus invites a re-examination of issues related to publishing, authorship, and scholarly inquiry. More broadly, the humanities can learn from the kairotic awareness of scientists, who are able to identify scholarly needs and disciplinary values and then harness technological power to achieve large-scale community goals. We would argue that the humanities can do the same—not by copying the sciences but by examining what actually works and how we can apply strategic thinking to our own field and disciplines.

The digital humanities could learn from science's progression from a print-based infrastructure to a more open, digitally based cyber-infrastructure. What follows, specifically, are some questions that help to define what such an approach would involve: What do humanities-based disciplines value? What are their research needs? How might technology enhance those needs? To what extent have these questions been answered before, in the age of print, and how will the answers change with the rise of digital publishing? Should the digital humanities be concerned about issues of rising subscription costs and the explosion of online publishing? Scholarship in the digital humanities is responding to changes brought on, in part, by digital technologies, but little research follows this progress with descriptive studies and defining treatises that identify issues like the "data" valued by digital humanities scholars and the "laboratories" they use. We would thus suggest that there is a need for more studies that show how humanities scholars create, distribute, aggregate, read, and rank scholarly publications.

Notes

1 The NIH is the largest single funder of medical research in the world, and their policy affects more than 300,000 researchers nationwide (NIH, 2011); the 2012 budget was nearly $32 billion.

2 In opposition to the policy, publishers and the music industry joined together to form the Copyright Alliance. In both 2008 and 2009, the organization sponsored a Congressional bill, the Fair Copyright in Research Works Act, to outlaw open-access policies like that of the NIH. However, these bills were dismissed, and Presidents Bush and Obama signed bills to make the NIH policy permanent. Finally, in February 2013, the White House's Office of Science and Technology Policy released a memo directly to all large federal funding agencies to pursue an open-access program like that of the NIH, effectively circumventing further legislative action by the Copyright Alliance.

3 It is worth noting that Oldenburg, despite his role as secretary of the Royal Society, was independently responsible for editing and publishing the journal. According to Willinsky (2006), "the Royal Society of London held back for almost a century before becoming more than nominally involved in the publishing of the *Philosophical Transactions*" (pp. 55–56).

4 Although ISI declines to publicize its subscription fees, one 2000 estimate (Arms, 2000) placed the yearly subscription at $100,000 per year, which has risen steadily since. At least one North American institution, the University of Prince Edward Island, canceled its subscription when the ISI announced a price increase of 120% in one year, and many libraries in developing countries simply cannot afford to have subscriptions (Willinksy, 2006). Furthermore, a 2011 estimate of ISI's parent company, Thomson Reuters, places yearly revenues at $800 million (Price, 2011).

5 Thomson Reuters offers at least two pieces of evidence for this claim. The first is Bradford's Law, which contends that only 1,000 journals make up the core literature of any given scientific discipline, and the second is Thomson Reuters' own internal analysis of 7,621 journals included in the 2008 *Journal Citations Report*, which found that "50% of all citations generated by this collection came from only 300 of the journals" (Thomson Reuters, 2012).

6 Preprints have not historically played a major role in humanities scholarship, but the dissemination of such manuscripts has been increasing throughout the sciences in the late twentieth and early twenty-first centuries. Scientists have leveraged emerging technologies to make this possible. In the 1960s, for example, the mimeograph provided scientists the opportunity to reproduce their work for dissemination more quickly. So vital was the work of preprints that Garvey and Griffith included them in their 1964 flow chart showing the academic publication cycle (Borgman, 2007; Garvey & Griffith, 1964).

• CHAPTER FOUR •

Hindered Hope: Shepard Fairey, the Associated Press, and the Missed Opportunity to Help Clarify U.S. Copyright Law

Ben McCorkle

> Copyright is in tremendous flux at the moment; governments all over the world are considering what their copyright systems should look like in the 21st century, and it's probably a good idea to nail down what we want copyright to do. Otherwise the question "Is copyright working?" becomes as meaningless as "How long is a piece of string?"
>
> —Doctorow (2010)

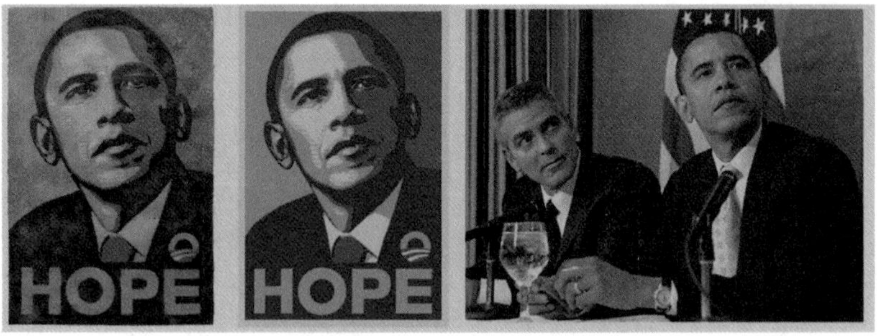

Figures 1, 2, and 3: Fairey's original mixed-media piece; Fairey's widely distributed "HOPE" design; Mannie Garcia's original 2006 AP photograph of then-Senator Barack Obama during a National Press Club event.

Shepard Fairey's iconic "HOPE" poster, which featured the likeness of Barack Obama and served as an enduring backdrop to the 2008 U.S. presidential election, will likely be remembered as one of the most impactful examples of visual rhetoric in contemporary American politics. Placed alongside examples such as the "I Like Ike" Eisenhower campaign button from 1951,

James Flagg's 1917 Uncle Sam recruitment poster, or the Lyndon B. Johnson campaign's infamous 1964 "Daisy" commercial depicting a young girl playing in a field juxtaposed with the ominous imagery of a mushroom cloud, Fairey's design—a remix of a newswire photograph of the then-Senator, heavily stylized and superimposed with a red, white, and blue color scheme, the word "HOPE" anchoring the design in all caps—evokes a similar sense of cultural heft, of *gravitas*, that has resonated with Obama supporters and detractors alike (see Figures 1, 2, 3). A sure sign of its cultural impact, the poster has been the subject of countless parodies and spoofs, targeting not only political figures such as Sarah Palin or John McCain, but people from the arenas of religion, such as the Pope, and popular culture, such as Amy Winehouse and Kanye West, as seen in Figures 4 and 5 (Barton, 2008; "Spoofing," 2008). It is largely on the strength of this cultural impact that Fairey's design also makes for a compelling potential case study concerning the legality of unattributed reappropriations used in derivative works, a test of Fair Use guidelines for the twenty-first century. That potential, as this chapter unfortunately details, has gone largely unrealized.

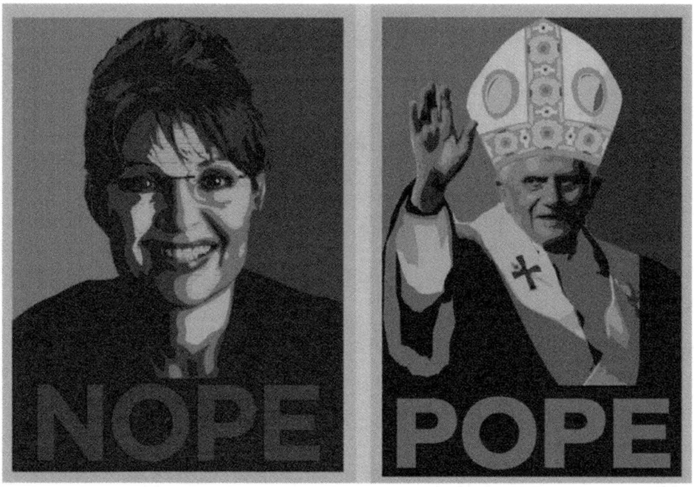

Figures 4 and 5. Two examples of some of the many parodies of Fairey's design, which circulate freely on the Web and typically target prominent figures from (L to R): religion (Pope Benedict XVI) and politics (Sarah Palin); other popular culture examples include Amy Winehouse ("Dope") and Optimus Prime ("CHANGE into a truck").

Fairey himself is no stranger to the visual aesthetic of the remix. He has long been a fixture in various youth subcultures, emerging as a kind of guerrilla graphic artist in the mid-1980s with his "Andre the Giant has a Posse" sticker campaign, a proto-viral, multi-city event that ironically featured the famous visage of the oversized professional wrestler. Fairey's designs served as a backdrop for the overlapping worlds of skateboarding, hardcore punk and hip-hop music, and activist politics. Even before the digital age, his collage-based designs anticipated remix-era styles, oftentimes reappropriating corporate logos, typefaces, imagery, slogans and other elements into new, parodic designs. More recently—and perhaps the surest indicator that he's fully arrived as an *habitué* of popular culture—Fairey made a cameo appearance in an episode of *The Simpsons* as part of an entourage of street artists who mentor Bart as he becomes a famous graffiti artist, arranging a gallery show of his work.

It's not a stretch to suggest that Fairey embodies the zeitgeist of today's mashup culture. A child of the 1970s and 1980s, his is the aesthetic of a pre-digital-age *bricoleur* who helped usher in a new era of remix, not unlike the transgressive filmmaker Richard Kern, deconstuctivist typographic designer David Carson, or punk rock fashion maven Vivienne Westwood. Yet in many ways, Fairey is a lot like the students we teach who produce digital media—someone who has the urge to bring together disparate items from the world around her in new, surprising combinations. In an interview for the web magazine *frontwheeldrive*, Fairey (who counts McLuhan, Debord, and Heidegger among his influences) explains that his artistic mission is ultimately phenomenological: "The first goal of phenomenology is to reawaken a sense of wonder about one's environment" (Christopher, 2007). Fairey's desire to blur the boundaries between highbrow and lowbrow, public and private, commercial and serious art, demonstrates that very sense of wonder.

The Birth of a Meme: Tracing "HOPE" Through Popular Culture

Fairey has become something more than just a boundary-muddling street artist within the last few years, largely owing to his 2008 "HOPE" poster. The image made an impact in the 2008 election, when it helped re-envision the genre of political art as something that can evoke feelings of idealism and transcendence in its viewers. Fairey's ultimate goal in his remixed design, according to an article for the "Arts & Living" section of *The Washington Post*, was to cast Obama as someone who was "wise, but not intimidating," a goal accomplished by the initial choice of photograph, the use of bold lines, geometric shapes, and a slightly tweaked patriotic color scheme (Booth, 2008). As Fairey himself described the poster's impact in a January 2009 interview with Terry Gross,

> Well, I think standard campaign posters are very safe. They use photographs. They don't take many liberties other than, you know, the usual patriotic American flag motifs and maybe a soft-focus blue background or something. And I think that people were just ready for something that had a little bit more of a unique approach and said, this is an iconic, confident image that isn't just about pandering to the lowest common denominator. I didn't make my image necessarily thinking that it would achieve the mainstream embrace that it has. I created it, in a lot of ways, for my usual audience, but

> hopefully, with the red, white and blue color palette, to be patriotic enough to transcend my audience of, I guess you could say, you know, progressive counter-culture types, because I really do believe that being patriotic is, you know, is about questioning your government when it's not making you proud, but also supporting it when it is. And with the opportunity to put Obama in the White House, you know, I felt like I needed to get behind that in a very patriotic way, and I needed an image that reflected that, but it still had to reflect my voice.

The cultural exposure of the image—and Fairey himself—has been extensive. The design's iconicity seems to invite remixes and reappropriations across the cultural landscape, for professionals and amateurs alike, and regardless of political affiliation. Since 2008, examples of this memetic play have percolated up from the lower strata of participatory culture to more established spheres of cultural significance, reflecting a strong desire to push at the traditional boundaries of copyright. In addition to the aforementioned examples of "HOPE" send-ups, variations of the image have spread to places as disparate as the cover design of columnist Robert Kuttner's 2008 popular political book *Obama's Challenge: America's Economic Crisis and the Power of a Transformative Presidency*, *The Advocate*'s Obama-critical, pink-and-lavender "NOPE?" cover from September 2009, and even a 2010 episode of the animated comedy *Futurama*, where the reanimated head of President Nixon (the thirty-first-century President of Earth) was accompanied by the caption "DESPAIR." That paragon of lampoonery, *MAD Magazine*, made the design a target in 2008 with a mock poster featuring mascot Alfred E. Neuman and accompanied by the caption "HOPELESS."

Fairey's own newfound celebrity has led to several notable media appearances, including street artist Banksy's 2010 mockumentary film *Exit Through the Gift Shop*, as well as *The Colbert Report*, where he designed a poster commemorating host Stephen Colbert; some of his other designs have appeared in a number of video games, including *Tony Hawk: Underground 2* and *CounterStrike*. In 2009, as Fairey's pop-culture stock was surging, he notably departed from his usual underground, anti-corporate antics to develop an advertising campaign for the department store Saks Fifth Avenue which, despite its commercial purpose, still managed to tweak corporate culture by aping Soviet-era Constructivist propaganda posters in its design language (Wilson, 2009).

Perhaps Fairey's biggest accolade, the original collage-style portrait on which the "HOPE" poster was based (see Figure 1) was put on display in the Smithsonian Institute's National Portrait Gallery in January of 2009. Yet despite such an exalted honor, "HOPE" has obviously struck a chord with the *hoi polloi* as well, transcending its function as a rarefied piece of political art and becoming, in effect, a durable cultural meme that circulates freely on the Internet and beyond. The design is eminently spoofable because it is so identifiable and relatively simple to replicate, especially with sites such as *Paste Magazine*'s Obamicon generator, which automatically adds a color overlay, filter, and caption to images that users decide to upload.

Flame and Fizzle: A Brief History of *Fairey v. The Associated Press*

In addition to its indisputable cultural impact, Fairey's design is also noteworthy as one of the digital era's first high-profile exhibits in the battle over intellectual property rights. In 2009, the iconoclastic graffitist and the Associated Press were entangled in what was initially shaping up to become a significant legal dispute hinging on whether or not the design was protected under Fair Use clause of U.S. copyright law, based largely on the purpose, market impact, and extent of transformation in the derivative work.

The way that Fairey's negotiations with the Associated Press have played out over the past 4 years has been, frankly, more than a little convoluted. In early 2009, the AP had been in talks with Fairey regarding credit and compensation for his unattributed appropriation of their wire photograph of Obama. In a preemptive move meant to curtail potential legal hassles from the AP, Fairey was the first to file suit, alleging that his poster is protected under Fair Use guidelines, asking a federal judge to rule accordingly (Kennedy, 2009, 2011). Right out of the gate, Fairey forced the issue, a seemingly bold strategic choice.

Fairey's argument, essentially, was that the poster constituted a Fair Use appropriation because not only was it sufficiently transformative–the stylization and superimposed color scheme resulted in a piece dramatically different from the source text–it also served a different purpose from the original photograph–political art as opposed to journalism. In a statement from Fairey's legal team, which included the Fair Use Project's executive director Anthony Falzone, the design only used the photograph as a starting point, that Fairey eventually created a "stunning, abstracted and idealized visual image that created powerful new meaning and conveys a radically different message" (Kennedy, 2009). Because of these factors, the poster did not threaten the original photograph's position in the marketplace. Additionally, the roughly $400,000 he generated in poster sales was all donated to the Obama campaign, so he didn't directly profit from the design (Wortham, 2008).

The Associated Press, on the other hand, sought credit and compensation based upon Fairey's use of their original photograph once they confirmed the design's provenance. Claiming that it was used without necessary permission, and that the poster had generated sales revenue to which the news service felt it had a claim, the AP initially attempted to reach a friendly agreement with Fairey; as AP media relations director Paul Colford said in an official statement in early 2009, "AP safeguards its assets and looks at these events on a case-by-case basis. We have reached out to Mr. Fairey's attorney and are in discussions. We hope for an amicable solution" (Italie, 2009). Fairey and his legal representation, however, felt that the AP's efforts were more coercive than amicable, which led him to file suit.

To further complicate matters, the legitimacy of the Associated Press's claim of copyright was called into question once the source image was definitively identified. Ironically, the self-same Internet that gifted Fairey with the image in the first place—he claims to have found it via a Google Image search—was also instrumental in solving the mystery of exactly which photograph and photographer Fairey used. A highly motivated community of bloggers eventually determined that Mannie Garcia was the original photographer (Kennedy, 2009). Garcia, technically a freelance employee for the AP at the time, alleged that he retained the rights to his work, maintaining in an interview for *Fresh Air with Terry Gross* that

> the dispute I have with AP and… the Associated Press has with me, is coming down to whether or not there was a contract or what kind of contract. Since I had never been a freelancer for the Associated Press prior to working with them on this, I don't have that freelance photographer's agreement.

Although he admitted feeling flattered by Fairey's appropriation of his image, Garcia also claimed in the same interview that he "was disappointed in the fact that, you know, someone had—was able to go onto the Internet and take something that doesn't belong to them and then use it." Garcia considered filing suit, and eventually intervened in Fairey's suit as a defendant alongside the AP, issuing cross-complaints that the AP itself had no grounds to claim ownership of the photograph. Additionally, he claimed that certain elements of his original work, among them the choice of moment, the shot angle, and framing, constituted the photograph's essence—according to Garcia, Fairey's appropriation did nothing to transform that essence (Boyden, 2009).

With a lawsuit pending and a decision imminent, what happened next surprised many of those who were following the case closely (this writer included). In a somewhat frustrating resolution to this fracas, Fairey and the Associated Press underwent mediation and in early 2011 hammered out a workable solution to the copyright dispute before a verdict on the case could be delivered. According to reporting by *The New York Times*, the terms of the out-of-court settlement meant that neither side conceded their viewpoints; furthermore, the would-be litigants would now share the rights of any HOPE-related creations moving forward (posters, t-shirts, stickers, etc.), would collaborate on a future project that will feature AP photographs redesigned by Fairey, and would abide by an undisclosed financial settlement (Kennedy, 2011). While the mediated agreement might work for the principal parties involved, it did not help clarify the oftentimes murky status of appropriating digital artifacts for the public at large. Those of us wanting a clear legal precedent pertaining to digital-era intellectual property/copyright issues will unfortunately be disappointed for the time being.

In fact, the last important legal statement on Fair Use is a product of the analog age. The "Betamax case" (*Sony Corp. of America v. Universal City Studios,*

Inc.) was decided by the U.S. Supreme Court in 1984. This case determined that the practice of non-commercial "time shifting," or recording televised content with a videocassette recorder to be viewed privately at a later time, was ultimately a legitimate exercise of Fair Use and did not constitute copyright infringement (Lee, 2005, pp. 147–148). Subsequent court decisions based upon this precedent in the Internet era, particularly those against peer-to-peer file sharing services like Napster, Aimster, and Grokster, concluded that such technologies *can* be held liable for inducing copyright infringement (Lee, pp. 154–155). These decisions partially eroded the Betamax argument that because a particular technology can be used for illegal purposes but otherwise facilitates appropriate Fair Use practices, this doesn't mean that the makers of that technology are to be held liable, any more than gun manufacturers can be held liable for a specific murder, or a manufacturer of cigarette lighters can be held liable for a particular instance of arson. Today, the incapability of the antiquated Betamax decision to deal adequately with the copying, dissemination, and transformation of digital content is becoming increasingly apparent. No longer is the cultural paradigm centered around copying and redistributing content simply for the sake of consumption; increasingly, we are shifting more and more into a period marked by practices of production, based largely on appropriation of pre-existing content, and our legal precedents should clearly demarcate when such practices are legitimate and protected, and when they stray too far.

Now What? The Aftermath of an Out-of-Court Settlement

For many different factions—digital artists, consumer advocacy groups, copyleftists, and so on—the Fairey/AP mediation was a deflating outcome. For rhetoric and composition scholars who specialize in digital media studies in particular, the deferment of a solid precedent places us in a kind of professional limbo. It is within such a limbo that concerns persist around the potential legal, ethical, and professional liabilities that we expose ourselves and our students to when producing digital media content. Clearer articulation of Fair Use cases would go a long way towards allaying those concerns. As we develop pedagogies and create scholarship based on real-world genres and practices of textual production, the real-world implications of such production need to be taken into account, even and especially those that might place our students at risk, legal or otherwise.

Those who create (or have their students create) mashups, remixes, parodies, collages, montages, and similar digital texts that often incorporate other content are understandably uncertain moving forward, as questions continue to revolve around the publication and dissemination of derivative works, regardless of their scholarly or artistic merit.

This isn't simply a matter of being able to have students create work using other people's source material for the fun of it. It also has to do with educating students on the issues surrounding these practices, especially since many of them participate in making remixed texts out in the wild, so to speak. Our students may be genuinely uninformed about Fair Use guidelines, in fact. Technology writer and Kickstarter co-founder Andy Baio (2011) recently wrote on what he recognized as an increasingly prevalent trend on YouTube: the use of vague, "no copyright infringement intended" statements in descriptions for remixed video. Baio's musings on this trend highlighted one user's statement in particular, which accompanied a chronologically re-ordered edit of *Pulp Fiction* and read in part, "the legendary movie itself placed into chronological order. If you'd like me to put the full movie itself up, let me know and I'll be glad to oblige. Please no copyright infringement. I only put this up as a project" (Baio; see also Nguyen, this volume). Baio goes on to describe the utter confusion that YouTube users exhibit when it comes to copyright concerns (not only in individual video descriptions, but in YouTube's own support forums, or in comments sections in their own attempt to inform users on the subject, the YouTube Copyright School). According to Baio, this confusion is to be expected, especially since the new normal of digital production for so many younger users is at odds with current interpretations of copyright law:

> Under current copyright law, nearly every cover song on YouTube is technically illegal. Every fan-made music video, every mashup album, every supercut, every fanfic story? Quite probably illegal, though largely untested in court.

No amount of lawsuits or legal threats will change the fact that this behavior is considered normal; I'd wager the vast majority of people under 25 see nothing wrong with non-commercial sharing and remixing, or think it's legal already.

Given such uncertainty, it makes sense for those of us in rhetoric and composition to devote attention to clarifying, advising, and weighing in on policy matters pertaining to copyright and guiding principles of fair use. In a recent CCCC Intellectual Property Committee report, Troy Hicks (2010) explained that a critical understanding of Fair Use is about far more than just insulating our students from potential infringement—it also facilitates a greater contextual and rhetorical understanding of what it means to appropriate material in the course of creating new arguments or analyses:

> As we invite students to create new media compositions, and use existing copyrighted materials to do so, we need [to] approach their work with the critical lens that fair use allows. Through discussions of fair use and the transformative nature of their own work, we ask them to be critical and creative thinkers, engaging them in discussions with one another about the ways in which they remix the work of others. Also, we need to reiterate that fair use does not mean unlicensed distribution of copyrighted materials.

> Teaching our students how to repurpose copyrighted materials in a transformative manner is the essence of applying fair use guidelines, and is an imperative skill when teaching them how to compose with new media.

Only within the last few years have we been truly attentive to these issues; we owe it to students we work with to become their advocates as well as their educators. The onus is largely on us to equip students, many of whom will leave our classrooms to join the ranks of participatory culture, with as great a sense of the ethical, logical, and critical dimensions informing intellectual property concerns as we are able. Moreover, in our roles as scholars, activists, policy advisors, and so on, we owe it to our field, our students, and our greater citizenry to advocate and demand clearer Fair Use freedoms and restrictions. For better or worse, we help preserve and propagate the continued health of culture by prescribing and proscribing conventions and practices of production; we mentor and teach the next generations of communicators. To a greater extent than we perhaps realize (or are comfortable admitting), we are in the culture business. It's time that we acted like it.

So what can we do? Where can we identify sites for resistance or spaces to effect change? For one, we can easily raise awareness about Creative Commons, public domain, and related open content resources in our own classes by designing assignments encouraging students to use (and give credit to) such content appropriately, thus fostering a culture more accommodating of derivative creation. Additionally, as my institution's first-year composition program has done, we can make open content, Creative Commons, and Fair Use an actual part of the first-year writing curriculum, to further educate students on the central issues surrounding intellectual property and give them occasion to consider these issues more fully. In my own case, I've even used Fair Use guidelines as a central component of assessment in a digital media composing course, an instrument that serves as a heuristic for students as they conceptualize and plan video remix projects, frames their rationales for creating the remixes, and informs my own evaluation of the finished product (Delagrange, Braun, & McCorkle, 2013). Even beyond our home departments, we should strive to be instrumental in helping to establish policies—with our campus libraries, our institutional administration, and larger consortiums—that articulate best practices for using, transforming, and acknowledging derivative works. Of course, we can also create scholarship—this present collection obviously being one example—that increases the visibility of intellectual property issues in contexts other than legal discourse, causing more people to feel empowered to weigh in on such pressing matters.

With bills such as SOPA (Stop Online Privacy Act), PIPA (Protect IP Act), and most recently CISPA (Cyber Intelligence Sharing and Protection Act) threatening to break the gravitation pull of the legislative process and become law, digital technology use promises to become an increasingly constrained, monitored activity. These constraints, however, are more concerned with the "what?" and the "how much?" of our digital practices rather than the "what for?" In the non-case of Fairey v. AP, we were teased with the unrealized promise of clarity concerning the limits of how we can use pre-existing content. This was a missed opportunity, and moving forward, we need clearer guidelines to help define the boundaries of Fair Use; we should remain hopeful that such a clarifying opportunity will present itself to us in the near future.

***

In a somewhat tragic postscript to this tale, albeit on a more personal scale, Shepard Fairey pled guilty to one charge of criminal contempt on February 24, 2012, a formal plea that came more than two years after Fairey admitted to the U.S. Attorney's Office that he had destroyed and fabricated evidence in the course of the official AP investigation (Ng, 2012). Facing a maximum penalty of 6 months in jail, one year of supervised release, and a $5,000 fine, Fairey was handed a sentence in September 2012 that was ultimately much lighter: 2 years of probation (Remizowski, 2012). Nevertheless, this coda highlights the squandered opportunity on Fairey's part to pursue the case more aggressively, to have a little more faith in the judicial system's ability to clarify the status of his work. That way, Fairey not only could have settled this matter for himself, no doubt bringing him some much needed peace of mind, he also could have become (excuse the pun) a kind of poster boy for an entire community of digital media producers in the remix era, present and future. As things stand now, however, he'll have to settle for the prospect of remaining one of the *enfants terrible* of the contemporary art world, while the rest of us will have to wait just a little longer for a resolution to these legal matters.

• CHAPTER FIVE •

New Digital Production Models: The Consolidation of the Copyleft

Joan Francesc Fondevila Gascón and Raúl López García-Navas

In this chapter we analyze digital production models and the changes experienced by the culture industries with a change in roles of production and distribution. The progress of approaches like copyleft generates a new framework for understanding cultural products. The history of international trade also reflects some progress that helps to explain the current situation of culture and entertainment industries. After the end of World War II, several countries began to seek trade liberalization; in 1947, as a result, a cluster of countries launched different measures, such as approving the General Agreement on Tariffs and Trade (GATT) or entering into negotiations on the Charter of the International Trade Organization (ITO). Three years later, succumbing to the ITO project, GATT became the sole multilateral framework regulating international trade.

Later, between 1970 and 1980, states began to consider certain issues to deal with the problems presented by new technologies (Pérez, 2004). The World Intellectual Property Organization (WIPO) offered a uniform movement forward, seen reflected in changes to national legislation of each country. From then until the mid-1990s rounds of negotiations were carried out to reduce tariffs and strengthen the multilateral system. The Uruguay Round, between 1986 and 1994, was the last and most important, as it gave rise to the current World Trade Organization (WTO) and a new set of agreements.

Of the 1994 WTO agreements, most relevant here is the Agreement on Trade-Related Intellectual Property Rights (TRIPS), made necessary due to the tensions between different countries because of an absence of a multilateral framework for dealing with international trade in counterfeit goods. The TRIPS Agreement, which launched January 1, 1996, sought to establish common rules concerning intellectual property and the proper recognition and enforcement of those rules. The ultimate goal was to overcome differences that existed in this area among the different member countries.

This agreement (Fernández Ballesteros, 2006; OMPI, 1996a, 1996b) also arose as a consequence of how the management mechanisms of IP rights could have a negative impact on the benefits of their owners, which in turn influenced the economics of their countries. Member States came to this conclusion after the massive influx of counterfeit products, the elimination of trade barriers, the lack of some states that penalize infringements, and the rapid development of new technologies. As a result, the priority of participating nations was the implementation of an effective mechanism of IP protection and control. The TRIPS Agreement appears to address three major challenges: emerging technology, the disappearance of global market barriers, and piracy (Del Río & Sagarduy, 2008; Gómez Aguiar, 2009; Prado, 2005).

The TRIPS Agreement was not enough to overcome the difficulties presented by new technologies, including digital networks and tools. In late 1996, WIPO developed a series of treaties that updated copyright and gained new strength (Fernández Ballesteros, 2006): the Treaty of the Internet; the WIPO Copyright or ALL (English WCT); and the Treaty of the WIPO Performances and Phonograms Treaty, or WPPT (in English WPPT).

In recent years, the world market has undergone some changes that follow the logic of capitalism (Sánchez Tabernero et al., 1993). One of the most important has been the wave of mergers that has occurred between powerful corporations (Grupo ETC, 2008) and the result has been a concentration of corporations. This phenomenon is illustrated by analyzing how the market is distributed. Patented seeds, for instance, account for 82% of that market, where the percentage of the top 10 companies account for 67% and the top three represent 47%. In the market for pesticides, the first six companies account for 74% of market share.

The 10 largest foods and beverage companies make up 35% of the income earned by the top 100 companies in the same sector. In 2007, these 100 companies earned 74% of total worldwide sales of packaged food products. The top 10 biotech industries earned 66% of industry revenues that same year. Clearly, companies are becoming fewer but larger, with more power to impose products and consumption patterns, determine working conditions, or shape conditions of unemployment. Further, they lobby U.S. Congress, world governments, and international institutions to achieve the standards and laws they deem necessary (Ribeiro, 2007).

These changes, in the framework of the Broadband Society (Fondevila Gascón, 2008, 2012), the Information and Knowledge Society (European Commission, 1994) and the Network Society (Castells, 1997), are a sign of change occurring in the global economy, which in turn could make us think that capitalism is being reconfigured (Rifkin, 2000).

New Digital Production Models: The Culture Industry

One of the paradigms best suited to answer questions that emerge with the changes described above can be found in the so-called culture industry, called, in the U.S., the entertainment industry. This term goes back to the 1940s (Adorno and Horkheimer are its greatest proponents). The culture industry is a

> set of branches, segments and ancillary production and distribution of goods with symbolic content, conceived by a creative, organized by a capital that is valued and intended ultimately to the consumer, with a playback function ideological and social. (Bustamante & Zallo, 1988; see, also, Zallo, 1992)

The term "culture industry" covers a wide range of means of cultural production and media (theater, television, dance, music, video or radio, etc.). Traditionally, the academic study of the culture industries focused on the sectors dedicated to the production or the commercialization of books, press, radio, television, and audiovisual products, but in the last years there has been a consensus to include in this classification activities like arts, theater, and music. In general, public policies about the culture industry connect local creation with the worldwide environment. We observe a mix of local reinforcement and commercialization spirit: creating and surviving, local and global, brick and mortar.

Global trading in culture industries is difficult to harmonize (Colbert, 2000). The spread could be in cultural handicraft sectors (selling a unique prototype in arts, or repeating a prototype in interpretive arts), in the product perspective (addressed to potential customers), in the culture industry sectors (improving thanks to technical progress and digitization) and in the market (from customer needs to the definition of product). With digitization, the production, commercialization, and marketing models—along with the management of these models—have changed. The convergence (Igarza, 2007) and the digital phenomena allow this kaleidoscopic sector a new exciting range of possibilities, like a constant flow of contents (e.g., cloud journalism; Fondevila, 2010a).

In this chapter we focus on music. A *priori* it may be an area that best represents transition, due to the different situations in recent years, as reflected by changes in media. The vinyl record, whose origins are in the late nineteenth century and whose existence continued almost throughout the twentieth century, gave prominence in the mid-1960s and early 1970s to the cassette, with more compact size and better sound quality. In the mid-1980s, the Walkman increased the rapid growth of cassette tapes, clearly leaving behind vinyl records in sales. However, the compact disc (CD) emerged in 1984, tentatively present in the worlds of music and computer science. The decline of cassettes was inversely proportional to the growth of CDs.

Moreover, and paradoxically, history repeated itself. In the mid-1980s, the digital audio format was developed, but it did not come to light until some 10 years later. Soon after, thanks mainly to programs like Napster (1999), the MP3 reached surprising heights of popularity and triggered a corresponding decline in CD sales. With this final technology, the case is more complex, as it became popular among users first, but was not fully taken into account in the commercial field. It took some years for the music industry to realize the profitability of digital music files.

The disappearance of the CD, therefore, will not be because of piracy, but rather will be due to a generational change toward music, and this isn't a particularly new change, when we look historically. However, the incursion of the digital age in the market is giving rise to new challenges—issues that require attention in our modern, digital times.

From Copyright to Copyleft

One of the challenges to appear in this new millennium and that has already generated considerable controversy is intellectual property. The culture industry wants to continue a business model and a concept of copyright established more than 20 years ago, without realizing changes in reality. However, currently other proposals different from and more flexible than copyright—such as the idea of copyleft—have emerged, and have been reflected in, for instance, the General Public License (GPL; Stallman, 1989). The origins of computers allow us to understand implications and possibilities that copyleft offers, as computer development is the area where the concept of copyleft emerged.

In the 1960s and 1970s, and hacker culture that arose around it, tools and source code were freely available for the vast majority of computer programs. Collaboration is part of old habits of the scientific community (Vidal, 2000). However, in the 1980s, this type of behavior begin to disappear, because the price of computers decreased at the same time computer power and storage capacity increased (see Moore's and Metcalfe's Law, in Gilder, 2002). The business of software changed shape.

Still, some developers continued to be faithful to the standard of the 1970s and early 1980s and opposed the privatization and commercialism of the software industry. That's when Richard Stallman (1989), a programmer at the Massachusetts Institute of Technology (MIT), decided to launch the GNU Project by the Free Software Foundation (FSF), with the aim of creating a completely free operating system and applications. Richard Stallman framed his approaches with four basic freedoms for software users: running, studying and adapting, distributing, and improving the program freely. On the GNU site (2011), that idea is summarized as follows:

- Freedom 0: freedom to run the program, for any purpose;
- Freedom 1: freedom to study how the program works, and adapt it to the user needs; access to source code is a precondition.
- Freedom 2: freedom to redistribute copies so the user can help others.
- Freedom 3: freedom to improve the program and release improvements, and modified versions in general, to benefit the whole community. Access to source code is a precondition.

The General Public License GPL (General Public License), promoted by the FSF in the 1980s, was created with the intention of protecting free software. The great importance of this license is that it is the embodiment of the copyleft concept, ensuring that the fruit of cooperation and collective intelligence be freely available public goods and that any development resulting from them becomes public and free.

Many definitions exist to explain copyleft. For instance, Joshua Gay (2002) explained copyleft as a *method* to convert a free software program, and to situate that all modified and extended versions of the program are also free. Arguably, copyleft is an idea similar to copyright, but much less restrictive than the latter. Difficulties of copying, modifying, and distributing the work disappear, provided that derivative works are under the same rights as the original and clearly expressed authorship (López, 2009a, 2009b). Furthermore, Vidal believed that

> Stallman invented the concept of copyleft, with the political purpose of ensuring the free movement of knowledge contained in the software and the possibility that all contribute to its improvement. Copyleft uses copyright international laws to give them back (all rights reversed) which protects the use of the property instead.

The appearance of copyleft opens new possibilities to participate in cultural life in a more free, democratic, and responsive way, as the stagnant copyright conventions and laws have been unable to adapt to new technologies.

As a result, a growing concern has emerged for finding a new model, able to adapt to new technological and social needs of the moment. Copyleft has other positive implications in the development process of society; by creating viable cultural markets, a wide variety of cultural events can be recovered by citizens, who can hold decision-making power over our culture (Smiers & Van Schijndel, 2008). Until recently, the term "free software" was rarely heard, and key issues do remain to be answered (Sádaba, 2005) to meet some of the factors that have helped the expansion of copyleft. These issues related to the existence of cooperative phenomena in cultural communication and free software, its emergence at this historical moment, or its existence in one context and not in another. Some answers are based on game theory, whose object is the analysis of the interrelationships between two or more individuals, and the search for optimal model performance (Martínez, 2009).

The first question about the reason for the existence of cooperative phenomena could be answered with the following conclusion drawn from game theory, as the number of iterations grows the level of collaboration between the various strategies (Martínez, 2009): In games, like "prisoner's dilemma," cooperation and long-term gains exist and are necessary, but on the other hand, the selfish, short-term skills emerge due to a small number of iterations or repetitions. This means that in a climate where there is lots of cooperation, the partners will eventually win; in a climate where cooperation is scarce, benefits will only be short term.

But if these cooperative phenomena are so beneficial for all, we must question why they have not been used before. According to Rodríguez Sádaba (2005), cooperation is beneficial and functionally adaptive when individuals share and generate enough profit for all. The rise and progress of information technology and communication, catalyzed by the Internet, suggest that the massive expansion and popularization of global access to new information technologies has created a context for the achievement of collaboration (Sádaba). Consequently, the more people cooperate with each other, the more it will help to keep alive collaborative strategies, which will benefit everyone involved, but how will such strategies get more staff? We next move to a discussion of this question.

The Copyleft and the Broadband Society

Today the production of knowledge has as a main purpose economic benefit, which results in knowledge understood solely as a commodity. Therein lies a major obstacle to both the expansion of copyleft and for the development of the knowledge society—that is, the need of universal and guaranteed broadband and the establishment of agreements between the telecommunication operators and the content providers to obtain micropayments.

Gradually changing, however, is the social, technological, and creative environment in the way of thinking and the way citizens interact with the world around them. All this has taken place because they have overcome traditional limitations, largely through the influence of information technology and communication technology (ICT) and the Internet (global interconnectedness). These, in turn, have created ideal conditions for the progress of the collaborative strategies of copyleft and free software, where the latter has fostered a different way to see and feel and, to point out the problems and opportunities of uncertainty (Alberich & Roig, 2008; Fondevila Gascón, 2010b).

Copyleft has been an engine of free software, but the latter, in turn, has had a major impact on other areas not related to computer science. There are other areas—including industrial, medical, audiovisual, scientific, economic, and social—that use software. As a result of the expansion of free software, activities in some areas have grown because the areas can access a larger number of tools best suited to their work (Abella, Sánchez, & Segovia, 2004). A large number of research, scholarly, and social areas are enhancing and improving their work thanks to the proliferation of free software.

If the idea of copyleft could be transported to the creation and management of content and cultural knowledge, we might imagine an unprecedented tool for the advancement of society. Currently, there are a number of licenses that allow users to apply the concept of copyleft to non-computer devices. Thus the advantages of free software can also be applied to creations of any kind, whether cultural, artistic, and scientific, all thanks to new licensing approaches based on copyleft.

The difficulties and controversies around ways to protect culture, creativity, copyright, remuneration, and distribution of note to copyleft include transformation and its role in the evolution of future models of creation, production, and cultural management. Benefits are starting to spread to small markets and, therefore, a market focused on a few products can no longer provide income (Del Río & Sagarduy, 2008). An example of this can be observed in Amazon.com, where there are several elements that have made their success possible, but one of them is the large number of products whose target audience is a few. Their strategy has led Amazon to benefit greatly from a small market (Miguel de Bustos, 2007).

The culture industries are not in danger because of piracy. From another perspective, some elements of the culture industry value chain are in danger of disappearing because alternatives have emerged that make them expendable. The case is illustrative of record labels, which, through a range of technological, social, and economic means, they controlled almost the entire process production and sales process—from album creation to store delivery. Most of these benefits were for them. This trend of revenues from the sale of recorded music is changing. Times Online Lab (2009) conducted a study and reported that the "best artists live in a world of illegal file sharing." The study concluded that the growth of live entertainment revenue showed no signs of decline and that live music was by far the most lucrative part of the income industry to the artists themselves, because they get a large percentage of money from the tickets. In the case of recorded music distribution, benefits are 90% companies and 10% artists. In the case of live music, this distribution is 10% promoters and 90% artists. The privileged position and control in the process of music creation and distribution is shifting.

Copyleft and Peer-to-peer Distribution

To date, the music industry at large has struggled with how to interpret the combined interests of consumers with the potential of new technologies to provide a business model adapted to the times. Even in a moment of "cloud" networking, the culture industries offer few portals from which users can easily and seamlessly acquire content. In the few cases, as of 2013, where this possibility is provided, prices aren't an economic advantage. If the means are available to buy are few and those few have abusive prices, consumers will likely not be willing to choose digital delivery or digital viewing options.

On the other hand, it is necessary to highlight that today the barrier of space disappears with the Internet. Torrent sites and peer-to-peer networks allow access to cultural property from anywhere in the world. The ease of access poses a range of options unthinkable until recently, for instance, variety allows users to break the homogeneity of cultural tastes that existed in the past. Groups like Stormy Mondays or Miss Caffeina gained popularity through digital spaces. Other musicians are exploring and experimenting with new ways of producing, broadcasting, and distributing their music (Albuu, 2010). And while this decision is a significant undertaking, many artists prefer to work in these conditions because they can potentially have more control over the artistic and economic aspects of their music. Many also consider record labels as an obstacle to their profession; for this reason, many of them acknowledge that they have been forced to seek alternative ways to deal with some of the difficulties in the recording industry.

Trends such as the ones we see in the music industry occur with torrent, peer-to-peer, and other Internet environments, which promote—along with, of course, Web 2.0 tools—a participatory approach and a range of sharing tools. Unidirectional communication potentially stops, and exchange and modification of information between users becomes the order of the day, in turn generating new data and tools. This encourages the participation of users who go from being mere spectators/consumers to becoming true content creators, with growth enhanced in proportion to the number of users (Fondevila Gascón, 2009a).

Below, we offer case studies to show that cultural content can be offered in a free and open access way that is economically viable. These examples have in common the platform from which their work is financed and distributed: digital networks.

Radiohead and NIN

The British band Radiohead decided to release *In Rainbows* in late 2007 in a peculiar way: Anyone could get the album at the price she thought best. Popular press reports of the monetization (or not) of digital content might indicate that the most logical thing would be for users to download the album for free, without paying anything for it. Not so: The average price paid was half the value of a traditional CD, and the album reached 1.2 million downloads.

The band Nine Inch Nails (NIN) worked with a record company and under typical copyright licensing until 2007. In 2009, Trent Reznor, at the helm of the band, published the album *Ghost I–IV* under a Creative Commons license (BY-NC-SA). As Nate Anderson (2008) reported,

> those who would pay nothing could download a free version of Ghosts I. For $5, there was a digital version 4 album.... For $75 and $300 deluxe versions were available, the latter limited to 2500 copies sold in 3 days.

Even with the variable-cost download offering, *Ghost I–IV* was the best-selling MP3 album on Amazon in 2008 (Benenson, 2009).

NIN decided to take that step in 2008 because of dissatisfaction with their record label. There are certainly other cases of bands other than Radiohead and NIN who have had disagreements with their label. La Excepción, for instance, decided to provide their album *The Real Truth* as a protest against Warner. As Laura Arambarri Ferrer (2009) pondered: "From each disk, The Exception gets a 10 percent split between three people. Do you think you can eat with that?" In her piece, Ferrer also pointed out that royalties are only distributed perhaps every six months, and checks often come late. Without a corporate intermediary, The Exception could potentially make 100% of their music's earnings, as was the case with Radiohead and NIN.

Tribe of Noise

There are, of course, examples of companies that have proposed a business model more in line with customers' digital demands, better leveraging new technologies and, in some cases, providing copyleft-oriented licenses. Tribe of Noise is one such example. The company provides a link between musicians and professionals who need access to music artists, facilitating contact between stakeholders and providing additional services (e.g., setting music files under specific licensing requirements for certain accounts; implementing useful management; providing sound engineering services). Tribe of Noise demonstrates a functional and fruitful connection between a web site and the daily work of composers, musicians, and those who rely upon access to music (publishers, film producers, television producers, video game designers, etc.).

Tribe of Noise was born publicly by the hand of Hessel van Oorschot and Sandra Brandenburg on July 14, 2008 (Bastille Day), with 350 musicians and 100 other members. Currently there are more than 7,000 participants, 80% of whom are musicians, songwriters, and composers from 40 countries. Tribe of

Noise has established strong physical contacts, for instance by visiting trade shows, and a strong digital network, through spaces like Twitter, Facebook, and LinkedIn; their work has been touted through newspapers, magazines, and radio.

The Tribe of Noise site uses a Creative Commons 3.0 BY-SA (authoring and sharing the same) license, which fits within the concept of copyleft. Therefore, they can protect the rights of both the authors/producers and also the end users. Tribe of Noise is an example that there can be a viable business model behind copyleft licensing. Tribe of Noise allows companies whose business models rely on copyleft a range of advantages, like having content immediately shared, saving months of negotiations. For a given project, as of 2013, Tribe of Noise coordinates the negotiations between the amount of viewing or copying allowed, the distribution media used, the time of use, and more. In most negotiations with Creative Commons licenses, it does not matter if a copy or a billion copies are distributed; if they are issued locally, nationally or internationally; or if they are in use for a day, a month, or 10 years.

Conclusion

The emergence of the current digital era was a clear change in the form of accessing, understanding, distributing, and managing literary and artistic works. These changes have been reflected in the difficulties that have emerged globally in managing intellectual property. The basis on which copyright was structured can, to some extent, now be considered obsolete. In awareness of this obsolescence, countries have necessarily adapted their IP laws, policies, and approaches.

Copyright, as it has historically existed and applied to physical artifacts, is often an unnecessary obstacle in the sharing and accessing of information, and of literary and artistic works. Copyright applies the brakes on the development of the knowledge society and creates a chasm of a digital divide between producers and consumers. The revolution created by the digital age—and by peer-to-peer networking, torrenting, and the Internet at large—has made obsolete many of our current intellectual property approaches. We urgently need new models to regulate this entire cultural conglomerate.

This new model could be based on the copyleft, because we now know the necessary conditions for its development, and because its effectiveness is already proven in the computer industry and in music distribution. If the concept of copyleft could be adapted to other areas, the benefits gained would surely be similar and would help, no doubt, in the development of the Broadband Society. Framing all of these changes and the potential for new models are shifts in our capitalist mentality. Knowledge is trending to be a commodity. That is, attitudes are changing; people are migrating away from having and more toward sharing.

CHAPTER SIX

"Not a Category of Constitutional Significance": *Golan v. Holder* and the Future of the Public Domain

Traci Zimmerman

On January 18, 2012, the Supreme Court handed down its decision in *Golan v. Holder*, a case centered on the question of whether Congress may retroactively restore copyright to foreign works in the U.S. public domain. The answer to this question? Yes, they can. For Lawrence Golan, a music professor and conductor, January 18, 2012, could quite possibly be the day the music died. For Golan, and other conductors like him, the removal of works from the public domain meant that he suddenly had limited access to pieces that he had been playing freely for years. "It was a shocking change," Golan said, "you used to be able to buy[1] Prokofiev, Shostakovich, Stravinsky. All of a sudden, on one day, you couldn't anymore" (Parry, 2011a).

If there has been any "sure thing" in the complex and often confusing world of copyright law and IP regulations, it has been this: Once information passes into the public domain, it is free for all to use. But the decision in *Golan v. Holder* casts even this surety into the realm of uncertainty (Zimmerman, 2012). In a rather striking statement, one that certainly challenges if not completely redefines the "traditional copyright balance between private and public interests," the Court declared that "neither the Copyright and Patent Clause nor the First Amendment... makes the public domain, in any and all cases, a territory that works may never exit" (McSherry, 2012).

This "now you see it, now you don't" definition is what inspired Anthony Falzone, one of Golan's lawyers and the executive director of The Fair Use Project, to argue to the Supreme Court in October 2011 that Congress violated the First Amendment and Copyright Clause when it pulled works out of the public domain and essentially re-copyrighted them. Falzone argued that the value of the public domain is destroyed if "the rug can be pulled out from you at any time" (Parry, 2011b).

Golan's fight is centered on the concept of the public domain—more to the point, how it is defined and defended—as such, it touches "a broad swath of academe for years to come, dictating what materials scholars can use in books and courses without jumping through legal hoops" (Parry, 2011b). Understanding the stakes in this case (and what precedent it sets for future decisions) is critical to understanding the culture of copyright in the United States. Consider that this 2012 Supreme Court decision was based on a model of copyright that was enacted well before the Internet existed in anything like its present form (McSherry, 2012). Consider the stark contrast between the timing of the SOPA/PIPA protests—protests that illuminated the public's outrage at overreaching copyright law—and the announcement of the decision of *Golan v. Holder*. It is too painfully poignant to be mere coincidence that both the protest and the decision occurred on the same day. In fact, Mike Masnick (2012), blogging for *Techdirt*, went so far as to say that the Supreme Court chose the SOPA/PIPA protest day to announce their decision to "give a giant middle finger to the public domain."

But the case of *Golan v. Holder* is not merely a philosophical argument about the value of public domain or the interpretation of the U.S. Constitution. It is a case about real people whose creative lives have been limited by Congressional action. Golan's concerns extend beyond the realms of sheet music and scores; they extend to libraries and archives, since the 1994 law he sought to overturn has "hobbled efforts to digitize and share books, films, and music" (Parry, 2011b). Beyond all of the parties affected is the sheer volume of works that have been pulled from the public domain by the 1994 law. Although the exact number of works is unknown, Marybeth Peters (then U.S. Register of Copyrights) noted in 1996 that it would "probably number in the millions" (Liptak, 2012). And with the 2012 *Golan v. Holder* decision, we have lost even the assurance that the works that *do* finally make it into the public domain will stay there.

The Road to the Supreme Court

To understand the decision in (and implications of) *Golan v. Holder*, it is necessary to understand where the case begins. First stop? Paris and the Berne Convention.

To the Berne Convention

The Berne Convention for the Protection of Literary and Artistic Works first came into existence in 1886, in part due to the insistence of a group of European authors led by Victor Hugo who sought to address the issue of international piracy. Since then, the convention has been revised and amended a number of times, with the last revision occurring on September 28, 1979. Before the Berne Convention, copyright laws applied only to works produced in their particular country. So a French writer could receive copyright protection for her work in her home country, but her works could be copied and sold outside of the protection of France. Under the Berne Convention, copyright was automatic once the creation was "fixed," and artists need not "apply" or "register" in member countries to receive full copyright protection.

This international agreement also set minimum levels of copyright protection that all member parties must provide and, most significant to an understanding of *Golan v. Holder*, required that member parties treat copyrighted works of the other Berne members the same as the copyrighted works of their own domestic authors, even providing for retroactive application to existing works. Article 18(1) requires protection for Berne member works in the new country which "have *not* fallen into the public domain *in the country of origin* through the expiry of the term of protection" (Hart, 2011, emphasis added). This is the central point of controversy in *Golan v. Holder*: retroactively applying copyright to foreign works already in the U.S. public domain.

The United States resisted joining the Berne Convention for over a century. After the passage of the U.S. Copyright Act of 1976, the United States experienced a great deal of international pressure to join the Berne Convention, because this act moved several important features of the Berne Convention into U.S. law: for example, relaxing standards on the formalities of copyright registration (essentially moving from an "opt-in" form of copyright, where you register works, to an "opt-out" form where copyright is automatic) and extending the duration of copyright protection to the Berne minimum of the author's life plus 50 years. Despite these changes, it would take more than a decade before the U.S. Congress would finally pass the Berne Convention Implementation Act (BCIA) of 1988.

Not surprisingly, the changes to U.S. copyright policy through the BCIA were very minimal and included no retroactive protection for foreign works that had fallen into the U.S. public domain. Congress essentially chose to ignore Article 18(1) when it implemented Berne, leaving these works in violation of the treaty (Hart, 2011). The member parties of Berne demanded reciprocity, but, as Karan Dhadialla (2012) pointed out, "in the absence of any meaningful enforcement mechanism, nothing was changed."

Five years later in 1994, the World Trade Organization (WTO) and the Agreement on Trade Related Aspects of Intellectual Property Rights (TRIPS) were created during the Uruguay round of the General Agreement on Tariffs and Trade (GATT). The United States joined both the WTO and TRIPS in 1994. TRIPS not only required implementation of the first 21 articles of the Berne Convention but also set up an international dispute resolution panel to enforce compliance. One of the first panels would be brought against the U.S. for failing to comply with Article 18(1) when it joined Berne. Section 514 of the Uruguay Round Agreements Act (URAA) was created as a result of this enforced compliance and is the key statute challenged in *Golan v. Holder*. The URAA was passed by Congress in 1994 to bring the United States into compliance with Article 18(1) of the Berne Convention.

To the District Court

In the wake of URAA, the Sonny Bono Copyright Term Extension Act of 1998 (CTEA) was passed. The CTEA extended the term of copyright an additional 20 years on currently protected works. These two acts inspired a group of artists, educators, and authors, including Lawrence Golan, to join together to challenge the constitutionality of the acts. In 2001, they filed an action in the U.S. District Court for the District of Colorado seeking declaratory and injunctive relief from these acts; that is, the suit was not brought forward for monetary gain, but instead to receive a "declaration" from the court that these acts were not constitutional and to also receive an "injunction" (directive) from the court that they would not have to follow the provisions of these acts. The plaintiffs involved in the suit had been "performing, copying, or distributing works" that had been in the public domain before URAA restored copyright protection in them; now, they were faced with "either paying royalties on the works, ceasing the use of them, or risking litigation" (Hart, 2011). Initially, Golan sought a declaration in the District Court of Colorado "that the CTEA and URAA were unconstitutional under the Copyright Clause and that the URAA was a restriction of free speech under the First Amendment" (Hart). But his case was "put on hold when the Supreme Court granted cert in *Eldred v. Ashcroft* to consider the constitutionality of the CTEA" (Hart).

The Supreme Court ultimately decided that the CTEA was within Congress' constitutional authority, though they noted that the act may have "extended copyrights long beyond what the framers of the Constitution envisioned" (Hart, 2011). Still, it was within Congress' authority to retroactively extend copyright, since Article I, Section 8 of the Constitution gives Congress the power to grant copyrights for "limited times." Extended copyright does not mean unlimited copyright. And so the District Court went back to Golan, ultimately denying Golan's motion. Golan then appealed to the United States Court of Appeals for the 10th Circuit.

To the Court of Appeals

Like the District Court, "the 10th Circuit found that URAA is within Congress' authority under the Copyright Clause" (Hart, 2011). Unlike the District Court, "the 10th Circuit devoted considerable time to examining the First Amendment issues raised by URAA" (Hart, 2011). If a work moves into the public domain, anyone may copy, distribute, perform, or otherwise use that work freely; the use of that work is protected by the First Amendment. Thus it should follow that "taking the work back out of the public domain [would] interfere with those vested First Amendment rights" (Hart). The 10th Circuit held that, while Section 514 of the URAA did not exceed Congress' power under the Copyright Clause of the U.S. Constitution, it did interfere with the First Amendment rights of those (like the plaintiffs) who routinely use and depend upon works in the public domain. It sent the case back to the U.S. District Court to determine whether Section 514 violates the First Amendment. And, in 2009, 8 years after the first action was brought to court, the District Court found in favor of Golan et al. on the remanded claim, finding that Section 514 of the URAA did violate the First Amendment.

But on appeal, the 10th Circuit reversed and held that the URAA did not, in fact, violate the First Amendment because it advanced the state's interest in protecting the copyrights of American works abroad. On March 7, 2011, the Supreme Court granted *certiorari* and arguments in the case of *Golan v. Holder* were scheduled to begin in October of 2011.

Golan v. Holder: Decision and Dissent

After a lengthy, bumpy, and acronym-filled journey, including several lively games of "hot potato" between the District Court of Colorado and the 10th Circuit, on October 5, 2011, the Supreme Court finally heard arguments in the case of *Golan v. Holder*. The central question was: "Are there circumstances when Congress can take works out of the public domain and recopyright them?"[2] The answer would come on January 18, 2012: Yes, they can.

The Supreme Court voted 6–2[3] to uphold the URAA and affirm that it was within Congress' right to retroactively copyright works in the public domain, ultimately claiming that "the public domain was not 'a category of constitutional significance'" (Liptak, 2012). For Lawrence Lessig—academic, activist, and copyleft advocate—this decision marked the day when "the Supreme Court shut the door, finally and firmly, on any opportunity to meaningfully challenge a copyright statute constitutionally" (qtd. in Hartline, 2012).

The ruling potentially also leaves the door open for Congress to make further changes to copyright law that we might find even more restrictive, said Kenneth D. Crews, director of the copyright advisory office at the Columbia

University libraries: "It is a grant of sweeping authority to Congress to shape copyright law in almost any way that it chooses," he said of the decision. "This should raise a red flag to be watchful about other developments in Congress" (Young, 2012).

The Court rejected all arguments that Congress acted outside its purview, holding that extended or retroactive copyright protection is still "limited" as per the terms of the copyright clause. In writing the majority opinion, Justice Ginsberg said that the law merely leveled out the international playing field, putting "foreign works on an equal footing with their U.S. counterparts" (qtd. in Liptak, 2012). Ginsberg's argument here echoes the central tenet of the Berne Agreement: that "members of the Berne Union agree to treat authors from other member countries as well as they treat their own" (*Golan*, 2012, p. 3). Nodding to Golan's particular dilemma as a conductor, Ginsberg cited the lack of balance in copyright protection for foreign versus domestic composers:

> Prokofiev's "Peter and the Wolf" could once be performed free of charge [while now] the right to perform it must be obtained in the marketplace. This is the same marketplace, of course, that exists for the music of Prokofiev's U.S. contemporaries: works of Copeland and Bernstein, for example, that enjoy copyright protection, but nevertheless appear regularly in the programs of U.S. concertgoers. (qtd. in Liptak, 2012)

Perhaps Justice Ginsberg's opinion can be read as "another step in a broader trend towards U.S. IP law compliance with international conventions and away from the cultural imperialism of yesteryear" (Dhadialla, 2012). Because U.S. copyright law has been so domestically oriented for much of our nation's history, the decision can also be viewed as "a step in the international direction" for our copyright law, but one that will require us to give up some of our protections to allow for and encourage the protections of others.

And, perhaps, as Chander et al. (2012) argue, the Golan decision allows for important progress to be made in both the internationalization of U.S. copyright law (in part by finally recognizing the rights of foreign creators) and in the redefinition of what counts as "incentive" to create. By rejecting the "narrow utilitarian understanding of incentives to create as the *sole* explanation for this law," the Court embraces a "pluralist view of copyright law [that is] not particularly European but, rather, [an] appreciation of the global context in which innovators today create, sell and share their works" (640).

In the dissent, however, Justice Breyer, joined by Justice Alito, assert that the Court's decision reflects more of a European view of copyright, rather than an Anglo-American utilitarian approach. It is this utilitarian view of copyright, Breyer argues, that has not only influenced the writing of the U.S. Constitution and its Copyright Clause, but also has historically influenced the Court's interpretation of the Copyright Clause (Band, 2012, p. 4). Breyer wrote that:

> This utilitarian view of copyrights and patents, embraced by Jefferson and Madison, stands in contrast to the "natural rights" view underlying most of continental European copyright law—a view that the English booksellers promoted in an effort to limit their losses following the enactment of the Statute of Anne and that in part motivated the enactment of some of the colonial statutes... that view, though perhaps reflected in the Court's opinion, runs contrary to the more utilitarian views that influenced the writing of our own Constitution's Copyright Clause. (qtd. in Band, 2012)

Ginsberg counters this dissent in a footnote to the majority opinion by invoking recent work that refutes the idea that the U.S. Copyright Clause mandates "isolationism" when it comes to "harmonizing our copyright laws with those [in] the civil-law tradition" (Band, 2012). If the United States is indeed the world's leading exporter of copyrighted works,[4] Ginsberg's argument makes sense. As Chander, Sunder, and Le (2012) observed, the U.S. can

> ill afford to be an international scofflaw as regards the intellectual property rights of foreigners. Continuing to flout the rights of some authors—simply because they were foreign—would prove to be a serious vulnerability for the United States in international negotiations. Congress accordingly concluded that honoring U.S. trade commitments was necessary, despite the loss to the public domain. (p. 641)

The Supreme Court, in rendering their decision in Golan, seemed to balance this loss with the gains that are made, such as "ensuring exemplary compliance with our international obligations, securing greater protection for U.S. authors abroad, and remedying unequal treatment of foreign authors" (*Golan*, 2012, p. 32).

But Justice Breyer saw no such gains. In fact, he questioned whether the copyright clause (as viewed through a utilitarian lens)

> empowers Congress to enact a statute that withdraws works from the public domain, brings about higher prices and costs, and in doing so seriously restricts dissemination, particularly to those who need it for scholarly, educational, or cultural purposes—all *without providing any additional incentive* for the production of new material? (*Golan*, 2012, p. 8)

Certainly Breyer's answer would be a resounding "no."

In his dissent, Justice Breyer highlighted the challenges (and costs) that the University of Michigan, the Institute of Museum and Library Services, and the HathiTrust Digital Library[5] (among others) have had in merely trying to determine the copyright status of works they wished to use. What will happen, he asked, to "film preservers, museums, universities, scholars, [and] database compilers" who face similar administrative costs[6] "associated with trying to locate foreign copyright owners?" (Golan, 2012, p. 12). He continued by noting:

> Consider the questions that any such individual, group, or institution must [now] answer: Is the work eligible for restoration under the statute? If so, who now holds the copyright—the author? an heir? a publisher? an association? a long-lost cousin? Whom

> must we contact? What is the address? Suppose no one answers? How do we conduct a negotiation?" (Golan, p. 12)

The answers to these questions "cost money," argued Breyer, but perhaps more importantly, they cost time. Breyer feared that many who have to face these questions will be "forced to curtail their cultural, scholarly, or other work-preserving efforts," which affects not only the creation of new works, but their dissemination to the public.

But Justice Ginsberg would argue that restrictions of copyright law can sometimes help creativity, by devising a clear system that allows authors to collect payment when their work is used: "Congress had reason to believe that a well-functioning international copyright system would encourage the dissemination of existing and future works" (qtd. in Young, 2012). Indeed, many prominent content owners and copyright holders applauded the ruling. The MPAA, for example, issued a statement saying that it is "pleased that the Supreme Court has again ruled that strong copyright protection is the 'engine of free expression' and fully consistent with the First Amendment" (Young, 2012).

Still, there remains something troubling in the *Golan v. Holder* decision: its ties to the legacy of *Eldred v. Ashcroft* (Jackson, 2012). In Eldred, no works were removed from the public domain, but existing copyright protections were extended by 20 years (keeping works out of the public domain that should have been made available). If Eldred allowed Congress the power to extend the length of copyright protection, Golan "adds a new snag: when the copyright protection ends, Congress can resurrect it again. 'Limited Times' is now the limited and limited again times" (Jackson, 2012).

One of the primary arguments of Eldred was that

> the Copyright Clause and the First Amendment were adopted close in time. This proximity indicates that, in the Framers' view, copyright's limited monopolies are compatible with free speech principles. Indeed, copyright's purpose is to promote the creation and publication of free expression. (Eldred qtd. in Hartline)

This argument was reinforced in Golan. But to argue proximity is to historicize the argument, and in so doing, it becomes clear that the original copyright clause allowed for very limited copyright protection (14 years) and not for the overextended and retroactive protection we currently have in the U.S.

Implications

In November 2010, Lawrence Lessig gave a keynote at the World Intellectual Property Organization's (WIPO) Global Meeting in Geneva. The theme of the meeting was "Facilitating Access to Culture in the Digital Age." In his talk,

Lessig addressed a number of things, but most interesting was his description of the role copyright should play in facilitating an "ecology of creativity."

Our ecologies of creativity can be loosely categorized, Lessig noted, as those that "have money at the core" (the professional ecology), those that "don't have money at the core" (the amateur ecology), and those where "people don't use money to express value" at all (the sharing ecology). These ecologies are not mutually exclusive and, in fact, must coexist to survive.

The professional ecology depends upon an "effective and efficient system of copyright" to assure that compensation can provide the incentive the artist needs to create; the amateur ecology depends on the opportunity for "free use and sharing," not on control and copyright and compensation. It is within this sharing ecology that children, lovers, friends, and family live—an ecology whose character would change radically if money were introduced as a mode of exchange. Our work as scholars "is and has always been" a kind of hybrid activity: We create "within a mixed economy of free and paid" and depend not upon "exclusive control, but both on free and fair use of creative work that is built upon and then spread" (WIPO). The "critical point" Lessig made with his examples is that a copyright system has to support each of these ecologies; it cannot privilege one and neglect the others. Of course, these ecologies are moving targets—government, technology, and economics change and redefine them for every age—so it is critical that our laws keep up with these changes.

In his address to WIPO, Lessig addressed the failure of the U.S. copyright system to work with(in) these emerging ecologies as not accidental to, but implicit in, "the architecture of copyright as we inherited it." It isn't that the law has grown more complicated, it's that the law has stayed the same, even though the nature and scope of what it regulates has changed dramatically:

> At the turn of the century, U.S. copyright law was technical, inconsistent, and difficult to understand, but it didn't apply to very many people or very many things. 90 years later, U.S. copyright law is even more technical, inconsistent, and difficult to understand. More importantly, it touches everyone and everything. Technology, heedless of law, has developed modes that insert multiple acts of reproduction and transmission—potentially actionable events under the copyright statute—into commonplace daily transaction. Most of us can no longer spend even an hour without colliding with the copyright law. (Lessig, 2010, quoting Litman, 1994)

What has also changed are our ecologies of creativity. Lessig argued that our laws have "failed to assure the adequate incentives in the professional culture, and failed to protect the necessary freedoms in the amateur and critical or scientific culture." It is because of this failure that Lessig implored WIPO to take the lead in reform (Zimmerman, 2010). In the short term, he asked that WIPO actively encourage systems of voluntary licensing (like Creative Commons) as they create a "better balance" between the ecologies of professional and amateur creativity. In the long term, Lessig asked that WIPO support a

"Blue Sky Commission"—a group that would have "the freedom to think about what architecture for copyright makes sense in the digital age, freed from the current implementation of copyright."

What is interesting in Lessig's appeal to WIPO is that he urged the U.S. to seek reform and balance on a world stage, not by merely adopting tenets of international treaties, but by developing and enacting a holistic understanding of "the commons." Lewis Hyde (2010), in his book *Common as Air*, might come closest to an adequate definition of the term: The commons is a "kind" of property, not "the opposite of property" or the absence of property (p. 24).

Hyde (2010) argued that property is a *right of action*, which is the idea that ownership rarely exists in a space where you can exercise the entire range of possible actions. Here's his example: If you own a house, you may paint your living room or redo the kitchen, but

> you cannot put a herd of cows in your backyard, you cannot build a tower ten stories high, you can't convert your home into a soap factory, and you can't rent out your office to a friend. (p. 25)

And these are things you cannot do even if you own the house outright; if you are paying a mortgage, your contract will probably restrict you even more.

So if property is a right of action, we can best understand the commons as a kind of property where more than one person has rights. This understanding allows us to imagine a definition of property and the commons that encourages agency rather than blocking or excluding it. As Hyde wrote:

> Invocations of the commons can carry with them a promise that more than air—can be *like* air, always there for the inhaling lung: infinite bandwidth, unlimited acorns and deer, all of literature available on the computer screen, unfenced prairie stretching to an unowned ocean—what John Locke would call "that great and still remaining common of mankind." (p. 24)

The Future of the Public Domain

With the decision in Golan, the public domain has simultaneously lost and gained. If the public domain exists only in the United States and within the limited understanding of the *Golan v. Holder* decision, then it has lost some ground. But if the public domain can be reframed as "the commons of mankind" (perhaps in one of Lessig's "Blue Sky" spaces), we may, literally, gain the world.

For many years, the United States freely copied from other countries to advance the education, culture, and industry of its citizens; thus, it seems oddly paradoxical (and perhaps blatantly hypocritical) that the country once known as the "Barbary coast of literature" (and its citizens, "the buccaneers of books") would now label other developing countries "pirates" because they want to produce and disseminate generic, affordable, lifesaving (and U.S.-patented) medications to their citizens, or reproduce (currently copyrighted) U.S. textbooks to educate their students (Chander et al., 2012, p. 640).

Although it may seem an odd role for the U.S. to pave the road to a "world commons," the roots are here. The same founding father who helped pen the "utilitarian" U.S. copyright clause also wrote that "the field of knowledge is the common property of mankind, and any discoveries we make in it will be for the benefit of yours and every other nation" (Thomas Jefferson, writing to Henry Dearborn in 1807). The concept of "fair use" was also made in the USA; it is a "uniquely U.S. concept, created by judges and enshrined in the law," and though it does not function as an exception to copyright compliance (rather, as a "legal defense"), it allows for copyrighted material to be used and built upon for "commentary, parody, news reporting, research and education" (Copyright Clearance Center, 2012). Both of these concepts—knowledge as the "common property" of all nations, and "fair use," as a distinctly U.S. understanding of "commoning" knowledge—may be places to start thinking outside the existing copyright structure.

James Boyle, who received the 2003 World Technology Award in Law for his theoretical work on the intellectual ecology of the public domain, has likened the efforts to establish a cultural commons to those of the environmental movement in its infancy:

> Like Rachel Carson in the years before Earth Day, the Copy Left is trying to raise awareness of the intellectual land to which they believe we ought to feel entitled and to propose policies and laws that will preserve it. Just as the idea of environmentalism became viable in the wake of the last century's advances in industrial production, the growth of this century's information technologies will force the country to address the erosion of the cultural commons. 'The environmentalists helped us to see the world differently,' writes Boyle, 'to see that there was such a thing as *the environment* rather than just *my* pond, *your* forest, *his* canal. We need to do the same thing in the information environment. We have to invent the public domain before we can save it.'" (Boyle, qtd. in Duke)

Certainly the public domain, as invented and articulated in the Golan decision, is not an ideal space to move forward. Academics and artists have already expressed concern that the Golan decision will make it that much more difficult to write books, create films, or assemble course readings without having to deal with a host of legal hurdles—or just prohibitively expensive fees—to avoid violating copyrights (Young, 2012).

The Supreme Court decision marks the end of Golan's fight but could signal the beginning of a new battle: "the only remedy now," according to Golan's lawyer, Anthony Falzone, "would be a change in U.S. law" though such a change would be "highly unlikely" (Young, 2012). Perhaps. But such changes are neither impossible nor unprecedented. What is past may very well be prologue, and "what to come, in yours and my discharge."[7] Almost 200 years ago, Thomas Jefferson wrote the following:

> I am certainly not an advocate for frequent and untried changes in laws and constitutions. I think moderate imperfections had better be borne with; because, when once known, we accommodate ourselves to them, and find practical means of correcting their ill effects. But I know also, that laws and institutions must go hand in hand with the progress of the human mind. As that becomes more developed, more enlightened, as new discoveries are made, new truths disclosed, and manners and opinions change with the change of circumstances, institutions must advance also, and keep pace with the times. We might as well require a man to wear still the coat which fitted him when as a boy, as civilized society to remain ever under the regimen of their barbarous ancestors. (Jefferson to Samuel Kercheval, July 12, 1816)[8]

Jefferson understood that the United States would outgrow the scope of a Constitution adopted in 1787; indeed, the Bill of Rights was added only 4 years later. What will our future be?

The *Golan v. Holder* decision was rendered on the same day that thousands of scholars and citizens across the globe joined together to protest the next generation of restrictive copyright laws: the Stop Online Piracy Act (SOPA) and the Protect IP Act (PIPA). Like the chilling effect that the Golan decision had on copyright reform, the effects of the massive online blackout in protest of SOPA and PIPA (H.R. 3261 and S. 968) were felt around the globe, when web sites including Google, Wikipedia, Mozilla, Wired, and others "joined in the global action against over-broad and overreaching copyright laws that would break the fundamental architecture of the Internet" (Rodriguez & Sutton, 2012). As Rodriquez and Sutton warned, however, SOPA and PIPA are merely the initial wave of proposed acts.

So, what's next? For teachers, scholars, artists, librarians, and others concerned with Congress' incessant expansion of the scope and duration of copyright, *Golan* makes clear that we can expect no help from the Supreme Court (Sprigman, 2012). As Corynne McSherry and Eric Goldman (2011) wrote:

> Justice Breyer got it. Too bad the majority didn't. Word to the Internet: this is why we must never again let copyright maximalists ram through legislation under cover of night. Word to Congress: we're staying vigilant, and if you won't protect the public domain, we will.

But if the SOPA/PIPA protests taught us anything, it was that perhaps we don't need to wait for the Supreme Court to "realize the error of its ways" (Jackson, 2012). Public domain advocacy is "far more immediate" than waiting for Congressional or legal intervention. After all, as Jackson eloquently put it:

> Congress cannot avoid the voices of millions, especially since social media websites give those voices megaphones. But it is not just sheer numbers of supporters, it is money too that influences the future of copyright protection. In the past, the more powerful entities—the MPAA, RIAA, to name a few—were on the side of copyright

protection. Now, there are large companies like Google and Wikipedia that are invested in the public domain and the free flow of information on the Internet. When these companies combine with millions of American citizens on social media websites, the public domain does not need the Supreme Court to save it.

Notes

1 The distinction between "buying" and "not being able to buy" an orchestral work under the provisions of the law upheld in *Golan v. Holder* is an important one. Lawrence Golan described it as follows:

> when something is rental only and under copyright, not only do you have to rent the music. On top of that, you have to pay a licensing fee to the publisher every time you want to play the piece. And that even goes for pieces that you purchased before the law came out. You actually have to pay a licensing fee on something you already own every time you want to play it. (qtd. in Bailey, 2011)

2 What is interesting about the question of whether Congress can restore copyright to works in the public domain is that one of the key composers used as an example in the Golan case, Dimitri Shostakovich, never enjoyed copyright protection for his work. The U. S. did not have copyright relations with the Soviet Union during the time of the composition of his symphonies, so the question of "restoring" or "recopyrighting" Shostakovitch is an odd one. As Lange, Weaver, and Reed (2011) asked: "How can one restore what never existed?"

3 The Supreme Court decided this case with only eight members; Justice Kagan recused herself due to her prior involvement with the Golan case as United States Solicitor General.

4 The U.S. is noted as such in Chander et al., p. 641.

5 A few months after the *Golan v. Holder* decision, the HathiTrust digital library won a copyright-infringement lawsuit brought against them by the Authors Guild et al. In his ruling, Judge Harold Baer Jr. of the U.S. District Court in Manhattan "threw out the authors' arguments that HathiTrust and its partners had trampled copyright law by preserving and making scanned works available for certain uses" (Howard, 2012). The decision was heralded as a victory for Fair Use.

6 Justice Breyer cited information from an *amicus curiae* brief submitted to the Court from the American Library Association in his dissent.

7 From Shakespeare's *The Tempest*, a play about the discovery of "new worlds."

8 These words are literally etched in stone on Panel Four of the Thomas Jefferson Memorial in Washington D.C.; a scanned copy of the original letter can be found online at The Library of Congress.

• PART TWO •

Cultures of Production

• CHAPTER SEVEN •

Permissions and Precedents: A Cautionary Tale from Art Publishing

Steve Westbrook and James Ryan

In this chapter, we examine the case of *Bridgeman Art Library, Ltd. v. Corel Corp*, which maintained that exact copies of public domain works of art are not original enough to be copyrightable under U.S. law, and discuss its influence—or, rather, its striking lack of influence—on the normative practices of art publishing. Although decided in 1999, the case has had little effect on altering the perception that publishers must seek permissions from photographers, museums, or related institutions in order to reproduce "their" copies of public domain artwork. In fact, the plaintiff that lost the case, Bridgeman Art Library, continues to collect permissions fees from publishers seeking to use images from its collection even though the court found that it has no legal basis to do so. Given the discrepancy between court ruling and industry policy, we argue that it is less the law itself and more the institutional and ideological practices within the culture of art publishing—the misunderstandings and misapplications of the law—that have established the most lasting, influential precedent for the proprietary treatment of images. Using our findings as a kind of cautionary tale, we explore the larger implications of this predicament for scholars across the disciplines and recommend they take the risk of *not* asking permission to reproduce visual material in certain questionable cases of appropriation, especially those concerning public domain works.

Art Books without Artwork

Susan Bielstein (2006) wrote that "the irony remains that in this late capitalist culture with its spectacle of images... as we turn more and more to the object of vision for information and learning, it is becoming harder and harder and impossibly expensive to include illustrations in books" (p. 9). The reason for this increasing expense, which extends not only to illustrations but also photographs and other visual media, has little to do with prices of raw materials or technological capabilities—theoretically, at least, innovations in digital printing have reduced the cost of publishing images. Rather, it reflects the permissions fees incurred by authors and publishers. As the culture of the fine arts industry has become increasingly proprietary over the last few decades, so too has the expense of obtaining licenses for publishing visual material. In a recent study commissioned by the Mellon Foundation, researchers who surveyed ten museums and four commercial image purveyors determined that the cost of purchasing licensing fees for reproducing images inside of a book ranged from \$35 to \$260 per illustration in color and \$20 to \$150 in black and white. According to the study's estimate, "a monograph with 100 illustrations might well cost its author \$5,000 or more in permissions costs" (Ballon & Westerman, 2006). Another university press editor found this estimate strikingly conservative, claiming that it is "not unusual" for an author "to pay \$10,000 to \$15,000 to illustrate a book that may only sell 400 or 500 copies" (Howard, 2006, p. 13). When the cost of permissions is added to other expenses faced by presses, a typical art or art history book may cost up to \$75,000 to produce. As Patricia Fidler has lamented, the *minimal* cost of producing a relatively basic art book at Yale University Press—arguably the top art publisher in the United States—is \$40,000 to \$50,000 (Howard, 2006).

While it may seem absurd to ask artists, art historians, and art critics to avoid reproducing images in their texts and instead settle for robust prose descriptions of art objects, the prohibitive cost of permissions has led publishers to issue exactly this advice. In *Permissions: A Survival Guide*, an aptly titled guidebook for emerging scholars seeking to publish in the visual arts, Bielstein (2006) offered the following directive regarding illustrations: "Don't use them. Concentrate on the writing... Chasing images is time-consuming and expensive. So if you can live without images, do it" (p. 101). She suggested with regretful humor that the staggering amount of money required for permissions might be better invested as a down payment on a house. To be clear, these sorts of statements—suggestions to avoid providing readers with images of artwork important to a particular study, joking asides that seek relief by making light of a serious, exigent problem for scholars—do not represent anomalies. They have become norms in the culture of art publishing.

Of course, these norms reflect something more than an economic problem; they also reflect a legal problem, one complicated by what might be described, at best, as a paradoxical application of copyright and, at worst, as a blatant abuse of the law. While this complication, with all of its nuances, deserves further address, we do our best to explain it here in a relatively short space. Often, the images for which museums, libraries, and image repositories charge hefty permissions fees are not copyrighted or copyrightable; they are, in fact, in the public domain. Some are ancient works created centuries before the cultural invention of intellectual property. Others are modern objects of art for which the term of the copyright has expired. Regardless, as public domain images, these works should be freely usable, at least according to the doctrine of U.S. law and the theory underlying it. The copyright clause of the U.S. Constitution not only provides exclusive rights to reproduction as an incentive for scientific and artistic creation but also specifically *limits* the terms of copyright to ensure cultural progress. Under Title 17 of U.S. Code, this limitation is currently 70 years after the death of the author or, for cases of anonymous and corporate authorship, 120 years after the time of creation (17 U.S.C. § 302). The idea of offering term limits to engender cultural progress is by no means limited to the United States. The Berne Convention, an international copyright agreement recognized by 164 countries, offers a default limit of 50 years (25 years for photographic works), but defers to the law of each particular signatory nation in cases of longer limits. Nationally and internationally, then, copyright is not, and has never been, granted in perpetuity. It expires, and works of intellectual property enter the public domain precisely so that creators can use, study, and build upon them in order to develop new insights and discoveries. Today, for instance, Darwin's scientific treatises and Shakespeare's plays can be used freely. Biologists can critique and build upon the theory of evolution by incorporating material from Darwin's *On the Origin of Species*; playwrights and screen writers can appropriate characters from *Hamlet* to develop their own dramas, and historians can use Shakespeare's work to develop new insights into the culture of Elizabethan England. It would seem puzzling—if not illegal—then, that museums, libraries, and licensing agencies would charge art historians to use an image of, say, a 17th-century painting to exemplify a particular point or prove an argument in a piece of scholarly writing.

Nonetheless, they regularly do so by claiming copyright on a particular layer of reproduction. According to a kind of circuitous logic, while the copyright of an original work of art may have never existed or have long expired, the copyright to the copy of that work may be active—or, rather, *claimed* to be active by a licensing agent. The College Art Association Committee on Intellectual Property (2004) has explained the problem as follows: "Even if a depicted work is in the public domain, a photographic reproduction of that work may carry additional layers of copyright protection claimed by photographers, publishers, or museums" (p. 4). Most often in the culture of fine arts, this copyright is claimed by museums under the work-for-hire doctrine. In short, the institution that owns a particular original artwork prohibits the public from photographing the artwork; it limits this practice to photographers under its own employ who sign contracts explicitly transferring rights of authorship to the institution. This way, the institution gains a kind of monopolistic control over copies of its holdings. It can sell photographs and transparencies—*copies* of the original artwork—and *claim* through a controversial application of copyright law that no other party has the legal right to sell or, in most cases, even use these copies without first securing permission. This monopoly on image control not only allows institutions to earn income by charging permissions fees for use of their photographic reproductions but also bolsters the value of the original artwork in their collections: that is, the more that people pay for reproductions of an artwork, the more valuable the original becomes. It is easy to see how this structural arrangement creates a boon for museums and archives while creating a burden for scholars.

This burden is not only reflected in the sheer expense of permission fees—in art history, the vast majority of scholarly publishers require their authors to bear the brunt of the raw cost—but also in the time and labor required to navigate the permissions process. According to the Mellon report, while an increasing number of institutions have attempted to streamline this process, "very few make it possible for the transaction to be handled through online price calculation and ordering without the intervention of a fees specialist" (Ballon & Westerman, 2006). Further, when commercial vendors, intermediary licensing agencies, or other organizations that simplify the permissions process are relied upon, the costs often dramatically increase from the numbers suggested near the beginning of this chapter, so that permissions fees may range from $300 per image to over $1,000. When publishers assist authors in the process of securing permissions, they estimate spending 20–80 hours per book, depending on the number of illustrations. One editor claimed that a book with 50 illustrations required "an average of 100 hours of permissions management by her assistant" (Ballon & Westerman). To be clear, these estimates reflect time spent by publishing professionals with expertise in navigating the permissions process. They do not reflect the research time required of authors unfamiliar with licensing procedures, nor do they reflect periods of time spent waiting for agencies to respond to requests, which can stretch from weeks to months. Regardless of the particulars, it is clear that authors and publishers in the discipline of art spend significant time, labor, and capital on the task of unraveling layers of rights—whether or not proprietary claims to the copyright of *copies* of public domain art are, in fact, legal in the first place.

Copies, Claims, and Case Law

The legal case that has most directly addressed this problem, or the rather postmodern component of this problem—the attempt to claim copyright of copies of uncopyrightable originals—is *Bridgeman v Corel*. In 1998, Bridgeman, an image licensing library, sued Corel, a software company, for reproducing, in CD-ROM form, 120 images presumed to be taken from their collection of transparencies, the rights to which it had acquired from museums across Europe and the United States. Because the museums it worked with strictly controlled access to their collections, and because, at the time, Bridgeman held exclusive contracts with these museums, the transparencies in its library were, Bridgeman claimed, the only existing high resolution images of the artworks in existence: that is, they had to have been the source for the images featured on Corel's CD-ROMs. The substance of Bridgeman's claim was that Corel must have surreptitiously acquired digital images made from Bridgeman's transparencies and then used these, without permission or payment, in its products. Bridgeman's entire business model was at stake in this case; if a software company could sell digital copies of its transparencies as "clip art," then high-resolution images of these artworks would be widely distributed and therefore easily obtainable and reproducible. Bridgeman would lose its status as exclusive owner of high-quality images of these works, and the print makers and publishers who formerly bought licenses from Bridgeman would need only purchase a copy of Corel's CD-ROM to print as many copies of these images as they liked. The very existence of an entity such as the Bridgeman Art Library was thrown into doubt, and this case was to answer the question of whether a seller of licenses to transparencies of photographs of public domain artworks could reasonably expect to conduct business in the digital age.

Bridgeman brought its case twice before the U.S. District Court of New York—a second time after the court granted Bridgeman's motion for reargument and reconsideration on the grounds that certain aspects of British and international law were not sufficiently considered during the first trial. In its two decisions (1998, 1999) the court made clear that, before it could decide if infringement had occurred, it had to settle the question of whether the plaintiff had grounds to claim copyright in the first place. The answer to this question depended on three related questions: (1) whether any photograph, which is always a "copy" of some "original," could ever have a claim to copyright; (2) whether a change in media, in this case from oil and canvas to photographic film and then transparency, constituted sufficient creative labor to justify copyright protection for the final product; and (3) whether the labor involved in producing a high-quality transparency entitled its producer to copyright of their work.

To clarify the existing legal answer to the first of these questions, the presiding judge, Lewis A. Kaplan, appealed to the precedent set by *Burrow-Giles Lithographic Co v. Sarony* (1884), a case in which a photographer filed suit against a company that was making and selling unlicensed lithographs of his portrait of Oscar Wilde. This case turned on the question of whether the copyright clause of the U.S. Constitution, which granted Congress the power to issue copyrights to "authors" for their "writings," could also be applied to photographers and their work. Burrow-Giles argued that photography was a mechanical and chemical process rather than an art and so no photographer could ever claim that their work was on par with that of an author expressing original ideas. The Supreme Court granted that Burrow-Giles' argument was sound when applied to photography in general but not when applied to Sarony's portrait or other photographs like it. Whereas most photographers engaged in "slavish copying," or the effort to avoid the introduction of original elements, Sarony had expressed much originality in his portrait, for example by arranging lines and lighting, by suggesting a pose and expression to Wilde, and by selecting a costume and setting for the image (*Burrow-Giles v. Sarony*, 1884).The precedent set by *Burrow-Giles v. Sarony* suggested, then, that when considering the applicability of copyright to a photograph, courts must consider the degree to which a photographer exercises control over his or her subject matter. If an image is sufficiently original, it can claim copyright. If not, it is merely a "slavish" copy.

"Slavish" copying is, of course, precisely what Bridgeman had prided itself upon: it made copies that were as faithful to their originals as current technology would allow. The only original quality to their work was the necessary alteration of media involved in making transparencies from original two-dimensional artworks, mostly of oil and canvas, and so it was to this point that the court turned its attention next, looking to the decision of the Second Court of Appeals in *L. Batlin & Son, Inc. v. Snyder* (1976) for guidance. In this case, Snyder, a toy manufacturer, filed copyright for a plastic coin bank modeled on a public domain design. When Baltin & Son, a competitor to Snyder, began selling a metal version of the bank based on the same public domain design, Snyder sued for infringement. Baltin argued that Snyder's copyright was invalid, and the Appellate court agreed, stating that reproductions were only entitled to copyright of those aspects that constituted "an original contribution not present in the underlying work of art" (*L. Batlin & Son, Inc. v. Snyder*, 1976). The medium of the reproduction did not itself represent such a contribution.

Like Snyder's piggy bank, Bridgeman's transparencies were not deemed original enough to merit copyright, and Judge Kaplan was rather direct in his language on this point:

> Absent a genuine difference between the underlying work of art and the copy of it for which protection is sought, the public interest in promoting progress in the arts...could hardly be served. To extend copyrightability to minuscule variations would simply put a weapon for harassment in the hands of mischievous copiers intent on appropriating and monopolizing public domain work. (*Bridgeman v. Corel*, 1999)

This is a harsh statement to be sure, especially as it associates the Bridgeman Art Library with "mischievous copiers" with malicious intent.

To answer the question of whether labor is sufficient grounds for copyright, Judge Kaplan called on *Feist Publications Inc. v. Rural Telephone Service Co.* (1991) to make clear that the labor involved in producing an image does not constitute the originality necessary for copyright. Rural Telephone Service Company was a local service provider that produced its own phone book; Feist Publications specialized in producing phonebooks that compiled data from multiple local services. When Feist approached Rural for a license to reproduce their listings, Rural refused. Feist printed their listings anyway, and Rural filed suit. Prior to this case, courts had relied on what was known as the "sweat of the brow" doctrine, which held that authors merit copyright by right of their labor in producing a work, rather than by the degree of that work's originality. While information could not claim protection, collections of information, like telephone directories, could do so under this doctrine, by merit of the hard work that went into collecting the information and producing the collection.

In the *Feist* decision, however, the Supreme Court rejected this doctrine, ruling instead that "the *sin qua non* of copyright is originality." A work needn't be wholly novel to qualify; rather, it need only possess "some minimal degree" or "spark" of creativity (*Feist v. Rural,* 1991). With originality as the basis for copyright rather than labor, the court could rule that phone books cannot claim protection. Likewise, reproductions of public domain works that do nothing at all original with the image are not protected no matter how much labor was involved in the production. In a sense, the public domain works Bridgeman copied were only so much "information"—material freely available to all that the library had labored to reproduce and therefore had no more claim to copyright than a phonebook. In closing his decision, Judge Kaplan stated simply that "there was no spark of originality" in Bridgeman's labors, "indeed, the point of the exercise was to reproduce the underlying works with absolute fidelity. Copyright is not available in these circumstances" (*Bridgeman v. Corel,* 1999).

In passing this judgment, the court decided not only that Bridgeman had no grounds to claim copyright over images of the public domain works in its collection but also, by extension, that there was no legal reason for publishers and print makers to pay for the use of these images. In effect, this decision should have ended Bridgeman's practice of charging permissions fees for non-transformative reproductions of public domain works. More broadly, it should have opened the door for art publishers to resist paying permissions or "use" fees to other institutions (e.g., museums and archives) attempting to charge for the use of exact or "slavish" copies. However, in this story, what should have happened did not happen. The result of the legal decision seems to have had almost no effect on the Bridgeman Art Library or the larger culture of art publishing.

Cavalier Copyright in the 21st Century

While accepting defeat in its legal case, Bridgeman ignored the implications of the verdict; to date, it has not changed its practice of charging permissions fees for what the court determined were uncopyrightable reproductions of uncopyrightable originals. Take Figure 1, a reproduction of Frans Hals' (1624) The Laughing Cavalier.

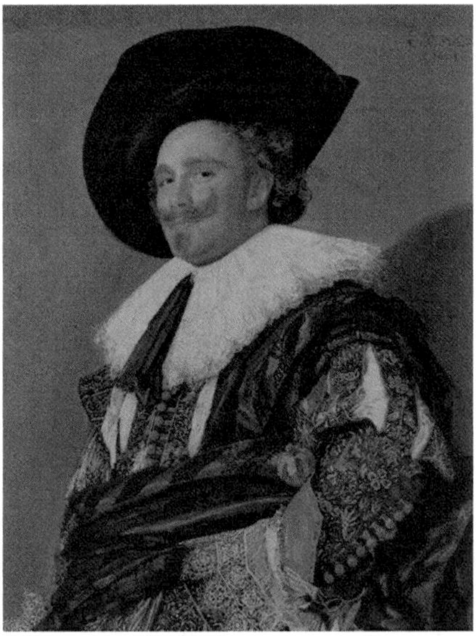

Figure 1: A reproduction of Frans Hals' The Laughing Cavalier (1624); credit: Public Domain

This image was among those originally included on the CD-ROM under investigation in *Bridgeman v. Corel*; indeed, it is one of the faithful photographic reproductions of a public domain work deemed a "slavish copy" by Judge Kaplan. Currently, Bridgeman issues licensing fees for the right to reproduce the image, despite its status as uncopyrightable, charging $150 for reproduction of a black and white copy (like the one above) in a scholarly book with a press run of under 5,000 copies (Kajette Bloomfield, personal correspondence, March 26, 2012). As legal scholars Colin T. Cameron (2006) and Mary C. Wojcik (2008) have separately pointed out, although Bridgeman holds no copyright to the image, the company continues—unequivocally—to claim that it does. The most recently updated Terms and Conditions (2009) listed on Bridgeman's web site offer the following warning regarding unauthorized use of "their" images:

> Unauthorized use of Content *constitutes infringement of copyright* and other applicable rights and shall entitle the Supplier to exercise all rights and remedies *under applicable*

> *copyright* and other laws, including monetary damages against all users and beneficiaries of the use of such Content.

In addition to making what appears to be a false claim to general copyright, Bridgeman's web site, more specifically, includes the following text under the image of The Laughing Cavalier: "©Wallace Collection, London, UK / The Bridgeman Art Library" (Bridgeman, 2012, "Laughing Cavalier"). The conspicuous absence of a year following the copyright symbol here suggests that Bridgeman would like—rather cavalierly—not only to assert a claim of copyright with no legal basis for doing so but, further, to assert this claim in perpetuity. And, it has found—if not in codified law, then in cultural practice—a means of doing so, for it requires licensed users to reproduce this exact phrasing when crediting their reproduction of The Laughing Cavalier. By perpetuating the myth of its intellectual property rights, Bridgeman sidesteps the law to serve its own interest: Even though the copyright does not legally exist, if it appears often enough, it may be perceived by potential users as valid. Bridgeman is not the only arts institution to capitalize on this strategy, as Bielstein (2006) has explained:

> Some institutions have the idea that if they just say they own the copyright to reproductions of public domain works and consistently put forth claims that not only go unchallenged but are acknowledged by writers who agree to use exact credit lines in exchange for rights to publish images, then it will eventually be accepted as so. (pp. 47–48)

Among others, Getty Images, the Chicago Art Institute, and the Metropolitan Museum of Art have followed this practice, which is now relatively widespread (see Bielstein, 2006; Cameron, 2006; Wojcik, 2008).

In fact, several institutions other than Bridgeman currently lay claim to the image of The Laughing Cavalier and charge accompanying permissions fees for its use. For example, Art Resource (ArtRes), a fine art stock photo archive that represents hundreds of museums, charges $45 for a black and white reproduction in print runs under 5,000 (Liz Kurtulik, personal communication, March 12, 2012), and the Wallace Collection, the museum that owns Hals' original oil painting, charges a reduced rate of £62 or approximately $99 to scholars, which includes a 30% discount from the regular price of $140 (Nell Carrington, personal communication, March 26, 2012). Both of these institutions also require that publishers of "their" images include mandated credit lines akin to the one above. In the case of ArtRes, the image must be captioned with the phrase "By kind permission of the trustees of the Wallace Collection, London / Art Resource" (ArtRes, 2012). These credit lines are buttressed by similar unfounded claims to copyright. For instance, the Wallace Collection includes the following conditions on the requisite Reproduction Application Form it provides potential clients on its web site:

> The Wallace Collection reserves copyright on all transparencies/digital images made in the Museum. Under no circumstances may duplicate transparencies, copy negatives or prints be made. Material may not be passed on to a third party. It is strictly prohibited to reproduce from 35mm slides or from any reproductions or copies of works of art in the Wallace Collection, for reasons of copyright and quality. (Wallace Collection, 2012, p. 2)

The number of institutions charging permissions fees for the use of a single public domain image and the forceful rhetoric of these institutions' terms and conditions reveal the misinformation, confusion, and corruption that define permissions chases within the culture of fine arts publishing. Faced with the circumstances of this single example—competing licensing agencies, various unfounded claims to copyright, and a virtual chasm separating practice from law—it is no wonder emerging scholars in the arts have a difficult time determining where they should begin seeking permissions and, further, given the status of this particular image as uncopyrightable, why they should even seek permissions in the first place. Underlying their predicament, of course, is a larger cultural question: How, in the wake of *Bridgeman v. Corel*, do entities like Bridgeman, ArtRes, and the Wallace Collection get away with charging permissions fees based on nonexistent or fabricated copyrights, and why do authors and publishers continue to pay them?

A Culture of Intimidation

While variegated and complex, the answers to this question can be located in at least three explanations that, taken collectively, combine issues of law, precedent, and power. The first and most immediate explanation concerns the courts and the structure of appeal. *Bridgeman v. Corel* was tried at the District Court level in the Southern District of New York. At this level, the court decision carries persuasive but not binding authority. In other words, the ruling may be used to form arguments in principle but not necessarily to comprise determinate judgments or hold parties outside of its purview accountable to its authority; justices of other courts may incorporate or reject its findings as they see fit. It may very well be that, as Cameron (2006) has argued, "the principle remains the same throughout the United States. Photographs that precisely reproduce public domain paintings are not copyrightable.... Any federal court, presented with the facts that arose in *Bridgeman*, would invariably reach the same result" (pp. 47–48). However, higher courts have not had the opportunity to hear these facts. Strategically, Bridgeman elected to accept the District Court's unfavorable ruling (and subsequently ignore this ruling) rather than appeal to the Second Circuit and risk receiving a binding judgment that would set federal legal precedent, thereby forcing Bridgeman to alter its unconstitutional practices in the U.S. (in theory, at least). By no means does the exploitation of this lack of appeal mean that what Bridgeman is doing is legal; the lower court has already determined it otherwise. It is simply a reality that without a higher court's binding judgment, Bridgeman and other arts organizations have an easier time, in one scholar's apt description, of "holding hostage" images within the public domain (McGill, 2006).

The second explanation would appear to concern contract law. The Terms and Conditions set forth on Bridgeman's web site combine claims to copyright with the language of common law contract. Here, Bridgeman uses a strange hodgepodge of discourse in an attempt to shore up what it cannot cover through copyright, namely by proclaiming to bind private parties in something akin to an exclusive user agreement:

> THE CLIENT AGREES TO BE BOUND BY AND COMPLY WITH ALL OF THE TERMS OF THIS AGREEMENT... The Reproduction of the Photograph is strictly forbidden without the specific written consent of the Supplier [Bridgeman]... This Agreement will inure to the benefit of and be binding upon the parties, their successors and assigns, except that the Client may not assign or transfer this Agreement without the Supplier's prior written consent. No term of this Agreement is intended to confer a benefit on, or to be enforceable by, any person who is not a party to this Agreement. (Bridgeman, 2009)

This rhetoric represents a clear attempt on the part of Bridgeman to sidestep the illegitimacy of its false copyright and bind not the general public but a private party (i.e., "the Client") to its terms of use through implied consent. If Bridgeman failed in court to legally secure rights to reproduce "its" public domain images through copyright, it has rebutressed attempts to secure the rights to reproduction through contract. As Wojcik (2008) has noted, this attempt, too, may lack any and all legal basis. Title 17 explicitly states that common law contracts cannot be substituted for or used to preempt federal copyright: "All legal or equitable rights that are equivalent to any of the exclusive rights within the general scope of copyright... are governed exclusively by this title. Thereafter, no person is entitled to any such right or equivalent right in any such work under the common law or statutes of any State" (17 U.S.C. § 301). According to Wojcik (2008), "there is no way, in other words, that Bridgeman can legitimately use the common law of contract to effectively bypass the Southern District's ruling" (p. 269).

Nonetheless, as Wojcik (2008) noted, the key word here is "legitimately." As Bridgeman continues to claim copyright over images to which it has no copyright, it misapplies contract law to a context in which it has no recourse to apply contract law. In all likelihood, it will continue to do so, for this strategy—however unlawful and paradoxical it may be—sustains Bridgeman's ability to charge permissions fees. It is not the law itself that is key here but, rather, the cultural perception of legality or, more aptly, the threat of litigation. The rhetorical conflation of copyright and common law contract—whether or not grounded in truth—all too often convinces authors and publishers to purchase rights to reproduce works they have the constitutional and legal right to use freely. And the more frequently authors and publishers purchase these rights, the more able Bridgeman and other arts organizations are to continue to charge illegitimate use fees.

The third explanation concerns just this issue: the threat of litigation. Or, to be perhaps less specific but more accurate, simply *threat*. Often museums and other image suppliers exploit the dependency of publishers on their institutions through a leveraging of institutional and economic power. In a word that the general public may not readily associate with museums but one that, within this context, art historians and art publishers frequently deploy, they rely on *bullying*. Although this kind of bullying manifests in different ways, it is often evidenced in threats of severed relations and retroactive billing, threats so pervasive within the culture of art publishing that evidence of them has begun to appear in publishers' guidelines for prospective authors. For instance, when discussing the subject of permissions, the University of Chicago Press encourages art historians not to assume they have the right to reproduce public domain images freely and, further, urges them to understand the consequences for neglecting to pay what it calls "Use Permissions" to a lending agency, whether or not this agency has a legitimate legal claim: "lenders may blacklist an author or a Press for using their images without having obtained a Use Permission from them or they may attempt to collect a fee and a penalty after publication" (University of Chicago Press, "More on Art Permissions"). In our example of The Laughing Cavalier, at least two institutions claim to charge retroactive penalties for unauthorized uses of "their" images. On its web site, the Bridgeman Library states that clients caught using images from their collection without authorization may be subject to pay ten times the original licensing fee "in addition to any other fees, damages and penalties the Supplier may be entitled to" (Bridgeman, 2009). Similarly, the Wallace Collection (2012) claims it will charge retroactively "a minimum fee of £150 as compensation, in addition to any other fees due" for unauthorized use of "its" images, thereby persuading publishers to pay what is in comparison a cheaper (though still unwarranted) permissions fee up front rather than risk additional expenses or institutional retribution. The latter, of course, is where the real threat lies.

The threat of severed relations resonates profoundly with publishers and scholars who depend not simply on museums' copies of public domain images but on access to museums' archives and original holdings, the documents and artifacts upon which, to a certain degree, they build their careers. Museums understand and exploit this vulnerability; within art publishing, stories of their threats of blacklisting abound. One university press editor has offered a narrative of what happened after she published a minor 18th century print—

undoubtedly in the public domain—without first seeking permissions. Upon learning of the publication, representatives of a museum that claimed the original print in its holdings,

> wrote a bullying letter threatening to sanction the *entire* university unless we paid a penalty for publishing the work without the museum's permission. In a menacing tone, they explained that if we refused, 'Steps would be taken': the faculty wouldn't be able to order slides from the museum or do research in the archives. In fact, any doings the museum was having with the university system would be suspended *immediately*. (Bielstein, 2006, p. 56)

The tone of the original letter may have resonated with baseless threat and hyperbole; nonetheless, for this editor, the potential consequences of defiance presented too great a risk. She paid the $100 cost of permissions retroactively rather than face the disproportionate retribution threatened by the museum. Bielstein admitted that although she is rather appalled by the intimidation tactics of museums and other image suppliers, she nevertheless finds herself in the position of routinely paying licensing fees that, frankly, either have no legal basis or, at the very least, occupy a "gray area" of copyright because she can find no immediate means of resistance (p. 50).

As we hope to have suggested, the culture of fear and bullying pervasive in art publishing has very little to do with *actual* law or litigation. The defining irony here is that while museums and image suppliers may be using legal rhetoric to advance their economic agendas and buttress their threats to blacklist presses and affiliated universities, they are not pursuing infringement lawsuits. In fact, they do not want to wind up in court at all. The exorbitant cost of going to trial for a copyright claim—close to $1,000,000 on average—outweighs the permissions fees they might garner from an individual client; more significantly, the risk of going to trial after *Bridgeman v. Corel* is simply too great. First, they are likely to face a losing verdict. As Wojcik (2008) has pointed out, in the wake of the Bridgeman case, at least two trials have reconfirmed the soundness of Judge Kaplan's decision. In *ATC Distribution Group v. Whatever It Takes Transmissions & Parts* (2005), the Sixth Circuit—an appellate court with binding authority—upheld a verdict that illustrations copied from photographs did not contain enough originality to be copyrightable. In *Meshwerks Inc. v. Toyota* (2008), a district court found that certain three-dimensional models of cars were not copyrightable because they attempted to reproduce an existing product "as closely as possible." Although concerned with the auto (rather than fine arts) industry, these cases reconfirmed the logic of Judge Kaplan's treatment of so-called "slavish" copying. Second, and more broadly, the consequences of a losing verdict would have long-term damaging effects for image providers. A loss would set further judicial precedent in favor of authors' and publishers' ability to use public domain images freely. If a loss were appealed and subsequently reconfirmed by a higher court, it would indeed set binding precedent in a case directly concerned with the arts—the very thing the Bridgeman Library sought carefully to avoid. In other words, the process of going to trial would most likely serve to develop an underdeveloped body of case law with a bias against the copyrighting of reproductions of public domain images. As Cameron (2006) has suggested, litigation that might result in this kind of unambiguous, binding precedent would be anathema to image licensors' agendas: "If a false claim to copyright can bully potential authors away from using uncopyrightable reproductions of public domain images, no museum need ever pursue an infringement action" (p. 52). Further, without taking this action, "museums and art libraries have found a way to... avoid both the ramifications of the *Bridgeman* decision and charges of copyright misuse. Indeed, they manage to maintain the rights of a copyright owner without having a valid copyright, without having to pursue litigation, and without having to pursue alternate theories of ownership" (p. 59).

Making the Public Domain Public Again

With image purveyors occupying the proverbial catbird seat, scholars in the visual arts have yet to find a way out of what may seem like an insurmountable problem. That said, several small steps toward change have already been made. For example, in 2007, Artstor began its program, Images for Academic Publishing (IAP), an automated web service that offers scholars at subscribing institutions a limited collection of images they may use freely in certain academic publications. The benefit of IAP is that its database makes scholarly searches for free, high-quality reproductions of public domain artwork more convenient and centralized. From a more cynical perspective, however, it succeeds only in presenting subscribers with copies of images that should already be freely usable. Furthermore, although the collection is growing in size, it presently contains copies of artwork from only ten institutions, each of which has contributed images on a voluntary basis. The Laughing Cavalier, for example, is not available.

While the IAP at least offers a variation from the cultural norms entrenched in art publishing, it represents a rather isolated anomaly and does not offer enough possibility for long-term, substantial change. Every day, authors and editors like those mentioned above continue to acquiescence to the demands of image purveyors charging for uncopyrightable copies. Their acquiescence reinforces a damaging cultural precedent, one of the consequences of which is the further erosion of the public domain. In light of this problem, we recommend that scholars in the fields of art, humanities, and jurisprudence join together in ongoing reform efforts to take more direct, forceful action in both legal and cultural arenas.

First, we suggest they address the problem of the law itself. As Mazzone (2006) and Wojcik (2008) have separately pointed out, one of the problems scholars face when contending with image providers is the bias of the Copyright Act, which is concerned much more heavily with copyright protection than copyright misuse or abuse. In fact, the law offers almost no recourse to victims of what Mazzone has deemed "copyfraud"— the practice of "claiming falsely a copyright in a public domain work" (p. 1027). Only two provisions of Article 17 address false claims to public domain materials: Sections 506(c) and 506(e). The former concerns the distribution of false copyright notices (such as the one displayed on Bridgeman's web site), and the latter concerns deliberate misrepresentation on applications for copyright. Both Sections set a maximum fine of $2,500 and carry an extremely high burden of proving false intent; that is, in order to issue this fine, the federal government must prove that a party deliberately made a copyright claim it "knows to be false" (17 U.S.C. § 506). While a defense of naiveté is not at all valid in infringement suits, which may carry civil penalties of up to $150,000 in statutory damages and criminal penalties of up to $250,000 and five years in prison, it is perfectly valid here, where the maximum consequence is, in comparison, the payment of a small sum. Furthermore, as Mazzone (2006) revealed, there is no private cause for action in Sections 506(c) and 506(e), and under the government's treatment, "these provisions are almost never enforced" (p. 1036).

Mazzone (2006) thus suggested that individuals lobby Congress to amend the Copyright Act and create new means of enforcing penalties for "copyfraud." More specifically, he recommended pursuing the creation of the following items: (1) an amendment that would make false claims to copyright actionable under civil law; (2) a civil penalty that would allow victims to collect damages from perpetrators of "copyfraud"; (3) a new agency—perhaps within the Department of Justice—charged with identifying and prosecuting parties who attempt to claim ownership of works in the public domain; (4) a national registry that would list public domain works (comparable to the U.S. Copyright Office's register of copyrighted works, or something akin to a radical expansion of the sort of searchable database offered by the IAP program); (5) a symbol to designate public domain works (similar to the © used to designate copyrighted works).

Echoing Mazzini's (2006) call to action, Wojcik (2008) recommended that the College Art Association, in particular, pursue these goals, specifically with respect to museums' and image lenders' assertions of false copyrights, through a program of what she has deemed "sustained lobbying" (p. 275). Building on Mazzone's work, we would like to second Wojcik's recommendation but suggest further that efforts at sustained lobbying not be limited to the College Art Association (CAA). Instead, we suggest forming a large coalition of scholars and organizations from across the disciplines, so that the CAA might join forces with, for instance, the Intellectual Property Caucus of the Conference on College Composition and Communication and the Association of Independent Video and Filmmakers and gather strength as a multi-disciplinary unified collective of scholars and educators.

Second, while launching this collective effort toward legal reform, we recommend that scholars and publishers do as much as they can in their daily practice. If possible, they should stop seeking permissions for exact copies of public domain works, embrace alternative means of acquiring images, refuse to reproduce credit lines that contain specious copyrights or other misinformation about ownership of public domain images, and resist image lenders' tactics of intimidation. Although museums and archives may seek to maintain a monopoly on copies of the images in their collection, in reality they have no such monopoly, as their attempts to control the circulation of public domain images cannot compete with the dynamism of culture. When we realized the necessity of including an image of The Laughing Cavalier within this chapter, we not only contacted Bridgeman, the Wallace Collection, and Art Resource; we also did a simple Google image search with the terms "Frans Hals Laughing Cavalier" that revealed 9,800 results, some of which were high-quality enough to be suitable for print publication. We also found scannable reproductions of Hals' painting in hardcopy art books. Having located these resources, we made the perfectly ethical and perfectly legal decision to use one of the uncopyrightable reproductions that we came across without paying fees to any of the three organizations claiming licensing rights.

By no means are we the only scholars to have taken a turn in this direction in an effort to redefine the precedent of image use. The Mellon Foundation's report suggested that "some publishers have in recent years become more inclined to scan images from previous publications without copyright permission, particularly if the images are of works that have long been in the public domain" (Ballon & Westerman, 2006). This trend has not been limited to fine arts publishers; authors outside the field of art have taken similar steps. When discussing the use of images in his recent book, one scholar in the discipline of rhetoric stated the following:

> I weighed how to respond to my publisher's request for permission information for some of the images reproduced in this book. In reviewing my use of others material within this text, I have arrived at the conclusion that all of my uses fall well within the orbit of fair use, as outlined in the U.S. Copyright Code... I have determined not to seek permissions for these obviously fair uses... It would be an absurd result if contemporary U.S. copyright law, descended from a 1790 law entitled 'An Act for the Encouragement of Learning...' were to be mobilized to strip a text like this of its few, necessary illustrations. (Logie, 2006, p. 149)

We find the position articulated here an aggressive and necessary stance, particularly with regard to copies of public domain images, and we suggest that more scholars and publishers adopt such strategies. Further, we recommend that when reproducing public domain images, authors refrain from attributing images to any particular lender and, instead, opt for the simple credit line we have used below our reproduction of The Laughing Cavalier: "Credit: Public Domain." Maintaining this consistency with credit lines will help to further establish an acceptable cultural precedent to help liberate images from the control of false or ambiguous copyright claims.

As we articulate our recommendations here, we understand that locating and reproducing images outside of the purview of museums and archives may represent the easier component of our trajectory for reform; resisting the bullying tactics of these institutions may be significantly more difficult. Nonetheless, we find it imperative that scholars and publishers do so to the best of their abilities, and we urge them not to fear threats of litigation but, rather, to welcome the opportunity of going to court to settle discrepancies over interpretations of copyright. If faced with menacing letters or threats of blacklisting, we suggest they, themselves, consider advancing this means of resolution rather than continuing to acquiesce to unlawful terms of use. Any move toward the *actual* law and away from the bullying rhetoric of "copyfraud" is a move toward democratic progress. While we understand that the risks of resistance for authors and publishers are high, we cannot state strongly enough how important it is to summon courage at this very moment in history. What is at stake is more than a series of isolated conflicts; it is the very existence of the public domain.

• CHAPTER EIGHT •

Authorship and Ownership of User Contributions on the Social Web*

Timothy R. Amidon and Jessica Reyman

More than ever before, users expect Internet experiences to be personalized, customized, and responsive to their interests, preferences, histories, and activities. The web in its current iteration—what we refer to as the social and participatory web—is not only a space for the passive transmission and reception of texts and information, but a dynamic environment within which users actively contribute. The social and participatory web facilitates a full range of activities among users, so much so that it is often lauded for promoting democratic discourse and a culture "co-created by and for the community of connected users" (O'Reilly & Battelle, 2009, p. 1). As the mission statements of popular social web services suggest, service providers posit that their sites occupy a facilitative role in global participation and communication:

- "Facebook's mission is to give people the power to share and make the world more open and connected" (Facebook, 2012).
- "Google's mission is to organize the world's information and make it universally accessible and useful" (Google, 2012).
- Twitter's mission is "to instantly connect people everywhere to what's most important to them" (Parr, 2011).
- "YouTube provides a forum for people to connect, inform, and inspire others across the globe and acts as a distribution platform for original content creators and advertisers large and small." (YouTube, 2012).

These mission statements make some common assertions: Social web technologies are for use by everyday people, everywhere, all around the world, and fa-

* *Portions of this essay appeared in Reyman, Jessica. (2013). User data on the social web: Authorship, agency, and appropriation.* College English, *75 (5), 513-533. Copyright ©2013 by the National Council of Teachers of English. Used with permission.*

cilitate access to information, enable connections with others, and foster participation in powerful and meaningful ways. Certainly, the missions sound promising, and many people do use these services with such aims in mind. Learners, for instance, enter terms into Google's search engine to find useful information; amateur videographers use YouTube to share their creations; everyday critics use Tumblr or WordPress to compose and share content; citizens worldwide use Twitter and Facebook to keep up with friends and family, professionally network with colleagues, engage fellow citizens, and even organize revolutions.

Nevertheless, these mission statements neglect to mention the costs users pay for access to the social web. Although social and participatory web technologies have the potential for unprecedented sharing, access, and connection, there is also an exchange system between technology service providers, who largely control information flow within these digital spaces, and users, who provide much of the content and information that makes them valuable. That is to say, users are provided "free" access to share information, view content, and network with others on the social web. In exchange, however, users consign to service providers a substantial degree of control over not only the visible content of contributions they make, but also the more hidden contributions of user data.

For instance, consider the vast array of data generated, collected, and stored when Twitter users author tweets. The data from a single tweet includes the tweet's unique IQ, the text of the tweet, the tweet's creation date, the author's user and screen names, the number of tweets the author has sent, the author's "location" (which may or may not be geocoded), whether the user has a verified Twitter badge, and much more information (see Krikorian's 2010 map of the data types embedded within a single tweet).

While these bits of information may not be surprising when taken alone, they reveal a substantial amount about individuals' online and offline activities and identities when the various forms of content, data, and metadata are recorded and aggregated. For example, this data affords a view of how frequently a user tweets, the time of day when a user tweets, and the degree and type of interactivity that occurs among multiple users. More importantly, a significant amount of the information that web users generate and transmit on the social and participatory web may be undetectable to most users. While Twitter users may carefully craft, pore over, edit, revise, and intentionally type each of the 140 characters they enter into a tweet, they may at the same time be unaware of the hidden contributions they are making to the social and participatory web.

Problematically, user data is often appropriated by site owners who retain the rights to collect, use, and control information contributed by users. At best, such ownership policies restrict users as coauthors within these spaces, failing to allow them access to or control over the substantive data they have helped to co-compose; at worst, user contributions are purposefully exploited and appropriated for the self-serving ends of site owners and/or service providers. Although the social and participatory web has the potential to provide increased access to tools for participation, more enriched online experiences, and nuanced interactions among humans and technologies, the exchange system set up through terms of use policies and common practices associated with data use, in fact, devalues users as authors and compels them to relinquish control over their contributions. As we seek to promote ethical, accessible, and sustainable online practices for communicating, participating, and creating digital culture on the social web, it is important to better understand what it means to author online and to explore the shifting nature of the cultural concepts of authorship and ownership on the participatory web.

How do we define authorship in an age of social media, when the web is written by users through their activities, behaviors, and interactions with other people, texts, and technologies; when individual writers do not own the range of contributions they make; and when writers do not necessarily act with intentional authorial agency when making both visible and invisible contributions? In asking these questions, we seek to explore the implications of data-mining for the concept of authorship on the social web. We argue that a wide range of activities that add value to the social web—including practices involved in the generation of user data—might be better understood as unique and situated acts of coauthorship. Such an argument has theoretical implications for the concept of authorship as digital humanists, literary scholars, and others in the humanities have to date understood it. On a practical level, such a reconceptualization of authorship supports more balanced ownership claims with respect to data contributions users make to and within the social web, and greater reciprocity in the design and management of culture online.

To begin, we delineate and define user contributions on the participatory web, which we posit are forms of coauthorship. Next, we examine specific examples of the ownership claims that site owners advance in their terms of use policies with respect to user content and user data authored in digital spaces. We conclude that data-mining practices and policies on the social and participatory web fail to recognize the shared author status of users for many types of composing and rely on an imbalanced ownership structure for managing user contributions. Last, we describe implications for users, for technology designers, and for humanities scholars studying the social and participatory web. Ultimately, we argue for deeper critical attention to the rights claims that surround all types of user contributions—especially the more hidden contributions that take the shape of data—and for protections that would provide technology users increased agency to manage the content and data they coauthor on the social and participatory web.

Authorship on the Social Web: A Taxonomy for User Contributions

Nearly every interaction within digitally networked spaces produces either content or data; thus, the user roles on the participatory web are always already productive. Many productive practices result in content: distinct, packaged artifacts or texts easily recognizable as authored works. At the same time, users also contribute hidden compositions in the form of data, which might—if recognized at all—be understood as fleeting utterances rather than formal products of authorship. User data creates a detailed narrative about what paths users have taken, what technologies they have used, how they have composed in such spaces, and with whom they have participated. Currently, acts of production on the social web are ill-defined, and the range of contributions made by users is frequently hidden behind interfaces and algorithms that can obscure acts of authorship. Table 1 delineates a wide range of types of user contributions possible on the social web, including an array of both user content and user data. The table illustrates the diversity of contributions users make to these spaces as well as the complexities surrounding how contributions are authored and managed on the social web.

Table 1. User visible and hidden contributions to the participatory web

User-Generated Contributions on the Participatory Web	Example(s)	Authorship/Ownership Issues
Visible Contributions		
User content. Content authored offline and uploaded to social and participatory web spaces.	Video, text, images, sound files. Photos taken with digital cameras and then uploaded to Flickr.	Content owners become site users as they agree to terms of use. Users are typically assigned copyright ownership, but site owners claim rights to display, store, and share content through their site services.
User–site content. Content authored using the tools and software offered through social and participatory web services.	Blog posts. Status updates. Comments on status updates/photos. Tweets.	Content owners become site users as they agree to terms of use. Users are assigned copyright ownership for some content but not all. Site owners claim rights to display, store, and share content through their site services.

User-inputted data. Data inputted by user activity on the site.	Profile information, including name, location, contact information. Tags. "Likes."	Data is created by specific user actions on the site. Sites retain the right to collect and use this user data.
Hidden Contributions		
Content-related data. Information associated with user content.	Date, time, and location of file creation. Data about the type of camera/lens/software used to take and edit a digital photograph. History of edits and changes made to a file.	Creators use hardware and software to produce content. User data is embedded in files by hardware and software, and shared when posted. Sites retain the right to collect and use this data.
User–site content-related data. Information associated with user–site content.	Date, time, and location of the user–site content generation. Keywords from Tweets and status updates.	Creators use social and participatory web services to produce content. User data is embedded in the content when created. Sites retain the right to collect and use this user data.
User–site data. Data created as byproducts of user interactions with the site. Does not require an active inputting of information by the user.	Log of links followed by users. Log-in times and duration of activity. Viewing histories. Activities performed in conjunction with social and participatory web services.	Created by user–site interactions. Used by site owners to refine and personalize services for audiences. Sites retain the right to collect and use this data.
Site-specific aggregate data. Data sets created as multiple users interact with a site on multiple occasions.	Facebook's "People you may know." Amazon's purchasing and viewing histories that inform recommendations.	Created by multiple users using one service. Used by site owners to refine and personalize services for audiences. Sites retain the right to collect and use this data. Can be packaged for third-party purchase and consumption.
Aggregate data across services. Data sets that are created as multiple users interact with multiple sites on multiple occasions.	History created when users log in and access any combination of sites that are owned by the same corporate entity (Gmail, YouTube, and Chrome are all owned by Google) or by services with partner agreements (Facebook and Socialcam).	Created by multiple users across services. Used by site owners to refine and personalize services for audiences. Sites retain the right to collect and use this user data. Can be packaged for third-party purchase and consumption.

We have chosen to emphasize the visibility of user contributions because it points to a fundamental problem in conceptualizing authorship on the social web. Many users are not aware of the different ways they add value: Five out of the eight user contribution categories are hidden contributions. Take Facebook, for example: Contributors might author content (e.g., a status update, a photograph), an activity that constitutes visible contributions. These actions also contribute elements such as keywords; embedded time, date, and location information; face-recognition data; IP address; identification of the browser used; and information regarding other members tagged in the content. Users might understand that photographs or status updates are authored works because they are more visible contributions, but they might not understand that they have also contributed hidden data inseparable from content, which operates below the surfaces of the social and participatory web. These contributions—such as keywords from status updates, date/time/location identifiers, and activity histories—are largely obscured from the view of everyday users as they interact with social media sites. These same user contributions, however, are central to the workings of the social web: Users populate social web sites and networks, adapt tools, access content, create user histories, navigate pages and travel through digital space, all the time adding value by creating an evolving tapestry of digital interaction. That a large degree of user contributions is hidden obfuscates the role of users as producers within these digital spaces.

Ownership of user contributions typically resides with site owners or technology service providers in all but two categories. As we explore further in the next section, ownership rights to user data, governed by terms of use agreements, are imbalanced in favor of site owners and/or technology service providers. For example, upon signing up and using Facebook (as of April 2014), users may retain ownership of their photographs, but the associated data, their personal messages, activity logs, chats, and other activities can be appropriated and used by Facebook (for target advertising, product development, etc.). This ownership structure allows corporate parties to track users so that companies are able to deliver customized goods, services, and engage in niche advertising campaigns. Moreover, as multiple users interact with the site, developers can aggregate and mine this data to produce even more sophisticated knowledge about users. *New York Times* columnist Charles Duhigg (2012) reported that Target Corporation uses data gathered from consumer web site activities to predict, with a surprising degree of accuracy, which users might be expecting a baby and also the due date of the child. Additionally, user data can be mined across services and sites and sold to third parties through data aggregation and analysis. For example, Acxiom Corporation, a database-marketing company, collects and sells what another *New York Times* reporter has called the "consumer genome"—consumer data analyses that reveal useful information about past, current, and potential purchasing activities, as well as about ethnic backgrounds, health issues, and even religious preferences (Singer, 2012a). In this way, user data provides a great benefit to technology service providers and other companies with vested interests by revealing who users are, how they use services, and what motivates those uses, information that can then be interpreted to improve the design, development, delivery, and sales of services and products.

If user data on the social web is widely collected, appropriated, and used, it is problematic that users themselves have not been extended a fair share of access and ownership to the more hidden forms of their contributions. Many user contributions presented in Table 1 may not take the form of a discrete text an author has purposefully shared, but they are nevertheless valuable goods and the result of a productive act. Both visible and hidden user contributions are valuable contributions that serve to "write" the social web into existence. Although users of social and participatory web services might understand that visible contributions (e.g., text, photographs, videos) shared on the social web are authored texts to which they retain ownership rights, they may not perceive their data contributions as coauthored, meaningful texts, or even worse, they may not even grasp that these contributions exist.

We recognize the significant differences among the productive acts of writing a status update on Facebook, liking a status update on Facebook, uploading a photograph to Facebook that includes a status update, tagging a photograph, and sharing a photograph posted by a friend; however, each of these contributions results from a unique and situated productive act that adds value to the social web. In attempting to illuminate the complexity that surrounds user contributions on the social and participatory web, we hope that this taxonomy might be used as a starting place for discussions regarding the management of both visible and invisible user contributions. This taxonomy elucidates a present imbalance in the ownership claims users might exert with respect to their contributions and reveals a particular exchange system established between technology owners, who provide access to tools and services for composition and participation, and users, who contribute content and user data that creates meaning and adds value to tools and services. Failure to recognize the wide range of contributions made by users as valuable products of coauthorship supports the appropriation of user contributions by site owners and service providers. With a richer understanding of the varied types of user contributions and greater attention to the situated processes of authorship through which these contributions emerge, we might develop more nuanced insight into the consequences of our current understandings of and approaches to managing user data. If user contributions are fundamental to the value of the social web, then management of user contributions is necessarily at the forefront of its sustainability.

Terms of Use Policies: Ownership Claims to Visible and Invisible User Contributions

Terms of use policies reveal the implicit and explicit agreements users enter into when authoring on the social web. Policies that describe data use and user data ownership are required by law, though these policies are often lengthy and difficult to understand. Further, many policies fail to account for the rich complexity of authoring online and rely on problematic assumptions about user roles on the social web. In this section, we analyze the user agreements governing user participation within several popular social and participatory web services, including Facebook, Twitter, and Pinterest. Through our analysis and examples, we uncover two problematic assumptions that underlie the terms of use agreements: 1) user data contributions are technology byproducts rather than authored texts; and, as such, 2) user data contributions are free to be appropriated and used by technology service providers. These assumptions are based on false distinctions between content and data, between authored texts and technology byproducts, and between agent-directed and agent-less activity. These binaries work to obscure the value of user contributions and to support claims of ownership of user data asserted by technology providers.

False Binary: Content and Data

As noted in the table, one category of user contributions is content (user content or user-site content). Content includes contributions typically perceived as authored works, such as status updates, posts, Tweets, and photographs. Each requires a direct action (e.g., posting a photograph or creating a photo album) by an individual (e.g., a Facebook user) that results in an immediately identifiable, packaged contribution (e.g., photographs available on a Facebook Timeline for others to view). These contributions are best understood as the visible contributions users make. Legal ownership of user content is governed by copyright law, and specific rights regarding use and distribution are assigned through terms of use policies established by technology providers. Facebook, for instance, assigns copyright ownership of "content that is covered by intellectual property rights, like photos and videos" to users, but stipulates that by posting it to Facebook users are granting Facebook "a non-exclusive, transferable, sub-licensable, royalty-free, worldwide license to use any IP content that you post on or in connection with Facebook" (Facebook, "Sharing your content and information," 2013). Pinterest has a similar copyright policy governing what it calls "member content." While Cold Brew Labs (owners of Pinterest) assert a right to "use, copy, adapt, modify, distribute, license, sell, transfer, publicly display, publicly perform, transmit, stream, broadcast, access, view, and otherwise exploit" member content on the site, at the same time they "do not claim any ownership rights," and state that users are free to share, distribute, and profit from their content elsewhere (Pinterest, "Copyright," 2012).

These examples illustrate terms of use governing ownership of what we might think of as traditionally authored content on participatory web platforms, and are informed by U.S. legal code. However, the terms of use statements cannot rely on copyright law for user contributions not traditionally considered "intellectual property," such as user data (which would include all user contributions identified in the table except user content and user–site content). Terms of use agreements reveal that the rights service providers claim toward user data typically exceed the rights granted for user content. Technology companies reserve the right to deliver or share user-generated content contributed by users, but they often reserve a wider, less regulated right to access, appropriate, exploit, and use the six types of data shared in digital spaces, and to do so without user knowledge.

For user data, terms of use policies rely on language that draws attention to user choices to relinquish rights to the data they generate. Policies acknowledge that some data relies on direct user action or input. Facebook refers to such data as "information you choose to share" ("Information you choose to share," 2012); Twitter calls it "information you provide to us" ("Public information," 2012); and Google terms it "information you share" ("Information you give us," 2012). This data includes, in part, profile information, such as a name, photo, lists of friends, birthdate, location, and contact information. These contributions also include information that users directly contribute when participating online, including "likes," tags, and locations. This user data is what we identify as user-inputted data in Table 1, and is typically visible to users upon creation, requiring a direct user action. According to the terms of use policies we analyzed, this is information that service providers understand users to have willingly relinquished ownership to (a user "provides" it or "gives" it or "chooses to share" it).

For largely invisible user data contributions (all categories of user contributions identified as "hidden contributions" in the table), site owners deemphasize users' productive roles in its creation but again rely on the concept of user consent when asserting rights to appropriate and use the data. A legal claim to appropriate and employ user data is, as for the user-inputted data described above, based on the idea that users willingly relinquish rights to it. Facebook states:

> While you are allowing us to use the information we receive about you, you always own all of your information. Your trust is important to us, which is why we don't share information we receive about you with others unless we have:
>
> - received your permission;
> - given you notice, such as by telling you about it in this policy; or

- removed your name or any other personally identifying information from it. ("Information we receive about you," 2012)

While this statement boldly asserts that users "always own all of [their] information," this assignment of ownership appears to be *pro forma* and Facebook reserves the right to use the information in many ways as long as at least one of the listed conditions is met (and one condition, of course, is an agreement the user accepts when using Facebook in the first place). Interestingly, in terms of use policies, site owners often make no explicit claim to own user data; in fact, the agreements posit that users retain ownership of their contributions, in both visible and invisible forms. However, the notion that users grant technology providers certain rights to data that they still "own" is misleading. Site owners automatically appropriate, upon creation, user data and use in wide-reaching and ill-defined ways, so much so that assignment of ownership to users appears to be close to meaningless. Therefore, while users retain meaningful ownership rights to their content contributions within participatory web platforms, site owners assume *de facto* control over user data.

This difference may be because user rights are protected by federal copyright law, while a legal claim to appropriate and employ user data is not. U.S. copyright law protects literary, dramatic, musical, and artistic works but not facts and ideas; it applies to expressions of ideas but not the ideas themselves. Data records may, in some cases, qualify for copyright protection, as arguments could be forwarded that the owner could be the record's creator (an individual user), the technology designer (who created the algorithm for aggregating data), the employer of the creator of the data or the algorithm (under work-for-hire), and/or some hybrid of all of these options. Data points alone, however, are not copyrightable, unless collected in a compilation or database based on unique coordination, selections, or arrangements that demonstrate sufficient originality (*Feist Publications v. Rural Telephone*, 1991). Although data alone cannot be copyrighted, forms of visible and hidden user contributions are inextricably bound, as the production of user data is tied to the production of content and vice versa. Because many types of user contributions are interconnected in complex ways, the rights extended to content and data are not easily separable. Problematically, terms of use policies rely on the assumption of a clear and meaningful distinction between user-generated content and data. Although they grant users a balanced set of rights to the content they contribute, they offer few if any meaningful rights to the data users generate. Terms of use policies that separate the rights to content and data, and falsely assert that users "own" all of their contributions, obscure the imbalanced management structure of user contributions on the social web.

False Binary: Authored Texts and Technology Byproducts

Within terms of use policies, types of user data typically invisible or obscured to users (user–site content-related data, user–site data, site-specific aggregate data, aggregate data across services in Table 1) are presented as byproducts of user interactions with technology rather than as authored products. Google refers to this information as "information we get from your use of our services" (2012) and Facebook calls it "information we receive about you" (2012).

A byproduct is a secondary and unexpected product that results from making a principal product. It is a derivative of the intended product but is not the intended result of a laboring effort, and it can even be undesirable in its outcome (think side effects). The user data described in terms of use policies does not appear to rely on an authorial agent responsible for a productive act. Rather, the generation of user data is seen as a technological outcome: The technology providers note that they "collect," "get," and "receive" information and data when users interact with the site, but such user data is not "produced" intentionally by the user. For instance, Google asserts that "when you use our services or view content provided by Google, we may automatically collect and store certain information." These types of user data (user–site content-related data, user–site data, site-specific aggregate data, aggregate data across services) differ from other types of user data (user-inputted data and content-related data) because, as presented in terms of use policies, they emerge as a result of user–technology interaction, neutrally available to be "received" by the technology provider and to be gathered and "collected." In these terms, the user's role is passive (collection is "automatic"), while the technology itself plays an active, generative role in what appears to be a neutral, even positive process of making good use of an otherwise wasted byproduct. Facebook, for example, claims to "receive" user data and then "put together data" in a meaningful way to offer higher quality, more efficient services. In this way, the terms of use statements position user data as technology byproducts without an owner or a human source, without meaning until it is put to use by the site owner.

The understanding of data derivatives as collected information—as objective facts that pre-exist rather than products of human agency—precludes an understanding of user data as texts to which users should retain some ownership and control. It is not within the scope of this chapter to explore in full the rich body of scholarship on the concept of authorship and its relationship to agency; it is, however, useful to note that Krista Kennedy (2010) challenged the notion of technologically automated tasks as unauthored in her analysis of Wikipedia bots as authors of encyclopedic entries. Kennedy urged scholars in the digital humanities to "recognize more and more that writing happens as an interactive process that involves exchanges between multiple agents, texts, and influences," and posited that automated bots performing "textual curation" and other mundane tasks be considered as authors, or at least as "a newly identifiable creature" (p. 308). The nonhuman agents at work on the social and participatory web compose through data solicitation, aggregation, and categorization. However, this technological agency is intertwined and articulated with human agency at key stages. Technology developers make decisions and implement choices as they design systems for data collection and mining, as well as when they develop interfaces that direct user interaction. Additionally, it is the interaction between humans and technology that results in the productive act of composing data: As users view, contribute, and share with social and participatory web technologies, with other texts, and with each other, they become collaborative agents in generating data. Despite the fact that data is produced by interactions among humans and technology, the terms of use policies noted above fail to recognize human agency in the generation of data. The treatment of data as authorless byproduct, a result of technological agency, precludes consideration of data as having creative and intellectual value, as well as the granting of ownership status to users.

The question is not whether social and participatory web technologies demonstrate some agency at strategic moments in the generation, collection, and use of data, but whether a technological agent is acting alone in the production of user data. According to the terms of use statements for social and participatory web technologies, user data is not a product of a human agent; the only agency demonstrated in its generation is a non-human, technological system. If we grant sole agency to technological systems, we should understand clearly the potential implications of excluding human agency from this aspect of digital composition. Carolyn Miller (2007) addressed the concept of agency in relation to automated computerized systems in her discussion of automated tools used for writing assessment. Miller recognized agency as that which requires "attribution" and asked important questions about the implications of granting attribution to automated systems. Marilyn Cooper (2011) recognized individuals' conscious and nonconscious rhetorical acts (as seem to occur in the production of social data) as acts of agency that have real consequences: "Rhetorical agency is a big responsibility. It means being responsible for oneself, for others, and for the common world we construct together" (p. 444). If attribution of agency is a gift of empowerment, as Miller argued, and if such empowerment places a high level of responsibility on the agent, as Cooper argued, then we must think carefully about whether we should be willing to grant social web technologies the power of agency in the generation of user data.

Separating a human author–agent from the productive act of generating user data, as do the terms of use policies for some social web services, privileges a structure in which the technology provider automatically assumes ownership and control over user information without knowledge or consent from a user. If user data is posited as a neutral byproduct of a technological system, it becomes impossible for users to claim ownership or control over it, or even to understand data contributions as a direct result of their activity online. Data becomes, at its inception, free to be appropriated and controlled by those responsible for the technology and not by users. Removing a human author–agent from the productive act of generating user data obscures the presence of an unfair exchange system established between users and technology providers. If use-related contributions are posited as neutral byproducts of a technological system (and indeed they are), it becomes difficult for users to claim any ownership or control over them. Instead, we argue that framing all user contributions as generative acts of collaborative agency, by recognizing the complexity of digital production and acknowledging the value that users contribute as data creators, is a strategic approach to combating a status quo wherein user contributions are misappropriated and devalued.

Managing User Data: Implications for the Future of the Social Web

Supporters of data appropriation by technology companies assert that users are active parties in giving up ownership of their contributions. For instance, Mark Zuckerberg, the founder of Facebook, claimed that,

> People have really gotten comfortable not only sharing more information and different kinds, but more openly and with more people. That social norm is just something that has evolved over time.... We view it as our role in the system to constantly be innovating and be updating what our system is to reflect what the current social norms are. (Kirkpatrick, 2010)

Zuckerberg reported that he was merely responding to social norms in the development of Facebook's data use policies. Based on the premise that "privacy is dead" in a networked era, he argued that users have little interest in retaining rights to or control over the user data they generate. However, we think that the problem surrounding user data is not a problem caused by how much people are sharing ("users are revealing too much"), or even by the type and nature of information they are willing to share ("if users are concerned about privacy, it's because they have something to hide"). Nor is it a problem that we should resign ourselves against ("we're all being tracked online all the time, so who cares?"). danah boyd (2008) reported that users have been surprised to find out that their information is being appropriated and applied toward commercial ends, breaching their expectations concerning privacy and information flow. Sherry Turkle (2012), based on an ambitious research study about human–technology interactions, reported on the general lack of privacy and resulting anxiety that adolescents, teenagers, and young adults feel when online. Arguing for the value of a more user-controlled space for communication, interaction, participation, and reflection, Turkle warned social media users that they should not ignore data-management practices. These studies and others support the idea that a solution to the data use problem on the social web requires more than user self-discipline or a change in user behavior to simply "be discreet" when online.

Further, individual user's actions to resist current practices of managing user data are likely to be met with roadblocks. Terms of use governing ownership of user contributions on social and participatory web technologies are based on agreements made between unequal partners—between uninformed users and powerful companies that hide much of their activities from users. Sites do have a legal duty to inform users how information will be collected and used, but the duty to inform can be fulfilled by simply posting terms of use on web sites. A 2008 study conducted by Carnegie Mellon researchers regarding the difficulty of reading and comprehending lengthy and complex terms of use agreements found that, based on an analysis of a large sample of terms of use policies, it would take an average user 76 work days per year to read all privacy policies on every web site visited (McDonald & Cranor, 2008). Potentially more problematic is that these user agreements may change at a moment's notice. Technology service providers reserve the right to make changes to privacy policies, and often do, which can leave users even more confused. Whether users have been fully informed of terms of use is debatable, and while service providers claim to only collect information with user consent, interpretation of what constitutes consent is questionable. As evidenced in the examples above, terms of use often assert that by using a service, users provide consent for the collection of information. Heidi McKee (2011) questioned the ethicality of this structure for consent, and called it "manufactured and illusionary" (p. 284).

In addition to the concept of consent, the concept of user choice in data use practices is also misleading. Users of social and participatory web services might believe that they have more control over their data contributions than they actually do. Facebook's Data Use Policy is introduced with the directive to users, "get to know the privacy settings that help you to control your information." Users are told that they have choices surrounding their information, and that they can customize settings to control the flow of their information. Users may be comforted by the notion of options and settings: Customization options give the illusion of user ownership and control over their own data, suggesting that users have the right to retain some ownership over some information types. However, default settings offered by technology companies largely determine the use of social media services by the vast majority of users. To choose different settings, users must be aware of the default settings, what their implications are, where to locate their controls, and how to change them.

User choice requires that users understand how the different settings affect their use of the service and which settings to implement to get specific results. In noting the problematic default settings in Google and the nature of "choice architecture," Siva Vaidhyanathan (2011) argued that "meaningful freedom implies real control over the conditions of one's life. Merely setting up a menu with switches does not serve the interests of any but the most adept, engaged, and well-informed" (p. 88). Because many users lack the understanding or the technical know-how to make different choices, default settings often result in most users allowing their data to be appropriated and used by technology companies, except in rare circumstances for the most informed and technologically adept users. Currently, users face a problematic situation: They are complicit in an arrangement in which they have been compelled to relinquish control over their own contributions, where consent carries little meaning and choice is illusory.

The issue of user rights to their contributions on the social web has not gone unnoticed by the federal government, which released a White House white paper in March 2012 signed by President Obama, titled *Consumer Data Privacy in a Networked World*. The report contained codes of conduct for technology developers and a call for Congress to pass legislation that applies a privacy "bill of rights" to commercial sectors. One month later, the Federal Trade Commission (2012) released its report on the topic, which encouraged technological fixes for the user data problem, such as the Do Not Track mechanism, a measure also supported by the Internet activism group the Electronic Frontier Foundation (Auerbach, 2012), but resisted by the Association of National Advertisers (Singer, 2012b). Such a mechanism would allow Internet users to participate online without leaving a trail of data behind, but it could also potentially prevent users from fully participating in networked environments. Further, it relies on a technological fix rather than encouraging a revised management structure with more reciprocity among technology designers, data managers, and users. Do Not Track is a set of pre-selected options rather than a thoughtful choice employed by individual users, much like the "customization" and privacy settings offered by individual social web services.

Certainly, privacy is a compelling social flashpoint for motivating government, trade, and user interventions to current approaches to data mining. As framed by the 2012 White House white paper, the issue of data-mining is largely about preserving "individual dignity" (p. 53) and the right to "be let alone" (p. 3). Still, for researchers, instructors, and students, especially in the digital humanities, the issue of owning user data is about more than "being let alone." Beyond privacy rights resides a larger issue that Internet users should be suspicious of: a structure of exchange that compels everyday users—often unaware—to give up control over their contributions for the right to participate. Digital humanists should be wary of a digital knowledge economy that stakes such large claims over something as valuable as user contributions. Yes, users are able to connect with others through social networking services, and they have the technical ability to contribute through participatory web platforms, but at what cost? Certainly, users trade tangible access to their personal information to garner access to technological platforms, yet what are the social and cultural costs that users pay? While Google tells users that new data use practices will make their lives better by creating a unified online experience, the fact remains that data-mining is, at the same time, pushing technology company stock values higher and challenging the boundaries of what users will—and should—accept as the cost for access. Management of user data determines the role and value of user contributions within a larger economy of cultural production.

Taken together, the terms of use policies governing social and participatory web services make false claims and problematic assumptions about authoring and owning user contributions online. While photographs and postings and other "member content" are considered to be copyrightable, owned by the user and used for particular purposes by the technology service provider, user data associated with such content and other interactions are not treated as user contributions. Rather, user data is presented as technology-generated material, or as a neutral byproduct of technology usage. Contrarily, user data might be considered coauthored texts and valuable compositions, produced by human agents acting collaboratively with other individuals and texts and technologies on the social web. User data results from a productive activity, a result of human interaction with a dynamic technological space. Further, it is inseparable from composing processes in the social web. Although the generation of user data might be regarded as ancillary to more traditional acts of online composing, the massive amount of information produced by users is central to the value of the participatory web, enabling collective intelligence, personalized experiences, and responsive technological spaces. User data, then, might be understood as providing the basis for a sustainable networked, participatory web.

As digital humanities scholars grapple with issues of privacy and ownership on the social web, we should work to educate ourselves, colleagues, and students about this unfair exchange system. The conditions of access to popular platforms for social networking and communication include submission to forms of surveillance and data use that support a particular view of the Internet: an Internet based on the logic of online commerce, data-driven mass customization, and target marketing. The danger presented is that contributions of everyday users will potentially be transformed into increasingly exclusive forms of proprietary data, available to the few. Instead, the social and participatory web might bring users greater social utility; it might promote more robust citizenry; it might facilitate more efficient markets; it might even add more accountability to the types of exchanges that occur—if it were managed with a more balanced approach to ownership of user contributions. If we hope for a social web that promotes increased participation, access, and citizenship, we must understand user contributions as authored texts collaboratively constructed among authors, texts, technologies, technology providers, and the sea of users who engage these spaces. By doing so, we might better recognize the value that users add to the social web as open and shared resources that produce digital culture.

• CHAPTER NINE •

No Copyright Intended

Nicole Nguyen

Many of the user-uploaded videos on YouTube have the phrase "no copyright infringement intended"—particularly on videos that are unique, fresh interpretations of mainstream culture. One such example is a full-length version of the film *Pulp Fiction* in chronological order posted on YouTube with the following description:

> The legendary movie itself into chronological order. If you'd like me to put the full movie itself up, let me know and I'll be glad to oblige. Please no copyright infringement. I only put this up as a project.

This YouTube video, posted by crimewriter95, could be the subject of a whole host of literary criticisms and may serve as a representation of the clash between the generation of content (and culture) remixers and the Institution of Copyright as we currently know it. The phrase "please no copyright infringement," and others like it reveals a key aspect of remix culture: Remixers believe that infringement turns *primarily* on intent. While courts consider bad faith under the Fair Use test, it is easy to imagine conservative courts construing the mere inclusion of such a disclaimer as evidence of the bad faith in the creation of the work.

In this chapter, I address the background of remix culture, focusing on definitions of various methods of remixing. Next, I discuss the case *Cariou v. Prince*, which addresses issues with appropriation art. Then, I analyze *Pulp Fiction* and a YouTube video of the film in chronological order, delving into the literary, cultural, and legal implications of each work.

Background

Remixing, Mashups, and Appropriation Art: Definitions

Remixing primarily refers to the practice of "sampling" music by other artists and incorporating it into new musical creations. More globally, remix "can be defined as the global activity consisting of the creative and efficient exchange of information made possible by digital technologies that is supported by the practice of cut/copy and paste" (Navas, 2012). More simply, a remix is a reinterpretation of an already existing work, such as a song. While the practice of remixing can trace its origins to Jamaican music, remixing has spread to other areas of culture, including the visual arts (Navas, 2012). Mashups may be considered a genre of remixing that takes two forms: regressive mashups (including music, such as those popularized by the television show "Glee"), and reflexive mashups (which could include fashion, film, television, video, and architectural elements; Navas, 2009, p. 2).

Appropriation art is an art history and art criticism term that refers to "direct taking over into a work of art a real object or even an existing work of art" (Beaven & Ward, 2012). Appropriation art "raises questions of originality, authenticity and authorship, and belongs to the long modernist tradition of art that questions the nature or definition of art itself," and has been used broadly since the 1980s (Beaven & Ward). Appropriation art often involves physical media, such as paintings, prints, drawings, or 3D objects, including personal and found objects.

Video Remix Culture

Vidding is the practice of creating music videos using the footage of one or more videos, in order to explore the original video in a new way. Vidding is typically done by fans who build videos around particular themes or characters; the practice is closely related in effect to fan fiction (Tushnet, 2011).

One notable genre of remixing that almost always qualifies as fair use is the political remix. Political remixer Jonathan McIntosh, creator behind the viral video "Buffy vs. Edward," noted about his experiences teaching others to remix that

> after engaging in remix culture, people young and old find it nearly impossible to experience media in a passive or uncritical way. As members of that remix culture even if we never make a remix video ourselves, we can't help but make imaginary mash-ups in our heads when watching television of movies. (Jenkins, 2010)

This sentiment expressed by McIntosh can be traced across all genres of remixing. McIntosh's remixes represent the epitome of remixing as fair use; he described his work as "remixing mass media narratives for critical purposes"

(McIntosh, 2012). McIntosh identified five essential criteria for determining whether a transformative video fit into the political remix genre:

1. Works appropriate mass media audiovisual source material without permission from copyright holders, and rely on the fair use doctrine;

2. Works comment on, deconstruct, or challenge media narratives, dominant myths, social norms, and traditional power structures;

3. Works transform the original messages embedded in the source material, as well as the source material itself;

4. Works are intended for general audiences or do-it-yourself (DIY) communities rather than academic or high-art audiences, and thus tend to use familiar mass media formats such as trailers, television ads, music videos, and news segments as vehicles for the transformed messages; and

5. Works are DIY productions and rely on grassroots distribution methods such as VHS tape duplicating circles, underground screenings, and, eventually, self-hosted Web sites. (McIntosh)

While distinct from Fair Use elements, these criteria shed some light on the divide between the legal perception of a remix video and the non-legal perspective. Criteria (1), (2), and (3), in particular, embody elements of the Fair Use defense, providing for specific aspects of the legal analysis: (2) requires that a remix comment on the original message, while (3) requires that the work transform the original message. These two elements parallel the considerations that a court takes into account when evaluating the first element of the fair use defense. While the legal world folds both of these elements—comment/criticism and transformation—into a single aspect of a four factor test (the character and nature of the use), the non-legal world recognizes that each of these tasks performed by a remixer is distinct and must be considered separately.

Cariou v. Prince: An Example of How Copyright Law Currently Affects Appropriation Art

Cariou v. Prince (784 F. Supp. 2d 337) is a 2011 case out of the Southern District of New York that held that artist Prince's appropriation of Cariou's copyrighted photos in paintings constituted infringement and was not protected as Fair Use, in part because the use was not transformative under the law. The district court concluded that Prince's work was not transformative because it did not "in some way comment on, relate to the historical context of, or critically refer back" to Cariou's work. However, on appeal, the Second Circuit reversed, and in the process, formulated a new Fair Use analysis.

Case Summary

The plaintiff in this case was Patrick Cariou, a professional photographer who took a series of photographs of Rastafarians in Jamaica for a book entitled *Yes, Rasta* (see also Evans, this volume). The photos included in the book were all taken by Cariou and he was the sole copyright owner of the photos in the book. Well-known appropriation artist Richard Prince, defendant, purchased a copy of *Yes, Rasta*, tore out the pages containing the photos, attached them to a wooden board, and painted over some portions of the photographs to make a series of collages entitled "Canal Zone."

The Southern District of New York held that Prince, the appropriation artist, infringed Cariou's photographs; his Fair Use defense failed because he did not meet the test for transformative use. Here, the defendant's intentions behind creating the works of art played an important role in the court's analysis of whether the defendant's use constituted criticism or comment of the copyrighted work. Prince testified during trial that he did not have an interest in the original photos, and that he did not "really have a message" to communicate through his works of art.

Ultimately, the court determined that Prince's uses were minimally transformative at best, and therefore the transformative use factor weighed "heavily" against a finding of Fair Use. The court also found that the other Fair Use factors weighed against a finding of fair use, though its analysis on the other factors was significantly shorter.

On appeal, the Second Circuit reversed the decisions of the District Court regarding transformation, the effect of the new work on the potential market for the original work, and found that 25 of Prince's works constituted Fair Use. (*Cariou v. Prince*, Docket No. 11-1197-cv; 2nd Cir. April 25, 2013). The Second Circuit held that

> the law imposes no requirement that a work comment on the original or its author in order to be considered transformative, and a secondary work may constitute a fair use even if it serves some purpose other than those (criticism, comment, news reporting, teaching, scholarship, and research) identified in the preamble to the statute.

Under this decision, a work can be transformative if it alters the original work through "new expression, meaning, or message" (Id. citing *Campbell*, 510 U.S. at 579 and *Blanch*, 467 F.3d at 253).

Additionally, the Second Circuit rejected the District Court's analysis on the third fair use factor, amount and substantiality of the original work taken, stating that "the law does not require that the secondary artist may take no more than is necessary." The Second Circuit remanded to the District Court to determine whether the remaining works met the new fair use test.

Implications

When the Southern District Court of New York issued its opinion in March 2011, the art and legal worlds had distinct reactions. From the art world's perspective, the District Court's decision in *Cariou v. Prince* was "the *Roe v. Wade* of the art world" (Sarmiento, 2012). The court's extreme focus on the issue of transformative use and the role that the defendant's intention played in the creation of the paintings seemed unusual and, at first blush, had negative implications for artists—appropriation artists, in particular.

It is notable that the Second Circuit's analysis of the Fair Use factors differed both from the analysis by the District Court *and* from Supreme Court jurisprudence (*Campbell* and *Blanch*, in particular). The Second Circuit's new formulation of the fair use analysis may have broader implications for appropriation artists because it expands the realm of how much of an original work can be used. At this point, it may still be too early to determine long-term effects of the *Cariou v. Prince* case, as it remains to be seen whether Cariou will appeal the Second Circuit decision to the Supreme Court.

Pulp Fiction: A Literary Analysis of Quentin Tarantino's Iconic Film

Pulp Fiction may be considered a prime example of postmodern film, though it is often alternatively described as either noir or neo-noir. The film's title refers to pulp magazines and hardboiled crime novels famous in the mid-twentieth century, and notable for their graphic violence and punchy dialogue. The nonlinear film follows three distinct, but interrelated storylines over the course of 27 hours. Each storyline concentrates on a single character, though the other characters weave in and out of the story. The three primary storylines are presented with a title card and with four, smaller narrative sequences filling in the gaps. Tarantino's original film presents the sequences in the following order:

1. Prologue—The Diner
2. Prelude to "Vincent Vega and Marsellus Wallace's Wife"
3. "Vincent Vega and Marsellus Wallace's Wife"
    (a) Prelude to "The Gold Watch"—flashback
    (b) Prelude to "The Gold Watch"—present
4. "The Gold Watch"
5. "The Bonnie Situation"
6. Epilogue—The Diner

In a 1994 interview with *The New York Times*, Tarantino described his motivation for writing the screenplay the way he did as stemming from a desire to do "something that novelists get a chance to do but film makers don't: telling three separate stories, having characters float in and out with different weights depending on the story" (Lowry, 1994). Despite Tarantino's desire to use what he considered a novel technique, there is ample evidence of such nonlinear storytelling in film dating back to the very first silent films (*Intolerance*, 1916), French avant-garde (*Un Chien Andalou*, 1929), and mid-twentieth-century films by Jean-Luc Godard and Robert Altman (Berg 2006). What Tarantino accomplished, however, was bringing the nonlinear narrative from a place in experimental film to straddling a line between art house, genre films and mainstream film: the "Tarantino effect" (Berg 2006).

Crimewriter95's *Pulp Fiction* in Chronological Order

A Literary Analysis

While Quentin Tarantino certainly had specific reasons for writing the film as a nonlinear narrative, changing that order from nonlinear to linear (chronological order) changes the experience of the film. The act of putting it in order is a standard analytical exercise for anyone delving deeper into the analysis of any non-linear narrative. For those *not* studying or analyzing the film, per se, the original film is still a puzzle—and the chronological order version the key to the puzzle. However, on a literary level, the bare action of re-ordering the film adds new meaning, new insights and understandings, and new value.

Crimewriter95's chronological-order version of the film followed the major delineations of the film, taking care to utilize the multiple prologues throughout, and divided the original film into the following segments (his own descriptions, making use of the major characters): (1) Butch getting the Golden Watch; (2) Vincent and Jules killing Brett and Flock of Seagulls; (3) The Bonnie Situation; (4) the intro scene mixed with the Vincent and Jules diner scene; (5) the bar scene with Marsellus and Butch; (6) the entire Mrs. Wallace diner and heroin overdose incident, Butch killing the other boxer, killing Vincent; (7) Marsellus and Butch getting captured; Zed and the other hillbilly's death, then riding off with Fabienne.

A Cultural Analysis

It is difficult to determine the full extent to which this YouTube video has affected popular culture, due in part to the fact that the video was removed several times. On January 23, 2012, crimewriter95 posted a video-blog (filmed such that the viewer could hear his voice, but not see his face), explaining why he removed his own videos, and seemingly admitting that they contained copyrighted material and that he could go to jail for a long time. In the video, crimewriter95 seemed the most upset about losing the large number of views on the Pulp Fiction video (around 300,000), and informed viewers that he would try to re-upload videos, starting with *Pulp Fiction*, within the week. The video was reposted on March 12, 2012, with the following comment: "I'm glad everyone's been enjoying this. Sorry I had to take the movie down in the first place. The SOPA and PIPA online piracy bills were threatening me and it gave me no choice. It's here to stay this time so enjoy!" However, by April 11, 2012 YouTube had removed the video, citing copyright violations.

It is also unclear what, precisely, he meant by the statement "the SOPA and PIPA online piracy bills were threatening me." He initially took down the videos—*all* of them, including several for which he had independently filmed and created the content—voluntarily, so any threats must have been perceived, rather than actual threats. This action reveals both a specific awareness of the proposed legislation and the threat they posed to such YouTube videos as uploaded by crimewriter95, as well as an acknowledgment that what he does is wrong—that his videos violate either existing laws or proposed laws.

A Legal Analysis

The following analysis will assume the following facts: that crimewriter95 purchased a DVD of *Pulp Fiction*, ripped it to his hard drive, completed all of the editing himself, and then uploaded the edited video to YouTube with the description,

> the legendary movie itself into chronological order. If you'd like me to put the full movie itself up, let me know and I'll be glad to oblige. Please no copyright infringement. I only put this up as a project.

Further, "put this up as a project" will be interpreted in two ways: (1) with "project" meaning as an educational or school-related assignment; and (2) with "project" meaning a personal, on-the-side hobby.

Infringement Analysis. Under the 1976 Copyright Act, a defendant may be liable for copyright infringement if the plaintiff owned a valid copyright in the work in question and that the defendant copied constituent elements of the work that are original (17 U.S.C. § 501). Originality in a copyright sense is a low threshold; to be original, a work must have been independently created by the author and have a minimal degree of creativity (see *Feist Publications v. Rural Telephone Service Company*, 499 U.S. at 345; 1991).

The underlying work, Quentin Tarantino's *Pulp Fiction*, is clearly the proper subject of a valid copyright, and whether that copyright belongs to Tarantino or the studio that produced the film is not relevant for this discussion. The underlying screenplay and the performance manifested in the film meet the minimum threshold for originality—that a work must have been independently created by the author and have a minimal degree of creativity. To complete the copyrightability analysis, the work must be fixed in a tangible medium of expression. Both the screenplay and the film meet this test; written works and works preserved on film are two standard examples of "fixed" works for purposes of the Copyright Act. The copying requirement in this situation is easily satisfied; crimewriter95 used the original, copyrighted film in its entirety. This constitutes direct copying; in the absence of direct copying, courts will look at circumstantial evidence to determine whether copying occurred.

Fair Use. Once a finding of infringement is made, the defendant (here, crimewriter95) would assert the Fair Use defense in order to avoid liability. The Fair Use defense consists of four factors: (1) the purpose and character of the use, including whether such use is of a commercial nature or is for nonprofit educational purposes; (2) the nature of the copyrighted work; (3) the amount and substantiality of the portion used in relation to the copyrighted work as a whole; and (4) the effect of the use upon the potential market for or value of the copyrighted work (17 U.S.C. § 107). Under the first factor, on which the court in *Cariou v. Prince* focused much of its analysis, there are three subfactors: (1) whether the use was transformative or supersedes the market for the original; (2) whether the use is commercial in nature; (3) the propriety of the infringer's conduct (essentially, whether the infringer acted in bad faith).

Here, with "Pulp Fiction in Chronological Order," the second and third factors are fairly straight-forward. Under the second factor, the original film is a published work of fiction—while there is more leeway for fair uses where the work is published (because the work has already been disseminated, the second use is not usurping the right of the original author to first publication), Fair Use is narrower for works of fiction. Under the third factor, amount and substantiality of the portion used in relation to the copyrighted work as a whole, the user-uploaded video clearly takes the *entire* film.

The fourth factor, the effect of the use upon the potential market for or value of the copyrighted work, is less clear cut. Courts have characterized this factor as "the single most important element of fair use" (*Harper & Row, Publishers v. Nation Enters.*, 471 U.S. 539, 566; 1985). This factor takes into consideration whether, if the challenged use "should become widespread, it would adversely affect the potential market for the copyrighted work" (*Sony Corp. of America v. Universal City Studios, Inc.*, 464 U.S. 417, 451; 1984). Courts are also concerned with whether a potential market for the derivative product could have existed (regardless of whether the rights holder contemplated expanding into that market), and whether the use deprives the rights holder of revenue/access/opportunities in that market (see *Roger v. Koons*, 960 F.2d 301; 2d Cir. 1992). Where the use is noncommercial, the plaintiff does not benefit from the presumption that the use would create a likelihood of harm to the derivative market, as it would if the use was primarily for commercial gain; rather the plaintiff must demonstrate that such likelihood exists (see *Campbell*, 510 U.S. at 591; *Sony*, 464 U.S. at 451).

Here, given the number of YouTube users who have attempted to create videos of *Pulp Fiction* in chronological order, along with the number of views, comments, and likes/dislikes that each video has, a court would likely find that some sort of market exists. What is not evident here is whether consumers of these YouTube videos would be willing to *pay* for a chronological-order version of the film. One further consideration is that these YouTube videos may generate interest in the original film and may drive users to purchase their own copies of the film for personal viewing and individual attempts at putting together the chronological puzzle.

The first Fair Use factor, purpose and character of the use, presents the biggest analytical challenge with its three sub-factors: (1) whether the use was transformative or supersedes the market for the original; (2) whether the use is commercial in nature; (3) the propriety of the infringer's conduct (essentially, whether the infringer acted in bad faith). Arguably, under the first sub-factor, the presence of YouTube videos at all, and in particular, this video, increases the market for the original, rather than superseding it. Without having viewed the original film, the viewing a chronological-order version of the film takes away the challenge and pleasure of the *Pulp Fiction* experience. Transformation in this situation requires more examination. One Fair Use guide suggests that users ask the following questions when taking portions of a copyrighted work: Has the material taken from the original been transformed by adding new expression or meaning? Was value added to the original by creating new information, new aesthetics, new insights, and understandings? (Nolo, 2010). Here, crimewriter95 took the entire film and re-edited it, adding nothing to the video itself—there is no obvious new expression. However, on a literary level, the bare action of re-ordering the film adds new meaning, new insights and understandings, and new value. Where the original film is a puzzle for the viewer to solve, the YouTube video provides the solution, and guides the viewer through a timeline that was otherwise not clear.

The next factor is whether work is commercial. Many courts have gone so far as to adopt the maxim that commercial uses are presumptively unfair. However, the court in *Rogers v. Koons* stated that though commerciality is a significant factor, "it is not itself controlling," and the determination of whether the use is fair must be made based on the totality of circumstances (*Rogers*, 960 F.2d at 309). Further, "the mere fact that a use is educational and not for profit does not insulate it from a finding of infringement, any more than the commercial character of a use bars a finding of fairness" (*Campbell v. Acuff-Rose Music*, 510 U.S. 569, 584; 1993).

Here, the video is presumably non-commercial in nature. The video does not have any advertisements and if the user was paid in some form for editing and posting the video, he did not disclose this. In all likelihood, the video squarely falls in the non-commercial realm, given the context—particularly that the user describes the video as a "project." Further, given his emphasis in his vlog on the number of video views, it appears that his value from the video derives primarily from popularity and followers. More views often translates to more subscribers, which is a larger potential audience for the user's self-created content.

Finally, we come to the hot-button issue in *Cariou v. Prince*: the propriety of the infringer's conduct, and whether the disclaimers employed by user-uploaders should be evidence of bad faith. In the YouTube context, the disclaimers typically attached to user-uploaded videos seem to be attempts at showing a subjective lack of bad faith. Notably, in *Campbell v. Acuff-Rose Music, Inc.* the plaintiff argued that the fact that the defendants had asked for, and were denied, permission to use the copyrighted work should be weighed against a finding of fair use (*Campbell* 510 U.S. 569, 585). The Court rejected this argument in dicta, reasoning that even if good faith were a central aspect of the Fair Use test, the action of requesting permission to use the song did not necessarily mean that the group believed that their version was not a fair use; the request may have been made in a good faith effort to avoid litigation (*Campbell* 510 U.S. 569, 585). Finally, the Court noted that "if the use is otherwise fair, then no permission need be sought or granted" (*Campbell* 510 U.S. 569, 585). Since the *Campbell* decision, courts have attempted to distinguish *Campbell* and allow consideration of bad faith motivation for copying under this factor, but the analysis has been "unconvincing," in the words of Nimmer (see, for instance, *Los Angeles News Service v. KCAL-TV Channel 9*, 108 F.3d 1119; 9th Cir. 1997; *Blanch v. Koons*, 467 F.3d 244, 256; 2d Cir. 2006; following the Supreme Court precedent in *Campbell* that being denied permission should not give rise to a presumption of bad faith).

On balance, this is a *very* close call for a finding against fair use and depends in large part on the first factor: purpose and character of the use. The second and third factors (nature of the copyrighted work and amount and substantiality of the use, respectively) both weigh against a finding of fair use. The fourth factor, effect on the potential market of the copyrighted work, is questionable; valid arguments can be made on either side, and thus may be considered a nullity. Regarding the first factor, while the use is non-commercial, its transformativeness is truly in the eye of the beholder. A literary or film aficionado judge may find that the use sufficiently transforms the original, but another judge could quite easily find the opposite way. Based on legal precedent, the final sub-factor of the purpose and character factor, propriety of the alleged infringer's conduct, will weigh against a finding of fair use.

What is troubling about this conclusion is that it glosses over added value that may not be obvious or clear to the casual viewer, and instead relies on the judge's subjective findings about value.

DMCA–Section 1201(a)(1). The Digital Millennium Copyright Act (DMCA) criminalizes the production and dissemination of technology, devices, or services intended to circumvent digital rights management (DRM) systems that control access to copyrighted works (17 U.S.C. § 1201, *et seq.*). The statute has built in safe harbors and exemptions, as well as a provision that requires the Librarian of Congress to issue additional exemptions that, when made, remain in place for three years (17 U.S.C. § 1201(a)(1)). In the September 2011 rulemaking suggestions, the Copyright Office added an exception to DMCA enforcement for the use of *short portions* of copyrighted motion pictures in videos created by film and media studies students and professors at colleges and universities:

> (1) Motion pictures on DVDs that are lawfully made and acquired [...] when circumvention is accomplished **solely in order to accomplish the incorporation of short portions of motion pictures into new works for the purpose of criticism or comment**, and where the person engaging in circumvention believes and has reasonable grounds for believing that circumvention is necessary to fulfill the purpose of the use in the following instances:
>
> > (i) Educational uses by college and university professors and by college and university film and media studies students;
> > (ii)Documentary filmmaking;
> > (iii) Noncommercial videos. (Billington, 2010; emphasis added)

Under this exception, crimewriter95 could only avoid liability under the DMCA if he (1) was a university or college professor, or (2) was a film or media studies student at a college or university. The fact that he described the YouTube video as "a project," without specifying whether it was for a *school* project may not be sufficient for him to benefit from the proposed exemption.

The Intent Factor

> "The legendary movie itself into chronological order. If you'd like me to put the full movie itself up, let me know and I'll be glad to oblige. Please no copyright infringement. I only put this up as a project."
>
> "Cover of Lady Antebellum's 'We Owned the Night.' No copyright infringement intended."
>
> "I don't own ___ or ____."

"I make no copyright claim to _____."

These above examples of disclaimers on user-uploaded YouTube videos are just a few of the iterations of essentially the same notion: that somehow the fact that the users do not *intend* to infringe the rights of the copyright owner will insulate them from liability. This notion may stem from several different sources: lack of knowledge about the nature of copyright law or the hope that copyright owners will see the disclaimer and decide not to pursue the user-uploader for liability because the user–uploader (1) has a good heart or (2) has no money and is therefore not a worthwhile target (or both). Alternatively, in some, but certainly not all, cases, these disclaimers may result from full knowledge of how copyright law operates and a desire to "get back" at the system—outright defiance, for political or social purposes (such as in a political remix).

To the extent that copyright infringement is a strict liability offense, intent is irrelevant. However, the Fair Use defense considers intent as far as concerns whether the defendant acted in bad faith. Further, even if the defendant is found not to benefit from the Fair Use defense, the court may consider whether the defendant acted willfully or whether the defendant was an innocent infringer in determining the amount of damages.

Intent: Good Faith, Bad Faith, and Innocent Infringement

Intent has a specific legal meaning that is different than in lay contexts. In a criminal context, "specific intent" means a person's intent to produce the consequences of that person's act; this generally includes the intent to complete the physical act itself. For example, to satisfy a requirement of specific intent, a person must only desire that their action occurs; it would not matter whether they knew that their action would produce consequences in violation of a law. In a copyright context, specifically where someone has uploaded a video to YouTube and disclaimed any intent of copyright infringement, the user would have had the specific intent to upload the video. Under Section 504(c), having such specific intent would expose the user-uploader to liability as a willful infringer, subject to the harshest penalties under the Copyright Act—statutory damages between $750 and $150,000 *per work*. (17 U.S.C. § 504(c)). However, as the Second Circuit noted,

> It is plain that "willfully" infringing and "innocent intent" are not the converse of one another. Thus, it is possible in the same action for a plaintiff not to be able to prove a defendant's willfulness, and, at the same time, for the defendant to be unable to show that it acted innocently. (*Fitzgerald Publishing Co. v. Baylor Publishing Co.*, 807 F.2d 1110, 1115; 2d Cir. 1986)

Further, "good faith," the converse of "bad faith," is normally equated with honesty of intention and equitable actions—but acting in good faith, and thus acting as an innocent infringer under the Copyright Act, is not a matter of simply *thinking* that the action is innocent: "Even where the defendant believes in good faith that he is not infringing a copyright, he may be found liable. More than simple 'innocence' is required" (*Peer Int'l Corp. v. Latin Am. Music Corp.*, 161 F. Supp. 2d 38; D.P.R. 2001). Traditionally, ignorance of the law is not a viable defense, and this is particularly true for a strict liability crime.

An innocent infringer under copyright is one who was unaware and had no reason to believe that his or her acts constituted an infringement of copyright (17 U.S.C. § 504(c)(2)). The Copyright Act presumes that any infringement is willful, however, so the burden of proving innocent infringement is on the alleged infringer (17 U.S.C. § 504(c)(2)). For example, an alleged infringer who reasonably believes that his or her use falls under the Fair Use doctrine may be an innocent infringer. However, what constitutes a "reasonable belief" is a fact-specific inquiry and courts may, upon consideration of all the relevant facts, still find that the belief was not reasonable and that the alleged infringer was not "innocent."

The catch for user-uploaders and remixers is the disclaimer itself—the mere fact of inclusion of such a statement of intent demonstrates that the uploader was aware, to some extent, that there was a potential copyright issue—aware of the possibility that the copyright owner would think that the uploader's action constituted infringement. A workable alternative to such (poorly worded) statements of "please no copyright infringement" is to assert that the use falls under the Fair Use exception. Such an assertion would (1) in the event that there *was* a finding of infringement, serve to edge the user into "innocent infringer" territory (if they truly believed that the use was fair, thus that they would not be liable), and (2) serve as some kind of reminder to the user/uploader him- or herself of what the Fair Use requirements are, and potentially allow them to mold the use to fit those elements, thus adding in an obviously significant and meaningful way to cultural discourse (as opposed to additions that are difficult for general audiences to appreciate). This suggestion, of course, is not ideal in terms of free culture and changing the mentality of how copyright *should* work with today's culture; rather it is a bandage, a temporary legal fix for a widely-occurring phenomenon.

User-uploaders who fail to successfully assert the Fair Use defense and/or those who employ disclaimers (without an assertion that the use is fair) will be as at risk for liability as "willful" infringers, who would be subject to the largest measure of statutory damages. The standard for "willfulness" has a distinct legal meaning in the context of statutory damages:

> It seems clear that as here used, "willfully" means with knowledge that the defendant's conduct constitutes copyright infringement.... This seems to mean, then, that one

> who has been notified that his conduct constitutes copyright infringement, but who reasonably and in good faith believes the contrary, is not "willful" for these purposes. (*Princeton Univ. Press v. Michigan Document Servs.*, 99 F.3d 1381, 1392; 6th Cir. 1996; quoting Melville B. Nimmer & David Nimmer, 3 Nimmer on Copyright § 14.04[B][3]; 1996)

Conclusion

The bottom line is that the strength of remix culture is strong and will continue to expand and grow. This is a remix culture—a culture of *engagement* with media and *anchored* in creativity—and this is exemplified by iconic films such as Quentin Tarantino's *Pulp Fiction* and crimewriter95's "*Pulp Fiction* in chronological order" YouTube video. Tarantino looked at all the creativity in film around him and created a critically and commercially successful genre film by taking the best elements of those films that inspired him and pasting them together, thus transforming them into a new vision—his vision of pulp fiction. Similarly, crimewriter95 looked at *Pulp Fiction*, with all of its homage and pastiche—its borrowing, stealing, and copying—and tried to understand it. In his attempt to understand the film, he also cut and paste, creating, whether consciously or unconsciously, a new meaning for each segment of the original film.

Legislation such as SOPA and PIPA, coupled with court decisions like the District Court decision in *Cariou v. Prince*, chill such engagement with the culture around us. However, the strong public reactions to SOPA, PIPA, and similar legislation show that those who support remix culture are willing and able to stand for their rights, fight back in any way possible. While the Internet has made it easy to stand up—by signing petitions, sending emails to legislators, and blacking out sites to awareness—it also makes other forms of protest more accessible. Even more important than accessibility of the means to engage in protests is the accessibility of the reasons behind the protest. News reports following the January 18 Internet blackout indicated that young people followed the progress of SOPA and PIPA more than they followed election news, in large part because if SOPA and PIPA passed, those laws would *directly* affect their online activities (Masnick, 2012).

Continuing to remix and mashup media and culture is to this time period what civil disobedience (for instance, sit-ins at lunch counters) was in other eras. Naturally, with some strong reactions, there is a veritable danger of needless over-reaction, spurred on by the bandwagon and mob mentalities. But with accurate information dissemination and vocal participation by legal, social, and art scholars (such as Lawrence Lessig) and powerful, pro-free culture players (such as the Electronic Frontier Foundation), we can be assured to some extent that the *real* problems and issues with such legislation and judicial decisions are brought to light for large-scale discussion and resolution. The key, as with many problems, is access to information, incentive to participate, and *actual* participation. Recent events suggest that all three of these elements are being met more often and on a large, public scale—a positive development for the preservation, encouragement, and expansion of remix culture.

• CHAPTER TEN •

Fracturing Digital Entertainment by Kindling Rivalries and Blowing Steam

Liza Potts, Dean Holden, and Katie Dobruse

Content producers are currently creating new kinds of economies that fracture entertainment experiences across digital and physical spaces. By limiting consumer activities, ostensibly to protect copyright-protected material, many content producers are restricting access to content as a form of inventing rivalrous commodities. Consumers are caught in a situation where resource scarcity either encourages platform loyalty and discourages competition or in which consumers must own and participate across multiple platforms if they are to access a varied set of content. Analyzing the experience of digital entertainment from consumer perspectives, this chapter highlights issues of materiality, ownership, and access.

Focusing primarily on digital entertainment content and devices, this chapter will look at issues involving how goods are exchanged between distributors and consumers. It is critical for digital humanities scholars—and other communication, legal, etc., scholars—to assess new modes of distributing content and resulting business models. Beyond assessment, we should work to influence policy makers, software developers, and executive decision-makers. This chapter provides some means for our doing so, by exploring how distributors have enforced cultural control through content channels on physical devices. Pointing to specific instances, this chapter will provide an analysis of content control—a model implemented in the gaming industry and now echoing across the publishing industry.

Digital Content and Copyright

Scholars must attended to the mechanisms by which digital content is produced, distributed, and consumed so that we can bring our knowledge of how these technologies work and how participatory cultures interact with them to bear on the corporate policies that bind these experiences. Understanding the distinctions between rivalrous and nonrivalrous goods is critical to such an understanding, as is having a shared set of definitions, descriptions, and concepts about these economies and the cultures that exist around them. This section will begin to outline this shared set, hopefully encouraging further exploration within the digital humanities and related fields.

Digital Content Producers, Distributors, and Consumers

In the context of this chapter, *content producers* are agents who create content; for the most part in this chapter, this term will reference agents who produce *digital* content. A content producer can be a person, corporation, or other organization tasked with producing digital products or services.

After content is produced, it then must be distributed if it is to reach the consumer market. *Content distributors* are agents who create, manage, and maintain the pathways by which material goods pass from producers to consumers. Content is often tied to various physical devices such as ereaders, computers, and console gaming systems. The term "content" can be rather nebulous; in this chapter, content can be any type of material that a consumer acquires from a content producer through a content-distribution mechanism.

Content consumers are typically people who have acquired, purchased, or borrowed digital content. Through brick-and-mortar stores such as GameStop, Target, and BestBuy, consumers can purchase video games, movies, and books. Online, they can access content through web sites such as Amazon or even their local library. The gaming community can purchase and access content from places such as Steam and Telltale, while the music community can use services such as Spotify and iTunes to access content. There are (quite literally) a host of other services, web sites, and mobile apps that allow content consumers to access new material—either to purchase or acquire it through other means.

Digital Humanities Engaging with Policy and Experience Design

As work in the humanities grows and expands outside the borders of our fields' more traditional artifacts (textual products, primarily, like essays and poems), we find further intersections between the digital and the humanist. Examining culture, policy, power, and experience is not new to these fields. Such investigations can problematize solutions already in place, uncover issues for policy implementations, and locate the deltas between business models that can be effective while also (and especially) supporting everyday people. Clearly, digital humanities scholars should be examining these conditions and conflicts further, delving into issues of policy as well as the overall architectures for experience design.

Rivalrous and Nonrivalrous Goods

One of the major arguments surrounding copyright and control has to do with the concept of rivalrous and nonrivalrous goods. At its core, *rivalrous objects* are physical goods that can be depleted and *nonrivalrous goods* are ones that can never be depleted. The former has a finite amount of use, the later infinite. Lawrence Lessig's *Future of Ideas* (2002b) made a stronger distinction with regards to copyright and control:

> 1. If the resource is rivalrous, then a system of control is needed to assure that the resource is not depleted—which means the system must assure the resource is both produced and not overused.
> 2. If the resource is nonrivalrous, then a system of control is needed simply to assure the resource is created—a provisioning problem, as Professor Elinor Ostrom describes it. Once it is created, there is no danger that the resource will be depleted. By definition, a nonrivalrous resource cannot be used up. (p. 95)

Cited often, Lessig's work is lauded as making a strong distinction between the two terms, but a close reading shows that Lessig saw many gray areas, rather than any strong divide. John Logie (2006) further complicated this argument when discussing how colloquial understandings of sharing are incompatible with most copyright restrictions, arguing that the concept of "sharing" is wholly rooted in the division or apportioning of rivalrous resources. Sharing physical objects, he argued, is clearly not the same as sharing an idea or sharing digital content:

> If I agree to share my car or my laptop with someone, I understand that there will be times that I will not have access to those resources. But if I share an idea, we both have the idea. And if I "share" an MP3 file by serving it to others via a peer-to-peer network, my resource is *never* depleted. Indeed, very nearly the opposite is true, as its presence on the network facilitates the creation of additional copies of that file." (Logie, p. 85).

Clearly, the binary opposition between rivalrous and nonrivalrous is not so simple when it comes to digital content. While teasing out this binary is useful, in this chapter we discuss these issues on a continuum, where the binary ends and the variations of content access can be explored, defined, and questioned. The remainder of this chapter will problematize these concepts further, discussing digital entertainment products as a site for current research with regards to distribution and personal control that demand further exploration within the digital humanities.

Opposing Ideologies of Copyright and Control

Many of the arguments about copyright tend to focus on the control of content itself, whereas in this chapter mechanisms that control *the access to* that content are discussed. Modern copyright law has its basis in 18th-century markets and technologies, when controlling content and controlling access to content were one and the same; the costs associated with the mass production of creative works limited their manufacture and distribution to a select group of dual producers and distributors, making them gatekeepers of creativity (Patry, 2011). Now, those same gatekeepers are no longer required: as means and modes of distribution are more accessible than ever before, and do not carry traditional costs (e.g., of ink, paper, delivery). As Patry put it, "in the world of digital abundance, one copy of a work is as good as the next, eliminating the need to source a work from a single, authorized gatekeeper" (p. 39).

One of the key traits of a nonrivalrous resource is that it is afforded protection to ensure the production of work—not to avoid its depletion. Not everyone has had the same reaction to the affordances digital media offer over traditional, physical forms of content. TyAnna K. Herrington (2001) described two opposing ideologies of interpreting current copyright law in terms of how it can be applied to new forms of media and media access:

> A community with a foundational, authoritarian ideology will support a protectionist interpretation of the law treating intellectual products, but a community whose dominant ideology is constructionist will be more likely to support greater public access to the intellectual products that influence knowledge creation. (p. 2)

Digital humanities scholars understand the necessity of freedom of information in constructing culture, and as such tend to fall into the constructionist camp. Content producers and distributors, on the other hand, take a protectionist position that strict access control is necessary to prevent piracy and to encourage creativity (and, often, to protect their economic interests and control). Currently, the dominant voices in the continued legal and legislative discussions of copyright law have been predominantly from the protectionist camp, arguing in favor of tighter mechanisms for access control.

One mechanism used to control the distribution of digital content is Digital Rights Management (DRM). DRM is a set of technologies present on digital devices deployed as a means to control access to content. DRM can be software-based or hardware-based, depending on the type of content distribution. Sometimes, these restrictions work to make it impossible to copy materials, as is the case with content scrambling on DVDs. Sometimes, they are used to restrict use to one type of hardware, as was the case with the pre-2009 versions of MP3s sold through iTunes. Many scholars have examined the issue of DRM, in articles (Allen, 2008; Arnab & Hutchinson, 2005; Erickson, 2003; Potts, 2010, Samuelson, 2003) and in books (Boyle, 2008; Lessig, 2008; Litman, 2006; Logie, 2006; Vaidhyanathan, 2005). Numerous laws governing DRM exist, varying in severity depending on the country and technology. Many of these laws came as a positive reaction to the United Nations' World Intellectual Property Organization Copyright Treaty signed in 1996, which required member nations to essentially enforce DRM by creating laws that would forbid the circumvention of DRM. For example, in the United States, the Digital Millennium Copyright Act (DMCA) was passed in 1998; the DMCA makes it illegal to circumvent DRM and limits the use of copyright materials on the Internet, among other restrictions.

Artificial Sweeteners

Unlike physical objects, digital artifacts can easily be copied, distributed, and shared: With a simple copy and paste, files can be duplicated across networks, sent in emails, or shared to various devices. Without the barriers of paper or CDs, games, music, books, and more can make their way to new consumers wherever and whenever. As a reaction to this ease of distribution, content producers and content distributors have created different kinds of artificial barriers by which they can prevent these consumer activities. In many cases, these barriers are created as a means to increase revenue, build new business models, and ostensibly protect the copyright held by the content producers.

In this section, two examples of these kinds of barriers are examined: *artificial scarcity* and *artificial exclusivity*. Artificial scarcity refers to the idea that content producers could somehow run out of digital objects. It is obvious that digital objects do not simply "run out"—while there are can be limits to bandwidth, storage space, etc., these limits have everything to do with cost rather than any actual loss of the digital object. The concept of artificial exclusivity is somewhat similar to scarcity, in that the digital objects are considered rare, *a priori* of any actual scarcity. The exclusivity comes from "special" content that can only be accessed through limited distribution channels on specific timelines dictated by the content producers and performed by the content distributors. The term "artificial" is used here to purposely problematize these implementation models. The implication is that these models are part of a broader set of false claims by content producers and their distributors.

It is this issue of economies created around the binary of rivalrous and nonrivalrous that is in desperate need of problematizing by scholars in the digital humanities. Binaries are easy; finding shades of gray is much more difficult. It is up to scholars who understand technology from the perspective of human beings to tease out the issues here. Digital humanities scholars, with their understandings of technology, use, policy, and—most importantly—people, can further the discussion and scholarship about rivalrous and nonrivalrous systems in unique and important ways because of this background and training. This section sets out to describe these two models in greater detail, and, later, discuss these concepts on a continuum, rather than a binary.

Artificial Scarcity

Gillespie (2007) argued that forms of cultural expression are defined by their capacity for "collective use of the same object, and duplication of one object into many" (p. 25). However, producers and distributors are now trying to use technological mechanisms to artificially impose the scarcity of the 18th century onto the 21st-century digital marketplace (Patry, 2011). While the scarcity of print books in the 18th century was a real situation, tied to the cost of production, the scarcity seen today is tied to business models where content producers are trying to create a need when these limitations do not exist.

Locking Down Free Content. Project Gutenberg's mission is "to provide as many eBooks in as many formats as possible for the entire world to read in as many languages as possible" (Hart, 2004). The boilerplate language included with most Project Gutenberg downloads exemplifies the potential of ebooks to be nonrivalrous:

> This eBook is for the use of anyone anywhere at no cost and with almost no restrictions whatsoever. A consumer may copy it, give it away or re-use it under the terms of the Project Gutenberg license included with this eBook or online at www.gutenberg.org. (gutenberg.org, 2012)

Theoretically, there is no limit to the number of times a given title can be downloaded, since copying a file does not exhaust the supply. The free, unlicensed distribution of these public domain texts is made possible because there is no author to support and no capital to raise for production. In this way, the digital content on Project Gutenberg can be said to be nonrivalrous. However, the need to have funding for technology (servers, access, etc.) is where Project Gutenberg blends the lines between rivalrous and nonrivalrous. And, unlike prefaced and/or annotated versions of classic texts produced by editorial teams of publishing houses, the versions on Project Gutenberg include only the original text. Key content distributors such as Amazon also offer these texts, but with DRM restriction. Neither charges for these ebooks; instead, they offer them up as examples of free "bonus" content that their respective digital devices have to offer. So, although the content is free (both of copyright and of cost to the consumer through these services), the content is restricted by DRM technology. Such a move takes works available without restriction through Project Gutenberg and locks them down via one distributor's platform, shifting the text from a nonrivalrous to a rivalrous good. This ignores the technical affordances of ebooks, which carry these works beyond the analog restrictions of the physical book, an issue that scholars in the digital humanities need to consider with regards to the future of publishing and distribution models.

Librarians and Ebooks. Librarians have come up against a kind of artificial restriction when attempting to secure ebooks for lending within their systems. Back in October 2011, "Big Six" publisher HarperCollins announced that it would reconfigure its system of library ebook rentals through its partner OverDrive, one of the primary platforms for library ebook distribution. Any ebook purchased under the new system could only be checked out by one patron at a time, and after 26 checkouts the book would disappear from the system unless the library paid for a "new" copy at a slightly reduced price, reflecting the price drop between hardcover and paperback releases (Hadro & Fialkoff, 2011). HarperCollins claimed that the 26 checkouts represented the life expectancy of a physical book, presumably based on a year's worth of 2-week checkouts (although frankly this does not remotely reflect the actual lifespan of a library book; McIntosh, 2011). In response to this move, the site www.boycottharpercollins.com was created, and almost 400 U.S. libraries have opted to stop future purchases of HarperCollins ebooks (Kelley, 2011). This is yet another example of artificial scarcity being introduced into a digital environment. There is no technological reason that a digital book should face the same restrictions as a physical book. Unlike a physical book, whose cover might tear or spine might crack (both of which libraries simply patch up), an ebook will not deteriorate over time. Yet, with HarperCollins' ebook lending policy, librarians are suddenly forced to adjust to a much shorter "shelf life" for their books.

A second blow to libraries came in November 2011, when Penguin Books (another of the "Big Six" publishers) removed all of its new titles from OverDrive (Coffey, 2012). As former *Publisher's Weekly* editor-in-chief Nora Rawlinson explained,

> Penguin cut off lending over the weekend, leaving library users first confused, then angry. Since libraries did not receive notification until mid-day Monday [Nov. 21], they were left blind-sided. (Albanese, 2011)

Penguin attributed the move to "security concerns," while OverDrive offered the excuse that its title availability is variable and dependent on the decisions of individual publishers. Librarians were vocal in their outcry on OverDrive's blog. One commented that patrons "want to know, rightly so, why they are funding the leasing of frequently unusable content via a frequently unusable product" (Albanese). The challenge libraries and users alike face going forward is deciding which platform and service to adopt, since both content producers and distributors have demonstrated their ability and willingness to change user access privileges with little to no warning.

Gaming Steam. In gaming, there are similar DRM issues—especially as applied to the user experience of purchasing, playing, and accessing digital entertainment. Many computer games are distributed digitally and managed independently from the original game producer. One of these systems is Steam, which refers to itself as the "ultimate entertainment platform" (Steam, 2012). Steam's version of DRM is implemented through an installed download manager. Before buying or downloading any games, users must download and install the Steam software, which then acts as a proxy to the Steam servers. When a user buys and downloads a game through Steam, it is added to the in-program "library," which then becomes the only way to access or play it. Accounts can be added to multiple devices, but only one device can be logged in to an account at a time ("Steam account use," 2012). Attempts to bypass or "hack" the Steam software can result in suspension of a user's account ("Suspended steam account," 2012), and therefore a loss of access to all of the user's purchased games (Walker, 2012). This raises questions about the "scarcity" of these resources. Because Steam allows a game to be downloaded an infinite number of times after a single purchase, the game in question is not a scarce resource. Yet Steam's model creates artificial scarcity despite infinite downloads by only allowing a single access point at a time.

This model is interesting because it seemingly makes games (or rather the licenses to play them) rivalrous while simultaneously admitting that they are not. As Lessig (2001) pointed out, "There is... no tragedy for nonrivalrous goods left in the commons—no matter how many times you read a poem, there's as much left over as there was when you started" (p. 22). Similarly, Steam proves the nonrivalrous nature of digital downloads by allowing for a game to be downloaded and installed on an unlimited number of systems, tying them to the user account and allowing that account to be accessed from anywhere ("Steam account use," 2012). However, Steam then superimposes a rivalrous model by only allowing access to an account (and thus game library) in one location at a time.

This model goes beyond just the download model. Users must have a Steam account to play games acquired via download, but some major market titles like *Fallout: New Vegas* require users to register even boxed retail copies of the game with the Steam client before playing with an activation key which prevents re-selling or linking with multiple accounts (DeCarlo, 2010). Consumers wishing to re-sell the games they buy through Steam (even physical copies) would have to sell the account that has access to the game itself, but Steam's terms of service make that impossible as well ("Suspended steam account," 2012). By disallowing a "used account" market, Steam is superimposing a rivalrous model on something as nonrivalrous as a user account, by threatening user account suspensions. The disc can be installed or even downloaded directly from Steam anywhere after activation, which is a necessarily nonrivalrous model; however, the game can never be detached from the original account and can only be used in a single location, which is arbitrarily rivalrous.

While there are inroads toward providing additional consumer content, there are still ways to further this access–especially when consumers are willing to pay for that content. It is important to investigate the policies that would punish consumers for upgrading their computers, shifting over to new devices, or simply purchasing easily mangled media types such as DVDs. Such licensing models call for further research into how content producers can build experiences that are centered on consumer experience where there is mutual trust and affinity. This research is perfectly suited for digital humanities work, where the focus is on human experience and where scholars with backgrounds in technology, culture, and policy can be empowered to propel discussions in this area.

Artificial Exclusivity

Another major issue concerning how people, culture, and policy collide in digital spaces relates to the concept of artificial exclusivity. Convincing consumers that one platform excels at delivering a certain kind of content and therefore must be the *de facto* provider of this content is another way for content distributors to impart rivalrous limitations on their content. The economic barriers of exclusivity are similar to scarcity in that it places an invented value upon digital content. In the case of exclusivity, it also carries the additional weight of restricting access based primarily on platform. The restrictions that come with DRM has a "history of frustrating consumers with compatibility problems, unreasonable restrictions on how legally acquired digital media can be consumed" (Allen, 2008, p. 5).

Exclusivity in Gaming. Artificial exclusivity has been a part of the console gaming industry since its inception in the 1970s. In the infancy of console games, console exclusivity was a function of differing programming and storage media. It was not so much that the Atari 2600 and ColecoVision were designed specifically to exclude one another, it's that the game cartridges, interfaces and controllers were physically different, and would not fit or read in a different system. Today, all three major consoles (Wii, Xbox 360, Playstation 3) use a combination of disc and digital-based content, much of which is already published across all three platforms. The Playstation 3 and Xbox 360 in particular are only semantically different, both utilizing not only the same content types but also controllers with near-identical layouts (both feature two analog joysticks, an eight-way digital joypad, six face buttons, four shoulder buttons and a "home" button). Yet, despite an increasing similarity between these consoles, platform exclusivity is as prevalent as ever.

Exclusivity in the video game console market has typically been not just accepted, but celebrated (Buchanan, 2009). For multiplatform games, nominal differences between console versions are discussed at length among fan communities, and many still discuss the merits (and nostalgia value) of the quality of past consoles ("Console wars," 2007). Spearheading these community discussions are the so-called "killer apps," software applications so desirable that they drive sales of the hardware system that run them. In the video game market, the "killer app" is the console-exclusive "must-have" game that creates demand for the console itself, much as *Halo* was for the Xbox (Juola, 2006). But the "killer app" games of today have nothing to do with which system can physically run the game, or which platform the game is designed for. It is about consoles, and the companies that back them, attempting to manufacture a competitive advantage by limiting the platforms where consumers can get their games. The companies backing these consoles also create first-party games with their own in-house development teams in the interest of driving both hardware and software sales at the same time, with Nintendo serving as a longtime example (Williams, 2002). These first-party games are kept limited to a single console in order to create exclusivity (and therefore demand), but given the relative similarity between today's consoles, there is little reason for these games to be limited to a single platform other than for marketing purposes. From a consumer point of view, having to purchase two different consoles to play *Halo 3* (Xbox 360) and *God of War 3* (PS3) is like having to buy one toaster for bread and another for bagels.

Though third-party games are trending toward multi-platform releases, this artificial exclusivity is beginning to appear in a new format: downloadable content, or DLC. DLC is add-on content released by a game's publisher after the game's initial release. Publishers may release additional stages/maps, quests, playable characters, equipment, modes of play, and other content that supplements the original game as shipped. These DLC packs can typically be downloaded for $10 or less, depending on the type of content (new stages or storylines tend to be more robust and valuable than characters or equipment). DLC is a relatively universal thing across today's consoles, but even DLC for multiplatform games is becoming subject to exclusivity, or at least temporary exclusivity. This appeared in games like *Batman: Arkham Asylum,* in which PS3 users got a special collection of stages with the Joker as a playable character (Clements, 2009), and in *The Elder Scrolls V: Skyrim*, which announced that DLC would be Xbox 360 exclusive for the first 30 days before announcing what that content consisted of (Sinclair, 2011). In some cases, games will introduce console-exclusive content, only to lift this exclusivity at a later date. *SoulCalibur 4* is an example of this when it introduced exclusive *Star Wars* characters, making Yoda and Darth Vader exclusive to the XBox 360 and

Playstation 3 releases, respectively, only to turn them into purchasable DLC months after the game's release (Beradini, 2008).

This content is not exclusive because of any technical limitations; the developers throw out that notion when it becomes multiplatform later. The "exclusivity" is a construct created by the game's developer to manufacture differentiation for two versions of the same product. By creating two versions of a game, the same yet slightly different, the publisher is attempting to make the media rivalrous against itself, in the interest of convincing consumers that one version of the media is better (or better yet, convincing them to buy both). And in the case of DLC, there is no technical reason for content to be exclusive, other than some negotiated business deal to limit content on certain devices for competitive advantage.

Device-based Content. With the advent of ereaders and tablet computers, artificial exclusivity has begun to emerge in publishing as well. With physical books, consumers could fill their shelves with books from any publisher, bought from any bookstore, in any format. They were not locked into buying from a single bookseller, or kept from buying titles from a specific publisher, simply because they did not have the necessary device. Currently, disputes between content producers and content distributors have kept that same freedom of access from emerging in the ebook market.

To promote the release of its Kindle Fire tablet, Amazon negotiated a deal with DC comics for the exclusive rights to distribute the digital versions of 100 popular DC titles; customers who used other devices would be unable to access these titles (unless they also purchased a Kindle Fire to download the title or used the Kindle app on their digital device of choice; Stuart, 2011). No other content distributor would be able to sell these titles for the first four months after the Fire's release (Fritz, 2011). Barnes & Noble's reaction to being denied the ability to sell digital versions of these titles was to remove the physical versions from the shelves of all their brick-and-mortar stores (Reid, 2011). Jaime Carey, Barnes & Noble Chief Merchant, defended the decision to pull the physical copies, stating "we will not stock physical books in our stores if we are not offered the available digital format" (Stuart). DC did not exclude the possibility of forming this kind of exclusivity arrangement with a different distributor, saying that while the titles in question "are currently exclusive to Amazon," DC will "continue to have discussions with our other valued partners as digital is a key growth area for DC" (Reid). Creating artificial exclusivity is an issue of concern for digital humanities scholars, whose work often involves examining issues of agency, power, and control within technology systems.

Futures of Digital Entertainment

New models of content distribution and restriction extend the concept of the continuum as well as question the practice of using DRM to create a closed system, where a consumer's interaction with digital content can be restricted, constrained, or censored. Scholars in digital humanities need to take note of these issues primarily because closed systems are inherently antithetical to scholarly commitments to the open exchange of information. Arnab and Hutchinson (2005) noted that "DRM does not actually implement the fundamentals of copyright law, and is rather a mechanism for enforcing license and contract restrictions on digital data" (p. 1). While content producers use piracy as a justification to convince people that DRM is necessary, DRM itself does not prevent the copying of content (and thus piracy). Instead, DRM is a means to control *access* to content by paying customers.

Emerging Business Models

Certainly new digital media distribution outlets in the gaming world are starting to rethink the way rivalrousness is measured. Consider a game like *Fallout: New Vegas,* which can be purchased as a physical copy and downloaded an unlimited number of times as a digital copy after registration, but is still limited to a single device at a time. The disc itself could be considered rivalrous, but it makes the game infinitely replicable and thus nonrivalrous upon initial install. Steam service then places restrictions on the game, making *access* to the game rivalrous. It is impossible to explain this example on a binary scale of rivalrous versus nonrivalrous; the game is not really being moved straight from one camp to another with each of these moves, but rather being pushed and pulled back and forth between them on a continuum. The physical object (the disc) makes the game *more* rivalrous, but the unlimited downloads via Steam make it *less* rivalrous. Steam then makes the game *appear* more rivalrous by paring the game's access to a single device. Here is where one finds a disconnect: Media distributors that utilize DRM are misplacing their media on the rivalrous continuum, trying to move their products toward the rivalrous end.

In response to some of these "artificially rivalrous" business models, companies like GOG.com have built their entire mission (and successful business models) around selling older content free from DRM. This falls right in line with Lessig's (2001) assertion that "new modes of distribution (including the removal of barriers to distribution) induce the creation of new markets for existing products" (p. 126). GOG founder Guillaume Rambourg (2011) claimed that the way to beat piracy is to treat it not as an enemy, but as a competitor, raising the question, "Your customers hate DRM... so why don't you?" Rambourg believes that piracy can be beaten by making the media that consumers pay for superior to the media that can be pirated:

> If you make the whole gaming experience more complicated and more frustrating for people who buy the game... if it's easier to play a game that is pirated because they removed all the technical restraints, then I think there is a big issue on the plate now. It should be easier to play a game that you bought legally than play a game that you pirated.

Rambourg's model at GOG makes no attempt to create a rivalrous model around content; it simply makes paying for content a preferable option to pirating. This model was employed by GOG for the first time on a new release game on *The Witcher 2*, and resulted in sales of 35,000 digital copies in the first 6 months (Yin-Poole, 2011). That falls well short of Steam's market share, but exponentially better than every other digital provider, which GOG considers to be a resounding success (Yin-Poole, 2011).

Ubisoft, perhaps on the opposite end of the spectrum from GOG, once called their DRM system "a success," in the sense that there was "a clear reduction in piracy of our titles which required a persistent online connection" (Hill, 2011). This does not begin to take into account consumer reaction and loyalty, which suffers greatly when games (for example) become unplayable for paying customers because Ubisoft's DRM servers go down, as they did in 2010 (Plunkett, 2010). Marcus "Notch" Persson, developer of indie game hit *Minecraft*, implicitly criticized Ubisoft when he tweeted, "Protip: if you pirate Ubisoft games instead of buying them, they will work fine if your internet connection goes down" (Yin-Poole, 2012). While Ubisoft is not yet willing to move away from DRM completely, they are beginning to look toward a more value-based approach to limiting piracy. Chris Early, Ubisoft's vice president of digital publishing, has a plan involving an attempt to integrate "companion gaming, which sees spin-off experiences on mobile devices and social platforms feed into their related core games" (Yin-Poole, 2012). The hope is that this would discourage piracy by only allowing access to these additional experiences to paying customers, thus (like GOG) giving the consumer more for purchasing the game, not less. As Early says, "the interesting thing will be, how do we create enough value that that need for DRM goes away?" (Yin-Poole, 2012). Such moves are of interest to scholars researching the impact of DRM on everyday people, as well as those who are investigating broader questions of impact and use from the perspective of the digital humanities.

Plotting the Continuum and Future Work

What is interesting to note about these models is that they work with the exact same media type—digital game downloads—yet they implement vastly different methods of distribution and content control making, all with differing measures of value and metrics for success. Yet Lessig (2001) would argue that all three are dealing with nonrivalrous content as there is no depletion of resources for a downloaded game. Ultimately, rivalrousness is being *assigned differently* for each of these three business models. If rivalrousness were a binary, it would be impossible to plot out three distinctly different models. Plotting them on a continuum of rivalrousness allows digital humanities scholars to accurately depict this multitude of distribution options and strategies. This concept of a continuum requires further study, calling on scholars in the digital humanities to continue to question the construction of various models of content production and distribution.

It is worth noting that sci-fi/fantasy powerhouse Tor Books recently announced that it will begin releasing all of its titles DRM-free as well. Given that Tor is an imprint of Macmillan, one of publishing's "Big Six," and that its publisher, Tom Doherty, has won the Locus Award for Best Publisher 23 years running, this is a significant move. If successful, this move may very well trigger a ripple effect among other publishers. Encouraging other kinds of business models that favor consumer experience is an activity that digital humanities research could take on, based on further investigation of these practices and prototyping of new experience types. In *The Future of Ideas*, Lessig (2002b) stated that

> the system of control that we erect for rivalrous resources (land, cars, computers) *is not necessarily appropriate* for nonrivalrous resources (ideas, music, expression). Indeed, the *same system for both kinds of resources may do real harm*. Thus, a legal system or a society generally, must be careful to tailor the kind of control to the kind of resource. One size won't fit all. (p. 96)

Clearly, future models of distributing digital content must be constructed such that consumers will not be caught in the middle, rather—they should instead be provided reasonable terms by which they can interact with digital content. And we, as humanities scholars, must engage here for all of the reasons discussed in this chapter. As humanists, it is imperative that we focus on these very human experiences, something often left out of discussions on technology, content delivery, and digital rights management.

• CHAPTER ELEVEN •

Taking IP Digital: A Personal Tale

Aaron Barlow

William Makepeace Thackery, in *Pendennis*, a novel of his from the late 1840s (and set a decade or so earlier), puts these words in his hero's mouth:

> No man shall tell me that a man of genius, as Shandon is, ought to be driven by such a vulgar slave-driver as yonder Mr. Bungay, whom we have just left, who fattens on the profits of the other's brains, and enriches himself out of his journeyman's labour. It makes me indignant to see a gentleman the serf of such a creature as that—of a man who can't speak the language that he lives by, who is not fit to black Shandon's boots. (p. 401)

This was much more the view for the first two centuries of copyright law: Copyright was seen as a protection of the creator from the unscrupulous exploiter. It had been established with just that in mind, at least in part, and it was something the creator could invoke—or not.

Yet, a new commonplace attitude, I would learn over the next few years, had replaced the older one almost completely well before the end of the twentieth century. The publishers and distributors, traditionally the gatekeepers of creative work in the public sphere, had taken on ownership as well, and were gathering most of the rewards. Writers, musicians, photographers, and other creators became mere supplicants, grateful for their royalty crumbs but seen by the industry as deserving little else. They no longer "owned" the work, not once it had been accepted for publication, but merely benefitted tangentially (and often at the sufferance of the new owner) from any success it might have, success dependent, in large part, on the efforts of the publisher, not the creator.

Rising corporate powers had taken advantage of temporary rights once intended for authors and inventors, rights designed to encourage creative effort and had turned them into what were becoming permanent property rights.

And I, like most, had accepted the change without awareness that it had happened. Then something happened to change that.

Like many in the early days of the web, I was fast becoming become an internet *flâneur*, a browser dropping in on any web site that struck my fancy. Eventually, my online wanderings led me to a site dedicated to the writer I'd written my doctoral dissertation on a decade earlier; philipkdick.com (now philipkdickfans.com) came into being in 1999, created by Jason Koornick, a long-time fan of Dick's science fiction. When I found the site, I quickly decided to offer my dissertation to it. Jason accepted and, after revising the chapters, I sent them to him as separate files. They became a series of academic essays on the site (parts of them, at least, are still there).

At that time, other things were happening on the web, of course. I was aware of a few of them, including the rise of Napster, and the problems it was creating for ownership of music, but I didn't really pay much attention. I remembered what had happened two decades earlier when the movie industry had tried to stop home videotaping. The case, *Sony Corp. of America v. Universal Studios, Inc.*, wasn't settled until 1984, but I believed—wrongly—that it had decreed that individuals could do whatever they wanted with whatever they had purchased. Downloading music that someone else had bought and was now offering for free or trade, I felt, should fall under the same ruling. The impact on creators, anyhow, would be minimal, my thinking went. After all, the vast majority of profits went to businesses that had little to do with the art of creation. Who cared if they lost a little of it?

Although I knew nothing about the Digital Millennium Copyright Act (DMCA) that had been signed into law by President Clinton the previous fall, I was vaguely aware that I did have certain rights over my own work, but I believed (falsely) that I still had to invoke them prior to their taking effect. To me, copyrighting something was a proactive choice, as once it really had been. I didn't realize that, now, the fact of publication invoked copyright automatically. I thought that doing nothing let greater rights migrate into the public domain, and I liked that idea.

In terms of my dissertation, well, I felt that it did not belong simply to me, anyway. I had earned my degree at a land-grant (public) university, after all, and felt that I had a bit of an obligation to share what the public, in part, had paid for.

In terms of copyright and IP, I was incredibly naïve.

Those were early days, though, in the transition to a digital age. If few of us outside of the industries dependent upon copyright, mainly publishers of print, sound and image, had known quite little about ownership of IP in the pre-internet age, the majority of us were now completely lost in the thicket of new digital possibilities. If few of us had known that, once, copyright had been a personal right, most of us now had no idea where it began and ended at all.

So, in general, we ignored it, considering copyright the domain of corporations and successful creative artists, with little impact on the rest of us. We had learned, through home Betamax and VHS video recorders and what had become the ubiquitous cassette tape recorders, that we could pretty much do as we pleased, anyhow—as long as we kept it to a small scale. Copyright laws didn't concern us, we believed, only affecting those unscrupulous who were trying to make profit off of the work of others.

The demise of Napster and prosecution of individuals for downloading music changed that—for me, and for many others. For the first time, we were really seeing what the ownership of IP now meant. In small ways, most of us had been breaking copyright laws for years, photocopying things that shouldn't be copied but, here again, none of us had ever suffered the consequences. Although the music industry first primarily pursued Napster itself, by 2003 it was also taking individuals to court—30,000 of them, either threatened or actually sued by 2008 (Kravets, 2008). But all of that, in 1999, was to come. Copyright, quite frankly, wasn't an issue most of us cared about.

Possibly, I was aware at the time of what the U.S. Constitution says about copyright, that Congress shall have the power "To promote the Progress of Science and useful Arts, by securing for limited Times to Authors and Inventors the exclusive Right to their respective Writings and Discoveries" (Article 1, Section 8). I certainly did not know what that meant generally, though or, certainly not on any conscious level, that "authors" and "inventors" no longer meant "individuals."

To me, as I have said, copyright had little to do with money anyway—that was the province of the publishers. It was only contractually that royalties could come to me, were I lucky enough to see a book of mine published, not really because of copyright itself. If anything, in my view at the time, copyright only protected that connection I described between me, were I to create anything, and my work. Implicit in that was the idea that I could sell the thing itself, and sell the rights to it—and that sell it I must, were I to make any money off of it. And that is all there was to it.

Sure, I could have paid to have something printed on my own, and would then own the copyright, but it really would have been meaningless: No self-published works, in those days, made any money and the likelihood that anyone would want to steal the work and publish it on *their* own was infinitesimal. It would just have cost too much.

Again, copyright made sure that no one else could take credit for what I had done. That was its primary function, as far as I was concerned. As a sometime writer, once the people who had contracted for it had paid me for my work, all I cared about was that my name stayed on it. I couldn't sell the work to another publisher, I knew, and I had no rights over who might buy it if my publisher decided to sell. The business of publishing was not mine, and I didn't care a whit for what it might or might not be able to do—once it had paid me for my work. I suspect that I didn't even really understand (never having thought about it) that the advances lucky authors do get are advances against royalties—or that royalties depend completely on sales.

When my dissertation chapters appeared on the web site, I did recognize that it was possible for anyone to download them or print them. That was fine; I had thought about it and had decided it should be available. Again, I didn't see the work as having monetary value, or didn't believe I had any way to monetize it. What I really wanted was for people to *read* what I had written and to *respond* to it. Few dissertations, I knew, ever made any money, or were meant to in anything but the writer's wildest dream. Most of them, in those days, ended up sitting on spools prepared by University Microfilms International and gathering dust. I didn't like that mine was sharing this fate. Or it had been, of course, until it appeared on philipkdick.com.

I had sent the chapters to Koornick as separate files simply because it had proven impossible to upload the whole thing singularly. I liked, though, that the chapters remained that way, with the web site presenting them as discrete units, for they really were independent of each other, each never building necessarily on the previous. Also, this moved the chapters away from "dissertation" status and, to my mind, made them a little more accessible to the average fan. Someone could read one without feeling that they had to read the others. One could download or print out one, something more manageable in those days of slow connections and slower printers.

About a year after the linked essays (as I now preferred to consider them) appeared on philipkdick.com, I got an email from someone in Spain, asking if one of those chapters could be translated, to appear in a journal there as a stand-alone piece. Tickled, happy that someone had seen at least a little value in what I had written, I immediately agreed. The only thing I asked was that a copy be forwarded to me once it was in print. If the people who wrote had published my essay without asking but had sent a copy, that would have been fine with me, too. All I wanted was to know about it, have my name on it, and be able to hold it in my hands.

The next year, the journal arrived. Called *VALIS: Ciencia Ficción y Fantasía* (No. 10, 2001), my article in it was titled "¿Cuánto te asusta el Caos...?: Introducción a la obra y filosofía de Philip K. Dick." That would translate as "How Much Does Chaos Scare You?: An Introduction to the Work and Philosophy of Philip K. Dick." Someone named Diana Catalán Ruescas was credited with the translation. I showed it around with a smile and went back to making espresso drinks, staffing the register and doing the bookkeeping.

Two years later, I got an email from someone named Arturo Villarubia in Spain. I had never heard of him and only chance kept me from sending it to spam. When I opened it, I saw that he was asking me if I knew that my *entire* dissertation had been translated into Spanish and published there as a book. Surprised, I did a quick search online. Sure enough, there it was, available for order. I was delighted. I printed out the cover image shown on the web and posted it on the bulletin board in the café.

By that time, I had begun to learn a little about modern copyright. Perhaps we all had, given the destruction of Napster and the first of those Recording Industry of American (RIAA) lawsuits. The problems presented by digital possibilities were certainly now getting broader attention. Not much, but enough so that I was even aware of the new Creative Commons concept of expansive ownership that was allowing authors to license "works freely for certain uses, on certain conditions" ("History," 2012) or even to clearly dedicate works to the public domain, something now not possible without some sort of clear and legal statement. I liked the concept of Creative Commons and its flexibility toward ownership, but I didn't really think about it much. I only wished that Creative Commons had been around a couple of years earlier, so that I could have made use of it when my chapters were posted on the web, for I would have liked to be able to have made that legal statement that my work was free for copying or other use, as long as I was given credit for writing it. Even though I now knew a little more about the law, my attitude toward my work and toward copyright had not changed.

That is why I wasn't too disturbed to find I had a book in Spanish, especially since it did have my name on it. Except for an edited collection of documents relating to my grandfather's World War I service that I had published myself with my family the only intended audience, this was my first book. I wanted to see it and was proud that it existed. So, I emailed Villarubia and asked if he had contact information for the publisher. I know no Spanish and there were no website translators on the web in those days, so I was having trouble getting information from the sites featuring the book. With Villarubia's help, I finally found contact information for the publisher and send off an email congratulating him for publishing it—and asking for a copy.

It took some 3 or 4 months to get a response. I sent off a number of follow-up messages, using alternate email addresses that I or Villarubia had managed to find. I suspect there was also a little bit of quiet prodding from Villarubia (who works in publishing himself) that he never told me about. Anyhow, I eventually did get a response from a highly embarrassed publisher. He was relieved, I am sure, to discover that I really did want nothing more than a couple of copies of the book, which he promptly sent.

The book is titled *Cuánto te Asusta el Caos?: Política, Religión y Filosofía en la obra de Philip K. Dick* after the earlier article, though the translator is different: Eva Verloop Van der Meij. The Granada publisher, Grupo Editorial AJEC, came out with a second edition the next year, 2004. I have never received royalties for the book but, then, I never expected to. After all, I did not write it for money, but for a degree.

Realizing that the book would never now be touched by an American publisher (if it ever had that possibility in the first place), I decided to use a Print-On-Demand service and publish it myself. After all, I had some familiarity with the process from my book about my grandfather. I used the English translation of the Spanish title, added an introduction, took out a chapter that had appeared in an anthology in the early 1990s, and inserted another I wrote specifically to replace it, one relating Philip Dick to contemporary events—a chapter which I also offered to Villarubia, who translated it and eventually included it as "La que está cayendo: Lecciones para el mundo posterior al 11-S en la obra breve de Philip K. Dick" in his annual *Jabberwock: Anuario de Ensayo Fantastic* (2007).

For a number of unrelated reasons, by the time I finally had my dissertation in book form in English, I was well on my way toward returning to academia. Not only was I now teaching part-time, but I was casting around for full-time positions and was involved in my first "real" book project, a study of home viewing of movies that centered on the impact of the DVD. The subject forced me to started learning about copyright in a way I never had before, for the DVD and digital editing possibilities were opening up copyright questions in ways never before considered. *The Phantom Edit* (Nichols, 2001), a reworking of George Lucas's 1999 *Star Wars Episode 1: The Phantom Menace* may have been one of the first, but it would certainly not be the last attempt at editing a commercially released movie in new ways—for the editor's own amusement or even with the hope of making money from it. Although most Americans knew by then that doing any of this contravened copyright, not too many of us cared. We just figured we needed to be a bit more careful than those poor people now being sued by the RIAA.

When it came out in 2005, my new book was titled *The DVD Revolution: Movies, Culture, and Technology*—and its final chapter was called "The Question of Ownership," my first serious exploration of copyright. In it, I wrote:

> One of the most radical aspects of virtual culture is the removal of control of the work itself from its creators to those who experience it, a change that copyright conventions, among other things, have not managed to adapt to in any sort of rational manner. Instead of recognizing that electronic media have instituted a fundamental shift in the way people interact with artifacts such as books, music, and images, the copyright holders have attempted to hold to a standard that not only cannot be enforced without the use of intrusive technology but also that no longer makes sense to most end users. (p. 145)

I was referring to film, and to the ability to alter it through digital tools—but I could just as well have been writing about my own experience with my dissertation. Thing is, though, I never had been thinking in terms of ownership or of profit—while corporate copyright holders most certainly were.

I had learned a great deal about copyright by then, but I was on track for learning more. The issues involved were more complex than I could have imagined, and involved law, culture, commerce, creation, and conceptions of ownership in a dance that I was having a hard time following—even though I had now spent enough time with the issue of have written a book chapter on it. Also, like most of us approaching copyright through our new digital possibilities, I was beginning to change my focus from the rights of owners to the rights of users, which made the issue even more complicated.

What I was seeing, though I didn't really know it at the time, not completely, was the start of a new trend in conceptions of ownership of IP. This trend was sparked by the start of the digital age, though it, too, had roots back in the print age.

Thomas Jefferson, of all people, provides a notable example of what would be coming through his *The Life and Morals of Jesus of Nazareth*. Jefferson, to make the New Testament keep pace with his own religious thought, cut up the Bible and pasted it back together, but with the parts he didn't like missing—much as Nichols would do almost 200 years later when he cut Jar-Jar Binks from his *The Phantom Edit*. Jefferson never published his work, but he did share it. Again, people do much the same with works today, but the line between sharing and publishing has blurred: send a file to a friend via email, and it may end up in public through very little effort... or, like my dissertation, something placed online might easily appear in another sort of media or language without the creator's knowledge.

Even then, though, Jefferson knew the dangers of sharing. A private letter of his had been excerpted and included in the first American edition of Tom Paine's *Rights of Man* in 1791. The excerpt was read as an attack on John Adams and got Jefferson in a bit of hot water. He likely took special care with his Bible, making sure that it would not be published without his approval—which, given the nature of the work, probably would not have been forthcoming. Today, of course, as I found out, almost anything anyone puts on the web stands the chance of "publication" elsewhere.

In his presage to digital possibilities *The Arcades Project*, Walter Benjamin (2002) took the Dada movement's uses of collage, the idea of incorporating extant artifacts into a new work, and extends it by looking back at the *flâneur* of Paris in the nineteenth century, a character that had been described at the time, by Baudelaire, as the person looking in shop windows and moving on. The *flâneur*, of course, is the great-grandparent of today's browsers of the web.

For creators, one of the scary parts of the digital revolution is that a work can now be so easily altered. It took patience and time for Jefferson to create his new work, as it did for Benjamin. Today, someone can even take something as complicated as a movie and change it with very little effort, making it into something quite different from what the initial creator meant it to be. The *flâneur* becomes creator.

If visions of copyright and IP had moved from protection of individual creators to protection of corporations in the twentieth century, they were now being forced to move in a new direction, one that includes protection for the end-user as herself or himself a creator, too. Or so I believed when I wrote my book on the DVD. As I said:

> When it was instituted, the copyright system was meant to encourage innovations while protecting prior creativity. It has become something else completely. Seen most cynically, it has simply become a device for insuring the profit stream of corporations. Earlier in the virtual age, people argued that the Internet was an example of information trying to be free. Control of intellectual property seemed to be slipping from governmental, corporate, and personal fingers. (p. 153)

This idealized vision could never manage to become reality, I came to believe over the years after the book came out, not in a political system dominated by corporate interests.

I was wrong, I also now believe, when I wrote at the end of the chapter that:

> If the past is any guide, the corporations are eventually going to have to find ways of coming to terms with consumer manipulation of copyrighted material without permissions. The weight of perceived individual prerogative is extremely high, and its pressure will be hard for the corporations to withstand—especially when technology constantly makes it easier and easier to circumvent controls. The corporations, however, are extremely powerful, and they perceive such manipulation as attacks on the basis of their very existences—so they will fight hard to protect themselves. (p. 156)

Given the cultural realities of the twenty-first century, I suspect I was a fool to let my own optimism run away with me, optimism resulting from my experience with my dissertation and exploration of Fan Art in relation to film. What looked like a possible birth of new possibilities for arts of all sorts now seems to have been strangled by its own umbilical cord, dying just as it seemed to be coming to life.

At the same time, my optimism refuses to die. Having been surprised by the possibilities of the web more than once (I have had other pleasant surprises because I do not protect my work on the web), I am certainly open to being surprised once again.

• PART THREE •

Cultures of Copyright

• CHAPTER TWELVE •

Copyright and Cultural Use: Tracing Tensions between Policy and Practice in Participatory Cultures

Dave Jones

Within online communities, people collaborate to find and share information and generate new knowledge (Diehl, Grabill, Hart-Davidson, & Iyer, 2008). In doing so, they become participants who use, share, manipulate, and replicate intellectual property across numerous social networking platforms, such as Facebook, Twitter, and many other services. In doing so, participatory cultures emerge wherein participants leverage their collective skills and abilities to create content, share ideas, and produce knowledge (Jenkins, 2006). As Henry Jenkins (1992, 2004, 2006) pointed out, the social and creative activities of participatory cultures often leverage copyrighted content. Participants extend storylines from television shows and movies in the form of fan-fiction, collaborate through blogs and forums to critically explore and repurpose these stories, and often recreate films, books, and stories in various modes. They distribute their work in the form of videos, written texts, audio recordings, and, sometimes, as fan-created computer and video games.

These social and creative practices, and their implications for collaborative knowledge work, are the focus of this chapter. Examining the ways that these cultures use IP for the knowledge work that often accompanies participation through social web tools allows us to better understand how and why these cultures appropriate IP as "differently abled, differently resourced, and differently motivated media producers" (Green & Jenkins, 2009, p. 216). We can then better understand how practices such as using IP often become "an important source of learning" within participatory cultures (Ducheneaut & Moore, 2005, p. 101). To do so, researchers must look at the full ecosystem[1] of people, groups, organizations, and technologies to trace the intersection between IP, the policies that govern its use in these ecosystems, and the practices of the communities that use copyrighted material in the production of their own cultural work (Jones, 2011). Tracing the tensions between cultural practices and governing policies will allow us to situate participation as a negotiation over the limits imposed on creative and social practices that employ IP.

This chapter outlines a methodology for exploring the intersection between the social and creative practices in which participants use copyrighted material and the implementation of policies that regulate such practices. I discuss LittleBigPlanet as a rich research space in which to explore participatory cultures and uses of copyrighted content. Next, I outline a methodology based on concepts from actor-network theory for tracing culturally situated participatory practices against policy regimes aimed at governing those practices. To do so, I use a case study that illustrates the use of copyrighted IP by people who play LittleBigPlanet and use its tools to produce characters and game levels. Through this case study, I illustrate the risks that participants take to become stronger participants with richer skill sets. Ultimately, I argue that the governing regime established by these policies creates a tension for participants that simultaneously enables their use of copyrighted content while also placing their social and creative work at risk because of these activities. From these insights, I discuss implications on policy implementation in the social web.

LittleBigPlanet as a Site of Research

As Douglas Eyman (2008) pointed out, "games can serve as objects of study" in which scholars "can learn about interface design, interaction design, and how users engage in complex communication tasks mediated by texts and data visualizations on a large scale" (p. 243). They can also serve as rich sites for exploring digitally mediated social and creative practices of participatory cultures (Sherlock, 2009; Sotamaa, 2010; Taylor, 2007). LittleBigPlanet is designed to facilitate and encourage the production and sharing of player-generated content, and the game's developer and publisher provide a strong ecosystem of tools and spaces to help players participate. As of June 2014, the official website for LittleBigPlanet listed more than 8.5 million player-produced game levels accessible through the PlayStation Network (PSN). In addition, LittleBigPlanet players can search for player-created levels using a web-based service, LBP.me. This service catalogues every player-produced level shared within the PSN, providing tools for players to comment on content, rate it, and even place it into a queue so that it can be readily accessed by players when they log back into the PSN with their consoles.

In addition, Media Molecule, Sony, and many fans within the LBP community use social web tools that are not part of Sony's proprietary network, including Facebook and Twitter, YouTube, and different forum and blogging services. There is no way to adequately track how much LittleBigPlanet-related content is produced and shared in these other spaces. Both Media Molecule representatives and gaming participants maintain very active presences on these services. A cursory keyword search of YouTube using "LittleBigPlanet" shows at least 270,000 results as of April 2014.[2] Participants often create fan pages, post videos, and build fan websites to support their participatory activities. Through digital systems owned by Sony and on a variety of third-party systems, people communicate in multiple and often complex ways. They produce and share content with friends and family members, with companies, government agencies, and other organizations. They share content, such as text updates, static pictures, and screen captures of other digital media, and video captures of game levels and fan reviews. This communication allows people to trace and coordinate a wide range of information and collaboratively develop knowledge relevant to them and the communities that they inhabit.

The original 2008 release of LittleBigPlanet allowed players to create side-scrolling experiences in which players largely move left or right on screen. Players could jump from one platform to the next, climb or leap over obstacles, or use various objects to combat other non-playable characters and objects within the environment. In 2011, LittleBigPlanet 2 updated these tools and in-game assets to include new objects, textures, and colors so that players could create a wider range of experiences. No longer limited to simply moving left or right, the LittleBigPlanet player community produces three-dimensional game environments that allow movement in any direction. With the ability to leverage three dimensions rather than just two, players can reproduce virtually any gaming experience possible on a modern video game console. Players can use different colors and textures to visually style their characters and game environments. Digital objects, some of which can be manipulated or customized, allow players to produce custom levels. Using the in-game interface, players can select objects, customize their look and some of their interactive behavior, and place them within an interactive space. Players can also customize the appearance of their digital avatars within the game—called "sack people"—to create characters.

Producing and sharing this content online is one of the central elements of the LittleBigPlanet experience. The digital infrastructure supporting the online networking experience is provided by Sony Computer Entertainment. Published for the Playstation 3 game console (PS3), the game taps into a Sony-owned networking service accessible exclusively through Sony-controlled portals. This service, the Playstation Network (PSN), can link with any PS3 whose owner has access to a broadband internet connection and is willing to create a PSN account. Generating such an account is as simple as creating a username, providing a valid email address, and setting a password. Through the PSN, LittleBigPlanet gamers can share the content that they produce using these proprietary tools.

Using the PSN's underlying architecture, LittleBigPlanet serves as a social networking service through which players interact with one another to learn more about producing in-game content, form working relationships and friendships, share both material assets and working knowledge, and even collaboratively build game levels and characters. To use Carolyn Rude's (2009) description of the importance of digital work that mediates communication, the content that players produce in the LBP ecosystem serves as "agents of knowledge making, action, and change" (p. 176). Thus, social web spaces such as LBP are critical research sites for exploring the intersection of creative and social practices and technological design.

In this chapter, I look at the terms of service and licensing policies that accompany the Little Big Planet (2008) and LittleBigPlanet 2 (2011) in conjunction with some of the key cultural practices carried by members of the participatory culture that has emerged around the game. According to the games' developer, Media Molecule, there are more than four million player-produced game levels across the LBP ecosystem (Media Molecule, 2011). Despite at least four separate policies that state some version of "do not create, transfer, share, send, submit, post or upload" any copyrighted content (Sony, 2011), participants are violating these policies and producing a wide variety of content. Recreating stories and characters from popular books, films, and other video games is a common practice across this community. The games' respective developer and publisher, Media Molecule and Sony Computer Entertainment, own and manage the proprietary networks. Thus, the ecosystem of actors[3] that support the participatory culture that emerges around these games provides a rich space in which to study the intersection of copyrighted material, governing policies, and cultural use.

Using the case of NyghtHawk (2008), I argue that these contradictions have significant ramifications for the social and creative practices of participatory cultures. NyghtHawk distributes his creations as playable levels within the Playstation Network (PSN)—owned and maintained by Sony Computer Entertainment—and as still images in a discussion forum owned and maintained by Media Molecule, LittleBigWorkshop.com. In doing so, his activities become subject to a complex web of policies that do not seamlessly align with one another or with the way Media Molecule constructs the notion of participation in other spaces. NyghtHawk's activities point to ways in which the local needs of participants are met through creative adaptations of already existing assets and copyrighted IP. As Clay Spinuzzi (2003) suggested, understanding and, as far as possible, supporting the innovations that participants produce in response to their needs is a critical requirement of researchers. In this case study, the local needs of participants include producing culturally meaningful content by improving their creative skills with the tools provided within LittleBigPlanet.

Methodology

Using the concepts of *inscription* and *prescription* from actor network theory (ANT), I construct a critical approach for examining the intersection between participation and policy. These two concepts provide a rich theoretical model for situating the practices of online participants within the policy regimes that govern the digital systems they use. In this approach, researchers can study governing policies designed and implemented by media companies alongside the creative and social practices of participatory cultures that use copyrighted IP. In ANT, prescriptions set the boundaries for what actors can and cannot do in actor networks (Akrich & Latour, 1992). Inscriptions are the traces of network activity left by a network's actors (Latour, 1987, 1999), providing a documented trace of the activities of actors within networks.[4] These inscriptions take the form of game levels, characters, and stories that players produce within the game, as well as many other images, videos, and texts that surround this creative work. Prescriptions can be traced through both the rules that establish what is and is not acceptable within a community and through the limitations and capabilities of technologies that apply those rules.

Examining inscriptions and prescriptions enables researchers to trace the possible tensions between participants' creative practices and industry-produced regulations that govern such practices. Tools and technologies must be flexible enough that they can adapt to the "local" (Spinuzzi, 2003) needs of network participants and communities within their own social and cultural contexts (Potts, 2009). Prescriptions and inscriptions highlight the ways in which media companies attempt to structure participatory practice through various means, including policy, as well as the meaningful activities that participatory cultures actually pursue. Looking at the inscriptions produced by participants enables researchers to trace the activities that participants use to produce digital content. Inscriptions are a type of record of participatory activity, allowing us to examine why some activities are meaningful, including sometimes tracing the mechanisms and tools through which participants mediate their social and creative activities. Exploring the tension between participatory activities of these cultures and the regulations that govern social web tools allows researchers to examine copyright policies in a new way. These policies become not only legal frameworks governing digital tools and their use, they are also critical components that shape the design of digital ecosystems intended to support cultural practice. We can begin tracing the tangible impact that such policies have on participatory cultures.

Inscribing Cultural Production

In an interview published on popular video game site IGN.com, Media Molecule executives state that one of the company's primary goals with LBP is to empower players to become "creators" (Robinson, 2008). As players become creators,[5] they become active contributors to the LBP ecosystem—adding content for others to play rather than simply playing content that already exists. LittleBigPlanet's manual describes LBP as "a world of infinite possibilities, where imagination becomes reality and the powers of creation are firmly in your hands" (Media Molecule, 2008, p. 4). Media Molecule markets LBP as a platform through which fans and players can produce their own stories, game levels, and characters—content that fans and players can then share with one another through the PSN.

The core interaction for player–creators in the LBP ecosystem is using the tools and assets provided within the games to make playable content that they then share publicly in the PSN. Once that content has been published to the PSN, any PS3 owner who has the LBP game, a PSN account, and an Internet connection can log on to the PSN and access this content. Player–creators in the LBP ecosystem are generating inscriptions, or an "archive" of the practices of player-creators and the information they produce (Latour, 1999). Through inscriptions, researchers can examine the content that participants produce as an archive of social and creative practices. For example, a forum post is not just an instance of text produced within a specific software. It can be explored as a record of the ways that content is converted and transformed so that a participant can transport digital content from one social web tool to another. Such knowledge helps researchers gain a greater understanding of the cultural importance of participatory activities.

It is useful to think of this "archive" as a collection of traces embedded within an inscription, which point to the practices, skills, and technologies used to produce that inscription (Akrich & Latour, 1992; Latour, 1999). According to Liza Potts (2009), inscriptions point out the ways information is transformed as it moves across the assemblage of people and technologies. Inscriptions are snapshots not just of content but also of practice. By tracing inscriptions, researchers can identify participatory practices in an actor network and trace the technologies that player–creators use to produce content. These inscriptions shed light into the ways participatory cultures use social web technologies as tools for cultural production and knowledge work.

NyghtHawk uses LBP's in-game tools to make costumes that recreate popular comic book, television, and video game characters. NyghtHawk makes costumes by modifying his sack person, a digital puppet that serves as the main avatar in LBP (Media Molecule, 2008). Media Molecule provides some costumes for the player–creator's sack person. Player–creators can also modify their sack person with different colors, textures, and images to produce their own costumes. NyghtHawk then posts screen captures of his costumes to the LittleBigWorkshop.com forum as a topic of discussion, a common practice in LBP.

NyghtHawk uses Sony's and Media Molecule's proprietary technologies to support his practices of reproducing copyrighted IP and sharing it with others. The screen captures he shares are, themselves, inscriptions, or "a sign, an archive, a document, a piece of paper, a trace" that record data about communication practices in an actor network (Latour, 1999, p. 306). The inscriptions, their technical details (such as file format), and connections to other people and technologies are all a part of this trace. In this case, NyghtHawk's costumes are an inscription that allows us to uncover the process described above so that we can identify some of his practices and the technologies he used. These are local practices that indicate both NyghtHawk's needs and the extent to which he and his fellow participants will work to support their local needs. By tracing the process necessary to produce the costumes within the game, capture static images of them, and share them in a discussion forum, we can uncover processes that support collaborative knowledge work among these participants.

Once he finishes his costumes, NyghtHawk can share them with other participants in different ways. First, he can publish them to the PSN in a game level, providing the different pieces of each costume—hats, shirts, pants, glasses, etc.—so that other player-creators can use them in their own game levels and mimic his designs. Or he can pursue a more cumbersome process: In this process NyghtHawk screen captures his costumes created within the game and saves the images locally on his PS3 hard drive as a JPEG image file. The PS3 provides several USB ports so that NyghtHawk can copy those JPEG files to a flashdrive, which will allow him to upload the images to a computer and post them in a discussion forum. Despite the common ownership between LittleBigPlanet and LittleBigWorkshop.com, there is no support for exporting images from within the game directly to NyghtHawk's account within the forum. Yet, with these technologies and the connections NyghtHawk forges among them, he can produce and distribute content in multiple ways, expanding his skills and the actor network in which he can work, as well.

To use Bruno Latour's (1999) words, NyghtHawk's activities are a type of "invention" by situating his character images within a "series of associations" with other people and technologies (p. 179). In doing so, NyghtHawk not only transforms the ways these costumes are used but forms new inscriptions by linking technologies so that he can move his costumes from the PS3 to the discussion forum. To support a local need—improving the creative skills that support participation, such as using a particular tool or feature set within the game—NyghtHawk and his peers use copyrighted content transformed through a complex process to support a rich discussion. This discussion is aimed at satisfying the local needs of this digital community. As the next section shows, using copyrighted content is a crucial tool for these participants to improve their creative practices. These inventions hint that using copyrighted IP within participatory cultures often supports learning improved creative skills, empowering participants as cultural agents within their communities.

NyghtHawk's inscriptions—the costumes he creates and the images of them he uses in the forums—become tools for facilitating social interaction among forum participants, a key component of participation in spaces such as LBP (Jenkins, 1992, 2004, 2006). This social interaction is characterized by discussions of the skills and practices documented within these inscriptions. For example, in the same discussion thread where he posted the costumes, NyghtHawk asked forum participants for feedback about his costumes, noting that he hopes to "inspire people to try out there [sic] skills as well" (NyghtHawk, 2008). The discussions documented in the LittleBigWorkshop.com forum thread are examples of knowledge work, or "analytical activity requiring problem solving and abstract reasoning" (Diehl, Grabill, Hart-Davidson, & Iyer, 2008, p. 414). Using copyrighted IP provides participants with a well-known and recognizable point of reference with which to critique the effectiveness of the skills they are discussing. This practice is a critical component of the knowledge work performed by NyghtHawk and his peers.

Spinuzzi (2008) argued that the relationships among network actors "change constantly" so that the "network tends to become more intricate, linking to and incorporating more groups, disciplines, fields, and trades as well as more technologies, regulations, legislation, and customers" (p. 198). The more work there is and the more complex that work becomes, the more intricate and unpredictable the connections among network actors become. Participants can respond flexibly to the intricacies of their local circumstances, especially where connections among people and technologies "may not be stable from one incident to the next" (2007, p. 268). Thus, understanding how to empower participant responses to local exigencies and participant needs in relationship to a larger cultural or political context is a critical element of the research and design of communication networks. For the LBP participants traced in this chapter, using copyright-protected IP can be understood as "unofficial, idiosyncratic, ad hoc solutions" (Spinuzzi, 2003, p. 19).

By using popular characters such as Batman, Captain America, and the Joker, NyghtHawk's costumes become points of reference for participants discussing the techniques, skills, and resources needed for making intricately detailed costumes. Social interactions that take place among NyghtHawk and his peers in the forums are critical components of knowledge work. In this knowledge work, NyghtHawk transforms the images from an interactive object of play, to a document that records traces of data, to a tool that presents information in creative and compelling ways. To return to Latour's (1999) concept, the "archive" of information about creative practices and skills is teased out of the inscription to produce knowledge useful for forum participants. NyghtHawk's activities transform the images through his "local innovations" (Spinuzzi, 2003, p. 19), wherein he adapts them to recreate copyrighted IP. NyghtHawk repurposes the copyrighted IP that he uses in his costumes, and then he repurposes the costumes as static images that become examples published within the forum thread. Forum participants then use these images as tools for developing and exchanging knowledge that expands their creative skills. By expanding knowledge and skillsets, the social interactions of these discussions expand the participatory skills of NyghtHawk, PhadedWun, Grifindor_seekr, and the other participants in the forum discussions: They are empowered to develop a stronger, more detailed understanding of how to use images to create costumes.

Prescribing Participation

As Potts (2010) stated, participatory activities in the social web often come "into conflict with various laws and regulations" governing proprietary technologies, copyrighted IP, and the ways participants use both across cultural, legal, and technological borders (p. 303). These participants are performing tasks not necessarily sanctioned by Sony and Media Molecule. Nearly all of NyghtHawk's activities utilize proprietary actors: the LittleBigPlanet game, the PSN, the PS3, and the LittleBigWorkshop.com forum.[6] All of these proprietary actors are governed by terms of service and licensing agreements that forbid the use of copyrighted IP. NyghtHawk's creative practices, inscriptions, and knowledge work are all intertwined with these policies. Because much of his creative work takes place within proprietary spaces or uses proprietary technologies, his activities are subject to policies that restrict or forbid these practices described above. According to these policies, NyghtHawk's reproductions of copyrighted characters violate the rules and regulations that govern the LBP ecology. Thus, NyghtHawk's practices within the LBP ecosystem are closely tied to the ways these policies intersect with his local innovations, including the knowledge work he and others perform in the forum discussions.

Returning to ANT, these policies can be understood as prescriptions, or "what a device allows or forbids from the actors" (Akrich & Latour, 1992, p. 261). In the LBP ecology, prescriptions can be identified in terms of service and licensing agreements. These are formal policies that participants often must agree to in order to use proprietary systems, networks, and technologies. These policies establish the boundaries of participation by asserting which activities are permissible and which are not. If the participant refuses to agree to such policies, then he may be denied access to important features of the technologies or to the spaces those policies regulate. For instance, if a participant does not accept the End User License Agreement (EULA) that accompanies the LittleBigPlanet game software, then the game will not connect to the PSN. This means that the participant cannot share content online or download content that other player-creators produce.

Table 1 below lists the policies (prescriptions) that apply to NyghtHawk's activities and content (inscriptions), provides a summary description of each policy, and lists the proprietary technologies that each policy applies to. The final column lists the activities and prescriptions that these policies most directly impact. Participating in the LBP ecosystem intertwines creative practices with a complex array of rules and regulations that define participation in contradictory ways. Once these rules are implemented as prescriptions, they become a sophisticated system for governing participation in the LBP ecosystem.

Table 1. Sony, Media Molecule, and NyghtHawk's activities

Policy	Summary Description	Proprietary Tech	NyghtHawk's Activities and Inscriptions
Terms of Service and User Agreement (TOSUA)	Includes policies regarding the use of the PSN, the types of content player-creators can produce for and share through the PSN, and copyrighted content.	Playstation Network	• Costumes • Costume creation • LittleBigPlanet game levels
Terms of Service (TOS)	Similar to the TOSUA in its restrictions and purpose. However, it applies to the "PlayStation family of web sites" (Sony, 2011) that are outside of the PSN but owned and maintained by Sony or one of its partners.	LittleBigWorkshop Forums	• Posting texts and images in forum posts • Discussing costume creation • Costume images
System Software License Agreement (SSLA)	Defines the restrictions PS3 owners face regarding the operating system's software.	Playstation 3 Operating System	• Use of the system to create costumes • Playing LittleBigPlanet
End User License Agreement (EULA)	Applies to the LBP 2 software and governs the use of the game and its content, as well any player-generated content.	LBP and LBP 2 software	• Costumes • Costume creation • LittleBigPlanet game levels
Whitelist	Not published and does not require the consent of player-creators; lists the third-party copyright holders who have expressed their wish that Media Molecule never moderate player-produced content that uses their IPs.	Player-generated levels	• Costumes • Costume creation • LittleBigPlanet game levels • Forum posts and discussions • Costume images

Each of NyghtHawk's participatory practices and the inscriptions he traces are affected by Sony's and Media Molecule's policies. As NyghtHawk creates costumes, captures images of those costumes, and moves those images over to a forum, he shifts his participatory work across the LBP ecosystem. He assembles numerous proprietary technologies and spaces to do so, such as LittleBigPlanet, the PS3, the PSN, and the LittleBigWorkshop.com forum. Shifting his work from one space to another (e.g., from the PSN to the LittleBigWorkshop.com forum), NyghtHawk also links each policy listed in Table 1 to his inscriptions and his activity. Assembling the actor network also assembles a complex array of prescriptions that govern his activity from multiple directions at once.

According to the EULA and other policies, player–creators are not permitted to create and share any levels, characters, or stories that utilize copyrighted content. For instance, the language of the EULA for LittleBigPlanet 2 tells player–creators that reproducing copyrighted IP in player-created levels is not permitted:

> To comply with the terms of this agreement, you will not submit any User Generated Content that... is protected by copyright, patent, trademark, trade secret or otherwise subject to third party proprietary rights, including rights of privacy and publicity (unless you are or have permission from the rightful owner). (Media Molecule, 2011)

The participant must obtain written permission from the copyright holder. Without this permission, practices such as NyghtHawk's can be deemed illegal. Because forum participants use copyrighted IP as part of their knowledge work, their activities expose their participation to the risk of moderation by Sony and Media Molecule, or even legal action by copyright holders of the characters in NyghtHawk's JPEG image.

The policies and technologies described in Table 1 form "a loosely regimented but highly cohesive, hybrid network" aimed at protecting Sony's and Media Molecule's creative and copyright interests (Gillespie, 2006, p. 652). As stated earlier in this chapter, for NyghtHawk to connect his game software to the PSN, he must first agree to the EULA. In addition, the PS3's operating system and its use are subject to the System Software License Agreement (SSLA), which describes the same restrictions (Sony, 2009). Once connected to the PSN, NyghtHawk's activities also become subject to the Terms of Service and User Agreement (TOSUA) that applies to Sony's network. And the TOSUA contains language similar to the previous two policies, stating that player–creators "may not upload, post, stream, access, or otherwise transmit any content" that is "known to be infringing" the IP rights of Sony, Media Molecule, or a third party (Sony, 2010). Further, the forums are subject to their own Terms of Service agreement (Sony, 2011). NyghtHawk faces four formal policies, all of which he must agree to in a way similar to the EULA, and all of which tell him his recreation of copyrighted characters is not permitted.

Yet, as this case study illustrates, this regimented network of policies does not serve as a strong deterrent to NyghtHawk and his peers. They still leverage copyrighted IP in their costumes and the knowledge work those costumes support. NyghtHawk's inscriptions are not only vital to the knowledge work of his participatory community, but his costumes also place these important player–creator activities at risk of moderation, or even outright banishment from Sony's and Media Molecule's services. His inscriptions are produced in systems owned by Sony and Media Molecule. His participatory activities leverage technologies and online spaces that those companies control. For this reason, NyghtHawk's inscriptions are entangled with prescriptions that forbid his practices, his creations, and by extension have the power to stall knowledge work he and his peers perform within the forums. As he expands his creative and social practices, his activities and his inscriptions are increasingly entangled with these policies and the limitations they define. In other words, the more he becomes a creator, the more he is exposed to Sony's and Media Molecule's governance.

A crucial contradiction arises from the presence of the Whitelist (Robinson, 2008) documented in Table 1; this Whitelist can contravene the copyright provisions of the other four policies shown. According to Media Molecule executive Alex Evans, this Whitelist contains a list of "IP owners who came up to us and said please whitelist us—we'll never ask you to pull infringing stuff" (Robinson, 2008). This policy provides a framework for contravening the other policies, such as the EULA or TOSUA—simply put, the copyright holder has the right to approve or disapprove any use of their IP. In this way, both phrases from the EULA help establish one view of the "morality of [the] setting" (Akrich & Latour, 1992, p. 261). Player-created content that uses copyrighted IP may be left public or taken down from Sony's and Media Molecule's proprietary networks and sites with no explanation given to the participants that gathered around the inscription.

What distinguishes the Whitelist from other policies in this ecosystem is that its prescriptions are not publicly visible. The names of copyright holders who have requested whitelisting are not publicized. The contradictions among policies in LBP are critical not because they can undermine one another, but because the player–creator cannot fully understand how or why one policy may override another. Local inventions, such as using copyrighted IP to explore costume-creation techniques, come to depend on the presence of the Whitelist to support the knowledge work of participants, such as NyghtHawk and his peers. The Whitelist offers provisions that may sanction such practices by creating an ambiguity in the morality established in the prescriptions.

In NyghtHawk's case, copyrighted IP also proves a useful resource for learning important participatory skills. New knowledge is generated from already-existing content. New creative practices are learned from the social interactions that form around inscriptions. NyghtHawk's multiple inscriptions support the knowledge work in the LittleBigWorkshop.com forum as a critical form of participation in this ecosystem. However, Sony and Media Molecule define acceptable participatory practices along two competing, mutually exclusive lines of thought, both of them seemingly endorsed by Media Molecule. The ambiguity that these two competing moralities create opens substantial space for participation because Sony and Media Molecule can avoid setting a clear precedent that defines where those boundaries lie. In addition, these competing prescriptions are under the direct control of Sony and Media Molecule.

Because these technologies are proprietary and Sony and Media Molecule establish the prescriptions that govern them and the use of copyrighted IP, these companies can shift the scope of the limitations around NyghtHawk's practices at any time. His local innovations can be deemed acceptable in one instance, and then unacceptable or even illegal in another. And this can happen in ways and for reasons that are not made clear to NyghtHawk. Policies may forbid his use of copyrighted IP in his costumes, but public statements from Media Molecule executives "refactoring" and turning players into "creators" (Robinson, 2008), the Whitelist, and activities by Media Molecule suggest he can use copyrighted IP. But he will never know with any certainty until he attempts to use copyrighted material and puts his activities and inscriptions at risk.

Conclusion

Regulatory policy regimes designed to govern the use of IP become deeply intertwined with the culturally situated use of such content. As this chapter illustrates, participatory cultures often leverage such content in order to better support their social and creative practices. Indeed, they may use such content to empower themselves as creative cultural agents. However, such policies create ever shifting boundaries in which participation takes place, sometimes disenfranchising important cultural activities that enable the development of critical social and creative skills. To participate in these ecosystems, those who produce and share content often have to place themselves at risk of moderation. The use of IP by participants can be situated within policy frameworks wherein such culturally rich practices oscillate between varying degrees of permission or censure.

As this chapter illustrates, policy regimes can be designed and implemented so that social web participants are invited to participate as those boundaries expand outward, yet they do not know when those boundaries contract inward until their content is removed. LBP illustrates how contradictions among different policies in these ecosystems can affect participatory practices. The boundaries that companies such as Sony and Media Molecule impose upon participation become elastic, able to expand and contract. Scholars with foundations in rhetoric and communication research are uniquely suited to study the tension between policy and cultural practice in the social web. We are equipped with a rich set of tools for exploring inscriptions, the practices they archive, and their importance for social interaction and knowledge work.

Notes

1 I use the term *ecosystem* to refer to the aggregation of individual people, groups and organizations, Media Molecule and Sony, the wide variety of digital tools and portals (such as the games, blogs, and forums), and practices that support this participatory culture. I explicitly selected this term for its implication that these actors are interdependently linked to one another in the production of knowledge and meaning.

2 Potts (2009c) illustrated that communities interacting through social web tools often use a wide variety of different keywords and terms that create problems for tracing and coordinating information. For LittleBigPlanet, online communities may also use other keywords, such as "LBP," "Media Molecule," or "MM" when referring to the game or the content they produce.

3 In ANT, the term *actor* is used to describe both human and non-human components of any network, including individual people, groups, technologies, physical objects, etc. (Latour, 1999; Law, 1999). Callon (1999) stated that "ANT... assumes the radical indeterminacy of the actor," leading to "no stable theory" of it (p. 181, Callon's emphasis). What constitutes an *actor* in any network is contingent, potentially different from one network to the next.

4 The term *participant* refers to any person not identified as a representative of Sony or Media Molecule who engages in the LBP ecosystem by producing an inscription of some kind: for example, game levels, comments and ratings added to games or forum discussions, or images, text, and video posted on social networking sites such as Facebook or YouTube.

5 After this point, I will refer to these specific participants as *player–creators* for the sake of clarity and brevity.

6 The term *proprietary actor* refers to any web site, digital technology, network, group, or person that is owned, maintained, or employed by Sony or Media Molecule.

• CHAPTER THIRTEEN •

Intellectual Property and Jewish Ethics: Scripture as a Resource for Socioeconomic Thought

Gabriel J. Michael

Religion is important in American culture: 71% of Americans profess an "absolutely certain" belief in God, and 56% percent describe religion as being "very important" in their lives (Pew Forum on Religion & Public Life, 2008). Pastors, priests, rabbis and imams are influential figures in the personal lives of large numbers of Americans, and the proper role of religion in public life remains a hotly contested issue. Religious values are invoked in moral, social, political, and economic debates by clergy and laity alike, on topics as varied as reproductive health, global warming, welfare policy, and the tax code. Given this broad influence, the dearth of explicitly religious thought about intellectual property comes as a surprise, especially given the long history of thought about property and other socioeconomic matters in both the Jewish and Christian traditions. Although intellectual property has long been a subject of inquiry for legal scholars and economists, and is increasingly becoming one for political scientists and anthropologists, there exist only a handful of scholarly articles examining intellectual property from an explicitly religious perspective (Andolsen, 2008; Berg, 2008; Carey, 2007; LenkaBula, 2005; Michael, 2010; Reed, 2006).

In this chapter, I argue that viewing intellectual property through the religious lens of Jewish scriptures has the potential to illuminate both academic and policy debates. Furthermore, lessons drawn from a religious perspective are not necessarily parochial: Whatever one's religious tradition or lack thereof, understanding what religion can say about intellectual property is important and useful. Even when considered separately from any religious understanding, Jewish scriptures are an especially rich resource of ethical and legal thought, documenting cultural attitudes present in antiquity, as well as centuries of rabbinical discourse pertaining to a broad swath of human activity, including socioeconomic activity. Understanding the attitudes and discourse present in this literature and considering their applicability to intellectual property can offer new ways to think about the role of intellectual property in modern society.

The Relevance of Scripture

Both the relevance and interpretation of ancient religious texts for modern socioeconomic inquiry present major conceptual hurdles. Jewish scriptures do not say any one thing (Rivkin, 1986); written, rewritten, and redacted, we cannot expect a consistent and simple treatment of any topic from these texts. Historicity is complicated by the fact that for the most part, we do not know to what extent, if any, the various codes of conduct discussed were respected.

Critical and historically conditioned reading is always necessary. At the same time, it is important to avoid the "trap of historicism... [that] tells us that a text or whatever document is worth studying only if it attests to history" (Illman, 1999, p. 89). In many cases, it is not necessarily the specific details of a text that interest us, but the ethical principles undergirding the text and the social message those principles convey. Whether or not the details of these texts are historically accurate, we cannot deny the influence that the texts, and the ethical principles the texts have been understood to convey, have had on religious and secular thought (Gustafson, 1984).

We also want to avoid an uncritical assessment of religious texts and concepts. One cannot simply look to a religion to find ready-made policies for the modern world. While admitting the difficulty inherent in asking what Jewish scriptures might say about intellectual property, those scriptures can tell us something about right action, justice, and mercy. If nothing else, it is reasonable to look to Jewish scriptures as a resource for ethical thought, and to view them similarly to how judge Richard Posner (1999) suggested a pragmatist ought to view past cases and decisions: as "repositories of knowledge, even, sometimes, of wisdom... as sources of potentially valuable information about the likely best result" (p. 242).

We can identify broad ethical principles present in Jewish scriptures, and we can and should consider how those ethical principles might apply to contemporary circumstances. Because "scripture provides an account of the sorts of human actions and events which the morally and religiously serious communities of the past have seen to be in accord and out of accord with the purposes of God for man" (Gustafson, 1984, pp. 170–171), it is valuable for ethical inquiry. Gustafson specified several ways of using scripture in the practice of ethical inquiry, the broadest of which involves critically examining human behavior "on the basis of reflective discourse about present events *in the light of* appeals to this variety of [scriptural] material as well as to other principles and experiences" (p. 165). The question, then, is not "what does Judaism say about intellectual property," but, rather, "how does understanding Jewish scripture and Jewish religious and legal culture affect the way we think about the role of intellectual property in modern society?"

In Judaism, religion and law were inextricably intertwined. For example, while the Ten Commandments contain some religious content, many of the commandments are similar in form to other ancient Near Eastern law codes. This mixing of religious and legal content is a familiar feature in other ancient writings, prompting some scholars to suggest that the commandments may have functioned as an early law code (Gnuse, 1985; Phillips, 1970). Similarly, while in a religious context the Torah's 613 *mitzvot* (precepts) are viewed as God's commandments, Jewish tradition has separated the *mitzvot* into different categories. Relevant to this discussion are the *mishpatim:* those *mitzvot* that are logical and self-evident, establish reasonable standards for governing conduct in society, and clearly have import even outside of a religious context. Thus, Jewish scriptures can sensibly speak to all kinds of readers. Conversely, ignoring one of the world's oldest and most important compilations of ethical and legal reasoning simply because it also contains religious material will require us to operate in a cultural vacuum.

Six Principles from Jewish Scriptures

Jewish scriptures contain numerous policies, regulations, and codes of conduct concerning socioeconomic matters, and specifically property. Before delving into a discussion of these, however, it is important to understand that property meant something different to ancient peoples, and particularly to ancient Israel. The early Israelites were a pastoral people for whom real property was necessarily highly important, and many features of Jewish scriptures reflect that importance. Some land was likely held in common, and even when land was held within a family, it could not be alienated arbitrarily. Animals such as cattle held a privileged position in relation to other forms of property; in general, the emphasis was on those types of property that sustained life. Besides land and livestock, this included goods such as millstones, which were capable of sustenance both literally and figuratively, and articles of clothing, such as a cloak, which protected a person from the elements (Gnuse, 1985). The difference is not so much between ancient and modern times, but between economically secure and economically fragile societies and individuals. In our own day, there are 830 million people who are consistently undernourished, 1.1 billion who do not have safe water, and 1 billion who do not have appropriate shelter (Pogge, 2008). For these people, basic goods really are life-sustaining. In examining the various policies about property in Jewish scriptures and in thinking about their application to intellectual property, we must keep in mind that they often may make the most sense in less-developed countries and for underprivileged individuals.

In keeping with a historically conditioned approach, we do not know to what extent, if any, many of the following policies were practiced. It is often unclear if the scriptures that relate such practices are utopian, imperative, or descriptive in nature. Still, the text provides an opportunity to view intellectual property in a novel way. In each section, I will provide a description of the practice and attempt to identify some of the ethical principles underlying the practice. Then I offer suggestions for how those principles might be applied to the modern institution of intellectual property.

Gleaning Rights

Apart from a widely recognized concern for the welfare of marginalized groups such as the widow, the orphan, and the stranger (Fensham, 1962; Malchow, 1996; Marsman, 2003; Patterson, 1973), Jewish scriptures also describe specific policies intended to ensure material subsistence for the poor. One of the most well-known of these is the practice of gleaning, or the right of the poor to gather leftover crops after a harvest. Gleaning has been practiced in many different societies over the centuries. Apart from the ancient practice described in Jewish scriptures, there are also references to gleaning in Sumerian and Egyptian sources, and the practice is well attested in both France and England (Baker, 2006; King, 1989, 1991; Soss, 1973; Vardi, 1993). The Torah specifies that landowners should refrain from harvesting the corners of their fields, not pass through their fields or olive groves twice (thereby stripping them bare), refrain from plucking all the grapes in their vineyards, and leave fallen stalks and grapes on the ground (Deuteronomy 24: 19–21, New Revised Standard Version). All of this produce was to be left behind for the benefit of the poor.

Turning to the Mishnah (a written compilation of Jewish oral traditions), we find an entire tractate devoted to gleaning and related practices. Tractate *Pe'ah* (which means "corner" in Hebrew and is a reference to the command to leave the corners of fields unharvested) describes in exacting detail how landowners should determine what portion of crops are left behind for the poor (Brooks, 1983). While all people had a claim to the necessities of life, some people were unable to provide for themselves. Gleaning and related practices ensured that even those who lacked the means to provide for themselves would still have access to the essential goods on which they had a legitimate claim. Similar gleaning rights can be traced to relatively modern times; for example, until 1788's "great case of gleaning," English villagers possessed a customary right to glean, and even after being outlawed, the practice continued (King, 1992). Gleaning continues in contemporary times; Oregon and other states have active gleaning programs that provide supplemental food to low-income households (Baker, 2006).

The ancient version of gleaning places several limits on the absolute property right of landholders. Some of these limits flow from the concept of God as the ultimate owner of the land, an idea that will be discussed in the following sections. On this matter, Roger Brooks (1983) wrote:

> Proper support of the poor constitutes part of the expression of God's ownership of the Land of Israel and acknowledges his right to determine how its yield is distributed. The householder thus must abandon his claim upon some of his produce, namely, that which God sets aside for the poor. (p. 34)

This limitation on appropriating all of the produce of a field or grove bears some connection with the Lockean proviso that people are free to appropriate things from nature, as long as there is "enough, and as good, left in common for others." Gleaning is thus one remedy to the situation where all real property—or all real property within a certain local area—has been appropriated and there are no other reasonable means by which someone can subsist. Furthermore, there are other necessary limitations of property rights, such as not claiming trespass when a gleaner walks on one's land and not denying access to gleaners by building a wall around one's plot or grove.

There are a number of features of intellectual property law that share the limiting aspects, if not the motivations, of gleaning rights. The most obvious of these is the concept of fair use in the United States, and the similar concept of fair dealing in Commonwealth countries. Both of these concepts are concerned with limiting the scope of a copyright holder's exclusive rights. In the United States, fair use is a flexible concept that permits many activities that would normally be considered a violation of copyright. For example, fair use permits a journalist or academic to use passages from a copyrighted work for the purposes of commentary or criticism without requiring the permission of the copyright holder, or even against the copyright holder's wishes. In this way, fair use is a limit on the extent to which a copyright holder can exclude others from a given work. Some room at the corners of the work must be left for others to use.

When it comes to patent law, the scope of limitations and exceptions is much narrower. Apart from testing required for regulatory approval of generic drugs during a certain period, the experimental use defense to infringement of patent rights, which in theory permits infringement for purposes of academic inquiry, is so limited as to be almost meaningless (Cai, 2004). The typical reasoning for why patents convey stronger protection and permit fewer exceptions than copyright is that patents convey those rights for a much shorter period of time, and the relatively short length of the patent term can itself be considered a limit on how much a rights holder can appropriate. Viewed in this light, limiting the length of exclusive rights that one individual can possess also guarantees future rights of access to others. Conversely, extending a copyright or patent term does not simply grant more rights to one person; it approaches a zero-sum equation: the rights of the individual are increased only by taking away the rights of others.

Compulsory licenses, which require a copyright or patent holder to allow others to use their work, usually in exchange for a set fee, may also be seen as analogous to gleaning rights. Compulsory licenses eliminate the right to exclude from the bundle of rights, but uphold the right to receive income from the use of property. In the case of pharmaceutical patents on essential medicines, compulsory licensing is highly analogous to gleaning rights. A resource that many people require to subsist remains under the exclusive control of someone else. Those people may not be able to pay the price set by the property holder, who in some cases may be the only seller of that item. A compulsory license established by the government creates conditions under which people can achieve a basic level of subsistence, and constitutes recognition that a property holder is not necessarily entitled to the right to appropriate all returns or the right to exclude in all cases.

The Shemittah

The *shemittah*, also known as the fallow year or Sabbatical year, refers to the practice of leaving fields and vineyards fallow or uncultivated every seventh year. Different aspects of the *shemittah* are described in various places throughout the Torah (the most familiar exposition is from Leviticus 25: 1–4). The *shemittah* demonstrates a certain respect for the land: To allow the land to lie fallow is to allow it time to rest and recover, partially for practical agricultural reasons, but also out of recognition that the land does not belong to Israel, and it is not a person's to do with as he or she pleases (Lemche, 1976). This is made clear by the text, which describes the land as "the land that I [God] am giving you" (Leviticus 25: 2).

There are two other important features of the *shemittah*. First, during the time that the land lay fallow, everyone, not just the person who owned the land, was permitted to eat whatever the land happened to produce. This included the poor and slaves, as well as livestock and wild animals (Leviticus 25: 6–7, Exodus 23: 10). A telling distinction is thus drawn between the produce from cultivated land and whatever food happened to grow naturally. While cultivated produce was subject to a number of restrictions such as the poverty tithe and gleaning rights, food that happened to grow naturally could be used by anyone who found it. In Talmudic vocabulary, it is considered *hefker*, or ownerless (Birnbaum, 1975). Any living thing had a claim to it. Second, the *shemittah* also involved release from debt. In the seventh year, creditors were to cancel any debts held against other Israelites, although they could still seek payment for debts owed by foreigners (Deuteronomy 15:1–3).

The view of land that the *shemittah* attempts to inculcate is complex. The deeming of fruit or produce that grows naturally as *hefker*, and thus freely available to any who will take it, is analogous to the view of unowned land or resources found in later thinkers such as Locke. In John Locke's (1887) view, real property and natural materials exist in a common state of nature from which any person, by means of labor, can remove them. The motivation behind the Jewish view of non-cultivated produce as *hefker* seems similar.

Attempts to apply the ideas of *shemittah* to intellectual property raise interesting questions for religious ethicists about the nature of creative work. Is creative work akin to cultivating a plot of land, in the sense that one takes an already existing raw product and works to change it into something vastly different and more valuable, but still something that owes its existence to the raw product in the first place? Should creative works that build upon the public domain (i.e., the vast amount of cultural material that is too old to be protected by copyright, but still relevant and valuable) recognize the *shemittah* principle that the use of property is not entirely at our disposal? When a creator reworks an uncopyrighted fairy tale into a major motion picture, what portion of the final value can be attributed to the raw cultural materials?

As early as Locke, thinkers have suggested that the vast portion of the value of human creations is generated by human activity, rather than the value inherent in natural materials. Thus, while goods existing in their natural state might be subject to principles of common use, as soon as human labor transforms those goods from their natural state into something more useful or convenient, common use no longer applies. This problem becomes even more acute with intellectual property, where there is no physical natural material involved. However, recent work on intellectual property and the sociology of knowledge highlights the extent to which human ideas are built upon the prior work of others (Benkler, 2006; May & Sell, 2006; Ostergard, 1999). Each person owes an incalculable debt to those who have come before, a fact particularly poignant to scholars. If we admit that "our" ideas are not ever wholly our own, we might also conclude that intellectual property cannot remain totally at our exclusive disposal. Along these lines, Andolsen (2008) suggested that because

> the scientists who developed the drugs, the researchers and clinicians who tested them, and the workers who manufactured and distributed them all owe a portion of their skills to myriad forms of social capital... The social capital embedded in AIDS drugs means that society has a basis for insisting that the drugs be made available in ways that are consistent with the common good. (p. 82)

Recognition of the cumulative and social characteristics of innovative and creative activity suggests that intellectual property policy ought to move away from the myth of independent creation and ideas of exclusive control, and begin to recognize the social capital in, and social claims on, intellectual property. As the *shemittah* indicates, when we recognize that much of the value of our property is in fact not due to our own activity, we are forced to expand the way we conceive of how that property should be used.

The Jubilee

One of the most well-studied property policies discussed in Jewish scriptures is that of the Jubilee. Described in Leviticus 25, the Jubilee was both an economic and a social phenomenon. Taking place in the 49th or 50th year, the Jubilee counseled, among other things, the return of all real property to its ancestral holders. The stated theological reason for this practice is to recognize that God is the true owner of the land, and thus the land cannot be claimed by humans. Real property was not to be held in perpetuity, but humans were tenants permitted to inhabit God's land. Any mass concentration of wealth in the form of land was to be only temporary. Practically speaking, the return of land every half-century may have been an attempt to limit the extent of latifundia, whereby wealthy landowners would buy up inordinate amounts of real property, a practice alluded to in Isaiah 5: 8, as well as other ancient texts (North, 1954).

Thus, while land could be bought and sold in the time between Jubilee years, every two generations or so conditions were supposed to return to their original, divinely ordained state. Rather than a permanent interest, a purchase of land would be more like a lease with length determined by the number of years remaining before the Jubilee. The biblical text recognizes this, counseling buyers and sellers to think of themselves as dealing with a certain number of "crop years," and to adjust the price accordingly (Leviticus 25: 14–17). Additionally, as with the *shemittah*, the Jubilee year required refraining from planting or cultivation of the land, theoretically forcing the Israelites to rely on whatever crops grew naturally (Leviticus 25: 11–12).

The Jubilee offers a prime example of the concept of stewardship. Because the land is seen as belonging to God, human use of it is bounded by certain regulations. It is one of many practices that recognize God as the source of sustenance and wealth. Economist and business ethicist Meir Tamari (1986) indicated that the entire scope of Jewish economic activity takes place under such an assumption. Tamari's description of Judaism's framework of economic activity is much broader than the specific assertion in Leviticus that God is the owner of the land. To support this expansive view of God's ownership, Tamari noted the Psalmist's declaration that "the earth is the Lord's and all that is in it"—a particularly interesting passage in light of the common objection that stewardship can only apply to material goods, or, at most, only to physical goods (Block, 1986; Finn, 2000). Intellectual property is an entirely human creation, owing nothing to nature or to God. But Jewish scriptures suggest that submitting intellectual property to a rubric of stewardship is not as problematic as it may seem: irrespective of labor, human capital, or ingenuity, one always has God to thank for one's property.

On the other hand, there is some scriptural recognition of the difference in nature between real property that derives its value primarily from God, and property that derives its value primarily from human activity. This distinction is particularly important for thinking about intellectual property, which arguably derives all or nearly all of its value from human activity rather than from naturally occurring material. For example, the Jubilee regulations differentiate between buildings constructed within walled cities and buildings in villages without walls or in the open country (Leviticus 25: 29–31). This difference can be explained theologically: The value of land itself is in many ways independent of its owner. The original owner did not create the land, but merely made use of what already existed, planting on it, or grazing livestock upon it. In this way, it is easy to view the land as a God-given resource. On the other hand, buildings within a city are much more the work of humans. They are not found and cultivated, but built by human labor. This distinction is further extended in other parts of the Jewish tradition. For example, although any improvements made to a field would be returned along with the field to its ancestral owner at the Jubilee, the ancestral owner was required to reimburse the current owner for the improvements that had been made (*Encyclopedia Talmudica*, 1969a). But apart from the theological explanation, as a practical matter, if real property was supposed to be returned to its ancestral owner, it only makes sense that the buildings on that property would also be returned even if those buildings were not originally there.

Whereas the *shemittah* encourages the recognition of the input and contribution of others (God, nature, or other people) to one's own property, the theological reasoning behind the Jubilee is based firmly upon the notion of God as the true owner of the land. As such, the application to intellectual property is not immediately evident. However, if we consider the practical impetus behind the Jubilee legislation (i.e., to avoid mass concentrations of property in the hands of a few, and to reset the clock on accumulation every two generations), a potential application emerges. Debt relief advocacy groups have already taken up the banner of the Jubilee apart from any theological meaning (Hanlon, 2000). Consider the practical aspects of the Jubilee with respect to copyright terms: Copyright terms have been repeatedly extended all over the world but particularly frequently in the United States. The initial 1790 Copyright Act established a maximum term of 28 years; in 1831, this was increased to a maximum of 42 years; and in 1909, to 56 years. In 1976, the term was changed to an indeterminate amount defined as the life of the author plus 50 years, and, in 1998, this was increased to the life of the author plus 70 years (Bell, 2000). Combined with changes in the requirements for copyright protection over time, the result is a knot of rules for determining whether a given work is in the public domain (Lessig, 2006), forcing those who wish to rely upon materials in the public domain to resort to badly outdated works. For example, Wikipedia incorporates a significant amount of text from the out-of-copyright 1911 edition of the *Encyclopaedia Britannica*. However, being more than a century old, the edition presents numerous challenges to its effective use in a modern encyclopedia (O'Sullivan, 2009). Unfettered, license-free access to a newer version of Britannica's text would prove quite valuable for Wikipedia, but even versions from the 1950s and 1960s, which no longer have any commercial value, will remain protected by copyright for several more decades. If copyright terms were limited to the 1909 standard of 56 years, a host of freely available information could be freely shared, duplicated, and translated, rather than remaining commercially valueless but legally inaccessible. Just as the Jubilee sought to return land to its ancestral holders, moderate copyright terms could have the effect of ensuring that copyrighted works eventually find their way to the public domain.

Bal Tashchit

In Hebrew, *bal tashchit* means "do not destroy," and this general command is widely considered to be one of the 613 *mitzvot* (Vogel, 2001). The phrase and its subsequent rabbinic interpretation and expansion are rooted in two verses from Deuteronomy that mention a practice prohibited in times of war:

> If you besiege a town for a long time, making war against it in order to take it, you must not destroy its trees by wielding an axe against them. Although you may take food from them, you must not cut them down. Are trees in the field human beings that they should come under siege from you? You may destroy only the trees that you know do not produce food; you may cut them down for use in building siege-works against the town that makes war with you, until it falls. (Deuteronomy 20: 19–20)

As a *mitzvah*, rabbinic interpretation expanded the command far beyond fruit trees and the battlefield, eventually viewing it as a prohibition on the destruction, waste, or reduction in value of anything useful to humankind. The prohibition included tearing clothes, demolishing buildings, stopping up springs, or wasting food. As is characteristic of Jewish law, there are a number of divergent opinions on the appropriate extent of the command, along with some necessary limitations. For example, destruction for the sake of improvement is permitted, as is burning a table to keep warm when there is no other suitable firewood (*Encyclopedia Talmudica*, 1969b).

Bal tashchit is frequently invoked in contemporary Jewish ethics as an environmental principle (Schwartz, 2001). If the principle of *bal tashchit* is broadly conceived as a prohibition against waste, it can also help us think in new ways about intellectual property. Imagine that someone holds a patent on an invention that would prove useful if incorporated into a larger product. You would like to build such a product, and license the use of the patent holder's invention. For whatever reason, the patentee refuses to grant you a license, but at the same time is not using the invention and has no intention of making the product. The result is that society is deprived of the useful product you would have made had the patentee granted you a license to the invention. Before the Patent Misuse Reform Act of 1988, one option would have been to use the invention without a license, and had the patentee sued for infringement, to raise an affirmative defense of patent misuse. With the passing of the Patent Misuse Reform Act, however, this avenue was foreclosed. U.S. law now expressly states that a patent owner cannot be found to have misused a patent even if he or she has "refused to license or use any rights to the patent" (Patent Misuse Reform Act).

From an economic perspective, the above situation seems implausible. If the patent were more than negligibly valuable, the patentee would either make or use the invention herself, or license it to someone else who found it valuable. If the patent were too valuable to the public to leave in the hands of a single supplier, or the patentee were only willing to license it at exorbitant rates, the government could intervene, exercising eminent domain to appropriate the patent *pro bono publico* while fairly compensating the patent holder, as India has recently done with the cancer drug Sorafenib (Love, 2012). However, the reality of the patent system is different. The proliferation of non-practicing entities, sometimes called "patent trolls," who acquire patents to offensively enforce them against others, as well as the response to this phenomenon in the form of defensive patenting, means that there are many enforceable patents whose owners have no intention of using them and will only license them at prices considered to be extortionate (Gregory, 2006). Asymmetries of information or resources may also mean that while obtaining a license would be extremely valuable for an individual or small firm, it does not appear worthwhile for a large patent holder to bother with the complexities of granting a license. If the current patent system's approach to patent misuse means that society is wasting resources because of unrealized gains in efficiency, as some evidence suggests (Lemley, 2007; Lemley & Shapiro, 2006), it may be time to reconsider the doctrine of patent misuse (Magliocca, 2006). Just as *bal tashchit* counsels against the wasteful annihilation of value, patent policy should ensure that downstream innovation is not being hindered by *mala fide* assertions of patent rights.

Bal tashchit may find a clearer application in the case of copyright, not least because of the much longer duration of copyright, of which the initial years are disproportionately valuable (Rappaport, 1998). It is a waste and disservice to society for thousands of orphaned works—that is, works still subject to copyright protection but whose owners are unknown or cannot be located—to languish in obscurity on a bookshelf somewhere (Hetcher, 2007). The technology to disseminate these works worldwide currently exists and is in use; it is only current copyright law that prevents such dissemination from happening. If the principle of *bal tashchit* exhorts us not to stop up a spring, why would we turn off a fountain of knowledge?

Hassagat Gevul

Of all the ethical resources to be found in Jewish scriptures, the concept of *hassagat gevul* ("encroachment") is likely to be the most immediately applicable to institutions of intellectual property. In fact, it has been directly referenced in various discussions about copyright, including an Israeli Court of Appeals case (Elon, 2007). The term comes from the biblical prohibition against the moving of landmarks, which is attested in numerous locations throughout Jewish scriptures (Deuteronomy 19: 14; Proverbs 22: 28; Hosea 5: 10) and in several instances is described in connection with neglect of widows and orphans or other abuses of the needy (Deuteronomy 27: 17–19; Job 24: 2–4; Proverbs 23: 10).

Historically, the prohibition dealt with land boundaries in a time before effective surveying mechanisms, when appropriating another's land could be as simple as moving a stone marker. Like the principle of *bal tashchit*, however, rabbinical interpreters have significantly expanded the literal meaning of *hassagat gevul*. Early glosses on the matter, such as that in the Sifre and Tosefta Bava Kamma 7:13, seem primarily concerned with correct attribution of ideas, sayings, and writings, a matter very different than copyright. With the invention of the printing press, however, *hassagat gevul* found some application as an early form of copyright: Warnings printed in books forbade others from "trespass" for various periods of time (Elon, 2007). The modern use of the principle shifted to a focus on source attribution when, in discussing the moral rights of a copyright holder, an Israeli Supreme Court justice made reference to Jewish legal sources that discuss *hassagat gevul* (Lim, MacQueen, & Carmichael, 2001).

The principle of *hassagat gevul*, despite having been invoked to support printers' exclusive rights and cited in modern legal discussions of copyright, has a very different approach to property in ideas and writings than is found in U.S. copyright law. As discussed above, the interpretation and application of the principle often has involved source attribution, suggesting an implicit theoretical framework of intellectual property that has a high regard for personhood. The claim is not that *hassagat gevul* reveals a systematic theoretical approach to intellectual property rights based on personhood, but rather that the concern with correct attribution of statements and texts indicates a focus on personality and moral rights.

U.S. copyright law lacks the same sort of protections of moral rights to be found in Continental law, but *hassagat gevul* and a personhood-based approach may lead us to think about intellectual property less in terms of exclusion, and more in terms of the role that intellectual property plays in an individual's life. Thinking with Hegel (1896) and Margaret Radin (1993) along the lines of "property for personhood," we can see that people may have a need to be recognized for their intellectual creations. However, the desire for recognition does not necessarily imply an economic right of exclusion. Although control over the dissemination of one's works could be considered an important element of personhood, the case is harder to make when the exclusion is premised upon economic gain. As for copyrighted works of corporate authorship, *hassagat gevul* may suggest that more attention should be paid to the individual contributors to the work, an approach that highlights the conflict between moral rights and the U.S. "work for hire" doctrine (Hayes, 2000).

The Commandment against Theft

In a way, the commandment "thou shalt not steal" forms a cornerstone of the Western institution of private property. Theft, after all, presupposes property, and the influence of the commandments on Western thought can hardly be denied. John Adams (1850) expressed the relationship between the divine commandment and human law succinctly: "If 'Thou shalt not covet,' and 'Thou shalt not steal,' were not commandments of Heaven, they must be made inviolable precepts in every society, before it can be civilized or made free" (p. 9). However, examining the commandment in its literary context reveals that Adams' view of the commandment, and indeed the prevailing modern interpretation of the commandment as a vindication of private property rights, may in fact be a gross misunderstanding.

"Thou shalt not steal" receives relatively little attention when compared with some of its fellow commandments, perhaps because of its brevity (it is even shorter in Hebrew) and seemingly transparent meaning. But as David Little (1980) reminded us, "what the Old Testament or, to be more precise, the various traditions of interpretation within the Old Testament mean by 'stealing' or 'theft' is itself far from self-evident" (p. 400). In fact, one Jewish tradition of interpretation has long suggested that the commandment refers specifically to kidnapping and enslavement—stealing persons (Little, 1980; Worley, 1971).

The context of the commandment suggests that rather than justifying the intemperate accumulation of wealth—a practice specifically condemned by the prophets (Isaiah 5: 8, Habbakuk 2: 5, Ezekiel 22: 29, Micah 2: 2)—it was designed to ensure a claim on the part of the needy against the holders of property for the basic necessities of life (Gnuse, 1985). That is, the purpose of the commandment was to protect people, not things. Given the context of the Israelite "tenant farmer, [who] works God's Land and enjoys its yield, with the result that a portion of all that he produces belongs to God," asserting the inviolability of private property and denying the property rights of the poor constitutes theft, both from God and from the poor whom God protects (Brooks, 1983).

Even biblical episodes that might be viewed as endorsing the importance of private property need not necessarily be read in such a way. Consider the story of Naboth's vineyard (1 Kings 21). On one view, King Ahab and his wife Jezebel are tyrants, intent on plotting to kill Naboth and acquire his vineyard. Unable to avoid God's justice, however, both Ahab and Jezebel suffer the consequences of their actions, and die gruesome deaths. Thus the inviolability of private property, and a man's right to it? Perhaps not. The story can also be viewed primarily as an instance where the law protects the weak and oppressed from the encroachments of the rich and powerful, and several scholars have adopted this interpretation (Miller, 2004; Rivkin, 1986; Rofé, 1988).

Given this person-centered interpretation of the commandment, the person who steals is not one who is hungry and takes a loaf of bread, but rather one who denies the needy person the essentials of life—that person is stealing years of life from the poor. Likewise, a person who invokes private property rights to deny sick people access to the patented medication that can heal them is stealing life from the sick person, and a person who invokes private property rights to deny poor people access to copyrighted educational materials from which they can benefit is stealing knowledge from them. In light of the ethical principles discussed throughout this part, the use of the commandment against theft to deny access of the needy to the private property of others, let alone intellectual property, is a total inversion of the commandment's meaning and ethical force.

Copyright as Theft

The problems with current policy are often highlighted when intellectual property rights conflict with human rights. A right to a certain level of medical care may conflict with the intellectual property right of a patent holder to prevent inexpensive generic production of a drug. A right to access and benefit from knowledge may be hindered by overly restrictive copyright enforcement.

One of the obstacles to untangling such disputes is that intellectual property rights and human rights live in separate legal worlds. The rights granted by a copyright and the remedies for infringement of that copyright are clearly spelled out in U.S. law. In contrast, there are no clearly defined rights to health or knowledge. Even if there were such rights, they would be toothless without clear provisions for enforcement and remedies for infringement.

Looking back to ancient policies in Jewish scriptures such as gleaning rights, we find property rights on the part of the poor. Gleaning represents not only an obligation on the part of the landowner; it represents a legitimate property right possessed by the hungry person (Gnuse, 1985). Instead of a murky, ill-defined human right to an adequate amount of food, conceptualizing the gleaning right as a property right gives it teeth. This way of viewing gleaning is part of a broader range of ideas referred to as just entitlement—at a certain basic level, giving alms and supporting the needy is not a voluntary act of charity, but a recognition of the legitimate claim of the needy person to property or wealth. As Meir Tamari (1986) wrote, "the giving of charity is not considered as an act of kindness on the part of the haves to the have-nots. The have-nots have by right a stake or share in the property of the haves, since it was given to the latter partially for that purpose" (p. 401). Both he and others point out that the Hebrew word translated as charity, *zedakah*, may be better rendered as justice or righteousness (Posner, Ben-Sasson, & Levitats, 2007; Tamari, 1986).

Thus, in the Jewish scriptural tradition, there is a balance of property rights: Landowners have a legitimate claim to the produce of their fields, but that claim is not absolute. At the limits of field lie the limits of the claim; the poor and hungry have a legitimate claim to a portion of that produce as well. The rights of the poor are not a matter of charity or goodwill, but a counterpoint to the property rights of the wealthy. In contrast, international law such as the Agreement on Trade-Related Aspects of Intellectual Property Rights (TRIPS; see also Daly and Farrand, this volume) specifies in detail the rights of intellectual property holders, but offers nothing to counterbalance these rights. The concept of just entitlement suggests that in establishing any property-related policy, the rights of the haves must be balanced with the rights of the have-nots. In the case of intellectual property, just entitlement suggests developing policies that ensure some measure of access to intellectual property, whether it be copyrighted educational material or patent-protected medicine.

To apply the idea of balanced rights to a modern situation, consider the debate over copyright and access to knowledge. Rights of access to knowledge or education are often classified by critics as "positive" rights, meaning that in order to be effected, they require intervention or support from others, as opposed to "negative" rights, which require only non-interference. But this dichotomy is misleading. A right of access to knowledge or education includes too many constituent rights to be deemed either positive or negative. While a right to attend school falls clearly into the category of positive rights, a right of access to knowledge might also include rights to read books and periodicals, or use software. If the prices and access restrictions of these media are prohibitive, then the prices and restrictions are interfering with one's right to access knowledge. In that case, the right of access to knowledge is a negative right.

Others scholars have already conceptualized human rights as negative rights with which others can interfere (Pogge, 2005). On the issue of copyright and access to knowledge, John Willinsky (2006) argued that the human right of access to science must be free of unwarranted costs. Here, I go one step further: rather than a human right of access to knowledge, I suggest that the accessor has a property right in the knowledge to be accessed. When copyright impedes such access, it violates more than a human right; it violates a property right, and the exercise of copyright becomes theft. (This line of reasoning is not unprecedented; other scholars have already suggested that Americans have a property right to medical care based on the enormous amount of publicly funded investments the U.S. makes in medical research and development; Earnest & Matthew, 2008.)

Conclusion

By now, I hope to have shown that looking to Jewish scriptures as a resource for ethical thought about intellectual property is a fruitful endeavor and has the potential to illuminate some of the ethical questions surrounding intellectual property in new ways. Looking to Jewish scriptures, we find that an ethically sound institution of property must enumerate not only the rights of property holders—the haves—but also the rights of the poor, the have-nots. Scripture records various policies designed to balance between the rights of the haves and have-nots. While it may be impossible to know how effective these policies were, or whether they were even implemented at all, they do offer a helpful ethical framework for thinking about intellectual property. Gleaning rights offer a concrete example of balancing property rights between landowners and the poor, and can be analogized to rights of access to intellectual property. The *shemittah* and Jubilee suggest thinking about intellectual property less in terms of individualistic creators, and more in terms of social capital and cumulative innovation. Principles such as *bal tashchit* promote a strong focus on the use of property for the common good, while the concept of *hassagat gevul* indicates that personal claims to intellectual property will be best served by due recognition of sources and contributions, rather than the ability to sell one's work. Finally, recovering historical interpretations of the commandment against theft reveals that a major strand of Jewish ethical and legal thought views property as a means to protect people from destitution, rather than as an end in itself. Viewing intellectual property through this religious lens offers new ethical and legal counterpoints to the way the debate over intellectual property is currently framed.

In thinking critically about intellectual property, it is important to avoid an all-or-nothing approach that sometimes prevails in the rhetoric of the debate. Different theoretical approaches will emphasize different social and ethical commitments, and yield different policy prescriptions. A focus on personhood emphasizes the importance of correct attribution of sources and elevates the relationship between the creator and his or her work, rather than privileging the economic exploitation of that work as the most important consideration. A focus on utility deemphasizes the notion of a natural or moral right to intellectual property, instead making the right contingent upon its serving a social function.

Whatever theoretical approach one is inclined to adopt, however, it is important to remember that the entire institution of property, intellectual or otherwise, is a social phenomenon. Various primary sources and scholars have demonstrated that in many Jewish scriptures there is no concept of an absolute right to property. Even if one believes that there is a natural law supporting a right to property, natural law says little about the specific vagaries of our current laws. As Thomas Pogge (2008) noted, it would be surprising if "a natural right of inventors should have precisely the contours enshrined in the TRIPS/TRIPS-plus agreements and implementing national legislation" (p. 227). Looking to other perspectives on property and intellectual property can help to remind us of the contingency of our own.

• CHAPTER FOURTEEN •

Scratching Out Authorship: The Creative Network of Hip Hop DJs

André Sirois (DJ food stamp)

The DJ is the "new rock star," a phrase the culture industries have latched onto and are exploiting. Smirnoff sponsors *Master of the Mix*, a DJ competition reality show that airs on VH1; Simon Cowell, one of the minds behind *The X Factor* and *Got Talent* franchises, has announced that he's developing a DJ competition show. The image of the DJ is visible in popular culture and the DJ technology industries are capitalizing.

Hip hop DJs have surely been a part of this commodification process. In this chapter, I look at hip hop DJ culture and its relationship to industry through intellectual property manipulation, exchange, and rights. Often, hip hop DJ culture is criminalized or valorized for music-sampling practices. I don't disagree with that, but here I show how hip hop DJs are themselves manipulated *as* intellectual properties as their ideas are encoded into DJ technology in the research and development (R&D) and the branding phases. Hip hop DJ culture is an open-source culture where ideas and techniques are shared and then built upon. It is a culture founded on *reinvention* and not necessarily the type of "invention" contemporary North American society rewards. Innovation in hip hop DJ culture comes from a creative network that is at its core decentralized; however, hip hop DJs achieve status in this hierarchy by building their subcultural capital through recognition as innovators. Innovation, though, is selectively recognized and rewarded and is also the product of a network and reinvention. Hip hop DJ culture thus problematizes romantic notions of authorship.

I situate hip hop DJ culture as a new media culture that began as one in the early 1970s. Before teenagers were remixing culture on computers, the remix logic was set forth by teenage DJs in the South Bronx using vinyl records and turntables. Hip hop DJs made the idea of remixing popular culture, and they did so by using read-only artifacts in defiance of the ideology of sound reproduction codified in decades of industrial behavior and law. Using interviews with 51 hip hop DJs and 16 industry professionals paired with critical historical and discourse analyses, in this chapter, I look at three dimensions of IP in relation to hip hop DJ culture: manipulation, exchange, and rights, explored through the lens of *technocultural synergism*, a concept I use to analyze how cultures guided by an open-source logic converge with companies interested in capitalizing on that logic. Technocultural synergism is also a process where industry and culture come together to produce a greater whole. What comes from this convergence are new technologies, and these technologies help to advance the culture by allowing for new creative techniques; in turn, this expands the market share for the manufacturers. Technocultural synergism, though, is political as it creates intellectual property haves and have nots, and it needs to be addressed critically.

I ground the impact of the hip hop DJ cultural production and then explore technocultural synergism. I present a historical analysis of the ideology of sound reproduction to highlight the socio-historical significance of hip hop DJ culture, and then address the logic of analog sampling driving hip hop DJ culture. Once hip hop DJ culture has been situated as a new media culture, I address intellectual property exchange and rights using case studies of technology R&D and branding, ending with the pioneering hip hop DJ Grandmaster Flash® as a case study.

Adventures on the Wheels of Steel

For much of the twentieth century, argued Lawrence Lessig (2008), technologies and media were read-only, thus the general cultural practice of consumers was read-only. Hip hop DJs, however, engaged in read–write practices well before the prominence of today's digital tools by turning consumption technologies—vinyl records and turntables—into tools for production (Souvignier, 2003). The hip hop DJ subculture subverted the read-only ideology encoded in sound playback technologies and codified in IP law. Hebdige (1979) suggested this is a characteristic of subcultures in general: "Recontextualizing commodities, by subverting their conventional uses and inventing new ones" (p. 102) is how oppositional meanings are given to those commodities.

The Ideology of Reproduction

Recorded sound began as a read–write medium. Edison conceived his Phonograph in 1878 as a sound transcription tool that allowed consumers to record and play their own recordings on cylinders. The Graphophone was another "talking machine" that came out in 1885, also a read–write device. In 1887, Emile Berliner patented the Gramophone, the first popular read-only sound playback technology. According to Simon Frith (2001), the Gramophone made it possible to "'play' a musical instrument without having any musical skills. Music could be made at home as a matter of consumption rather than technique" (p. 31). And many of the talking machine companies marketed their players as genuine instruments, although consumers simply reproduced recordings. Recordings for the Gramophone were mass produceable—an innovation that set forth and established an ideology of the reproduction of sound that dominated popular culture until hip hop DJs subverted it in the 1970s.

Due to monopolies granted by patents in the late 1800s, entrance into the market was extremely difficult, and often independent inventors who showed their innovations to other manufacturers would sell them or have them stolen by larger corporations. The industry was the "wild, wild west" of IP rights, where innovation was trumped by patent rights and "ongoing espionage" (Welch & Brodbeck Stenzel Burt, 1994, p. 72). According to Steve Wurtzler (2007), patent rights were the linchpin in the consolidation of economic power in this time period, and the association of an invention with known trademarks allowed for the extension of consumer loyalty after the expiration of the patent (Slack, 1984). Edison-as-brand was far more valuable than Edison-as-inventor; he had a lab of machinists and engineers—a creative network—that interpreted and executed his ideas in products, but his brand name gave inventions credibility.

When most patents for talking machines began expiring around 1917, established companies began focusing on selling copyrighted music, as it was easier to create and exploit in the market. This ideology of sound reproduction and read-only consumption perpetuated until the cassette tape, itself a read–write medium. Cassettes allowed consumers to make copies of their vinyl records—reflecting the fact that record labels "did not satisfy the demands of consumers" (Morton, 2000, p. 137), rupturing the economic laws that the record companies exploited because it "promoted the circulation of recorded music outside the market" (Chanan, 1995, p.154). The cassette, like the Phonograph and Graphophone before it, allowed consumers to manipulate and repurpose recordings. I want to argue, then, that the consumer empowerment ushered in ideologically by the cassette set the stage for hip hop DJ uses of vinyl records and turntables (tokens of read-only, proprietary culture) to produce music and culture.

Analog Sampling

Hip hop culture, what Jeff Chang (2005) called an "idea machine" and what Nelson George (1998) described as a "capitalist tool," has given fruit to a multi-billion-dollar market. I consider hip hop DJ culture a valuable tool for capitalism because it is an *idea machine*. The core themes of DJ culture are that "creativity rests in how you recontextualize the previous expression of others" (Miller, 2004, p. 33) and recorded texts "become the raw material for the DJ's art" (Cox & Warner, 2004, p. 329). Dick Hebdige (1987) described this compositional methodology as a "cut 'n' mix attitude... that no one owns a rhythm or sound. You just borrow it, use it and give it back to the people in a slightly different form" (p. 140). Ulf Poschardt (1998) wrote that "DJ composition is the interpretation and reconstruction of something that has been deconstructed at the turntable" (p. 163); although initially considered "the violation of technology," the DJ "recodes modern technology" (p. 358) by using the turntable as means of production.

Hip hop culture and music came from the South Bronx in the early 1970s. Surrounded by social, racial, and economic inequities, teenage African Americans and Puerto Ricans gravitated towards a breakbeat style of music orchestrated by the DJ. These DJs set up their sound systems in recreation centers and parks and gave "jams" for their neighborhoods. At these jams, DJs isolated and manipulated small phrases of music, known as "breaks," using two turntables, a mixer, and vinyl records. Eventually, the DJs—gatekeepers to the culture and celebrities within it—brought on emcees, later known as rappers, to the jams.

DJ Kool Herc is credited as the first breakbeat DJ, when he developed a method for playing breaks back to back. By transforming the artifacts of previous musical history into his own derivative compositions, "Herc made the DJ an author, the originator" (Poschardt, 1998, p.163). Herc and other DJs demonstrated that "it was possible to isolate parts of a complete work and to use these in the creation of an original piece of music" (Smith, 2000, p. 76). Although there are numerous hip hop DJs who were vital to the development of hip hop's network of innovation, such as Afrika Bambaataa and Grand Wizzard Theodore, it was Grandmaster Flash who took Herc's style and turned hip hop DJing into a scientific discipline.

Grandmaster Flash made technicality and skills in record manipulation a key element of hip hop DJ culture. Flash was one of the first hip hop DJs whose brand name and subcultural capital were exploited by cultural industries, and Grandmaster Flash® is still being used on various DJ-related products today. Flash was also one of the first DJs to retrofit electronics to materially realize his ideas. Notably, Flash modified his DJ mixer so that he could use headphones to cue up one record as another played over speakers to the crowd. By the end of the 1970s, when rap records started coming out, Grandmaster Flash was the most prominent DJ in the South Bronx.

When breakbeat music was commodified as rap in 1979, the DJ was displaced as an author, because rap music pushed hip hop to conform to standard practices of the recording industry. Moving into the 1980s, the hip hop DJ was pushed into the background as the market for rap music grew (Chang,

2005; Charnas, 2010). The new star in the industry was the rapper, and rappers could author works because they wrote lyrics and could receive song publishing royalties. The only way for DJs to become authors recognized by copyright was by transforming into record producers, and therefore the compositional method of DJs was remediated by using digital sampling technology to cut and loop breaks. Aside from achieving authorial status, Joseph Schloss (2004) suggested that the innovation of DJs using digital sampling technology was accepted because it conformed to the preexisting aesthetic of hip hop DJ analog sampling, but subtly changed it: "Sampling was initially embraced because it allowed DJs to realize their turntable ideas with less work" (p. 42).

Digital sampling, IP, and rap have been addressed in numerous scholarly works (see, for instance, McLeod & DiCola, 2011; Vaidhyanathan, 2001), but analog sampling and hip hop DJs' problematization of authorship has been underemphasized.

Convergence, Collective Authorship, and Subcultural Capitalism

I want to flip the scholarly script and address how hip hop DJs themselves are intellectual properties manipulated by cultural industries. First, I look at the new media characteristics of convergence between corporations and grassroots culture in the case of product research and development (R&D) of DJ-related products. Then I turn to addressing the use of prominent DJs in product endorsement, another way in which hip hop DJs are manipulated intellectual properties. This analysis highlights the exchange of intellectual properties, as well as the rights to exploit them in a market, what I call *technocultural synergism*.

Over the course of its 40-year history, credit for innovation and "invention" has been a major antagonism within hip hop culture. There are all sorts of documented instances of cultural members claiming authorship over a particular style, technique, or the naming of both. Authorial credit has usually been granted to those who have fixed the idea or its naming into a tangible medium (audio or video recording). The problem with hip hop is that it is all built on something else—it is the reinvention of everything, and its authorship is inherently collective. Innovation in hip hop culture is the product of a creative network. However, in a society that rewards, credits, and privileges individual genius, it is no wonder that some people in the network feel like they have been left out of the story. Collective intelligence and authorship in hip hop DJing is another way we can consider hip hop DJs as new media.

Convergence Culture

In *Convergence Culture* (2006), Henry Jenkins looks at convergence culture as a phenomenon largely based on social interactions between people. For Jenkins, convergence is a process that occurs at the various intersections between media technologies, industries, content and audiences. Convergence is changing the relationship between producers and consumers. Jenkins believes that convergence occurs on two levels: corporate and grassroots. While media is produced and distributed at the corporate level, at the grassroots level, "digitally empowered consumers" shape the production, distribution, and reception of media. An important part of empowerment has to do with the hardware itself.

Jonathan Sterne (2003) considered any medium of sound reproduction to be part of a network, which is "a whole set of relations, practices, people, and technologies" (p. 225). Scholars suggest convergence helps create innovative flat and non-hierarchical networks, essentially decentered and lacking the socio-economic power struggles that we see in other structures. That said, Tiziana Terranova (2004) critiqued how the Internet materializes collective intelligence and argued that music and information are "all produced collectively but are selectively compensated" (p. 84). So, although more ideas are being produced through a network, those who can "farm" and harvest those ideas can capitalize on them in a marketplace. Using interviews with DJs and manufacturers, I look at how collective intelligence and convergence are used in product research and development.

It should be clear that the most important technology in all of this discussion is the hip hop DJ, the human. DJ technologies adapt to, encode, and try to reflect advancements in DJ technique. "But the biggest technological advance has been the DJ technique and then scratching, I guess," says DJ Quest. "The thing that has advanced the most is that DJs have been practicing and just fuckin' scratch techniques have evolved beyond what a lot of people can comprehend... but the thing that has advanced the most, and I'm proud to say, has been the hand" (personal communication, December 26, 2009). Technologies follow the innovations of DJs.

The Vestax 05Pro

In the 1980s, manufacturers were designing products for DJs with no input from the market they served. Product engineers had little idea about what DJs wanted and thus manufacturers either copied the successful design concepts of competitors or put products in the market and hoped people would buy them. The end-users of these products, DJs, had all sorts of ideas for making better technology, but manufacturers weren't listening.

In 1989, after winning the DMC Technics European DJ Championships, the UK's DJ Trix approached Vestax, then a small Japanese electronics manufacturer, about demonstrating the company's products at trade shows. Trix had been using Vestax's PMC-05mkII mixer, but he thought that its layout design was all wrong. He had a better design that he showed to Vestax company executives: "I drew a design using the components of the PMC-05mkII but laid the mixer out as I wished, I also included the Vestax logo and my sig[nature]" (personal communication, April 20, 2011). Trix admitted that he did not think anything would come of it, but in 1990 Vestax released the PMC-05 TRIX battle mixer, a "carbon copy" of his initial concept. The mixer made Trix the first DJ to have a signature mixer, and thus began the important trend of manufacturers listening to DJs, implementing their ideas into products, and then using DJs to brand and sell technology. Today, DJ Trix is an executive at Vestax Europe.

In 1993, DJ Shortkut was 18 years old and was demonstrating products for Numark, an American manufacturer, at trade shows. He noticed the only other company at these trade shows with a DJ at its booth was Vestax. One day Shortkut was eating lunch with a Numark representative and suggested that Numark would sell a ton of mixers to hip hop DJs if they would simplify their layout and make a smooth crossfader. Shortkut drew a sketch on a napkin, but the Numark rep blew him off. Shortkut told me:

> Numark wasn't really feeling me. You know, I was just a little kid. I was working one of these trade shows and Vestax had a booth in the next hall. So during my breaks I'd go to Vestax and see their stuff, and I would feel their equipment and it was real nice. They actually had the loosest fader possible that I had seen so far. I started talking to them.... Then we just developed a relationship and they kept asking for some ideas. (personal communication, January 11, 2010)

In 1994, out of an exchange of ideas, came the Vestax 05Pro mixer. Shortkut introduced Vestax to other DJs in his crew (i.e., Qbert, Mix Master Mike, and Rhettmatic) to help with research and development, and Vestax also consulted notable Japanese DJs, Takada and GM Yoshi.

The Vestax 05Pro was a game-changer for hip hop DJs, and also for Vestax as a manufacturer. Vestax put a smooth crossfader in the mixer, which allowed DJs to create new scratch techniques. Initially, Vestax produced 50 grey 05Pro model mixers as a test run, but the company eventually sold between 300,000 to 400,000 units of the iconic gold and black 05Pro. "At first when we made it," said Qbert, "they were like 'oh, this mixer is not going to sell, no I don't think anyone is going to buy it, it's too expensive,' and then they made it... and all of a sudden, they sold thousands" (personal communication, January 7, 2010). Because of its popularity, other manufacturers started designing mixers that imitated the 05Pro. The 05Pro showed how profitable creative networks could be. Aside from listening to DJs like Shortkut in the R&D phase and then interpreting ideas into products, the Japanese manufacturer relied heavily on Skortkut's crew, the Invisibl Skratch Piklz (ISP)—the most popular hip hop DJ crew in the world at the time—to brand and authenticate the mixer and the company.

Although Trix had a signature mixer, he lacked the brand value within the hip hop DJ market that a crew like ISP had. After the success of the 05Pro, it became standard to use DJs as intellectual properties in both R&D and branding. Unfortunately, many times DJs involved in the R&D process lacked brand value, so manufacturers would use other DJs in the marketing stage, which often led to the brand name DJs being credited as the "inventor" or designer of a mixer. An interesting case of this is the successor to the 05Pro, the Vestax 07Pro, where Qbert and ISP were used heavily in marketing and often mentioned as the inventors; however, the mixer was designed by a lesser-known DJ from the UK, DJ Go.

Shortkut never got any royalties or credit for his role in 05's development, but he humbly said that "to me, it was for the better good of the DJ." Shortkut admitted that he did not even think about protecting his ideas or seeking some sort of patent or contract protection because he was just happy to have a manufacturer listening to him. "Yeah if I did learn how to put a fuckin' patent down on a mixer then sure I'd be fuckin' well-off right now," Shortkut said.

It is doubtful, though, that Shortkut's design would have been patentable. Although the design could possibly have met the utility requirement for patentability, it would have been a challenge to show that the design was non-obvious. Although some manufacturers, such as Rane Corporation and Stanton Magnetics, have successfully received patents on crossfaders for mixers, most DJ mixers are made of public domain audio components and therefore most mixers cannot receive patent protection. Furthermore, because Shortkut's design dealt mainly with the function of the mixer, it's also unlikely that he could have applied for a design patent. Shortkut may have been able to protect his design through nondisclosure or non-compete contracts, but during the early 1990s when DJs started being used as intellectual properties, most of them were young and not particularly business savvy. However, Shortkut did tell me that he had an endorsement deal and healthy relationship with Vestax, and being at the forefront of the company's marketing campaign helped to bring him income.

An Exception to the Rule

Protecting the ideas of DJs in this industry is a significant challenge because, well, they are *ideas* and tend to miss the requirements for patentability. Beyond that, most DJs lack the resources to execute their ideas in a product because they are not engineers, and even if they could actually "invent" a technology, manufacturing and marketing it would be the next challenge. Therefore, most hip hop DJs have exchanged ideas with manufacturers; for the well-known DJs, compensation has come in the form of endorsement deals. However, credit for innovation has been rare.

The exception to this rule is DJ Focus, who actually invented numerous tools and technologies for hip hop DJs. He had simple ideas that were both revolutionary and genius. In the late 1990s, Focus invented a product for DJ mixers that changed the industry: a contact-less crossfader. Using infrared emitters and some epoxy, Focus designed a crossfader that would never wear out. To get the crossfader out in the market, Focus partnered with the American manufacturer Stanton. With Stanton, Focus was able to patent a crossfader that worked like his original design and entered into an exclusive licensing agreement with Stanton. Stanton put the crossfader in all its higher-end mixers and also sold it as a third party replacement crossfader for other mixer brands. Before Focus' invention, crossfaders would wear out quickly for hip hop DJs and manufacturers had built up a strong aftermarket for replacement faders; the change was welcomed by DJs, but manufacturers were forced to adapt because of this innovation.

Elliot Marx, the owner of Audio Innovate (AI), a company whose innoFADER is currently one of the leading aftermarket crossfaders, said that "patents in the DJ market are worthless" and are a way of "sinking money" into something that has no benefit to end-users (personal communication, March 11, 2010). Marx continued, noting that:

> The market is small enough that I think DJs will get much better variety and quality of products if companies work more on a trade secret basis to protect technology rather than with patents... The best thing to do is develop relationships with people you trust. You can license ideas without patenting.

Marx explained that DJs simply having product ideas are valuable, but not enough in and of themselves: "Well look, if you scribble a picture on paper for an hour or so a manufacturer, for good reason, would probably laugh at you if you asked for royalties." He also stated that if a DJ has spent months testing and consulting on a project, they should be compensated, but DJs should try to actually prototype their ideas before they just bring an idea to a manufacturer. DJ Babu said that he and other DJs in the Beat Junkies crew have given "tech advice" to manufacturers and been involved in endorsing them. However, these endorsement deals are usually considered mutual marketing opportunities where no cash exchanges hands (compare that, for instance, to the endorsement deals athletes like Tiger Woods or LeBron James ink). Babu said: "We get free gear and they put ads out for us, and stuff like that, and they definitely ask us about the stuff they are making." Babu explained that he and his crew members have made contributions but have never designed a technology from the "ground up." He also felt that he has been fairly compensated for his ideas. Disk, who was involved with Vestax in the mid-1990s, said, "you give them a little idea, they give you a bunch of free mixers" (personal communication, November 24, 2009).

Manufacturers get ideas from all over the place. So, how does credit and compensation happen within creative networks? While hip hop DJ culture has problematized the notion of the romantic author when it comes to musical texts and the manipulation of intellectual properties in sound playback technologies, R&D and product design highlights another way this network defies the notion of an individual genius. But a DJ mixer is just a bunch of knobs and faders. So, how do corporately produced electronics gain credibility in the marketplace amongst hip hop DJs, a group bound by notions of authenticity? Using the brand value, or subcultural capital, of DJs on products or in marketing campaigns is an attempt at authenticating technical innovations. In the next subsection of this chapter I explore instances of the DJ as brand being a manipulated intellectual property.

Experiences in Product Endorsement

A DJ's name is one of his/her most valuable assets. Hip hop DJs who have been used in signature DJ products have worked to build their subcultural capital. The name-as-brand is what gets a DJ gigs, what helps bring people through the doors, and what helps to open other doors for them. Sometimes the brand name is just hype, such as celebrities who take up DJing to use their mass cultural capital as a draw; however, for professional hip hop DJs, skills, musical selections, and style make up the their subcultural capital.

Manufacturers rely on what Sarah Thornton (1996) called "subcultural capital"—basically, brand value and credibility within the hierarchy of a subculture. It has become standard practice with DJ technology manufacturers to use the names of DJs with the highest levels of subcultural capital to market products. By attaching the names and likenesses of DJs with high levels of subcultural capital to products, manufacturers authenticate their products in the market. While distinctiveness is a key element in trademark protection, Thornton's concept of subcultural capital distinction is about difference that entails some claims to "authority and presumes the inferiority of *others*" (2005, p. 185; original emphasis).

For DJs with subcultural capital, they become brand ambassadors for manufacturers. In his study, Bill Herman (2006) suggested that a DJ gets authorship by the ways in which s/he is represented within the capitalist system, and thus becomes a "brand-name author-god" (p. 22). Herman said that DJs' names are a function of their authorship, and that by using DJs' names on signature products, manufacturers use the DJ as "the ultimate brand name, the moniker under which almost everything is sold" (p. 31). Instead of subcultural capital, Herman concluded that the "social capital of authorship becomes a tool for generating financial capital" (p. 33).

For most companies, there no set standards for compensating endorsees; some manufacturers pay in cash, but most pay in product and support. Endorsement is viewed as a mutual marketing opportunity for both manufacturer and brand name DJ. That is, as the DJ's subcultural capital is used in a company's marketing materials or at trade show demonstrations to authenticate the manufacturer's brand, the visibility of the DJ in those materials also helps to market the DJ and build his/her brand. In the case of signature DJ products, in some instances DJs will receive royalties based on sales or cash sums, but this is rare because even signature products are viewed as mutual marketing. Regardless, the relationship between both the manufacturer's and DJ's brands, if marketed right, engages in a powerful feedback loop.

Most of the DJs I interviewed were used in research and development, while a smaller percentage of my collaborators were used as brands. DJ Babu, who has had numerous endorsements with Rane, Vestax, and Shure, said that, "as far as endorsements go I've always looked at that as a relationship and never expected to get paid." Although Babu said manufacturers "break bread" with him,

> it really means more for me to have that official relationship and have them recognize who they included on the roster.... It's the visibility and perception angle of it is how we get paid.

Chuck Ono, VP at Vestax, said

> having these people backing up your product and using your product definitely shows an importance to the brand, and not only that, it does show that there is a strong bond and an understanding between the brand and the DJ and why he is using it.

Rane's Mike May knows that having DJs endorsing Rane products adds credibility; he commented that manufacturers look to harness a DJ's "star power and their recognition in the industry" and stressed that "you want them to have your gear and you want them to use your gear... without them you don't have the genuine aspect of the products that you are trying to get in their [consumers'] hands."

Endorsements show another way in which hip hop DJs have been manipulated as intellectual properties. When DJs are manipulated like this, IP is exchanged. Where DJs are credited as authors is as a brand, and, therefore, on the surface, that is where they are most important. Branding aids in the fetishization of technology, essentially masking the creative labor that goes into design and production. Like Edison-the-brand, DJs-as-brand can complicate the creative network that goes into product design by confusing brand name authorship with technical innovations. Thus, branding becomes a signifier for "invention." While this happens in most industries, it is interesting to explore in a micro industry that caters to a niche market. In the next section of this chapter I analyze product endorsement and the politics of name ownership using one of the founding fathers of hip hop culture, Grandmaster Flash®, as a case study.

Case in Point: Grandmaster Flash

I have tried to highlight convergence and collective intelligence to demonstrate technocultural synergism and depict hip hop DJ culture as new media necessarily ensconced in intellectual property issues. The purest example of technocultural synergism is the pioneering hip hop DJ Grandmaster Flash®, who is the focus in this section.

In the late 1970s as hip hop culture matured, Joseph Saddler worked to establish his DJ moniker, Grandmaster Flash, as a recognizable name within the culture. Flash innovated, named, and popularized his tricks; he also retrofitted technology using the parks of the South Bronx as his R&D laboratory. He is, in my opinion, one of the first hip hop DJs to really "author" works and create intellectual properties. Grandmaster Flash and The Furious Five had a string of hit singles from 1980 to 1983 on Sugar Hill Records, although Flash was displaced in the studio by a session band. For all of the group's hits, Flash was not part of the production and therefore received no royalties for publishing and presumably for actual record sales. However, Sugar Hill Records used Grandmaster Flash and The Furious Five as the artist name on all of their records, fully exploiting the value of the Grandmaster Flash® brand name. Because Flash had very high levels of subcultural capital and was highly regarded within the scene, Sugar Hill Records duped consumers into thinking that Flash was the author of the music. After years of seeing his brand exploited by Sugar Hill without compensation, Flash left the group and the label in 1983.

Saddler filed a $5 million lawsuit against Sugar Hill Records, where he fought for back royalties on records bearing his name. Thus, Saddler was fighting for his identity as Grandmaster Flash and to maintain and have the right to use Grandmaster Flash®. He said, "Sugar Hill also claimed to own the words 'Grandmaster' and 'Flash' and said that I couldn't use them together for any reason" (Saddler & Ritz, 2008, p. 200).

A judge in the lawsuit ruled in favor of Flash, as there was no clear evidence that Sugar Hill owned Grandmaster Flash®, and concluded that Flash owned a common law trademark on his name by being the first to use it in commerce in park jams and clubs. The judge explained that Flash had put considerable effort into building his brand and that he should be able to exploit that name. Likely in an attempt to prove ownership of Grandmaster Flash prior to litigation, a Grandmaster Flash & The Furious Five® trademark was registered in 1983; after Sugar Hill lost the lawsuit, the mark was abandoned. With the primary purpose of trademark protection being to use marks to distinguish the source of goods/services, Sugar Hill Records was likely diluting the distinctiveness of Grandmaster Flash® by blurring it by applying the name to goods not produced by Flash, with the intention of confusing consumers.

Saddler did not obtain a federally registered trademark on Grandmaster Flash® until 2004 when it was registered for use on apparel. In 2004, he also federally registered Grandmaster Flash® as a service mark for DJ performances; he later registered Grandmaster Flash® for "DJ slipmats; audio circuit boards and audio mixing boards" in 2005, giving him a total of three federally protected trademarks.

Prior to the 2000s, Grandmaster Flash® supposedly invented a box that allowed DJs to perform one of the most popular and complicated scratches of the day, the transform, a technique that Flash could not do well. To make his DJ ideas a reality, he used his electrical engineering skills to make the box, which eventually became the FF-1 Flashformer, manufactured by the American company Gemini. The Flashformer was a "cheat" because it allowed DJs to perform a transform scratch without using the crossfader. For skilled hip hop DJs caught up in authenticity, the Flashformer was corny, and needless to say it didn't fare well in the market. But, having a pioneering hip hop DJ's name and credibility associated with Gemini was more important in the long run. The selling point on the Flashformer was that it featured Flash on the box, and the product itself bore the signature of Grandmaster Flash®, which made it the first signature DJ product featuring a signature on the technology itself. Flash opened the floodgates for DJ product manufacturers using the signature, likeness, and subcultural capital to authenticate their products (Trix came a bit later). The Flashformer shows the significance of Flash winning the right to use the Grandmaster Flash® trademark.

The adventures of Grandmaster Flash® on the wheels of steel is a case study of how DJs are manipulated as intellectual properties, as well as how exchange and rights play into manipulation. This adventure in subcultural capitalism shows how a DJ's brand—a function of a DJ's authorship—is a valuable commodity. Flash, whose genius is produced through collective intelligence and IP manipulation, is an example of the ways in which convergence allows for culture to be manipulated as IP. In the final section, I draw some conclusions based upon what we've learned from Grandmaster Flash® and other hip hop DJs in these larger collaborative and creative networks.

Conclusion

Networked innovation within a new media culture operates under the capitalist construct of authorship. Importantly, a culture whose style is usually discussed as criminal and criminalized in respect to intellectual property has contributed intellectual properties to industry. Through numerous case studies, we see that a DJ's brand/subcultural capital is the easiest function of his/her individual authorship to be recognized under the capitalist mode of authorship. In research and development, however, we clearly see how networked innovation problematizes traditional notions of invention and recognition of authorship.

Social, cultural, and economic power inequities arise through convergence and collective intelligence. There is also a complex relationship between culture and industry—usually pitted against one another as distinct oppositional entities. This chapter demonstrates what Raymond Williams (1977, 1981) theorized many years ago as "cultural materialism," which is that culture takes place in both the material base and the ideological superstructure. In the case of hip hop DJs, culture takes place in a similar dialectical realm of intellectual property manipulation, exchange, and rights in a process of technocultural synergism, where culture and industry interact and combine to produce a total effect that is far greater than the sum of the individual parts. Technology manufacturers have benefitted greatly from hip hop DJs' intellectual properties, and conversely hip hop DJ culture has benefitted from the use of these technical innovations. Technocultural synergism highlights cultural uses and uses of cultures with no end result—these cycles of subversion and co-optation will continue in the name of "progress."

A central component of technocultural synergism is that culture and corporations work together toward a similar goal. In this chapter that goal is better technology. For hip hop DJs, the goal is technologies that aid in improving and expanding technique and creativity. Manufacturers seek to make better technology to improve sales and expand market share, which relies heavily on the creativity of the network. Technocultural synergism, then, begins with culture's manipulation of intellectual properties and continues with its manipulation *as* intellectual property. This process relies heavily on the exchange of IP and associated rights. These rights are not limited to those granted by law, but also the resource-based rights of developing and marketing the byproducts of manipulation and exchange.

Lastly, I want to stress that technocultural synergism brings to light how the greatest creativity comes from a strong network, where ideas bounce around and are reinvented by the network. The ethos of individualism fostered by capitalism and how it rewards authorship are long engrained, but ultimately as a society we'd benefit more by accepting the fact that the best ideas and innovations come from sharing and a healthy creative commons. Hip hop DJs are an example of how a creative commons is socially valuable and economically viable. Once we begin to recognize that creations come from a collective intelligence in a network, then we can look to implementing IP laws, systems, and processes that reward this type of authorship.

Hip hop DJ culture, however, serves only as an example of technocultural synergism. Another example could be digital game modding, where users of games modify game content and sometimes hardware (for related examples, see Potts, Holden, & Dobruse, this volume). Often, this cultural manipulation of intellectual properties leads to game developers/publishers incorporating these mods into future games or working with these modders on game development. Furthermore, game mods can result in the increased sales of older games because of the new content and gameplay. In modding, users modify games to allow for better uses of them and for the notoriety among their peers and other gamers; money is not the end goal, much like hip hop DJ culture. Vidding and other acts of fandom may also arise through technocultural synergism. Some fanvid stories have been incorporated by media conglomerates. Surely, in other media industries, corporations rely heavily on the feedback from focus groups or harness the collective intelligence shared on online forums. Future scholarship should investigate technocultural synergism in other media industries.

Technocultural synergism may help humanities scholars better understand the politics of cultures being manipulated *as* intellectual properties, rather than giving primary focus to the cultural subversion of corporate texts. In the future, technologies that are the byproduct of technocultural synergism, such as DJ mixers, will continue to be a part of our collective human history. If we fail to explore these creative networks and tell their stories, only brand names and packaging will be remembered, rather than the rich processes of research, development, distribution, and use.

• CHAPTER FIFTEEN •

Biocultural Diversity and Copyright: Linking Intellectual Property, Language, Knowledges, and Environment

Gabriela Raquel Ríos and Donnie Johnson Sackey

Boatema Boateng (2011) noted that there is an "uneasy fit" with respect to how folklore meshes with traditional notions of intellectual property. Her study of the production and circulation of adinkra and kente textiles within and outside of Ghana cuts across issues of cultural nationalism and sovereignty in the age of globalization, which encourages the dismantling of cultural boundaries "thus offering foreign media and marketers transcultural wedges for forging affective links between their commodities and local communities" (Kraidy, 2005, p. 148). This highlights an interesting tension as cultural productions function between two competing poles: a) private ownership for profit and b) public availability to spur either innovation or creativity. These varying interests seem only to underscore the fact that notions of "ownership" and "usefulness," largely from an economic standpoint, undergird the logics of copyright law and occlude the noneconomic terms by which Indigenous peoples regard and *make use* of life sustaining artifacts. Following Boateng's pursuit, we build upon growing speculation of what copyright cannot address. Specifically, we offer a paradigm that presents a different way of envisioning the complexity of how Indigenous cultural products function outside of Western tropes of intellectual property.

What would it mean to do away with traditional notions of copyright driven by the exigencies of modernity in favor of paradigms that are more culturally sensitive and appropriate? With this question we explicitly inquire into the importance of ecological dimensions (e.g., landbases and biodiversity) toward rethinking how we understand "intellectual property" through an Indigenous worldview. Furthermore, what would it mean to recognize tribal governments not as cultural stakeholders in the litigation process, but as sovereign states on par with any internationally recognized government? Indeed, the question of legal subjectivity largely looms over any discussion of copyright. Perhaps more importantly, what can working from the limitations of copyright law expose with regard to the production of knowledge in an age of globalization?

In this chapter, we proffer biocultural diversity (BCD) studies as a corrective to the apparent inadequacies in copyright law with respect to Indigenous cultural production. Biocultural diversity studies emerged as scholars in various fields began to notice overlap in the mapping of biodiversity and linguistic diversity, which led to a series of research projects aimed at understanding and recognizing the ways in which nature, language, and Traditional Ecological Knowledge (TEK) are interlinked. Additionally, Luisa Maffi (2010) noted that the increased breakdown of perceived links between humans and nature is the root of not only many environmental problems but also social issues we collectively face today. The loss of connectivity is often attributed as a derivative of globalization, which offers growth and prosperity, while posing substantive social and environmental challenges. As a corrective, Maffi (2010) urged that scholars undertake research initiatives that "understand the connections between biodiversity and cultural diversity, and to act on this understanding, in both policy and practice" (p. 4).

It is our belief that work in the area of biocultural diversity presents a novel approach whereby we can rethink how we understand copyright issues. As we have noted above, most research on intellectual property issues relies upon a Western methodological interrogation of the relationship between culture and law. The move toward biocultural diversity as an analytic is an inquiry into how non-Western (primarily Indigenous-centered) approaches can alter the way we see cultural production and protection of intellectual property by marking copyright as a culturally-situated practice that often omits essential constituents from the purview of scholarly investigation. Indigenous conceptions of knowledge are primarily ecologically-centered, whereas Western conceptions of knowledge (or "intellectual property") mobilize and continue a colonial relationship to knowledge that is rooted in capitalism and either ignores or implicates relationships between land and peoples into a monetary-based agenda.

To explore the importance of an Indigenous model of biocultural diversity to research on intellectual property, in this chapter we make clearer through a case study what a biocultural diversity lens offers to the way we understand issues of copyright by complicating notions of intellectual commons; raising the question of what happens when we think about overlooked aspects of cultures (e.g., textile designs) as a kind of "intellectual commons," or shared, "community-owned knowledge"; and finally, highlighting how appropriation can often divest cultural practices of their ecological foundations. It is our position that the relationship of law to knowledge is predicated upon the nation-state that creates a colonial imposition whereby people have difficulty conceiving of a relationship of land to knowledge. The rhetorical frames that undergird copyright law privilege textual production in a way that both disembodies knowledge and only acknowledges a specific kind of materiality as having intellectual merit. Siva Vaidhyanathan (2004) argued that we cannot create a better copyright system "as long as we continue to work within the limited rhetorical frameworks that we have inherited" (p. 251). Clearly, we need to create a better system for understanding the production and valuing of knowledge. We believe that a look toward biocultural diversity is a step toward that direction. Ultimately, inquiring into copyright law *vis a vis* an Indigenous model for BCD exposes the connections between copyright law and a nation-state agenda predicated on the politics of representation and capital that exists over and against biocultural diversity. In other words, the means by which a people determine their humanity under the organizing principles of a nation-state suggest or manifest a separation between humans and the natural world.

John Tomlinson (2003) noted that "cultural identity is at risk everywhere with the depredations of globalization, but the developing world is particularly at risk" because very few adequate protections exist to stop the proliferation of cultural forms considered sacred and important to one's community (p. 270). As the story goes, Indigenous peoples around the world have had to fight to protect their traditional knowledges for years from governments and pharmaceutical companies. Bioprospecting, or the process of exchange of Traditional Ecological Knowledge (TEK) between Indigenous peoples and corporate entities with the promises of community development or royalties, has often been touted as not only a way to develop new medicines and technologies but also a means of preserving cultural diversity and knowledge (Hayden, 2003). Compensation, however, is often inequitable or even nonexistent as Indigenous knowledge of nature is often acquired without consent from and compensation to Indigenous peoples. This amounts to what some have termed "biopiracy" (Shiva, 1997). There have been efforts by the United Nations through its General Assembly and the World Intellectual Property Organization (WIPO) to protect Indigenous traditional knowledge from misuse (Convention on Biodiversity, 1992; United Nations, 1993, 2004). Still, these efforts arise from a largely Western legal tradition that employs culturally irrelevant heuristics (e.g., time) in the protection of cultural artifacts that most Indigenous peoples do not understand as "property" in the traditional free-market capitalist sense of the word.

Intellectual property law (copyright, patent, trademark, trade secret) is often governed by particular time constraints. The problem for Indigenous peoples is how is it possible to use time-governed systems to protect culturally-sustaining knowledge that has been orally transmitted across generations. Our discussion regarding copyright is framed by one contemporary moment in the United States that, although on the surface they appear different from the issue of biopiracy, can only be seen as a story that documents the continuing struggles of Indigenous peoples to protect their knowledges and cultures.

The Navajo Nation et al. v. Urban Outfitters, Inc.

On Columbus Day of 2001, Sasha Houston Brown, a member of the Santee Sioux Nation (or Eastern Dakota) wrote an open letter to Glen T. Senk, CEO of Urban Outfitters Incorporated. The letter chronicled her experience visiting a local Urban Outfitters in Minneapolis. Brown (2011) described the store: a cheap, vulgar and culturally offensive retail collection. Plastic dreamcatchers wrapped in pleather hung next to an indistinguishable mass of artificial feather jewelry and hyper sexualized clothing featuring an abundance of suede, fringe and inauthentic tribal patterns. At the heart of her comments is a pointed critique of Urban Outfitters' appropriation of American Indigenous cultural forms in a "mass marketed collection of distasteful and racially demeaning apparel and décor" (Brown, 2011). Historically, this would not be the first time that the issue of appropriation of Native American culture has arisen as an issue for public debate. One would need only recount the range of controversies that span anywhere from the naming of collegiate and professional sports teams (e.g., University of North Dakota "Fighting Sioux") to popular commercial products (e.g., Jeep Grand Cherokee). Brown's letter was a response to Urban Outfitters' "Navajo" collection, which featured a range of "Navajo" branded items that included clothing, flasks, blankets and bracelets. Responding to the growing controversy surrounding the brand, Ed Looram, Urban Outfitter's PR Director, wrote that the company, like other retailers, was merely interpreting a trend and that the

> Native American-inspired trend and specifically the term "Navajo" have been cycling thru [sic] fashion, fine art and design for the last few years [and that the company had] no plans to modify or discontinue any of these products. (Sauers, 2011)

The Navajo Nation—protected under the Federal Indian Arts and Crafts Act of 1990—holds a trademark on the name "Navajo" and, through its Department of Justice, sent a cease-and-desist order to the company in hopes that they would "adopt another name and trademark for its products" (Sauers, 2011). After several months of unsuccessful arbitration in the matter, the Navajo Nation Department of Justice filed suit against Urban Outfitters.

American Indians and U.S. Intellectual Property Law: A Troubled Legal History

The foundation for our turn to biocultural diversity (BCD) is the inadequacy of a Western-based culture of copyright at protecting Indigenous peoples' TEK. There have been attempts to protect Indigenous cultural forms within the United States through enacting a series of "Indian-made" laws geared at promoting the development and marketing of Native American arts and crafts and creating a board that would assist tribes and artisans in the production and distribution processes (Indian Arts and Crafts Act, 1935). The intentions of these acts were not to protect Native cultures on account of their own value. Instead, they were created to bring American Indians into commercial markets under the auspices that economic development would best insure cultural survival. Drafters of the legislation could only see the value of Native cultures through Western eyes.

For example, the Indian Arts and Crafts Act of 1990 (IACA), an improved version of the Act of 1935, was signed into law as a means of protecting American Indian artists and craftspeople from those who would falsely market products as an Indian product or affiliated with a tribal government. The act was a "truth-in-advertising" law that outlined stiff penalties for misrepresenting products as "Indian made." Many hailed the IACA as progressive because it aimed at the political recognition of Indigenous peoples in dominant culture; centered on principles of economic justice; and tended toward cultural preservation; however, the Act of 1990 proved to do more harm than good. Shortly after its passage, the Museum of the Five Civilized Tribes closed indefinitely as officials were uncertain as to whether displayed art would pass the legal test of being "Indian-made" (Sheffield, 1997; Thacker, 1991; Watts, 1990). The problem with the IACA is that it defined Native designed crafts through a strict understanding of identity. One has to be an Indian under the law, and in order to be an Indian under the law, one has to be a member of a federally recognized tribe. Section 309.2 of the IACA (1990) stated "Indian tribe" to mean:

> (1) Any Indian tribe, band, nation, Alaska Native village, or any organized group or community which is recognized as eligible for the special programs and services provided by the United States to Indians because of their status as Indians; or (2) Any Indian group that has been formally recognized as an Indian tribe by a State legislature or by a State commission or similar organization legislatively vested with State tribal recognition authority.

Because the museum never made inquiries into whether artists were officially recognized by a tribe, they ran the risk of both civil and criminal proceedings. Yet, politicians only managed to add to the complexity regarding tribal membership and who can identify as an Indian by choosing to protect

Native artisans through identity recognition. The IACA's identity requirements conflict with other understandings of "Indian" based on rubrics of kinship and/or blood quantum. Under these processes, a person can classify themselves as Indian either "ethnically or racially but not [necessarily] politically or legally" (Hapiuk, 2001, p. 1012). This is to say that even if a person has complete Indian ancestry, they can still be denied legal recognition since they have no relation to a tribe. The IACA entirely disregards other more expansive cultural definitions of "Indian" as it simplistically attempts to regulate a market. We find William Hapiuk's (2001) description of the act's effects to be gripping as he wrote, "when it comes to making and selling Indian arts and crafts, a non-enrolled Indian ceases to be Indian" (p. 1012). Thus, the problem with copyright is not merely a struggle with respect to cultural property but also encompasses a struggle over identity.

U.S. copyright law also engages in a politics of knowledge that marks some Indigenous People's cultural artifacts as intellectual property and relegates others to a dubious and unprotected categorical distinction. Congress designed the Native American Graves Protection and Repatriation Act (NAGPRA, 1990) to protect communal ownership that governed the "removal of human remains, funerary objects, sacred objects or objects of cultural patrimony on Federal, Indian and Native Hawaiian lands." On the surface, this law has had the power to force museums, universities, and collectors to restore artifacts to their respective tribal communities. NAGPRA is no more a blessing than a bane to Native communities because it makes a distinction between cultural property and intellectual property. Tribes have the power to regain their artifacts, but they do not have the power to stop production of derivative works used as replicas in museum settings. David Jordan (2000/2001) offered the example of Iroquois Wampum belts where tribes can request the repatriation of specific belts obtained illegally through collectors, but they are virtually powerless to stop the selling of reproductions to museums by members affiliated with the tribe. The issue here is that the intellectual knowledge of Wampum belt production largely circulates in the public domain and tribes are incapable of stopping reproductions.

Through this brief rhetorical read of legal history, readers get an idea of how U.S. intellectual property laws frame how we understand Native peoples and their cultural effects. There is real cause to argue that these laws do not protect Native cultures as much as they cause them harm either because of their authoritative identity constraints or their forcing Indians to adopt notions of market value, ownership, and what counts as "intellectual," largely Western ideas. If we revisit the case of the Navajo nation, we can clearly see how the laws recognize that there is a monetary value to culture but ignore the sacred aspects of cultural resources that help to form identity. While reproduction of "inauthentic" forms can cause financial harm, the greater risk for tribal communities is the loss of meaning. Even if the Navajo win their suit against Urban Outfitters, Inc., what will prevent the company (or other companies) from making products inspired by Navajo culture without the name "Navajo" attached to the product? Furthermore, "Indian-made" laws name tangible aspects of culture as worth protecting, but ignore non-material forms, such as story or ceremony (Osborne, 2003/2004). These concerns are not new, as American Indian, Hawaiian, and Alaskan Native intellectuals have pointed our attention to them for decades (Cajete, 1999; King, 2008; Smith, 1999; Trask, 1991). We, however, wish to add another concern that highlights the importance of the relationship between land and knowledge, which the current system does not recognize. Cultural preservation through copyright cannot take place if it fails to recognize that in the Indigenous worldview, knowledge emerges from the land in which it is created. To address this issue, we turned to biocultural diversity.

Biocultural Diversity

In 1996, a group of scholars and activists created Terralingua, a non-governmental organization committed to preserving and promoting what they have termed biocultural diversity (BCD). According to Terralingua, BCD is the "'true' web of life: the interlinked diversity of nature and culture," to the degree that cultural diversity is understood as part and parcel of biodiversity. BCD as a concept emerged out of the mapping of an overlap between linguistic diversity and biodiversity, and for BCD scholars, language stands as a proxy for culture because language is the primary means by which we transmit and store knowledge, in this case land-based cultural knowledge. These mappings cite that the areas of the world that exhibit the most biodiversity and linguistic diversity are those areas populated by Indigenous peoples whose TEK has helped to cultivate and sustain the biodiversity of their land bases. Though the interconnectedness of humans and our natural environments is foundational to Indigenous world views, it is a concept that has only recently gained currency in academia. For Terralingua specifically, a host of diverse studies and methodologies in BCD have generated some rhetorical velocity since its creation in 1996, and studies in global and regional mappings, and analyses of distribution patterns of BCD have taken form. Ultimately, BCD inquiry operates on the belief that language, knowledge, and the environment are inextricably connected.

One area of focus in BCD studies that bears relevance to our discussion here is the formation of a theory for BCD that is predicated on the ways in which land-based cultural knowledge is mediated through language. Initially, in making their arguments for cultural preservation, linguists and anthropologists in BCD studies primarily drew parallels between the loss of biodiversity and the world's languages as a matter of convenience in order to stress that the loss of languages was "comparable damage to humanity's heritage" (Maffi, 2001, p. 7). Researchers soon came to realize that there was indeed a crucial correlation between so-called endangered species and endangered languages (Harmon, 1995; Harmon & Loh, 2004; Lizarralde, 2001; Nettle, 1996, 1998; Skutnabb-Kangas, Maffi, & Harmon, 2003). This correlation suggested a more material connection between biodiversity and language, and by extension, between language and (environmental) knowledge, or TEK.

Explanation

To better understand how Indigenous languages and biodiversity could be linked, first-wave scholars attempted to understand the link between language and knowledge, a relationship that they believed to be *framed* by culture. Maffi (2001) drew from early scholars of Indigeneity, culture, and the environment like Alfred Kroeber to make this claim. In observing and studying Indigenous peoples and their lands, Kroeber (1939) argued that his work did not perpetuate the antiquated idea that culture is produced by the environment, claiming,

> While it is true that cultures are rooted in nature, and can therefore never be completely understood except with reference to that piece of nature in which they occur, they are no more produced by that nature than a plant is produced by the soil in which it is rooted. (p. 1)

He offered a critical claim, however, that culture is (re)produced primarily by other cultural phenomena, which recognized that the relationship between nature and culture can only help enhance a "full" understanding of culture. In later studies, scholars like Eric Smith (2001) argued against the "myth of the pristine wilderness," claiming studies indicate that "any understanding of contemporary biodiversity change in the Americas is likely to be uninformative and misleading if it employs a prehistoric baseline imbued with pristine characteristics" absent the influence of culture (p. 109).

Scholars (Maffi &Woodley, 2010; Posey, 1999) noted that although it is true that increased human activity poses the prime threat to biodiversity, recognizing the role that anthropogenic impact has had on the natural environment must not obscure the fact that human relationships with the environment are complex and should be understood on the basis of a wide range of social and political variables. In fact, research suggests that smaller, localized societies have been able to enhance or even develop accurate knowledge about local ecology and biodiversity, and have been able to use that knowledge to further enhance and maintain the local biodiversity (Berkes, 1999; Hunn, 1999; Shepard, 2004). Using systems theory, scholars began to understand the relationship amongst language, culture, and environmental knowledge as a complex system. Though complex systems theory is generally taken up in the study of biological systems, BCD theorists have inserted culture and language into a matrix for understanding the emergence and maintenance of biodiversity. In this way, scholars are now attempting to better understand the possible link(s) among culture, nature, and knowledge by privileging the TEK of Indigenous peoples, whose land bases house the world's greatest areas of biodiversity (Maffi, 2001). BCD became theorized as a complex socio-ecological adaptive system composed of the "biosphere," "logosphere," and the "ethnosphere" (Maffi & Woodley, 2010, p. 4), with the logosphere and the ethnosphere representing language and culture, respectively.

Discussion of Complexity

BCD scholars have intimated that because BCD emerges from on-the-ground experiences, the idea is thus in many ways still emerging and evolving as case studies arise. Nevertheless, there have been some trends that allow scholars to operate off a set of core beliefs:

1. Humans are an intrinsic part of the natural environment, even while they have adapted to their natural environments.
2. Cultural beliefs, practices, and knowledge manifest this relationship between humans and their natural world.
3. Cultural diversity does not merely parallel biodiversity—these phenomena are interdependent.
4. The perception of this link is weaker in industrialized societies, and this lack of awareness underlies many environmental and social problems in the world today.
5. Awareness of this link remains stronger in Indigenous or other localized communities whose worldviews maintain direct ties to the natural world.

BCD policy case studies focus on only policies that affect or are affected by policy that engages BCD in direct and literal ways. In other words, looking to projects that are "integrative and synergistic" is of utmost importance. Projects that focus on only one part of the BCD system without relating it to another are considered outside of the purview of BCD studies.

BCD studies articulate these series of connections through complex systems theory, citing culture as merely one point of entry for understanding how the connections among language, land, and knowledge manifest. However, even when scholars attempt to disrupt the sharp dichotomy between nature and culture, they resist the push, much like Kroeber (1939), to assume that cultural phenomena *do* arise from natural phenomena. This represents hesitation on the part of scholars who hypothesize that humans, nature, and culture "co-evolve" but are only willing to posit this as a likely hypothesis rather than an actuality in the absence of more definitive research. It also represents a point of departure for an Indigenous understanding of BCD.

Critique

Because Indigenous peoples have historically been linked with the environment in a variety of problematic ways (Vizenor, 1999) it has been difficult to discuss the ways in which Indigenous people's TEK has affected biodiversity. Indigenous peoples are caught in a binary understanding of their role as either the ecological stewards of humanity's survival (Daes, 2008) or as passive, unconscious inheritors of biodiversity due to unintentionally maintaining small populations and utilizing low-impact technologies (Maffi & Woodley, 2010). For Indigenous peoples, the idea that humans and nature "co-evolve" is a given, and TEK is predicated on that truth. It may be argued that researchers' hesitancy to acknowledge the coevolution of humans and nature grows out of the culture of Western science, which operates on experimentation and observation as an objective practice. Additionally, while BCD studies do at least challenge us to see the formation of knowledge as co-evolving alongside culture and the environment, the notion of culture is still understood in limiting, sometimes problematic terms (i.e., when the ethnosphere stands in for racial difference).

Nevertheless, these findings have very broad ramifications for not only Indigenous peoples, but also for scholars who borrow from Western ideologies that understand knowledge to be a byproduct of cultural phenomena that are divorced from natural phenomena. In fact, the Western production of knowledge functions on a very necessary distinction between these categories, given that knowledge grows out of the observation of natural phenomena through cultural apparatuses. For example, language is used as a proxy for culture in much of BCD studies; however, the Western orientation to language is always-already logocentric (or text-based) (Derrida, 1997). If we recall the systems model used in BCD studies previously mentioned, we can see that the "space" in/from which knowledge and language function is referred to as the "logosphere." Logocentrism functions as a cultural apparatus from which to better understand everything in the natural world. In other words, we aim to turn natural phenomena into "texts" that can be "read" or con*text*ualized.

So, while BCD studies challenges copyright law to consider the ways in which intellectual property may also house TEK, it remains text-centric. As a corrective, we make use of Gabriela's articulation of an Indigenous model of BCD as an alternative analytic that further complicates the notions of intellectual property that privilege the production of text and that understand cultural production only in terms of textual production that is divorced from TEK. Furthermore, we illustrate how an Indigenous model of BCD challenges notions of an "intellectual commons" insofar as it makes visible the material, biocultural consequences of cultural appropriation.

Discussion

An Indigenous model for BCD challenges the premises upon which BCD studies grounds itself, namely that even if we use language as a proxy for culture, we must understand language as a non-textual practice and we must look to practices that may not be easily recognized as "ecological" from the perspective of Western science. Additionally, using an Indigenous model of BCD to advance an analytic for understanding copyright law challenges a Western production of knowledge that operates separately from, and often times over and against, the environment. Furthermore, it challenges the very categories and taxonomies of knowledge privileged by Western legal discursive practices. For Indigenous peoples, "cultural property" is both "intellectual property," and "environmental knowledge." Indigenous "art" is also at once a techne *and* an episteme *and* an epistemology. Ultimately, using an Indigenous form of BCD as an analytic distinguishes TEK as emerging from a reciprocal relationship between bodies/peoples, land, and culture that ultimately posits nature as a site of origin.

What we are stressing here is that there is a fundamentally different orientation to knowledge that does not separate epistemology from ontology. For Indigenous peoples, nature most certainly produces culture, just as culture also helps to produce nature; however, an Indigenous paradigm of sustainability understands our relationship to nature through engagement and practice, not merely through observation. TEK is formed consciously through engaging nature on a relational, *familial* level via dance, storied practice, and art. We want to make clear, however, that when we use the word "traditional," in this context, we refer to the traditional ecological knowledges carried in oral (his)stories, languages, textile designs, and other art forms carried on by Indigenous peoples. These traditions are not static; they are enduring. Therefore, when Maffi and Woodley (2011) cite a gap in policy regarding "the need to promote a more in-depth understanding of the importance of supporting local and traditional knowledge and languages for the maintenance of both biological and cultural diversity, and thus for sustainability," we believe that a necessary point of entry for addressing this gap is at the intersection of copyright law, the environment, and Indigenous "intellectual property." The Urban Outfitters case shows not only how Western copyright practices cannot account for a relationship between knowledge and TEK, but also how understanding the causal links between local tradition and biodiversity pushes us to extend our analysis to forms of cultural production such as textile designs, which are traditionally out of the purview of what are deemed ecological practices.

Eric Cheyfitz (2011) argued that Western copyright law forces Indigenous peoples' epistemological/ontological practices into a system based primarily on capital gain and notions of *property*. These notions complicate Indigenous intellectual traditions in two primary ways: (1) They force Indigenous peoples into legal battles over issues of representation that are divorced from environmental or land-based concerns, and often times from concerns over knowledge (like TEK). Ultimately, this means that intellectual or cultural property can only have *monetary* value (as opposed to cultural or environmental value), and they can only have that value when they are tied to representation. However, Indigenous intellectual productions ground them to their particular land bases, and carry within them TEK. (2) The very notion of "property" constitutes a kind of ownership that does not readily translate into Indigenous culture, especially considering that TEK is an integral part of Indigenous art-based intellectual traditions. This is why Urban Outfitters can simply remove the name "Navajo" from their "Native-inspired" designs and still continue to reproduce designs in a way that forgets the TEK with which they are created, because the traditional designs cannot be copyrighted as intellectual or environmental knowledge. Western copyright culture, as it applies to American Indians, can only protect the U.S.-authorized authenticity of their "artifacts" or "cultural property." Even when copyright law becomes an "issue" in debates over Native artifacts or cultural production, legal discourses frame the concern as *either* one of representation or profit. However, the notion of profit does not protect TEK. Even if American Indians are compensated for the use of their art or cultural property, this does not ensure that their TEK is being protected.

Indigenous peoples' relationship to their land bases is kincentric, in other words, Indigenous peoples see themselves related to their landbases in a literal, familial way (Cajete, 1999; Cheyfitz, 2011; Salmón, 2001). If copyright law is enacted as a matter of justice with respect to knowledge (i.e. as a form of protecting peoples and their intellectual "property") it does not do so in a way that can protect the environment, which for Native peoples is always-already an integral part of not only intellectual property, but also of identity and lifeways. To protect TEK is to protect the relationship between the people and the environment. What copyright law does is turn intellectual and cultural property into a commodity. Cheyfitz (2011) argued that "from an Indigenous perspective, we can understand commodity fetishism as the displacement of kinship relations by object relations" (p. 303). The relationship between nature, culture, and knowledge is lost on Western copyright practices. What an Indigenous model of BCD affords, then, is a critique of Western copyright culture's objectification of the environment in a very real, *material* way. In a way that ultimately affects us all.

The problem with *Navajo Nation v. Urban Outfitters* is that the case hinges upon the issue of representation. Accordingly, the U.S. legal system affords the Navajo Nation protection of its culture through control of its name. The Navajo Nation holds twelve trademarks on the use of "Navajo" on products that range from sportswear to jeans. As the owner of the registered trademark, the Nation can readily commence legal proceedings in order to prevent unauthorized use that may affect its image. What the law does not prevent is reproduction of "Native" designs. The problem here is a question of who controls the commodity not so much that a cultural resource is being commodified. In this case, Native "authors," as the titleholders of intellectual property, have the right to prevent others from accessing certain resources with the benefit of retaining or maximizing a product's value (Osbourne, 2003/2004). Urban Outfitters, however, is not really invested in the name "Navajo" itself as much as it is interested in the cultural aesthetic attached to the name. And this is where intellectual property laws do not work in Indigenous peoples' best interests.

It is difficult to talk about the implications of Urban Outfitters' commodification of Navajo culture without briefly referencing the history of the American Indian trade blanket, the language of the blanket, and its importance to tribal communities. The term "Indian blanket is misleading" because the blanket did not originate inside Native cultures (Kapoun, 1997). This artifact, which in various forms is often associated with Indigenous Americans of the Southwest and Great Plains, initially emerged as a commercially produced product by Europeans for trade. Over time, however, the woolen blanket gained increasing use and importance within Native communities as they replaced robes made from various natural materials (e.g. fur, bark, feathers, etc.). The blanket did not retain a static form. Throughout its adoption Native American users have "recast" it in order to "meet the needs and acceptance" of their respective cultures (Houlihan, 1997). Soon both Native peoples and commercial producers exclusively understood the blanket as a garment that bestowed a sense of Indianness and citizenship within a tribal community for its owner. Yet, if the blanket emerged as a European creation that Indigenous Americans adopted and remixed for their own use, how can the Navajo find fault with Urban Outfitters? The answer is simple in that the Navajo trade blanket is actually an "Indian" blanket. This artifact is part of a weaving tradition that extends as far back as the 14th century. Navajo artisans for centuries have used upright looms to weave blankets exclusively for Indian people long before European fur traders or commercial mills. So, the history of this blanket can easily get lost within the larger story of the American Indian trade blanket. Both the motifs found on the blanket and the cultural practice of weaving together bear great significance within Navajo cosmology. The instructions for how to build the first loom and how to weave were given to Navajo women by Spider Woman (Na'ashjéii asdzáá), a supernatural being that factors prominently in Navajo spirituality. It is these material dimensions of the blanket that exist outside the realm of protection of copyright. The fight over the blanket is not just about the name "Navajo." It is also about all the other elements of Navajo culture and intellectual property that the blanket signifies.

Removal of the name, while it satisfies copyright laws, accomplishes nothing. Regardless of whether the word "Navajo" appears on Urban Outfitter's "Truly Madly Deeply Navajo Print Tunic" or its "Navajo Hipster Panty," shoppers will still recognize designs such as those found on Indian trade blankets as representing a southwestern tribal aesthetic. Therefore, the clothes will always represent a belief of an Indigenous culture that is based on geography in the average consumer's imagination. Geography here is key. And with the issue of location we cannot ignore the history and sacredness of the blanket's designs as its production by the Navajo was often a derivative of the world around them as these designs were regularly referential of geography, and by extension, of BCD. To this point, Rain Parrish (1992) wrote of the connection between the trade blanket and land citing the varying connections:

> as the light from the fire illuminated the moving bodies and blankets, the swirling shapes, lines, patterns, and colors sprang to life. I no longer saw blankets, but rather the familiar designs of the Holy People coming to life from the sand paintings. I saw moving clouds, glowing sunsets, varicolored streaks of lightning, rainbow goddesses, sacred mountains, horned toads, and images like desert mirages—all dancing before my eyes. (p. 2)

This excerpt shows the level of importance of not only trade blankets but also the designs found on them as representations of people, events and places. These are not merely art forms or creative works. These are meaningful cultural resources in the form of material objects that the Navajo rely upon to fortify their identities and relationships with others. We could easily argue that the Navajo Nation is entering into the wrong fight or protecting the wrong thing; however, they are simply working in the only way that the system allows. Reproduction of certain forms, regardless of whether they carry a tribe's name, is still as harmful because as a product is reproduced and disseminated along a production cycle it increasingly becomes disassociated from the aspects that imbued it with meaning. Furthermore, by reproducing these forms for consumption, retailers and consumers imbue these products with their own cultural conception of fashion and then transfer this aesthetic back to Indigenous Peoples. In this case, Indigenous culture becomes a derivative of the Western imagination.

Conclusion

The Urban Outfitters case study exemplifies Cheyfitz' (2011) argument that the "commodity fetishism" of American Indian cultural/intellectual production displaces kinship relations with object relations. But, as we have shown, they also make visible the relationship between a Western production of knowledge and the colonial enterprise that enables that commodity fetishism. The consequences of this displacement extend beyond the concept of cultural appropriation, as it is understood from within the legal dimensions of copyright law, and challenge Western legal practices with respect to copyright law and intellectual property to interrogate the ways in which the current system cannot fully protect not only American Indian rights, but also the TEK that essentially all of humanity is dependent upon. Considering and reflecting on an Indigenous model for BCD as it intersects with copyright law allows for scholars in the humanities to engage the cultural implications of intellectual property issues. A Western cultural model of copyright law commodifies culture and identity, but it also operates on an ontological premise that does not see possible connections between identity, knowledge production, and land. A more gripping concern, then, is the potential for copyright law to *overwrite* ecological knowledge, and more specifically, TEK that houses information and practices for sustainable living here in the Americas. In addition, this analytic can allow scholars in the humanities to better address the role/s that language practices play in the global distribution of culture and knowledge, namely the ways in which particular cultural orientations to language either inhibit or enhance biodiversity, and as a result, biocultural diversity.

As attractive as the model looks for adoption, we do want to issue a caveat with respect to a potential limitation of BCD as a heuristic. BCD retains a text-centric approach to the analysis of language and subsequently culture. In the pursuit of preserving language through artifacts like dictionaries, the identity of a culture stabilizes and remains unchanged. The problem here is that scholars adopting BCD might look at texts as being stable objects that they then turn back onto language and subsequently culture. Such stability that comes from textual hermeneutics does not encompass the many practices that exist around a text and often in opposition to a text. Therefore, there is a risk that culture can remain unchanged in the eyes of scholars. We urge those interested in BCD as a heuristic to engage in complexity by considering the multiple ways in which textual and nontextual practices of cultures are linked across space and time to create the conditions they research. So we close with a simple corollary: The adoption of BCD comes with a commitment to networks.

• CHAPTER SIXTEEN •

Toward a Reflexive Approach to Remix—or—What Hawai'i Creole English and Corporate Tourism Can Teach Us about Copyright

Jennifer Sano-Franchini, Robyn Tasaka, and Lehua Ledbetter

Kirby Ferguson's (2012) "Everything is a Remix" argues that all forms of creativity come from pre-existing ideas; however, *which* ideas are protected under copyright is much more limited. Ferguson claimed that all culture evolves through a three-part process: copy, transform, and combine. This process dismantles notions of originality, a fundamental concept in the discourse on copyright. In this chapter, we engage this premise from the vantage point of postcolonial theory and cultural rhetorics. As Michael Brown (2003), Kimberly Christen (2005), and Boatema Boateng (2011) have argued, neither U.S. copyright law in its current state nor much of the scholarly discussion surrounding copyright in the U.S. accounts for the complexities of cultural flow in the production of knowledge and goods.

We extend the work of Brown (2003), Christen (2005), and Boateng (2011) by shifting the boundaries that define what is protected under copyright law. Moving beyond fixed artifacts, we examine cultural practices and processes of cultural production as intellectual work and shared knowledge, or a kind of "commons." More specifically, we disentangle the complex social relations and political histories that have accompanied processes of cultural production in Hawai'i, with issues of intellectual property in mind. Using historical, rhetorical, and literary methods of analysis, we examine cultural production in Hawai'i in two cases: First, we explore Hawai'i Creole English (HCE) as a kind of "remix." Then, we examine how corporate tourism "remixes" local and Hawaiian culture on gohawaii.com, Hawai'i's official tourism web site, along with how such representations have, themselves, been remixed.

Ultimately, we show how these cases provide opportunities for re-examining notions of copyright and ownership in ways that better account for issues of shared identity, cultural survivance, cultural appropriation, and ideological colonial violence. We conclude by providing steps toward a reflexive approach to remix.

We center on Hawai'i because we believe its unique yet fraught history of cultural mixing via legacies of colonialism, immigration, military occupation, and tourism offers an opportunity to examine some of the implications of this mixing in a politicized context. In less than 250 years between Captain Cook's "discovery" of Hawai'i in 1778 and today, Hawai'i has seen several waves of outsiders enter the islands, bringing cultural practices and knowledges to mix with Hawaiian culture. This movement of bodies across geographical space created the conditions that allowed for "remixes" of what were once—and are sometimes still—thought of as distinct cultures. That is, there are aspects of local Hawai'i culture that cannot be parsed out to distinct racial, ethnic, or national origins—for instance, local foods like shave ice or lomi salmon, and practices like taking one's shoes off when entering a person's house or making too much food for a party. Here, Kirby's (2011) notion of "copy, transform, and combine" resonates: Lines between cultures blur, the cultures themselves change, and new cultural practices emerge through processes of hybridization. While copyright law privileges certain kinds of intellectual work, protecting "original," fixed artifacts such as musical recordings, books, and other print and digital materials, we suggest that cultural processes and languages are "intellectual commons" or shared, "community-owned knowledge"—forms of intellectual work that have not traditionally been considered intellectual property. In taking this perspective, we respond to and extend Christen's (2005) recognition of increased debates over what constitutes—and who owns—intellectual property and cultural knowledge (Brown, 2003; Boateng, 2011).

Our attention to Hawai'i also springs from our having been born, raised, and in part educated there as Asian American and mixed-race Asian/white women of settler origin. Yet we are not "Hawaiian," as the term is used in Hawai'i; in Hawai'i, a person local to the state is considered "Local," but not Hawaiian, as Hawaiian is reserved for the indigenous people and cultures of Hawai'i. For example, literature written in Hawai'i may be considered "Local literature" or "Hawai'i literature," but "Hawaiian literature" is reserved for literature written by people of Native Hawaiian ancestry. We disclose this background because we understand ethnicity and cultural subjectivity as critical in discussions of politics in Hawai'i, and worth taking into consideration in discussions of intellectual property. The examples that follow show the entanglement of identity, settler politics, and survivance, while also raising questions of who has the right to speak when it comes to remix.

Our move to consider intellectual work beyond fixed artifacts follows the work of several scholars in postcolonial studies who have critiqued the privileging of alphabetic text and material culture in the EuroAmerican tradition. For example, Mignolo (2003) showed how the "belief that only alphabetic literacy allowed for a reliable recording of the past" allowed "imperial agencies [to] inscribe the idea that people without writing were people without history and that people without history were inferior human beings" (pp. 127, 128). Such processes are not unlike the privileging of fixed artifacts in contrast to everyday language practices, cultural concepts, or orality in discussions of what is protected under the purview of copyright.

Furthermore, the scholarship on hybridity is useful for understanding how processes of "remix" unfold, with implications for power and privilege (Ang, 2001; Bhabha, 1994; Lowe, 1996; Mao, 2006; Mignolo, 2003; Thomas, 1991, 1997). For instance, Lisa Lowe (1996) defined hybridity as

> the formation of cultural objects and practices that are produced by the histories of uneven and unsynthetic power relation… Hybridity, in this sense, does not suggest the assimilation of Asian or immigrant practices to dominant forms but instead marks the history of survival within relationship of unequal power and domination. (p. 67)

Homi Bhabha (1994) articulated a similar process that takes place in colonial contexts using the concept of mimicry, which he said,

> emerges as the representation of a difference that is itself a process of disavowal. Mimicry is, thus, the sign of a double articulation; a complex strategy of reform, regulation, and discipline, which 'appropriates' the Other as it visualizes power… the discourse of mimicry is constructed around an ambivalence; in order to be effective, mimicry must continually produce its slippage, its excess, its difference. (p. 266)

Mignolo (2003) likewise explained that colonization is a "coexistence of languages, literacies, memories and spaces" (p. 4). That is, "colonial situations imply a plurality of traditions" (p. 19). Nicholas Thomas (1997) illustrated this process by explaining how values that are today perceived by Fijians as key aspects of their culture "either originated in the colonial period (1874–1970) or were transformed by it" (p. 177). This view is possible because of divergent definitions of "authenticity" in "European" and Fijian culture—while "Europeans" take particular physical artifacts as key symbols of Westernization in Fiji, Fijians are concerned with whether one uses introduced objects to continue traditional practices. Through this description, Thomas highlights how different epistemological emphases on object versus use result in different understandings of what is authentic and what is Fijian.

As Christen (2005) observed, "cultural and intellectual property are managed and mediated within social relations and produced through histories of ongoing political tensions" (p. 336). Yet, despite the argument that cultural mixing is ubiquitous and always embedded in webs of power, complex social relations and political histories are often neglected in discussions of copyright in the U.S. In what follows, we examine how cultural knowledge has been managed and mediated in a moment of complex social and political relations through a historical analysis of Hawai'i Creole English.

Case 1: Hawai'i Creole English as Remix

Hawai'i Creole English (HCE), the first language of a majority of Hawai'i locals, is a confluence of languages that initially merged for communication and cultural expression. Like remix culture, HCE is a form of cultural mixing that has surfaced new forms of communication and cultural practices. In this section, we draw on the history of HCE to complicate the idea of remix, extending the rhetorical situation beyond textual modes of production to language as shared experience. In reviewing HCE's shifting status across time, we engage the scholarship on settler colonialism to raise questions about ownership as it pertains to culture and to think about remix as a means of cultural survivance and shared identity.

HCE first developed in plantation-era Hawai'i when laborers from China, Puerto Rico, Japan, Korea, and the Philippines, alongside management from the continental U.S. and Europe, came to work in sugar cane and pineapple fields, where an indigenous culture already existed. The gathering of laborers from a variety of cultural and linguistic backgrounds was strategic, as plantation owners believed that culturally and linguistically segregating workers would increase productivity through competition. These groups worked and lived in close proximity, developing a culture and a system of communication from their various root languages that came to be known as "pidgin" in Hawai'i (though HCE is not a pidgin language as the term is used by linguists). HCE, then, is a remix language drawing on vocabulary, syntax, pronunciation, idioms, speech rhythms, and other elements from home languages. For instance, words commonly used by HCE speakers of diverse ethnicities are sometimes borrowed from specific languages—for instance, *haole*, *kapakahi*, *ono*, *high makamaka*, *holoholo*, *bachi* (Hawaiian and Japanese). HCE pronunciation is often rooted in the pronunciation of immigrants, for example, *da* (the), *kine* (kind), *Podagee* (Portuguese). In creating this remix language, speakers took part in strategic cultural authorship, constructing new practices from pre-existing languages.

While HCE effectively facilitated communication across people of diverse linguistic backgrounds, this remix language has also been used to divide and control. Lisa Kanae (2001) explained that "plantation 'masters' used [HCE] to create class stratification between 'master' and 'servant' laborer... by keeping the laborer ignorant of the 'master's' ruling class language." Perceptions of

HCE were later shaped by local education system policies, which led to HCE being "perceived as a corrupt form of Standard English... used as a marker of race and class and proof of the unassimilability of Asians into American life" (Young, 2002, p. 424). HCE has historically been "associated with low academic achievement and low socioeconomic status" (Kanae qtd. in Sato, 2001):

> Dey say if you talk Pidgin you no can... / communicate / eat at fine dining restaurants / enter a beauty pageant (and win) / flirt / function / go out tonight / go to job interviews / go mainland / go mainland school / go opera or someplace elegant / go forward. (Tonouchi, 2004, p. 78)

This history points to the significance of literacy and access in discussions of remix culture.

In 1999, Da Pidgin Coup, a collective of community members and faculty and graduate students from the Departments of Second Language Studies, Linguistics, and English at the University of Hawai'i, expressed concerns that when children enter schools with HCE as their first language, and when that language is dismissed as "broken" or unintelligent, this disrupts the learning process as children "withdraw and choose not to speak and participate in class rather than risk saying something 'wrong,'" and they "develop negative academic self-concepts labeling themselves as 'bad students' and behave accordingly." Such concerns sound akin to Lawrence Lessig's (2004) and other proponents for digital remix culture's concerns for "our youth"; remix is, in both situations, attached to political and ethical implications for people—particularly young people—who adopt it as their own.

The inscription of HCE in material artifacts, as with other forms of remix, played a key role in legitimating historically marginalized identities. For instance, local author Lois-Ann Yamanaka has on more than one occasion quoted Darrell Lum, who "'always says that until you see yourself in print, you don't really exist'" (Coleman, 1999, p. 6). That is, when authors began writing in HCE in Local literature, Local people were finally able to identify with literature in a way that was never possible before. In this way, HCE has been used for purposes of resistance—first in the plantation setting, and as an ongoing protest to the implementation of standard English as the "official" language of the State—and played an important role in overturning stereotypes. This function of HCE relates to the notion of remix as shared identity and cultural survivance. By *survivance*, we mean acts of survival and resistance (Powell, 2002; Vizenor, 1998, 1999), such as the persistence of Local language use and identity (rather than a return to "authentic" identity).

Despite these attributes of HCE in particular and remix more generally, we are remiss if we celebrate them without attending to some of their inherent problems. The scholarship on settler colonialism problematizes the characterization of HCE as "authentically" Local, arguing that readers are given a false sense of authenticity through nonnative writers' reverence for Local culture, which often fails to distinguish between indigenous and non-indigenous (Fujikane, 2008; ho'omanawanui, 2008; Trask, 1999). According to Candace Fujikane (2008)

> literature focusing on the immigrant experience ignores... that such texts are symbolic of the erasure of a Native Hawaiian presence in settler literature [which] enacts a depopulation that renders Hawai'i an "emptied" space open to settler claims of "belonging." (qtd. in Luangphinith, 2006, p. 55)

Correspondingly, Haunani-Kay Trask (1995) argued that this creates "a false nostalgia... A celebration of Pidgin English becomes a gloss for the absence of authentic [Hawaiian] sounds and authentic voices" (p. 170). Thus, while remix is often celebrated as encouraging greater creativity (Lessig, 2004), HCE's erasure of Hawaiian shows that remix can cover over important traditions. In fact, Lee Tonouchi (2009) discussed how HCE draws from Hawaiian more than English, citing Kimura's (1983) "Language Section of Native Hawaiian Study Commission Report." According to the report, HCE is greatly influenced by Hawaiian "grammar, intonation, stress, and vocabulary" and is more accurately characterized as "broken Hawaiian" than "broken English." From this perspective, even the popular history of HCE covers over indigenous contributions, neglecting to attribute to Hawaiians their immense contribution to a language that is a source of such pride in the islands and viewed as central to Local culture and identity.

To address the risk of remix covering over other cultures, we need to identify who the cultural authors are and who/what is being remixed, and we should locate the remix within larger patterns of cultural appropriation and/or erasure. ho'omanawanui (2008) argued that the inclusion of Hawaiian literature as part of Local Hawai'i literature covers over the "centuries-long Native literary tradition" (Fujikane, 2008). Furthermore, she argued that this has consequences for how Hawaiʻi is represented. For instance, "there is a distinction between representations of *ʻāina* in Kanaka Maoli [Hawaiian] literature and Asian and other settler or 'local' literature" that results from their use of HCE and Hawaiian respectively (ho'omanawanui in Fujikane, 2008). When Hawaiian language is subsumed under HCE and Hawaiian literature under Local literature, the representations of Hawaiʻi created by Hawaiians are also covered over. As kuʻualoha ho'omanawanui said,

> the inclusion of Kanaka Maoli literature under the generic term 'local' is problematic because there are political tensions between Kanaka Maoli and non-Natives, the consequence of the inability of haole and Asian settlers to understand that Kanaka Maoli have a different relationship to Hawaiʻi. (Fujikane, 2008)

Likewise, the covering over of Hawaiian language by HCE can also be said to cover over the significant distinctions between Local and Hawaiian.

ho'omanawanui (2008) also discussed the cultural misappropriations and epistemological inconsistencies that arise when certain terms—for instance, *'āina*, *mo'okū'auhau*, or *'ohana*—are translated from Hawaiian to HCE. For example, *hapa*, a Hawaiian word meaning half-Hawaiian, half-Caucasian, has been appropriated by the Asian American community to describe a person who is half-Asian and half-Caucasian. This use is now popular in both Hawai'i and the continental United States, and "many Native Hawaiian people object... to how it ["*hapa*"] is applied to anyone of mixed Asian and or Pacific Islander heritage, when it implies Native Hawaiian mixed heritage" in the original Hawaiian context (Dariotis, 2007). Wei Ming Dariotis stated many people with whom she interacted assumed *hapa* was Japanese in origin. Although she focuses on the use of *hapa* in the continental U.S., the shift in how the word is used stems from an HCE definition that covers over Hawaiian. As result, the original meaning of *hapa* and its link to Hawaiian language is all but erased.

The supplanting of Hawaiian language by HCE is not an isolated phenomenon, but works hand in hand with other "Local"—especially Local Asian—cooptation of Hawai'i, with consequences for Hawaiian self-determination. Fujikane argued that although Asian political and economic "successes" in Hawai'i have been represented as evidence of Hawai'i's exceptionalism as a multicultural state, this history glosses over Hawaiian efforts to regain independence from a colonial power. As Fujikane and Jonathan Okamura (2008) have shown, Asian settler colonialism via language and information design has had consequences for not just intellectual property, but physical property (i.e., land) as well, as Local culture has supplanted Hawaiian concerns. They recount that

> in the struggle to make the Ethnic Studies Program permanent on the University of Hawai'i campus, for example, different ethnic groups employed a terra nullius argument of land in Hawai'i being 'empty' or 'belonging to no one,' erasing Native peoples and places in order to celebrate their role in the "building" of the settler colony. A 1976 poster announcing an Ethnic Studies Program rally reads, "We working people of Hawai'i cultivate the land and harvest the sea. We build every home, harbor, airport and industry. Through the centuries we've fought loss of lands, evictions, low pay, unemployment, and unsafe working conditions. Yes, we working people struggled for and built Hawaii!" (p. 2)

This example illustrates not only how land is implicated in discussions of cultural mixing, but also how Hawaiian models of ownership and property are another kind of cultural knowledge that has been overrun by capitalist models. The scholarship on settler colonialism shows that we must recognize that there are material consequences to language use and cultural borrowing, suggesting that discussions of remix should attend to issues of cultural appropriation and erasure, both in the ideological and material sense. Remix is not only about intellectual property as an abstraction, but the material consequences of these abstractions. Through this discussion of Asian settler colonialism in Hawai'i via HCE, we raise the following questions: How might remix gloss over the efforts and mask concerns of marginalized peoples in other contexts? Does our overwhelmingly positive celebration of remix do similar things? If so, what is being masked?

Case 2: Corporate Tourism in Hawai'i and Cultural Appropriation

> Just five hours away by plane from California, Hawai'i is a thousand light years away in fantasy. Mostly a state of mind, Hawai'i is the image of escape from the rawness and violence of daily American life. Hawai'i–the word, the vision, the sound in the mind–is the fragrance and feel of soft kindness. (Trask, 1999, p. 136)

In this section, we examine how the Hawaii Tourism Authority (HTA) "remixes" Hawaiian culture through a rhetorical analysis of gohawaii.com, Hawaii's official tourism web site. In our analysis, we examine how, through "remixes" of Hawaiian land, bodies, language, and imagery, Hawaiian culture is appropriated to support the state, an especially problematic practice in light of the history of Hawaiian efforts to restore independence from the U.S. We then examine how HTA's representation of Hawai'i has been critiqued via remix in Sean Connelly's (2009) "In-between Paradise: Alternative Postcards—Views from Waikīkī, Ignored," thinking about how remix also speaks back to cultural appropriation.

Scholars like Edward Bruner (1991) have framed tourism as a neocolonial enterprise, a moment of contact between dominant and other, offering "authentic" experience for economic capital—an "authentic" experience that has been purposefully and rhetorically constructed for the tourist. Often, these experiential constructions are built from a "remixing" of indigenous and local cultures. In the case of gohawaii.com, the site remixes images of Hawaiian land, culture, bodies, and language to sell the idea of "legendary Hawai'i—a space constructed primarily for non-Hawaiians and especially Americans, to experience Hawai'i as exotic and primitive while beautiful and welcoming" (Bacchilega, 2007, p. 61).

Visually, images of Hawaiian land are featured throughout gohawaii.com. With its warm brown, greens, and blues, reminiscent of nature, clear skies, lush greenery, and the ocean, the main images on the home page show gorgeous landscapes and exciting activities available for tourists to experience across the islands: a small group of people horseback riding along a mountainside to Kalaupapa; a woman and couple kayaking across a clear blue ocean in Hulope Bay; a couple watching fiery red lava run down a volcano into the ocean from an intimate boat; people canoeing and surfing in Waikīkī, iconic Diamond Head in the background. Each of these images features activities deeply tied to land, activities through which one might not only come "closer to nature," but perhaps even conquer nature. Moreover, there is little that might remind one of urban life, inflecting a sense of "Hawaii" as primitive. The main images, along with a weather widget on the right panel, provide a reminder of Hawai'i's warm, balmy weather. Through these visual and textual representations, gohawaii.com remixes Hawaiian land so that tourists may experience "legendary Hawai'i," a place where there's "not a problem in the world." Below the main images reads: "The fresh, floral air energizes you. The warm, tranquil waters refresh you. The breathtaking, natural beauty renews you. Look around. There's no place on earth like Hawaii." Both this text and the imagery used on gohawaii.com reduce the lives and concerns of the people who actually live and work in Hawai'i to being at the service of the tourist. Although HTA may not necessarily be required to pay for the copyright-protected use of the images of land, land has cultural and political significance; portrayals of Hawai'i as primitive have the potential to affect the way people from Hawai'i are viewed by people outside of Hawai'i, and open invitations for outsiders to "consume" Hawai'i. Land is not typically perceived as cultural within EuroAmerican views, and images and experiences of land are often regarded as free for the taking, for both personal and commercial use.

If we scroll down, we find two smaller images of hula dancers in bright floral dresses. The visitor captures a glimpse of "authentic hula throughout the islands at seasonal festivals and competitions as well as live performances at hotels and resorts." In case merely consuming the Other visually does not suffice, the web site offers information on how the visitor might come to "own" a piece of hula via embodied practice: "Visitors can get a free lesson at places like the Royal Hawaiian Center or the Waikiki Beach Walk on O'ahu. Some luau shows even let you take the stage to show off your new hula skills." Missing from these pictures and descriptions is a historical account of the systematic banning of hula, a form of history that Hawaiians practiced to ensure that younger generations would be able to recall and relay past events. Visitors are not told that as missionaries exerted control over Hawaiians and decimated the population with disease, the language and songs dwindled, and histories became myth and legend. Even as HVCB and HTA offer tourists an opportunity to experience "authentic" hula, the history of the hula as a primary means of communicating and of conveying history is lost, as the notion of hula-as-history does not exist beyond the islands, where it is seen as little more than a sexualized, exoticized novelty for tourists to consume and perform.

Titling below the main images reads, "the people of Hawaii would like to share their islands with you," a sign of the friendly locals who graciously welcome visitors to their lovely islands. This rhetoric of hospitality and the oft-cited "aloha spirit" is pervasive in tourism media in Hawai'i and other parts of the Pacific. As Paul Lyons (2005) explained, hospitality is one of the "aspects of Oceania most attractive to tourists" (p. 123). Below the titling reads

> whether you're a new visitor or returning, our six unique islands offer distinct experiences that will entice any traveler. We warmly invite you to explore our islands and discover your ideal travel experience.

Yet who this "we" refers to is ambiguous. Would potential visitors imagine the staff of the HTA in their business attire awaiting them with fragrant leis as they deplane in Honolulu? More likely, the "we" refers to "the people of Hawaii," whose bodies are appropriated for mass consumption.

We also find a superficial nod to the Hawaiian language via the use of *aloha*, alongside "exotic"-sounding place names in main image captions—Kalaupapa, Hulope Bay, Waikiki—even while much of the web site largely neglects the Hawaiian language. For instance, there is no use of Hawaiian diacritical marks, and HTA directly addresses this issue in the footer of the HTA (2013) web site (hawaiitourismauthority.org): "these diacritical markings have been omitted throughout the website to ensure the best online experience *for our visitors*" [emphasis ours]. They continue, "HawaiiTourismAuthority.org recognizes the importance of using these markings to preserve the language and culture of Hawaii and respectfully uses them in all communications beyond the online platform"—in other words, in all communications except for what is likely a significant form of advertisement with a global reach. This treatment of language speaks to Trask's statement that "tourists flock to my Native land for escape, but they are escaping into a state of mind while participating in the destruction of a host people in a Native place" (Trask, 1999, p. 137).

Beneath the tab "About Hawaii" is the text: "*Discover* Hawaii," and visitors may sign into "*My* Hawaii" [emphasis ours], an online planner that allows site users to "save all [their] vacation ideas." This language conceptually positions Hawai'i—its land, its culture, and the bodies in it—as something that individual tourists can own. In Trask's (1999) interpretation, "to most Americans... Hawai'i is theirs: to use, to take, and, above all, to fantasize about long after the experience" (p. 136). Through "My Hawaii," corporate tourism uses language to take ownership of the intellectual property—the identities and ideas—of the Other so that it can be sold for further consumption by the tourist.

Remixed representations of Hawaiian culture through a limited and reductive image of "legendary Hawai'i" have significant ideological and material consequences for the people who live and work there, as it masks complex problems ongoing in the state. As Bruner (1989) noted, "tourism prefers the reconstructed object, and indeed, this preference for the simulacrum is the essence of postmodern tourism, where the copy is more than the original" (p.

438), pointing to the ideological colonial process by which native cultures and concerns are covered over by the tourism industry. Remix as cultural appropriation, in this case, masks such issues as the rising cost of land and housing, low wages, a recent rise in crime, lack of sustainable resources, and a homelessness epidemic, not to mention the denigration of Hawaiian culture.

Political and social implications accompany not only reductive representations of Hawai'i via corporate tourism marketing, but also an over reliance on the tourism industry as the state's economic backbone. Organizations like HVCB and HTA have pushed tourism to the fore of Hawai'i's economy, persuading Locals that tourism is an essential industry despite its repercussions on residents. As a result, the state is victim to fluctuations in the tourist market and therefore especially vulnerable to outside markets. In addition, the over emphasis on tourism detracts from the problems many Locals face on a daily basis (i.e. the high cost of living, education for their children), and takes capital away from Local concerns, as much of the state's budget goes into projects like the recently developed Waikīkī Beach Walk rather than, say, the local school system.

More significantly, Hawaiians are placed in a particularly compromised position, as their culture is appropriated for a structure that keeps them subjugated (Trask, 1999). Representations of Hawai'i and Hawaiians do little to benefit Hawaiians, yet there are no structures in place to protect Hawaiian ownership of cultural practices and imagery. Through this case, it is clear that the act of remix can be reductive and problematic when not conducted carefully, respectfully, and responsibly. In the case of corporate tourism via gohawaii.com, for example, we need to ask who is doing the remixing, what is being remixed, for what purpose, and for what audience. Purpose is a key category in copyright law as well as in Creative Commons in terms of commercial and educational use respectively, but the analysis here shows that we need to additionally account for the ideological effects on those whose culture is being remixed.

Yet, in some instances, remix has been used for what Malea Powell (2002) has called a rhetoric of survivance (survival + resistance). We understand survivance as acts that undo the systemic structure that upholds oppressive institutions by enabling what Powell refers to as the absent presence—the presence that has been overwritten as nonexistent by neocolonial institutions like the HTA. We explore remix as an act of survivance: a means of using images and language to explore alternative vantages and shift gazes as a means of survival and resistance, bringing into view presences and histories that have been erased and/or hidden as part of colonial processes that have literally eroded Hawai'i's natural geography for the sake of tourism.

Connelly's (2009) alternative postcards featured in "In-between Paradise: Alternative Postcard Views of Waikīkī, Ignored" point to a problematic institutional presence (the corporate tourism industry), on the land upon which Waikīkī and its hotels sit. Connelly visually remixes the imagery that often appears in corporate tourism marketing by redirecting the gaze of the viewer away from the lush, tropical imagery to the presence of hotels and overdevelopment in Waikīkīland on land once used for sustainable Hawaiian agricultural practices. By remixing these images, Connelly argues for "a more nuanced way of seeing Hawai'i," which, he said, "will, hopefully, promote an awareness of the ignored conditions that fall in-between those that are more popularly acknowledged"—bringing into view the hidden, absent presence of a geography and landscape that will never return to its former state.

One of Connelly's postcards remixes the iconic image of Diamond Head crater, most often photographed from a vantage that disguises the jagged skyline of hotels, condos, and luxury resorts that make it nearly impossible to actually view the geographical landmark from Waikīkī. The warm, saturated colors of typical postcards depict a pristine Waikīkī fronting a serene ocean, framed by coconut fronds and cast in the pink and purple hues of sunset. The postcards invite viewers to partake in the consumption of a spectacularly beautiful location and culture and beckons tourists to participate in the ideological making of "legendary Hawai'i," as it takes part in the "simultaneous and mutually informing production and consumption of the exotic and erotic Other" in tourism (Aitchison, 2001, p. 134)—a site that appears temporally and geographically frozen in time. Hidden from view is a "beach that has been modified extensively" (Wiegel, 2008, p. 3) —that is, the geographical characteristics of the beach are largely artificial and have been cosmetically enhanced to meet the desires of tourists. Waikīkī is largely a cultural construction that has become a geographical reality and did not exist just a century ago (Wiegel). Connelly's remix of the postcard genre points to the absence of this geography, which has been erased by various commercial and cultural processes, in making explicit the practices that have (problematically) shaped Waikīkī and Diamond Head. The remixed postcard frames a view of Leahi (the Hawaiian name for Diamond Head) from a vantage much more familiar to O'ahu residents; it emphasizes the proliferation of high rises that front the shoreline of the south coast of O'ahu. Remixing a genre that is used primarily by the tourism industry addresses the erasure that has taken place as part of colonial processes in Hawai'i, and functions as an act of survivance by altering the function of the postcard from a mode of erasure and silencing to a mode of discussion and critique. Connelly's images represent a remixed genre and treatment of history and geography that is both *responsible* and *respectful* in that Hawai'i's geographies, histories, and people are not erased from the scene, but brought into it as active, agentive participants.

Discussion

The two cases presented in this chapter offer a multifaceted look at culture, remix, and copyright. Case 1 highlights some of the positive outcomes of an open culture approach, including the potential for facilitating communication across cultural and language barriers, and the emergence of a new, dynamic, multi-layered local culture. At the same time, settler colonialism makes visible how HCE is itself a colonial language that has largely displaced Hawaiian. Case 2 adds to this complex depiction of remix as it presents ethical issues that result from cultural remix via the HTA website, particularly as one set of stakeholders profits at the expense of the Other. This analysis is contrasted with an example that shows how remixes of the Hawai'i postcard genre and imagery of legendary Hawai'i can begin to undo the damage of cultural appropriation by making the hidden acts of erasure in appropriation explicit for dialogue and discussion. Moreover, while the case of HCE begins to unravel the complex web of relations that exists in instances of cultural borrowing, the case of the HTA website shows how this web can be reduced to a binary relationship between tourist and local, or colonizer and colonized, wherein "tourist" and "local" are each cast in a singular light. In other words, the site does not take into account the varied groups of people impacted by tourism or their overlapping, conflicting, and diverse concerns. Finally, our discussion of these cases, together, draw on the cultural mixing that is part of Hawai'i's past and present to provide valuable lessons on what paying attention to culture can help us understand about copyright, remix, and intellectual property. Based on the cases presented in this chapter alongside the scholarship on intellectual property and culture discussed above, we present a set of practices that we refer to as a reflexive approach to remix:

Learn about and respect the cultural values, practices, and epistemologies of those from whose cultures you draw—on their own terms. At the same time, recognize your own position—do not forget that you are learning about these cultures as an outsider, and that learning about them does not change that. While culture is always implicated in any discussion of copyright, the epistemological consequences of privileging certain types of intellectual work are often not considered. Boateng's (2011) discussion of intellectual property in Ghana, for example, makes clear that intellectual property law is insufficient as it protects only individual creators and is irrelevant to the ubiquitous "cultural flows" that Bhabha (1994), Lowe (1996), Mignolo (2003) and Thomas (1991, 1997) describe.

Engage in open communication and transparency when drawing from other cultures. Be transparent about how you are using Others' culture, as well as the purpose of your remix and the benefit to all parties that may come from it. When we do not attend to diverse epistemologies that exist across cultures, it becomes dangerous to freely "borrow" and remix according to our own systems of knowledge production. For this reason, some of the copyright literature has critiqued the celebration of the cultural commons, or the open sharing of cultural knowledge and artifacts, especially for the purpose of creative development—a position implied by HTA's representation of Hawai'i and its appropriation of Hawaiian culture. For instance, Brown (2003) argued, "From an indigenous rights perspective, the public domain is the problem, not the solution, because it defines traditional knowledge as a freely available resource" (p. 237). There is a problem in the assumption that "culture wants to be free" (Lessig, 2004). Christen (2005) argued that while the commons is often celebrated for promoting creativity and its capacity to produce "knowledge, innovative ideas, and democratic disobedience" (p. 332), such perspectives ignore "the multiple disparities between those assumed to make up the commons" (p. 334). She continued:

> Calling for a commons where culture is generalized around first-world notions of public/private accountability denies the multiplicity of both the objects/ideas under culture's umbrella and the social modalities in which they circulate. Empowering local communities to invigorate their own Maoli literature under the generic term local information regimes means recognizing that information, in fact, does not want to be free. (p. 336)

Thus, although "creative commons" may work to an extent in the narrow context of the contemporary, capitalist, European American, middle-class West, this context does not exist in a vacuum, nor are there clear boundaries separating this context from other cultural values and practices. The examples presented above show how there exists knowledges and practices that should be approached with care, and an effective approach is one of open communication and transparency when borrowing from Other cultures.

Examine access from multiple vantage points. Do those from whose cultures you draw benefit from remixes of their culture? Do audiences of your remix have access to the context from which you are borrowing? The implications of remix across cultural lines are mired in issues of access. For example, Brown (2003) explained, "the economic injustice associated with the imitation of indigenous music and art" is not the result of cultural borrowing, but of the "appropriators' social capital" that "leaves them better positioned than their indigenous counterparts to reap financial reward" (p. 236). As we argued above, many Hawaiians do not have access to the benefits of corporate tourism. Instead, corporate tourism appears to be more interested in how it can use Hawaiian culture and Hawaiian bodies to provide particular experiences benefitting visitors, so that corporations in the tourism industry may reap its economic benefits. Furthermore, the gohawaii.com website does not provide its audience access to a more complex understanding of Hawai'i or Hawaiian concerns. The site does not provide links, for example, that might provide a fuller account of Hawai'i's history of colonization, or to the sites of nonprofit organizations that might help educate visitors about the lives of people in Hawai'i. As Christen (2005) put it, "the cultural commons solution buys into a mutated colonial logic that once produced the museum of mankind ideal of cultural collection; innovation and preservation for some, erasure for others" (pp. 333–334). This observation is applicable to HTA's use of Hawaiian culture on gohawaii.com, and its "free for the taking" logic toward cultural knowledge, much akin to the frontier metaphor.

Be cautious about taking cultural practices and artifacts out of context. Understand that when cultural practices and artifacts are taken out of context, erasure inevitably takes place. Be cognizant of what's being left out. In certain ways, remix can be compared to cultural tourism in that it draws from local and indigenous cultures in often decontextualized ways (Bruner, 1989); such acts make possible the appropriation of cultures without a process of learning about larger cultural contexts, histories, and political conditions. Even while appropriators may be aware that there is a context from which they are drawing, those who access the culture only through the remix may have difficulty accessing the original context from which the remix was "borrowed." As Bruner (1989) noted, this phenomenon is particularly common in photographic images wherein the

> major sensory mode for the perception of the native other is... through the viewfinder of a camera. Such a perspective isolates the native people from their larger social context, in that everything outside the frame of the viewfinder is removed from view, including the politics of the situation. (p. 441)

Acknowledge that culture is shifting and complex–that cultural artifacts and embodied identities are grounded in histories, and that decisions and acts that take place now impact the status of people in the future. Acknowledging the shifting and complex nature of cultural identity is an important step in a reflexive approach to remix. Our discussion of the scholarship on hybridity, above, illustrates this complexity. As Lowe (1996) explained, cultural identity,

> is a matter of "becoming" as well as of "being." It belongs to the future as much as to the past. It is not something which already exists, transcending place, time, history and culture... they are subject to the continuous "play" of history, culture, and power. (p. 64)

In many ways, this understanding of cultural identity is comparable to creative process, particularly from the lens of remix. Although we focus on two cases—HCE and corporate tourism—in Hawai'i specifically, this view of cultural identity as a process that is constantly in flux and unfolding across time and place is useful in understanding remix in other contexts; see, for example, Tasaka's 2009 discussion of "Hawai'i clubs," interest-based clubs on academic campuses that focus on perpetuating Hawai'i culture and remixing it for a continental audience. Although the web site of these clubs can engage in problematic cultural appropriation and can also constitute acts of colonial violence, they are mediated by subjects who hold different stakes in the preservation of Hawai'i's cultural and geographical attributes, and may just as well generate useful cultural critique and foster potentially beneficial collaborative relationships.

Use remix as a starting point for future discussions that highlight the concerns of the cultures from which you draw. As seen in our analysis of Connelly's postcards, acts of remix should be presented as starting points for discussions that may have ramifications beyond issues of ownership; when access to culture is negotiated with an understanding that remix can cause harm, the trauma of past colonial damage can be addressed and acted upon. This step should go hand in hand with open communication and transparency, as an understanding of Others' cultures should be based on communication—on talking with people who identify with those cultures. Because people who identify with those cultures are themselves diverse with varied experiences and concerns, it is important to be deliberate when making decisions of who and how many people we communicate with. When used responsibly for facilitating and encouraging dialogue among past producers and current users, remix offers a means for productive cultural mixing. Such an approach creates possibilities for shared identity and cultural survivance, while reducing the likelihood that cultural appropriation and ideological and/or colonial violence will result.

The cases presented above, together, offer insights about the complex, gradient relationship between cultural borrowing and appropriation: As Christen (2005) pointed out, rather than approach cultural sharing and appropriation as a binary, it can be more productive to acknowledge that acts occur along a continuum that is mediated by "material and social networks" (p. 336). Furthermore, we must ask who has access to and who constitutes these networks, rather than assume that such networks are readily accessible to all stakeholders. Remix facilitates and encourages relationships formed and maintained by acts of borrowing and the dialogue that those acts produce. Because attention to relationships is key to the indigenous epistemologies that we bring into our approach to intellectual property, we argue for the necessity of this attentiveness to any act of cultural and intellectual borrowing. When approached in this way, acts of borrowing can create and fortify relationships. The relationships formed around acts of borrowing should be characterized by respect for cultural values and practices as well as by transparency, with the understanding that remix can also cause harm to cultures and people.

Finally, cultural borrowing and remixing are themselves romanticized notions; in many indigenous knowledge networks, "past producers must be acknowledged and accounted for" (Christen 2005, p. 333). In systems of Western thinking, this is not always the case, and, in virtual spaces, relational accountability becomes a challenge. When not consciously enacted into remix activities, it is easy to neglect to account for past producers, and when we erase the ideological and material conditions of decontexualized Others, we contribute to even more systemic violence. Remix necessitates care, education, and cultural sensitivity from all parties. Only then can it function as a means of undoing cultural erasure.

• CHAPTER SEVENTEEN •

Authorship Abroad: Considering Copyright Across Cultures

Angela M. Shetler

With writing, we are taught—and we teach others—to adapt writing styles according to audience, purpose, use, and context. That same kind of careful consideration needs to happen when working in a culture with differing notions of intellectual property. Something as seemingly simple as word choice can obscure the role of the author in favor of the role of the producer, and thus accommodate group society norms. It can be careful documentation and attribution of sources to protect oneself against plagiarism or copyright infringement. It can even be informed violation of copyright laws to create a visually rhetorical argument against those very laws. Understanding how various cultures perceive authorship and copyright is essential for protecting the creative process and final work, both inside and outside the classroom. It is imperative that humanities disciplines be aware of basic IP laws and the relation to cultural contexts and values beyond the U.S. copyright paradigm.

This short chapter is a reflection on my personal experiences with copyright and authorship in education in three countries: the United States, Japan, and Australia. In this narrative, I reflect on my learning and teaching experiences with international and cross-cultural communication to support the need for academic experiences to include a basic understanding of copyright issues. I focus on the idea of "property" from cultural perspectives of authorship, particularly in regard to remix, fair use, and plagiarism. Through this personal reflection, I show how IP perspectives vary depending on a country's cultural values, and how an understanding of those values is crucial to understanding rights of authorship and successfully navigating cross-cultural situations in communication, whether as students, teachers, or professionals.

I use "culture" in three ways that correlate to intellectual property and copyright law. The first use is in the sense of workplace culture, or "the set of shared attitudes, values, goals, and practices that characterizes an institution or organization" (*Merriam-Webster*, 2012), specifically that of academia. The second use is related to the country in which a work is produced, and thus is defined as "that complex whole which includes knowledge, belief, art, morals, law, custom and other capabilities and habits acquired by man as a member of a society" (Bowe & Martin, 2009, p. 2). The third use is that of remix culture, as framed by Lawrence Lessig (2008) to describe a societal value in the creation and distribution of derivative works. My experiences with IP laws interweave these definitions in considering copyright across cultures and the ways in which creativity and authorship are situated in the cultures in which it is produced. To conclude, I postulate how cultural perspectives of IP may be altered or challenged in the near future given the political climate around U.S. legislation and multi-nation trade agreements, which have international ramifications on copyright regardless of differing cultural contexts and values.

Copyright in the United States

During my time as an undergraduate student at Michigan State University, I heard the words "copyright," "fair use," and "authorship" on a regular basis. At the time, my knowledge of copyright was topical at best, and it was this limited understanding that influenced the work I produced in my courses. To show how my experience with the doctrine of Fair Use evolved over time, let us go back in time to 2004 when I decided to design a remix web site for a class presentation.

The assignment was fairly straightforward: Each student was assigned a particular section or set of rules in Anthony Weston's *A Rulebook for Arguments* to present to the class. I knew that I wanted to do something other than a slideshow presentation or a handout. The previous semester, I had begun learning basic web design and I was eager to put what I knew into practice. Thus I designed a simple web site consisting of four webpages: the homepage, relevant quotes from the text, select rules from the text, and discussion questions. I wanted the site to serve as a new form of presentation, but I also wanted to create something that would be accessible to my classmates afterwards. In the process of constructing the site, I made the conscious design decision to imitate the design of the book itself. I chose a web font that was similar to the title font, and I chose a color scheme similar to that used in the cover design. I also found an image of the book cover online and manipulated it in a graphic-design application through the use of the crop tool, filters, and layers to create a new, remixed image that I added to the home page for visual effect.

Throughout the creation process, I operated under the assumption that whatever work I produced in the classroom as a student was covered under Fair

Use. The web site was for educational purposes, and I did not see my act of remix or use of text to be a violation of copyright. Instead, I regarded it as a creative approach to an otherwise standard presentation assignment. However, the web site didn't stay in the educational sphere. Prior to graduation, I designed the first of many iterations of my digital portfolio. In it, I included synopses and links to student work that represented my skills and abilities to potential employers. One of these works was the Weston web site.

To frame the work for use in my digital portfolio, I wrote a brief explanation of the purpose of the web site and the design choices I had made. This explanation existed solely on my portfolio web site with a link to the Weston presentation site, all of which was initially hosted on my allotted university server space. I didn't think about whether or not this was "allowed" or "okay"; I was still a student, and even after I graduated, this was student work created for educational purposes. It wasn't until 3 years later that I considered the work in relation to copyright law, and then only because of an email from someone I had never met: a professor at the university where I had created the work.

The email was sent to my university email address and began without a greeting. The professor informed me that she had come across the site and that my use of material from Weston's text was copyright infringement because it lacked attribution. I was advised to remove the site immediately and to ask the university's technology services to remove it if I no longer had access to the hosting space. The email concluded with the note that the professor would "check back later in the week to see whether the site has been removed before reporting it to anyone official" (Shetler, personal communication, November 24, 2008). Along with this, the professor explained why she was concerned with my use of the material on my site:

> My interest in the matter is that I often assign the book. When my students search the Web to find cheap copies and see your site, they may mistakenly think you provide them with all they need to know—which is misleading. A new edition will be published before next semester begins, causing an additional problem for students who mistake your site for the real thing. (Shetler, personal communication, November 24, 2008)

This email raised a lot of questions for me: Was my site really in violation of copyright? Did this professor have any rights to assert copyright infringement on behalf of Weston? What steps did I need to take to keep it active as a portfolio piece? I turned to Martine Courant Rife for advice, acknowledging in my email that I had created the Weston site before I knew much about copyright, and thus it never occurred to me as being anything other than for educational purposes. She agreed that it was important to provide context and references within the site itself instead of relying on my portfolio site. I moved all the content off the university space and on to my own hosting service. I changed the attributions across the site to ensure consistency; altered the image text to include the assignment, course, and date; and created an "about" page to provide context for the site. After this was finished, I responded to the professor's email and thanked her for bringing the matter to my attention as it allowed me to revisit my work. I explained what changes I had made to provide purpose and context for the shift in audience, and I also reiterated that the work was protected under the Fair Use clause of U.S. Copyright Law. This latter statement included a link to the clause in the event the professor wanted to refer to it. The professor responded by thanking me for removing the site from university space and assuring me that her tone was not meant to imply policing of the web. The email concluded:

> I read the section of the copyright law you sent by url, but I see nothing exculpatory in it. If the only salient issue were "educational purposes" there would be no publishers of textbooks, for we'd all be happy to make material freely available to our students. I didn't want to see my university implicated in copyright infringement, and especially not with a publisher I respect, Hackett, and an author I admire, Weston. You may not know that when an author signs over copyright in her/his contract, the publisher assumes *responsibility* for pursuing copyright infringements. (Shetler, personal communication, November 26, 2008)

This was the last correspondence on the matter, and the site in question no longer serves as a portfolio piece given its creation date. But this experience serves as an excellent example of why it is necessary for students and educators across disciplines to understand the basics of copyright law. For students, copyright knowledge provides context for the work they produce while in university and how that work is presented to the public. It also serves as a reminder of how copyright considerations change as the status of the creator changes; educating students about the contexts in which fair use applies will prepare them for dealing with copyright outside of academia, as well as how to situate their work in terms of remix culture. What is acceptable in the culture of academia may not carry over to the culture of the workplace, from the way work is produced and how it is published to what is copyrighted and what can be repurposed. For educators, it is vital to be aware of copyright basics in order to assist students with any concerns or questions as well as to be able to recognize appropriate and inappropriate use of materials, whether in the classroom or in the public sphere.

This experience also reflects U.S. cultural values in regards to copyright law and perspectives on authorship. Although copyright law began as a means of encouraging innovation, it has grown into a system that operates in the interest of controlling and enforcing authorship. The U.S. copyright paradigm in particular has a history of being imposed on other countries by being developed into international property rules without regard to cultural differences. As Woodmansee and Jaszi (1994) noted:

> Since it is derived from Western, especially Continental, 'authors' rights' principles, the international copyright regime that governs relations between developed and developing nations inevitably exhibits much the same biases [...] while the traditional, folkloric, and collaborative productions of these countries circulate internationally, becoming subject to appropriation by the culture industries of the developed world. (p. 12)

As I would later learn while working overseas, and as evident in current legislation and international agreements, culture can either be protected or eroded through IP. It is essential to consider cultural contexts in the development of a balanced international copyright paradigm.

Copyright in Japan

In 2008, I left my job in communications to move to Japan. As an English teacher in a public high school in northern Japan, I was immersed in the culture and language. When working in a different culture, there are several issues to consider in regards to authorship and copyright. For me, it was necessary to transition out of the U.S. mindset where importance is placed on the individual, whether on individual talent or individual recognition. The group culture of Japan is evident throughout both personal and public spheres, and it was in the workplace where I learned how this cultural value is reflected in attitudes and behaviors. Instead of approaching a task or project as an individual author, the work took on the context of a contribution to the group. This is different from contributing to a project in the U.S. workplace in that praise or blame is assigned to the entirety of the group, not necessarily the single author or creator. I saw this demonstrated in the classroom as well. It was typically very difficult to get students to raise their hands and participate in a lesson focused on a single contribution. But if the lesson contained an activity where the focus was on teamwork or partner work, students were much more likely to be active. The pressure of being singled out from the group was thus lessened.

For both teachers and students, the importance of acting in collaboration carried over to the creative and decision-making processes. Everyone was allowed to contribute their opinion or idea, but at the same time, opinions or ideas that varied from the group majority were not well received. A strict hierarchal structure distributed power and authority. This brings to mind the Japanese proverb that translates to "the nail that stands up is hammered down." In the interest of keeping the cultural society intact, individuals are encouraged to conform to the group.

These cultural values are reflected in how intellectual property is dealt with in Japan, and the result is a different idea of what constitutes authorship and, subsequently, plagiarism. For students, it was common practice to copy other students' work, or to include word-for-word passages from copyrighted material.

Rather than being seen as an infringement of copyright or an act of stealing, copying in this manner was regarded as a means of paying respect to the work of those who have come before; it was a way of honoring the cultural value of that work. For those interested in Japanese popular culture, this practice is frequently seen in *manga*, the comic book industry of Japan. *Doujinshi* is a form of *manga* appropriation where amateur artists or fans of a particular *manga* will take the original characters and recreate them in their own storylines and illustrations. However, unlike the genre of fan fiction in the U.S., *doujinshi* creators will then display, distribute, and even sell their *manga* at the large conventions (Pink, 2007). As Kouichi Ichikawa, one of the organizers of *doujinshi* gatherings acknowledged, the acceptance of this practice relates to the group culture:

> This is something that satisfies the fans, and that the publishers understand that it does not diminish the sales of the original products, but it may increase them. This is something very Japanese. (qtd. in Pink)

Like with copying in the classroom, *doujinshi* was viewed as paying homage to the artist, and it furthers the value of the cultural property.

In my experience as an undergraduate student in the U.S., I spoke about how my work and my approach to my work were influenced by my understanding of both Fair Use and fair use. Copyright law in Japan does not currently include a fair use provision. While U.S. copyright law protects originality and creativity, Japan's copyright law protects creativity, focusing on the moral rights of the author (Copyright Research and Information Center, 2011). With a culturally rich society that values the group over the individual, copyright law in Japan is structured to balance authors' interests in monetary gain with the public's interests in enjoying the cultural contributions. According to Keiko Tominaga (2009):

> Explaining that copyright is cultural property, Japan has one of the most complete systems for the promotion of culture in the world. General legislation for cultural property, the Fundamental Law for the Promotion of Culture and Arts, was enacted on November 2001 for the purpose of providing a comprehensive mechanism for promoting culture and the arts in Japan. It includes the enhancement of cultural facilities and the protection and use of copyrights. Thus, the aspect of cultural promotion of copyright is ensured not only in the Copyright Act itself, but in General legislation for the promotion of culture.

If Japan were to change its current copyright law to more closely reflect U.S. copyright law, there would be complications in how work and authorship are culturally viewed in Japan, as well as how cases of infringement are handled. Japan's traditional values are deeply rooted in its collaborative culture, and appropriation of those values in the form of an international IP law would be highly problematic.

Copyright in Australia

After teaching in Japan, I transitioned to the role of postgraduate student in Australia. I initially assumed that Australia had similar copyright laws to the U.S. regarding Fair Use for educational purposes. I was surprised to learn that not only is there no Australian equivalent of the U.S. Fair Use provision, but the laws in place are not nearly as extensive. Rather than a general fair use defense, Australian law allows "fair dealing" with copyright material for specific purposes, including research or study. The Australian Copyright Council (2012) identified five factors that are taken into consideration when determining whether or not use is fair in a reproduction:

(1) the purpose and character of the dealing;

(2) the nature of the work;

(3) the possibility of obtaining the work within a reasonable time at an ordinary commercial price;

(4) the effect of the dealing on the potential market for, or value of, the work; and

(5) the amount and substantiality of the part copied in relation to the whole work.

Australia also added moral rights for authors in 2000, which requires attribution for any material copied and does not require copyright ownership for an author to file an infringement claim. My understanding of Australian copyright law in the context of remix culture came about during the creation of my final project for my remixable media postgraduate course. I chose to construct a remix video, and in the process I was required to justify any intentional infringements.

In my *Hermione Granger and the War of the Wizards* remixed trailer, I used re-editing techniques to craft a new narrative where Hermione Granger, who plays a sidekick role in the Harry Potter books and films, is upgraded to heroine status. My goal with this remix was to highlight Hermione's strengths and visually demonstrate how she could have been written as the main character of the series. To do this, I incorporated video and audio clips from all eight *Harry Potter* films to create an authentic-as-possible movie trailer. The remix used both copyright-protected studio trailers and copyright-protected fan videos (even though the fan videos themselves infringed on copyrighted work). The creation and distribution of this remixed trailer was done with conscious copyright infringement in regards to J.K. Rowling, the author of the *Harry Potter* series; Warner Bros., the distributor of the films; and John Williams, the composer and conductor of "Hedwig's Theme." While I would have liked to distribute my remix under a Creative Commons CC BY license, which allows for further remix and reuse with attribution, YouTube only allows this licensing for works consisting entirely of content owned by the uploader, other CC BY licensed videos, or videos in the public domain.

Without a general fair use defense, my remix video could have been challenged as copyright infringement in Australian courts, particularly because current copyright law only considers remix in relation to music, not video. The most I could do to protect myself was to document the creative process, attribute all source materials, and learn about the current legislation. Even in a course about remix culture, the focus was on the history and theory of remix rather than the legal aspects. Thus it is not surprising that the absence of a general fair use provision for educational purposes and a lack of understanding about copyright are keenly felt in the classroom from a teaching perspective as well.

In the writing courses I have taught or tutored, I have found that students are generally unaware of copyright and attribution when it comes to using images in class projects. When students are given an assignment to create a visually rhetorical argument for their essay topic, many do a keyword search on Google Images and choose an image they like. The approach to protecting oneself against plagiarism charges seems to be one of simply including the source URL, and there is little consideration as to whether or not the images are in the public domain or are copyright protected. Rather than remix or repurpose an image that is available for use and then layer it with text or employ editing techniques, students will often find an image that already includes these elements, such as an advertisement, and submit it as their own work. Unlike my undergraduate writing courses where basic copyright knowledge was taught, it seems that these writing students were expected to already know what acceptable use is. The result is a gap in knowledge that affects how students approach written works versus visual works with regard to intellectual property.

As I witnessed first-hand while teaching in Japan, there are culturally diverse ways of thinking about copyright and ownership that diverge from the construct of the solitary author and owner of the work. According to The University of Sydney Strategic Planning Office (2009), international students make up 6% of the undergraduate student body. In multicultural classrooms, varying cultural perspectives of copyright must be addressed to ensure students are not simply appropriating another author's work. The various enactments of culture in Australia must also be taken into account, with regards to a group society, a culturally diverse population, and an indigenous culture. In Australia, "tall poppy" is a pejorative term used to describe individuals whose talents and achievements cause them to stand out from the group. Instead of being celebrated, they are resented or criticized for their success. Thus cultural perspectives on plagiarism may be more closely aligned with other cultures where conformity to the group is valued. The postcolonial social identity must also be considered in regards to how the "other" is viewed, along with how Aboriginal and Torres Strait Islander perspectives on cultural property conflict with Australian copyright law. These all affect how IP is regarded and codified in Australia, and while there have been progressive amendments enacted in the past 12 years, Australia's participation in several trade agreement negotiations has led to an overall weakening of its copyright law.

International Intellectual Property

Cultural IP perspectives will continue to be challenged and may even be altered in the near future given recent developments in both U.S. and international legislation. In the past year, the U.S. government has proposed legislation that endangers innovation and creativity through more restrictive IP law with wider enforcement parameters, including the Stop Online Piracy Act (SOPA, H.R. 3261), Protect Intellectual Property Act (PIPA, S 968), and Cyber Intelligence Sharing and Protection Act of 2011 (CISPA, H.R. 3523). While SOPA and PIPA have been shelved, as of this writing, CISPA is currently still under consideration. These acts are examples of U.S.-based legislation that would have international copyright ramifications, as they propose a tightening of control of borderless digital spaces through U.S. policing of the Internet. There are also international treaties being developed that would impose blanket IP agreements on countries regardless of differing cultural contexts and values.

In late 2011, two separate trade agreements began negotiations on treaties that, if enacted, will change how IP is regarded and enforced internationally. Eight partnering countries, including the U.S., Australia, and Japan, signed the Anti-Counterfeiting Trade Agreement (ACTA) in October 2011. The goal of the plurilateral agreement was to "strengthen the international legal framework for effectively combating global proliferation of commercial-scale counterfeiting and piracy" (Office of the United States Trade Representative). ACTA has been compared to SOPA and PIPA in its lack of transparency and the damaging effects on digital rights, including innovation and IP. Shortly after ACTA was signed, nine countries outlined the Trans-Pacific Partnership (TPP) agreement that would "enhance trade and investment among the TPP partner countries, promote innovation, economic growth and development, and support the creation and retention of jobs" (Office of the United States Trade Representative). The U.S. and Australia are two of the nine partners in this agreement, and Japan has announced its intention to begin consultations towards joining as well.

While it may not be immediately apparent, a partnership agreement such as TPP does have ramifications on copyright. In the framing of the agreement, the partnering countries have included a section on IP in which the partners will "reinforce and develop existing World Trade Organization Agreement on Trade-Related Aspects of Intellectual Property (TRIPS) rights and obligations

> with discussion on many forms of intellectual property, including trademarks, geographical indications, copyright and related rights, patents, trade secrets, data required for the approval of certain regulated products, as well as intellectual property enforcement and genetic resources and traditional knowledge. (Office of the United States Trade Representative)

However, the claim that TPP will develop its IP rules based on TRIPS has been called into question amid a lack of transparency.

In March 2012, the stakeholders in the TPP gathered in Melbourne, Australia, for an eleventh round of negotiations. On the agenda were several speeches dedicated to the issues and concerns raised by a leaked, U.S.-authored intellectual property proposal. David Campbell, president of Pirate Party Australia, stated that

> the US draft intellectual property chapter will only benefit a few companies in the United States and will have a negative impact upon the culture and health of all signatory countries. (Pirate Party Australia, 2012)

Professor Sean Flynn, Associate Director of the Program on Information Justice and Intellectual Property at American University Washington, also spoke, and while his statements are not publicly available, he and his colleagues co-authored an article in December 2011 in response to the TPP intellectual property chapter. In the article, Flynn, Margot Kaminski, Brook Baker, and Jimmy Koo highlighted that

> the U.S. proposals, if adopted, would upset the current international framework balancing the minimum standards for exclusive rights for media and technology owners, on the one hand, and the access rights of the public, competitors, innovators and creators, on the other. (p. 2)

The article also points out that the provisions in the proposed IP chapter are inconsistent with, and in some instances expand on, the current IP laws of the TPP partner countries, including the U.S. Tim Conway (2012), Senior Policy Advisor for the World Information Technology and Services Alliance, echoed these concerns from the viewpoint of the ICT industry over the lack of consultations in the preparatory stage of the TPP, calling for: "an evidentiary basis to the provisions of any agreement that impose greater regulation on any sector... IP rules and regulations must be a global development, not regional or bilateral" (p. 9).

These international trade agreements are not the first instances in which U.S. IP perspectives have been forced upon other countries. After the Australian and United States Free Trade Agreement was enacted in 2004, "critics argued that the U.S. had imposed its copyright rules on Australia; a consistent theme was one of real disquiet at the loss of sovereignty and freedom to determine matters of economic, cultural, and social policy" (Meese, 2010, p. 175). While the Australian government later amended copyright law to lessen the criminalization of some acts set forth in AUSFTA, there is the concern that the trade agreements currently under negotiation would further impose U.S. IP law on Australia and the other partnering countries.

Conclusion

Through my reflection on personal experiences with intellectual property in three diverse countries, I have shown how perspectives toward copyright are rooted in cultural values. Understanding those values is crucial to understanding rights of authorship and being able to successfully navigate international and cross-cultural situations. According to Martine Courant Rife, Steve Westbrook, Dànielle Nicole DeVoss, and John Logie (2010),

> the hybridity that can emerge as cultures rub together in a globalized world is a complex thing. Too often, this cultural convergence results in one culture cannibalizing another—that is, one culture dominating and devouring aspects of the other culture. Rather than true hybridity, one culture is left, in some ways, skeletonized. Intellectual property can, to some extent, protect against such cannibalism; in others ways, however, it contributes to cultural cannibalism. (p. 161)

The lack of cultural understanding in the development of the previously mentioned acts and treaties has led to a fear of this kind of cultural cannibalism as the role of enforcement and legislation is taken on unilaterally by a dominant country rather than considering differing cultural contexts and values in a balanced, international approach. As Carys Craig (2011) noted, "The author is socially situated and necessarily dependent upon the texts, languages and discourses already at play in the cultural domain" (p. 40). Rather than a progressive tightening of national and international IP law, copyright and authorship must be situated within social and cultural contexts in the continuing debate on how creation and distribution of works are regulated in the digital space and across borders.

• CHAPTER EIGHTEEN •

The Mutual Interests of Multicultural Studies and Some Rights Reserved Copyright

Jill M. Parrott

The culture of copyright has often been one of repression and exclusion. In fact, exclusion is embedded in our current intellectual property paradigm: The default all rights reserved system the United States currently uses sets up any individual who is not the author as a potential threat to the author's inviolate work. In this way, IP has been a tool by which the power structure has been able to deny many non-hegemonic authors the benefits of authorship by seeing them as objects rather than subjects able to create their own IP. Viewing these interactions through the framework of subject/object is useful because the subject/object binary parallels the current all rights reserved/no rights reserved binary of our current copyright system, and we are led to see ways these binary structures are flawed and to see that other options are preferable.

A some rights reserved copyright that rejects the binary copyright system offers unique opportunities for creators from various cultures, backgrounds, and formerly perceived objectivities by providing an alternative to strongly subject-focused copyright. A some rights reserved system, wherein authors have the option to choose the type and level of copyright protection for their individual work, has become preferable to many people because its utilization would strengthen the authorship awareness of users through its volition-based implementation and would provide the amount of protection and/or collaboration appropriate for the (con)text. For these reasons, some rights reserved copyright supports the types of non-singular, non-binary, collective authorship projects so many authors from varied cultural backgrounds have been creating for generations. In many contexts involving authors from multicultural backgrounds with little to no societal power, authors have been using these same tactics to subvert the copyright authority of entities that wish to exclude them. As a reaction to the historical problems with the practical application of IP for women's cultural artifacts, for example, many contemporary female authors have challenged the IP culture that had excluded past generations through non-traditional narrative techniques and textual critique. Some rights reserved copyright acknowledges the value of such strategies that could negate old binaries of subject/object that parallel all rights reserved and no rights reserved copyright. Authors' contributions to these discussions lend to the potential of some rights reserved to provide further evidence of the existence of a consciousness alternative to subject/object. In this, there are two major ways that the purposes of the some rights reserved movement parallels multicultural studies: in the rejection of binary logic and in the protection of the right to create textual critiques.

The Rejection of the Binary

The idea of subjectivity is essential to understanding the relationship between the author and his text. Moreover, it is essential to a post-colonial consciousness. Hegel, from whom we have inherited the vocabulary of the subject/object framework, claimed, "universal history goes from East to West. Europe is absolutely the *end of universal history*. Asia is the beginning. Africa is in general a closed land, and it maintains this fundamental character. It is characteristic of the blacks that their consciousness has not yet even arrived at the intuition of any objectivity" (as cited in Villanueva, 2003, p. 841). In light of this perceived (or—we could argue—falsely and forcefully created) power differential, then, equally important is our responsibility to question and deconstruct the subject and its subjectivities:

> we have little idea of the potential that a variety of subjectivities—operating with honor, respect, and reasonable codes of conduct—can bring to critical inquiry or critical problems. What might happen if we treated differences in subject position as critical pieces of the whole, vital to thorough understanding, and central to both problem-finding and problem-solving? (Royster, 2003, p. 615)

The view of subjectivity as an elite status available only to the few and unavailable to everyone else leaves those to whom it is supposedly unavailable without publishing outlets validated by the controlling power structure.

The argument to protect and support those who fall outside the all rights reserved/no rights reserved system is undergirded by theorists such as Mike Rose, Maxine Hairston, and Victor Villanueva who have long argued that the relationship between a person's writing (or not-writing) and his or her perceived place in academia specifically and the world generally is strong. Rose (2003) said, for example, "to be literate is to be honorable and intelligent. Tag some group illiterate, and you've gone beyond letters; you've judged their morals and their minds" (p. 561). This predisposition to belittle and invalidate those non-hegemonic voices has been the force attempting to negate multicultural voices for generations. In her popular essay "When the First Voice You Hear is Not Your Own," Jacqueline Jones Royster (2003) claimed that

> subject position is everything. I have come to recognize, however, that when the subject matter is me and the voice is not mine, my sense of order and rightness is disrupted. In metaphoric fashion, these 'authorities' let me know, once again, that Columbus has discovered America and claims it now, claims it still for a European crown. (p. 613)

Her insight shows that questions of authority and subjectivity are still very relevant in the minds of many who have that subject "status" being kept from them maliciously.

The idea of being a subject and being able to control one's own intellectual property are inextricably linked. A look at Walter Benn Michaels' (1995) *Our America* lends an analogy relating national identities to individual identities often used in maximalist copyright arguments. Michaels claimed that nativism and modernism both represent a commitment to identity: "In nativist modernism, identity becomes an ambition as well as a description" (p. 3). By making a replacement, the sentence could just as easily read "in [all rights reserved copyright licensing] identity becomes an ambition as well as a description," as all rights reserved copyright has a tradition of relating to the moral rights and personality of the author. Again, Michaels is not concerned with copyright issues in this text, but the nativist impulse comes from a similar place of self-preserving individualism—the desire to keep an(other) out. We can see this nativist impulse play out in the perpetuation of racially based ideologies about slaves writing their own captivity narratives and the desire to impede others from telling the stories (creating an identity) for the nativist (white) subject while simultaneously attempting to keep the object from his or her own subjecthood. To alleviate the tension caused by such juxtaposition, an introduction, preface, or letter is required from within the nativist circle to make assurances that the text poses no threat to their own subjectivity.

The history of the colonized world is rife with objectification and exclusion. There is no need to recount here all the many ways underrepresented groups have been ill-treated. The ways that objectified groups have been excluded from or forced to submit to certain rules surrounding publication, however, shows a particular pertinence to the current conversation about culture and copyright law. As Sarah Robbins (2003) noted, "tools such as social class, race, and gender in our studies of intellectual property can help us complicate the picture" (p. 158) of the subjectivity of authors and its relationship to copyright. Women's authorship, for example, has always been challenged under the auspices of clearly inferior intelligence and natural affinity for things of the home rather than things of the mind.

Often, only female works that were about the "home" were deemed appropriate for female authorship. Not until the nineteenth century did American female authors and editors uphold a strong position in the literary economy. Robbins (2003) explained that

> nineteenth-century American women's texts provide an especially fertile ground for intellectual property case studies, partly because of U.S. culture's tendency to position a woman's labor as both private (belonging to her family in the home) and public (belonging to the community), and, in either case, *not* clearly possessed by her individually. (p. 158)

Elizabeth Flynn (2003) said that studies of women's feelings about intellectual development have also shown that the attempt to find subjectivity often transforms or interrupts "women's ways of knowing" and that "this sense of self is embedded either in external definitions and roles or in identifications with institutions, disciplines, and methods" (p. 576). Women have been viewed as objects; under such an ideology it is incredibly difficult for men *and* women to adjust ideology and accept a female author's subjectivity in that same subject/object ideological framework. In other words, for a person of this understanding, either you are an object (woman) or you are a subject (author)—you can't be both. This binary thinking makes conceptualizing outside of the two options difficult. It also makes challenging the binary with your actions practically impossible because of resistance and hostility.

Slave Narratives and the Intellectual Property Binary

In particular, captivity narratives seem excellent examples of the "need" for a perceived subject to vouch for the perceived object's experiences in order to perpetuate the power differential. What better example of a human object than a slave or captive viewed as chattel to sell or barter or garner power? When the slave's or woman's body is already culturally commodified, no clearer example of a subject/object relationship exists. What more powerful way for a human subject to impress his subjectivity upon an(other) than to fill the object's lack of subject with his own subjectivity, in essence taking ownership of the text himself? Indeed, some of the most famous captivity narratives in American literary history exhibit this strange subject/object relationship in the cultural sub-conscious. They exhibit how, in some cases, the identity of an author can become political capital and, therefore, can be used to benefit the all rights reserved system. In this history, there are many examples of white men (or, in the case of black female authors, white women) vouching for the author in order to supply the female object—whose work is "*not* clearly possessed by her"—with white (male) subjectivity by proxy. Racial differences present similar subjectivity complications. In other words, in the public consciousness, a black male author, a white female author, or a black female author could not possibly exist because they each lacked the subjectivity associated with authorship and intellectual property. Their subjectivity had to be given to them in some outside way.

For example, Olaudah Equiano's 1789 (reprinted in 1999) *The Life of Olaudah Equiano, or Gustavus Vassa, the African* contains a preface vouching for the accountability of the text. Praising Equiano's role in advancing the British movement to stop the slave trade (called the Bill for the Abolition of the Slavetrade). The preface author calls Equiano's text a "round unvarnished tale" and a "true relation of occurrences which had taken place" (p. 3) in an attempt to replace any doubt of Equiano's veracity with the preface author's own. Surely the publisher realized that no "civilized" audience could read a text written by a savage (object) because that confused the culture's sociolinguistic paradigm and, in doing so, would have questioned their own powerful subjectivity.

Throughout the work, Equiano continues to acknowledge his awkward role as both subject and object in his case: He recounts his time as an object of the slave trade, necessarily embracing his subjectivity as author to tell his story, but simultaneously recognizing that many who will read will continue to see him as an object and question his ability to author this work. In this, he attempts to achieve some kind of *ethos* with his audience by shirking the cloak of subjectivity:

> I am not so foolishly vain as to expect from it either immortality or literary reputation. If it affords any satisfaction to my numerous friends, at whose request It has been written, or in the smallest degree promotes the interests of humanity, the ends for which it was undertaken will be fully attained, and every wish of my heart gratified. Let it therefore be remembered, that, in wishing to avoid censure, I do not aspire to praise. (1999, p. 10)

In this passage, Equiano shows that he feels he must convince his reader that he does not desire subjectivity through his authorship, that it has been forced upon him by others and that his aspirations lie in the good of humanity, not himself. He feels that they will only accept his subjectivity as an author if he rejects it—that is, *knows his place*.

This first slave narrative written in English about the trans-Atlantic slave trade set the standard for future American slave narratives to come in its arrangement and obligatory renouncement of desire for subjectivity through the authorship of the captive. As Houston Baker (1985) told us in "Autobiographical Acts and the Voice of the Southern Slave," in "'transmuting an authentic, unwritten self—a self that exists outside the conventional literary discourse structures of a white reading public—into a literary representation' the ex-slave loses an 'authentic' self" (as cited in Herndl, 1999, p. 263). Diana Price Herndl goes on to explain that the slave narrative tradition met requirements of the "prescribed form" (p. 263). In meeting that prescribed form, they were denied the opportunity to create their own text, informed by the experiences and pre-existing traditions of their own culture, forced to mold their experiences to the culture of others. In other words, they were forced to meet standards to publish in an infrastructure that required it.

Frederick Douglass's 1845 *Narrative of the Life of Frederick Douglass, an American Slave* (2000) and Harriet Jacobs's 1861 *Incidents in the Life of a Slave Girl* (2000) follow this format using a letter, preface, or introduction from a well-known and respected member of the white community to achieve *gravitas* enough for publication. Wendell Phillips, who completed the recommendation letter for Douglass by writing *to* Douglass, declared to Douglass that he and the reader can

> put the most entire confidence in your truth, candor, and sincerity. Every one who has heard you speak has felt, and, I am confident, every one who reads your book will feel, persuaded that you give them a fair specimen of the whole truth. (p. 14)

This letter to Douglass provides support for Douglass and for the reader that Douglass's authorship can be trusted. Douglass alone cannot be trusted in the mind of many of his contemporaries; in the cultural framework in which he published, Douglass *lacks* because he is a black man. He needs the white man's addition to reach the "full" authorial standard.

Likewise, Harriet Jacobs is provided with her own certificate of authenticity in the form of an introduction from a white person sharing her socially recognized subjectivity with Jacobs. Like Equiano and Douglass, Jacobs necessarily acquiesces her authority by begging the reader to believe the representation of her account. She said: "Reader, be assured this narrative is no fiction," and then later, "I wish I were more competent to the task I have undertaken" (p. 119). Like Equiano, she inhabits a negotiated space between the subject her readers would have expected from an author with intellectual property and the object her readers in social power would have projected upon a person of her social and cultural standing. Lydia Maria Child's introduction addresses what she perceived as the readership's questions about the author's ability to "write so well," which might "excite surprise" (p. 121). Child, by then a famous name in the abolition movement, lent her reputation to Linda Brent (Jacobs's pseudonym), to convince readers of the appropriateness of reading the story. Although it holds some gruesome details about Jacobs's sexual abuse over years of slavery, Child is able to give the work the needed authority by taking this "indecorum" upon herself (p. 122). The audience's expectation would already create a perceived lack in Brent—in her case doubly because she is a woman *and* black—which needs to be filled to achieve authority.

These sociocultural power differentials necessarily perpetuate hostile, fearful, resentful environments. The prominent cultural rhetoricians of the last few decades have written extensively about rhetorical choices writers can make that reject the binary and favor the active over the reactive, the productive over the reductive. Many have written about the rejection of binary systems in a multicultural context, which often involves collective authorship or authorship with many voices. For example, in the introduction to the 1999 collection *Beyond the Binary*, editor Tim Powell suggested that the Self/Other dynamic as laid out by Hegel and then expounded upon by Freud, Lacan, and others is no longer appropriate for the exploration of cultural dynamics. He is, of course, referring to racial and national ideologies, but no reason exists to negate its application to other venues. The Self/Other binary is a symptom of structuralist diacritical difference—that is, anyone who is not me is the "Other" and should, therefore, be viewed suspiciously and, often, aggressively. We can also see this fear of difference in the implementation of traditional copyright law. The "Self" side of the binary coin can represent all rights reserved copyright and its tendency to elevate the individual/creator/subject, while "Other" becomes those literary intruders who might violate the copyright and manipulate the "Self"'s text. In this binary situation, the "Self" must protect himself and his proxy work from outside invading forces. Yet, this self is no longer appropriate in a postmodern world. In fact, it seems anachronistic.

Indeed, these intellectual property frameworks have become ill-fitted to the contemporary multicultural, multimedia West. Walter Ong (1982) described a type of secondary orality wherein, because of visual and audio media, we have come once again to rely on communications alternative to the written word and all its abstractions (although also relying on it) to build new media. The ever-growing exposure to and acceptance of unfamiliar languages, cultures, foods, music, dress, and lifestyles necessarily negate an insular view of self as many people embrace their multiple subjectivities. This multiplicity of identity scares many, as evidenced in violence against other races, the deaths of homosexuals at the hands of heterosexuals, or laws that have forbidden marriages of different races or similar genders. Yet, theories exist to support and adopt these multiplicities, insisting that a singular, coherent subject is neither achievable nor desirable.

For example, throughout her works Gloria Anzaldúa pushes the boundaries of the binary to negate the subject's power. Through her *mestizaje écriture*, Anzaldúa validated and provided a vocabulary for the rhetorical choices of people who live in the Borderlands and have mixed identities, and she entreated them to action. *Mestiza* (Anzaldúa, 2001) is the idea of all at once being different from and separate from others while also being the same as and connected to others, representing multiple identities at once. Modeled in a non-linear fashion, Anzaldúa's work exemplifies her assertions as she challenges herself (and all humanity) to see the world not as either/or but to include and validate all facets, especially those that exist in the "borderlands." In her work, Anzaldúa delves into the geographical, linguistic, and cultural spatialities that govern these Borderlands, which are not only formed by geographical demarcation but by the cultural spaces in which society allows the interminglings to occur.

Although Anzaldúa rebels against linear and binary ideologies, she acknowledges their existence and the need to work with their existence. Rather than creating an equal and opposite new set of these demarcations, she called for herself and others to "be proactive rather than reactive" (as cited in Reuman, 2000). She does not desire a revolution of ideas that requires two sides to resist against each other: "It is not enough to stand on the opposite river bank, shouting questions, challenging patriarchal, white conventions" (Anzaldúa, 2001, p. 1597). Rather, she said that we must work with what we have been given and change ideologies from the inside out. To avoid the use of binary oppositions, which would just perpetuate the hegemonic logic, Anzaldúa encouraged writing and resistance not "entirely *outside* the dominant culture's inscriptions. To do so would participate in the dualistic thinking that subordinates women of color and other oppressed groups" (Keating, 1996, p. 133). By acknowledging and sometimes working within the language of mainstream society, she creates the opportunity for a non-binary paradigm shift.

Alternative copyright protection such as a some rights reserved copyright provides a unique opportunity to embrace the mindset Anzaldúa represents because it rejects the old power structure without opposing it. Some rights reserved and the efforts of feminist and cultural critics complement one another's objectives. Because these authors and theorists do not need an outside structure telling them how to copyright or publish their works or that they must or cannot, the recent history of multicultural literatures shows that many authors already question the all rights reserved paradigm.

The Protection of Cultural Critique

In light of the contemporary movement concerning intellectual property, which has seen mainstream ideas of authorship expand because of the ubiquity of communication outlets on the internet, we should continue to value and protect those texts that use forms of derivation or appropriation to provide cultural critique. As strengthened maximalist copyright policies are applied, we will have less legal right to negotiate cultural legacies through creative texts and to use critique as a negotiation tool. Those individuals who might consider IP something to be vehemently protected—because it is an extension of their own subjectivity through authorship—will be threatened by the textual critique and appropriation. Although copyright fair use guidelines give us all the right to these forms of expression, the more the system is pulled toward all rights reserved by the power structure, the more that right will be challenged. Looking at examples of cultural critique, we can see how this tactic has been valued as a tool to challenge intellectual property claims in the past and should be protected in the future to preserve this right to critique.

The canon inherently resists transgression within its own borders because of the mostly mainstream and hegemonic makeup of the authors in it. The controversy around Alice Randall's (2001) *The Wind Done Gone* shows us protectionism of mainstream texts and reveals how we must continue to vehemently protect the right to appropriate texts in a critical and responsible way. In 2001, SunTrust (the trustee of *Gone With the Wind* author Margaret Mitchell's estate) brought suit against Houghton Mifflin for making plans to publish Alice Randall's *The Wind Done Gone,* which provides a narrative criticism of *Gone With the Wind.* As Australian copyright expert Matthew Rimmer (2003) explained, this novel "belongs to a distinguished literary tradition of shadow texts which seek to re-write and subvert canonical texts from fresh perspectives and view-points."

However, SunTrust was able to get the court to grant an injunction against Houghton Mifflin to prevent them temporarily from publishing *The Wind Done Gone.* Houghton Mifflin then appealed to have the injunction lifted and subsequently to publish the work.

The appellate did lift the injunction, mainly because of its transformative nature:

> A later work is "transformative" of an earlier work when it uses that earlier work in a manner that gives new meaning to that earlier work, i.e. it enables us to see the earlier work in a different manner than might have been originally intended. (Hoffman, 2001).

The four-factor Fair Use criteria were applied and, in this case, the court lifted the injunction, for they agreed with Houghton Mifflin that the parodic and critical nature of *The Wind Done Gone* not only benefitted from the use of *Gone With the Wind* but necessitated it. Randall's commentary directly addressed the particulars of Mitchell's novel

> *Gone With the Wind* has become an icon and a pervasive point of reference for people's understanding of the Civil War-era South, but the picture presented by *Gone With the Wind* is inaccurate and extremely racist. Just as troubling is our culture's continued acceptance of the work. (Houghton Mifflin, 2001)

In this way, her commentary could not exist without the direct use of Mitchell's text for it would not engage the appropriate literary and cultural themes. The nature and purpose of the work required a critical engagement with *Gone With the Wind* directly because of the iconic nature of *Gone With the Wind.*

For these reasons, the court supported Randall's right to use Mitchell's work in a transgressive and critical way. The only difference in this case from, for instance, appropriations of Shakespeare was that an entity still "owned" the text being remastered. Had the court not lifted the injunction, Randall's book would have been delayed until 2032, when the copyright extension granted to SunTrust will expire—unless, of course, the copyright is extended again. The court's findings, however, were based not on a theoretical conceptualization of an artist's tendency to speak to works before her but on the premise that "copy-right does not immunise a work from comment and criticism" (as cited in Rimmer, 2003). As many work to strengthen all rights reserved, these fair use guidelines are constantly under negotiation—as recently as July 2010, Congress recognized the need to update Fair Use guidelines for some digital productions.

Looking at *The Wind Done Gone* shows how under-represented and frequently under-estimated people have long used the appropriation of canonical or hegemonic texts as tools with which to critique mainstream culture. As appropriations are often used as criticism of previous texts, they are protected under Fair Use guidelines as such. Yet this protection makes an important distinction: Criticism is protected while other potentially creative and meaningful remixes, appropriations, and manipulations are not. Criticism *should* be protected, but we should also question the reasons why other forms of textual derivations are not covered under Fair Use. Criticism is the protected *exception*, not the norm, as far as the law is concerned. As of now, the courts have not labeled remixes or other narrative alternatives Fair Use. Were distributed authorship not considered abnormal, deviant, or dishonest it might not be frequently accompanied by physical, monetary, or social punishment. Rhetorical play, such as talking back or signifying, has taken (and will certainly continue to take) an irreplaceable roll in the continuing conversation of deconstructing cultural implications in a multicultural world. The opportunity is upon us to recognize, nurture, and protect these and other variances of word play that can extend and complicate these conversations. Some rights reserved copyright can support such an endeavor because its licenses foster a community that uses these alternatives freely.

A constant back and forth of action and reaction such as that encouraged in a binary copyright system is not the only option for authorship. As discussed above, an extended conversation trajectory involving textual remixing and some rights reserved could show that a text can contribute deeply to the knowledge base, be productive, or be powerful and creative building off a prior text without being critical of it. In that, authors such as Sandra Cisneros have chosen to work within their own narrative structures to challenge the idea of the singular author-god productively but not reactively. Rather than criticize others' works, they use a built-in system whose internal logic upholds what I like to think of as a *pantheistic* notion of authorship. Rather than presenting a picture of themselves as omnipotent, subject, author-god, they show themselves to be a more pantheistic author-deity, willing to make room for others with authority to build a complete picture, a communal work in progress. This paradox is successful for Cisneros in her novel *Caramelo* (2002) because her narrative style effectively convinces the audience that it accepts these values of negotiated narrative style and challenged binaries. Cisneros's narrator speaks and acts in accordance with the overriding norm of the text: textual remixing outside the traditional system as an appropriate form of text creation.

Other authors also use this tactic. Kathy Acker, for example, envelops others' works into her own. As Andrea Lunsford (1999), writing about Acker's work, noted:

> the conventional crime of writing—plagiarism—is consciously deployed to call attention to what she sees as the current impossibility of "owning" language and to the need for alternative rhetorical practices for enacting multiple selves in discourse. (p. 539)

Although the two take very different tones and topics for their works, each use their creative texts to challenge strict notions of authorship, providing vivid prose that distributes authorship among themselves and others. When the internal logic of the narrative includes evidence of distributed authorship and that internal logic is accepted by the reader, distributed authorship becomes less deviant. Although many have come to expect singular authorship and assume its superiority or normalcy, multicultural authors have shown evidence that alternatives exist through cultural critique and are equally interesting and valid.

Conclusions

We can see a move against the singular subject and toward a more flexible definition of authority. Possibly, the authors whose work is described above are *most* apt to present this kind of change *because* they already exist outside the norms of "authority" in American culture. Further, these authors show that the some rights reserved mindset is not all that novel nor is it abnormal, although its manifestation in the legal world may be. As more intellectual property options become available, the need for responsible interrogation of the relationship between culture and IP grows. Anupam Chander and Madhavi Sunder (2004) argued in "The Romance of the Public Domain" that "the commons... is not always kind to the commoners" (p. 1338). They claimed that while many have deconstructed all rights reserved copyright for its frequent control by corporations and potential exploitation of the weak or powerless, the opposite complete support of no rights reserved also shows evidence of exploitation. As Chander and Sunder explained, most of the contemporary conversation about copyright and the commons

> presumes a landscape where each person can reap the riches found in the commons. This is the *romance* of the commons: the belief that because a resource is open to all by force of law, it will indeed be equally exploited by all. But, in practice, differing circumstances—including knowledge, wealth, power, and ability—render some better able than others to exploit a commons. (p. 1332)

In addition to strict all rights reserved copyright, which often puts power into the hands of corporations rather than individuals, the public domain/no rights reserved also has exploited "the labor and bodies of the disempowered—namely, people of color, the poor, women, and people from the global South" (Chander & Sunder, p. 1335).

On the other end of the spectrum, the powerful have also found benefit in plundering the public domain, which is filled with traditional cultural expressions, and reaping for benefit. Wend Wendland (2008) told us that

> open sharing does not automatically confer a right to use the knowledge (of indigenous people)... traditional cultural expressions are not in the public domain because indigenous peoples have failed to take the steps necessary to protect the knowledge in the Western intellectual property system, but from a failure of governments and citizens to recognise and respect the customary laws regulating their use. (p. 172)

In other words, because traditional cultures do not recognize and work within the Western copyright system, their works are often co-opted from those within the system. Intellectual property is favored by a Western system and favors those who work within the Western system. Therefore, to ignore the lengthy history that publishing and copyright has in relationship with non-hegemonic groups who have been exploited, from American Indians to African Americans to women from any background and too many others, would be negligent and short-sighted.

The American Folklore Society claims that strict intellectual property laws might inhibit community efforts to protect traditional cultural expressions (Wendland, 2008, p. 151). This inconsistency happens mainly because the information of traditional knowledge and art, when taken out of its community, "works to the systematic advantage of a few identifiable constituencies" (Chander & Sunder, 2004, p. 1337). As Chandler and Sunder pointed out, "the movement to privatize the commons generally involved breaking down a more communal social order and concentrating wealth in the hands of the power" (p. 1340). And, although the romantic conception of the commons often sees its "emancipatory" potential, "it is also naïve, idealistic, and removed from reality" (p. 1341). The global IP system as it is currently set up actually moves wealth from the poorest countries in the world to the richest (through art, holistic medicine, minerals, genetic information and more) while simultaneously arguing that the exploitation of these resources is a good thing because a wide public domain benefits everyone.

These examples provide evidence that those wishing to promote an IP model that also promotes values conducive to multiculturalism in a postcolonial world *should* support a some-rights-reserved copyright system. Some rights reserved presents an ideological framework that has long been used and supported by authors from various cultural backgrounds as tools to claim rhetorical traditions that more appropriately represent their lived multiple selves. Understanding some rights reserved this way reinforces its importance as a tool in situations where singular authorship becomes inappropriate or undesirable.

As the examples presented above show, the choices many authors from various cultural and social backgrounds use to challenge oppressive binary logic and to represent the multiple identifications of a *mestiza* existence bely the all rights reserved/no rights reserved binary. Some rights reserved provides the opportunity to change the binary copyright system from the inside out. Villanueva (2003) said that "there are attitudes from those we have revered over the centuries which we inherit, that are woven into the discourse that we inherit" (p. 840). And while some of this discourse is valuable, some of it supports an inherently excluding power structure that attacks from both sides. Rather than destroying the copyright system or aligning with one (potentially dangerous) side, some rights reserved acknowledges that multiple copyright possibilities are more appropriate than an opposing two just as our lived multicultural existence shows a multiplicity of selves.

An all rights reserved copyright represents the interests of the subject being protected against potential intrusion/miscegenation from an outsider. Nativist impulses often lead to protectionism of personal or national identity, which can also be extended into authorial identity. With the singular author, the text is often an extension of the author's subjectivity. When the text is seen as the extension of the subject, the protectionist impulse is strong. When the text is a representation of many selves not connected to some authorship ideology, the text is released from the burden of nativism. Authors can reject the notion of protectionism by embracing the texts of others and exemplifying *mestiza* narration, showing the negotiation between individualism and community-based authorship, and reflecting the contingencies of today's multicultural environment wherein many selves require recognition. In the twentieth century, as individuals rejected the idea that they must choose, we saw hybrid characters and authors become even more complex and more challenging. We saw the adoption of new vocabulary; for example, rather than the "tragic mulatto" of the nineteenth century, we have Gloria Anzaldúa's powerful image of *mestiza* consciousness. Our current twenty-first century has potential to create our own paradigm of authorship and IP that accurately represents the wide array of authorship potentialities.

The traditional Western subject *can* be excised from a text and the text can still be left standing—meaningful, interesting, authoritative, and relevant. Al-though a legally sanctioned some rights reserved copyright option did not exist when many of these texts were written, they show that authors from various multicultural backgrounds have both historically and contemporarily used strategies that parallel some rights reserved such as the sharing and manipulation of texts whose origins lie elsewhere. Their narrative structures challenge the reader's idea of the role an author should play in the text—mainly that the creator of a text must rule as author-god over it, the text must be an extension of the author's very being and come from the author's own genius, thereby deserving strict protection. We can also see in these examples the promise that the proliferation of some rights reserved copyright might encourage authors from non-hegemonic backgrounds to compose. Yet as Chander and Sunder (2004) described, no rights reserved can be as harmful as all rights reserved because it opens sacred texts up to exploitation. Some rights reserved and other non-binary copyright options "break the binary" and reject the fundamentalism on either side. Lunsford (1999) suggested that we find "methods [that] work toward a balance between protecting individual dignities and rights—especially those *not* protected by earlier regimes of intellectual property—and protecting the public good" (p. 536). The flexible nature of some rights reserved provides a venue for more authors to compose this way and for more understanding of the validity of this narrative play. A non-binary, some rights reserved copyright system acknowledges—in fact, encourages—a system where multiple voices interact together.

• PART FOUR •

Implications, Actions, and Pedagogical Work

• CHAPTER NINETEEN •

A Culture of Sharing: The U.S. Nonprofit Sector and Intellectual Property

Guiseppe Getto and Jessica Getto-Rivait

Encouraged by public relations firms and law firms, as well as the successes of their for-profit counterparts, many U.S. nonprofits are exploring how branding can aid them in weathering the current philanthropic climate ("Charitable giving drops," 2010). Often, nonprofit organizations (or NPOs) and their in-house or consultant allies couple branding practices with the use of digital media (such as organization web sites and social media accounts) to stand out to potential stakeholders (e.g., donors, members, and volunteers). To attract stakeholders, these organizations attempt to "sell" what makes them different from other NPOs. Unfortunately, this interest in branding has also led to some infighting over which organization owns what brand materials—in extreme cases, this has led to lawsuits. In response to this new level of competition over intellectual property, some NPOs are turning to law firms and are actively recruiting lawyers to sit on their executive boards in an effort to protect their organizations from financially devastating legal disputes.

Despite this spike in various forms of competition within the recent history of the nonprofit sector, however, we argue that a "culture of sharing" still exists among small NPOs. Further, we maintain that this culture may be key to the survival of some NPOs—even in the face of the many current economic and legal challenges to this culture. As opposed to the publicly lauded culture of sharing that existed 100 years ago, however, in which nonprofits banded together financially to create some of the infrastructure that makes this economic sector possible today, the new iteration of a culture of sharing in the nonprofit sector is largely a private endeavor encouraged by grant funders who support nonprofit mergers and nonprofit resource-sharing behind closed doors (Chui, 2011).

Despite this, as we will demonstrate in this chapter, NPOs themselves are also sharing intellectual materials—such as mission statements, web site templates, elements of logos, and brochure mock ups—to help one another start new community initiatives. In addition, nonprofits who successfully engage in this sharing of intellectual property often form mutually beneficial sharing networks with other nonprofits, much like organizations at the turn of the last century shared financial donations. This still-surviving culture is a starting point for a kind of cooperative branding, we claim, or an attitude towards distinctiveness that doesn't hurt the branding efforts of other local organizations. At the same time, as we will point out, there are significant barriers to maintaining and expanding this culture of sharing—barriers that humanists who understand intellectual property law can aid NPOs in overcoming.

Humanists are uniquely positioned to aid nonprofits with managing intellectual property issues for several reasons. Like many NPOs, humanists are largely interested in investigating and representing societal inequalities. Also like humanists, many NPOs create identities that revolve around what has not been done and said regarding a social issue. And, most pointedly, arts and culture NPOs—those that most represent and carry forth the public agenda of the humanities—have been the most defunded 501(c)3 organizations in the U.S. during the last decade. This is not surprising, given that government resistance to financially supporting organizations like the National Endowment for the Arts and the National Endowment for the Humanities (which fund both NPOs and academic projects) has mirrored higher educations' divestment from humanities departments since the 1960s.

Yet, to embark on this work in a critical way, humanists first need to understand the multitude of factors that impact branding-related knowledge work (a.k.a., intellectual property) in the U.S. nonprofit sector. In this chapter, we sketch out the nonprofit culture of IP creation, management, and circulation as we have experienced it, through research and experience working with a variety of nonprofit organizations and service-learning partnerships in the community of Lansing, Michigan. We provide a case study of how one organization, the Women's Center of Greater Lansing, attempted to brand themselves, and how these kinds of attempts by local nonprofits are frequently at odds with the best practices of U.S. IP policies and regulations. Ultimately, our goal is to introduce heuristics to humanists for studying and working with nonprofits they are partnered with to encourage and perpetuate a culture of sharing. The aim of a culture of sharing should be the promotion of IP as communally generated and owned knowledge work that is produced with the intent of being revised and distributed in ways that are respectful, non-competitive, and mutually beneficial.

Corporatization as Deficits Approach to NPO Intellectual Property

Although the U.S. nonprofit sector works actively for social welfare, it is also an industry that has a significant impact on national and local economies in the United States ("Nonprofit Growth Engine," 2011). Dubbed as the "third sector," it closely follows the retail and manufacturing industries as the third largest employer of Americans ("Nonprofit Employment," 2012). And despite general economic decline in the U.S. between 2001 and 2010, the U.S. nonprofit sector maintained an average job gain of 2%—even during the "Great Recession" caused by the 2008 New York Stock Exchange crash ("Nonprofit Growth Engine," 2011).

Despite these deservedly celebrated successes, the U.S. nonprofit sector encounters significant struggles that serve as barriers to sustainability. Even though NPOs serve as a major employer in all regions of the U.S., the decline of donor support, the recent imposition of government fees, and the increased number of NPOs applying for the same resources has caused many NPOs to tighten their budgets ("Nonprofits pay fees," 2011). To maintain staff positions, some nonprofits opt to freeze salary, decrease benefits, and demand a higher rate of production from remaining employees ("Recession toll," 2010). To leverage better working conditions, high-performing employees at middle-level administrative positions leave positions for better opportunities approximately every 2–7 years ("Nonprofit turnover," 2008; "Jump ship," 2012).

Development professionals, or nonprofit employees who do a combination of marketing and fundraising, are especially likely to abandon ship because they are in short supply and often face unrealistic pressure to perform as "money machines" as nonprofit senior staff and executive boards search for quick fixes to their economic struggles ("Jump ship," 2012). Not only is this costly for nonprofits because of costs associated with job searches for replacements (see Flandez, 2012), but it also does substantial damage to stakeholder and donor relationships and a nonprofit's long-term financial health (Joyaux, 2012).

Although deciding upon and displaying organizational identity does not inherently need to be about staking territory, within this context it all too often is framed in terms of scarcity. In the parlance of community development, such framing is in line with a "deficits approach" to community problem-solving efforts. Critics maintain that a deficits approach to community problem-solving emphasizes the scarcity of community resources and focuses mostly on the differences between groups. In short, community groups operate with a fear of "losing out" to other community groups who may "outcompete" them for precious resources.

Within this framework, individual nonprofit organizations often create public organizational identities and compete with other NPOs through advertising their mission, goals, and projects in very specific ways, and by creating a brand identity. Branding is a term that originally arose in corporate culture to describe the ways in which for-profit organizations and products are presented to the public-at-large. Branding includes the creation of unique names, logos, font type, mottos, and symbols (Zaichowsky, 2010). Although NPOs have much different operations and needs than businesses, they often adapt corporate practices and repurpose them to serve their needs. NPOs do this because, like businesses, they want to stand out in the sea of information consumers and stakeholders swim in and they correctly view symbolic impact as the first steps to making a material impact. For this reason, they value brand iconicity, or "the degree to which a brand symbolizes the values, needs, and aspirations of the members of a particular cultural group," (Torelli, Chiu, Keh, & Amaral, 2005, p. 108). NPOs believe that achieving brand iconicity is key to gaining community recognition and anchoring trust—a means to establish organizational sustainability in local communities.[1]

Although some humanists may be disheartened by NPO adoption of corporate practices (see Blake Scott, 2010), NPOs can use branding best practices to ethically represent themselves. For example, authenticity is one branding best practice. Organizations should have "clarity about [their] reason for being... unique vision, goals, values, voice, and personality" (Wheeler, 2006, p. 22). NPOs, whose missions usually involve addressing societal problems to create more equitable conditions for those who are marginalized, have a natural affinity for this practice. However, for reasons outlined above, NPOs may not always have the in-house expertise to brand themselves and may turn to outside consultants for help.[2]

Although much information about IP best practices is available free online, as is often the case, freely available information is not enough. No scholar or organization has conducted a wide-scale research study concerning nonprofit knowledge about public domain and creative commons, but early research suggests that few organizations know about open-source licensing options like Creative Commons. A small survey of 200 nonprofit organizations, for instance, revealed that most copyright their materials rather than licensing them using Creative Commons (Tomlinson, 2011). While this survey is not necessarily representative or conclusive, it does correlate with what IP experts know about how licensing has been advertised: Copyright and Fair Use are front runners, while knowledge of the public domain and Creative Commons lags behind within public consciousness.

There are also some issues with way the public domain and Creative Commons currently works that we wish to highlight. First, as DeVoss (2009) has pointed out, the public domain is threatened by prolonged protections of copyrighted material, which corporations have rallied for in recent years. The public domain is limited because of these prolonged protections, and material that is likely to resonate with potential nonprofit organization donors that could have been used in the past without fear of retaliation is now not legally usable. Second, as John Tomlinson (2011) argued, the Creative Commons "Non-Commercial" license is problematic for nonprofit organizations because they are trying to gain financial support via their marketing materials. Also, because the Creative Commons "Non-Commercial" license is heavily used, nonprofits are limited to the kinds of Creative Commons materials they can use to market themselves.

What's more, some nonprofits may think of IP as copyrighted or "copyrightable" material, and not consider the possibility that what they consider to be typical "branding" practices actually fall under the purview of trademarking and servicemarking. Law professionals, like those at Public Counsel Law Center (2010), provide IP "boot camp" materials to explain these distinctions: Although artistic, "original" works (such as photographs) are copyrightable items, trademarks and service marks are organizational boilerplate (in the form of specific words, images, numbers, symbols, designs, color, sounds, and the combination thereof) that represent consistent and planned organizational identity on a good or service—or advertising for a good or service (see also San Francisco Bar Association, 2011 for freely available PDFs targeted for nonprofit organization use). In practical terms, a URL, logo, or motto can be used by a nonprofit to invoke community recognition and loyalty to their organization.

While these strategic goals do not themselves promote competition, ensuring uniqueness of branding can be stressful and involved. To ensure the 10-year protection of their brand identity through official trademarking, for instance, U.S. nonprofits must rely on IP lawyers who charge hundreds of dollars on average to search for and register each kind of trademark with the United States Trademark and Service Mark Office. This process takes an average of 10–24 months to complete, and nonprofits still may lose their trademarks for reasons outside of their control—such as their motto suddenly becoming a common one in the nonprofit sector. For small NGOs running consistently under budget, this move may not make sense in terms of time and financial investment. But as Bambi, Faivre, and Walters, PC, assert, nonprofits can also trademark free, customized social media account names (on sites like Facebook) and customized online fundraising account names (on sites like razoo.com) that have "D/B/A"s (or "do business as" names that are slightly different than the organization name) or project or service names that qualify them as "Service Marks."

Due to this mire of technicalities, NPOs are often afraid of involuntarily "going out of business" because of not being able to obtain enough resources to sustain their efforts. While some public relations firms, development consultants, and IP specialists have aided nonprofit organizations in navigating these issues, some leaders in the nonprofit sector liken these professionals to "vultures" preying on nonprofit professionals' fears to make a profit off of them. Yet, despite this deficits approach to resources, the nonprofit sector has another, older legacy of resource sharing that stems from an assets-based approach to community problem-solving, an approach that foregrounds communal capacity-building.

Origins of a Culture of Sharing

In contrast to the deficits-based model of community problem-solving articulated thus far, an asset-based model of community problem-solving emphasizes coalition-building. That is, instead of community groups focusing on their differences and working as individual units, an assets-based approach requires community groups to identify common goals and to seek to form mutually beneficial partnerships to meet goals—even if only temporarily or periodically. When resources are limited, community groups using an assets-based approach discover how to share them fairly and how to assemble assets everyone can use. Although individual and organizational tensions and conflicts may still exist, community groups using this approach value solidarity above these tensions and aim to put aside differences long enough to achieve common goals.

Nonprofit organizations in the U.S. survived through the development of vast social networks in which community resources are shared by numerous organizations. This began at the turn of the twentieth century, when nonprofit organizations decided to pool their fundraising efforts after realizing that they were each seeking financial resources from the same potential donors. For example, community members in Cleveland, Ohio formed "Community Chest" in 1913, which was a precursor to the United Way, the purpose of which was to represent each local nonprofit organization and collect donations to be evenly distributed between these organizations (United Way, 2008). Such joint fundraising efforts have allowed nonprofits to focus on resolving community issues rather than competing for resources. In other words, nonprofits in this country have developed a culture of sharing over the past century, a culture which has allowed them to mobilize their efforts in collective rather than competitive ways.

But 100 years later, this culture of sharing is being threatened by recent developments in the implementation of IP. This is due in part to the very mechanism that first enabled nonprofits to work together for survival. As fundraising efforts like the United Way evolved, inevitable conflicts arose, as no centralized fundraising system or regulatory agency developed to prevent competition between nonprofit organizations over resources. Fortunately, the United Way and other umbrella nonprofit organizations have continued to promote solidarity and smaller nonprofit organizations have followed suit in less public, but no less profound, ways.

Because nonprofits have largely weathered the financial difficulties they have faced in recent years, we have hopes that they will also weather increased competition fostered by fears over intellectual property. Toward this end, we present below a model of what a culture of sharing around IP might look like, in the hopes that readers will help foster this culture within nonprofits that they partner with. Toward this end, this model contains not only successful practices to be emulated, but challenges to nonprofit adoption of these successful practices.

A Model of a Culture of (Intellectual Property) Sharing

Borrowing with Permission

One successful practice that small nonprofit organizations engage in is borrowing branding materials with permission from one another. This practice is often fostered when nonprofits engage in social networking within a specific community that they all serve and come to recognize a common need for something like an effectively designed logo. Needs like this can arise because, as organizations often struggling just to stay in operation, nonprofits have little capacity to produce marketing materials like logos, brochures, and professionally designed web sites in-house because many do not have full-time trained development staff, as we mentioned above. Due to the issue of not having permanent in-house human resources that can aid in the branding process, many small nonprofit organizations search for successful models of organizations that have established good marketing practices. Not only are these mostly new nonprofits looking for ways to avoid mistakes that could render them obsolete, they are also starting to build social networks for themselves as they attempt to establish their organizations.

The Women's Center of Greater Lansing (WCGL) is a nonprofit organization in Lansing, Michigan that has used social networking to build their organizational identity in terms of their physical location, external and internal relationships with other nonprofits, and branding via various media. In what follows, we'll explain why the WCGL is a shining example of how social networking can support a culture of sharing via the practice of borrowing with permission, a practice that enables local nonprofits to collectively succeed.[3] The WCGL is a brick-and-mortar, direct-service nonprofit organization in Lansing's East Side neighborhood along Michigan Avenue (a main throughway that connects Michigan State University in East Lansing and the state capitol building in Lansing). The WCGL was started by Cindie Alwood and Manuela Kress, two second-wave feminist social workers and long-time Lansing-area residents. Alwood and Kress started the WCGL in response to years of hearing their clientele discussing the inadequacies of government agencies to respond to women's needs as they retooled themselves for the workforce. The WCGL just celebrated their fifth birthday, which is quite an accomplishment for any nonprofit organization (given the high degree of turnover that occurs). But what most of their clients don't know is that Alwood and Kress spent 3 years doing feasibility research before ever applying for 501(c)3 status.

Alwood and Kress spent those 3 years examining what already existed in the local area and beyond. They collected data on what kinds of job-seeking services and women's health services were already provided to Lansing-area and Ingham County residents. They took advantage of opportunities to meet with East Side neighborhood leaders to find out more about prospective physical locations for the center. But what they needed the most help with was discovering how to brand themselves as a women's center that focused on women's career and mental health services, rather than on domestic violence issues. Not surprisingly, they did not find such services available to them anywhere in the Lansing area. They needed to go outside of the geographical area to find what they were looking for, which they found in other urban centers in Michigan.

By conducting a statewide search for nonprofit organizations with missions similar to their own, Alwood and Kress discovered that six such organizations existed in the upper and lower peninsulas of Michigan. Alwood and Kress made site visits with two organizations in Grand Rapids and Ann Arbor. They were most impressed by their visit to the Women's Center of Southeastern Michigan (in Ann Arbor) and were pleased when this organization offered their materials (including their mission statement, brochures, and other marketing materials) as start up materials for their own center. Because Alwood and Kress saw their mission and practices as aligned so closely with that of the Women's Center of Southeastern Michigan (WCSM), they used many of the materials directly until their mission and practices started to become more distinct and materials needed to be customized.

There are several circumstances that make this example of borrowing unique. First, Alwood and Kress were in talks with an organization that was a few counties away. Even if they were competing for the same national and state funding, they would not be courting the same local donors. Also, the WCSM had already been established, whereas the WCGL was an emerging nonprofit organization; the WCSM staff saw themselves as mentoring the emerging WCGL rather than being on equal footing. Finally, these organizations were fairly unique in mission compared to other types of nonprofit organizations. While nonprofit organizations like domestic violence shelters have proliferated, there are relatively few nonprofit organizations like the WCSM and the WCGL.

Thus, they saw themselves more in solidarity than in competition. These conditions are ripe for producing a culture of sharing in which borrowing with permission can be so graciously offered rather than being painstakingly sought.

Even though this particular instance of borrowing with permission is unique, it is also a clear-cut way around IP restrictions. Because permission is granted by the creator of the IP (albeit orally in the case of the WCGL), there is no question about who owns what and how it can be used. There is no formal agreement, but permission has been offered freely and without expectation of recompense.

Borrowing without Permission

Because smaller nonprofit organizations often lack staff members trained in marketing, they may not be familiar with IP laws; in some instances, this may cause them to unintentionally use some copyrighted materials incorrectly. This may be due to incorrect interpretations of Fair Use standards, which allow copyrighted materials to be used for "educational" or not-for-profit purposes; in short, nonprofits may assume that Fair Use means "fair use" and that the private sector is willing to share their work and allow it to be used or modified for any nonprofit purpose. But, as any humanist interested in IP knows, even though a nonprofit does not produce profits the same way a private organization does not mean that nonprofit organizations can use copyrighted IP that they do not own for commercial purposes. When they do so, often without the knowledge that they are violating copyright law, they put themselves at risk for a host of nasty penalties, ranging from a simple cease-and-desist notification to a full-fledged lawsuit by a large business or nonprofit that can afford to sue for damages.

Given all this, it is not surprising that the WCGL borrowed without permission in their early days as a nonprofit organization because they had no in-house, full-time development staff and no money to pay outside consultants to produce marketing materials for them.[4] When they were advertising a grief counseling seminar, for instance (in 2007), they used a Charlie Brown animation with the caption "Good Grief!" to emphasize that the meeting would describe how grieving was part of a healthy process.

When Jessica found this flyer during data collection for her dissertation research and asked Alwood why WCGL had chosen a copyrighted image, Alwood replied that "it was for nonprofit purposes" and "we couldn't have put it better ourselves. It communicated, in a humorous way, what we wanted to say to women about the grieving process" (Alwood, 2010). The grief seminar being advertised was also a fundraising event for the WCGL, an organization that offers services to women on a sliding scale, so this is a clear example of borrowing without permission and an unintentional violation of copyright. Based on

Alwood's response, it is also safe to assume that she was unaware that this communication moment and product violated copyright law, knowledge that might have caused her to reconsider the use of the image, or at least would have influenced how she thought about her promotion of the seminar via this image.

Today, nonprofit organizations that take similar risks are more likely to be caught than they would have been a few years ago. Users who download copyrighted images from a search engine like Google are tracked (Ehrmann, 2010). Google Images, for instance, embeds code into catalogued images, which makes the tracing of those images easier than ever. Additionally, the entertainment industry has announced their intentions to develop a Center for Copyright Information that would "discourage illegal file sharing" and "send a series of letters to customers" who are continually found to be "downloading unauthorized content" (Sandoval, 2012). Even though IP laws are increasingly being publicized to the general public and the nonprofit sector, NPOs do not always have ready access to this knowledge, nor do their staff members always understand how to apply this knowledge to their branding efforts. In fact, as we saw in the above instance, it may be an afterthought for many organizations whose missions center on social issues rather than media literacy.

Alternative Borrowing Practices

As pressures to conform to IP law increase, more nonprofit organizations are being schooled in the intersections of IP and technology—mostly because of the support of nonprofit umbrella organizations (like Techsoup). During technology workshops sponsored by these umbrella organizations, nonprofit organizations learn about using and producing media effectively—which includes learning about IP laws and which digitally shared materials they can use with permission. As a result, nonprofits have become more aware of public domain materials and creative commons licensed materials and have started to use these in their work.

While law firms may educate nonprofit organization clients about public domain and creative commons works they can borrow, development consultants and researchers can also aid nonprofit organizations in learning how to use and adapt these licensed materials. For example, the WCGL recently paid a development consultant-in-training to redesign their web site to make it more sustainable; they wanted to translate their static web site into a Wordpress-based site that staff and volunteers could maintain without having extensive technological expertise. As the consultant was redesigning the website, she used a "Rosie the Riveter" image as a placeholder on the front page—a public domain image perfect for representing the WCGL, as it is a female figure that represents strength, confidence, and capacity to adapt to difficult work conditions. During this process, the WCGL staff learned more about public domain materials and how to access them because this consultant knew about those materials and offered to educate staff and interns during the web site redesign process.

In this case, the consultant acted in the organization's best interest, but another challenge to the culture of borrowing comes when organizations hire consultants who put profit first. Countless organizations we've worked with over the years have had experiences very different from the WCGL's. Recently, in fact, Guiseppe encountered a web designer who had charged a small nonprofit over $1500 to design a web site, that, upon examination, was not even designed with current web standards in mind. When the organization asked the designer to add four links and one page to the site, the designer reportedly replied that though he engaged in community service, he would have to charge them more for the additional work.

Like this individual, most consultants and public relation firms like to own the IP that they create for nonprofit organizations so that they can charge for additional services that they offer. And though we do not wish to demonize consultants for charging for their services, we do wish to highlight the high costs that nonprofits endure to make sure that they are borrowing correctly, which often put them in worse financial straits than if they just took their chances by borrowing incorrectly (at least from their point of view). Once again, there is lots of room for motivated humanists to consult with nonprofits in their local area, for a price or as an act of service, in order to help them negotiate the branding minefield.

Implications for Encouraging a Culture of Sharing

Encouraging a culture of sharing within a nonprofit community via the practices of borrowing with permission and educating nonprofit leaders as to alternative borrowing practices made available via public domain storehouses is no easy task, and neither is helping nonprofits through the mire of trademarking. In our own work toward this end we have encountered resistance, some maliciousness, and a decent amount of wrong-headedness amongst nonprofit leaders who sometimes, despite our best efforts, continue to try to operate "under the radar" of IP laws rather than deal with them head-on. Although it is beyond the scope of this chapter to visit the motivations of these individuals, suffice it to say that education related to best practices is sometimes not enough.

Like IP practices themselves, then, helping to foster increased knowledge about IP is best approached via an assets-based mindset. The first step is always to find *willing* nonprofit leaders in one's own community, leaders that are interested in fostering communal branding practices. These do not necessarily have to be highly motivated individuals like the founders of the Women's Center of

Greater Lansing, but *should* be pragmatic people who understand the seriousness of intellectual property violations.

Next, organizing workshops, forums, and service-learning partnerships that foster a culture of intellectual property sharing takes time. Besides being open to the development of this kind of culture, humanists will need allies in the local community willing to do the hard work of organizing events, promoting opportunities, and even helping to build community-run databases and archives of available materials. Though such an effort should not be taken up lightly, as we hope we have demonstrated, the cultivation of a thriving nonprofit sector that is knowledgeable about and able to successfully negotiate intellectual property law is in everyone's best interest.

Notes

1 When their brand iconicity is threatened, NPOs may take legal action. For instance, the Susan J. Komen Foundation took legal action when other NPOs used their motto "for the cure."

2 For this reason, for-profit ventures like the Nonprofit Branding Institute have been very successful. However, many local marketing firms and a small, rising number of NPOs have specialized in helping NPOs create their public faces.

3 We're using, with permission, data from chapter 4 of Jessica's dissertation (2011) to discuss how the WCGL's use of intellectual property has changed over time. WCGL has allowed us to use identifying information.

4 Although Kress was an experienced grant writer in academia (as a social work professor) prior to her work at the WCGL, she received her formal training as a social worker and social science researcher; during her tenure at the WCGL, she became a development professional. However, only half of her full time appointment involved marketing and fundraising work; half of her assigned tasks involved training social work interns to work with clients.

• CHAPTER TWENTY •

Oppositional Copyright Curricula in the K–12 Classroom

Clancy Ratliff

Effective July 2007, California enacted the following state law for primary and secondary schools that receive funding for technology:

> The guidelines and criteria shall include a component to educate pupils and teachers on the appropriate and ethical use of information technology in the classroom, Internet safety, the manner in which to avoid committing plagiarism, the concept, purpose, and significance of a copyright so that pupils are equipped with the skills necessary to distinguish lawful from unlawful online downloading, and the implications of illegal peer-to-peer network file sharing.

To meet this mandate, California schools have two prefabricated curricula to teach if they choose. One is from the Recording Industry Association of America (RIAA), created in 2006 for third through eighth grade. Titled "Music Rules!," the curriculum centers on copyright as granted to works of music, and students engage in activities that include writing songs and solving math problems about how much money recording companies lose through illegal downloading using numbers provided by the RIAA. The other, "Teaching Copyright," is from the Electronic Frontier Foundation (EFF), created in 2009 for ninth through twelfth grade, and it features reading assignments, videos, discussions, and writing prompts where students inhabit the positions of various stakeholders affected by copyright law.

In this chapter, I rhetorically analyze each curriculum using terms introduced by Jessica Reyman (2010) in *The Rhetoric of Intellectual Property: Copyright Law and the Regulation of Digital Culture*–specifically, "the property stewardship narrative" to refer to the content industries' argument and "the cultural conservancy narrative" to refer to the counterargument. I situate these curricula in a broader cultural context that includes new music distribution mechanisms and use law scholar Jonathan Zittrain's (2008) idea of generativity to suggest an answer to Reyman's call for change in the rhetoric of copyright.

Pedagogy and Culture

It is commonplace that good pedagogy hails students as future leaders, encouraging them to critique received knowledge and participate in creating new knowledge, and that bad pedagogy treats students as passive receptacles whose job it is to unquestioningly repeat what they learned in drill-type exercises. Admittedly, this is a generalization, but if we at least provisionally accept it, it extends to any subject, including copyright, technology, and culture. Presenting content (in this case, copyright law) as open to question and interpretation will stimulate student intellect more than presenting them with rules they must obey and tasks they must complete without understanding the reasons or purposes they serve.

As far back as 1987, Paul Olson found that children in underprivileged schools learned about technology in a very "rote" and "mechanical" way, whereas children in "middle-class schools" were expected to interact with computers in a more sophisticated way, one that called for "cognate skills, industry, generalizability, and language and programming skills" that had "transferability across content" (p. 195). A democratic approach to pedagogy would give all students access to teaching and learning that helps them to flourish as active, engaged, empowered agents—and citizens. Such an aim is also aligned with cultural studies, and my use of the terms "culture" and "digital culture" is informed by a cultural studies approach to writing pedagogy, which situates students not just as consumers, but as scholars who engage in "culture analysis and critique into the rhetoric of public discourse" (George & Trimbur, 2001, p. 86).

Before looking closely at the rhetoric used by each copyright curriculum, I'd like to situate them in the larger context of the K–12 education system, in which (as of June 2014) 43 states have adopted the Common Core State Standards (CCSS), an initiative designed to ensure that students are college- and career-ready upon graduating from high school. To be sure, these standards have come under criticism from education scholars (e.g., Gilyard, 2012). Nonetheless, most schools are implementing them during or shortly after the 2014–2015 school year. The scope of this chapter does not permit an analysis of the CCSS as a whole; I only want to show a potential gap in student understanding of intellectual property issues not addressed in the CCSS: These standards seemingly require students to publish their writing on the Internet, which would provide an appropriate occasion for discussing copyright, but only mention IP in the context of plagiarism. In the table below are Common Core State Standards numbers six and eight under "Writing," applicable to all grade levels. Number six falls under the heading "Production and Distribution of Writing," and number eight falls under the heading "Research to Build and Present Knowledge."

Table 1. Common Core State Standards

Grade Level	Writing Standard #6	Writing Standard #8
6	"Use technology, including the Internet, to produce and publish writing as well as to interact and collaborate with others; demonstrate sufficient command of keyboarding skills to type a minimum of three pages in a single sitting."	"Gather relevant information from multiple print and digital sources; assess the credibility of each source; and quote or paraphrase the data and conclusions of others while avoiding plagiarism and providing basic bibliographic information for sources."
7	"Use technology, including the Internet, to produce and publish writing and link to and cite sources as well as to interact and collaborate with others, including linking to and citing sources."	"Gather relevant information from multiple print and digital sources, using search terms effectively; assess the credibility and accuracy of each source; and quote or paraphrase the data and conclusions of others while avoiding plagiarism and following a standard format for citation."
8	"Use technology, including the Internet, to produce and publish writing and present the relationships between information and ideas efficiently as well as to interact and collaborate with others."	"Gather relevant information from multiple print and digital sources, using search terms effectively; assess the credibility and accuracy of each source; and quote or paraphrase the data and conclusions of others while avoiding plagiarism and following a standard format for citation."

The CCSS assume a text-based model of writing and cast IP only in academic terms: citing sources, quoting, paraphrasing, and avoiding plagiarism. Although the CCSS emphasize academic norms of IP as well as collaborative writing with peers, they don't extend those ideas into an outcome statement about understanding the consequences of publishing writing online, which involve some knowledge of copyright law.

Those in higher education, especially composition studies, have argued for years that if we're going to require students to publish their writing online, particularly if that writing includes images, sounds, or video, we must educate students about copyright and fair use. Dànielle DeVoss (2007) noted that "digital composing practices are typically at odds with digital (and material) protection practices" and that "if we ask students to compose and create, we bear the responsibility of teaching students about how they work, play, and live in the larger copyright system" (p. 207). TyAnna Herrington (2009) commented that "students whose instructors demand that they create blogs published to the Web also make their work accessible and at risk for copyright violation" (p. 163)—a reminder that at the same time students need to learn about fair use of others' materials, they also need to understand their rights to their own work and how to recognize when their rights have been violated. Stephen Westbrook (2011) explained the consequences of publishing work online: "when texts traverse academic and public arenas, they radically complicate the question of fair use; this is especially true for non-print genres that rely on appropriated images or audio clips" (p. 161). Although the CCSS are certainly flexible with regard to content, enabling teachers in English Language Arts and other subjects to assign essays about copyright and fair use, the standards themselves don't recognize what connects collaborative writing, publishing writing on the Internet, and understanding academic norms of IP: the underlying ideas of authorship and copyright.

Enter the copyright curricula. Many K–12 teachers, along with most of the general public, may not have a deep familiarity with copyright law themselves. In addition, they are often under pressure from school, district, or state administration to teach certain pre-selected texts. Tarleton Gillespie (2011) explained that the content industries get their curricular materials to schools through direct mail campaigns and partnerships with "established scholastic publication[s]," including Channel One (an ongoing student-oriented video series with embedded advertising). It is under these educational circumstances that students learn what they learn, if anything, about copyright and fair use.

Copyright Rhetoric: Patterns and Problems

To inform my analysis of the RIAA and EFF's curricula, I have found Reyman's and Zittrain's work especially useful. Reyman identified broad rhetorical patterns on both sides and called for "a new rhetoric of copyright" that would embody a four-part schema of "democratic," "user focused, not technology-driven," "action-oriented," and "unified" (pp. 148–149). Zittrain's study of the Internet, with its rhetorical frame of "generativity," offered an important step toward a new rhetoric of copyright.

Reyman's (2010) "property stewardship narrative" refers to content industry arguments about copyright law. In this narrative, property stewards are official distributors (e.g., record companies) who disseminate creative and intellectual work. We pay the property stewards for these recordings, who in turn pay the authors and artists. Copyright law's purpose is to help property stewards such as the RIAA, which "are essential for protecting artists from exploitation and ensuring that creators get paid for their contributions" (Reyman, p. 59). The problems with the property stewardship narrative are familiar to those studying the discourse about copyright: It demonizes new technologies as piracy tools and misrepresents the intended purpose of copyright law (i.e., to further the arts and sciences, not only to ensure that creators are paid for their work).

In the "cultural conservancy narrative," the conflict is not between artists and would-be pirates, but between artists and corporate rightsholders who keep creative and intellectual work out of the public domain, which artists depend on for material to enable them to create new works. This narrative attempts to show the balance between copyright holders and the public and to claim that artists are in the best position to create new intellectual and creative work if they are able to use others' content. The implication is that culture is conserved and enriched by maintaining and continually replenishing a commons, or a public domain of content. Copyright law decrees that after the specified time limit, the work must go into the public domain to be distributed freely and used in the creation of new work. Like the property stewardship narrative, the cultural conservancy narrative has problems. Reyman (2010) noted that

> the discourse of the commons has failed to establish a coherent message that sufficiently argues against the heightened rhetoric of theft and morality from the entertainment industries. One reason for this failure may be that the cultural conservancy narrative appears only at dispersed points in varied forms of the discourse of the debate, oscillating between analogies to an environmental movement ("endangered gizmos"), political freedoms (providing access "where suppression of particular material might be attempted"), and even feminist ethics ("sharing" and "responsibility"). (p. 92)

The discourse of copyright reveals a larger problem in U.S. political discourse: We have a simple argument—in this case, the good guys/bad guys message of the property stewardship narrative—that, though misleading, registers clearly with the public and thus appears stronger and more compelling. Although the cultural conservancy narrative is more accurate on copyright law, it's a complicated argument that, in its refusal to oversimplify, sounds weaker and less organized.

In *The Future of the Internet and How to Stop It*, Zittrain (2008) set up an opposition between the Internet as "generative PCs attached to a generative network" and "sterile appliances tethered to a network of control" (p. 3). Zittrain's analysis focused not on copyright law directly but on the architecture of the Internet: the availability or locking down of software code and its implications for innovation, online security, freedom of speech, the economy, education, and more. However, his rhetorical frame of generativity can be useful for copyright rhetorics. Zittrain defined generativity as, broadly speaking, "a system's capacity to produce unanticipated change through unfiltered contributions from broad and varied audiences," and he continued, "terms like 'openness' and 'free' and 'commons' evoke elements of it, but they do not fully capture its meaning, and they sometimes obscure it" (p. 70). Here, it seems, Zittrain hinted at problems with the cultural conservancy narrative. He listed five qualities of generative systems:

> (1) how extensively a system or technology leverages a set of possible tasks; (2) how well it can be adapted to a range of tasks; (3) how easily new contributors can master it; (4) how accessible it is to those ready and able to build on it; and (5) how transferable any changes are to others—including (and perhaps especially) nonexperts. (p. 71)

It's not difficult to see how these five factors can be applied to copyright law. The concept of generativitiy simplifies discourse about copyright in a helpful way, clarifying without oversimplifying. Generativity is less ideologically and historically loaded than "commons." Generativity anchors the discourse by prompting the important questions about copyright: Is copyright generative? Why may we want it to be generative? Who may generate and under what conditions? What may be generated, and how? Generativity lifts the stakes to the surface without dragging so much of the complexity of copyright law along with them (the minutiae of fair use, the successive extensions of the terms of copyright, and digital rights management, to give some examples).

In the next section, I summarize each of the lessons in "Music Rules!" and "Teaching Copyright" and then focus more closely on specific artifacts in each curriculum, including key visuals and prompts for students. I intend to show that the curricula, especially "Music Rules!" embody the property stewardship narrative and the cultural conservancy narrative, and that neither one credibly situates students as producers of digital culture.

The Curricula

The Electronic Frontier Foundation's curriculum consists of five lessons. The first one, titled "Definitions of Copyright: What Do They Know?," is intended to be given after a preliminary assessment called "Copy Quiz," the results of which serve as a baseline of the group's copyright knowledge. The lesson provides a basic sketch of copyright law, covering the terms "public domain," "fair use," and "copyright." FAQ documents give students more information about the circumstances under which works are copyrighted, the length of the terms of copyright, the First Sale exception, licensing, plagiarism, and the ways that copyright can be transferred from one person to another. The RIAA's first lesson, out of a total of four, is titled "Music Rules!" In the lesson-by-lesson comparison I'm about to provide, I have used the RIAA's lessons for sixth through eighth grades so that the age groups for the two curricula would be more closely aligned. The lesson's main objective is to familiarize students with the term "songlifting," with an ancillary objective of helping them learn to use spreadsheet software. Students learn the various forms of "songlifting":

accepting a copied CD from someone, downloading music illegally, and making a copy of a CD for someone else. They are also given dollar figures for how much the music industry loses from "songlifting."

The EFF's second lesson is called "A Brief History of Copyright and Innovation," and it shows students the ways that copyright law has changed since its inception, as well as the ways that technology has changed—specifically, those technologies that copy creative works, such as the printing press and the rewritable CD. The title of the RIAA's second lesson is "Meet the Music Makers," and in it, students learn about the types of jobs in the music industry.

Lesson three for the EFF's curriculum is "Fair Use: Remix Culture, Mashups, and Copyright." Students learn, through exercises stemming from a "Stakeholders Worksheet," that copyright law affects academia, government, business, the legal profession, nonprofit organizations, and others. They practice doing the four-factor analysis for judging whether or not a use falls under Fair Use. The curriculum frames Fair Use as a matter of free speech versus censorship. The RIAA's lesson three is titled "It's the Law," and it gives some basic information about copyright law: that its intent is to encourage people to create new works, that copyright does not require the work to have a copyright © symbol, and that it means people must secure permission to make copies of that work and distribute them. Neither Fair Use nor fair use are not mentioned, but the lesson does point out that someone who buys music is permitted to transfer those song files to an MP3 player or a blank CD for personal use.

The fourth lesson in "Teaching Copyright" is "Peer-to-Peer File Sharing." The EFF uses the term "file sharing" as a frame rather than "piracy" or the "songlifting" of the "Music Rules!" curriculum. The lesson seems designed to impress upon students that the technology itself is not illegal, only that some of its uses are. The curriculum gives the teacher a "fictionalized composite RIAA case" to present, and it encourages students, using the idea of stakeholders, to express their views about file sharing, including those views that support the RIAA's position.

I exhibit the fourth lesson in "Music Rules!" alongside the fifth lesson in "Teaching Copyright" because both are intended to be capstone experiences for students. The "Music Rules!" capstone exercise is called "Make Your Own Music," and students are asked to write songs about songlifting. The curriculum materials give this verse from a rap as an example:

> Music is worth it, if you're asking me—
> True words, new rhythms, sweet melody—
> Just tell me where to get it and I'll gladly pay
> For a song that says what my heart wants to say.

> But don't try to fool me with a phony copy,
> 'Cause songlifting's wrong, and it's got to stop, see?

Once the students write and record their songs onto CDs, they design a CD cover and posters to promote the artists and songs, enacting the roles of designers and publicists, among other roles. The teacher and students then have a "music party" to perform the songs and discuss how it might affect them if someone were to "songlift" their songs. One could argue that in giving students this experience, "Music Rules" is taking students seriously as producers of culture. I would agree that this activity gives students the opportunity to be creative and to be in charge of a project; however, the way culture is presented does not make this claim convincing. Culture, understood as music, is cast as a career that one does or does not pursue; there is no representation of amateur, not-for-profit production. Students essentially pretend that they are real producers of real music, and by extension producers of culture.

"Teaching Copyright's" capstone activity is a mock trial. The lesson is titled "Fair Use: You Be The Judge," and students are instructed to take a side in the case of *Walt Disney Studios v. Faden*, invoking a real-life situation in which Eric Faden, a professor at Bucknell University, created a clever short film about Fair Use by splicing together short clips of Disney movies. Students are designated as plaintiff, defendant, and lawyers for each side; once they present their arguments and have opportunities for examination and cross-examination, other students discuss the case as jurors, and the teacher acts as judge. This activity is laudable in that it, like the music activity, requires students to lead a project; unlike the music activity, it allows students to engage a variety of perspectives and arguments about copyright. But this project (as well as other shorter activities embedded in earlier lessons) puts students in the role of judge, deciding whether a particular case—something that someone else has produced—is Fair Use or copyright infringement. The only exercise in the curriculum that asks students to produce is an ancillary one in lesson three under the heading "Extension Activities," in which students create parodic or critical collages about a celebrity.

Cultural Variables

The RIAA

In pursuit of a more complete rhetorical analysis of these curricula, I'd like to contextualize the RIAA's role in the copyright debate. The organization is arguably less powerful and culturally relevant than it once was. Their property stewardship narrative, to use Reyman's (2010) term, is still more rhetorically coherent and catchy than the more disjointed cultural conservancy narrative, but changes in music distribution technology are affecting both narratives. The property stewardship narrative is easier to learn and recite, but it may no longer be as persuasive; certainly the rise of new major industry players (Google, Facebook) affects the balance of power. We see this most recently in the withdrawal of the Stop Online Piracy Act (SOPA) and the Protect Intellectual Property Act (PIPA), both of which the RIAA lobbyists supported with both public rhetoric and money to its main architect, Representative Lamar Smith of Texas.

In late 2008, the RIAA decided to stop suing individuals for downloading music, as that strategy "created a public-relations disaster for the industry, whose lawsuits targeted, among others, several single mothers, a dead person and a 13-year-old girl" (McBride & Smith, 2008). Instead, they decided to seek a partnership with Internet services providers, such that ISPs would cut off users' Internet access if they downloaded music illegally. The ISPs refused to cooperate. Both the RIAA and the EFF are cultural variables, in fact, though I would argue that the RIAA's role has changed more than the EFF's; while the RIAA was once formidable but now lacks some of the power it once had, the EFF has always been a grassroots organization without a lot of cultural influence. The RIAA, as evidenced by the arguments in the "Music Rules!" curriculum, is in a retreating position. As McBride and Smith reported,

> In 2003, the industry sold 656 million albums. In 2007, the number fell to 500 million CDs and digital albums, plus 844 million paid individual song downloads'—hardly enough to make up the decline in album sales.

In the years since the industry collected this data, album sales have likely declined more. RIAA president Cary Sherman (2012) wrote that

> music sales in the United States are less than half of what they were in 1999, when the file-sharing site Napster emerged, and that direct employment in the industry had fallen by more than half since then, to less than 10,000.

The RIAA is relying more heavily now on other fear tactics instead of litigation to persuade users not to download music illegally: for example, the increased likelihood of encountering online predators, viruses, and spyware.

Technological change and cultural change are intertwined here; while the technology changed from vinyl records to cassette tapes to compact discs to downloaded files played on small devices, I would argue that the move from discovering new music at record stores to discovering it online is a cultural (not just an economic or technological) shift. Perhaps users who buy single songs on iTunes or Amazon, or who view the advertisements on online streaming services, feel that they do their part to compensate the music industry, so they refuse the "pirate" label, and that message is less effective. The RIAA's rhetorical tactics have not acknowledged these new practices that demonstrate the middle ground between paying for a CD and illegally downloading music files. In a

February 2012 *New York Times* op-ed, Cary Sherman wrote that the aims of SOPA/PIPA were to "protect American property from theft, to shield consumers from counterfeit products" (he cited pharmaceuticals in particular, which do not fall under copyright law) and fraud, and to combat foreign criminals who exploit technology to steal American ingenuity and jobs.

Music Distribution and Digital Culture

The years since "Music Rules!" was originally published have seen dramatic changes in music distribution. While technology does not determine culture, I would agree with Reyman (2010) that distribution "based on exclusivity and centralized control by powerful content industries" is "a *cultural model* for producing and distributing content" (p. 7, emphasis mine). This model is now much more complex than hearing a song on the radio and buying the CD. The taxonomy of terrestrial radio, satellite radio, and Internet radio is now familiar. We can, obviously, still download music illegally through BitTorrent and other venues, and we can still buy music on CD. However, users have grown increasingly accustomed to buying individual songs from iTunes, Amazon.com, and other services. Also, there are popular services like Spotify, MOG, last.fm, Grooveshark, and Pandora that allow users to listen to streaming music. With some of these services, users can listen to songs on demand for no cost, legally, as these sites—and the purchasing of rights to play the music—are funded by advertisements.

With others, such as Napster and Rhapsody (technically the same company), users pay a monthly subscription fee for unlimited listening, with the option to download MP3s without Digital Rights Management copy protection technology. These streaming services are becoming as portable as CDs; we can now use Pandora in cars, as the Hyundai Veloster is designated "Pandora friendly," meaning that we can use the Internet connections on our smartphones or tablets, sync them with the Veloster, and—if we have an Apple iPhone—control Pandora using the car's buttons and dials. In fact, users can automagically use their smartphones to make Pandora play in any vehicle that has Bluetooth; they just have to control Pandora using the buttons and touchscreens on their devices.

About the technology in the Hyundai Veloster, Bill Howard (2011) of ExtremeTech wrote: "This is what you'll see on all cars once automakers stop believing CDs are the core of the entertainment experience." Indeed, many 2013- and 2014-model vehicles have Bluetooth but no CD players, such as the Kia Soul and Chevrolet Spark. Still, the RIAA's curriculum tends to assume a CD model, as they have not updated "Music Rules!" since it was created in 2006.

In curriculum materials, they list six categories of jobs in particular that they claim are affected by illegal downloading:

1. Talent Spotters: club owner, music scout, record company executives, mom.
2. Tune Crafters: music producer, songwriters, arrangers, singer.
3. Recording Artists: music producer, sound engineers, backup vocalists, instrumentalists, singer.
4. Buzz Builders: music producer, publicist, designer, photographer, magazine publishers, poster distributors, music critics, radio DJs, music video broadcasters, TV talk show hosts, singer.
5. Disc Wranglers: CD manufacturer, machine operators, printers, packagers, shipping manager, truck driver.
6. Hit Merchants: store managers, sales clerks, cashiers, online vendors, online order handlers, mail carriers. (Teacher Guide, p. 5)

The last two in particular are linked with a CD distribution (and cultural) model—a culture their curriculum's target audience does not inhabit now: I would argue that many third through eighth graders are more familiar with online streaming music than CDs. It should be noted that the RIAA approves of services like Pandora and Spotify. On the "Resources" page of "Music Rules!" there's a link to "Legal Music Sites," which leads to a page on the riaa.com domain that lists 23 online music services, including all the ones I've mentioned.

So it would seem that we have a compromise that's acceptable to both sides: Users are no longer forced to pay upwards of $20 for a CD of several songs they don't want bundled with the one song they do want, and the content industries are reassured that they can make money in the pay-per-song and paid-by-ads distribution model. However, a deeper problem in the rhetoric remains: Digital culture and users are misrepresented. The RIAA assigns

> binary roles for students in their digital copyright narratives, on the one hand, as amoral or unethical criminals, making them villainous characters, or, on the other, as responsible consumers who pay for all content on digital networks. (Reyman, 2010, p. 114)

The problems, still, are these: The content industries' rhetoric does not accurately represent copyright law, digital culture, or users, and the counter-industry rhetoric is not yet a simple, easily communicated message.

A New Rhetoric of Copyright

Neither of these curricula quite embodies Reyman's (2010) idea for a new rhetoric of copyright. For Reyman, a rhetoric of copyright that avoids the problems of the property stewardship narrative and the cultural conservancy narrative would have to meet four criteria: it would have to be *democratic*, *user-focused*, *action-oriented*, and *unified*.

Democratic

Reyman (2010) argued for starting with the fact that both sides—cultural conservancy and property stewardship—want to encourage the production of creative and intellectual work, a value she rightly characterized as democratic. The new rhetoric of copyright would locate this value in (and emphasize) early copyright law and focus on the creative works that are produced in everyday digital culture. We saw some of this highlighting of early copyright law during the *Eldred v. Ashcroft* case in 2002 and 2003, when bloggers displayed buttons on their blog sites that said "Create like it's 1790!" and we see it in the availability of Founders' Copyright terms facilitated by Creative Commons. To the EFF's credit, "Teaching Copyright" does engage early copyright law, as does the cultural conservancy narrative generally. The RIAA's curriculum only states that copyright is in the United States Constitution, not specifying the difference between the original copyright terms and those of today.

User-based, not Technology-driven

The current rhetoric of digital copyright leaves us with binaries, as Reyman (2010) explained: "theft versus originality and free copying versus paying royalties" (p. 147). She argued that the discourse has been preoccupied with emerging technologies and their implications for copyright law, labeling these new technologies as liberating or threatening. Users' everyday practices—their digital culture—is far more complex than these binaries suggest. "Teaching Copyright" acknowledges this culture in lesson three about Fair Use, claiming that people are "using copyrighted content to build a culture of remixes and mashups—essentially multimedia collages—exercising a great deal of wit and creativity in the process," and they give several examples of such users in true-or-false questions in their "Copy Quiz":

> Adam recorded a video for his YouTube channel about the upcoming Senate elections and includes an official photo taken by a government employee and four bills authored by the incumbent that Adam found on the Senate's website.
>
> That's copyright infringement.
>
> False. Works produced by the U.S. government, or any U.S. government agency, are in the public domain. The texts of legal cases and statutes produced by the federal government are also in the public domain.
>
> Kathy downloaded a few photos of local organic farms from Flickr.com's Creative Commons (CC) pool. She follows the rules of the photographer's specific CC license and uses them in her digital video about sustainable agriculture. That's OK.
>
> True. Kathy can legally use the photos as long as she follows the rules of the license.

Certainly these examples show users as contributors to digital culture, but not all users create videos using other people's content. "Teaching Copyright" offers this example as well, though:

> Amy tells Daniel about her summer vacation, and he says he'd love to see her pictures. Amy uses a peer-to-peer (P2P) file-sharing program to upload the photographs she took at camp so he can download them. That's copyright infringement.
>
> False. Sharing your own original work using peer-to-peer file-sharing technology is legal.

A user doesn't have to make videos, podcasts, or collage-style projects in order to make a contribution to digital culture; even sharing vacation photographs is among these everyday practices of building and embodying culture.

Action-oriented

Here, Reyman (2010) argued that a new rhetoric of copyright needs visible, ethical actions, and she cited Flickr and Facebook as businesses that make money based on the availability and sharing of free content. To these I might add Reddit, Boing Boing, Wikipedia, and other sites that participated in the January 18, 2012, blackout in protest of SOPA and PIPA. Awareness of larger, more organized actions such as these is missing from both curricula.

Unified

The arguments in the cultural conservancy narrative have been disjointed, and Reyman (2010) called for a unified focus on "the very future of cultural production on the Internet" (p. 149), as well as more explanation about how specific groups are affected by changes in copyright law. The EFF's curriculum, with its consistent emphasis on stakeholders, meets this quality of the new rhetoric somewhat.

Although Reyman (2010) named and briefly explained these criteria, she does not actually show what this new rhetoric would look like. I believe Zittrain's (2008) ideas might, though. When setting forth her criterion of "democratic," Reyman argued that a new rhetoric of copyright would be grounded in the goal shared by both poles in the copyright debate: creating more new creative and intellectual work. She explained that this new rhetoric would focus "on the productive processes online and the ways in which participation in creative activity has the potential to increase with the use of digital technologies" (p. 148). Zittrain's framing device of generativity satisfies the democratic aim in the simple question, or test, implied in the frame: is copyright generative? Both sides want generativity, and Zittrain's five qualities show the emphasis of generativity on productive processes. We see democratic ideals here as well, as Zittrain remarked of generativity,

> the first good is its innovative output: new things that improve people's lives. The second good is its participatory input, based on a belief that a life well lived is one in which there is opportunity to connect to other people, to work with them, and to express one's own individuality through creative endeavors. (p. 80)

In the second good especially, the focus on people (users, in Reyman's schema) is apparent.

Zittrain's frame also meets the "user-based, not technology-driven" criterion. He does not lapse into fallacious technological determinism, or attaching "inherently progressive or destructive" labels onto technologies (Reyman, p. 148). A technology is more generative or less generative, and while more generative is the preferred route, it can result in viruses, malware, and other undesirable outcomes. Generativity asks what users already do and what else they're able to do (or not do)—good questions for a rhetoric of copyright.

Reyman's (2010) third point is that our rhetoric should be "action-oriented," meaning that it foregrounds positive, ethical actions and users identifying as contributors to digital culture in a "participatory Internet" (p. 148). Again, this idea aligns well with Zittrain's (2008) notion of generativity, which implicitly asks: What is generated, and by whom?

The final criterion for a new rhetoric of copyright in Reyman's schema is that it must be "unified"—that is, that it illustrate the stakes of copyright law, "the very future of cultural production on the Internet." To that I would also add the future of cultural production *not* on the Internet. The rhetoric from the "copyleft, copyfight" set has attempted to show these stakes, but perhaps not clearly. Generativity looks simply at possibility—what can and cannot be done in a particular system. I would argue that the term "generativity" is less ideologically charged than "commons," thus serving as a reminder of the shared goal between the opposing camps, "saving digital culture" (Reyman, 2010, p. 149). That goal might be open to question. The RIAA president recently wrote that "we all share the goal of a safe and legal Internet," adding, with unintentional irony, that "we need reason, not rhetoric, in discussing how to achieve it" (Sherman, 2012). In any case, finding common ground is much needed in the copyright debate.

Conclusion

I have no numbers for how many California schools are using "Music Rules!" or "Teaching Copyright," as opposed to creating their own curriculum to meet their state's mandate. The uptake of these curricula in other schools outside California is also unclear (the "Music Rules!" site has a page titled "Teacher Comments" with blurbs from teachers in Laguna Niguel, CA; Bellerose, NY;

Concord, CA; San Diego, CA; Chicopee, MA; Clarksdale, AZ; Amityville, NY; Kettering, OH; and Springfield, TN. Teachers' full names aren't listed, nor are the school names, however). What is clear is that the RIAA's curriculum is not representing copyright law accurately, and that both of these curricula fail to position students explicitly and seriously as users who already make legitimate contributions to digital culture: users who make, produce, and generate. Zittrain (2008) remarked that "generativity itself is, at its core, not a technology project. It is an education project, an exercise in intellect and community, the founding concepts of the university" (pp. 244–245). The humanities are commonly associated with the preservation and advancement of culture, and each curriculum seems concerned with that goal. Teachers using these curricula are implicated as the standard bearers of support for the arts, as differently as that idea is defined in the property stewardship narrative and the cultural conservancy narrative, and must maintain a critical balance as they influence students' conceptions of intellectual property.

• CHAPTER TWENTY-ONE •

Using Eco-feminism to Sustain the Open Educational Resources Movement in a Corporatized Culture

Laural Lea Adams

> What is at stake is the impact of technologies on the quality of our lives. Because the rate of technological change is remarkably faster than in the past, we no longer have the luxury of slowly, organically evolving our practices to catch up... We must deliberately consider our technology choices and changes to our practices in light of our values. (Nardi & O'Day, 1999, p. 210)

Ecofeminism, with its ecology focus, can be used to promote the sustainability of open education by recognizing, involving, and fostering a culture in the "community of development" that considers and involves the "community of use." This chapter proposes eco-feminism as a framework to help coordinate open educational resources (OER)[1] initiatives that resist the business-model approaches threatening to render many digital resources as income strategies rather than as modes for extending access to education. Every realm of society, from childbearing to dying, has become increasingly corporatized in the wake of neoliberal reform and economic strain in contemporary U.S. culture. Educational institutions have not been exempt from the shift to privilege economic outcomes over social ones. Since the late 1990s, even primary and secondary public schools are increasingly employing for-profit educational management organizations, which structure children's educational experiences in terms of business operations. Similarly, the bulk of management practices in post-secondary education is now characterized by business-model approaches, spurred largely by privatization and the need to respond to reduced state support with cost-saving and income-producing measures. Framed as a service industry, higher education privileges efficiency and effectiveness, and tailors much of its curriculum and research around market demand, designing new programs to capture niches for professional degrees and certification and eliminating programs and services that contribute little return on investment. Today, higher education is regarded less as a social institution tasked to provide education as a "public good" and more as one necessarily competing in a fiercely competitive market that now spans the globe (Rovai, 2009). As a result, many colleges and universities undertaking OER initiatives do so primarily as a means to expand their presence in the global education marketplace, threatening to leave OER's original, more humanist aims—opening education to disadvantaged and life-long learners—unfulfilled. I argue in this chapter that an eco-feminist lens, with its synthesis of ecology and feminist principles, can help humanities scholars resist the corporatization of OER by framing responses to cultural factors in the academy in both national and global contexts.

Eco-feminism: Responding to Successes and Excesses

Eco-feminism emerged in the mid-1980s as a social movement that combined both ecological and feminist perspectives to respond to the links between the oppression of both women and the natural environment. At its most productive and inclusive, eco-feminism works against oppressions of gender, race, class, and nature, implicitly recognizing their interdependence. The principles of eco-feminism are concerned not just with preserving environmental ecologies but supporting sustainable human communities by responding to the "successes and excesses of… the dominant social paradigm" (Naess, 1973/2007, p. 471). Eco-feminism, spearheaded by Ariel Salleh (1984), is an ecological lens that arises out of a critical stance toward the limitations of the "deep ecology" perspective advanced by Aerne Naess and Bill Devall (1980). The approach calls for the recognition that not only are environmental resources subject to human exploitation, but so too are fellow human beings. Eco-feminism challenges underlying assumptions, such as the privileging of growth at any cost, that enable the exploitation of some members of a system through technology, and favors instead cooperative activities in a more complex, mutually beneficial, sustainable environment. In cultures that privilege growth, technological expansion is predicated on the notion that increasing production creates a higher standard of living. In such cultures, a utopian regard for technology's capacity to assuage problems is coupled with the idea of change as an end-in-itself, and these factors fuel excessive rates of production and consumption. Through an eco-feminist lens, when the corporatized institution of higher education is structured to participate likewise in an "academic capitalism" by producing goods and services for the consumer market, it is to the detriment of more sustainable humanist aims that contribute to the larger ecology.

Eco-feminism's ecological perspective is hopeful, however, in that it enables us to recognize and "transcend the shortsighted instrumental pragmatism of the resource-management approach to the [global] environmental crisis" through education (Salleh, 1984, p. 480; Devall, 1980). However, resisting pressures to frame and measure social initiatives like education in economic terms is not an easy task, particularly in a climate characterized by a neoliberal faith in a free market system's ability to regulate social needs. Maintaining an OER movement that privileges openness to education and education for the development of personhood over corporatized sponsors' commercial interests is difficult in this culture. It requires championing the creation of a cooperative endeavor that extends the idea of ecology beyond metaphor.

Extending the Ecology Metaphor for OER

An eco-feminist perspective can aid humanities scholars in preserving humanist aims for OER by extending the ecology models that have already been applied to it. Stephen Downes' (2007) well-known article, "Models for Sustainable Open Educational Resources," explored sustainability from the perspective of an organization's ability to locate its advantages in funding or cost savings, technological expertise, or expertise in and access to content. These factors are useful to institutions considering OER endeavors because advocates can look to their own context and build on their strengths. However, Downes recognizes that the potential for economic sustainability is but one facet of a more extensive set of factors; he implicated cultural factors when he noted

> it also seems clear that the sustainability of OERs—in a fashion that renders then at once both affordable and usable—requires that we think of OERs as only part of a larger picture, one that includes volunteers and incentives, community and partnerships, co-production and sharing, distributed management and control. (p. 41)

Charles Lowe (2010) took up the idea of ecology more broadly in his exploration of the advantages of copyleft. Lowe described the potential for reciprocal relationships among numerous constituents, many with commercial aims. These possibilities suggest that corporate motives to engage in OER are not necessarily antithetical to humanist aims for opening access to free education. In his analysis of the factors that drive OER developers' copyright decisions and their implications for openness, Lowe described share-alike, wherein all subsequent versions carry a copyright that is "alike," or rather, replicates the original resource's restrictions and allowances for the way in which they may be reused, revised, remixed, or redistributed. Lowe delineated how copyright choices can enhance sustainability by allowing a single resource to proliferate in numerous iterations. When juxtaposed with traditional copyright, which cordons off ownership to a single entity, this alternative facilitates more open use of resources.

As Lowe said, "those who support copyleft prioritize the importance of preventing enclosure of software/content in building and sustaining a commons." However, there is no clear consensus on the role of commercial participants and whether they advance or threaten OER's sustainability. Many feel licensing should prohibit commercial interests from adopting an open resource and then closing off its use to subsequent developers who impose their own licensing restrictions, thus violating the spirit of openness with which the educational resources were first shared. What is evident from Lowe's analysis of copyright culture among developers is its complexity. The same can be said for the other sectors, such as higher education, that participate in OER's ecology as well.

OER's Place in Higher Education's Cultural Terrain

Humanities scholars who wish to advocate for privileging OER's humanist rather than commercial aims must recognize the complex cultural terrain in which OER is emerging in order to cultivate sustainable initiatives. The OER movement has represented an opportunity to enable open access to knowledge across the globe. The William and Flora Hewlett Foundation defines OER as "teaching, learning, and research resources that reside in the public domain or have been released under an intellectual property license that permits their free use or re-purposing by others," and OER can include full courses, course materials, modules, textbooks, videos, tests, software, and techniques "used to support access to knowledge" (Atkins, Brown, & Hammond, 2007). In 2007, the Shuttleworth Foundation crafted and signed the Cape Town Education Declaration, which they described as a "statement of principle, a statement of strategy and a statement of commitment" in order to advance OER initiatives across the globe. However, several cultural factors complicate fulfilling these principles, strategies, and commitments, not just at the global level, but in local contexts. They include the high costs of course development; faculty's role in the culture of knowledge production; a multicultural global ecology; a traditional student body resistant to carrying the financial burden of privatized education; and a non-traditional student body seeking alternatives to traditional degrees.

Development Costs

The expense of developing open resources is a powerful cultural factor. Currently, MIT estimates that its OpenCourseWare (OCW) project, which is international in scope and offers over 2,000 courses, some featuring expensive video content, costs approximately $3.5 million annually to sustain, and this includes distributing, collecting, digitizing, and addressing copyright issues in course content and the maintenance of a "considerable technical infrastructure to manage content and distribute it through a worldwide network to a global audience" ("Why Donate?"). OER can generate revenue to cover costs in multiple ways, such as add-ons, fee-based premium services, and advertising opportunities. Some institutions foot the bill for OER because it can enhance institutional brands.[2] They may also charge students nominal fees. Others garner fees from corporate recruiters and placement services, or, similar to the University of Michigan's arrangement with Coursera, sponsor the platform and content but hold their corporate partners responsible for monetization. As the latter model shows, closing off all commercial relationships and opportunities is short-sighted, given the extensive financial and co-operative investment required for OER initiatives. However, partnerships and practices designed to cover development costs or generate revenue streams in ways that exploit other partners in OER, whether they are developers or users, threaten its sustainability.

Faculty and the Culture of Knowledge Production

Faculty are crucial for OER's content and pedagogical expertise but are generally still subject to largely traditional promotion and tenure processes, and those who cannot articulate how their work with OER contributes to the economic well-being of the university can find it undervalued. They also feel the sting of a public that possesses a "caricatured vision of higher education faculty as 'unproductive' and privileged (which often hides an ideological distaste for critical research and teaching)" (Rosow, 2007, p. 17). Many faculty are contracted via a work-for-hire arrangement, so that educational institutions with commercial aims take ownership of their intellectual work. Lowe (2010) described the accompanying dynamics: Work-for-hire faculty fear losing control over the content they have created and feel exploited, not by the fact that they do not earn monetary compensation for contributions toward educational resources fundamentally designed to be free, but that the university reaps this compensation.

Further, many faculty believe that knowledge generated in the public academy has already been paid for by the state and other constituents, which makes publishing companies' revenues a form of unethical profiteering on what, by rights, should already be in the public domain (Fitzpatrick, 2011). However, as Laura Taylor and Brendan Riley (2006) pointed out, an open source model for publishing, which features a "collaborative developer base and the emphasis on peer review [that] establishes a community of development and innovation" appeals to academics, if they can get past a culture that has traditionally valued individual contributions, has regarded the publishing industry as central to the credentialing process and is wary about the implications of alternative copyright arrangements. Discussions about OER should therefore contextualize a resistance to strictly commercial goals for the dissemination of knowledge in OER's other affordances. For example, Taylor and Riley (2006) noted how an open-source model includes collaboration with talented others working from globally distributed locations, extensive and independent peer review, opportunities for user feedback and parallel development, as well as rapid release, all of which positively inform both academic teaching and research. Appeals for humanist OER initiatives should also call on other faculty motivations and concerns, such as interest in improving course content and feedback, concerns with the potential to positively or negatively impact an instructor's reputation, the realignment of instructors' professional goals by an OER-based agenda, and the benefits and disadvantages of having to work with other developers (Preston, 2012).

Global Cultures

With the "global reach of distance education and the emergence of a market structure as a means of regulation" (Rovai 2009, p. 63), higher education now aggressively pursues an international student market where cross-cultural factors complicate considerations of intellectual property and copyright law. OLnet, the Open Learning Network, which serves as "an international hub for aggravating, sharing, debating and improving" OER, noted that licensing is a central issue and that "differences between Creative Commons across countries and contradictions between some laws within countries results in users not contributing as they would rather be 'safe than sorry'"(Kozinska, 2011).

The factors that complicate OER in a global context are not limited to intellectual property law, as "differences in culture and teaching methods may turn out to be the greatest barrier to global and international distance education" as course developers ignore or develop courses according to these differences (Rovai, 2009, p. 50). Many developers enlist Hofstede's five dimensions of national culture, such as power distance, an individual-versus-collective orientation, gender-related cultural characteristics, and other factors, to inform their OER design. However, in a corporatized environment, there will be pressures to standardize a product toward maximizing efficiencies, which can run counter to the idea of accommodating a multicultural student body. Humanities scholars are experienced in accommodating cultural and ideological diversity through sites such as culture, language, and women's studies, and are perhaps better prepared than other disciplines in the academy to protect OER initiatives from pressures to commercialize. Further, an eco-feminist orientation can help those in the humanities extend ecological thought to considerations of diversity and cultural accommodation.

Traditional Student Culture

Students also shape the general academic culture, and student issues—such as debt and college completion—can shape national agenda as well. Students are troubled by the fact that they "spend an average of $1,168 a year on textbooks and course materials, and prices have been rising more than four times the rate of inflation for the past two decades" ("Make Textbooks Affordable," 2012). The Student Public Interest Research Group (SPIRG) advocates for open-source textbooks as a solution; they have a campus and web presence that includes collecting student signatures, and they are also represented nationally in conversations about the future of OER. Universities will need to address student concerns with costs, defending the value of accreditation, accommodating changes in learning with online and hybrid courses, and adopting their own OER initiatives.

Non-traditional Students and For-profit Alternatives

For-profits, who see marginalized learners—such as women, minorities, foreign-language speakers, older learners, and life-long learners—as untapped markets, are generally credited with adapting educational offerings to these groups better than traditional, bachelors-granting institutions. OER appeals to these groups, largely due to economic and scheduling factors, but most institutions have yet to fully consider them in their strategic visions. Further, many of these potential OER users aim not just to supplement their own knowledge, but to earn certifications that can assist these constituents in the job market, and OER developers are beginning to respond to this. Certification also plays an important role in developing countries where, for example, "this certificate is often the difference between being hired or not hired for educators in sub-Saharan Africa" (Moriarty, 2010). The badge system, which would also entail multimodal eportfolios with transcripts, CVs, sample work, and more, has been proposed not just as a resource for prospective employees, but as a way to

> structure the process of education itself. Students will be able to customize learning goals within the larger curricular framework, integrate continuing peer and faculty feedback about their progress toward achieving those goals, and tailor the way badges and the metadata within them are displayed to the outside world. Students won't just earn badges—they'll build them, in an act of continuous learning. (Carey, 2012)

Certificates and badges offer yet another opportunity for revenue. However, they threaten to erode the branding by which many traditional institutions have marketed their education. Further, when students design their own a la carte education with only future job prospects in mind and when OER is increasingly linked to technical vocational education and training (TVET) efforts, many of the critical and humanist aims of more traditional curricula are shortchanged, leaving these important factors out of the cultural mix. An eco-feminist perspective can respond to these factors by assuring that the needs of marginalized learners are fully accounted for and that TVET does not displace humanist and critical components of higher education.

What Eco-feminism Can Enable Us to Do for OER

Make "Ecology" More than Metaphor

Understanding the basic features of an ecology model, including the concept of "sustainability," can yield insights and opportunities for developing and retaining humanist OER initiatives, because metaphors have the power to govern the way we see and respond to the world. As George Lakoff and Mark Johnson (1980) noted: "Since metaphorical expressions in our language are tied to metaphorical concepts in a systematic way, we can use [them]... to gain an understanding of the metaphorical nature of our activities" (p. 2). The ecology metaphor has the power to shape OER's culture and activities too, if we more fully assert it. For example, by figuring a knowledge *ecology* in place of the knowledge *economy*, we can bring attention to the idea that we and our corporate sponsors necessarily function in an interdependent system. By revisiting the term "sustainability" through an eco-feminist lens, we can reestablish its roots in natural ecology, overcoming its now conventional use as a signifier for revenue generation in order to recognize the emphasis on mutuality and reciprocity among and between stakeholders in the community of development and the community of use. However, humanities scholars must proactively extend the ecology metaphor in their discourse on OER, in part by appealing to OER as a "movement" that extends beyond the single institution and involves much larger, more communal roles suggested by early advocates. This emphasis on returning to OER's more cooperative origins is articulated by Caswell, Henson, Jensen, and Wiley (2008), who asserted that

> to be sustainable, OCW [open course ware] will have to look back to its roots in open source software—to a model where the community works together and principles of openness and sharing guide the development of technologies, content, and financial support.

Eco-feminism, with one foot in the foundations of deep ecology and another in feminism, can help us to recognize that an ecology exists beyond the metaphors. Furthermore, work in the digital humanities can serve as an example of how discursive practices can organize contributors around a semi-stable set of values.

Produce a Statement of Values that Reflects Principles of Ecology

Lisa Spiro (2012) has argued cogently that the digital humanities, which represents a confluence of communities with overlapping values—a humanities that includes libraries, museums, and cultural heritage organizations, and networked culture—has become a mature community that must now "develop a flexible statement of values that it can use to communicate its identity to itself and the general public, guide its priorities, and perhaps heal its divisions.... the DH community needs to develop a keener sense of what it stands for and what is at stake in its work " (p. 17). Spiro argued that producing a single values statement can enable the community to confront issues such as "the lack of open access to information and hidebound policies that limit collaboration and experimentation" (p. 17). At its best, the process of creating such a statement is open and iterative, focusing on closely held beliefs and ideals rather than on ethical codes of behavior, and "may be as important as the statement itself, since that process will embody how the community operates and what it embraces" (p. 18). Spiro connected the digital humanities to its humanist origins, reminding us that

> knowledge of the Humanities as constituted in the modern university has shaped lives, conveyed critical skills, provided a moral compass... given pleasure and satisfaction, inspired acts of generosity and heroism. (p. 21)

Historically, OER's aims and professional codes are similar to DH's, including the valuing of openness and knowledge sharing, as well as collaboration, cross-disciplinarity, innovation, and participation. While the desire to democratize knowledge that undergirds our professional culture can support OER initiatives, it may also make us quick to collaborate in open-access projects that compromise our central aims.

To avoid having intellectual and pedagogical efforts repurposed primarily for profit, we must respond to Spiro's (2012) urging that we develop a values statement, but one specific to OER. Such a statement can advise members of the development community on their participation in OER projects. In the interests of pursing a genuine ecology, this requires we involve all contributors to the development community and all stakeholders in the use community, and that we do not shy from points of conflict but seek common ground instead. We must actively engage corporate sponsors in our discussions of values and trust that these conversations will produce the kinds of synergies that enable sustained OER initiatives. Importantly, Spiro noted that DH has historically been "exclusive," failing to recognize the contributions of participants working in less noticeable ways. OER's similarly unrecognized contributors, such as administrators who champion digital pedagogies and publication, must be included in conversations. Further, we must resist barriers to participation, proactively finding ways to invite those with less experience or opportunity into the community of development.

The values of openness, collaboration, diversity, and experimentation that Spiro identifies as central to the DH represent a starting point for a values statement specific to our participation in OER. However, the larger ecology for OER includes a whole array of contributors to the community of development whose professional cultures may not coincide with the values that Spiro identifies in the DH. For example, contributors from business disciplines may believe strongly that market-based models can best produce quality OER, or that market-based solutions will address the educational needs of the economically disadvantaged. Contributors from the STEM disciplines will probably vary widely in their commitment to knowledge as public good. Equally, we can expect dissent among diverse contributors affiliated with the social sciences. If the stakeholders in higher education's OER initiatives are to come into alignment about retaining humanist goals for OER, efforts from the local context must run parallel with efforts in the broader education ecology. Nationally, the U.S. Department of Education recognizes that the high costs of college education have created a "gap—between aspirations and opportunity—[and it] must be closed" (Duncan, 2013). This concern is coupled with a renewed emphasis on post-secondary education not as a luxury, but as a necessity. Further, many worry that, "in a space of a generation, the U.S. has dropped from leading the world in college attainment to being ranked 12th in the world in college attainment among young adults. That is unacceptable" (Duncan 2013). The rallying cry to reduce the costs of education and extend access may well present an opportunity. However, this national context also includes discussions about common core standards and TVET that risk skewing OER initiatives towards instrumentalist aims and displacing critical and humanist ones. Further, discussions about national initiatives to expand global markets must consider questions about social justice; building local, national. Global alliances and developing values statements from within MLA or NCTE, for example, can guide these conversations and hold us accountable to the community of use, particularly if they are produced in concert with international organizations like OLnet.

Foster a Responsive Faculty and Student Culture

Interest in OER can coalesce more readily if humanities scholars begin to recognize it as a mode to enhance pedagogical practices, particularly as they increasingly experiment with hybrid courses which offer partial immersion into online teaching environments. Further, when humanities scholars realize that the demands of designing new courses might be countered by sharing teaching resources, the merits of open knowledge models will become apparent. As Spiro (2012) noted, this benefits humanities disciplines, because "rather than cheapening knowledge by making it free, embracing openness recognizes the importance of the humanities to society" (p. 25). Conversations about copyright can help shift the culture to one more comfortable with OER's principles of openness to develop the culture of trust that Wiley calls for.

Involving the Student PIRG advocates for open source textbooks in conversations about democratizing education will enable students to play a role in more than just advocating open textbooks. It will foster their participation in

OER as a social issue with humanist aims. Student platforms can provide forums for advancing education that is broader than TVET, and the Student PIRG's national and campus presence affords opportunities for this. Moreover, through alliances with student groups like this one, for-profit institutions that offer cheaper educational alternatives and threaten the standing of more costly traditional institutions can be framed in terms of their instrumentalist aims. Discussions such as these can present students with a more hopeful and inclusive ecology perspective so they can advocate for education as a basic human right.

Refigure Education as a Basic Human Right

OER is at its heart a social movement, an effort to provide free education as the fulfillment of a basic human right. It has been affiliated with the United Nations Educational, Scientific, and Cultural Organization (UNESCO) since 2002 when the term was coined (Johnstone, 2005). As David Wiley (2006) noted,

> all human beings are endowed with a capacity to learn, improve, and progress. Educational opportunity is the mechanism by which we fulfill that capacity. Therefore, free and open access to educational opportunity is a basic human right.

This right appears in Article 26 of the 1948 *Universal Declaration of Human Rights* and also in Article 13 of UNESCO's *International Covenant on Economic, Social and Cultural Rights*, a multilateral treaty for enabling economic, social, and cultural rights for all (United Nations General Assembly, 1948). The covenant includes commitments to labor rights, the right to health, education, and an adequate standard of living. The right to education is predicated on the notion that it is a necessary condition for the "full development of the human personality and the sense of its dignity" as well as civic participation and the realization of all other human rights (United Nations General Assembly, "Article 13," 1948). The covenant also lays out the expectation that all signatory bodies must strive to make education free at all levels, including higher education. A justification for open education as a way to further economic growth can at times conflict with these more humanist rationales, but an eco-feminist perspective can help re-establish and foster the connection between OER and the right to education by cultivating a culture that openly and frequently vocalizes its aims toward open access. With its emphasis on feminist principles, eco-feminism can keep members of OER communities trained on the ethical foundations and goals for OER, and help them retain a regard for the multicultural factors that should inform their development. Feminist approaches to human rights have spurred mainstream human rights groups to reconsider gender's relationship to human rights issues and combining human rights with feminism has enabled its advocates to challenge power structures (Reilly, 2007). The ecology and feminist foci of eco-feminism contribute to the idea that we must champion diversity and symbiosis in human systems, and these emphases can enable us to maintain an inclusive and multicultural scope in OER.

An eco-feminist lens can also enable contributors to retain a critical stance in relation to the assumptions and assertions we might make about ourselves and our projects. For example, as Knox (2013) noted,

> despite the general claims to openness and independence...major stakeholders in OER have a tendency to revert, paradoxically, to the authority of organisations, systems and structures in the production of reliable academic "content." (p. 1)[3]

This critique about the movements' continued affiliations with institutional systems of power underscores the need for rigorous self-examination that a feminist lens can bring to OER's project. Further, as Mary Queen's (2010) article "Transnational Feminist Rhetorics in a Digital World" demonstrates, feminists can usefully interrogate the intersectionality between race, gender, class, and culture in ways that help us retain sensitivity for our own cultural assumptions and biases, particularly if we naively slate OER to solve global issues for access to education. Ultimately, the feminist thread of eco-feminism can foreground our relational status in the larger ecology.

Conclusion

According to human systems ecologist Paul Shepard, the ideological status of *ecology* is that of "resistance movement," because the framework enables critiques of the major premises that undergird the dominant paradigm (Devall, 1980, p. 475). Ultimately, an ecology lens can aid humanities scholars in an advocacy role for OER, not only to avail others of their basic right to education, but to call into question the stronghold that corporatization has over the role of higher education in a national and transnational culture. In an eco-feminist approach, the tensions between business model aims and humanist aims can be productively managed by ensuring that we privilege the principle of mutuality in human ecologies (Selfe, DeVoss, & McKee, 2011).

To conclude with the words of MIT President Susan Hockfield (2012):

> we do not yet know the full potential of OCW and its ultimate impact on global education. But it is clear to us that by thinking of knowledge as a public good for the benefit of all, and acting on this philosophy through OpenCourseWare, we can make a difference...in ways we have not yet imagined.

Notes

1 The author wishes to acknowledge Charles Lowe and Kristine Blair for directing her to this important topic.

2 MIT, for example, has noted that students reported that a familiarity with their OER initiatives influenced the choice to attend and also positively influenced their educational experiences at MIT, which included advising and coursework mediated by OER (Caswell, Henson, Jensen, & Wiley, 2008).

3 For example, open courses frequently advance their legitimacy by foregrounding the institutional status/affiliations of instructors.

• CHAPTER TWENTY-TWO •

Borrowed Images: A Studio Arts Conundrum

Lisa Evans

What is the most effective way to teach studio arts to aspiring artists? Activities structured to allow creative experimentation with materials, methods and concepts? That seems logical. Probably expose students to lots of imagery; some from distant cultures and histories, but also some current examples—contemporary art creates the liveliest discussions. A visual cornucopia of imagery to show students is available thanks to the Internet. The Fair Use Doctrine protects teachers' rights to use copyrighted imagery for teaching purposes and pedagogues can distribute images within their student network. Students can also use these copyrighted images in their art under the educational provisions of Fair Use. Life is good!

Armed with a lay understanding of fair use practices for educators, you boldly plunge forward lecturing, demonstrating, and illustrating with found images from the web. Your students create art—some inspired by art of the past, some inspired by contemporary culture—drawing from the vast repository of images they accessed online.

Perhaps an advanced student interested in fashion is inspired by your presentation about collage. To fulfill a class assignment, he creates a collage inspiration board for a line of paramilitary-style clothing he has designed. His board references visual inspiration sources with photos. One photo shows the entirety of an image found on the web: a photograph taken by an Associated Press photographer featuring Afghan citizens with American soldiers. The use of the photo, unaltered and in its entirety, seems allowable, because it is part of a new work created within an educational context. Later, this enterprising student tells you he has posted this collage to his personal blog, a fashion blog with links to purchase his clothing. His blog features paid advertising. Is there a copyright problem?

Well, maybe...

You begin to ponder examples of artists using found images in order to put your student's activities in the larger context of appropriated art. But, before you slip into a philosophical reverie, a colleague notifies you that he thinks one of your students has violated copyright on a poster design for the school's fall play.

These scenarios illustrate the tangled issues that arts educators regularly traverse. This essay touches on the history of appropriation art, reviews high-profile legal cases, and discusses the educational climate regarding the use of borrowed images. A classroom project involving found images reveals the complexity of copyright and illustrates how educators enjoy greater latitude regarding fair use. The opinions of working artists regarding copyright are presented, and then the role studio art educators assume (or choose to ignore) in the complex, litigious and confusing world of copyright and fair use is addressed.

Found Images: A Mini-primer on Art Appropriation

Deliberate, strategic use of imagery not originally created by the artist is often described as "appropriation art." The use of copyrighted imagery for satire, parody, or political commentary is a strong thread in contemporary art by professional artists. This type of use is protected by the Fair Use Doctrine and is available to everyone, not just students and educators.

The methods and meanings of artists using appropriation are impressively varied and creative. Appropriation art can range from usurpation of an entire physical object or image, to oblique, partial references, perhaps in combination with other imagery. Sometimes the image is used but unaltered. Sometimes it is mechanically reproduced (e.g., via photography) and sometimes it is virtually unrecognizable because of artistic manipulation. Occasionally the artist intends this incorporation of imagery as a critical part of the content of the piece. But not always—it may just be part of the creation process and not an intentional comment on the original imagery. A change in context may be all that an artist adds to the mix to make it their art. A few notable practitioners—such as Duchamp and Warhol—are touchstones for contemporary art students.

Use of "found" objects blossomed when inexpensive (or free) images became widely available due to advances in printing technology. Found images can be traced back at least as far as the Cubists and their collages, but the boldest provocateur of modern art was Marcel Duchamp. He pioneered the "readymade" concept whereby the artist need only choose the object and deem it art in order to make it art. Duchamp put this concept into play with his piece "The Fountain," a urinal reoriented and signed R. Mutt; with this piece, he shocked the art world. His actions expanded the role of the artist from the one who *makes* the art to the one who *selects* what is art. His assertion of a new intellectual authority for artists was perfectly in keeping with the advent of industrialization. Duchamp's bold act, which privileged premise over technique, has been a dominating concept in twentieth-century art, influencing artists such as Andy Warhol and Jeff Koons.

Andy Warhol's Campbell's soup cans and Brillo boxes are part of the canon of popular art. Warhol appropriated these commonplace images from advertising and popular culture to create art that addressed themes of everyday life, thereby creating a new genre of art. How did Andy Warhol fare legally? According to National Public Radio's Joel Rose (2012), "Warhol was himself sued for taking other people's images without permission, although he always settled out of court." But Warhol was ideologically consistent about copying. He let other artists copy him, even providing his silkscreens to one artist, Elaine Sturtevant. In the 1960s, Sturtevant was a respected contemporary of several soon-to-be famous New York artists and known for her painstaking study of artists' techniques to produce exact replicas. Her work questions originality and authorship. For instance, "when a Johns flag that was part of 'Short Circuit,' a 1955 Rauschenberg combine, mysteriously went missing, Rauschenberg asked Sturtevant to produce a new one" (Russeth, 2012). "Short Circuit" is now in the permanent collection of the Art Institute of Chicago and Sturtevant is currently enjoying career resurgence.

Sometimes appropriated imagery has been mediated by the hand of the artist, but not always. A case in point is Sherrie Levine's photographs of Walker Evans' depression-era photographs. Art critic Roberta Smith (2011) stated that

> for more than 30 years Ms. Levine has been slyly lifting images and forms from works by well-known Modernist artists and photographers, using them, her admirers maintain, in ways that undermine conventional notions of originality, artistic mastery and authorship. Her goal has apparently been to expose evils like the commodification or fetishization of the unique art object and to chip away at the myths of individual creativity that have historically served male artists and their markets.

Levine even addressed Duchamp's "Fountain," casting a urinal in bronze and transforming it into a sculptural niche for religious statuary. According to Ann Temkin (1993), Levine's work addresses the "inevitable condition of belatedness." Not surprisingly, in 2001 another artist, Michael Mandiberg, did essentially the same thing as Sherrie Levine, but to Levine's own photographs of the Walker Evans' photographs.

Is That Legal?

Appropriation art has raised many thorny legal issues about intellectual property, ownership, copyright, and fair uses. One example is the litigious world of Jeff Koons, an art world luminary known for his sculptures of banal objects made through casual, initially un-credited use of found imagery as source material.

One notable case resulting from Koons' work, *Rogers v. Koons*, involved a sculpture called "String of Puppies," which was based upon a photograph Koons found on a greeting card. Koons made minor changes to the image, including changing the puppies' noses to clown noses and altering some of the colors. After removing the copyright notice on the card, he instructed his fabricators to sculpt the altered image in the photograph as closely as possible. The greeting card photographer sued Koons. Koons' parody defense, based upon his assertion that his intention was to use the imagery to show the banality of contemporary life, was rejected and he lost the case. He tried a similar defense with essentially the same result when United Features Syndicate sued him for his use of their Odie character in his sculpture "Wild Boy and Puppy." With both cases, the specific image Koons used was judged to be insufficiently linked to his parody concept.

Another of Koons' experiences with copyright law came about because of a photograph in a magazine advertisement featuring of a pair of legs with sandals dangling from the toes. The photograph, "Silk Sandals by Gucci," was taken by Andrea Blanch and published in *Allure* magazine. Its sensual appeal caught Koons' eye. He chose to use it to provoke viewers to think about how they relate to and use these types of products and images. Koons used the image as part of a larger composition of many pairs of legs in a painting that he entitled "Niagara."

Koons prevailed in court because his use of Blanch's imagery was found to be transformative. He was deemed to have added new information to the original image. The copyrighted image was one part of a larger piece and was reoriented and re-contextualized, but, most importantly, he added a different interpretation of the image (Bielstein, 2006).

Studio Arts Education and Appropriation

Serious art students (including high school students) are informed of these artists and their work from classroom lectures, museum visits, pre-college classes, and casual discussions with faculty and peers, not to mention their own Internet surfing. The afore cited art stars shape not only the gallery and museum world, but contemporary art discourse too.

Borrowing others' material (often without attribution) is endemic in studio arts education. In the visual arts, student reproduction of style, technique, and imagery of revered artists is a basic educational approach, especially in a traditional technique-based studio arts curriculum. Is the visual arts educational culture more forgiving of this borrowing than other fields, viewing it as a natural part of the maturing process of young artists? Do specific training needs contribute to this differing attitude? Would an alternative attitude or system be more fair, more realistic, or even implementable?

Art history is filled with examples of artists who found their own voice by melding qualities they admired in other artists. Perhaps because so much of art education involves synthesis, the visual arts seem to enjoy a more fluid relationship between original source material and derivative works. The adage "copying is the most sincere form of flattery" fits many student efforts as they struggle with technique, personal iconography, and style. Undergraduate art shows typically feature the "Lucian Freud painter" or the "Egon Schiele draftsman." The educated eye can usually spot the artistic predecessors very easily.

In an Evanston, Illinois, coffee shop where I wrote this text, I noticed an anonymous photo collage layering multiple images of the coffee shop from slightly different viewpoints. The anonymous collage clearly owes a debt to David Hockney's photomontage technique. But is Hockney's technique a manifestation of an idea about photography and simultaneity? If Hockney's technique is an idea, then it isn't copyrightable. And, to situate Hockney's work in a larger context, it might be argued that his technique is hardly new, but just an application of late twentieth-century technology to the concepts pioneered by the Cubists earlier in the century and as practiced by Braque and his peers.

What about exact copying? Copying a masterwork is well documented in art history. For example, the Romans copied Greek statuary for study and admiration. Sometimes artists even copy themselves for financial reasons (e.g., DeChirico). Copying of imagery and techniques has long-held educational value for artists as learning methods. Who hasn't visited an art museum and seen artists busy at work copying a masterwork? The School of the Art Institute of Chicago even has a course for students interested in copying paintings in the museum. And, of course, copying has been a way to celebrate and promote the personages portrayed, as well as the ideas and the culture of a society or religion.

But copying has many flavors. There is copying to fool someone (or forgery, which is clearly illegal), copying of a style but not exact imagery, copying as homage (e.g., Picasso's copies of Velazquez's "*Las Meninas*"), copying for learning purposes, and copying out of just plain laziness and lack of originality. Copying a masterwork may be perfectly legal if the copyright has lapsed. If not, there is probably protection for the student under the Fair Use Doctrine.

My experience is that art students are very comfortable with copying to unlock the technical knowledge exhibited by art they like—so comfortable, in fact, that they rarely think too much about it. The practice is ubiquitous, but in my art education no mention was made about its legalities. Book publishers' perfection of photographic reproductions aids the artist in analyzing the art, and allows virtually unlimited time to study the work in question. It is not unusual to find paint-splattered art books littering studios, facilitating painterly vivisections large and small. And now we have Google Art Project.

Besides gaining technical knowledge, borrowing—or "artistic quotations"—by student artists often situates their work within a richer conceptual context. These "artistic quotations" communicate interests and the territories they wish to engage. As an art student in the 1990s, instructors encouraged us to incorporate materials, processes, and visual references to heighten associative meanings in our art. Further back in history, followers of Leonardo da Vinci would incorporate his signature hand gesture of an index finger pointing to heaven into their compositions to reference the master. This type of borrowing (particularly borrowing without attribution) is part of art culture. It presumes a knowledgeable audience that knows the reference.

It is easy to see how contemporary artists schooled in this culture are unprepared for the realities of copyright law. When removed from the educational shield provided by the Fair Use Doctrine, the use of copyrighted imagery can be contentious, especially when corporate-controlled IP is involved. Susan Bielstein (2006), an art book editor, writes that:

> More than ever, art offers a host of self-conscious challenges to the concept of authorship. What I am driving at is that in the United States visual artistic property was, and to a degree still is, caught in a thicket of inadequate legal discourse that is inherently biased toward text and not images.

I am an art educator, not a lawyer, but as I reviewed court cases for this article I found baffling non sequiturs in logic between the art and legal world (e.g., the role of artistic motivation, the importance of physical changes). The operating methodologies and priorities of these groups are apparently so distinctly different that, at times, they seem to ignore salient issues in each other's arguments (particularly with conceptually based art).

Of course not all artists view appropriation art equally enthusiastically. Some do not welcome copying, especially if the copy is of poor quality and could harm their reputation. The Ringling Museum in Sarasota, Florida, featured an exhibition in 2012 exploring Peter Paul Rubens' strategies to assert quality control over the reproductions of his paintings. Rubens was so distressed at the poor quality of prints made to represent his paintings that he took it upon himself to obtain a copyright of his imagery so that he could control and maintain accurate reproductions. Today, photographers seem to be the most vexed category of artists regarding copyright, feeling their work particularly vulnerable to usurpation. The American Society of Media Photographers and the Professional Photographers of America are two groups actively lobbying for more copyright protection for photographers.

What Do Artists Do?

Discussion about copyright issues amongst artists usually creates more dissention than consensus. The business of acquiring permission to use imagery is often beyond the legal expertise of the average artist. Artists are cultural sponges. They want to create art (which may involve building upon another person's copy-righted work) without consulting an attorney. Much of an artist's work is personal, experimental, and doomed to failure (both financial and conceptual). Artists don't want to be constantly impeded from exploring ideas because of copyright problems. Additionally, the distinctions between patent, trademark, licensing, and copyright are not broadly understood and add to general confusion. Some artists intentionally self-censor their explorations to avoid any risk of copyright infringement. Others bury their heads in the sand, do what they want, and hope that even if they do violate copyright, legal repercussions are unlikely. Following the law has never been a strong artistic motivation.

Although some well-known visual artists have encountered legal problems associated with their appropriation activities, the discussion of their work in art education circles usually circumvents legal issues and instead focuses on discussion of the philosophical implications of their practices. Perhaps this is because as artists and educators we are more interested in these issues, but I suspect that it is also because lawsuits take time to work through the courts and because the results are sometimes hard to understand, based on singular situations that are not broadly applicable or are cloaked in secrecy. Case law is interpretive, guided by the law (of course), but applied by individuals to unique circumstances. Court cases sometimes reveal strange, unexplained, or conflicting details. Additionally, behind-the-scenes activities, as well as personalities, financial resources, psychological stamina, and personal agendas influence outcomes. Adding to the confusion are the many instances where copyright infringement has taken place, but no legal action has been taken by a potential plaintiff either due to ignorance or lack of interest. Perhaps it is not financially worthwhile, or perhaps it is also a realization that copying gives cachet to the original work (or the ideas the work represents) that keep copyright owners from pursuing legal action. One such case is Alberto Korda's famous photograph of Che Guevara.

In My Classroom

The ubiquitous silkscreened image by Jim Fitzpatrick of the handsome activist Che Guevara is part of the lexicon of popular political imagery—a sign of rebellion that is worn by political revolutionaries as well as angst-filled teenage mall shoppers. I showed this image to students as I developed a new unit for my studio art class at University Laboratory High School in Urbana, Illinois. The majority could name Che; although they were a bit less specific about his politics, most intuited that he was a leftist political activist.

The image is aesthetically, technologically, and motivationally linked with older political propaganda art. In this lesson, students learn about, explore, and utilize the visual language of activism by portraying a humanitarian of their choice in a relief print. The Che Guevara image is an excellent example of effective propaganda art—simple, forceful, and high contrast. This stylistic language has been utilized for political art so often that the style alone connotes political activism. Unbeknownst to me at the time, the Fitzpatrick portrayal of Che was based on a photograph taken by Alberto Korda, a Cuban photographer. Korda never challenged Fitzpatrick's use of his photograph, for a variety of reasons, but perhaps because he was pleased that it popularized the cause and history of Che.

In this unit, my students found images of their subjects on the web and copied them onto a printing block. Next, students carved their humanitarian's image into the rubber block and experimented with inks and printing techniques to produce new works of art. The projects were aesthetically and conceptually powerful.

Hope-lessly Confusing

Meanwhile, in the non-academic world, another artist had undertaken a similar project, albeit with different means. Shepherd Fairey, a street/graffiti artist, produced the ubiquitous "Hope" image of Barack Obama for his 2008 presidential campaign (see McCorkle, this volume). Although Fairey claimed his primary motivation was to assist Obama's campaign, he also profited from the sales of souvenirs and clothing featuring the image.

Controversy about the image ensued when the Associated Press claimed that the image was based upon a photograph taken by AP photographer Mannie Garcia and demanded compensation. Fairey had neither paid for nor acknowledged the reference, even obscuring evidence that pointed to his use of the specific photograph. Eventually Fairey admitted that his image was based upon Garcia's photograph, but claimed it was fair use. Fairy elaborately detailed his artistic process for the court. He discussed the political motivations underlying his creation—an image that melds the conventions of heroic political portraiture and patriotic iconography with the stylistic power of Soviet Agitprop. After much publicity and legal wrangling the parties settled their disagreement out of court in a confidential arrangement in January 2011. Fairey wrote in the *Harvard Journal of Law and Technology*:

> Though I believed the principles of the case were strong, I was very concerned that my spoliation had harmed my credibility in a way that would taint the case regardless of

> the fact that the spoliation occurred later and did not change the principles of the Hope poster case.... Also, the AP's calculus for the legal fees and damages it sought to collect from me was quite daunting. The figure would have completely bankrupted me. (Cost et al., 2012)

Fairey's decision to settle sent a chilling message to all artists using appropriation methods.

When beginning to develop the printmaking unit for my classes, I did not consider the copyright implications of the strategy students would use for capturing their source image. The Fairey "Hope" controversy was not settled at that point (and its subsequent murky conclusion has not clarified fair use of copyrighted images). My goal was simply for students to learn more about propaganda art and relief printmaking.

The implication of wrongdoing conveyed by the lawsuit and Fairey's settlement sent an alarm to me that perhaps I was encouraging a wrongful use of copyrighted imagery. It led me to an exploration of fair use—and Fair Use—concepts and I was grateful to find that educators and students enjoy greater latitude of use than strictly commercial uses. I now include a discussion of fair use concepts in this unit.

Familiarity with fair use is imperative for students, educators, and all those creating and using intellectual property, but it is an elusive and moving target. As technologies evolve and creative people push the boundaries, the law needs flexibility to factor in the context, content, and dynamics of each unique situation. But the price for this flexibility is to operate in an arena of some uncertainty.

Some breathing room for appropriation artists was forthcoming when the U.S. Court of Appeals for the Second Circuit ruled in April 2013, on a high-profile case that has slowly been working its way through the system: *Patrick Cariou v. Richard Prince*.

New Expression?

Patrick Cariou, a professional photographer, lived and worked among Rastafarians in Jamaica over the course of 6 years. In 2000, he published his photos in a book called *Yes, Rasta* (see, also, Nguyen, this volume). Richard Prince created a collage utilizing portions of 35 photographs from *Yes, Rasta* (without permission), blocking and altering some features of Cariou's subjects. Prince went on to create another 30 artworks in the series, entitled "Canal Zone," incorporating whole or parts of Cariou's photographs into all but one piece in his series. Cariou's images were taken in whole or in part, enlarged, ink jet printed, and affixed to (sometimes large) painted canvases, and (sometimes) painted over and combined with other appropriated imagery. Prince showed 22 of his paintings in

New York at the prominent Gagosian Gallery, where the show grossed over $16 million (Gilbert-Egglesten, 2011).

In 2011, Cariou succeeded in his copyright infringement suit against both Prince and the Gagosian. At the U.S. District Court for the Southern District of New York, Judge Batts' decision relied most heavily upon two of the four Fair Use factors, namely the market effect on the original underlying work, and, most critically, the question of transformative use. The court's definition of transformation was tied to work that "comments on, relates historically to or critically refers to the original work" (*Patrick Cariou v. Richard Prince*, 2013). Under this definition of transformation, aesthetic manipulations via materials and methods as transformation devices are seemingly ignored in favor of a narrowed focus on the conceptual intent of the artist. Prince was vague about his reasons for choosing Cariou's photographs, but admitted that it was not to comment on Cariou's specific work. The implications of the court's narrow transformation standard alarmed the visual art world. Prince appealed the ruling.

In April of 2013, the U.S. Court of Appeals for the Second Circuit ruled that the district court applied an incorrect standard for Fair Use, and further found all but five of the 30 paintings constituted Fair Use. It sent the remaining five back to the district court to reconsider. The appeals court said there is no requirement for a work to comment on the source material to be transformative:

> The artworks were transformative because they manifested an entirely different aesthetic from the photographs since the artist's composition, presentation, scale, color palette, and media were fundamentally different and new compared to the photographs as was the expressive nature of the artist's work. (*Patrick Cariou v. Richard Prince*, 2013).

Additionally, the court found the artist's comments about the intent of his work irrelevant, instead preferring to judge how the art may be perceived by a reasonable observer. The market loss claim made by Cariou was discounted because the court found Prince's elite clientele distinctly different from Cariou's.

Of course this decision has also been criticized. The Court's Judge Wallace wrote a partially dissenting opinion stating that "if the district court is in the best position to determine fair use as to some paintings, why is the same not true as to all paintings?" Others (including me) criticize the dismissal of artist intent because it seems to privilege physical differences, thereby ignoring conceptual art (that may be physically similar but conceptually or contextually different). Cariou appealed his case to the Supreme Court, which determined in November 2013 that it will not hear the case. In March 2014, Prince settled with Cariou regarding the remaining five paintings.

Prince, meanwhile, has decided to continue his provocations. For instance, he re-tweeted a photo of himself selling copies of Salinger's *Catcher in the Rye*. The book Prince is selling is identical to the one Salinger wrote with one critical difference—he substituted his name for Salinger's name.

In August 2013, another closely watched case involving the question of transformation validated the role of artist intent. The court upheld commercial juggernaut Green Day's Fair Use claim. Green Day's video backdrop (that played during a song they performed in concert) prominently incorporated the image of a screaming face created by Dereck Seltzer without his permission. This case hinged in part upon the artist's (Seltzer's) statement about his original artistic intent. In general, Seltzer (who posted the image on the street) said he was making a statement about street and youth culture. Green Day used Seltzer's full image (with the addition of a red cross over the face) intending to create a message about religious hypocrisy, thereby differing radically from Seltzer's intended message. Although Seltzer claimed Green Day's use had tarnished the original image, the radical distinction between their messages allowed Green Day to succeed in court. Luckily for Seltzer, the court vacated Green Day's award for attorney fees (over $200,000; *Dereck Seltzer v. Green Day Inc.*, 2013).

New Territories

A recent exhibition entitled "Free" at the New Museum in New York City was dedicated to artists exploring the new space created by the Internet:

> "Free" takes its name from free culture, a social movement that acknowledges the revolution the internet has caused in industries like music and print publishing, and argues that it be dealt with as an opportunity for greater sharing and distribution of knowledge, rather than a threat. (New Museum, 2010)

Artists are expected to push boundaries and challenge the status quo. Their sometimes casual attitude toward copyright and attribution creates a culture of disregard about the need for such practices. But this freedom also means there is less protection for the small producer, too—look at who has been winning the court cases, and who has the resources to sustain expensive legal battles.

This is the cultural milieu that art educators operate within. Although my colleague's worry over the use of a copyrighted image by my student to promote the fall play is easy to defend as fair use, I am not as confident about the use of copyrighted imagery in a student blog that sells products and accepts advertising. Teachers and students need to understand and discuss fair uses and Fair Use. And, although educators and students have greater Fair Use latitude, students should be informed about the standards they will face outside of academia. Discussing the Fair Use Doctrine with examples from case law allows students to grapple with the ethical questions underlying the doctrine. According to the court that decided the Green Day case, "the question presented in a case where a defendant makes a winning fair use defense is whether the successful defense of the action furthered the purposes of the Copyright Act." Does copyright law actually promote the greatest public good and create an equitable and workable balance between the interests of creators and those of the public? Ultimately, classroom discussions will lead students to better decisions about their rights and responsibilities in the complicated arena of borrowed images.

• CHAPTER TWENTY-THREE •

Cultural Critique, First-year Composition, and Copyright

Jen Ware, Ashley Hall, and Sydney Stegall*

Particular writing technologies, especially the technology of alphabetic literacy that has dominated western culture since the Renaissance, have contributed to the development of what legal scholar Lawrence Lessig (2008) called a "read-only" culture. In a read-only culture, the roles of consumers and producers are rigidly bifurcated. In a read-only culture, the act of producing cultural artifacts is reserved for highly trained professionals with access to the technologies of production and the concomitant literacies necessary for composing. For example, in *Free Culture*, Lessig (2004) discussed the nineteenth century technology of photography, noting that in its infancy, "the process was complicated and expensive, and the field was thus limited to professionals and a few zealous and wealthy amateurs" (p. 31). This depiction of the initially limited access to the technologies of photographic production stands in stark contrast to the digital composing technologies widely available in contemporary American culture. Although access issues persist, we have far greater access to a wider range of composing technologies than ever before. What's more, the literacies needed to work with digital composing technologies are steadily expanding.

Taken together, these relatively recent techno-social developments could be seen as the signal of a cultural shift toward a "read-write" culture in which the sharp distinctions between consumer and producer elided. Yet, despite rapid developments in writing technologies and related digital literacies, one crucial thing remains unchanged: Cultural critique remains largely confined to the

* With contributions from the following student-authors: Claudia Amand, Marin Matchinske Brehmer, Brianna Chavis, J. Forrest Finch, Benedict Grauman, Nick Kessig, Maya Kruse, Cameron Lawson, Erika Locklear, Jeffrey Merrill, Holly Roberts, Brittany Rountree, Erik Rys, Allison Marie Turner, Jonathan Villanueva, Charlie Wilcher, and Jack Witty.

highly professionalized domain of the humanist. Although digital composing technologies are often lauded for their democratizing potentials, within the humanities it is still the professional, not the novice (the ordinary citizen, or the college student, for example) who produces (and is recognized as a producer of) cultural critique.

The long-standing tradition of read-only culture within the humanistic disciplines has privileged a separation between consumer and producer on the basis of credentials, training, and expertise acquired through apprenticeship and extended practice resulting in a relatively limited scope of who is allowed to speak from the position of a cultural critic and in what ways they are able to express their work. Existing digital composing technologies could be leveraged to foster a cultural shift toward a read-write culture in which cultural critique is opened up for a wider range of participants using more varied means (technologies and modes) of production. However, complex institutional forces—including curricular expectations and assumptions about the roles students, especially undergraduates play—often resist such change.

A typical goal of a liberal arts education is to help students develop critical thinking skills, which in turn helps them become more informed citizens and consumers. However, the liberatory aims envisioned for students when they move outside of the academy are not frequently embraced (and are even sometimes resisted) within academia. Despite the potentials digital composing technologies might afford for humanists to complicate the traditional division between consumer and producer of cultural critique, such a shift has not yet fully occurred. For example, within the humanities, first-year students are not generally thought of as producers of cultural critique, an activity still reserved for the highly trained professional humanist. Instead, students are assumed to be novices—consumers of the refined critiques produced by trained specialists, often their professors. This observation can be extended across the humanities including even the field of rhetoric and composition, a disciplinary community with a longstanding investment in student-centered pedagogies.

Rhetorician Steve Westbrook (2006) observed that "education in writing instruction too often teaches students to accept their subject position within a culture of corporate consumerism" (p. 476). Although students may often be asked to analyze aspects of the culture of corporate consumerism Westbrook described, they are rarely engaged in public practices of cultural critique meant to reshape that culture. And, as Westbrook explained, changing these dynamics is not only a question of technology and culture, but also a legal question—one in which copyright is central.

Copyright in the Humanities

Up to this point in time, humanities scholars have been able to perform cultural critique while remaining relatively insulated from debates about copyright because typically their critiques have been produced with the technology of alphabetic writing. This mode of critique has shielded professional humanities scholars from copyright debacles in two ways. First, well-established alphabetic citation conventions allow scholars to borrow thoughts, ideas, and words from others and provide an accepted method for such borrowing to be acknowledged. Second, the Fair Use exception to copyright enables teachers and scholars to work with copyrighted materials for educational purposes. Thus, the technology of alphabetic prose coupled with the allowances provided by the Fair Use exception have typically afforded humanities scholars a great deal of flexibility even when working with copyrighted content for the purposes of critique.

Yet, as we demonstrate in this chapter, artists, humanities scholars, ordinary citizens, and students all confront the same set of challenges when they compose with copyrighted materials in multimodal forms even while adhering to copyright exceptions. Working collaboratively with first-year students, as we are doing in this chapter, can be an avenue for blurring producer/consumer roles and transgressing the legacy of read-write culture. Through these practices, students can be valued as collaborators working in tandem with humanists to negotiate complex copyright laws so as to provide a well-balanced and legally sound framework for understanding what it means to be an active participant within the public sphere. This is one way we can expand the understanding of who is "authorized" to create cultural critique. Then we can, with students, simultaneously begin to create working and recognized systems of attribution (such as those developed long ago for alphabetic texts) that further advance our freedom to compose multimodal cultural critiques with copyright images, videos, and sounds in ethical and legal ways.

In the remainder of this chapter, we present three case studies intended to provide an initial framework for humanities scholars and students beginning to confront questions about how copyright issues intersect their work, especially in light of the expanding range of composing tools and practices. The first case study provides an example of derivative use. Our discussion of this example will explain why derivative use can lead to serious complications and even legal challenges for composers who fail to obtain necessary permissions from copyright holders. The second case study outlines an example of potentially transformative use. In our analysis of this example, we focus on the challenges of ensuring that our composing choices meet the legal guidelines for transformative use and the problems that uncertainty about what constitutes fair use can cause when we want to circulate our work to public audiences. The third case study demonstrates that even when we are confident in the legality of our composing choices, our ability to circulate legitimate cultural critiques to wider public audiences can be hindered or systematically impeded by automated copyright filters. We share the experiences of a student who attempted to post a parody video composed for a class assignment to Facebook to illustrate a widespread cultural assumption behind automated anti-piracy filters on social networking sites. We argue that these filters sometimes incorrectly censor legitimate work that appropriates copyrighted content in a transformative—and legally protected—manner. We further maintain that automated anti-piracy filters limit our ability to publicly display digital compositions that conform to the legal framework provided for transformative use by Fair Use because they assume that any use of copyrighted content is unauthorized and therefore illegal appropriation.

Derivative Use versus Transformative Use

Case Study One: Derivative Use

In *Remix*, Lessig (2008) presents the example of Candice Breitz, a young South African artist working in London, to show how derivative use renders copyrighted content "off limits" to composers, even professional artists who seek to showcase their work in galleries and museums. Breitz sought to create an art exhibit that consisted of fans singing their favorite John Lennon songs

> to shift the focus away from those people who are usually perceived as creators so as to give some space, some room, to those people who absorb cultural products—whether it's music or movies or whatever the case may be (p. 6)

Breitz's articulation of the goals she set for her project reveals that she viewed her work as a way of appropriating copyrighted content to reshape culture by making the boundary between consumers and producers of popular music more permeable. However, despite her artistic and theoretical motives for working with copyrighted content, the gallery requested that she contact the copyright holders to "secure permission" (Lessig, p. 9). Upon doing so, Breitz was denied permission by Yoko Ono, who holds the copyrights to Lennon's work. Consequently, Breitz's ability to display her work was thwarted until the copyright issues could be addressed.

After being denied permission to work with Lennon's songs in her project, a "major international curator" and supporter of Breitz's work intervened on her behalf, explaining to Ono "that, as he understood the situation, Breitz could in fact have paid the relevant copyrights and gone ahead with the project" (p. 10). Ono disagreed with the curator: "'Permission,' Ono insisted, 'was vital, legally'" (p. 10). This response from Ono illustrates that professional artists, and even those who may be willing and able to pay costly fees to work with copyrighted content, may still run into problems and be challenged or denied the ability to circulate their work if it is deemed to be derivative use.

Breitz's use of copyrighted content can be defined as derivative because her project involved fans singing John Lennon songs, appropriating the original copyrighted content not for the purpose of staging a cultural critique but as a performance of conceptual art interrogating the consumer–producer relationship. Although Breitz's rhetorical purpose was both scholarly and artistic, her use of copyrighted content was not transformative and therefore she encountered considerable complications when trying to show her work publicly. Humanists—both professional scholars and humanities students—are likely to encounter similar problems if their use of copyrighted content is derivative.

Case Study Two: A Potentially Transformative Use

The ability to engage in cultural critique—to observe and comment upon our government, our educational system, and our corporate environment—is the cornerstone of our first amendment right to freedom of speech. Parody is a genre of critique increasingly being used by non-specialists (ordinary citizens and students) as a way of expressing such commentary. Yet, it remains unclear what forms of digital texts may be appropriated to create a parody that necessarily relies upon a previously existing text to make new meaning. Although parody is a legally protected form of critique, uncertainty about how to differentiate between derivative use and fair use is a deterrent to some composers. We can see an example of this in Westbrook (2006), where he reports being unable to actually show an image described as a "spoof ad" created by one of his undergraduate students. He explained, "On the right is an image that I will have to ask you to imagine, for the ambiguous definition of 'fair use' under current copyright law prevents me from showing it" (p. 458). Westbrook wrote *about* the student's "absent text," describing it as a "feminist counter-advertisement" and "a complicated text that responds satirically to a Maybelline advertisement through a combination of appropriated digital images and original poetry" (p. 458). It is clear from these descriptions that the student's work was rhetorically effective, but Westbrook's inability to actually show the image points to one of the ways in which uncertainty about what constitutes fair use limits our ability to fully engage in cultural critique in the public sphere.

Why was it permissible for the student to produce the composition for a class assignment but not to print it in one of our field's most respected journals? If the student's parody was appropriate for the classroom audience without violating copyright, why shouldn't he and the student be able to share the text with a wider scholarly audience in the public sphere? As Westbrook noted,

> the sheer cost of legal representation (easily absorbed by a large and successful corporation but not necessarily by an individual citizen or educational organization) is often persuasive enough to dissuade multimedia producers and publishers from disseminating texts when the issue of infringement remains even questionable. (p. 475)

At precisely the same moment when parody is creating an opportunity for cultural critique to become more mainstream and be conducted by "ordinary citizens" who are non-specialists, legal concerns about copyright infringement present a rhetorical constraint to composers even when their work would most likely be considered fair use in a court of law.

Case Study Three: Transformative Use and a Takedown Notice

In the previous case study, we saw that uncertainty about whether our use of copyrighted content falls within the legal guidelines for transformative use can lead to the stifling of creative expression and cultural critique. Yet, even when we have studied the guidelines and are certain that our composing choices are aligned to the legal framework for protected speech, problems can arise when we attempt to display our work in the public sphere. One of the students who is a collaborating author on this project encountered the challenges posed by Facebook's anti-piracy filter when he attempted to post to his Facebook account a parody video he composed for a class assignment.

This student, along with his classmates, took up the question of how to work with copyrighted content in a transformative way as part of a first-year writing course. In a 16-week composition course, students were introduced to copyright law, carefully examined the Fair Use exceptions specified in Section 107, and conducted research on legal cases involving fair use and parody. With a foundational understanding of how to differentiate between derivative use and fair use, students took on the challenge of creating cultural critiques through parody by appropriating copyrighted content (images, sounds, texts, etc.) and subverting their meaning for the purpose of producing a research-based multimodal argument. Throughout the composing process, students documented their thinking process and tracked their composing choices so that they were prepared to defend their work and justify its legality if called upon to do so. In addition to preparing students to respond to legal challenges they might encounter, documenting their thinking and composing choices in this way enabled students to gain critical awareness of how their work was situated within complex networks involving issues of power, authority, and technology. Consequently, these students were able to question and challenge the well-established consumer–producer relationship in the humanities. Here is what one student has to say about his experience:

> A couple weeks ago, I had to post a parody for my English class. My parody was based on a highly controversial topic and I didn't want anyone else outside of my class to see

> it. For this reason, I posted it to Facebook but made sure that I was the only person who could see it.
>
> An hour later I checked my Facebook account and I was surprised to find a notification from Facebook saying that they had taken down my parody due to copyright violation. The message said that if I continued to try and post my parody, my Facebook account would be deleted. My first reaction was to chuckle because not only was my parody within the fair use part of copyright law, but the settings for it were made so that only I could see it. In other words, in no way could it be said that I was redistributing the content I used in my parody. Apparently this did not matter to Facebook. Everything on the Internet can be broken down into numbers and when the audio data from my parody matched that of a copyrighted work, it was immediately removed by the (anti-piracy) program. While it is true that this program does prevent illegal uses of copyrighted works, it also prevents the legal use as well.

Here we see an example of how automated anti-piracy filters enforce a cultural logic that assumes copyrighted content is "off limits" for ordinary citizens, regardless of whether their use of such content is derivative or transformative. Facebook's anti-piracy filter left no room for discussion about the nature of the student's work or whether it conformed to the guidelines established in the Fair Use exception.

Section 5 of Facebook's "Statement of Rights and Responsibilities" is titled "Protecting Other People's Rights." At first, this section looks benign; it begins with the statement "we respect other people's rights, and expect you to do the same." That seems fair enough. But within the sub-points of this section, things get a bit murkier. Item one states: "You will not post content or take any action on Facebook that infringes or violates someone else's rights or otherwise violates the law." With the volume of content appearing on Facebook every minute of every day, it would be simply impossible for the company's human staff to maintain the sole responsibility for insuring user compliance with this policy. Therefore, the watchful eye policing Facebook's user-generated content to make sure that it doesn't violate copyright is non-human automated software. In fact, as social media industry analyst Josh Constine (2011) has pointed out, relying primarily on human labor to monitor copyright would put Facebook at risk of losing the safe harbor from copyright liability status granted by the Online Copyright Infringement Liability Limitation Act (17 U.S.C., Sec. 512).

Under pressure from elite and powerful copyright holders threatening massive lawsuits, such as the billion dollar challenge Viacom brought against YouTube in 2010, many social networking sites have installed similar anti-piracy filters. These filters operate on the cultural logic that copyright holders work to instill in composers, namely, that if copyrighted content is present in a user-generated file, it must be illegal. This logic is reaffirmed even in Facebook's "Help Center," where users are strongly cautioned to refrain from posting content if they are unsure whether that content may violate copyright. Facebook ("What if?," 2012) presents the following question and answer pair:

What if I want to upload content to Facebook but I'm not sure whether that would infringe someone's copyright?

If you're not certain that you are legally authorized to use the content, do not upload it to Facebook. If you have done so already, you should remove it. If you don't own the copyright to the content you wish to post, posting it without permission of the copyright holder might be a violation of the law.

Fair use is neither mentioned in this recommendation nor in the "Statement of Rights and Responsibilities." Presumably, this is due to what Westbrook (2006) and Lessig (2004) observed: Fair use is ambiguous. Facebook's intellectual property policy doesn't have room for ambiguity; therefore, they err on the side of caution. Unfortunately, this also means erring on the side of copyright holders instead of composers and it means imposing unnecessary restrictions on users who might compose works fully legal under the Fair Use exception.

Because anti-piracy filters are essentially search algorithms, their technical operation is less rhetorical than a human decision-making process would be.[1] To filter content, files are scanned and processed comparing user-generated content against a database of copyrighted content in multiple file formats (video, images, text, audio, etc.). When a user uploads content, the filter compares the user's file to records in the database searching for matching or closely related patterns. If a match is found, the user's content is flagged as a copyright violation and, in many cases, the content is removed automatically. Such logic is problematic, though, because it assumes that any match is an attempt by a user to upload copyrighted content illegally with no regard for *how* that content is actually being used within the context of a composition.

The default assumption of Facebook's anti-piracy filter is that if content posted by a user contains copyrighted content, the file is automatically in violation of the "Statement of Rights and Responsibilities"—even though this is not always the case. Following the incident of having his content removed by Facebook's automated anti-piracy filter, this student reflected on the broader implications for his learning in a university setting:

This encounter with Facebook made me realize that copyright does not only influence my ability to share my creations, but the way I go about getting my education. At [our university], the honor code is shoved down everyone's throat and every professor advises students against plagiarism and copyright infringement. Not only this, some students say they do not record their classes because they are afraid of running into an issue of copyright with the professor. Is this the type of education system where the students are allowed to reach their full potential? Putting such a large emphasis on copyright without knowing what is fair and what isn't and without teaching students how to figure this out is actually hindering the education process.

The student's comments above demonstrate a desire for authentic and meaningful learning contexts.

Techno-poet and rhetorician Daniel Anderson (2008) persuasively argued that assigning new media compositions and supporting students as they acquire a broad spectrum of literacies is an effective way of heightening student engagement. Our classroom experiments composing parodies with new media (graphic-editing software, HTML editors, and video-editing software) have affirmed many of Anderson's claims. Student engagement in the composing process was high and many students expressed becoming more invested[2] in their projects (compared to more traditional alphabetic analysis essays) because they were thinking deeply about the arguments they wanted to make and realized the consequences of their decisions could mean the difference between creating a legal parody or a derivative and therefore illegal appropriation of someone else's work. As the students revised their composing strategies to make them more effective, they also made sure that they were following the framework outlined by the U.S. Fair Use provision. And they realized throughout the entire process that their ability to articulate and justify their choices was critical to their success within the classroom for the purpose of the assignment, and also to our shared success later when we eventually collaborated on this chapter together.

Conclusion

Negativland's Mark Hosler discusses cultures in/of/and around copyright, saying:

> When you turn around 360 degrees, how many different ads or logos will you see somewhere in your space? [O]n your car, on your wristwatch, on a billboard. If you walk into any grocery store or restaurant or anywhere to shop, there's always a soundtrack playing. There's always... media. There's ads.... It's the world we live in. It's the landscape around us. (in Lessig, 2008, p. 71)

Lessig (2002a) made similar observations, describing "a picture of culture." Ours is a culture of copyright.

We live in a branded society where notions of "private property" are used to regulate and control both public and educational spaces. FBI warnings appear when we watch movies at home. Complicated terms and conditions must be acknowledged to view article PDFs in academic databases. Signs posted above photocopiers and scanners in libraries warn us that someone else owns the content we are using, that our use of that content may be surveilled, and that the ramifications for unauthorized uses could be severe.

Our physical environments are media saturated. Everywhere we turn, copyrighted cultural artifacts surround us; we are also constantly reminded that we are supposed to passively consume these (supposedly) fixed and static cultural artifacts. We can watch a movie or read an article but, according to powerful copyright holders, we are deterred from duplicating, re-purposing, or recreating them to make new meaning beyond what was initially intended and authorized even though the law makes certain allowances for us to do so. In other words, powerful copyright holders would prefer for us to observe and respect the traditional roles of consumers and producers. Social networking sites typically facilitate the sharing of user-generated content. However, as our third case study shows, the ability to freely and fairly circulate texts containing copyrighted content on these same sites may be stifled by the cultural logic encoded into antipiracy filters. Consequently, the reach and impact of such forms of legitimate and legal cultural critique are diminished, especially for ordinary citizens and students who are assumed to be consumers of culture and critique but not necessarily producers of either.

Notes

1 The decision to implement the filter and establishing processes for configuring the filter or processing content flagged by the filter is all certainly rhetorical but the process itself of matching the digital signatures of two files is an automated process. The problem we see with such automation is that it simply can't account for the rhetorical ecology in which the copyrighted content appears and therefore can't accurate determine whether the copyrighted content is being used fairly.

2 Another student commented at the end of the semester that a few weeks into the parody project he found himself forgetting about the grade. He understood that the point of what we were doing was to say something meaningful and something that we believe in to the point of risking a challenge to the legitimacy of our work. This, he said, "changed the game." Figuring out what he wanted to say and how he wanted to express that while composing legally with copyrighted content became more meaningful than worrying about the grade.

• CHAPTER TWENTY-FOUR •

Asking the Right Questions

Nancy Schrock

During the last half of the twentieth century and into the twenty-first, society's products have been increasingly intellectual products enabled by changes in technology. The ability to produce and share intellectual products globally has changed human relations in fundamental ways and brought about a global *cultural* climate change. Wealth created from intellectual products is known as intellectual capital, and legally protected intellectual capital is intellectual property. The holders of wealth use IP as an exchangeable commodity on a global scale and finance its production, but not indiscriminately.

For workers in the humanities to continue to produce IP, they will have to compete with other disciplines for funding. In some ways, workers in the humanities are disadvantaged versus STEM workers (those in science, technology, engineering, and math) because the monetary value of intellectual products from the humanities is generally harder to quantify and, therefore, less likely to attract investment. However, they have an advantage in that their intellectual products have a stronger connection with a society's culture, so the products are less likely to be commoditized. For example, a worker in India can be hired by a U.S. firm to write computer software, but a worker in India is unlikely to write *To Kill a Mockingbird.* Understanding how and why corporations, particularly those based on STEM products, have been successful in generating and leveraging IP may hold some value for workers in the humanities. But these same corporations can have weaknesses related to cultural issues where the humanities have strengths.

Examples of funding decisions that deselect the humanities are not hard to find. A controversy was sparked in October of 2011 when Florida Governor Rick Scott announced that the state of Florida did not need any more anthropologists, and that he was diverting funds from the liberal arts to STEM (Anderson, 2011). Governor Scott was simply accelerating a trend that has been ongoing since the 1960s when degrees in the humanities began declining (Reitz, 2011).

With fewer workers and less funding, intellectual products will likely also decline. The products of intellectual thought are the precursors to IP. In the corporate environment, IP is a fundamental tool used for leveraging revenue generation, and, consequently, smart companies manage it like an asset. IP can provide similar leverage to workers in the humanities, but they will have to make it their own. Their intellectual products are different, and they will have to find new ways of generating and protecting their intellectual products and, even more critically, of putting a recognized value on their contributions.

In some respects, the best practices of multinational corporations may need to be adopted in part and then adapted for the strengths of the humanities. While in the corporate environment, I led a group of 50 to 60 people who managed IP for the Dow Chemical Company. And now, after residing in the humanities, I understand some of the differences between the two cultures related to how IP is generated, used, and squandered. In this chapter, I address some relevant aspects for the humanities of how corporations are managing intellectual capital, turning it into IP, and then extracting value for those assets. Some practices of corporations are considered "best practices" and should be understood and adapted to the humanities, but then others should be avoided. The opportunities associated with IP in the twenty-first century need to be understood and managed not just by large multinational corporations but also by those who give voice to alternative ideas and ways of thinking and who may not have as a primary driver corporate profit motives.

Understanding

Definitions

The genesis of intellectual property starts with intellectual products, the products of human intellectual effort. For corporations, much of an organization's knowledge resides in the employees' heads in the form of skills, know-how, and capabilities. *Human capital* is frequently the term used to refer to the implicit employee knowledge that contributes to the wealth or assets of the organization, hence the term *capital*. When employees generate intellectual products that have the potential to contribute to revenue, then the term *intellectual capital* (IC) is used, defined by Patrick Sullivan (1998) as "knowledge that can be converted into profit" (p. 21). Sullivan defined codified knowledge as *intellectual assets* (IA). Information that has been codified is more easily managed and protected as company confidential information. *Intellectual property* (IP) refers to the intellectual assets that have legal protection such as copyrights, patents, trade secrets, and trademarks. *Intellectual capital management* is often a term associated with IP because intellectual capital precedes IP, as it includes the human capital and intellectual assets that lead to intellectual property: IC → IA→ IP (see Figure 1).

Human Capital →	**Intellectual Assets →**	**Intellectual Property**
Generating new ideas, talking with customers, engaging the marketplace, solving problems, analyzing competitors	Ideas, notebooks, emails, summaries of work performed, business plans, customer lists	Patents, copyrights, trademarks, trade secrets

Figure 1. Intellectual capital leading to intellectual property

In the mid-1990s, an industry group coalesced around the common interest of understanding best practices associated with IP management, and the founding members called themselves the Gathering for Intellectual Capital Management (or ICM Gathering; Harrison & Sullivan, 2012). I was privileged to be a member of the ICM Gathering as the representative of the company that I worked for. This group chooses to focus on intellectual capital management rather than IP management for a very good reason: The most effective IP management starts with intellectual capital management. The pipeline from ideas to IP should be managed in order to generate assets that have the most potential value to the owner. The intellectual products of employees become intellectual assets when documented and IP when legally protected.

Let us consider a parallel schematic for the humanities: In the humanities, rather than thinking of intellectual capital as "knowledge that can be converted into profit," intellectual capital might be thought of as knowledge that adds potential value to the organization or individual. What that value is and how it is extracted is situation dependent, but all knowledge is not of equal utility. Knowledge that can contribute to the goals of individuals or organizations is by definition intellectual capital whether it eventually leads to IP or not.

Consider in Figure 2 an example within the humanities related to the process of generating a piece of visual art. An artist creates intellectual capital in the form of ideas for future work (e.g., by visiting new places, talking with other artists, or viewing the work of others). An individual artist has many experiences, and some fraction of them become documented in the form of notes, reference photos, sketches, or inventory spreadsheets. These documented ideas are the artist's intellectual assets. IP is generated when a piece of art is completed and signed, giving the artist a copyright and ownership of the work. Without the proactive generation of ideas and a process for reducing them to a communicable form, the final piece of artwork may never be realized. A very similar process could be drawn for a writer, or a filmmaker. With this grounding in the terminology used in industry, I next outline how IP generation and management have been evolving and the state of the current industry practices. But, first, I situate industry practices within a global context.

Human Capital →	**Intellectual Assets →**	**Intellectual Property**
Idea generation, finding/inventing images, visiting new places, viewing the work of others	Notes, reference photos, sketches, applications to art shows, inventory of works, web site	Finished pieces, copyrighted work

Figure 2. Intellectual capital pipeline for the artist

The Corporate Global Environment

The book *The World Is Flat* by Thomas Friedman (2005) was widely read in the business world because of its erudite condensation of the factors contributing to the dramatic changes in the global marketplace during the last quarter century. Friedman attributed the changes to a "triple convergence" of conditions: "new players, on a new playing field, developing new processes and habits for horizontal collaboration" (p. 181). All of these changes had significant impact on intellectual capital and consequently IP.

The global socioeconomic changes that occurred during the last half of the twentieth century were famously (and sometimes reluctantly) termed the *postmodern era* (Hardt & Negri, 2000; Jameson, 1991; Lyotard, 1984). Jean-Francois Lyotard described the contemporary role of knowledge in *The Postmodern Condition* and noted, "knowledge is and will be produced in order to be sold, it is and will be consumed in order to be valorized in a new production: in both cases, the goal is exchange" (p. 4). He termed the production and sale of knowledge in a manner similar to material goods as the "mercantilization of knowledge," which he said has affected the hegemony of nation-states and produced a new entity on the global scene: multinational corporations. Fredric Jameson further described the effect that late capitalism has had on culture and intellectual productions like art, architecture, and literature. And Michael Hardt and Antonio Negri termed economic postmodernization as informatization wherein industrialization gave way to "services and information" (p. 280). The changes happening to intellectual capital fit within a context of these postmodern definitions (Schrock, 2011). The discourse of postmodernism captures the cultural signifiers in society, and some intellectual products are highly dependent on culture.

Taking perspectives from the business world, I would like to explore what these changes mean for a worker in the humanities for the foreseeable future. Three of the major changes that have directly impacted intellectual capital are the increase in global interconnectedness; the commodification of knowledge; and the competing sovereignties of nation states, transnational corporations, and international non-governmental organizations.

Global Interconnectivity. The global environment has seen an unprecedented increase in connectivity between people and nations. Video, audio, and text can be transmitted anywhere globally to mass audiences. For transnational corporations in particular, the ability to communicate instantly around the globe has been game changing. Increased collaboration has become not only possible, but also mandatory to survive in the competitive marketplace. Global communications made intellectual capital a resource more easily tapped into than ever before. Companies scramble to mine intellectual raw materials. Innovators can be anywhere, not just in the company offices or labs. Networking between innovators received well-known articulation by Henry Chesbrough (2003), who built a case for how collaboration furthers innovation. Probably nowhere is collaboration more necessitated than in the computer and electronics industry, and IP ownership is an ante to entry.

Marshall Phelps and David Kline (2009) related the market conditions that led a large transnational corporation like Microsoft to move away from a closed business model and toward a collaborative business model. Phelps and Kline said that

> technology development had become too widely dispersed and heterogeneous, the pace of innovation too rapid, and the competition for markets and customers too multifaceted and demanding for any one firm to go it alone anymore (p. 4)

Highly complex technology requires a breadth of skills on the part of developers, and, further, the speed at which implementation must occur to meet market needs precludes companies from incubating all of the skills internally if they are to stay ahead of the competition. The need to collaborate was clear, and the tool used to leverage collaboration became IP.

To succeed with innovation, companies began using IP in ways that transformed it—making it a new form of social capital with entirely new uses and abuses. Prior to the 1970s, IP was used mainly to ensure that intellectual producers were compensated for their efforts by excluding others from practicing the intellectual products for a period of time, as in the case of patents. More recently, the complexity of high-tech devices has led to complicated patent landscapes. Companies found themselves unable to produce a highly complex device that did not fall within the claims of a competitor's patents. Patent landscapes around many products became minefields or as some have described "anticommons" (Heller, 1998). As one colleague at the ICM Gathering explained the situation to me, to produce a device like a printer, hundreds if not thousands of patents must be considered. As a result, since the 1980s, patents have been used as leveraging tools to facilitate and even force collaboration between firms. As Phelps and Kline (2009) stated,

> intellectual property was becoming the sine qua non of open innovation itself. It provided the legal scaffolding upon which firms could share their most innovative research and partner together to create new products and services. (pp. 5–6)

Many forms of partnerships and licensing agreements have emerged in response to this competitive environment. An anticommons has been turned back into a commons, but with a high fee for entry.

The Commodification of Intellectual Capital. The increase in global interconnectivity drove global collaboration and open innovation, but it also had the effect of commoditizing intellectual work and workers, to use Marxist terminology. Dan Hunter (2005) laid the groundwork, saying that the rights to content can be seen as a class struggle between corporate interests and the interests of the public as both creators and users of content; he described how IP has become the new wealth of a bourgeoisie. The clash over IP rights between the haves and the have-nots is a form of class struggle—and the class struggle also exists over jobs that create IP.

During the first few years of the twenty-first century, many white-collar workers began feeling that a new type of world war had begun, and the spoils were not geographical but intellectual. The battle for jobs and the good life was being fought in the fields of intellectual capital. As an employee in a large transnational corporation, I witnessed a steady stream of outsourcing to Asia. From the management perspective, why not source work out of Asia? A growing segment of the population was educated, skilled, and a fraction of the cost of workers in the U.S. or Europe. In previous decades, jobs emigrating to developing nations were physical labor jobs (e.g., factory assembly lines). With education levels rising in countries like India and China, these same countries became sources for cheap intellectual capital. This high-priced specialty product of the developed countries became commoditized. Modern telecommunications and the Internet made it possible for corporations to mine intellectual products globally and cheaply.

By 2007, one of the responsibilities of my job was to manage several people in India. I spent time in India getting to know them, and I came away changed by the experience. The Indian workers became friends who, like all of us, were trying to earn a living for themselves and their families. The same transnational corporation I worked for was their vehicle to a better life. They had equipped themselves with the skills to compete in the global marketplace, and they were collecting their due. As workers producing intellectual capital, we were all proletariat.

Competing Empires. Competing empires relevant to IP are in the domains of knowledge use and the sociopolitical climate. Of the former, Lyotard (1984) said that

> knowledge and power are simply two sides of the same question: who decides what knowledge is, and who knows what needs to be decided? In the computer age, the question of knowledge is now more than ever a question of government. (pp. 8–9).

For Lyotard, the "merchantilization of knowledge" has affected the sovereignty of nation-states relative to multinational corporations and created a second type of competing empires, with the net effect of increasing privileging of work that can justify capital expense. If contributions to the organization cannot be quantified, the producers of the contributions may not be maintained. In a highly connected, global marketplace where human intellect can be mined from diverse sources, the flow of capital is used to generate IP for the holders of capital. Most countries are now members of WIPO (World Intellectual Property Organization), an organization that brings rationalization and consistency to IP processes, making it easier for IP rights to span the globe. To foster foreign business investments, even communist countries like China have taken WIPO seriously and have modified behaviors and laws to gain acceptance into the WIPO states.

The changes in China are an example of the importance of IP driving cultural behavior. When western companies began doing business in China, the new Chinese employees had little understanding of company confidential information—that not all information could be in the public domain. Chinese companies and organizations were accused of violating patent and trademark rights routinely. However, when Chinese companies began to have their own company confidential information and wanted to enforce their own patents, the Chinese government began prosecuting abusers. The Chinese began adopting IP practices common to the capitalist economies, and they learned from the best practices of others. Recent decades have seen innovations in the management of IP as assets, and these practices and behaviors are instructive for managing the future generation of intangible assets.

Adopting

Five Levels of IP Management

In *Edison in the Boardroom, Revisited,* Suzanne Harrison and Patrick Sullivan (2012) described the evolving role of IP and many of the best practices shared by members of the ICM Gathering. Pulling from the original book by Davis and Harrison (2001), *Revisited* describes five levels of IP management. For companies, the ultimate objective should be to first manage intellectual capital and then IP in a manner consistent with business strategy. Every business should have a clearly articulated strategy that plans for the utilization of business assets. Each piece of IP is a business asset; therefore, its generation and disposition should be managed like other business assets, at least in theory.

Level One is termed "Defend Position"—using IP to defend the current business position. Managers file for patents and copyrights to protect the intellectual products generated; they document trade secrets; they educate employees on the protection of intellectual products; and they insure they have the proper agreements in place with business partners to protect IP rights.

Level Two IP management is "Manage Costs": IP costs money, and IP managers should consider the cost of maintaining and defending it in light of the value to the business. For example, managing costs may mean abandoning patents that the firm will no longer use in order to avoid maintenance costs. At Level Three, companies "Capture Value" from their IP and generate revenue streams, for example, through selling, licensing, or litigating. For some companies, the sale or litigation of intellectual property *is* the business model. For others, the sale or licensing of intellectual property originally obtained for defensive purposes becomes a significant revenue stream.

Level Four management involves a more strategic use of IP. A company operating at Level Four utilizes IP to position itself in the marketplace. IP is a lever for gaining profitable business growth through partnerships, business negotiations, or other "tactical positioning" (p. 119). Companies have been driving collaboration through their IP as described above.

Managers of IP at firms operating at a Level Five create futures within which the firms want to do business. They are forward looking and develop IP in anticipation of markets or even in creation of markets. IP is managed proactively, strategically, and consistently within the current business strategy or extrapolated future business strategies.

Few corporations, according to Harrison and Sullivan (2012), "have mastered all five levels" (p. 17). In my experience within a large transnational corporation, the management of IP varies across the corporation from Level One to Level Five depending on the business and its management. Some of this variance is a result of the varying business strategies and is appropriate. A business that sells a large, commodity product with no patents or trademarks should give little attention to the generation of IP unless a business strategy can be developed where it can be used to transform the business. Conversely, the managers of a business undergoing strategic growth into new products or markets should spend a significant amount of time planning branding, patents, trademarks, and the protection of trade secrets—globally. But attention to IP management costs resources, and time is money. The costs in resources—people's time—can be quantified, and usually the actual value of the return in the future cannot be quantified, so there is a tendency to under-resource the management of intellectual capital in general, which is another reason why few businesses operate at Levels Four or Five.

To summarize through a specific example applied to a worker in the humanities, consider the artist whose intellectual capital was described in Figure 2. What the levels reflect is the adoption of a culture where intellectual property is managed like a business asset. A visual artist might consider operating in varying ways within these five levels of IP management:

> Level 1: The artist starts by recognizing existing intellectual capital. Ideas for future works are documented and catalogued; photos are taken of places visited and stored in a secure location; sketches are saved; works of art are generated and protected from damage; works are signed and dated; in some cases, copyrights might be sought.
>
> Level 2: The artist understands cash flow out. Costs associated with supplies, storage of art, advertising, and production processes are considered and kept to a level that allows for profit from the sale of the work; the costs versus value of pursuing formal copyrights are considered and decisions made based on types of work and markets; time toward branding and marketing is spent when value can be realized.
>
> Level 3: The artist understands the market and how to generate revenue. Artwork is sold in markets or galleries where the best price can be extracted; rights to reproduce images are sold; sales occur through artist's website; copycats and illegal copying by others is brought to their attention and possibly litigated; the production, reproduction, and sale of the artwork is run like a business.
>
> Level 4: The artist profits through interaction with a community of artists. The artist is a member of a community of artists and networks with other artists through various social media; the artist stays current on what's selling in the world of art, themes, media and collaborates with others on new works particularly in adjacent media or subject matter to broaden work and reach; artist mentors and teaches others.
>
> Level 5: The artist works to create new markets or evolve exiting ones. Artist wants to raise awareness of a cultural issue or problem in society and tries to bring about changes in public opinion through his or her artwork; or the artist is concerned with some aspect of IP rights and works through government or industry decision-makers to effect changes in laws; or the artist develops and promotes a new form of artistic expression because it accomplishes or conveys something new or creates a new market.

The practices above require various skills and behaviors on the part of the IP owner whether the owner is a corporation or an individual. These behaviors are consistent with a culture where IP is managed like a business asset. But the culture of managing IP like an asset is not only enabled by certain behaviors within a corporation, it also may be disabled by corporate behaviors. The enabling behaviors may be admirable and worthy of imitation, but other behaviors should be avoided.

Adapting Yet Avoiding

How Strengths Become Weaknesses

Because of the drive for profit, companies have engineered and honed many positive behaviors related to the generation of IP. In fact, they are so good at some behaviors that strengths become weaknesses. In identifying the following strong and weak behaviors, I pull from personal experiences, experiences related to me from colleagues at other companies, and the many books written on corporate management practices. In doing so, I make generalizations that I have found mostly true for transnational corporations (although, as with all generalizations, one can find exceptions). For privately held firms some of the following behaviors may not necessarily apply. I outline these strengths to aid in understanding why corporations are so successful at generating and utilizing IP, and how they can struggle to realize its full potential. For many of these characteristics, the humanities present a complement that creates opportunities.

Communication. Corporate employees who have aspects of their jobs related to knowledge generation or management live or die based on the ability to communicate. An "elevator speech" is important to have mentally tucked away for the occasion when a 30-second verbal synopsis is needed of work in progress or planned and its importance. Experts in a specific field may have precise vocabulary that they speak among themselves, but to get their messages out, communications have to be on a level that, for example, a general studies major can understand. If management does not understand what individuals or groups are doing, then the output of those workers will be undervalued. Funding flows in routes deemed worthy of maintenance based on contributions to the corporation. Bright people can sometimes struggle to succeed in a corporate environment because of poor communication skills.

Corporate employees are experts at connecting and communicating. Instant, global communications are so easy, that now they have the opposite problem: to restrict information flow. Documented corporate information comprises a significant segment of the intellectual assets. Much of this information is confidential and should be disseminated only on a need-to-know basis. A company would not want business plans or customer lists falling into competitors' hands. Even more important, many countries have import/export laws to restrict the flow of information deemed important for national security. Export-restricted technology cannot legally flow to certain countries where other employees of the same company may be working. Restricting information flow within a corporation can be as important as preventing information flow out of the corporation.

Restrictions around copyrighted material are not dissimilar; both require controlled information flow. For instance, although a publisher needs to recover costs and make enough profit to justify future business efforts, increased costs to users can be viewed as exploitation. A recent boycott of Elsevier's pricing for mathematics journals caused a reversal of its policy to raise prices as reported in *New Scientist*:

> Journal publisher Elsevier has announced changes in the pricing of its mathematics titles, and withdrawn support for a controversial, proposed US law, which has subsequently been scrapped. Both moves follow a boycott of the company's journals, which was led by mathematicians who objected to Elsevier's prices and its support for the legislation. (Aron, 2012).

According to Jacob Aron, the mathematicians were finding other ways of sharing information that did not involve the publisher. The many tools available for global communications are providing some checks in the ability of large publishers to control access to information.

Creating a Brand. IP around branding can be some of the most valuable, but also some of the least permanent. Company names, brand names, and the image associated with each can be worth far more than the physical assets of a company. Harrison and Sullivan (2012) noted that,

> for P&G [Procter & Gamble], their brands and trademark names have always been the crown jewels of the company. "Our brands make an ongoing promise that when consumers buy Tide or Pampers or Gillette, they also are buying a promise of quality and value." (pp. 177–178).

Corporations spend a lot of time and money branding not only their products, but also themselves.

A publically traded corporation is always positioning its image so that stock will be viewed as a good investment to Wall Street. Investors have choices on how to invest their money, so the corporation's stock must be viewed as returning more profit than other potential investments. Corporations are so good at branding and image that like politicians, they project an image based on how they want to be perceived. For example, to give confidence to investors that they have a profitable future, they champion an image of innovative growth whether that image is accurate or not. One way that IP is used in managing image is through the accumulation of massive patent portfolios. Because patents can be highly complex and value is context dependent, no one has a definitive method of calculating real value. A large patent portfolio may indicate innovation, or it may be creating a simulacrum of innovation. In the latter case, the problem is not so much that they have created a simulacrum, but that they begin to believe and act within the simulacrum that they created, leaving the marketplace to eventually administer correction.

Universities are adopting the behaviors of branding when budgets tighten. The image of the college or university attracts students whether that image is based on athletics or academics or both. In *The University in Ruins*, Bill Readings (1996) described "the University as a corporation" (p. 11) and the student as a consumer. The reality of the current economic climate is that branding is critical to obtaining funding even in university settings. IP that supports positive brand recognition becomes important and must be managed strategically.

Boundaryless Behavior. Corporations have become creative in mining diverse sources of intellectual capital. Jack Welch, CEO of General Electric during the 1980s and 1990s, called global idea-mining "boundaryless behavior." During the 20 years that he was CEO of GE, Welch championed four major initiatives, one of them was globalization, which involved inculcating global thinking in GE's employees. He attributed the success of these initiatives to his insistence on "boundaryless behavior." Welch expected specific types of behaviors in employees to elicit boundaryless behavior. In 1991, GE began grading managers on boundaryless behavior: Every manager received a rating from Type 1, a manager who delivers on commitments and shares the GE values, to Type 4, a manager who delivers on commitments but does not share the values. Type 4 managers were released from employment.

GE is still a leader in tapping into ideas globally. From mid-July until September 30, 2010, GE launched *Ecomagination*, challenging anyone worldwide with access to the Internet to submit ideas in three areas: renewables, grid efficiency, and eco homes/eco buildings. For submitting an idea, the innovator was in the running for one of five $100,000 awards. *Ecomagination* is a good example of what Welch meant by the term "boundaryless behavior."

Corporations can be excellent at tapping into intellectual capital from all sources and converting it into IP, but they do so within a defined ideology. And residing within that ideology, employees frequently do not realize how narrow the thinking actually is. Personnel internal to the corporation are caught in the web of corporate ideology, so new ideas are rarely out-of-the-box thinking. Intellectual capital is within specific boundaries: ideas with an obvious route to a revenue stream are privileged over ideas that *prima facie* do not have an obvious route to revenue. Consequently, corporations only pursue innovative thinking that relates to profitable growth. As far as society is concerned, this privileging of the profitable leaves a huge hole in the intellectual heavy lifting and self-transformation that human culture must continually do to survive. Fortunately, borderless ideas are not confined to corporations.

Workers in the humanities outside of corporations are also collaborating in shorter time frames and across geographies in ways not achievable before email and the Internet. Collaboration on intellectual products like texts can occur instantaneously across the globe. Web sites and forums like blogs or Twitter allow access to one's intellectual products. Digital media helps to juxtapose images and ideas, creating the seeds for new inventions (e.g., as demonstrated in Garrett, Landrum-Geyer, & Palmeri, 2012). Frans Johansson (2006) described how innovation often occurs at the intersections of disciplines; bringing together disparate subject matter fuels new ways of thinking, new ideas, and consequently the potential for IP.

Innovate to Address Needs in the Marketplace. New ideas are the genesis of intellectual property. Typically, the innovations that corporations excel at are line extensions and variations of the current product line. Previously successful corporations can struggle with disruptive innovations, and this struggle leads to failure. The reasons why successful organizations fail is explained by Clayton Christensen (2003) in *The Innovator's Dilemma*: "there is something about the way decisions get made in successful organizations that sows the seeds of eventual failure" (p. xv). In other words, the behaviors that made the company successful are frequently not the same behaviors that allow it to sustain success into the future. Corporations that do not adapt to a changing environment become extinct, and there are many examples of corporate dinosaurs. The humanities outside of the corporate environment are where disruptive ideas can arise and thrive because worker's behaviors are not as constrained by having to utilize expensive infrastructure like manufacturing plants or by having to satisfy stockholders. Innovation is less risky financially.

Understanding Value. When two polar opposites on the political and economic spectrum agree on a point, then it probably has some validity. Joel Bakan (2005) argued that both Milton Friedman and Noam Chomsky agree that the purpose of corporations is—in Friedman's words—to "make as much money as possible for their shareholders" (p. 34), or in Chomsky's words, "they really have only one mission, and that is to increase shareholder value" (p. 35). Corporations put an economic value on nearly everything they do. Projects are funded based on economic value to the bottom line. This type of financial rigor helps to control bureaucracy and to focus efforts on activities that contribute to profitability. A well-run organization has clarity on priorities, purpose, and goals—all of these being based on financial health. Although the drive to maximize shareholder value creates a burning deck on clarity of organizational purpose, it comes at a cost.

Just as focusing on utilizing current assets and satisfying paying customers creates a kind of tunnel vision, focusing on maximizing profits causes a kind of myopia. Activities and projects favored are those that have a clear economic advantage, so business decisions privilege the type of work that has hard economic value. In order to justify resources for any group of people to be employed, management must understand the purpose served to the organization and the return on investment. The environment created is one based on a philosophy of teleology. Budgeting processes can make it difficult for some organizations to focus on intangibles.

For some IP, like patents, the value is far enough in the future to have a high degree of value uncertainty. No one has a crystal ball to predict market direction. Consequently, the generation of IP as Harrison and Sullivan (2012) stated, "is an option on an investment" (p. 30). Companies that experience swings in profitability corresponding to economic cycles can have difficulty sustaining strategic maintenance of IP in the long term. In ancient times, when a ship was beset by a violent storm, cargo was jettisoned, for example cannon balls, in order to help save the ship from sinking. The uncertainty of future use is subordinated to present needs similar to corporate assets during rough economic times. IP is particularly susceptible to being jettisoned because of the corporate need to conserve cash and the property's uncertain link to future cash generation. The strong teleological funding link causes short-term focus and difficulty in far-sighted vision.

Making an Example of Big Bird

Bringing all of the above behaviors to bear on Big Bird may help to illustrate the difficulty amid success faced by an icon of the humanities in contemporary culture where viability is judged based on return on investment. In the fall of 2012, I watched a debate of the U.S. presidential candidates and heard Mitt Romney make a comment that received a lot of publicity post-debate. He said the U.S. should not borrow money from China to pay for Public Broadcasting and Big Bird. Whether the U.S. government should or should not contribute to PBS is not what I plan to focus on here. The point I would like to illustrate is that when organizations are run like a business, every expense has to be justified. So, would Big Bird be laid off if the government were run more like a business? How could Big Bird, one of PBS's biggest brand images and communicator of intellectual products, end up in the unemployment line? The answer is that ultimately when organizations are run like businesses, *every* resource has to show a return on investment *in hard numbers* (in dollars and not intangibles) in order to receive funding, even Big Bird.

Public Broadcasting posted a response to Mitt Romney's comment (PBS, 2012), and in the response were specific numbers related to the audience and the cost: 91% of adults and 81% of children ages 2 to 8 tune into PBS sometime during the course of a year, making the cost per viewer $1.35 per year. But the communication did not contain hard numbers related to return on investment—probably because these numbers are very difficult to obtain. The data related to audience and cost suggest value but not in terms that are necessary to justify investment from a business standpoint. More compelling numbers for keeping Big Bird around from a business standpoint might be dollars saved in educational resources by school systems as a result of having access to PBS's digital content, dollars saved in the classroom as a result of content learned at home, or dollars earned in revenue from sales tax of *Sesame Street* toys and games. If the government were run like a business, even Big Bird will need to quantify his contributions.

Managing Perception

Workers in the humanities bring unique skills, and their voices need to be heard independent of profit motives. Corporations cultivate behaviors that promote the generation of specific IP, yet within those positive behaviors are limitations. Workers in the humanities outside of for-profit organizations provide a complement to workers in a corporate environment. One of those skills is the ability to deal with complexity without having to drive to simplicity or reduction to an easy answer. In fields where there are often no easy answers and possibly no right answers, the ability to deal with complexity and to work through cultural issues is an asset. In the March 17, 2012, issue of *New Scientist*, Noam Chomsky was asked in an interview if human nature was too complicated to be researched and he replied,

> take, say, physics, which restricts itself to extremely simple questions. If a molecule becomes too complex, they hand it over to the chemists. If it becomes too complex for them, they hand it to biologists. And if the system is too complex for them, they hand it to the psychologists… and so on until it ends up in the hands of historians or novelists. (p. 28)

Human nature can evade simple explanations or mathematical predictions. The humanities embrace complexity and explore it through intellectual products that may never be profitable in a market sense. The challenge for workers in the humanities is to position their efforts as having value in order to receive funding even though a dollar figure cannot be calculated.

A corollary to handling complexity is thinking out-of-the-box. Corporations may believe they encourage "boundaryless behavior," but they do not. They work to stimulate targeted ideas and innovations—ones with potential to generate revenue and meet corporate objectives. Workers in the humanities are far less constrained in their thinking because the connection to profit is less obvious, necessary, or desired. The driver to generate capital is a two-edged sword. For industry, it creates a burning deck, a sense of urgency and common purpose, but it also narrows the focus, thinking, and behavior. There is far less tolerance for diversity of thought in a corporation than outside of the corporate environment. Employees who generate IP for corporations are working within an ideology that is not questioned because it is not profitable to question it.

The abilities to deal with human complexity, to think out-of-the-box, and to challenge the dominant ideology are all traits that are needed in order to ensure that we are asking the right questions. In fact, knowing how to ask the right questions is at the heart of Level 5, visionary IP management. Working to create a future in which we want to live requires vision and the ability to ask the right questions, which should generate opportunities for capturing and utilizing IP.

Asking the Right Questions

In a recent television ad, the Chief Technology Officer of a Fortune 100 company made the following statement: "Science is definitive. There is a right answer out there." For science, this statement is generally true depending on the question asked, but if we want to thrive as a society, we should be fostering the disciplines that help to ensure the right questions are being asked. Especially for problems in the humanities, there are frequently no "right" answers. The ability to understand the complexity of abstract human problems is demanded of individuals schooled in the humanities, but the difficulty in attaching a value to this intellectual work causes these efforts to be undervalued, which in difficult economic climates leads to underfunding. If the trend continues where universities and governmental organizations are run more like businesses, workers in the humanities are going to have to become innovative at understanding how to value their work and communicating that value to the funding decision makers. Increasingly, during the last quarter of the twentieth century, intellectual products and IP have evolved into commodities. For some industries, the generation and management of IP has become a type of commodity fetishism. In a society driven by late stage capitalism, the humanities must manage IP like the commodity that it has become or be able to define the use value inherent in their intellectual products that distinguish those products from commodities. Science may be a definitive tool, but it needs the humanities to ensure application toward answering the "right" questions.

References

Abella, A.; Sánchez, J.; & Segovia, M. A. (2004). *Libro blanco del software libre en España*. Retrieved from http://www.oei.es/salactsi/254-2004.pdf

Academic Coursepacks. In *Copyright & fair use: Stanford University Libraries*. Retrieved from http://fairuse.stanford.edu/Copyright_and_Fair_Use_Overview/chapter7/7-a.html

Adams, John. (1850). *The works of John Adams, second president of the United States with a life of the author, notes and illustrations* (Vols. 1–10, Vol. 6). Boston: Little and Brown.

Aitchison, Cara. (2001). Theorizing Other discourses of tourism, gender, and culture: Can the subaltern speak (in tourism)? *Tourist Studies: An International Journal, 1*(2), 133–147.

Akrich, Madeleine, & Latour, Bruno. (1992). A summary of a convenient vocabulary for the semiotics of human and nonhuman assemblies. In W. E. Bijker & J. Law (Eds.), *Shaping technology/building society: Studies in sociotechnical change* (pp. 259–264). Cambridge, MA: MIT Press.

Alberich, J., & Roig, A. (2008). *Creación y producción audiovisual colaborativa. Implicaciones sociales y culturales.* Universidad Oberta de Catalunya. Retrieved from http://www.uoc.edu/uocpapers/7/dt/esp/alberich_roig.pdf

Albuu (2010). Interview with Miss Caffeina. Retrieved from http://talvezconunpocodemusica.blogspot.com/2010/04/hace-mas-o-menos-un-mes-el-magnetica.html

Allen, Peter. (2008). Rip, mix, burn...sue...ad infinitum: The effects of deterrence vs. voluntary cooperation on non-commercial online copyright infringing behavior. *First Monday, 13* (9). Retrieved from http://firstmonday.org/ojs/index.php/fm/article/view/2073

American Chemical Society. (2011). SciFinder Web. Retrieved from http://cas.org/products/scifindr/index.html

Anderson, Daniel. (2003). Prosumer approaches to new media composition: Consumption and production in continuum. *Kairos, 8* (1). Retrieved from http://endora.wide.msu.edu/8.1/index.html

Anderson, Daniel. (2008). The low bridge to high benefits: Entry-level multimedia, literacies, and motivation. *Computers and Composition, 25*(1): 40–60.

Anderson, Nate. (2008). *Reznor makes $750,000 even when the music is free.* Retrieved from http://arstechnica.com/old/content/2008/03/reznor-makes-750000-even-when-the-music-is-free.ars

Anderson, Zac. (2011, October 10). Rick Scott wants to shift university funding away from some degrees. *Herald-Tribune.* Retrieved from http://htpolitics.com/2011/10/10/rick-scott-wants-to-shift-university-funding-away-from-some-majors/

Andolsen, Barbara Hilkert. (2008). Essential goods for AIDS widows: Property, including intellectual property, in Catholic social teachings. *Journal of the Society of Christian Ethics, 28*(1), 67–86.

Ang, Ien. (2001). *On not speaking Chinese: Living between Asia and the West.* New York: Routledge.

Anti-piracy strategies questionnaire - conclusion. (2010). Retrieved from http://www.vigilantdefender.com/QuestionnaireCon.php

Anzaldúa, Gloria, & Keating, AnaLouise. (Eds.). (2001). *This bridge we call home.* New York: Routledge.

Anzaldúa, Gloria. (1990). *La concienca de la mestiza:* Towards a new consciousness. In Gloria Anzaldúa (Ed.), *Making face/Making soul: Haciendo caras* (p. 379). San Francisco: Aunt Lute Foundation.

Anzaldúa, Gloria. (2001). *Borderlands / la frontera.* In Patricia Bizzell & Bruce Herzberg (Eds.), *The rhetorical tradition: Readings from classical times to the present* (pp. 1582–1604). New York: Bedford.

Arnab, Alapan, & Hutchinson, Andrew. (2005). Fairer usage contracts for DRM. *Proceedings of the 5th ACM workshop on Digital Rights Management.* Alexandria, VA: ACM.

Aron, Jacob (2012, February 28). Elsevier vows to keep price of mathematics journals low. *New Scientist.* Retrieved from http://www.newscientist.com/blogs/shortsharpscience/2012/02/elsevier-announces-changes-to.html

Aron, Jacob. (2012, February 14). Web freedoms fuel "academic spring" journal protest. *New Scientist.* Retrieved from http://www.newscientist.com/article/dn21467-web-freedoms-fuel-academic-spring-journal-protest.html

Art Resource. (2012). ArtRes web site. Retrieved from http://www.artres.com

Atkins, Daniel E.; Brown, John Seely; & Hammond, Allen L. (2007). *A review of the open educational resources (OER) movement: Achievements, challenges and new opportunities.* New York: The William and Flora Hewlett Foundation.

Atkinson, Dwight. (1999). *Scientific discourse in sociohistorical context: The philosophical transactions of the Royal Society of London, 1675–1975.* Mahwah, NJ: Erlbaum.

Auerbach, Dan. (2012, October 12). Ad industry's assault on "do not track" continues at the W3C Amsterdam meeting. *Electronic Frontier Foundation.* Retrieved from https://www.eff.org/deeplinks/2012/10/ad-industrys-assault-do-not-track-continues-w3c-amsterdam-meeting

Australian Copyright Council. (2012). Information sheet G053v08: Research or study. Retrieved from http://www.copyright.org.au/admin/cms-acc1/_images/17257045814f3b3aa41d472.pdf

Bacchilega, Cristina. (2007). *Legendary Hawai'i and the politics of place: Tradition, translation, and tourism*. Philadelphia: University of Pennsylvania Press.

Baio, Andy. (2011, December). No copyright intended. *Waxy*. Retrieved from http://waxy.org/2011/12/no_copyright_intended/

Bailey, Rich. (2011, October 7). Lawrence Golan speaks about *Golan v. Holder* and his Fight to Protect the Public Domain. techdirt. Retrieved from: http://www.techdirt.com/articles/20111006/12220616236/lawrence-golan-speaks-about-golan-v-holder-his-fight-to-protect-public-domain.shtml

Bakan, Joel. (2005). *The corporation: The pathological pursuit of profit and power*. London: Constable & Robinson.

Baker, David L. (2006). To glean or not to glean... *Expository Times, 117*(10), 406–410.

Baker, Houston. (1985). Autobiographical acts and the voice of the southern slave. In Charles T. Davis & Henry Louis Gates, Jr. (Eds.), *The slave's narrative* (pp. 192–261). New York: Oxford University Press.

Ballon, Hilary, & Westermann, Mariet. (2006). Art history and its publications in the electronic age. *Connexions*. Retrieved from http://cnx.org/content/col10376/1.1/

Band, Jonathan. (2012). A farewell to constitutional challenges to copyright laws. Retrieved from http://www.librarycopyrightalliance.org/bmdoc/golan_summary_06feb12.pdf

Barthes, Roland. (1977). *Image, music, text*. New York: Hill and Wang.

Barton, Laura. (2008, November 9). Hope—the image that is already an American classic. *The Guardian*. Retrieved from: http://www.theguardian.com/artanddesign/2008/nov/10/barackobama-usa

Bazerman, C. (1988). *Shaping written knowledge: The genre and the activity of the experimental report in science*. Madison: University of Wisconsin Press.

Beaven, Kristie, & Ward, Rebecca. (2012, October 18). Tate debate: When is appropriation homage and when is it plagiarism? Tate Blog. Retrieved June 9, 2014 from http://www.tate.org.uk/context-comment/blogs/tate-debate-when-appropriation-homage-and-when-it-plagiarism

Bell, Tom W. (2000). Escape from copyright: Market success vs. statutory failure in the protection of expressive works. *University of Cincinnati Law Review*, 69, 741.

Benenson, F. (2009). *NIN's CC-Licensed best-selling MP3 album*. Retrieved from http://creativecommons.org/weblog/entry/11947

Benkler, Yochai. (2006). *The wealth of networks: How social production transforms markets and freedom*. New Haven, CT: Yale University Press.

Benjamin, Walter. (2002). *The arcades project*. (Rolf Tiedemann, Ed.; Howard Eiland and Kevin McLaughlin, Trans.). Cambridge, MA: Belknap Press.

Bently, Lionel; Davis, Jennifer; & Ginsburg, Jane C. (2010). *Copyright and piracy: An interdisciplinary critique*. New York: Cambridge University Press.

Beradini, César. (2008, October 17). *Soulcalibur IV Darth Vader is no longer a ps3 exclusive*. Retrieved from http://news.teamxbox.com/xbox/17884/Soulcalibur-IV-Darth-Vader-is-No-Longer-a-PS3-Exclusive/

Berg, Charles Ramirez. (2006). A taxonomy of alternative plots in recent films: Classifying the "Tarantino Effect." *Film Criticism, 31*(1), 5–61.

Berg, Thomas C. (2008). Intellectual property and the preferential option for the poor. *Journal of Catholic Social Thought, 5*(1), 193–233.

Berkenkotter, Carol, & Huckin, Thomas. (1995). *Genre knowledge in disciplinary communication: Cognition/culture/power*. New York: Routledge.

Berkes, Fikret. (1999). *Sacred ecology: Traditional ecological knowledge and resource management systems*. Philadelphia: Taylor and Francis.

Berne Convention for the Protection of Literary and Artistic Works. (Last amended 1979). Retrieved from http://www.wipo.int/treaties/en/ip/berne/trtdocs_wo001.html

Bhabha, Homi. (1994). *The location of culture*. New York: Routledge.

Bielstein, Susan M. (2006). *Permissions, a survival guide: Blunt talk about art as intellectual property*. Chicago: University of Chicago Press.

Billington, James H. (July 26, 2010). Statement of the Librarian of Congress relating to Section 1201 rulemakings. Retrieved from http://www.copyright.gov/1201/2010/Librarian-of-Congress-1201-Statement.html

Birnbaum, Philip. (1975). *A book of Jewish concepts* (rev. ed.). New York: Hebrew Publishing Company.

Björk, Bo-Christer; Welling, Patrik; Laakso, Mikael; Majlender, Peter; Hedlund, Turid; & Guðnason, Guðni. (2010). Open access to the scientific journal literature: Situation 2009. *PLoS One, 5*(6). Retrieved from http://www.plosone.org/article/info:doi/10.1371/journal.pone.0011273

Blanch v. Koons, 467 F.3d 244 (2d Cir. 2006).

Block, Walter. (1986). Comment on "Judaism and the Market Mechanism." In Walter Block & Irving Hexham (Eds.), *Religion, Economics, and Social Thought* (pp. 430–449). Vancouver, B.C.: Fraser Institute.

Boateng, Boatema. (2011). *The copyright thing doesn't work here: Adinkra and kente cloth and intellectual property in Ghana*. Minneapolis: University of Minnesota Press.

Body of European Regulators for Electronic Communication. (2012, March 9). BEREC preliminary findings on traffic management practices in Europe show that blocking of VoIP and P2P traffic is common, other practices vary widely. Retrieved from http://ec.europa.eu/digital-agenda/sites/digital-agenda/files/Traffic%20Management%20Investigation%20BEREC_2.pdf

Bollacker, Kurt; Lawrence, Steve; & Giles, C. Lee. (1999). A system for automatic personalized tracking of scientific literature on the web. *DL'99 Digital Libraries, the 4th ACM Conference on Digital Libraries*, 105–113.

Booth, William. (2008, May 18). Street artist Fairey gives Obama a line of cred. *The Washington Post*. Retrieved from http://www.washingtonpost.com/wp-srv/artsandliving/style/features/2008/obama-poster-051808/graphic.html

Borgman, Christine. (2007). *Scholarship in the digital age: Information, infrastructure, and the internet*. Cambridge, MA: MIT Press.

Borgman, Christine. (2009). The digital future is now: A call to action for the humanities. *Digital Humanities Quarterly*. Retrieved from http://works.bepress.com/borgman/233/

Bowe, Heather, & Martin, Kylie. (2007). *Communication across cultures: Mutual understanding in a global world*. Melbourne: Cambridge University Press.

Bowker, Geoffrey. (2006). *Memory practices in the sciences*. Cambridge, MA: MIT University Press.

boyd, danah. (2008). Facebook's privacy trainwreck: Exposure, invasion, and social convergence. *Convergence*, *14*(1), 13–20.

Boyden, Bruce E. (2009, July 13). The Obama "Hope" poster case—Mannie Garcia weighs in. *Marquette University Law School Faculty Blog*. Retrieved from http://law.marquette.edu/facultyblog/2009/07/13/the-obama-hope-poster-case-mannie-garcia-weighs-in/

Boyle, James. (2008). *The public domain: Enclosing the commons of the mind*. New Haven, CT: Yale University Press.

Bradley, Jean-Claude. (2008). Chemistry crowd-sourcing and open notebook science. *Nature Proceedings*. Retrieved from http://precedings.nature.com/documents/1505/version/1/files/npre20081505-1.pdf

Bridgeman Art Library, LTD. v. Corel Corporation, 25 F.Supp.2d 421 (S.D. New York 1998).

Bridgeman Art Library, LTD. v. Corel Corporation, 36 F.Supp.2d 191 (S.D. New York 1999).

Bridgeman Art Library. (2009). Terms and conditions (U.S.). Retrieved from http://www.bridgemanart.com/terms-and-conditions-us

Brooks, Roger. (1983). *Support for the poor in the Mishnaic law of agriculture: Tractate peah*. Chico, CA: Scholars Press.

Brown, Michael. (2003). *Who owns native culture?* Cambridge: Harvard University Press.

Brown, Sasha H. (2011, October 10). An open letter to Urban Outfitters on Columbus Day. *Racialicious*. Blog post retrieved from http://www.racialicious.com/2011/10/10/an-open-letter-to-urban-outfitters-on-columbus-day/?utm_source=feedburner&utm_medium=feed&utm_campaign=Feed%3A+Racialicious+%28Racialicious+the+intersection+of+race+and+pop+culture%29

Buchanan, Levi. (2009, March 20). *Genesis vs. SNES: By the numbers*. Retrieved from http://retro.ign.com/articles/965/965032p1.html

Burrow-Giles Lithographic Company v. Sarony, 111 U.S. 53 (1884).

Cai, Michelle. (2004). Madey v. Duke University: Shattering the myth of universities' experimental use defense. *Berkeley Technology Law Journal, 19*, 175.

Cajete, Gregory. (1999). *Native science: Natural laws of interdependence*. Santa Fe, NM: Clear Light Publishers.

Callon, Michel. (1999). Actor-network theory—the market test. In J. Law & J. Hassard (Eds.), *Actor network theory and after* (pp. 181–195). Malden, MA: Blackwell Publishing.

Cameron, Colin T. (2006). In defiance of Bridgeman: Claiming copyright in photographic reproductions of public domain works. *Texas Intellectual Property Law Journal, 15*(1), 31.

Campbell v. Acuff-Rose Music, Inc., 510 U.S. 569 (1993).

Carey, David H. (2007). *The social mortgage of intellectual property*. Christian Social Thought Series. Grand Rapids, MI: Acton Institute.

Carey, Kevin. (2012, April 8). A future full of badges. *The Chronicle of Higher Education*. Retrieved from http://chronicle.com/article/A-Future-Full-of-Badges/131455/

Cariou v. Prince, 784 F. Supp. 2d 337 (S.D.N.Y. 2011).

Case C-275/06, Productores de Musica de Espana ("'Promusicae") v. Telefonica de Espana SAU, [2008] ECR I-00271.

Case C-70/10 Scarlet Extended v Societe Belge des auteurs, compositeurs et editeurs (SABAM) 2011.

Castells, M. (1997). *La era de la información. Economía, sociedad y cultura.* Madrid: Alianza Editorial.

Caswell, Tom; Henson, Shelley; Jensen, Marion; & Wiley, David. (2008). Open educational resources: Enabling universal education. *The International Review of Research in Open and Distance Learning.* Retrieved from http://www.irrodl.org/index.php/irrodl/article/view/469/1001

Center for Community Solutions. In *The encyclopedia of Cleveland online.* Retrieved from http://ech.case.edu/ech-cgi/article.pl?id=CFCS1

Chanan, Michael. (1995). *Repeated takes: A short history of recording and its effects on music*. London & New York: Verso.

Chander, Anupam, & Sunder, Madhavi. (2004). The romance of the public domain. *California Law Review*, 92(5),1331–1373.

Chander, Anupam; Sunder, Madhavi; & Le, Uyen. (2012). International decision: Golan v. Holder. *American Journal of International Law, 106*, 637–642.

Chang, Jeff. (2005). *Can't stop won't stop: A history of the hip-hop generation.* New York: St. Martin's Press.

Charitable giving fell 3.6 percent in 2009, "Giving USA" finds. (2010, June). *Philanthropy News Digest.* Retrieved from http://foundationcenter.org/pnd/news/story.jhtml?id=296700002

Charnas, Dan. (2010). *The big payback: The history of the business of hip hop.* New York: New American Library.

Chaucer, Geoffrey, & Benson, Larry D. (1987). *The riverside Chaucer.* Boston: Houghton Mifflin.

Chesbrough, Henry W. (2003) *Open innovation: The new imperative for creating and profiting from technology.* Boston, MA: Harvard Business School Press.

Cheyfitz, Eric. (2011). Native American philosophies and the limits of capitalism's imagination: A brief manifesto. *The South Atlantic Quarterly, 110*(2), 291–307.

Christen, Kimberly. (2005). Gone digital: Aboriginal remix and the cultural commons. *International Journal of Cultural Property, 12*, 315–345.

Christopher, Roy. (2007). Shepard Fairey: Giant steps. In Roy Christopher (Ed.), *Follow for now: Interviews with friends and heroes* (pp. 277–282). Seattle, WA: Well-Red Bear Press.

Chui, Lisa. (2011, April). IRS figures show charity creation may be slowing after years of fast growth. *The Chronicle of Philanthropy.* Retrieved from http://philanthropy.com/article/Charity-Creation-Appears-to/126962/

Cisneros, Sandra. (2002). *Caramelo.* New York: Knopf.

Clements, Ryan. (2009, April 23). *The Joker playable in Batman: Arkham Asylum.* Retrieved from http://ps3.ign.com/articles/975/975942p1.html

CNBC special: A history of video game industry. (2006, November 30). Retrieved from http://www.msnbc.msn.com/id/15734058/ns/business-cnbc_tv/t/cnbc-special-history-video-game-industry/

Colbert Report, The. (2010, February 11). Comedy Central. Television.

Colbert, F. (2000). *Le marqueting des arts et de la culture.* Montréal-Paris: Gaëtan Morin Éditeur.

College Art Association Committee on Intellectual Property. (2004). Q & A. CAA *News: Newsletter of the College Art Association, 29* (1).

Connelly, Sean. (2009). In-between paradise: Alternative postcards—Views from Waikīkī, ignored. *Vice-Versa, 5.* Retrieved from http://viceversajournal.com/2009/10/18/connellalternativepostcards/

Console wars—the good ol' days. (2007, March). Retrieved from http://forums.penny-arcade.com/discussion/18012/console-wars-the-good-ol-days

Constine, Josh. (2011). In trying to follow copyright law, Facebook takes down innocent pages. Retrieved from http://www.insidefacebook.com/2011/04/28/copyright-law-infringement.

Convention on Biodiversity, Signed at the United Nations Conference on Environment and Development 29 December 1992 (No. 30619). (1993). *United Nations Treaty Series* 1760, pp. 79–308.

Conway, Tim. (2012). Fulfilling the promise of the digital age: Balancing IP interests. Retrieved from http://www.witsa.org/gpac/Presentation_to_TPP_StakeholdersForum_WITSA_tconway_vFINAL.doc

Cooper, Marilyn. (2011). Rhetorical agency as emergent and enacted. *College Composition and Communication*, *62*(3), 420–449.

Copyright Act, 17 U.S.C. § 301, 302, 506.

Copyright Clearance Center. (2012). Fair Use. Retrieved from http://www.copyright.com/content/cc3/en/toolbar/education/resources/copyright_basics.html#fairuse

Copyright Research and Information Center. (2011). Copyright Law of Japan. Retrieved from http://www.cric.or.jp/cric_e/clj/

Cox, Christopher, & Warner, Daniel (Eds.). (2004). *Audio culture: Readings in modern music*. New York: The Continuum International Publishing Group Inc.

Craig, Carys. (2011). *Copyright, communication and culture: Towards a relational theory of copyright law*. Cheltenham: Edward Elgar.

Crimewriter95. YouTube Channel. Retrieved from http://www.youtube.com/user/crimewriter95

Creative industry hits out at delay to workings of anti-piracy code. (2012, April 26). Out-Law.com. Retrieved from http://www.out-law.com/en/articles/2012/april/creative-industry-hits-out-at-delay-to-workings-of-anti-piracy-code/

Cusack, Nick. (2011). Is the Digital Economy Act 2010 the most effective and proportionate way to reduce online piracy? *European Intellectual Property Review*, *33*(9), 559.

Da Pidgin Coup. (1999). Pidgin and education: A position paper. University of Hawai'i. Retrieved from http://www.hawaii.edu/sls/pidgin.html

Dariotis, Wei Ming. (2007). Hapa: The word of power. Mixed Heritage Center. Retrieved from http://www.mixedheritagecenter.org/index.php?option=com_content&task=view&id=1259&Itemid=

David Geffen: Net Worth 5.5 B. (2012). *Forbes*. Retrieved from http://www.forbes.com/profile/david-geffen/

Davis, Julie L., & Harrison, Suzanne S. (2001). *Edison in the Boardroom: How leading companies realize value from their intellectual assets*. New York: John Wiley & Sons.

DeCarlo, Matthew. (2010, June 9). *Fallout: New Vegas will use Steam for drm*. Retrieved from http://www.techspot.com/news/39250-fallout-new-vegas-will-use-steam-for-drm.html

Defoe, Daniel. (1704). *An essay on the regulation of the press*. London.

Del Río, C., & Sagarduy, J. L. (2008). *El impacto de la piratería digital.* Retrieved from https://siappii.planavanza.es/es-ES/Herramientas/bibliotecavirtual/Documents/IMPACTO%20DE%20LA%20PIRATER%C3%8DA%20DIGITAL.pdf

Delagrange, Susan; Braun, Katie; & McCorkle, Ben. (2013). Stirred, not shaken: An assessment remixology. In Dànielle N. DeVoss & Heidi McKee (Eds.), *Digital writing assessment and evaluation.* Logan, UT: Computers and Composition Digital Press/Utah State University Press. Retrieved from http://ccdigitalpress.org/dwae/

Dereck Seltzer v. Green Day Inc., 2013 U.S. App. LEXIS 16322 (U.S. Court of Appeals for the Ninth Circuit, Pasadena, CA. August 7, 2013).

Derrida, Jaques. (1997). *Of grammatology.* (Gayatri Chakravorty Spivak, Trans.) Baltimore, Maryland: Johns Hopkins University Press.

Devall, Bill. (2003). The deep ecology movement. In Robert C. Scharff & Val Dusen (Eds.), *Philosophy of technology: The technological condition, An anthology* (pp. 471–479). Malden, MA: Blackwell Publishing Ltd.

DeVoss, Dànielle N. (2009). English studies and intellectual property: copyright, creativity, and the commons. *Pedagogy: Critical Approaches to Teaching Literature, Language, Composition, and Culture.* (10/1). 201–215.

DeVoss, Dànielle N., & Porter, James E. (2006). Why Napster matters to writing: Filesharing as a new ethic of digital delivery. *Computers and Composition, 23*, 178–210.

DeVoss, Dànielle N., & Webb, Suzanne. (2008a). Grand theft audio. *Computers and Composition Online.* Special issue: Media convergence. Available: http://www.bgsu.edu/cconline/CConline_GTA/

DeVoss, Dànielle N., & Webb, Suzanne. (2008b). Media convergence: Grand theft audio: Negotiating copyright as composers. *Computers and Composition, 25*, 79–103.

Dhadialla, Karan. (2012). *Golan v. Holder* and the URAA's impact on the public domain. Retrieved from http://btlj.org/2012/04/09/golan-v-holder-and-the-uraas-impact-on-the-public-domain/

Diehl, Amy; Grabill, Jeffrey T.; Hart-Davidson, William; & Iyer, Vishal. (2008). Grassroots: Supporting the knowledge work of everyday life. *Technical Communication Quarterly 17*(4), 413–434.

Directive 2001/29/EC on the harmonisation of certain aspects of copyright and related rights in the information society [2001] OJ L167/10

Directive 2011/77/EU of the European Parliament and of the Council of amending Directive 2006/116/EC on the term of protection of copyright and certain related rights.

Doctorow, Cory. (2010, November 23). What do we want copyright to do? *The Guardian.* Retrieved from http://www.theguardian.com/technology/2010/nov/23/copyright-digital-rights-cory-doctorow

Douglass, Frederick. (2000). *Narrative of the life of Frederick Douglass, an American slave*. New York: Modern Library.

Downes, Stephen. (2007). Models for sustainable open educational resources. *Interdisciplinary Journal of Knowledge and Learning Objects, 3*, 29–44.

Drahos, Peter, & Braithwaite, John. (2002). *Information feudalism: Who owns the knowledge economy?* New York: The New Press.

Drexl, Josef; Hilty., R.; & Kur, A. (2003). Proposal for a directive on measures and procedures to ensure the enforcement of intellectual property rights—a first statement. *International Review of Intellectual Property and Competition Law, 34*(5), 530–535.

Drucker, Susan J., & Gumpert, Gary. (Eds.). (2010). *Regulating convergence*. New York: Peter Lang.

Ducheneaut, Nicolas, & Moore, Robert J. (2005). More than just 'XP': Learning social skills in massively multiplayer online games. *Interactive Technology & Smart Education, 2*(2). 89–100.

Duhigg, Charles. (2012, February 16). How companies learn your secrets. *New York Times Magazine*. Retrieved from http://www.nytimes.com/2012/02/19/magazine/shopping-habits.html

Duke Law Magazine. (2004, Fall). Protecting the information ecology, pp. 40–41.

Duncan, Arne. (2013, July 9). The coming crossroads in higher education: Remarks of U.S. Secretary of Education Arne Duncan to the State Higher Education Executive Officers Association Annual Meeting, July 9, 2013. Retrieved from http://www.ed.gov/news/speeches/coming-crossroads-higher-education

Earnest, Mark, & Matthew, Dayna Bowen. (2008). A property right to medical care. *Journal of Legal Medicine, 29*(1), 65–80.

Education Code Section 51870-51874 (2012).

Ehrmann, Dan. (2010, June 24). Beware of copyrighted images used without permission. *NonProfit Conversation.* Retrieved from http://nonprofitconversation.blogspot.com/2010/06/beware-of-copyrighted-images-used.html

Eisenstein, Elizabeth. (1983). *The printing revolution in early modern Europe*. Cambridge: Cambridge University Press.

Electronic Frontier Foundation (2009). Teaching copyright.

Elon, Menachem. (2007). Hassagat Gevul. In Michael Berenbaum & Fred Skolnik (Eds.), *Encyclopaedia Judaica*, Gos-Hep. Detroit: Macmillan Reference.

Emerson, Ralph Waldo. (1883). *The works of Ralph Waldo Emerson: Essays*. London: Routledge.

Encyclopedia Talmudica: A digest of Halachic literature and Jewish law from the Tannaitic Period to the present time. (1969a). (Vols. 1–5, Vol. 2). Jerusalem: Talmudic Encyclopedia Institute.

Encyclopedia Talmudica: A digest of Halachic literature and Jewish law from the Tannaitic Period to the present time. (1969b). (Vols. 1–5, Vol. 4). Jerusalem: Talmudic Encyclopedia Institute.

Equiano, Olaudah. (1999). *The life of Olaudah Equiano, or Gustavas Vassa, the African*. Mineola, NY: Dover.

Europa Press Release. (2003). Proposed directive on enforcement of intellectual property rights—frequently asked questions, MEMO/03/20.

European Commission. (1994). *Europa y la sociedad global de la información. Recomendaciones al Consejo Europeo (Informe Bangemann)*. Retrieved from http://mbecerra.blog.unq.edu.ar/modules/docmanager/get_file.php?curent_file=27&curent_dir=9

European Commission. (2005). *Legislative document* COM/2005/0276.

Exit through the gift shop. (2010). Dir. Banksy. Producers Distribution Agency. DVD.

Eyman, Douglas. (2008). Computer gaming and technical communication: An ecological framework. *Technical Communication* 55(3), 242–250.

Facebook. (2009, October 29). Information we receive. *Facebook's Privacy Policy-Full Version*. Retrieved from http://www.facebook.com/note.php?note_id=%20322194465300

Facebook. (2011). Statement of rights and responsibilities. Retrieved from http://facebook.com/legal/terms.

Facebook. (2012) Sharing your content. *Facebook: Terms of use*. Retrieved from http://www.facebook.com/legal/terms

Facebook. (2012). About. Retrieved from http://www.facebook.com/facebook

Facebook. (2012). Information you choose to share. *Facebook: Data use policy*. Retrieved from http://www.facebook.com/about/privacy/your-info

Facebook. What if I want to upload content to Facebook but I'm not sure whether that would infringe someone's copyright. Retrieved from http://facebook.com/help/?faq=308895412492789

Fairey, Shepard. (2009, January 20). Interview with Terry Gross. *Fresh Air with Terry Gross*. WHYY, Philadelphia, PA.

Farrand, Benjamin. (2010). The Digital Economy Act 2010: A cause for celebration or a cause for concern? *European Intellectual Property Review*, *32*(10), 536–541.

Federal Trade Commission. (2012). *Protecting consumer privacy in an era of rapid change: Recommendations for businesses and policymakers*. Retrieved from http://www.ftc.gov/os/2012/03/120326privacyreport.pdf

Feist Publications, Inc. v. Rural Telephone Service Co., 499 U.S. 340. (1991). Retrieved from http://www.law.cornell.edu/copyright/cases/499_US_340.htm

Fensham, F. Charles. (1962). Widow, orphan, and the poor in ancient near Eastern legal and wisdom literature. *Journal of Near Eastern Studies, 21*(2), 129–139.

Ferguson, Kirby. (2011). Everything is a remix. Retrieved from http://www.everythingisaremix.info/watch-the-series/

Fernández Ballesteros, C. A. (2006). Marco jurídico internacional del derecho de autor y los derechos conexos: de Berna (1886) a los tratados de la OMPI (1996). *Revista Jurídica De Deporte y Entretenimiento*, 773: 481–500.

Ferrer, Laura Arambarri. (2009). *Hemos lanzado el disco gratis por internet porque las discográficas te esclavizan.* Retrieved from http://www.diariodeibiza.es/pitiuses-balears/2009/12/02/hemos-lanzado-disco-gratis-internet-discograficas-esclavizan/376718.html

Film-makers seek injunction to block pirate site. (2011, June 28). *BBC News*. Retrieved from http://www.bbc.co.uk/news/technology-13927335

Finn, Daniel Rush. (2000). Creativity as a problem for moral theology: John Locke's 99 percent challenge to the Catholic doctrine of property. *Horizons, 27*(1), 44–62.

Fiss, Karen. (2006, Jan/Feb). Eating the other. *Print*, pp. 57–61.

Fitzgerald Publishing Co. v. Baylor Publishing Co., 807 F.2d 1110 (2d Cir. 1986)

Fitzpatrick, K. (2011). *Planned obsolescence: Publishing, technology, and the future of the academy*. NYU Press.

Flaim, Sean M. (2011). Copyright conspiracy: How the new copyright alert system may violate the Sherman Act. *NYU Journal of Intellectual Property and Entertainment Law*. Retrieved from http://jipel.law.nyu.edu/2012/11/copyright-conspiracy/

Flynn, Elizabeth. (2003). Composing as a woman. In Victor Villanueva (Ed.), *Cross-talk in comp theory: A reader* (pp. 571–585). Urbana, Illinois: National Council of Teachers of English.

Flynn, Sean M.; Kaminski, Margot; Baker, Brook K.; & Koo, Jimmy. (2011). Public interest analysis of the US TPP Proposal for an IP Chapter. Northeastern University School of Law Research Paper No. 82-2012; American University, WCL Research Paper No. 2012-07. Retrieved from http://ssrn.com/abstract=1980173

Fondevila Gascón, J. F. (2008). *La alianza entre el periodismo digital y tradicional y los operadores de telecomunicación: hacia un rendimiento óptimo de la red.* Barcelona: II Congreso Nacional Ulepicc-España.

Fondevila Gascón, J. F. (2009a). Adaptació dels gèneres periodístics al periodisme digital: estudi empíric comparatiu. *Trípodos* (Extra 2009-V Congrés Internacional *Comunicació i realitat, La metamorfosi de l'espai mediàtic*, Universitat Ramon Llull), *1*, 657–666.

Fondevila Gascón, J. F. (2009b). El papel decisivo de la banda ancha en el Espacio Iberoamericano del Conocimiento. *Revista Iberoamericana de Ciencia, Tecnología y Sociedad-CTS*, 2 (Portafolio CTS), 1–15.

Fondevila Gascón, J. F. (2010a). El *cloud journalism*: un nuevo concepto de producción para el periodismo del siglo XXI. *Observatorio (OBS*) Journal*, 4(1), 19–35.

Fondevila Gascón, J. F. (2010b). Visual impact in the digital press: A Spanish empirical research. *Brazilian Journalism Research*, 6(2), 120–137.

Fondevila Gascón, J. F. (2011). *Cable and broadband in Spain, 2010*. Terrassa: CECABLE.

Fondevila Gascón, J. F. (2012). *The broadband society in the world*. Terrassa: CECABLE.

Friedman, Thomas L. (2005). *The world is flat: A brief history of the twenty-first century*. New York: Farrar, Straus and Giroux.

Frith, Simon. (2001). The popular music industry. In Simon Frith, Will Straw, & John Street (Eds.), *The Cambridge companion to pop and rock* (pp. 26–52). Cambridge, UK: Cambridge University Press.

Fritz, Ben. (2011, October 7). Barnes & Noble to pull DC graphic novels in digital spat. *L.A. Times*. Retrieved from http://latimesblogs.latimes.com/entertainmentnewsbuzz/2011/10/dc-graphic-novels-to-be-pulled-from-barnes-noble-in-digital-spat.html

Fujikane, Candace. (2008). Introduction. In Candace Fujikane & Jonathan Okamura (Eds.), *Asian settler colonialism: From local governance to the habits of everyday life in Hawai'i*. Honolulu: University of Hawai'i Press.

Garcia, Mannie. (2009, February 26). Interview with Terry Gross. *Fresh Air with Terry Gross*. WHYY, Philadelphia, PA.

Garfield, Eugene. (1955). Citation indexes for science: A new dimension in documentation through association of ideas. *Science*, *122*, 108–111.

Garfield, Eugene. (1956). Response to "Citation indexes for science." *Science*, *123*, 61–62.

Garrett, Bre; Landrum-Geyer, Denise; & Palmeri, Jason. (2012). Reinventing invention: A performance in three acts. In Debra Journet, Cheryl E. Ball, & Ryan Trauman (Eds.), *The new work of composing*. Logan, UT: Utah State University Press/Computers and Composition Digital Press. Retrieved from http://ccdigitalpress.org/nwc/chapters/garrett-et-al/

Gay, J. (2002). *Free software, free society: selected essays of Richard M. Stallman*. Boston: GNU Press. Retrieved from http://www.gnu.org/philosophy/fsfs/rms-essays.pdf

Geiger, Christophe. (2003). "Constitutionalising" intellectual property law? The influence of fundamental rights on intellectual property in the European Union. *International Review of Intellectual Property and Competition Law*, 37(4), 371–406.

General Electric Company. (2010). Ecomagination. Retrieved from http://www.ge.com/about-us/ecomagination

George, Diana, & Trimbur, John (2001). Cultural studies and composition. In Gary Tate, Amy Rupiper, & Kurt Schick (Eds.), A *guide to composition pedagogies* (pp. 71–91). New York: Oxford University Press.

George, Nelson. (1998). *Hip hop America*. New York: Viking Penguin.

Gilbert-Eggleston, Jennifer. (2011). *Cariou v. Prince*: Painter or Prince of Thieves? *University of Denver Sports and Entertainment Law Journal*, *11*(117) p. 3.

Gilder, G. (2002). *Telecosm: The World After Bandwidth Abundance*. New York: Touchstone.

Gillespie, Tarleton. (2006). Designed to "effectively frustrate": Copyright, technology and the agency of users. *New Media & Society*, *8*(4), 651–669.

Gillespie, Tarleton. (2007). *Wired shut: Copyright and the shape of digital culture*. Cambridge, MA: MIT Press.

Gillespie, Tarleton (2011). Characterizing copyright in the classroom: The cultural work of antipiracy campaigns. In Mario Biagioli, Peter Jaszi, & Martha Woodmansee (Eds.), *Making and unmaking intellectual property: Creative production in legal and cultural perspective*. Chicago: University of Chicago Press.

Gilyard, Keith. (2012, Feb. 9). NCTE president Keith Gilyard talks about NCTE and Common Core Standards. Retrieved from http://www.ncte.org/standards/commoncore/kg_2-9-12

Glazer, Gwen. (2008). Online scientific repository hits milestone. Cornell University Library. Retrieved from http://news.library.cornell.edu/content/online-scientific-repository-hits-milestone

GNU. (2011). *La definición de software libre*. Retrieved from http://www.gnu.org/philosophy/free-sw.es.html

Gnuse, Robert Karl. (1985). *You shall not steal: Community and property in the biblical tradition*. Maryknoll, NY: Orbis Books.

Golan v. Holder. (2009) Civil Case No. 01-cv-01854-LTB.

Golan v. Holder. (2012). 565 U.S.

Goldstein, Paul, & Hugenholtz, P. Bernt. (2012). *International copyright: Principles, law, and practice* (3rd ed.). New York: Oxford University Press.

Gómez Aguiar, J.C. (2009). Nuevas ilegalidades en el orden global: piratería y la escenificación del estado de derecho en méxico. *Foro Internacional*, *196*, 403–424.

Google. (2012). Company overview. Retrieved from http://www.google.com/about/company/

Google. (2012, July 27). Information we get. *Google: Privacy Policy*. Retrieved from http://www.google.com/policies/privacy/

Google. (2012, July 27). Information you give us. *Google: Privacy Policy*. Retrieved from http://www.google.com/policies/privacy/

Gowers, Andrew. (2006, November). The Gowers review of intellectual property. Retrieved from http://www.hm-treasury.gov.uk/d/pbr06_gowers_report_755.pdf

Green, Joshua, & Jenkins, Henry. (2009). The moral economy of web 2.0: Audience research and convergence culture. In J. Holt & A. Perren (Eds.), *Media industries: History, theory, and method* (pp. 213–225). Malden, MA: Wiley-Blackwell.

Gregory, Jennifer Kahaulelio. (2006). The troll next door. *John Marshall Review of Intellectual Property Law*, 6, i.

Grifindor_seekr. (2008). Re: Custom character creations. Forum thread at *LittleBigWorkshop.com*. Retrieved from http://forums.littlebigplanet.com/t5/General-Discussion/Custom-Character-Creations/m-p/13244/highlight/true#M5624

Grosart, Alexander. (Ed.). (2012). *The prose works of William Wordsworth*. Charleston, SC: Nabu Press.

Gross, Alan G.; Harmon, Joseph E.; & Reidy, Michael S. (2002). *Communicating science: The scientific article from the 17th century to the present*. Anderson, SC: Parlor Press.

Grupo ETC. (2008). ¿De quién es la naturaleza? El poder corporativo y la frontera final en la mercantilización de la vida. Retrieved from http://www.etcgroup.org/upload/publication/709/03/etc_won_report_spa23dic08.pdf

Gustafson, James M. (1984). Scripture in Christian ethics: A methodological study. In Charles E. Curran & Richard A. McCormick (Eds.), *The use of scripture in moral theology* (pp. 151–177). New York: Paulist Press.

Halloran, S. Michael. (1984). The birth of molecular biology: An essay in the rhetorical criticism of scientific discourse. *Rhetoric Review*, *3*(1), 70–83.

Hanlon, Joseph. (2000). How much debt must be cancelled? *Journal of International Development*, *12*(6), 877–901.

Hapiuk, William J. (2001). Of kitsch and kachinas: A critical analysis of the Indian Arts and Crafts Act of 1990. *Stanford Law Review*, *53*(4), 1009-1075.

Hargreaves, Ian. (2011). *Digital opportunity: A review of intellectual property and growth*. Retrieved from http://www.ipo.gov.uk/ipreview-finalreport.pdf

Harmon, David. (1995). Losing species, losing languages: connections between biological and linguistic diversity. *Southwest Journal of Linguistics*, *14*, 1–28.

Harmon, David, & Loh, Jonathan. (2004). The IBCD: A measure of the world's biocultural diversity. *Policy Matters*, 13, 271–280.

Harper & Row, Publrs. v. Nation Enters., 471 U.S. 539 (1985)

Harrison, Suzanne S., & Sullivan, Patrick. H. (2012). *Edison in the boardroom revisited: How leading companies realize value from their intellectual property* (2nd ed.). Hoboken, NJ: John Wiley & Sons, Inc.

Hart, Michael. (2004). *Project Gutenberg mission statement by Michael Hart.* Retrieved from http://www.gutenberg.org/wiki/Gutenberg:Project_Gutenberg_Mission_Statement_by_Michael_Hart

Hart, Terry. (2011). *Golan v. Holder. Copyhype.* Retrieved from http://www.copyhype.com/2011/02/golan-v-holder/

Hartline, Devlin. (2012). From Eldred to Golan: The 'Traditional Contours' Test – Part I. *Copyhype.* Retrieved from http://www.copyhype.com/2012/02/guest-post-from-eldred-to-golan-the-traditional-contours-test-part-i/

Harvey, David. (2007). Neoliberalism as creative destruction. *Annals of the American Academy of Political and Social Science,* 610(21), 22–44.

Haunss, Sebastian. (2011). The politicisation of intellectual property: IP conflicts and social change. *WIPO Journal, 129,* 129–138.

Hawai'i Tourism Authority. (2013). Hawaii Tourism Authority. Retrieved from http://www.hawaiitourismauthority.org

Hawai'i's official tourism site. (2012). Hawaii Tourism Authority. Retrieved from http://www.gohawaii.com/

Hayden, Cori. (2003). *When nature goes public: The making and unmaking of bioprospecting in Mexico.* Princeton, NJ: Princeton University Press.

Hayes, Benjamin S. (2000). Integrating moral rights into U.S. law and the problem of the works for hire doctrine. *Ohio State Law Journal, 61,* 1013.

Hebdige, Dick. (1979). *Subculture: The meaning of style.* London: Routledge.

Hebdige, Dick. (1987). *Cut 'n' mix: Culture, identity, and Caribbean music.* London: Routledge.

Hegel, Georg W. F. (1896). *Philosophy of right.* (Samuel Walters Dyde, Trans.). New York: George Bell & Sons.

Heins, Marjorie, & Beckles, Tricia. (2005). *Will fair use survive? Free expression in the age of copyright control.* New York: Brennan Center for Justice at the NYU School of Law/Free Expression Policy Project.

Heller, Michael A. (1998). The tragedy of the anticommons: Property in the transition from Marx to markets. *Harvard Law Review 111* (3), 621–688.

Herman, Bill D. (2006). Scratching out authorship: Representations of the electronic music DJ at the turn of the 21st century. *Popular Communication 4,* 21–38.

Herndl, Diana Price. (1999). Miscegen(r)ation or mestiza discourse?: Feminist and racial politics in *ramona* and *Iola Leroy.* In Tim Powell (Ed.), *Beyond the binary: Reconstructing cultural identity in a Multicultural Context* (pp. 261–275). New Brunswick, NJ: Rutgers University Press.

Herrington, TyAnna K. (2001). *Controlling voices: Intellectual property, humanistic studies, and the Internet.* Carbondale: Southern Illinois University Press.

Herrington, TyAnna K. (2003). A *legal primer for technical communicators, multimedia developers, graphic designers, and other creative communicators*. New York: Allyn and Bacon/Longman Publishers.

Herrington, TyAnna (2009). Blogging down: Copyright law and blogs in the classroom. In Stephen Westbrook (Ed.), *Composition and copyright: Perspectives on teaching, text-making, and fair use* (pp. 154–171). Albany, NY: SUNY Press.

Herrington, TyAnna K. (2010). *Intellectual property on campus: Students' rights and responsibilities*. Carbondale: Southern Illinois University Press.

Hetcher, Steven. (2007). Orphan works and Google's Global Library Project. *Wake Forest Intellectual Property Law Journal*, *8*, 1–38.

Hicks, Troy. (2010, January). Transforming our understanding of copyright and Fair Use. Conference on College Composition and Communication IP Caucus report. Retrieved from http://www.ncte.org/cccc/committees/ip/ipreports/transforming

Hill, Owen. (2011, July 28). Ubisoft: Our DRM "is a success." Retrieved from http://www.pcgamer.com/2011/07/28/ubisoft-our-drm-is-a-success/

Hilty, Reto, & Nérisson, Sylvie. (2012). *Balancing copyright–A survey of national approaches*. Munich, Germany: Springer.

History. Creative Commons. Retrieved on April 6, 2012 from http://creativecommons.org/about/history

ho'omanawanui, ku'ualoha. (2008). This land is your land, this land was my land: Kanaka Maoli versus settler representations of 'āina in contemporary literature of Hawai'i. In Candace Fujikane and Jonathan Okamura (Eds.), *Asian settler colonialism: From local governance to the habits of everyday life in Hawai'i*. Honolulu: University of Hawai'i Press.

Hoffman, Ivan. (2001). The *Seinfeld* and *The Wind Done Gone* cases: Studies in fair use. *Ivan Hoffman*. Retrieved from http://www.ivanhoffman.com/seinfeld.html

Hogge, Becky. (2006, July). The future of intellectual property: Andrew Gowers interviewed. *Open Democracy*. Retrieved from http://www.opendemocracy.net/media-copyrightlaw/gowers_4160.jsp

Houghton Mifflin Harcourt. (2001). *The Wind Done Gone*: Questions and answers about this dispute. *Information about Suntrust Bank v. Houghton Mifflin Company*. Retrieved from http://www.houghtonmifflinbooks.com/features/randall_url/qandas.shtml

Howard, Bill. (2011, September 19). Review: Hyundai Veloster gets tech right with Bluetooth, USB, Pandora. *Extreme tech*. Retrieved from http://www.extremetech.com/extreme/96513-review-hyundai-veloster-gets-it-right-with-bluetooth-usb-pandora

Howard, Jennifer. (2006). Picture imperfect. *Chronicle of Higher Education*, *52*(48), 13.

Howard, Jennifer. (2012). Digital library's win in court continues run of rulings for academic fair use. *Chronicle.com. Retrieved* from http://chronicle.com/article/Digital-Librarys-Win-in-Court/135020/

Howe, Helena R. (2011). Copyright limitations and the stewardship model of property. *Intellectual Property Quarterly, 2*, 183–214.

Hugenholtz, P. Bernt. (2000). Why the Copyright Directive is unimportant, and possibly invalid. *European Intellectual Property Review, 22*(11), 499.

Hugenholtz, P. Bernt. (2011, June 4). O no, not again: Term extension. Kluwer Copyright Blog. Retrieved from http://kluwercopyrightblog.com/2011/04/06/o-no-not-again-term-extension/

Hunn, Eugene S. (1999). The value of subsistence for the future of the world." In V. Nazarea (Ed.), *Ethnoecology: Situated knowledge/located lives* (pp. 2–36). Tucson: University of Arizona Press.

Hunter, Dan. (2005). Culture war. *Texas Law Review, 83*(4), 1105–1136.

Huxley, Thomas. (1866). On the advisableness of improving natural knowledge. Retrieved from http://aleph0.clarku.edu/huxley/CE1/AdINKn.html

Hyde, Lewis. (2010). *Common as air: Revolution, art, and ownership*. New York: Farrar, Straus and Giroux.

Igarza, R. (2007). *Convergencia de medios.* Buenos Aires: Universidad Austral.

Illegal downloaders to have Internet connections cut under new government plans. (2009, August 25). *Telegraph.* Retrieved from http://www.telegraph.co.uk/technology/news/6086778/Illegal-downloaders-to-have-internet-connections-cut-under-new-government-plans.html

Illman, Karl-Johan. (1999). Response to "The Rich and the Poor as a Theme in the Biblical Prophets." In Jacob Neusner (Ed.), *Religious belief and economic behavior: Ancient Israel, classical Christianity, Islam, and Judaism, and contemporary Ireland and Africa* (pp. 87–89). Atlanta, GA: Scholars Press.

Indian Arts and Crafts Act of 1935, Pub. L. No. 74-355, 49 Stat. 891 (1935).

Indian Arts and Crafts Act of 1990, 18 U.S.C. §1159, 25 U.S.C. §305 (2012).

Italie, Hillel. (2009, April 2). AP accuses Obama artist Shepard Fairey of copyright infringement. *The Huffington Post.* Retrieved from http://www.huffingtonpost.com/2009/02/04/ap-accuses-shepard-fairey_n_164045.html

Jack, David. (1998). Confessions of a journal junkie. *The Lancet, 352*, S23–S24.

Jackson, Elizabeth. (2012, Spring). A look at the supreme court justices' individual biases toward copyright law: Prediction and reflection on the *Golan v. Holder* decision. *American University Intellectual Property Brief* (pp. 22–29).

Jackson, Steven J., & Hokowhitu, Brendan. (2002). Sport, tribes, and technology: The New Zealand all Blacks Haka and the politics of identity. *Journal of Sport & Social Issues, 26*(2), 125–139.

Jacobs, Harriet. (2000). *Incidents in the life of a slave girl.* New York: Modern Library.

Jameson, Fredric. (1991). *Postmodernism or, the cultural logic of late capitalism.* Durham, NC: Duke University Press.

Jefferson, Thomas. (1813, August 13). Letter to Isaac McPherson. In P. Kurland & R. Lerner (Eds.), *The founders' constitution.* Retrieved from http://press-pubs.uchicago.edu/founders/documents/a1_8_8s12.html

Jenkins, Henry (2010). DIY video 2010: Political remix (Part Three), MIT Center for Civic Media. Retreived from http://civic.mit.edu/blog/henry/diy-video-2010-political-remix-part-three

Jenkins, Henry. (1992). *Textual poachers: Television fans and participatory culture.* New York: Routledge.

Jenkins, Henry. (2004). The cultural logic of media convergence. *International Journal of Cultural Studies,* 7(1), 33–43.

Jenkins, Henry. (2006a). *Convergence culture: Where old and new media collide.* New York: New York University Press.

Jenkins, Henry. (2006b). *Fans, bloggers, and gamers: Exploring participatory culture.* New York: New York University Press.

Johansson, Frans. (2006). *The medici effect: What elephants and epidemics can teach us about innovation.* Boston: Harvard Business School Press.

Johns, Adrian. (2010). *Piracy: The intellectual property wars from Gutenberg to Gates.* Chicago: University of Chicago Press.

Johnson, Steven. (2010). *Where good ideas come from: The natural history of innovation.* New York: Riverhead Books.

Johnson-Eilola, Johndan. (1998). Intellectual property: Questions and answers. *Kairos,* 3(1). Retrieved from http://english.ttu.edu/kairos/3.1/binder2.html?coverweb/johndan.html

Johnstone, Sally M. (2005). Open educational resources serve the world. *Educause Quarterly,* 28(3). Retrieved from http://www.educause.edu/ero/article/open-educational-resources-serve-world

Jones, Dave. (2011). *Black boxes and Co-Creation in* LittleBigPlanet 2. In *Selected Papers of IR12: Performance and Participation.* Seattle, WA.

Jonson, Ben, & Gifford, William. (1879). *The works of Ben Jonson.* New York: D. Appleton and Company.

Jordan, David B. (2000/2001). Square pegs and round holes: Domestic intellectual property law and Native American economic and cultural policy: Can it fit? *American Indian Law Review, 25*(1), 93–115.

Joyaux, Simone (2012, March). Are you slowly going out of business? *Nonprofit Quarterly*. Retrieved from http://www.nonprofitquarterly.org/management/19903-are-you-slowly-going-out-of-business.html

Judge, Peter. (2010, March 25). UK digital bill enters "wash up" despite protest. *TechWeek Europe*. Retrieved from http://www.techweekeurope.co.uk/news/uk-digital-bill-enters-wash-up-despite-protest-6089

Juola, Patrick. (2006). *Killer applications in digital humanities*. Unpublished manuscript. Duquesne University, Pittsburgh, PA. Retrieved from http://www.mathcs.duq.edu/~juola/papers.d/killer.pdf

Kanae, Lisa. (2001). *Sista tongue*. Honolulu: Tinfish Press.

Keating, AnaLouise. (1996). *Women reading women writing: Self invention in Paula Gunn Allen, Gloria Anzaldúa, and Audre Lorde*. Philadelphia: Temple University Press.

Kennedy, Krista. (2010). Textual machinery: Authorial agency and bot-written texts in Wikipedia. In Michelle Smith & Barbara Warnick (Eds.), *The responsibilities of rhetoric* (pp. 303–309). Long Grove, IL: Waveland Press.

Kennedy, Randy. (2009, February 9). Artist sues the A.P. over Obama image. *The New York Times*. Retrieved from http://www.nytimes.com/2009/02/10/arts/design/10fair.html?_r=0

Kennedy, Randy. (2011, January 12). Shepard Fairey and the A.P. settle legal dispute. *The New York Times*. Retrieved from http://www.nytimes.com/2011/01/13/arts/design/13fairey.html

King, Peter. (1989). Gleaners, farmers and the failure of legal sanctions in England 1750–1850. *Past and Present, 125*, 116–150.

King, Peter. (1991). Customary rights and women's earnings: The importance of gleaning to the rural labouring poor, 1750–1850. *The Economic History Review*, 44(3), 461–476.

King, Peter. (1992). Legal change, customary right, and social conflict in late eighteenth-century England: The origins of the great gleaning case of 1788. *Law and History Review*, 10(1), 1–31.

Kirkpatrick, Marshall. (2010, January 9). Facebook's Zuckerberg says the age of privacy is over. *Readwrite Social*. Retrieved from http://readwrite.com/2010/01/09/facebooks_zuckerberg_says_the_age_of_privacy_is_ov

Knox, J. (2013). Five critiques of the Open Educational Resources movement. *Teaching in Higher Education*, 1–12.

Kono, Toshiyuki. (Ed.). (2012). *Intellectual property and private international law: Comparative perspectives*. Portland, OR: Hart Publishing.

Kozinska, Kasia. (2011, June 3). International workshop on open educational resources and intellectual property rights, Moscow, Russia. *Olnet.org*. Retrieved from http://www.olnet.org/node/592

Kraidy, Marwan M. (2005). *Hybridity: Or the cultural logic of globalization*. Philadelphia: Temple University Press.

Kranich, Nancy. (2004). *The information commons: A public policy report.* Retrieved from http://dcommon.bu.edu/xmlui/handle/2144/53

Kravets, David. (2008). File sharing lawsuits at a crossroads, after 5 years of RIAA litigation. *Wired.* Retrieved on April 2, 2012 from http://www.wired.com/threatlevel/2008/09/proving-file-sh/

Kravets, David. (2012). A SOPA/PIPA blackout explainer. *Wired.* Retrieved from http://www.wired.com/threatlevel/2012/01/websites-dark-in-revolt/

Kretschmer, Martin. (2003). Digital copyright: The end of an era. *European Intellectual Property Review, 25*(8), 333–341.

Krikorian, Raffi. (2010, April 10). Map of a Twitter status update. Retrieved from http://www.slaw.ca/wp-content/uploads/2011/11/map-of-a-tweet-copy.pdf

Kroeber, Alfred L. (1939). Cultural and natural areas of Native North America. Berkeley: University of California Press.

Kroes, Neelie. (2011, November 19). Who feeds the artist? *Forum d'Avignon.* Retreived from http://europa.eu/rapid/pressReleasesAction.do?reference=SPEECH/11/777&fo%20rmat=HTML&aged=0&language=EN&guiLanguage=en

Kuttner, Robert. (2008). *Obama's challenge: America's economic crisis and the power of a transformative presidency.* White River Junction, VT: Chelsea Green Press.

L. Batlin & Son, Inc. v. Snyder, 536 F.2d 486 (2d Cir. 1976).

La Quadrature du Net. (2011, March). IPRED versus the sharing of culture: Moving away from enforcement. Retrieved from http://www.laquadrature.net/files/LQDN-20110331-SubmissionIPREDconsultation.pdf

Lakoff, George, & Johnson, Mark. (1980). *Metaphors we live by.* Chicago: University of Chicago Press.

Lange, David L.; Weaver, Risa J.; & Reed, Shiveh R. (2011). *Golan v. Holder*: Copyright in the image of the first amendment. *The John Marshall Review of Intellectual Property Law, 11*(1), 84–132.

Latour, Bruno. (1987). *Science in action: How to follow scientists and engineers through society.* Cambridge, MA: Harvard University Press.

Law, John. (1999). After ANT: Complexity, naming, and topology. In J. Law & J. Hassard (Eds.), *Actor network theory and after* (pp. 1–15). Malden, MA: Blackwell Publishing.

Law Society of the UK. (2006, August). Proposal for a directive on criminal measures aimed at ensuring the enforcement of IP rights: Comments by the Law Society of England and Wales. Retrieved from http://ec.europa.eu/prelex/detail_dossier_real.cfm?CL=en&DosId=193131

Lee, Edward. (2005). The ethics of innovation: p2p software developers and designing substantial noninfringing uses under the Sony doctrine. *Journal of Business Ethics, 62*(2), 2005, 147–162.

Lemche, Niels Peter. (1976). Manumission of slaves - the fallow year - the sabbatical year - the jubilee year. *Vetus Testamentum, 26*(1), 38–59.

Lemley, Mark A. (2007). Are universities patent trolls. *Fordham Intellectual Property, Media & Entertainment Law Journal, 18*, 611.

Lemley, Mark A., & Shapiro, Carl. (2006). Patent Holdup and Royalty Stacking. *Texas Law Review, 85*, 1991.

LenkaBula, Puleng. (2005). The social and ethical implications of article 27 of the Agreement on Trade Related Aspects of Intellectual Property Rights (TRIPS) on African Communities, Biodiversity and Indigenous Knowledge. *Journal of Theology for Southern Africa*, 122, 36–56.

Lessig, Lawrence. (2002a). *<free culture>*. Retrieved from http://randomfoo.net/oscon/2002/lessig/free.html

Lessig, Lawrence. (2002b). *The future of ideas: The fate of the commons in a connected world.* New York: Vintage Books.

Lessig, Lawrence. (2004). *Free culture: How big media uses technology and the law to lock down culture and control creativity*. New York: Penguin Press.

Lessig, Lawrence. (2006). Re-Crafting a public domain. *Yale Journal of Law & the Humanities, 18*, 57.

Lessig, Lawrence. (2008). *Remix: Making art and commerce thrive in the hybrid economy*. New York: Penguin Press.

Lessig, Lawrence. (2010, November). WIPO keynote. Retrieved from http://dotsub.com/view/d354cf7e-835e-464d-b171-ef1463ed15ee/viewTranscript/eng

Liptak, Adam. (2012). Public domain works can be copyrighted anew, Supreme Court Rules. *New York Times.com.* Retrieved from http://www.nytimes.com/2012/01/19/business/public-domain-works-can-be-copyrighted-anew-justices-rule.html

Little, David. (1980). Exodus 20:15, "Thou shalt not steal." *Interpretation, 34*(4), 399–405.

Locke, John. (1887). *Two treatises on civil government* (2nd ed.). London: G. Routledge and Sons.

Logie, John. (2006). *Peers, pirates, and persuasion: Rhetoric in the peer-to-peer debates*. West Lafayette: Parlor Press.

López, R. (2009a). *Internet: por una democratización de la cultura y del conocimiento.* Retrieved from http://copyleftlicencias.blogspot.com/2009/05/internet-por-una-democratizacion-de-la.html

López, R. (2009b). *La filosofía del Copyleft: un impulso para el desarrollo de la Sociedad del Conocimiento.* Chile: Universidad Católica San Antonio.

Los Angeles News Service v. KCAL-TV Channel 9, 108 F.3d 1119 (9th Cir. 1997).

Love, James. (2012, March 12). KEI Statement on India's granting of compulsory license to patents on cancer drug sorafenib. Retrieved from http://keionline.org/node/1384

Lowe, Charles. (2010). An issue for open education: Interpreting the non-commercial clause in Creative Commons Licensing. CCCC *Top Intellectual Property Developments of 2009*. Retrieved from http://www.ncte.org/cccc/committees/ip/2009developments

Lowe, Lisa. (1996). *Immigrant acts*. Durham, NC: Duke University Press.

Lowry, Beverly. (1994, September 11). Criminals rendered in 3 parts, poetically. *New York Times*.

Luangphinith, Seri. (2006). Homeward bound: Settler aesthetics in Hawai'i's literature. *Texas Studies in Literature and Language*, 48(1), 54–78.

Lucchi, Nicola. (2006). *Digital media & intellectual property: Management of rights and consumer protection in a comparative analysis*. Berlin, Germany: Springer.

Lunsford, Andrea. (1999). Rhetoric, feminism, and the politics of textual ownership. *College English*, 61(5), 529–544.

Lyons, Paul. (2005). American pacificism: Oceania in the U.S. imagination. New York: Routledge.

Lyotard, Jean-Francois. (1984). *The postmodern condition: A report on knowledge*. Minneapolis: University of Minnesota Press.

Maffi, Luisa (Ed.). (2001). *On biological diversity: Linking language, knowledge, and the environment*. Washington, DC: Smithsonian Institution Press.

Maffi, Luisa. (2005). Linguistic, cultural, and biological diversity. *Annual Review of Anthropology*, 29, 599–617.

Maffi, Luisa, & Woodley, Ellen (Eds.). (2011). *Biocultural diversity conservation: a global sourcebook*. Washington, DC: Earthscan.

Magliocca, Gerard N. (2006). Blackberries and barnyards: Patent trolls and the perils of innovation. *Notre Dame Law Review*, 82, 1811.

Malchow, Bruce V. (1996). *Social justice in the Hebrew bible: What is new and What is old*. Collegeville, MN: Liturgical Press.

Mao, LuMing. (2006). *Reading Chinese fortune cookie*. Logan, UT: Utah State University Press.

Marsman, Hennie J. (2003). *Women in Ugarit and Israel: Their social and religious position in the context of the ancient near East*. Oudtestamentische studiën = Old Testament studies. Leiden; Boston: Brill.

Martínez, J. A. (2009). *Software libre: una aproximación desde la teoría de juegos*. Retrieved from http://oasis.dit.upm.es/~jantonio/documentos/revistas/teoriajuegos/teoriajuegos.html

Masnick, Mike. (2010, March 18). Courts stretching computer hacking law in dangerous ways. *Techdirt.* Retrieved from http://www.techdirt.com/articles/20100305/0404088432.shtml

Masnick, Mike. (2012, January 18). Supreme Court chooses SOPA/PIPA protest day to give a giant middle finger to the public domain. Retrieved from http://www.techdirt.com/articles/20120118/09090217454/supreme-court-chooses-sopapipa-protest-day-to-give-giant-middle-finger-to-public-domain.shtml

Masnick, Mike. (2012, February 2). Young people followed SOPA news more than election news. *Techdirt.* Retrieved from http://www.techdirt.com/articles/20120202/02405117634/young-people-followed-sopa-news-more-than-election-news.shtml

May, Christopher, & Sell, Susan K. (2006). *Intellectual property rights: A critical history.* Boulder, CO: Lynne Rienners Publishers.

Mazzone, Jason. (2006). Copyfraud. *New York University Law Review, 81* (3), 10–26.

McBride, Sarah, & Smith, Ethan. (2008, December 19). Music industry to abandon mass suits. *Wall Street Journal*, B.1.

McCreevy, Charlie. (2008, May 13). Comments. Conference on Counterfeiting and Piracy, Brussels. Retrieved from http://europa.eu/rapid/pressReleasesAction.do?reference=SPEECH/08/237&format=HTML&aged=0&language=EN&guiLanguage=en

McDonald, Aleecia M., & Cranor, Lorrie Faith. (2008). The cost of reading privacy policies. ACM *Transactions on Computer-human Interaction, 389*(3), 1–22.

McGill, Lawrence. (2006). The state of scholarly publishing in the history of art and architecture. *Connexions.* Retrieved from http://cnx.org/content/m13985/latest/?collection=col10377/latest

McIntosh, Jonathan. (2012). About Jonathan McIntosh. http://www.rebelliouspixels.com/jonathan-mcintosh

McKee, Heidi A. (2011). Policy matters now and in the future: Net neutrality, corporate data mining, and government surveillance. *Computers and Composition, 28*(4), 276–291.

McLeod, Kembrew. (2007). *Freedom of expression®: Resistance and repression in the age of intellectual property.* Minneapolis: University of Minnesota Press.

McLeod, Kembrew, & DiCola, Peter. (2011). *Creative license: The law and culture of digital sampling.* Durham, NC: Duke University Press.

McSherry, Corynne, & Goldman, Eric. (2011, July 18). The "graduated response" deal: What if users had been at the table? Electronic Frontier Foundation Deeplinks Blog. Retrieved from https://www.eff.org/deeplinks/2011/07/graduated-response-deal-what-if-users-had-been

Media Molecule. (2008). *LittleBigPlanet.* Sony Computer Entertainment.

Media Molecule. (2011). *LittleBigPlanet 2.* Sony Computer Entertainment.

Michael, Gabriel J. (2010). Catholic thought and intellectual property: Learning from the ethics of obligation. *Journal of Law and Religion, 25*, 415.

Michaels, Walter Benn. (1995). *Our America: Nativism, modernism, and pluralism*. Durham, NC: Duke University Press.

Mignolo, Walter. (2003). *The darker side of the Renaissance: Literacy, territoriality, and colonization* (2nd ed.). Ann Arbor: University of Michigan Press.

Miguel de Bustos, J. C. (2007). *Cambios institucionales en las industrias culturales. Hacia una economía directa o reticular*. Portal de la Comunicación. Institut de la Comunicació UAB. Retrieved from http://www.portalcomunicacio.es/esp/pdf/aab_lec/27.pdf

Miller, Carolyn R. (1994). Opportunity, opportunism, and progress: Kairos in the rhetoric of technology. *Argumentation, 8* (1), 81–96.

Miller, Carolyn R. (2007). What can automation tell us about agency? *Rhetoric Society Quarterly*, 37(2), 137–157.

Miller, David. (2010). How neoliberalism got where it is: Elite planning, corporate lobbying and the release of the free market. In Ken Birch & Vlad Mykhnenko (Eds.), *The rise and fall of neoliberalism: The collapse of an economic order* (pp. 23–41). London, UK: Zed Books.

Miller, Patrick D. (2004). Property and possession in light of the ten commandments. In William Schweiker & Charles Mathewes (Eds.), *Having: Property and possession in religious and social life* (pp. 17–50). Grand Rapids, MI: W.B. Eerdmans.

Miller, Paul D. (2004). *Rhythm science*. Cambridge, MA: MIT Press.

Mitchell, Joni. (1974). Free man in Paris. *Court and Spark* [audiorecording]. Los Angeles: Asylum.

Moncayo von Hase, A. (1998). The application and interpretation of the Agreement on Trade-Related Aspects of Intellectual Property Rights. In C. M. Correa & A. A. Yusuf (Eds.), *Intellectual property and international trade: The TRIPS Agreement* (pp. 83–122). Alphen aan den Rijn, Netherlands: Kluwer Law International.

Moriarty, Glen. (2010, Sept 15). Certification with OER: Considerations and examples. Open Courseware Consortium. Retrieved from http://www.ocwconsortium.org/en/community/blog/page/19/

Morton, David. (2000). *Off the record: The technology and culture of sound recording in America*. New Brunswick, NJ: Rutgers University Press.

Naess, Arne. (2003). The shallow and the deep, long-range ecology movement. In Robert C. Scharff & Val Dusen (Eds.), *Philosophy of technology: The technological condition, an anthology* (pp. 467–470). Malden, MA: Blackwell Publishing Ltd.

Nardi, Bonnie A., & O'Day, Vicki L. (1999). *Information ecologies*. Cambridge, MA: MIT Press.

National Governors Association Center for Best Practices, Council of Chief State School Officers. (2010). Common Core State Standards writing. Retrieved from http://www.corestandards.org/ELA-Literacy/

National Institutes of Health. (2011). About NIH. Retrieved from http://www.nih.gov/about/

National Institutes of Health. (2011). *Fiscal year 2012 budget request.* Retrieved from http://www.nih.gov/about/director/budgetrequest/index.htm

Native American Graves Protection and Repatriation Act, 25 U.S.C. §3001 (2012).

Navas, Eduardo. (2009). Regressive and reflexive mashups in sampling culture. In Stefan Sonvilla-Weiss (Ed.), *Mashup cultures.* Retrieved from http://remixtheory.net/remixImages/NavasMashups_2010.pdf

Navas, Eduardo (2012). Remix theory >> Remix defined. Retrieved from http://remixtheory.net/?page_id=3

Nettle, Daniel. (1996). Language diversity in West Africa: An ecological approach. *Journal of Anthropological Archaeology, 15,* 403–438.

Nettle, Daniel. (1998). Explaining global patterns of linguistic diversity. *Journal of Anthropological Archaeology,* 17, 354–374.

New Museum. (2010) Exhibition: "Free." http://archive.newmuseum.org/index.php/Detail/Occurrence/Show/occurrence_id/1092

Ng, David. (2012, February 24). Shepard Fairey enters guilty plea in criminal case with AP. *Los Angeles Times: Culture Monster Blog.* Retrieved from http://latimesblogs.latimes.com/culturemonster/2012/02/shepard-fairey-enters-guilty-plea-in-criminal-case-with-ap.html

Nielsen, Michael. (2012). *Reinventing discovery: The new era of networked science.* Princeton, NJ: Princeton University Press.

Nimmer on Copyright § 13.05 (2011).

Nolo. (2010). Copyright and fair use overview. Retrieved from http://fairuse.stanford.edu/Copyright_and_Fair_Use_Overview/chapter9/9-b.html#1 (April 11, 2012).

Nonprofit employment outpaced private sector during "decade of turmoil," report finds. (2012, January). *Philanthropy News Digest.* Retrieved from http://foundationcenter.org/pnd/news/story.jhtml?id=367800015

Nonprofit sector among few growth engines of Michigan economy, report finds. (2011, January). *Philanthropy News Digest.* Retrieved from http://foundationcenter.org/pnd/news/story.jhtml?id=322000008

Nonprofit turnover lower than for-profit. (2008, March). *Philanthropy Journal* Retrieved from http://www.philanthropyjournal.org/news/nonprofit-turnover-lower-profit

Nonprofits pay fees despite tax-exempt status, survey finds *(2011, April). Philanthropy News Digest.* Retrieved from http://foundationcenter.org/pnd/news/story.jhtml?id=337100014

North, Robert Grady. (1954). *Sociology of the biblical jubilee*. Analecta Biblica. Rome: Pontifical Biblical Institute.

North, Robert Grady. (2000). *The biblical jubilee, after fifty years*. Analecta Biblica. Roma: Editrice Pontificio Biblico.

Now on view: Portrait of President Barack Obama by Shepard Fairey. (2009, January). Smithsonian Institute's National Portrait Gallery. Retrieved from http://www.npg.si.edu/collection/obamaportrait.html

NyghtHawk. (2008). Custom character creations. Forum thread at *LittleBigWorkshop.com*. Retrieved from http://forums.littlebigplanet.com/t5/General-Discussion/Custom-Character-Creations/m-p/13244/highlight/true#M5624

O'Reilly, Tim & Battelle, John. (2009). Web squared: Web 2.0 five years on. [White paper]. *Proceedings from Web 2.0 Summit*. San Francisco: O'Reilly Media, Inc. Retrieved from http://www.web2summit.com/web2009/public/schedule/detail/10194

O'Sullivan, Dan. (2009). *Wikipedia: a new community of practice?* Burlington, VT: Ashgate Publishing, Ltd.

Office of the United States Trade Representative. Trans-Pacific Partnership. Retrieved from http://www.ustr.gov/tpp

Olson, C. Paul. (1987). Who computes? In D. W. Livingstone (Ed.), *Critical pedagogy and cultural power* (pp. 179–204). New York: Bergin & Garvey.

OMPI. (1996a). *Tratado de la OMPI sobre Derecho de Autor (TODA)*. Retrieved from http://www.wipo.int/clea/en/text_pdf.jsp?lang=ES&id=4050

OMPI. (1996b). *Tratado de la OMPI sobre Interpretaciones o Ejecuciones y Fonogramas (TOIEF)*. Retrieved from http://www.wipo.int/clea/en/text_pdf.jsp?lang=ES&id=4051

Ong, Walter J. (1982). *Orality and literacy: The technologizing of the word*. London: Methuen.

Ostergard, Jr., Robert L. (1999). Intellectual property: A universal human right? *Human Rights Quarterly, 21*, 156.

OverDrive. (2012). About. http://www.overdrive.com/About/.

Oxford Dictionaries (2012). Oxford University Press. http://oxforddictionaries.com

Parr, Ben. (2011, January 10). Twitter's new CEO finally nails down the company's long-term vision. *Mashable Social Media*. Retrieved from http://mashable.com/2011/01/10/twitters-new-ceo-finally-nails-down-the-companys-long-term-vision/

Parrish, Rain. (1997). A woman's experience. In Robert W. Kapoun and Charles J. Lohrmann (Eds.), *Language of the robe* (pp. 1–3). Layton, UT: Gibbs-Smith.

Parry, Marc. (2011a). Library rights are at stake in new Supreme Court copyright case. *Chronicle.com.* Retrieved from http://chronicle.com/blogs/wiredcampus/library-rights-at-stake-in-new-supreme-court-copyright-case/30222

Parry, Marc. (2011b). Supreme Court takes up scholars' rights. *Chronicle.com.* Retrieved from http://chronicle.com/article/A-Professors-Fight-Over/127700/

Patent Misuse Reform Act, 35 U.S.C. § 271 (1988).

Patrick Cariou v. Richard Prince, 2013 U.S. App. LEXIS 8380; (U.S. Court of Appeals for the Second Circuit of New York April 25, 2013).

Patry, William. F. (2009). *Moral panics and the copyright wars.* New York: Oxford University Press.

Patry, William F. (2011). *How to fix copyright.* New York: Oxford University Press.

Patterson, Richard D. (1973). The widow, the orphan, and the poor in the Old Testament and extra-biblical literature. *Bibliotheca Sacra, 130*(519), 223–234.

PBS Statement Regarding October 3 Presidential Debate. (2012, October 4). Retrieved from http://www.pbs.org/about/news/archive/2012/statement-presidential-debate/

Peer Int'l Corp. v. Latin Am. Music Corp., 161 F. Supp. 2d 38 (D.P.R. 2001).

Pérez, C. (2004). *Revoluciones tecnológicas y capital financiero.* México DF: Siglo XXI editores.

Peukert, Alexander. (2011). Intellectual property as an end in itself. *European Intellectual Property Review, 33*(2), 67–70.

Pew Forum on Religion & Public Life. (2008). U.S. religious landscape study. Retrieved March 15, 2012, from http://religions.pewforum.org/comparisons#

PhadedWun. (2008). Re: Custom character creations. Forum thread at *LittleBigWorkshop.com.* Retrieved from http://forums.littlebigplanet.com/t5/General-Discussion/Custom-Character-Creations/m-p/13244/highlight/true#M5624

Phelps, Marshall, & Kline, David. (2009). *Burning the ships: Intellectual property and the transformation of Microsoft.* Hoboken, NJ: John Wiley & Sons, Inc.

Pink, Daniel H. (2007). Japan, ink: Inside the Manga industrial complex. *Wired 15*(11). Retrieved from http://www.wired.com/techbiz/media/magazine/1511/ff_manga?currentPage=all

Pinterest. (2012). Copyright. *Pinterest: Copyright and Trademark.* Retrieved from http://pinterest.com/about/copyright/

Pirate Party Australia. (2012). Pirate Party Australia's presentation to Trans-Pacific Partnership Stakeholders Meeting in Melbourne. Retrieved from http://pirateparty.org.au/2012/03/04/pirate-party-australias-presentation-to-trans-pacific-partnership-stakeholders-meeting-in-melbourne/

Plunkett, Luke. (2010, March 8). Ubisoft's new DRM system falls down, locks out paying customers. Retrieved from http://kotaku.com/5487918/ubisofts-new-drm-system-falls-down-locks-out-paying-customers

Pogge, Thomas. (2005). Severe poverty as a violation of negative duties. *Ethics & International Affairs, 19*(1), 55–83.

Pogge, Thomas. (2008). *World poverty and human rights: Cosmopolitan responsibilities and reforms* (2nd ed.). Cambridge, MA: Polity.

Poschardt, Ulf. (1998). *DJ Culture*. (Shaun Whiteside, Trans.). London: Quartet Books.

Posey, Darrell A. (1999). *Cultural and spiritual values of biodiversity*. London: Intermediate Technology Publications.

Posner, Raphael; Ben-Sasson, Haim Hillel; & Levitats, Isaac. (2007). Charity. In Michael Berenbaum & Fred Skolnik (Eds.), *Encyclopaedia Judaica*, Blu-Cof. Detroit, MA: Macmillan Reference USA.

Posner, Richard A. (1999). *The problematics of moral and legal theory*. Cambridge, MA: Belknap Press of Harvard University Press.

Potts, Liza. (2009). Using actor network theory to trace and improve multimodal communication design. *Technical Communication Quarterly, 18*(3), 281–301.

Potts, Liza. (2010). Consuming digital rights: Mapping the artifacts of entertainment. *Technical Communication, 57*(3) 300–318.

Powell, Malea. (2002). Rhetorics of survivance: How American Indians use writing. *College Composition and Communication, 53*(30), 396–434.

Powell, Tim (Ed.). (1999). *Beyond the binary: Reconstructing cultural identity in a multicultural context*. New Brunswick, NJ: Rutgers University Press.

Prado, J.C. (2005). *Piratería digital: la tecnología desarma a la industria. En Distribución Actualidad*, 333, 26–30.

Price, Richard. (2011). Richard's answers about Web of Science. *Quora*. Retrieved from http://www.quora.com/Richard-Price/answers/Web-of-Science

Princeton Univ. Press v. Michigan Document Servs., 99 F.3d 1381 (6th Cir. 1996).

Proposal for a European Parliament AND Council Directive amending Directive 2006/116/EC of the European Parliament and of the Council on the term of protection of copyright and related rights, COM/2008/464 final (16/07/2008) at section 1 of the Explanatory Memorandum.

Proposition infinity. (2010). *Futurama: Volume 5*. (David X. Cohen, Prod.). 20th Century Fox. DVD.

Public Counsel Law Center. (2010, May). Copyright and fair use basics for nonprofits. Retrieved from http://www.publiccounsel.org/tools/publications/files/fairuse.pdf

Queen, Mary. (2008). Transnational feminist rhetorics in a digital world. *College English*, 70(5), 471–489.

Radin, Margaret Jane. (1993). *Reinterpreting property*. Chicago: University of Chicago Press.

Rambourg, Guillaume. (2011). *Three reasons selling DRM-free content is the future*. Retrieved from http://www.youtube.com/watch?v=AKZjz0nwHf4

Randall, Alice. (2001). *The wind done gone*. New York: Houghton Mifflin.

Rappaport, Edward. (1998). *Copyright term extension: Estimating the economic value* (No. 98-144E). Washington, DC: Congressional Research Service. Retrieved from http://digital.library.unt.edu/govdocs/crs/permalink/meta-crs-727:1

Ray, Amit, & Graeff, Erhardt. (2008). Reviewing the author-function in the age of Wikipedia. In Caroline Eisner & Martha Vicinus (Eds.), *Originality, imitation, and plagiarism: Teaching writing in the digital age* (pp. 39–47). Ann Arbor: University of Michigan Press.

Readings, Bill. (1996). *The university in ruins*. Cambridge, MA: Harvard University Press.

Recessions continues to exact toll on nonprofits, survey finds. (2010, July). *Philanthropy News Digest*. Retrieved from http://foundationcenter.org/pnd/news/story.jhtml?id=301300008

Recording Industry Association of America. (2009). Music rules! Retrieved from http://www.music-rules.com/

Reed, Esther D. (2006). Property rights, genes, and common good. *Journal of Religious Ethics*, 34(1), 41–67.

Reid, Calvin. (2011, October 7). B&N pulls 100 DC graphic novels from shelves over Kindle Fire deal. *Publishers Weekly*. Retrieved from http://www.publishersweekly.com/pw/by-topic/digital/retailing/article/49008-b-n-pulls-100-dc-graphic-novels-from-shelves-over-kindle-fire-deal.html

Reilly, N. (2007). Linking local and global feminist advocacy: Framing women's rights as human rights in the Republic of Ireland. *Women's Studies International Forum*, 30(2), 114–133.

Reitz, Stephanie. (2011, November 26). Colleges defend humanities amid tight budgets. *Business Week*, Retrieved from http://www.businessweek.com/ap/financialnews/D9R8HVUG0.htm

Remizowski, Leigh. (2012, September 7). Obama poster artist gets probation for evidence tampering. *CNN: Justice Blog*. Retrieved from http://www.cnn.com/2012/09/07/justice/obama-poster-artist-probation/index.html

Reuman, Ann E. (2000). Coming into play: An interview with Gloria Anzaldúa. *MELUS, 25*(2), 3–45.

Reyman, Jessica (2010). *The rhetoric of intellectual property: Copyright law and the regulation of digital culture*. New York: Routledge.

Ribeiro, S. (2007). *El 2006 y la plutocracia.* Retrieved from http://www.rebelion.org/noticia_pdf.php?id=44374

Rife, Martine Courant; Slattery, Shaun; & DeVoss, Dànielle N. (Eds.). (2011). *Copy(Write): Intellectual property in the writing classroom*. West Lafayette, IN: Parlor Press.

Rife, Martine Courant; Westbrook, Steve; DeVoss, Dànielle Nicole; & Logie, John. (2010). Introduction: Copyright, culture, creativity, and the commons. *Computers and Composition,* 27(3), 161–166.

Rifkin, J. (2000). *La era del acceso.* Barcelona: Paidós.

Rimmer, Matthew. (2003). Gone with the wind: Copyright law and fair use. *Australian Library and Information Association.* Retrieved from http://archive.alia.org.au/incite/2003/04/wind.gone.html

Rimmer, Matthew. (2007). *Digital copyright and the consumer revolution.* Bodmin, Cornwall: MPG Books.

Ringling Museum of Art. Peter Paul Rubens: Impressions of a Master. Retrieved from http://www.ringling.org/Exhibitions2.aspx?id=11790

Rivait, Jessica L. (2011, April 15). *The impact of the coordinator role on public-making: Assembling local publics in the digital age.* Unpublished dissertation. Lansing, MI: Michigan State University.

Rivait, Jessica L.; Getto, Guiseppe; & Leon, Kendall. (In press). Service-learning partnerships as distributed knowledge work: Community media within local infrastructures. *Community Literacy Journal.*

Rivkin, Ellis. (1986). Judaism's historical response to economic, social and political systems. In Walter Block & Irving Hexham (Eds.), *Religion, Economics, and Social Thought* (pp. 376–387). Vancouver, BC: Fraser Institute.

Robbins, Sarah. (2003). Distributed authorship: A feminist case-study framework for studying intellectual property. *College English,* 66(2), 155–171.

Robertson, Michael. (2008). Property and privatisation in *RoboCop*. *International Journal of Law in Context,* 4(3), 217–235.

Robinson, Martin. (2008). LittleBigPlanet interview. *IGN.com*. Retrieved from http://ps3.ign.com/articles/940/940711p1.html.

Rodriguez, Katitza, & Sutton, Maira. (2012, January 19). Internet black-out day fires up digital rights activism around the world. Retrieved from https://www.eff.org/deeplinks/2012/01/internet-black-out-day-fires-digital-rights-activism-around-world

Rofé, Alexander. (1988). The Vineyard of Naboth: The origin and message of the story. *Vetus Testamentum,* 38(1), 89–104.

Rohter, L. (2011, December 9). Europe extends copyright on music. *New York Times.* Retrieved from http://www.nytimes.com/2011/09/13/arts/music/european-union-extends-copyright-on-recordings.html?pagewanted=2&_r=1

Rose, Joel. (2012, May 16). "Canal Zone" collages test the meaning of fair use. http://www.npr.org/2012/05/16/152844727/canal-zone-collages-test-the-meaning-of-fair-use

Rose, Mike. (2003). The language of exclusion: Writing instruction at the university. In Victor Villanueva (Ed.), *Cross-talk in comp theory: A reader* (pp. 547–569). Urbana, IL: National Council of Teachers of English.

Rosow, Steven J. (2007). *Globalization and corporatization in higher education: A report on the changing structure of the university.* Retrieved from http://uupinfo.org/research/GlobalizationReport07.pdf

Rovai, A. P. (2009). *The Internet and higher education: Achieving global reach.* Cambridge, UK: Chandos Publishing.

Royal Society Publishing. (2012). Transactions of the Royal Society. Retrieved from http://rstb.royalsocietypublishing.org/

Royster, Jacqueline Jones. (2003). When the first voice you hear is not your own. In Victor Villanueva (Ed.), *Cross-talk in comp theory: A reader* (pp. 611–622). Urbana, IL: National Council of Teachers of English.

Rude, Carolyn. (2009). Mapping the research questions in technical communication. *Journal of Business and Technical Communication, 23*(2), 174–215.

Russeth, Andrew. (May 8, 2012). The original: Doing the elastic tango with Sturtevant. http://galleristny.com/2012/05/the-original-doing-the-elastic-tango-with-sturtevant/

Sádaba Rodríguez, I. (2005). *La cultura en un mundo global e hipertecnologizado.* Retrieved from http://www.edicionessimbioticas.info/spip.php?article328&debut_articles_rubrique=10

Salleh, Ariel. (1984). Deeper than deep ecology: The eco-feminist connection. *Environmental Ethics,* 6(4), 339–345.

Salmón, Enrique. (2000). Iwígara: A Rarámuri cognitive model of biodiveristy and its effects on land management. In Paul E. Minnis & Wayne J. Elisens (Eds.), *Biodiversity and Native America* (pp. 180–206). Norman: University of Oklahoma Press.

Samuelson, Pamela. (2003). DRM [and, or, vs.] the law. *Communications of the* ACM, *46,* 41–45.

San Francisco Bar Association. (2011, February 1). Intellectual property law basics for nonprofits. Retrieved from http://sfbar.org/forms/vlsp/corp_ip_legal_alert_2011.pdf

Sánchez Tabernero, A., et al. (1993). *Concentración de la comunicación en Europa. Empresa comercial e interés público.* Barcelona: Centre d´Investigació de la Comunicació de la Generalitat de Catalunya.

Sandoval, Greg. (2012, April 2). New copyright center to target online piracy. *CBS News Techtalk.* Retrieved from http://www.cbsnews.com/8301-501465_162-57408106-501465/new-copyright-center-to-target-online-piracy

Sato, Charlene J. (1990). The syntax of conversion in interlanguage development. Germany: Muller Bass.

Sauers, Jenna. (2011). Urban Outfitters and the Navajo Nation: What does the law say? *Jezebel: Celebrity, Sex, Fashion for Women.* Blog post retrieved from http://jezebel.com/5849637/urban-outfitters-and-the-navajo-nation-what-does-the-law-say

Schloss, Joseph G. (2004). *Making beats: The art of sample-based hip-hop.* Middletown, CT: Wesleyan University Press.

Schrock, Nancy. (2011 May/June). Postmodern IAM. *IAM Magazine*, 13–19.

Schwartz, Eilon. (2001). Bal Tashchit: A Jewish environmental precept. In Martin D. Yaffe (Ed.), *Judaism and environmental ethics: A reader* (pp. 230–249). Lanham, MD: Lexington Books.

Scott, J. Blake (2009). Civic engagement as risk management and public relations: What the pharmaseutical industry can tell us about service-learning. *College Composition and Communication, 61*(2), 343–366.

Selfe, Dickie; DeVoss, Dànielle Nicole; & McKee, Heidi A. (Eds.). (2011). Collectives, common worlds and the idea of sustainability: An introduction. In Dànielle Nicole DeVoss, Heidi A. McKee, & Richard (Dickie) Selfe (Eds.), *Technological ecologies and sustainability* (pp. 1–7). Logan: Utah State University/ Computers and Composition Digital Press. Retrieved from http://ccdigitalpress.org/tes/00_intro_selfe_devoss_mckee.pdf

Sergio Muñoz Sarmiento. (2012, January 29). Cariou's lawyers file response. Retrieved from http://clancco.com/wp/2012/01/cariou-fair-use-appropriation-transformative/

Sheffield, Gail K. (1997). *The arbitrary Indian: The Indian Arts and Crafts Act of 1990.* Norman: University of Oklahoma Press.

Shepard Fairey. *Wikipedia, The Free Encyclopedia.* Retrieved from http://en.wikipedia.org/wiki/Shepard_Fairey

Shepard, Glen H. (2004). Ethnobotanical ground-truthing and forest diversity in the western Amazon. In J. S. Carlson and Luisa Maffi (Eds.), *Ethnobotany and conservation of biodiversity.* Bronx: New York Botanical Garden Press.

Sherlock, Lee. (2009). Genre, activity, and collaborative work and play in World of Warcraft: Places and problems of open systems in online gaming. *Journal of Business and Technical Communication, 23*(3), 263–293.

Sherman, Cary (2012, Feb. 7). What Wikipedia won't tell you. *The New York Times*.

Shiva, Vandana. (1997). *Biopiracy: The plunder of nature and knowledge*. Boston, MA: South End Press.

Shuttleworth Foundation. *The Cape Town Open Education Declatation*. Retrieved from http://www.capetowndeclaration.org/

Simpson-Jones, Katie. (2010). Comment: Unlawful infringement or just creative expression? Why DJ Girl Talk may inspire congress to "recast, transform, or adapt" copyright. *John Marshall Law Review, 43*, 1067.

Sinclair, Brendan. (2011, August 26). Skyrim dlc to be Xbox 360-exclusive for 30 days. Retrieved from http://uk.gamespot.com/news/skyrim-dlc-to-be-xbox-360-exclusive-for-30-days-6331158

Singer, Natasha. (2012a, June 16). You for sale: Mapping, and sharing, the consumer genome. *New York Times*. Retrieved from http://www.nytimes.com/2012/06/17/technology/acxiom-the-quiet-giant-of-consumer-database-marketing.html

Singer, Natasha. (2012b, October 13). Do not track? Advertisers say "don't tread on us." *New York Times*. Retrieved from http://www.nytimes.com/2012/10/14/technology/do-not-track-movement-is-drawing-advertisers-fire.html

Skutnabb-Kangas, Tove; Maffi, Luisa; & Harmon, David. (2003). *Sharing a world of difference: The Earth's linguistic, cultural, and biological diversity*. Paris: UNESCO Publishing.

Slack, Jennifer Daryl. (1984). *Communication technologies & society: Conceptions of causality & the politics of technological intervention*. Norwood, NJ: ABLEX Publishing Corporation.

Smiers, J., &Van Schijndel, M. (2008). *Imagine... no copyright*. Barcelona: Gedisa.

Smith, Eric A. (2001). On the coevolution of cultural, linguistic, and biological diversity. In Luisa Maffi (Ed.), *On biological diversity: Linking language, knowledge, and the environment* (pp. 95–117). Washington, DC: Smithsonian Institution Press.

Smith, Linda T. (1999). *Decolonizing methodologies: Research and indigenous peoples*. New York: Zed Books.

Smith, Roberta. (2011, November). Flattery (sincere) lightly dusted with irony. *New York Times*. Retrieved from http://www.nytimes.com/2011/11/11/arts/design/sherrie-levine-mayhem-at-whitney-museum-review.html?pagewanted=all

Smith, Sophie. (2000). Compositional strategies of the hip-hop turntablist. *Organised Sound, 5*(2), 75–79.

Snow, C. P. (1961). *The two cultures and the scientific revolution*. New York: Cambridge University Press. Retrieved from http://www.questia.com/googleScholar.qst?docId=58108775

Sony Corp. of America v. Universal City Studios, Inc., 464 U.S. 417 (1984).

Sony. (2009). System software license agreement (version 1.3) for the PlayStation 3 system. *UK.Playstation.com*. Retrieved from http://uk.playstation.com/ps3/support/system-software/detail/item384082/Update-features%28ver-3-66%29/

Sony. (2010). Terms of service and user agreement. *Playstation.com*. Retrieved from http://us.playstation.com/support/termsofuse/index.htm#PSNToSUA

Sony. (2011). Terms of service. *Playstation.com*. Retrieved from http://us.playstation.com/support/termsofuse/index.htm.

Soss, Neal M. (1973). Old Testament law and economic society. *Journal of the History of Ideas*, *34*(3), 323–344.

Sotamaa, Ollie. (2010). Play, create, share: Player production and agency. *Fiberculture, 16*. Retrieved November 22, 2010 from http://sixteen.fibreculturejournal.org/play-create-share-console-gaming-player-production-and-agency/

Souvignier, Todd. (2003). *The world of DJs and the turntable culture*. Milwaukee, WI: Hal Leonard Corporation.

Spinuzzi, Clay. (2003). *Tracing genres through organizations: A sociocultural approach to information design*. Cambridge, MA: The MIT Press.

Spinuzzi, Clay. (2007). Introduction: Technical communication in the age of distributed work. *Technical Communication Quarterly, 16*(3), 265–277.

Spinuzzi, Clay. (2008). *Network: Theorizing knowledge work in telecommunications*. New York: Cambridge University Press.

Spiro, Lisa. (2012). "This is why we fight": Defining the values of the digital humanities. In Matthew K. Gold (Ed.), *Debates in the digital humanities*. Minneapolis: University of Minnesota Press.

Spoofing Shepard Fairey's Obama poster. (2008, November 10). *The Guardian*. Retrieved from http://www.theguardian.com/artanddesign/gallery/2008/nov/10/art-uselections2008

Sprigman, Christopher. (2012). Copyrights and wrongs. *Chronicle.com*. Retrieved from http://chronicle.com/article/CopyrightsWrongs/130422/

Standeford, D. (2011, December 9). EU extends copyright protection from 50 to 70 years. *IP Watch*. Retrieved from http://www.ip-watch.org/weblog/2011/09/12/eu-extends-copyright-protection-from-50-to-70-years/

Steam about. (2012). Retrieved from http://store.steampowered.com/about

Steam account use. (2012). Retrieved from https://support.steampowered.com/kb_article.php?ref=8963-EIKC-3767

Sterne, Jonathan. (2003). *The audible past: Cultural origins of sound reproduction*. Durham, NC: Duke University Press.

Stormy Mondays. (2009). *Stormy Mondays y la distribución libre por internet.* Official Web Stormy Mondays. Retrieved from http://www.stormymondays.com/biblioteca

Stuart, Matt. (2011, October 7). Barnes & Noble pulls every graphic novel exclusive to Kindle Fire. Retrieved from http://cnnmoneytech.tumblr.com/post/11141640153/barnes-noble-pulls-every-graphic-novel-exclusive-to

Suber, Peter. (2004). Promoting open access in the humanities. Retrieved from http://www.earlham.edu/~peters/writing/apa.htm

Sullivan, Patrick. H. (1998). *Profiting from intellectual capital: Extracting value from innovation.* New York: John Wiley & Sons.

Susan G. Komen Foundation. (2008, August 14). Terms of use policy. Retrieved from http://ww5.komen.org/AboutUs/TermsofUse.html

Suspended steam account. (2012). Retrieved from https://support.steampowered.com/kb_article.php?s=ef3d701f17c0fcefba795c86f6b8c890&ref=5406-WFZC-5519

Tamari, Meir. (1986). Judaism and the market mechanism. In Walter Block & Irving Hexham (Eds.), *Religion, economics, and social thought* (pp. 393–421). Vancouver, BC: Fraser Institute.

Tapscott, Don, & Williams, Anthony D. (2010). Macrowikinomics: New solutions for a connected planet. New York: Penguin.

Tasaka, Robyn. (2009). Challenges and privileges, entanglement and appropriation: Rhetorical practices of Asian Americans from Hawaii. Unpublished dissertation. Lansing, MI: Michigan State University.

Taylor, Laurie, & Riley, Brendan. (2006, February 21). Open source and academia. *Computers and Composition Online*. Retrieved from http://www.bgsu.edu/cconline/tayloriley/intro.html

Taylor, T. L. (2007). Pushing the borders: Player participation and game culture. In J. Karaganis (Ed.), *Network_netplay: Structures of participation in digital culture* (pp. 112–130). New York: Social Science Research Council.

Temkin, Ann, & Levine, Sherrie. (1993). *Sherrie Levine: Newborn*. Philadelphia: Philadelphia Museum of Art

Terranova, Tiziana. (2004). *Network culture: Politics for the information age.* Ann Arbor, MI: Pluto Press.

Thacker, Kathi. (1991, February 18). Museum reopens as fear of Indian art rule eases. *The Oklahoman*. Retrieved from http://newsok.com/article/2347995

Thackeray, William Makepeace. *History of Pendennis: His fortunes and misfortunes, his friends and his greatest enemy*. New York: Thomas Nelson and Sons.

Thomas, Nicholas. (1991). Entangled objects: Exchange, material culture, and colonialism in the Pacific. Cambridge, MA: Harvard University Press.

Thomas, Nicholas. (1997). In Oceania: Visions, artifacts, histories. Durham, NC: Duke University Press.

Thompson Reuters. (2012). History of citation indexing. Retrieved from http://thomsonreuters.com/products_services/science/free/essays/history_of_citation_indexing/

Thornton, Sarah. (1996). *Club cultures: Music, media, and subcultural capital*. Hanover, NH: University Press of New England.

Thornton, Sarah. (2005). The social logic of subcultural capital. Ken Gelder (Ed.), *The subcultures reader* (2nd ed.; pp. 184–192). New York: Routledge.

Times Online Lab. (2009). Do music artists fare better in a world with illegal file-sharing? Retrieved from http://labs.timesonline.co.uk/blog/2009/11/12/do-music-artists-do-better-in-a-world-with-illegal-file-sharing

Tomlinson, John. (2003). Globalization and cultural identity. In David Heald & Anthony McGrew (Eds.), *Global transformations reader: An introduction to the globalization debate* (pp. 269—277). Malden, MA: Blackwell Publishing Inc.

Tomlinson, John. (2011, November 2). Encouraging a culture of reuse? Copyright policies of nonprofit organizations in international development. Retrieved from http://www.johntomlinson.com/docs/culture_of_reuse.pdf

Tonouchi, Lee. (2004). Da state of pidgin address. *College English, 67*(1), 75–82.

Torelli, Carlos; Chiu, Chi-yue; Keh, Hean Tat; & Amaral, Nelson. (2005). *Brand symbolism and reference groups: perspectives on the identity value of brands symposium*. Minneapolis: University of Minnesota.

Trask, Haunani-Kay. (1991). Lovely hula hands: corporate tourism and the prostitution of Hawaiian culture. *Contours, 5*(1), 8—14.

Trask, Haunani-Kay. (1995). De-colonizing Hawaiian literature. In V. Hereniko & R. Wilson (Eds.), *Inside/out: Literature, cultural politics, and identity in the New Pacific*. Oxford: Rowman & Littlefield Publishers.

Trask, Haunani-Kay. (1999). *From a native daughter: Colonialism and sovereignty in Hawai'i*. Honolulu: University of Hawai'i Press.

Turkle, Sherry. (2011). *Alone together: Why we expect more from technology and less from each other*. New York: Basic Books.

Tushnet, Rebecca (2011). Symposium: Creativity and the law: Scary monsters: Hybrids, mashups, and other illegitimate children. *Notre Dame Law Review, 86*, 2133.

Twitter. Public information. *Twitter: Privacy Policy*. Retrieved from https://twitter.com/privacy

Tyfield, David. (2010). Neoliberalism, intellectual property and the global knowledge economy. In Ken Birch & Vlad Mykhnenko (Eds.), *The rise and fall of neoliberalism: The collapse of an economic order* (pp. 60–76). London, UK: Zed Books.

U.S. Constitution, Art. I, § 8, cl. 8.

United Nations General Assembly. (1948a). Article 13. *International Covenant on Economic, Social and Cultural Rights* 1948. Retrieved from http://www.un.org/en/documents/udhr/index.shtml#a13

United Nations General Assembly. (1948b). *Universal Declaration of Human Rights*. 1948. Retrieved from http://www.un.org/en/documents/udhr/

United Nations. (2004). *Resolution adopted by the General Assembly: 59/174 Second International Decade of the World's Indigenous People*. (No. Fifty-ninth session. A/RES/59/174).

United States Copyright Office. (2010). Highlights of copyright amendments contained in the URAA. (Circular 38B.1110). Washington, DC: US Government Printing Office.

United States Government Accountability Office (GAO). (2006, June). Faith based and community initiative: improvements in monitoring grantees and measuring performance could enhance accountability. Report to congressional requesters. Retrieved from http://www.gao.gov/new.items/d06616.pdf

United Way. (2012). History. Retrieved from http://www.unitedway.org/pages/history

University of Chicago Press. (2012). Author's permission guidelines. Retrieved from http://www.press.uchicago.edu/infoServices/permissions.html

University of Sydney Strategic Planning Office. (2009). Statistics 2009. Retrieved from http://sydney.edu.au/staff/planning/statistics/publications/Statistics2009.pdf

Vaidhyanathan, Siva. (2003). *Copyrights and copywrongs: The rise of intellectual property and how it threatens creativity*. New York: New York University Press.

Vaidhyanathan, Siva. (2011). *The Googlization of everything (and why we should worry)*. Los Angeles: University of California Press.

Valle, Ellen. (2006). Reporting the doings of the curious: Authors and editors in the Philosophical Transactions of the Royal Society of London. In Nicholas Brownlees (Ed.), *News discourse in early modern Britain: Selected papers of CHINED* (pp. 71–90). Bern, Switzerland: Peter Lang AG.

Vardi, Liana. (1993). Construing the harvest: Gleaners, farmers, and officials in early modern France. *American Historical Review*, 98(5), 1424–1447.

Vidal, M. (2000). *Cooperación sin mando: una introducción al software libre*. Retrieved from http://biblioweb.sindominio.net/media/pujats/informacion/55a9e31cb24266e89bfdbaaa6302e8a1511.pdf

Villanueva, Victor. (2003). On the rhetoric and precedents of racism. In Victor Villanueva (Ed.), *Cross-talk in comp theory: A reader* (pp. 829–845). Urbana, Illinois: National Council of Teachers of English.

Vizenor, Gerald. (1998). *Fugitive poses: Native American Indian scenes of absence and presence*. Lincoln: University of Nebraska Press.

Vizenor, Gerald. (1999). *Manifest manners: Narratives on postindian survivance*. Lincoln: University of Nebraska Press.

Vogel, David. (2001). How green Is Judaism? Exploring Jewish environmental ethics. *Judaism*, *50*(1), 66.

Walker, John. (2012, February 1). *Thought: Do we own our steam games?*. Retrieved from http://www.rockpapershotgun.com/2012/02/01/thought-do-we-own-our-steam-games/

Wallace Collection. (2012). Reproduction application form. Retrieved fromhttp://www.wallacecollection.org/thecollection/imagesandphotography/imagesandrightsforpublication

Warburton, William, & Hurd, Richard. (1811). *The works of the Right Reverend William Warburton, D.D. Lord Bishop of Gloucester*. London: Luke Hansard & Sons.

Watson, James, & Crick, Francis. (1953). A structure for deoxyribose nucleic acid. *Nature, 171*, 737–738. Retrieved from http://www.nature.com/nature/dna50/archive.html

Watts, James. (1990, December 8). New Indian art law affects Oklahomans: Act stresses tribal listings. *Tulsa World*. Retrieved from http://www.tulsaworld.com/news/article.aspx?no=subj&articleid=180740

Webster, Noah. (1826, September 30). Letter to Daniel Webster. In L. Bently & M. Kreschmer (Eds.), *Primary sources on copyright (1450–1900)*. Retrieved from http://www.copyrighthistory.org

Welch, Jack. (2001). *Jack: Straight from the gut*. New York: Warner Books, Inc.

Welch, Walter L., & Brodbeck Stenzel Burt, Leah. (1994). *From tinfoil to stereo: The acoustic years of the recording industry 1877–1929*. Gainesville: University of Florida Press.

Wendland, Wend B. (2008). It's a small world (after all): Some reflection on intellectual property and traditional cultural expression. In Christoph Beat Graber & Mira Buri-Nennova (Eds.), *Intellectual property and traditional cultural expressions in a digital environment* (pp. 150–181). Northampton, MA: Edward Elgar.

Westbrook, Stephen. (2009). What we talk about when we talk about fair use: Conversations on writing pedagogy, new media, and copyright law (pp. 159–177). In Martine Courant Rife, Shaun Slattery, & Dànielle Nicole DeVoss (Eds.), *Copywrite: Intellectual property in the writing classroom*. Clemson, SC: Parlor Press.

Westbrook, Steve. (2006). Visual rhetoric in a culture of fear: Impediments to multimedia production. *College English*, *68*(5), 457–480.

Wheeler, Alina (2006). *Designing brand identity: a complete guide to creating, building, and maintaining strong brands* (2nd ed.). Hoboken, NJ: John Wiley and Sons, Inc.

White House. (2012, February). Consumer data privacy in a networked world: A framework for protecting privacy and promoting innovation in the global digital economy. [White paper]. Retrieved from http://www.whitehouse.gov/sites/default/files/privacy-final.pdf

Why do development professionals jump ship? (2012). Retrieved from http://www.iteachfundraising.com/articles/Jumpship.html

"Why donate?" Massachusetts Institute of Technology. Retrieved from http://ocw.mit.edu/donate/why-donate/

Wiegel, Robert L. (2008). Waikiki Beach, Oahu, Hawaii: History of its transformation from a natural to an urban shore. *Shore and Beach*, 76(2), 3–30.

Wiley, D. A. (2006). About COSL. *Center for Open and Sustainable Learning*. Logan: Utah State University.

Wiley, D. A. (2007). On the sustainability of open educational resource initiatives in higher education. OECD's Centre for Educational Research and Innovation (CERI). Retrieved from http://www.oecd.org/edu/ceri/38645447.pdf

Williams, Raymond. (1977). *Marxism and literature*. New York: Oxford University Press.

Williams, Raymond. (1981). *Culture*. London: Fontana.

Willinsky, John. (2006). *The access principle: The case for open access to research and scholarship*. Cambridge, MA: MIT Press.

Wilson, Eric. (2009, January 7). Consumers of the world unite. *New York Times*. Retrieved from http://www.nytimes.com/2009/01/08/fashion/08ROW.html

Wojcik, Mary. (2008). The antithesis of originality: Bridgeman, image licensors, and the public domain. *Hastings Communications & Entertainment Law Journal (Comm/Ent)*, 30(2), 257.

Women's Center of Greater Lansing. (2012). Retrieved from http://www.womenscenterofgreaterlansing.org/

Women's Center of Southeastern Michigan. (2012). Retrieved from http://womenscentersemi.org/

Woodmansee, Martha, & Jaszi, Peter. (1994). *The construction of authorship: Textual appropriation in law and literature*. Durham, NC: Duke University Press.

World Intellectual Property Organization. (1979). The Berne Convention for the Protection of Literary and Artistic Works. Retrieved from http://www.wipo.int/treaties/en/ip/berne/trtdocs_wo001.html

World's Indigenous People. (No. Forty-eighth session. A/RES/48/163.): UN General Assembly.

Worley, David R. (1971). God's gracious love expressed: Exodus 20:1—17. *Restoration Quarterly*, *14*(3—4), 184–204.

Wortham, Jenna. (2008, September 21). "Obey" street artist churns out "Hope" for Obama." *Wired.* Retrieved from http://www.wired.com/underwire/2008/09/poster-boy-shep/

WTO. (OMC). (1994). *Acuerdo sobre los Aspectos de los Derechos de Propiedad Intelectual relacionados con el Comercio, inclusive el comercio de mercancías falsificadas (ADPIC).* Retrieved from http://www.wto.org/spanish/docs_s/legal_s/ursum_s.htm#nAgreement

Wurtzler, Steve J. (2007). *Electric sounds: Technological change and the rise of corporate mass media.* New York: Columbia University Press.

Yin-Poole, Wesley. (2011, November 11). Cd projekt: Witcher 2 gog.com sales vindicate DRM-free decision. Retrieved from http://www.eurogamer.net/articles/2011-11-10-cd-projekt-witcher-2-gog-com-sales-vindicate-drm-free-decision

Yin-Poole, Wesley. (2012, March 23). Ubisoft wants to offer PC gamers so much value the need for DRM "goes away." Retrieved from http://www.eurogamer.net/articles/2012-03-23-ubisoft-wants-to-offer-pc-gamers-so-much-value-the-need-for-drm-goes-away

Young, Jeffrey. (2012). Supreme Court upholds law that pulled foreign works back under copyright. *Chronicle.com.* Retrieved from http://chronicle.com/article/Supreme-Court-Upholds-Law-That/130376/

Young, Morris. (2002). Standard English and student bodies: Institutionalizing race and literacy in Hawai'i. *College English, 64*(4), 405–431.

YouTube. (2012). About YouTube. *YouTube.* Retrieved from http://www.youtube.com/t/about_youtube

Zaichkowsky, Judith Lynne (2010). Strategies for brand identity. *Journal of Brand Management, 17*(8), 548–560.

Zallo, R. (1992). *El mercado de la cultura (estructura económica y política de la comunicación).* Donostia: Tercera Prensa.

Zimmerman, Traci. (2010). Think locally, act globally: Taking US copyright reform to a world stage. *NCTE Inbox.* Retrieved from http://www.ncte.org/ccccc/committees/ip/ipreports/thinklocally

Zimmerman, Traci. (2012). One step forward, two steps back. *The CCCC-IP Annual: Top Intellectual Property Developments of 2011.* Retrieved from http://www.ncte.org/library/NCTEFiles/Groups/CCCC/Committees/TopIP2011Collection.pdf

Zittrain, Jonathan (2008). *The future of the Internet and how to stop it.* New Haven & London: Yale University Press.

Index

B

D

E

H

I

J

K

L

N

O

P

Q

R

S

V

W

X

Y

Z

COMMUNICATION LAW

SUSAN DRUCKER
Series Editor

Acknowledging the variety of ways in which the disciplines of communication and law converge, the aim of this series is to publish books at the nexus of these two areas with particular attention paid to communication in law in the changing media landscape.

Utilizing both qualitative and quantitative methodologies, volumes in this series provide analysis of issues at the interdisciplinary and international level such as free and responsible speech, media law, regulation and policy, press freedoms and governance of new media.

For additional information about this series or for the submission of manuscripts, please contact Dr. Drucker at susan.j.drucker@hofstra.edu.

To order other books in this series, please contact our Customer Service Department:

(800) 770-LANG (within the U.S.)
(212) 647-7706 (outside the U.S.)
(212) 647-7707 FAX

Or browse online by series at www.peterlang.com.

COMMON DENOMINATORS IN ART AND SCIENCE

COMMON DENOMINATORS IN ART AND SCIENCE

edited by
MARTIN POLLOCK
with the assistance of Keith Brown
Aubrey Manning and
Barrie Wilson

The proceedings of a discussion conference
held under the auspices of
the School of Epistemics
University of Edinburgh
November 1981

ABERDEEN UNIVERSITY PRESS

First published 1983
Aberdeen University Press
A member of the Pergamon Group

The Publisher acknowledges subsidy from the Scottish Arts Council towards the publication of this volume.

British Library Cataloguing in Publication Data
Common denominators in art or science
1. Knowledge, Theory of
I. Pollock, Martin
121 BD761

ISBN 0-08-028457-4

Cover Design by Ivor Davies

PRINTED IN GREAT BRITAIN
THE UNIVERSITY PRESS
ABERDEEN

FRANK MALINA
(1912–1981)

Founder-editor of Leonardo *and a devoted and experienced protagonist of the 'dialogue' between art and science*

A shadow was cast on the conference by the tragic news of the sudden death of Frank Malina only a matter of hours before he was due to leave Paris for Edinburgh to join the meeting, where the loss of his invigorating presence was deeply felt.

At the end of the conference his friend and colleague, Peter Lloyd Jones, paid the following tribute to his memory.

* * *

Frank Malina pursued brilliant careers in both art and science. As a young graduate student he espoused an interest in the then eccentric subject of rockets and together with Von Karman the great fluid-dynamicist and two other colleagues started the first commercial rocket company—Aerojet General, which, coming as it did at the opening of World War II, had a spectacular growth in the area of rocket assisted take-off for military planes. Later Malina was the driving force behind the first US sounding rocket to escape the atmosphere and truly penetrate outer space and he was for a time Director of what had come to be known as Jet Propulsion Laboratory.

Malina was however a man of peace and deeply disliked the military applications of a rocket technology that had grown so fast. After World War II he suddenly left Jet Propulsion Laboratory and, a comparatively wealthy man, went to work for UNESCO on projects to harness technology for peaceful purposes. His interest in space engineering continued unabated however and he was the first Chairman of the International Academy of Astronautics. But, from his student days, he had been a talented artist and, after settling in Paris, devoted himself to this activity which evolved rapidly from abstract easel paintings to the kinetic-optical constructions for which he was famous.

For the past eleven years however he devoted most of his time and energy to his journal *Leonardo*. Based on his belief that artists should have the kind of truly academic and strictly non-commercial journal long familiar to their colleagues in the sciences, he worked tirelessly to establish *Leonardo* as an essential organ of communication in many fields where valuable work would otherwise go unpublished. Its truly international character was very important to him and he strove to solicit articles from all parts of the world, ignoring political diversions with characteristically Texan determination. Himself a brilliant man in many directions, he was a model of generosity to all those who had anything original and honest to say in their own fields.

CONTENTS

PARTICIPANTS

DR JONATHAN BARD, MRC Clinical & Population Cytogenetics Unit, Western General Hospital, Crewe Road, Edinburgh

DR LARRY BRISKMAN, Dept. of Philosophy, University of Edinburgh, David Hume Tower, George Square, Edinburgh

DR KEITH BROWN, Deputy Director, School of Epistemics, Edinburgh University, 2 Buccleuch Place, Edinburgh

VANDA COOK, 13 Apsley Road, Clifton, Bristol

PROFESSOR CHRISTOPHER CORNFORD, Spring House, Conduit Head Road, Cambridge (formerly Head, Dept. of General Studies, Royal College of Art, Kensington, London)

DR IVOR DAVIES, Gwent College of Higher Education, Faculty of Art and Design, Clarence Place, Newport, Gwent

DR TOM ELSDALE, MRC Clinical & Population Cytogenetics Unit, Western General Hospital, Crewe Road, Edinburgh

PROFESSOR MICHELE EMMER, Istituto Matematico, 'Guido Castelnuovo', Università di Roma, Citta Universitaria, 00100 Roma

PROFESSOR ERIC FORBES, History of Medicine and Science Unit, Dept. of History, University of Edinburgh, High School Yards, Edinburgh

DR JOHN GAGE, Dept. of Art History, Cambridge University, 1, Scroope Terrace, Cambridge

PROFESSOR PHILIP GELL, FRS, Dunn School of Pathology, Cambridge University.

PROFESSOR RICHARD GREGORY, Laboratory of Brain and Perception, Medical School, Bristol University.

PROFESSOR ROM HARRÉ, Sub-Faculty of Philosophy, University of Oxford, 10 Merton Street, Oxford.

HOMME HELLINGA, Dept. of Molecular Biology, Edinburgh University, Mayfield Road, Edinburgh

DR ALEX KELLER, Dept. of History of Science, University of Leicester

DAVID KINMONT, Head of Extra-mural Art Dept., Bristol University, 32 Tyndall's Park Road, Bristol

DR DAVID KNIGHT, Dept. of Philosphy, University of Durham, 50 Old Elvet, Durham

DR BRIAN LLOYD, High Wall, Pullen's Lane, Oxford (formerly Director, Oxford Polytechnic)

DR PETER LLOYD JONES, Director, 3D Design Centre, Knights Park, Kingston Polytechnic, Kingston-upon-Thames, Surrey

PROFESSOR AUBREY MANNING, Dept. of Zoology, University of Edinburgh, West Mains Road, Edinburgh

PROFESSOR ARTHUR MARWICK, Dept. of History, The Open University, Walton Hall, Milton Keynes

GERARD MERMOZ, City of Liverpool College of Higher Education, Liverpool Road, Prescot, Merseyside

DR ANTHONY MICHAELIS, c/o Spectrum House, Hillview Gardens, London (Editor, *Interdisciplinary Science Reviews*)

DR SPEDDING MICKLEM, Dept. of Zoology, University of Edinburgh, West Mains Road, Edinburgh

GRAEME MONTGOMERY, Dept. of Physics, Edinburgh University, late of Edinburgh College of Art, 23 Hillpark Avenue, Edinburgh

CLAIRE MORRIS, 18 Pembroke Green, Lea, Malmesbury

PROFESSOR MARTIN POLLOCK, FRS, Emeritus Professor of Biology, University of Edinburgh. Margaret Marsh, Shaftesbury, Dorset

DR JOSÉ REISSIG, Genetics Laboratory, C. W. Post College, Long Island University, Greenvale, NY

DR BARRY RICHARDS, Director, School of Epistemics, University of Edinburgh, 2 Buccleuch Place Edinburgh

DR JUDITH RICHARDS, 13 Gloucester Place, Edinburgh. Faculty of Technology, The Open University

PROFESSOR GILES ROBERTSON, Dept. of Fine Art, Edinburgh University, 4 Saxe-Coburg Place, Edinburgh

PROFESSOR MARTIN ROBERTSON, 7a Parker Street, Cambridge (formerly of the Dept. of Classical Archaeology, Oxford University)

DR NICHOLAS RUPKE, University Museum, Oxford

PROFESSOR ALAN TORMEY, Dept. of Philosophy, University of Maryland, Baltimore County, Catonsville, Md. 21228, USA

PROFESSOR BARRIE WILSON, Dept. of Architecture, Edinburgh University, 20 Chambers Street, Edinburgh

DR ANTHONY WINTERBOURNE, Dept. of Philosophy, City of Birmingham Polytechnic, Margaret Street, Birmingham

PROFESSOR LEWIS WOLPERT, FRS, Dept. of Biology applied to Medicine, Middlesex Hospital Medical School, London

ACKNOWLEDGEMENTS

Grateful appreciation is due: first, and above all, to the School of Epistemics, Edinburgh University (Director, Dr Barry Richards) not only for Academic sponsorship of this meeting, but for the direct and indirect practical help so generously given by their staff in the manifold aspects of its organisation: secretarial assistance, xeroxing, catering and arrangement of accommodation for participants etc.; to the Seminars Committee of the Faculty of Social Sciences for financial assistance; to the British Academy for provision of travelling and subsistence funds for Dr Nicholas Rupke; to the Richard Bradford Trust for a generous grant towards travelling and subsistence expenses for several other participants (through the good offices of Dr R. B. McConnell); and to the Aberdeen University Press for their cooperation in publishing a full report of the proceedings of the conference and defrayment of the expenses of providing a transcript of the Discussion.

INTRODUCTION

Art and Science are usually assumed to be distinct aspects of culture, with differing aims and results requiring contrasting talents, skills and personal characteristics for their successful pursuit. But this has not always been so and even nowadays it is questionable whether the distinction is really as deep as is often supposed. Common denominators should be identifiable beyond the relatively superficial level at which the practice of either art or science is simply an expression of human activity in general: there may be aspects within the processes of scientific discovery and artistic invention which are shared by both practices either when science or art take particular forms or indeed in their deep structures. Once the products of scientific or artistic activity have taken their place as distinct elements in science or art, any similarities may be quite faint—shadows extinguished by the bright lights of cultural categorisation—but as we track them back through the hands and minds of their makers within the historical context of their creation, the common denominators begin to appear.

This is something of a hypothesis and it was the aim of this conference to explore it with reference to the work of artists and scientists in the history of mankind. In doing so, we hoped to learn something about the structures of artistic and scientific activity, about those aspects which art and science have in common and about the ways in which they are both manifestations of human expression; and particularly to go some way towards questioning the depth of the contemporary split between science and art.

It began in the form of a proposal presented to the Steering Committee of the School of Epistemics at Edinburgh University in November 1979 which provoked considerable interest and led to the committee accepting the role of academic sponsor for the project and the formation of a 4-member sub-committee (see below) responsible for its organisation.

The primordium of the idea for a debate to explore the significance of common ground amongst scientists and artists appeared first in an article (by one of us) in the journal *Trends in Biochemical Sciences* much earlier (Jan. 1977). This later hardened into a suggestion that the issue might be one suitable for an organised discussion amongst scientists and artists themselves. As a general proposition, this was not, of course, entirely original. Indeed, the cultural climate had for some time been conducive to a 'reconciliation' between art and science, at least in the sense of an increased desire, on both 'sides' to understand better the aims and methods of the other.

It would, in fact, be appropriate to recognise the enthusiasm and influence of the late Professor Waddington of this University in that respect. 'Wad' would surely have approved of this meeting and his participation would have greatly added to its interest and value. The idea, then, was not revolutionary, but the specific element of focusing attention on a limited period of time in a restricted cultural and geographical area and placing emphasis primarily on an historical approach, had not previously been exploited.

The proposed structure of the meeting went through a number of stages in its development. One of the earliest proposals was that its coverage should be narrowly restricted to a single, relatively short period in the cultural history of one country. The latter half of the nineteenth century in France seemed one possibility: an era of rapid and fundamental scientific development both in the physical and biological sciences, in literature, in philosophy and in visual art. This was abandoned in favour of a much wider coverage, dealing with examples from all over the world and at very different epochs: classical Greece, for instance, China during the first millenium AD, Islamic art and science in the Middle Ages, the European Renaissance, contemporary developments etc. But this rapidly showed itself to be impossibly ambitious for the two-day conference which was the most we felt to be practicable and we finally opted modestly for a compromise covering the relatively small area of the last 200 years in Western Culture. Even this proved, in the end, to concentrate itself rather on the period of the turn of the nineteenth century and mainly confined to this country—for the simple reason that most of those approached and who were available were inclined to specialise on some aspect of that particular epoch. And so, ironically, we returned, forcibly, to something rather similar to the first original proposal. In the event we do not feel that this was unfortunate; more important is that contributors were concerning themselves with areas and aspects of the subject with which they were truly competent to deal. Moreover it always seemed vital to limit the areas being considered, as well as the levels of approach, quite drastically in order to prevent participants wandering off in all directions and to keep discussion reasonably coherent.

From the very beginning there was easy agreement that the meeting should be considered as a 'workshop' to *explore* freely the proposition that 'common denominators' for art and science existed and were of significance and importance, and that it should therefore function informally and that participants, all or most of whom would be expected to be actively engaged in debate, should not exceed 40 in number, and should therefore be chosen by invitation. With cooperation of the Editors concerned, a brief notice of the meeting was inserted in *Leonardo* and in *Interdisciplinary Science Reviews*. Quite a number of interested people wrote to ask for invitations and in no case was it necessary to refuse such requests on the grounds that numbers had reached our set maximum. The final total of all participants was 37 and the proportions of art-orientated and science-orientated were remarkably equal, a rather surprising and very satisfactory balance being thus achieved without any manipulations!

In our approach to prospective participants, the objective of the 'workshop' was described as an attempt to 'uncover similar operative factors in art and science through a study of the work and working methods of selected artists and scientists in the historical period chosen'. And emphasis was placed on the need to focus on the idea that one of the most important features common to great art and great science is 'the sequence of breaks with tradition from time to time, leading to the development of revolutionary concepts of interpretation and the reorganisation of perception to create a new form of reality'.

During the early stages of organisation much needed encouragement, together with many suggestions of useful people to approach, was provided by Dr Frederic Samson (formerly of the Royal College of Art) and this was greatly appreciated. Later on Professor Rom Harré gave much valuable advice on the structure of the meeting and possible participants.

We believe that the standard of papers prepared by the major contributors is remarkably high; their efforts and achievement are deeply appreciated. We are grateful, indeed, to all participants: the principle speakers, those who took part in the debate and the few who just listened.

The report of the discussion, upon which we had set great store, may not prove to be quite so complete and valuable as had once been thought possible. This is partly due to shortage of space and the need for drastic editing and partly because the set-up for a transcribable recording was not entirely satisfactory and we had to rely too much on the relatively few voluntary write-ups by discussants of what they thought they had said; these are inevitably, with the best will in the world, very difficult to procure and not truly representative of the discussion as a whole. Beyond that, the editors have encouraged contributors to the discussion to accept abbreviations and even paraphrasing in order to clarify the meaning as well as, if necessary, to revise what they said, in the light of further thoughts on the subject after the meeting.

We hope that most readers will find something useful and interesting in this book. And we hope that they themselves may pursue the dialogue between artists and scientists here shown to be not only possible, but stimulating and productive. As a long-term objective it is also hoped that it may find its way into the course structure of universities and other centres of higher education to help break the present rigid polarisation between the so-called 'two cultures'.

MARTIN POLLOCK
KEITH BROWN
AUBREY MANNING
BARRIE WILSON

1

WHAT IS THE 'ZEITGEIST'? PROSPECTS AND PROBLEMS FOR THE INVESTIGATION OF THE INTERACTION OF ARTS AND SCIENCES

Rom Harré

Sub-Faculty of Philosophy, Oxford University

SUMMARY

If we are able to identify certain common factors or similar themes in the arts and sciences of a period, two questions arise. What is the nature of the similarities and how does it happen that they come about in diverse fields at the same time? I suggest that there are three ways in which the arts and sciences can be thematically coordinate: through explicit content, through metatheoretical beliefs which show up in similar or identical methods and finally through deep structural identities, being based as it were upon a common plan. The question of historical change and of origins cannot be solved with a single theory and I believe that dialectic, evolutionary and structural theories are all required.

I take it that most of the contributors to this volume would be reluctant to take the concept of 'Zeitgeist' literally. I introduce it merely as a term standing in for the proper way to refer to an as yet undiscovered mechanism by reference to which we might look for an explanation of certain facts in the history of civilisation. In particular it would stand in for a cluster of proper explanatory concepts needed to make intelligible to ourselves the cultural coherence of those eras in European history which are sufficiently far removed from us to appear as some kind of wholes.

So far as I follow the examples discussed in this volume, the coherence of a culturally distinctive era can be, at least partially, abstracted as certain correlations between some features of scientific activity (techniques, concepts, etc.) and some apparently similar features of the products of an art form (say painting or music) or even the method of their production. I postpone for the moment discussion of the puzzle about how we could reasonably make judgements of similarity or difference between such highly disparate activities. Keller (see p. 97) offers us the 'granularity' of scientific atomism and pointillisme as generic correlations. Emmer (p. 90) discloses quite specific simultaneous invention of similar forms by artists and mathematicians (Bill and the Moebius strip; Escher and the Penrose triangle). These are correlations between quite different kinds of matters, a theory and a technique in the one case and two instances of the same geometric structure in the other. Perhaps both could be accommodated under some sort of idea of 'common concept' if we could get that notion straight.

This rather vague beginning seems to condense into two questions:

What is it that can be found in each of music, art, chemistry, mathematics, garden design etc., that can be seen to have common form in the arts and sciences of an era?
Why do the diverse productions of at least some ages share common features?

Many further questions are presumed in answering these. For instance, is there some kind of temporal gradient or slope so that innovations of the kind we are trying to identify appear at one focus in a culture (say amongst poets) and diffuse at some discernible rate to other parts and persons? Did innovations in fashion start in Paris and diffuse to London and Rome? Or was it somehow that in Paris designers of clothes were particularly sensitive to the 'spirit of the age', exemplifying rather than creating 'it'?

If the fact of correlation is regarded as established, and all its presumptions clarified, there seem to be two problems to which students of culture might address themselves.

(i) The 'Zeitgeist' problem: what is (are) the mechanism(s) of correlation?
(ii) The problem of cultural change: what is (are) the origin(s) of the phenomena whose correlations pose the puzzles to the solution of which this volume is addressed?

Kepler was the first author I know of to undertake to construct a comprehensive theory of cultural coherences. His answers to my two leading questions above were simple to state, but needed great detail in their working out. His *Harmonices Mundi* is a massive study (Kepler, 1618). According to Kepler, architecture, music, mathematics and astronomy have certain mathematical proportions and harmonies in common. Commonalities of form could be exemplified in practically anything that has structure. Certain ratios are particularly pleasing to a Neo-platonic God who can be expected to have incorporated them in his productions. In so far as we can grasp His nature we can understand the world in His terms. There is a weaker version of this general viewpoint, a kind of Kantian and mundane version. *We* love certain mathematical harmonies and so we recognise as structured only those things which exemplify them. But Kepler would not have accepted that interpretation of the *Harmonices Mundi*. For him the Renaissance was not just a moment in history, but *the* moment. It was just then that Johannes Kepler himself glimpsed the eternal mathematical and architectonic verities and made them available for the rest of mankind in the form of mathematical theories of the structure of the world.

Before we proceed to a detailed examination of cases, it might be advisable to set out some possible ways in which cultural matters (and I include the sciences in culture) could be correlated.

(1) A scientific theory and an art form could share a common content. Rupke (see p. 30) shows how in the early nineteenth century, geologists and painters shared a common belief in a flood (or floods), a common diluvialism. Secularisation of ancient theological dogmas could perhaps be identified as the locus of a system of shared beliefs animating both painters and geologists. Direct and explicit borrowings from geology to painting (and vice versa, cf. the painterliness of early geological illustrations) are easily demonstrable.
(2) More difficult to establish is what I might call 'commonality of style'. Keller offers us the tantalising historical parallel between the return of physics to atomism after its long dallying with fields, partly through the establishment of the existence of 'atoms' of electricity (electrons) by J. J. Thomson, and the appearance of a kind of atomism of light and colour in the pointillisme of Seurat. Pointillisme is, I suppose, a kind of painterly technique that leads to what one might properly call a 'style'. (I think Gombrich, 1960, has shown that distinctions of style are by no means always a matter of distinctive technique.) Chiaroscuro is another example of a technique-cum-style, I think. One might be inclined to see atomism in physics as a very high level theory which dominated the period and resulted in something like a style in physics, though I am not so sure that style is as apt a word for what happened in physics as it is for the commonality of method, subject, etc. that the term picks out in painting. Can a technique and a theory be juxtaposed in this way? Keller shows how pointillisme as a technique was the product of a theory of the nature of colour, so in the end in this case a comparison of like with like is being undertaken.
(3) The theories in (2) are not theories *of* art or science, they are theories *in* art and science. However, commonalities might occur in the products of an age by virtue of a shared metatheory, a theory about science and art. In the chapters discussing the Romantic movement in art and science, certain very general thematic terms like 'polarity', 'unity' are not so much high level general concepts in science, like *mass*, but rather determinants of the desiderata by which anything is to count as explanatoriness in science and profundity in literary productions.

Eric Forbes has suggested a fourth way in which artistic production and scientific theories can be alike, by virtue of certain analogies. Probably this suggestion should not be taken as drawing our attention to a special way in which disparate productions can 'have something in common'. It could be taken as reminder that it is not just homologies that are in question, that along with likenesses we must pay attention to differences. Each of the above three modes of commonality could be refined by following Forbes' suggestion. For instance, if to the question, 'What is the analogue of "polarity" in electrical studies' we answer 'Positive and negative charge' this should prompt a re-examination of the literary uses of the idea of polar opposition.

But what of the mechanisms by which any of the above kinds of correlations could be established in an era? What, in detail, is Rupke's 'common pool of cultural resources'?

A deep-structure form of explanation of correlations treats the correlations of the products of human activity as superficial similarities, having no productive or causal connections between them. Each is produced by one 'deep structure' or underlying template. It is because each is produced from the one common template that accounts for their similarity (see Figure 1).

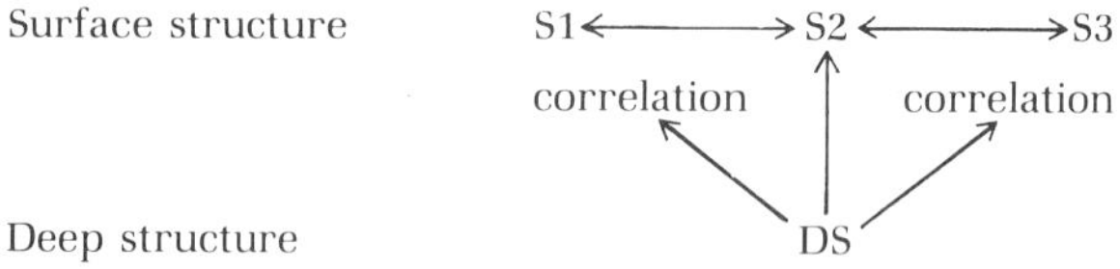

FIGURE 1

It would be natural to take DS and the operations of the productive process to be unconscious. The problem of the nature and location of DS, the common template, becomes pressing if this sort of theory is to be realised concretely in explanations of particular historically given correlations. The idea that the processes of production must be unconscious suggests that they are sited in individual persons. But it could be that what count as deep structures are located somehow in collectives, groups of people perhaps with some kind of social structure. I will return to elaborate this thought below.

I have already suggested that a commonality between cultural products may be no more than a common metatheory (that is a theory about the form or content required of theories in a common domain). But a metatheory could be the basis which maintains correlations in some cases. A metatheory might be metaphysical, that is it might be a systematic way of expounding the virtues of a linked system of concepts, as it was I believe in the Romantic era. But it could be a set of methodological prescriptions. It was in that way that Positivism engendered a set of like cognitive products and social practices. This would explain the similarities between certain forms of economics, literary productions, therapies (behaviour) in the immediate past.

Why does a certain metatheory attract subscribers to itself at a certain period? Why, for instance, is there a history of recurring episodes of science declining into postivism? The oscillations between positivism and realism have been rocking away for at least two thousand years. Some further level of analysis of the metatheory seems to be needed. It might take the form of a psychological study of the kinds of persons who form up in these opposing camps. It might be a kind of hermeneutical winkling out of the inner political assumptions of those points of view (cf. the works of J. Habermas, particularly *Knowledge and Human Interests,* 1972).

This rough sketch of the general character of cultural resources does not solve the problem of the location of these sources. *Where* are they? The arts and sciences of the Romantic period are recognisable, unified and coherent, and it is the persistence of certain beliefs and obsessions that explains it, I believe. But, as modern thinkers, we cannot accept any kind of Neo-platonic answer to the question as to the nature and location of these themes and of the common 'something' that explains why these themes and obsessions are shared. Without its men and women the universe would have no aesthetic qualities and the very concept of seeking to realise an ideal would have no place. So whatever the answer to why there are persisting themes, it must be human. I shall argue that it lies in something the French call *réprésentations sociales*. I throw in this pregnant French phrase to make it clear that I repudiate any naive suggestion that people just learn certain modes of doing things and ways of thinking from each other. Experience tells us that people can learn, in a way, only what they already know. Someone is a guru to a movement only because he is already being copied. *Réprésentations sociales* exist prior to anyone appearing as their particular embodiment. But if that dogmatic statement is to be made good one must at least show how.

In any civilisation there seem to be two realities encompassing enough to be the sources of its idiosyncratic style. As Marx saw, there is the system of material production and its social organisation which enters overtly or covertly into every social relation, and so into every social product. But I think it is nothing like so prepotent an influence as Marx seems to have believed. There is another all encompassing and permanent but ever-changing human reality, the endless conversation that binds human beings into a society and to which in small or large measure we are all contributors (Rorty, 1980). I believe that it is the quality and demands of that conversation that is the most potent influence in forming our minds. The human conversation is conducted in so many semiotic modes. It is from this discourse, be it linguistic or conducted in terms of some more primitive symbolic system, say through the food and drink we offer and accept, that we appropriate whatever we need for our personal projects. I believe that the very possibility of framing such projects and the purposive or intentional actions that we use to realise them, is a product of our participation in the conversations of mankind. I hold the conversation to be primary and the social system of material production to be a secondary and often dependent reality. By talking of *conversation* I mean to emphasise the essentially semiotic form of every cultural product (cf. the contributions of Lloyd Jones and Richard Gregory in this volume pp. 149 and 164). We are enabled to talk of the syntax (form) of all such products, of their semantics (content) and of the conversational themes which they subserve (realised in what I have called 'meta-theories').

The problem for the historian and sociologist of culture is, I believe, posed by the fact that the conversation, though it is the fundamental human reality, is ephemeral. It leaves behind only our occasional appropriations; works of art, memories, old cars, motets, scientific theories, potsherds, yellowing menus and concert programmes. To reach the heart of the historical process we must try to reconstruct the conversation that was babbling on during the production of the works in which we have taken an interest.

Were the forms of all human products always the same we could look for the principles of their production at any time, including our own. But the fact that style seems to be as labile as anything in our culture suggests that not only should we try to construct a classification of styles, modes and so on, but also try to explain their succession. To catalogue the common factors that appear from time to time in the arts and sciences is to offer only a kinematics of change. We should try for a dynamics.

But to try to construct a theory of the forces or mechanisms of change is hopeless without some sort of solution to the problem of the nature of social invariants and the criteria for their identification. If there is to be change, rather than a mere succession of different beings, it must be possible not only to say what is different about a new state of affairs but what has remained the same. The point is of some immediate consequence. On the lunatic fringe of the philosophy of science the idea has been put forward that the history of science is a discontinuous sequence of autonomous moments (Feyerabend, 1975). These moments might roughly be called 'theories', each of which by determining the meaning of its own vocabulary defines its own form of evidence. Theories cannot be compared one with another, particularly with respect to such epistemic goods as truth. On this view science is not a progressive revelation of the inner workings of the processes of nature, but a drunkard's walk, having no direction and no terminus. Scarcely any serious person would subscribe to such a view, but it does force our attention on to something we have not perhaps sufficiently studied, namely what it is that is conserved when one theory supersedes another. The same question could be posed for the history of an art form. What is it that unifies into a progression the successive ways of painting that went on in, say, English ateliers from 1780 to 1880? What is it that makes them all 'painting'? If we could say what it is that makes a succession of theories all scientific theories, we might be some way towards answering the question of what it is that makes them all theories of inheritance.

Philosophers of science have proposed two main kinds of invariant, to link successive theories into a progression, presuming that our intuitions that each is a scientific theory is well grounded. One kind of invariant we could perhaps call 'cognitive'. Theories are linked into a progression by virtue of the fact that certain important terms in the theories of the sequence have overlapping meanings (Papineau, 1979). This could perhaps be expressed in terms of a partition of rules of use, into core rules and peripheral rules. Between any pair of successive theories some of the core rules for important terms must be the same. The other kind of invariant is non-cognitive, lying, it is supposed, outside any moment of human theorising. It is that to which the terms in the theory refer, some entity, property or process in the world, which is independent of men (Putnam, 1975). It might be argued that the Pacific Island Continent is the common referent of both *Terra Australis* and Australia, and that during the last millenium a great deal has been found out about that *thing*, and that we have gradually corrected our ideas about *it*. In short philosophers of science have proposed both an internal and an external invariant to define what it is for there to be scientific change.

A thorough-going study of common factors in arts and sciences must take some account of the problem of invariants. Do common styles, contents, etc. wax and wane together? If so what is it in painting, music and so on that unifies the sequence of different moments into a progression? We must be able to identify the arrival and departure of a stylistic variant, so to speak. I hope that in the substantive chapters of this work it will be possible to make out what sorts of criteria are implicit in the judgements of historians as to whether there has been a stylistic or other innovation, that determine whether there could be said to have been a historically continuous practice.

If all that has gone well, we might be in possession of a description of that which is to be explained. The fact of change as well as the prior fact of correlation between arts and sciences has so to speak been established. If I may remind us of the tests Mill suggested to tell whether a relationship of correlation was causal: if there is not only correlation but co-variation then we are strongly inclined to judge a relationship causal. This is why period studies are so important in this field, since if we show that some common factor has come to both the arts and the sciences at about the same time, and has disappeared from both more or less together, we have good grounds for suspecting a more than accidental connection. But as a preliminary we should take heed of the warning issued by Rupke (p. 30). It would be altogether too facile to look for 'linear' explanations in which, say, a social phenomenon (industrialisation) was offered as the one and efficient cause of a cultural phenomenon (Romanticism) say by a Blakean reaction against the 'dark, Satanic mills'. Rupke's phrase 'borrowing from and contributing to a general pool of cultural resources' sounds right to describe the process, but how are we to explain changes in that pool?

I think that there are three main ways available for explaining change: dialectic (based on a tension-resolution format); evolutionary (based on a mutation-selection format) and finally structural (based on a transformational format—cf. Harré, 1979). If we are to hope for anything like a comprehensive theory of social change (and indeed change of any cultural product whatever) we shall find ourselves calling on all three. A rough outline of how they interrelate to provide an overall theory goes as follows.

Mutations appear because of the resolution of certain tensions that have arisen within a practice, a group, a theory, etc. But not all innovations spread. Some modifications to, or innovations in, practices are not copied by anyone outside the immediate circle of the innovators. One must presume a selection environment which favours or does not favour the spread of a mutant practice, be it poetic metaphor, novel form of greeting, new way of classifying plants and animals, etc. I take the basic selection environment to be the endless and pervasive human conversation carried on by the structured ensemble that makes up the human population. That conversation has certain persisting forms which are not easily set aside and it is these that determine what spreads and what perishes. For instance, the social distinction between men and women has persisted through all the recent changes and attempted changes in social relations between the sexes. Though sartorial symbols marking the social distinctions between human beings of different sexes have altered, they have done so in such a way as to preserve the possibility of marking the distinction. Here we have the transformation format.

A research programme that would look for an understanding or explanation of change (and its equally fascinating sibling, invariance) should be directed at answering three questions for any identifiable practice.

Between what elements would one expect tensions to exist, in any field of human endeavour and how are these resolved?

Which resolutions are read by the folk involved as novelties, and against what background of invariance are they so read?

What are the selection conditions which determine whether or not a novel practice will spread, and what invariants do these selection conditions reflect?

Finally one must have some idea as to why the selection mechanisms of a social order abort some but encourage other innovations. It seems reasonable to think in terms of a concept of adaptation suitable to the context and the subject matter involved. In social matters one can say roughly that a mutant practice is well adapted if it serves to enhance what people of that subculture take to be their honour and the marks of their dignity. A practice is ill adapted if it tends to lead to their humiliation. Since societies are complex it is necessary to ask in specific cases whose dignity we have in mind. It may be adaptive to insist on social practices that humiliate most people if we are thinking in terms of explaining the encouragement of a practice that advantages the few. The point I am driving at with this example from outside the field of interest of this volume, is that what counts as adaptation is to be decided relative to the projects of the people concerned. There could not be a generic concept of adaptiveness which would serve to explain the fate of every kind of innovation in every field. This raises the question of the extent to which we can think of both scientists and artists as having common projects or at least projects of the same kind. Some such assumption needs to be made if we are to try to treat the appearance of a novel form, idea, structure, technique etc. in both the arts and the sciences of a period (cf. Davies, p. 107). Were the projects of the artists and the scientists wholly different and quite independent of one another it would be the most astonishing coincidence that each moiety of a culture felt itself and/or its power to carry out its projects enhanced by the very same innovation.

REFERENCES

Feyerabend, P. K. (1975) *Against Method,* N.L.B. London.

Gombrich, E. H. (1960) *Art and Illusion.* Phaidon, London.

Habermas, J. (1972) *Knowledge and Human Interests.* Heinemann, London.

Harré, R. (1979) *Social Being.* Blackwell, Oxford.

Kepler, J. (1618) *Harmonices Mundi.* Linz.

Papineau, D. (1979) *Theory and Meaning.* Clarendon Press, Oxford.

Putnam, H. (1975) *Philosophical Papers,* vol. II, pp. 235–8. Cambridge University Press, Cambridge.

Rorty, R. (1980) *Philosophy and the Mirror of Nature.* Blackwell, Oxford.

2

GOETHE'S VISION OF SCIENCE

Eric G. Forbes

History of Medicine and Science Unit, Department of History, University of Edinburgh

SUMMARY

Goethe, in his *Farbenlehre*, made an uncompromising attack upon Newton's optical experiments which was seen by David Brewster as an attempt to supplant the inductive stream of newtonian natural philosophy with the *Naturphilosophie* of the German Romantic school of thought. Goethe criticised the mathematical physicists for their preoccupation with quantifiable phenomena and consequent neglect of qualitative attributes. The advantage of his colour theory over the newtonian one was that it perceived colour subjectively as well as objectively and in a wider physiological and psychological context: its prime disadvantage was that while accounting qualitatively for many observable phenomena, it failed to yield accurate quantitative predictions. This historical example raises the question of the adequacy of current scientific enquiry as *the* means by which we seek to attain Truth, and exemplifies the need for a study of the history of science that will reveal both the limitations of its hypothetico-deductive methodology and the role of imagination in scientific creativity.

It is not my purpose, in the short space at my disposal, to attempt an analysis of Johann Wolfgang von Goethe's scientific works (Kuhn, 1971) nor, more specifically, to interpret his views on the theory of colour which many persons, more qualified than I, have already sought to do (Richter, 1938). Rather, my intention is simply to draw attention to the difference in attitude between the restrictive mechanistic view of nature accepted by the newtonian physicists of the early nineteenth century, and Goethe's own all-embracing vision of God's creation. In view of the complexity and extensiveness of his scientific writings, I shall refer particularly to his theory of colour (Judd, 1970). As far as his detailed investigations in botany, geology, and zoology are concerned, suffice it to say that Goethe was seeking nothing less than a theory that could explain all living forms; and usually extrapolated generalisations that were far broader in scope than his observations warranted.

Goethe's belief in the continuity, organic and divine unity of nature (with man an essential element in it) was moulded by the philosophy of Spinoza and his reading of the German edition of *Contemplation de la nature* by Charles Bonnet (1783) where the implications of the Chain of Being concept are explicitly developed. Instead of a unilinear hierarchy of Being, however, Goethe envisaged it as 'holistic', with each organic whole contained within another that was larger than itself. His constant quest for wholeness and continuity in nature, and acceptance of this hierarchical principle, place him in the neoplatonic tradition of European thought. The direct influence upon him, however, was Herder and, through him, Leibniz to whose writings he owed his preoccupation with analogies. These, coupled with his holistic view of nature, caused him on different occasions to draw comparisons between plants and animals, chemical and human behaviour, electrical forces and the human qualities of attraction or repulsion, and perhaps even led him to the study of comparative anatomy.

One analogy he did not accept was the mechanistic notions fostered during the eighteenth century by newtonian scientists, the French Encyclopaedists, the mathematicians Lagrange, Laplace, Clairaut and Euler, to mention but a few, that man is a machine and the universe a celestial clock. The successful application of Newton's three laws of motion and inverse-square law of gravitation to the problems of planetary astronomy seemed to vindicate the rationalist view that one could dispense with God altogether as the causal agent of changes in the mechanical workings of the solar system. Goethe's own view was that mathematical formulae and symbols were no substitute for the phenomena of nature, and that by schematising the world of nature in this way one is obscuring rather than illuminating it. In other words, he preferred to adhere to an organic interpretation rather than subscribe to the rationalist tendency to translate everything into quantitative terms.

These anti-rationalist and neoplatonic attitudes were already firmly implanted in Goethe's mind when, in the early 1790s, he began to extend his scientific studies beyond natural history into the field of the physical sciences (Nisbet, 1972). Herder had already introduced him some time previously to the empirical tradition of Francis Bacon, and he had been particularly attracted to the latter's discussion of 'idols'—prejudices that prevent men from perceiving nature accurately—in the first part of the *Novum Organum* (1620). When writing his essay *Der Versuch als Vermittler* in 1792, Goethe believed that the procedure of using experiments to prove hypotheses is pernicious, and that no theoretical constructions should be set up until observational data themselves are assembled and known. Thus his intention at that time was to gather all available experiences in optics and to conduct all experiments himself . . . 'then to frame such propositions as one can term experiences of the highest kind and wait to see how far it is possible to arrange these in turn under a higher principle'. Only a large number of phenomena viewed together and ordered methodically could, in his opinion, finally provide something that could be classed as a theory. Notice how closely this parallels Bacon's method of examining a multitude of instances before seeking to find a quality shared by them all, and eventually formulating a general definition of that quality. Goethe's continuing concern with the relationship between experiment and theory is well-testified by his correspondence during 1798 with Friedrich Schiller, in the course of which he praises Boyle's *Experiments touching colour* (1664) published, as he remarks, before Newton 'tyrannised' optics with his hypothesis in a completely anti-Baconian manner.

By the time Goethe came to write his *Farbenlehre* (1805), however, he was referring to Bacon as a 'Hercules . . . who cleanses a stable of dialectic dung, only to let it fill up again with empirical dung'. The reason for this switch in attitude is that he had meanwhile made intensive historical studies in the history of the theory of colours, including Thomas Sprat's *History* of the Royal Society of London (1667) from which he came to realise that this body had *not* followed its motto 'nullius in verba'. Its condoning of Newton's theory of optics was a case in point. Goethe regarded Bacon himself as being partially to blame, since the attempts of others to follow his radical empiricism by dispensing with all theory had been responsible for the acceptance of ill-considered theories or *ad hoc* hypotheses.

In all his scientific work, Goethe's aim was to penetrate the *mind* of Nature. He was not content merely to explain her *workings* in terms of the laws which scientists of his and previous generations had discovered. Contemporary scientists were in general sympathetic to this attitude—particularly in his native Germany, where the ideology of German Romanticism was reacting strongly against the popular mechanistic world-view (Anderson, 1941). Indeed, as David Brewster tells us in his anonymous review of Charles Eastlake's translation of Goethe's colour theory, even British scientists were rather disposed to welcome into their sombre territory 'the bold, though unbidden minstrel, who could set to music the abstractions of science' (Brewster, 1840). But this spirit of toleration ceased to exist when Goethe in his *Farbenlehre* dared to 'assail the mild precepts of Newton with the shafts of sarcasm and ridicule', and marshalled against them 'all the mysticism of an unbridled imagination—all the ambiguities of allegory and symbol—and all the sophistries of German metaphysics'. It then became necessary 'to protect our Inductive Philosophy from the inroads of a new School [German Romanticism], in which the reason and the imagination were permitted to exercise a mingled and a dangerous control' (Brewster, 1840). The main reason for Brewster's concern, apart from his indignation at the outright rejection of Newton's description and interpretation of his optical experiments (Newton, 1704; Whiteside, 1973) was that Goethe was stepping outside the recognised boundaries of natural science by seeking explanations which transcended the realm of application of the hypothetico-deductive method of reasoning. The accompanying allegory and symbolism were, of course, necessary means of achieving this.

There was a real need, in Goethe's view, to unite the various branches of human knowledge. He recognised that he had to understand what faculties and virtues in his own intellectual make-up would help him to obtain a unified vision of the world of nature; but was aware that he had no methodological criteria or formula for understanding how he managed to create his own poetry—other, perhaps, than his habit of meditating long and executing his literary work rapidly which, he felt, might have given his productions animation and energy (Young, 1813–14). Since he could not recognise any principles of his own that could be applied to other fields of cultural endeavour, he decided to learn and apply the rules of painting in the hope that he would thus be incited to more passionate exertions. His lack of natural artistic talent would, he believed, be an advantage to him since it would force him to abide by such rules. His journey to Italy to learn the techniques of the fine arts indeed had the beneficial effect of making him aware of the errors in his previous artistic attempts, and to begin again from elementary principles. As far as the theory of colouring itself was concerned, he discovered that the practice of the best artists was really a matter of taste formed by habits which often reflected a prejudiced attitude of mind or of study.

The phenomena of colour greatly attracted Goethe, and he borrowed some optical instruments from Court Councillor C. W. Büttner of Jena in order to investigate prismatic spectra. When he eventually came to project sunlight through one of Büttner's prisms on to a white wall, he found that instead of observing the seven colours of the rainbow he saw only blue-violet at one end of the spectrum and orange-red at the other, while the middle of the spectrum still appeared white. It is interesting to note, in this connection, that when conducting a similar experiment in 1665, the young Newton had expected to obtain a circular image of the hole in the shutter through which the sunlight was entering his room, but found instead that the spectrum was five times as long as it was broad (Shapiro, 1980). Fundamentally, this was why he himself interpreted the observed phenomenon as due to the superposition of co-axial circles of differently-coloured light, to which his analysis of white light into rays of differing refrangibility was but a logical corollary. Goethe, on the other hand, had no hesitation in asserting that the newtonian doctrine of colours being split up then overlapping so as to destroy the appearance of colours was a 'perverse theory', a 'joke', an 'unbelievable folly', 'strange', and 'baroque' (Wells, 1967–8). It led him to pursue his own experiments on colour independently, even though a physicist friend who was assisting him tried to convince him that the appearances could be explained on Newton's principles (Grassman, 1853).

The crux of this ideological issue is well grasped, in my opinion, in an article published a decade ago by George Wells bearing the simple but apt title 'Goethe's Qualitative Optics' (Wells, 1971). Here it is stressed that Goethe's main objection to Newton, or to mathematical physicists in general, was that any numerical or geometrical representation of the world of nature must necessarily ignore many of the details and properties of physical phenomena, and hence produce distortion. Goethe recognised that in order to solve a physical problem by mathematical methods one had first to express the physical data in mathematical form, manipulate the mathematical formulae, then interpret the final result of this manipulation back into terms of physical reality. For him, however, the weakness in this procedure was that it took account of quantity but not of quality; and since he regarded these attributes as polar opposites by which reality appears to us, he argued that many physical appearances can never be represented quantitatively.

Goethe also uses polar opposites as the basis of his theory of colour, supposing these to be light and darkness. A turbid medium (such as smoke or dust) was supposed to make them reconcilable. At first sight, this notion appears to have the merit of being visually perceptible and less complex than the derived notions of refrangibility of light rays or their refractive index.

Yet they are dogmatic assertions that can be upheld only by ignoring or distorting some of the observable facts. More fundamentally, however, the acceptance of Goethe's 'axioms of explanation' implies that the truth about Nature is to be derived from sense-experience, a presupposition that was later to be destroyed by the distinguished German physiologist Johannes Müller when he demonstrated that sensation is no guide to the nature of the stimulus (Müller, 1826). In other words, reasoning inductively from effect to cause is no guarantee that the conclusions obtained are valid.

It was nevertheless his unquestioning adoption of this Baconian attitude which accounts for the vehemence of Goethe's rejection of Newton's interpretation of the visible spectrum; for his own purpose in conducting his optical experiments was to seek each time a few more facts and gradually accumulate sufficient data from which to draw a theoretical inference. That is, to record a multitude of related observable facts without formulating a prior hypothesis; or, as one of his contemporaries puts it when singing the praises of Aristotle: 'catching Nature in the act, without attempting, after modern fashion, to put her to the torture' (Gillies, 1797). In contrast, Goethe criticised Newton for 'putting Nature to the rack' (Wells, 1967–8), and did not fully appreciate that the latter's optical experiments were deliberately designed to isolate the most crucial factors on which his theory depended—not to reveal the entire range of optical phenomena, as Goethe himself was intent on doing.

A crucial distinction which was not made by Goethe but by his distinguished contemporary Hermann von Helmholtz, was between mental images (or pictures) that must resemble the reality they represent, and symbols (or signs) that need not, but could do so (Wells, 1971). Goethe himself divorced the world perceived through the senses from that derived from the manipulation of the symbols used in mathematical equations, and was led to the belief that physics should use all of its resources to penetrate the properties of nature, whereas mathematics must proclaim its independence from all external reality. In contrast to Immanuel Kant, who regarded the truths of mathematics as knowledge stemming from innate ideas, Goethe ascribed the certainty of mathematics to the logical rigour of the deductive operations carried out with arbitrary symbols and regarded the results obtained by manipulation of these symbols as mere tautologies that never transcended the definitional premisses from which they had been obtained. A late medieval philosopher accustomed to relating views of the nature of knowledge to the context of the problem of universals, would have dubbed Kant a 'Nominalist' and Goethe an 'Extreme Realist'. This same mental attitude was largely responsible for Goethe's lack of appreciation of the advantages of a mathematical approach to Nature, inasmuch as it stifled his appreciation of the fact that the various optical phenomena described in the *Farbenlehre* are dependent upon the size of atmospheric particles (for this measureable quantity is intimately related to the quality of turbidity), and that the nature of light waves can be analysed into the quantitative elements amplitude, frequency, and velocity. Thomas Young himself, for example, had measured particle size and interference fringes in order to determine wavelength (Peacock and Leitch, 1855).

On the other hand, the traditional physical interpretation of colour as the result of a splitting-up of white light (in which darkness is dismissed as 'nothingness'), though capable of providing an adequate quantitative scientific interpretation of the observable phenomena, makes no distinction between spectral colours and colour pigments; neither does it encourage any attempt to conceive the nature of colour in its physiological or psychological contexts, nor to capture the aesthetic and emotional roles of colour in creative works of art. Thus I was particularly pleased to note, while preparing this brief lecture, that the spirit of independent enquiry which Goethe epitomises still lives on in a relatively recent book which professes to apply Goethe's theory of colour to works of art (Schindler, 1964). The method advocated for developing one's creative instincts is to witness the creation of prismatic colours and then to make practical experiments and exercises in colour. The results of these, as depicted in Schindler's accompanying plates, illustrate the point that a 'dead' scientific theory can still be a stimulus to creative art.

A similar, but somewhat more general approach to the understanding of colour is described by Josef Albers, who asserts that distinct colour effects are produced not by the mechanical application of laws or rules of colour harmony, but through: 'an awareness of the interdependence of color with form and placement; with quantity (which measures amount, respectively extension and/or number, including recurrence); with quality (intensity of light and/or hue); and with pronouncement (by separating or connecting boundaries)' (Albers, 1975). For him, the only way to achieve a complete comprehension of the nature of colour is to couple an empirical approach—using what he terms 'sample studies'—with fantasy and imagination.

These subjective elements, so necessary to the creation of artistic productions, are generally regarded as inadmissible in the currently-accepted method of scientific enquiry. It seems to me, however, that a creative scientist likewise requires a leap of imaginative insight in order to transcend the realm of experience from which his generalisations have been derived, and that the fundamental dichotomy lies rather in the inadequacy—as opposed to the error—of the scientist's approach. Through the assimilation of data, application of the hypothetico-deductive method of reasoning, and mathematical formulations, he will create an image of some natural phenomenon (such as colour) which other scientists may independently seek to verify. Yet, even if the *intrinsic* qualities of that image should be faithfully reproduced by such objective tests, the kind of *relational* qualities to which Albers was referring in his study of the interaction of colour lie outwith the scope of the traditional scientific method. As a general rule, therefore, the scientist's conception of Truth and criteria for attaining it are more restrictive than those of the artist.

To conclude: Goethe's theory of colour is nowadays generally discredited, for reasons such as have been given. It nevertheless provides an historical example of how an independent and original thinker coming face to face for the first time with a traditionally-accepted theory may, depending on his philosophical attitude regarding the nature and purpose of experimental method and logical standpoint on the theory of knowledge, experience a conflict with the accepted norms (or paradigms) which characterise it. At the same time, it raises the live issue of the adequacy of current scientific enquiry as the means of seeking Truth, and the possible need to make deliberate departures from the traditional mode of thinking to which our minds are conditioned through our schooling and higher education. Although it would be wrong to discredit science or reduce its dominance in academic curricula, we do need to encourage studies of the history of science and scientific method in order to increase awareness of the fact that many crucial scientific discoveries of the past have depended as much upon subjective factors such as fantasy or imagination as upon objective criteria such as the rigorous application of the hypothetico-deductive system of logical inference (Heisenberg, 1959).

REFERENCES

Albers, J. (1975) *Interaction of Color,* p. 2. Yale University Press, New Haven and London.

Anderson, E. N. (1941) German Romanticism as an Ideology of Cultural Crisis, *J. Hist. Ideas* **2,** 301–17.

Brewster, D. (1840) Goethe's Theory of Colours. Translated from the German, with Notes, by Charles Lock Eastlake, R.A., F.R.S. 8vo London 1840, *Edinburgh Review* **72,** 99–131. See, in particular, p. 99.

Gillies, J. (1797) *Aristotle's Ethics and Politics,* London, vol. 1, Introduction, p. 139.

Grassman, H. G. (1853) Zur Theorie der Farbenmischung, *Annalen der Physik und Chemie* **89,** 69–84.

Heisenberg, W. (1959) Die Goethesche und die Newtonsche Farbenlehre im Lichte der modernen Physik, *Wandlungen in den Grundlagen der Naturwissenschaften* **9,** erw. Aufl. Stuttgart.

Judd, D. B. (ed.) (1970) *Goethe's Theory of Colours, translated by C. L. Eastlake.* London and Cambridge, Mass.

Kuhn, D. (1971) Goethes Schriften zur Naturwissenschaft, *Goethe* **33,** 123–46.

Müller, J. P. (1826) *Zur vergleichenden Physiologie des Gesichtssinnes des Menschen und der Tiere nebst einen Versuch über die Bewegung der Augen und über den menschlichen Blick.* Leipzig.

Newton, I. (1704) *Optiks.* London.

Nisbet, H. B. (1972) *Goethe and the Scientific Tradition.* London.

Peacock, G. and Leitch, J. (eds.) (1855) *Miscellaneous Works of the Late Thomas Young, M.D., F.R.S.,* 3 vols. vol. 1, pp. 140–69. London.

Richter, M. (1938) *Das Schriftum über Goethes Farbenlehre.* Berlin.

Schindler, M. (1964) *Goethe's Theory of Colour.* East Grinstead.

Shapiro, A. E. (1980) The Evolving Structure of Newton's Theory of White Light and Colour, *Isis* **71,** 211–35.

Wells, G. A. (1967–8) Goethe's Scientific Method and Aims in the Light of his Studies in Physical Optics, *Publications of the English Goethe Society* **38,** 69–113. See p. 88.

—— (1971) Goethe's Qualitative Optics, *J. Hist. Ideas* **32,** 617–26.

Whiteside, D. T. (ed.) (1973) *The Unpublished First Version of Isaac Newton's Cambridge Lectures on Optics 1670–1672.* Cambridge.

Young, T. (1813–14) Review of *Zur Farbenlehre* in the *Quarterly Review* **10,** 427–41. See, in particular, Goethe's Confession, pp. 430–1.

3

NEWTON AND PAINTING

John Gage

Department of Art History, University of Cambridge

SUMMARY

Newton's *Opticks* was the most widely accessible of his works in the eighteenth century, and the one on which it was thought his reputation would chiefly rest. It was also the book in which he was prepared to frame hypotheses of the most wide-ranging kind. The eighteenth century was, too, the period when painters were for the most part members of academies, which sought to establish the principles of art, and in particular to fill the major gap in artistic theory by providing artists with a comprehensive theory of colour.

This paper attempts to outline the ways in which painters tried to reconcile the newtonian doctrines with their own experience, and takes as its foci theories of colour-mixing and of colour-harmony. It also traces the growing preoccupation with colour-perception during the century.

That God is Colouring Newton does shew,
And that the devil is a Black outline, all of us know.

Blake's words refer, of course, to a newtonian extension of the notion of God as light, and their context, an attack on Sir Joshua Reynolds and the Venetian style, suggest that, at the close of the eighteenth century, Newton's *Opticks* had become as much a pre-occupation of the painters as it had already been so abundantly of the poets (Nicolson, 1946; Greene, 1953; Murdoch, 1958; Guerlac, 1971; Gage, 1971). Long before the Romantic period it had been regarded as essential reading for landscape artists, who were themselves seen as something of experimenters in natural philosophy (Turnbull, 1740); but I propose in this paper to deal not with the general background to the acceptance of Newton's work among painters, but to look briefly at two more precisely documented instances of its effect. One is rather practical, and concerns methods of colour-mixture; the other is almost purely theoretical, and deals with a newtonian phase in the search for principles of colour-harmony. Both involve the concept of primary colours.

Newton's theory of colours, which was first published in the 1670s in the *Philosophical Transactions of the Royal Society*, appeared at a time when painters, especially in Rome and Paris, were seeking some firmer basis for the study of this aspect of their art. Nicholas Poussin, in an early self-portrait now in East Berlin, painted the year after the foundation of the French Academy of Painting and Sculpture (1648), shows himself holding a book *De*

Lumine et Colore; this is certainly not the most up-to-date treatment—by Descartes (1637)—but an eclectic and conservative compilation by Matteo Zaccolini (Blunt, 1966; Pedretti, 1973); it nevertheless proclaims an interest which was to play a prominent role in the discussions of the Academy after it became primarily a teaching institution in 1664 (Teyessèdre, 1957). It was an interest which united the Poussinistes and their rivals the Rubènistes within that institution, and it was the chief spokesman of the Rubènistes, Roger de Piles, who best outlined the problem facing the painter in his *Dialogue sur le Coloris* of 1672:

> During the all-but three hundred years since the revival of painting we can hardly reckon half-a-dozen painters who have used colour well; and yet one could list at least thirty who have been outstanding draughtsmen. The reason for this is that drawing has rules based on proportion, on anatomy, and on a continual experience of the same data (*de la mesme chose*: i.e. the human figure); whereas colouring has as yet hardly any well-known rules, and, since the studies made have differed according to the different subjects they treated, no very precise body of rules has yet been established.

A French didactic print of 1677/83 after the influential Roman teacher Carlo Maratta sums up this situation: students busy themselves with the study of drawing, perspective, anatomy, and, above all, ancient sculpture, while a palette and brushes stand idly by (Kutschera-Woborsky, 1919). Since the French Academy was the mother of all the many art academies founded during the the eighteenth century, and the large body of theoretical writing it engendered the model for most subsequent theory, these colouristic concerns carry a good deal of weight.

Doctrines of mixture

It may at first sight seem surprising that Newton's theory had any part to play in these developments, for it was chiefly concerned with the causes of colours, and only marginally with those subjective effects which were the central concern of painters. This is especially so in the case of the notion of primary colours, which had been clarified over the previous half-century or so through the experience of mixing paints (Gage, 1981). Robert Boyle, in a treatise of 1664 which stimulated Newton to make some of his earliest colour-experiments, had written:

> . . . much of the Mechanical use of Colours among Painters and Dyers, doth depend upon the Knowledge of what Colours may be produc'd by the Mixtures of Pigments so and so Colour'd. And . . . 'tis of advantage to the contemplative Naturalist, to know how many and which Colours are Primitive . . . and Simple, because it both eases his labour by confining his most solicitous Enquiry to a small Number of Colours upon which the rest depend, and assists him to judge of the nature of particular compounded Colours, by showing him from the Mixture what more Simple ones, and of what Proportions of them to one another, the particular Colour to be consider'd does result.

Boyle had already stated that these few primitive or simple colours of the painter were black and white, and red, yellow and blue (Boyle, 1664; cf. Hall, 1955, Hendry, 1979/80).

But Newton had thrown this neat symmetrical scheme of simple colours into confusion in his first paper of 1672 by showing that there were as many 'simple' (or 'primary', 'primitive', 'uncompounded', 'original', or 'homogeneal') colours as there were wavelengths of light (Newton, 1958; Westfall, 1962); and that these same colours (e.g. green, and even yellow) might occur in both a simple and a compounded form. Newton's leading opponent on this occasion, Robert Hooke, who had himself developed a radically reductive theory of only two primary colours, understandably sought to apply Occam's razor (Newton, 1959); and during the eighteenth century Newton's number of primaries (which was generally and erroneously thought to be seven) continued to present something of an obstacle to students with painterly connections. And yet the circular diagram of colour mixtures which Newton introduced into the *Opticks* of 1704 (Book I, Part II, Proposition VI, Problem II; our Figure 1) gave promise that a white might indeed be compounded from two or three of the colours lying opposite each other, which could thus be regarded as primary by themselves (Shapiro, 1980). Newton claimed in the text to this figure that he was never able to mix more than a 'faint anonymous Colour' by means of the proportions indicated; but in his experiments with the mixture of coloured powders (Book I, Part II, Proposition V, Theorem IV, Experiment 15), he had succeeded in making a mouse-colour (his surrogate for white in pigment-mixtures) with only two: one part red lead and five of copper-green, which he concluded, to save his theory, must themselves be compounds of other colours.

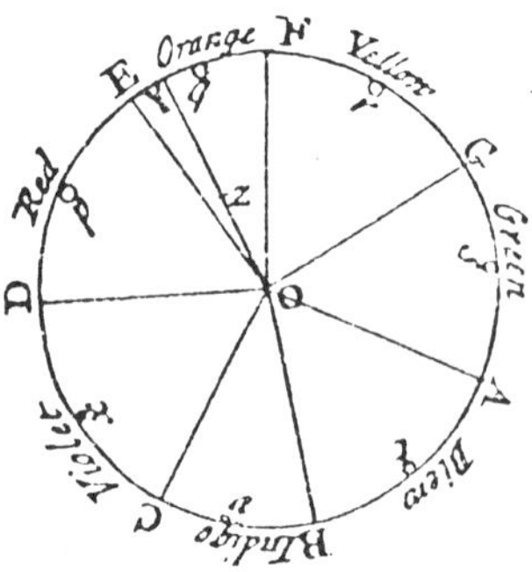

FIGURE 1

This circular diagram became the model for many colour systems in the eighteenth and nineteenth centuries, from the supplement to the *Traité de la Peinture en Mignature* attributed to Claude Boutet, in the Hague edition of 1708, where the seven-colour division (with two reds) seems clearly to reflect the newtonian arrangement of four years earlier, to the first completely symmetrical and complementary colour system of Moses Harris, *The Natural System of Colours*, published about 1776. Newton's scheme provided, too, the starting-point for the first attempt to apply the newtonian system to the practical problems of colour-mixture, published by the Cambridge mathematician Brook Taylor in the second edition of his treatise on linear perspective in 1719. Taylor amplified Newton's conception of mixture to emphasise the co-ordinate functions of hue, value and saturation in each colour; and he observed that white 'breaks' (i.e. desaturates) colours far more than black, hence the prime importance of the lightest pigments, for 'it is easier to make clean dark tints with light Colours and Black, than to make the bright light ones with dark Colours and White'. Taylor also noted that because of the impure nature of pigments, mixtures could not always be accurately predicted; and, although he seems to have been an amateur painter himself, he concluded, 'these Properties of particular Materials I leave to be consider'd by the Practitioners in this Art' (Taylor, 1719).

Three- and four-colour engravings

The establishment of an irreducible number of primary colours and their embodiment in available colorants became of practical significance in a new development in colour-engraving introduced about 1715 by the German artist J. C. Le Blon. The earliest reference to Le Blon's process, which employed the technique of mezzotint, suggests that he was chiefly interested in manipulating hues and values according to newtonian principles in order to achieve harmony (Haskell, 1980). This account refers to his period in Holland about 1715, but the emphasis is renewed in his treatise, *Coloritto: or the Harmony of Colouring in Painting*, published in London about 1723, after the failure of his large-scale English enterprise, The Picture Office (Byam Shaw, 1967). *Coloritto* also makes it clear that Le Blon's printing methods were themselves a matter of newtonian principle:

> Painting can represent all visible objects with three colours, yellow, red and blue: for all other colours can be compos'd of these three, which I call primitive. . . . And a mixture of those three original colours makes a black, and all other colours whatsoever; as I have demonstrated by my invention of printing pictures and figures with their natural colours.
>
> I am only speaking of material colours, or those used by painters: for a mixture of all the primitive impalpable colours, that cannot be felt, will not produce black, but the very contrary, white, as the great Sir Isaac Newton has demonstrated in his Opticks.

Le Blon thus removed black and white from the category of primary colours (as, indeed, had Boutet, and even Alberti before him), and invoked the authority of Newton, for whom black and white had also been a compound of the same species of colour, just as red, for example, might be either light or dark. By the late 1720s Le Blon had begun to supply the 'Curious' with colour-separations of his prints: the three constituent colours, plus an example of a mixture of two of them, to demonstrate the process (Singer, 1901; Wildenstein, 1960); one such set, after a self-portrait by Van Dyck, is now at Yale (Franklin, 1977; Friedman, 1978). This particular example seems, however, to show the use of a fourth black plate, and there is ample evidence, including a number of references in *Coloritto* itself, that at least as early as his period in England, Le Blon was prepared to adopt this expedient in order to make the process faster and hence cheaper. This became a matter of controversy after his death in 1741, when a former pupil, Jacques Gautier d'Agoty, was anxious to protect *his* patent for this four-colour process, and disputed the claims of Le Blon's workshop that the master had never used more than three. The debate was long and tedious, but it is of some interest to us because Gautier d'Agoty sought to bolster his method with a vigorously argued anti-newtonian theory of colour, which was essentially a revival of the traditional Aristotelian view that all hues are generated by the interaction of black and white, or light and darkness (Gautier d'Agoty, 1749). The apologists for Le Blon in this exchange argued that their master never spoke of his fourth plate precisely because he used it in spite of himself, and felt that it would dishonour his system. If we cannot establish the formative effect of theory on the practice of these print-makers, it was certainly in the forefront of their public relations. Le Blon's appeal to Newton was not itself essential to his three-colour system, for that had already been proposed by Boutet in his treatise of 1708, where Le Blon, as a miniature painter himself, may well have found it. Perhaps what had really attracted him to Newton's theory of colours was the promise it presented of a quantifiable theory of colour-harmony. The Venetian writer Antonio Conti, to whom we owe the first record of Le Blon's ideas, reported:

> . . . the newtonian theory of colours has given many [painters] the opportunity of determining their compositions by the mechanical rule of the centres of gravity [a concept deriving from Newton's circular mixture diagram], (our Figure 1). That German painter who prints pictures [Le Blon] derived his secret from this source. . . . I met [him] at the Hague, and he assured me that following Newton's principles of the immutability and unequal refrangibility and reflexabilty of the rays of light, he had established the degrees of strength and weakness which colours required to be harmonized . . . (Haskell 1980).

The principles of harmony: colour and music

Newton's great achievement in optics was, of course, to have quantified the components of white light, and his mixture diagram was based on this quantification. It was also arranged according to the proportions of the colours in the spectrum of white light, which, for Newton (see Birch, 1757) was a musical proportion (Figure 2); and it was this analogy which gave a new impetus to the ancient attempt to assimilate the aesthetics of sight to those of hearing, and to give the new science of colour the benefit of the many centuries of investigation into the principles of musical harmony. In the *Opticks*, the analogy between aural and visual harmonies, based on that between the vibratory characteristics of light and sound, is relegated, in a very summary form, to Query 14; but Newton had given a fuller exposition in a letter to the Royal Society of 1675, which remained unpublished until the middle of the following century:

> . . . as the harmony and discord of sounds proceeds from the proportions of the aereal vibrations, so may the harmony of some colours, as of golden and blue, and the discord of others, as of red and blue, proceed from the proportions of the aethereal. And possibly colour may be distinguished into its principal degrees, red, orange, yellow, green, blue, indigo and deep violet, on the same ground that sound within an eighth is graduated into tones. For, some years past, the prismatic colours being in a well darkened room cast perpendicularly upon a paper two and twenty foot distant from the prism, I desired a friend to draw with a pencil lines across the image, or pillar of colours, where every one of the seven aforenamed colours was most full and brisk, and also where he judged the truest confines of them to be, whilst I held the paper so, that the said image might fall within a certain compass marked on it. And this I did, partly because my own eyes are not very critical in distinguishing colours, partly because another, to whom I had not communicated my thoughts about this matter, could have nothing but his eyes to determine his fancy in making those marks. This observation we repeated divers

> times, both in the same and divers days, to see how the marks on several papers would agree; and comparing the observations, though the just confines of the colours are hard to be assigned, because they pass into one another by insensible gradation; yet the *differences* of the observations were but little, especially towards the red end . . . (Newton, 1958, 1959).

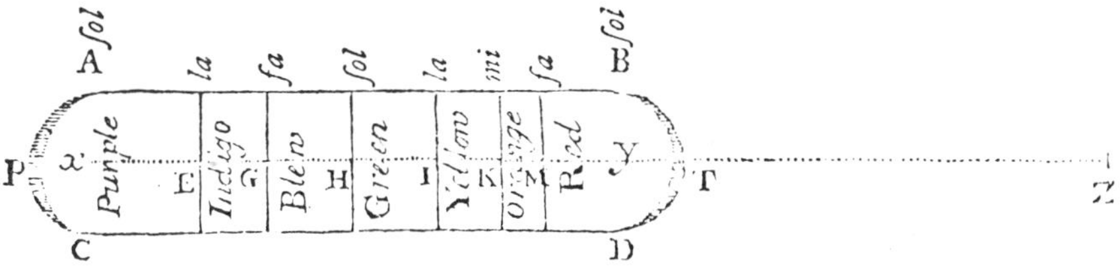

FIGURE 2

It seems clear that, in spite of Newton's efforts to make the experiment 'objective', the isolation of seven prismatic colours was itself the result of the musical analogy, in which he had been interested for some years (Newton, 1959; Westfall, 1963; Sabra, 1967; Shapiro, 1979/80). The conception of the especially harmonious character of a combination of gold and blue (which shifted to indigo in the *Opticks*, as purple was re-named violet), and the discord of red and blue, have no justification other than their relative places in Newton's scale. The general conception of numerical harmonies in colours had an Aristotelian origin, but Aristotle (*De Sensu* 439b) had confined it to the light and dark components of single hues rather than an assortment of hues; and the closest precedent for Newton's view is in a remarkable study of the rainbow published by Marin Cureau de la Chambre in 1650. Cureau de la Chambre, however, did not use a prismatic spectrum, but an Aristotelian scale between black and white, and he was not able to give each colour a precise numerical value. But he agreed with Newton that blue was dissonant with red and consonant with yellow (Teyssèdre, 1967).

It was Newton's suggestion in Query 14 of the *Opticks*, however tentatively expressed, which provided the chief stimulus to the study of colour in the first half of the eighteenth century, both for Le Blon, and for another unsuccessful projector who sought to materialise the theory of correspondences, the French Jesuit Louis Bertrand Castel, the inventor of the ocular harpsichord, which became a *cause célébre* throughout Europe in the latter part of the century. In the first brief outline of his idea in 1725, Castel traced its inception to some hints by the mid-seventeenth century polymath Athanasius Kircher, but more immediately to Newton's *Opticks*, 'that excellent book', which had 'verified' the link between sound and light. He secured professional help to design an instrument embodying the analogy by means of a keyboard controlling coloured glass filters and mirrors; but the prototype, which was ready by 1730, appears to have been rather simpler. Castel began the building of a full-scale version in 1734, but the account which he published the following year shows that he had by now moved away from any newtonian scheme. He had come under the influence of the composer and theorist of harmony Jean-Phillippe Rameau, who had encouraged his project from the first, and he had adopted a scale based on the three primary colours, red, yellow and blue, of which blue, which Castel regarded as close to both white and black, the origin of all colours, was analagous to a musical ground-bass (*basse fondamentale*). Blue he gave the note-value of C, yellow of E, and red, 'the dominant colour of nature', G. Rameau had published his first treatise on harmony in 1722, and also regarded the base as fundamental; he, too, had developed a triadic theory of harmony in which the consonances of the fifth and the two thirds were primary, and gave rise to the three secondary consonances, the fourth and the two sixths (Ferris, 1959). It may well be that Castel adopted his scale of three colours from Le Blon, whose printing process he had witnessed in 1732, for, as he noted in a review of *Coloritto* a few years later, that process also treated blue as the fundamental colour, with which the sequence of impressions began. But, notwithstanding Le Blon's newtonian pretensions, by the time of his most important publication, *L'Optique des Couleurs* of 1740, Castel had become the most extravagant of anti-newtonians, and had rejected all prismatic studies in favour of the exclusive investigation of colouring materials. The ocular harpsichord, which was now based on a twelve-colour circle and a chromatic scale of twelve notes over twelve octaves, was finally completed in the 1750s, and demonstrated in London and Paris before unenthusiastic audiences (von Erhardt-Siebold, 1931/32; Schier, 1941). But it was the ancestor of the many instruments which have sought to present colour in motion, with or without a musical analogy, until our own times (Klein, 1937; Jones, 1972).

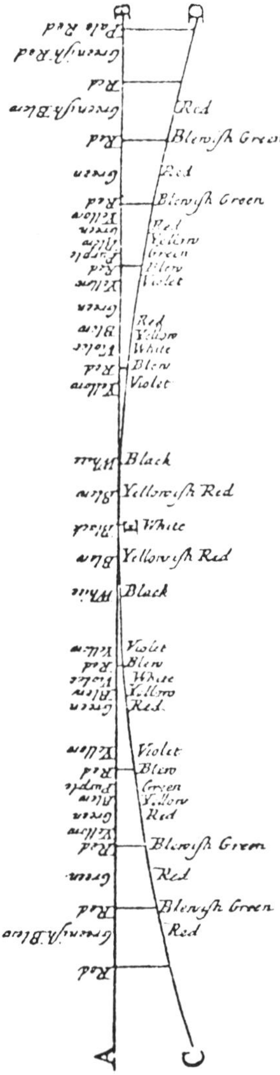

FIGURE 3

Harmony and complementarity

A rather more durable theory of the harmony of colours, current among painters, was based on the idea of complementary colours, and this, too, derives from Newton, In his experiments on the colours of thin plates he had long recognised that certain colours were 'opposite or 'contrary' (Newton, 1958; Westfall, 1965); and the diagram in his classic exposition of what came to be known as 'Newton's rings' (Newton, 1730) in the *Opticks* (Figure 3) became the starting-point for the study of complementarity in the latter half of the century (Darwin, 1785; Matthaei, 1962). The experiment with the mixing of red and green powders, mentioned above, could also be interpreted in terms of the complementarity of these colours. By about 1800, both scientists (Young, 1793; Rumford, 1802; Milner, 1803) and painters (West in Forster-Hahn, 1967; Hayter, 1815; Phillips, 1829; Howard, 1833) had come to believe that the simplest form of colour-harmony was the juxtaposition of complementaries. This view became canonised for the nineteenth century in Chevreul's *Principles of Harmony and Contrast of Colours* (1839), and through him became a decisive stimulus to the developing painterly methods of Seurat, for whom, too, harmony was implicit in contrast (Homer, 1964). It is appropriate that what is perhaps the only series of paintings to be based directly on newtonian ideas about colour, Frank Kupka's *Discs of Newton* of 1912, should look back to these influential experiments on the colours of thin plates (Spate, 1979).

Conclusion

I have tried to show that during the late seventeenth and eighteenth centuries the scientific and the painterly students of colour, under the dominant influence of Newton, shared several common interests, and were each prepared to draw on the experience of the others. These interests were not yet considered to be antithetical, although, by the middle of the eighteenth century some writers, like Castel, and Gautier d'Agoty (who owed a good deal to him), sought to drive a wedge between the quantative study of the colours of light and the qualitative study of colorants. Both controversialists were much used by Goethe. It was not until the close of the century that Wünsch in Germany and Young in England brought clarity to the notions of additive and subtractive mixtures, and not for another half-century again that these ideas became widely accepted. As late as Mondrian in the 1920s the whole universe of colour could be symbolised in terms of the subtractive primaries, red, yellow and blue. The fascinating question of the harmony of colours also led Newton to propose some far-reaching but ultimately unsuccessful hypotheses about the relationship of colours to musical sounds; but it was a notion of complementarity, latent but unexpressed in his work, that came to have the greater resonance in the history of painting.

REFERENCES

Birch, T. (1757) *The History of the Royal Society of London*, vol. III, p. 263.
Blunt, A. F. (1966) *The Paintings of Nicholas Poussin: a Critical Catalogue.*
Boyle, R. (1664) *Experiments and Considerations touching Colours.*
Byam Shaw, J. (1967) General Guise and J. C. Le Blon, in *Paintings by Old Masters at Christ Church, Oxford.*

Darwin, R. W. (1796) On the Ocular Spectra of Light and Colours (1785), in E. Darwin, *Zoonomia* (2nd ed.), vol. I.
von Erhardt-Siebold, E. (1931/2) Some Inventions of the Pre-Romantic Period and their Influence upon Literature, *Englische Studien,* lxvi.
Ferris, J. (1959) The Evolution of Rameau's Harmonic Theories, *Journal of Musical Theory,* iii.
Forster-Hahn, F. (1967) The Source of True Taste'. Benjamin West's Instructions to a Young Painter, *Journal of the Warburg and Courtauld Institutes,* xxx.
Franklin, C. (1977) *A Catalogue of Early Colour Printing, from Chiaroscuro to Aquatint.*
Friedman, J. M. (1978) *Color Printing in England, 1486–1870.*
Gage, J. (1971) Blake's *Newton, Journal of the Warburg and Courtauld Institutes,* xxxiv.
—— (1981) A *Locus Classicus* of Colour-Theory: the Fortunes of Apelles, *Journal of the Warburg and Courtauld Institutes,* xliv.
Gautier d'Agoty, J. (1749) *Chroagenesis, ou génération des Couleurs, contre le système de Newton.*
Greene, D. J. (1953) Smart, Berkeley, the Scientists and the Poets, *Journal of the History of Ideas,* **14.**
Guerlac, H. (1971) An Augustan Monument: the *Opticks* of Isaac Newton, in P. Hughes and D. Williams, *The Varied Pattern: Studies in the Eighteenth Century.*
Hall, A. R. (1955) Further Optical Experiments of Isaac Newton, *Annals of Science,* **11.**
Haskell, F. (1980) *Patrons and Painters* (2nd ed.).
Hayter, C. (1815) *An Introduction to Perspective, Drawing and Painting,* (2nd ed.).
Hendry, J. (1979/80) Newton's Theory of Colour, *Centaurus,* **23.**
Homer, W. I. (1964) *Seurat and the Science of Painting.*
Howard, H. (1833) *A Course of Lectures on Painting,* ed. F. Howard, 1848.
Jones, T. D. (1972) *The Art of Light and Color.*
Klein, A. B. (1937) *Coloured Light: An Art Medium.*
Kutschera-Woborsky, O. (1919) Ein Kunsttheoretisches Thesenblatt Carlo Marattas und seine ästhetischen Anschauungen, *Mitteilungen d. Gesellschaft f. vervielfältigende Kunst.*
Matthaei, R. (1962) Complementäre Farben. Zur Geschichte und Kritik eines Begriffes, *Neue Hefte zur Morphologie,* **4.**
Milner, I. (1803) Theory of Colours and Shadows, in H. Repton, *Observations on The Theory and Practice of Landscape Gardening.*
Murdoch, R. T. (1958) Newton and the French Muse, *Journal of the History of Ideas,* **19.**
Newton, I. (1730) *Opticks* (4th ed.), Bk. II, pt. 1, obs. 9.
—— (1958) *Papers and Letters on Natural Philosophy,* ed. I. B. Cohen.
—— (1959) *Correspondence,* ed. H. W. Turnbull, vol. I.
Nicolson, M. H. (1946) *Newton Demands the Muse.*
Pedretti, C. (1973) The Zaccolini Manuscripts, *Bibliothèque de Humanisme et de Renaissance,* xxxv.
Phillips, T. (1833) *Lectures on the History and Principles of Painting* (1829).
Rumford, Benjamin Thompson, Count (1802) Conjectures respecting the Principles of the Harmony of Colours, in *Philosophical Papers.*
Sabra, A. I. (1967) *Theories of Light from Descartes to Newton.*
Schier, D. (1941) *L. B. Castel, Anti-Newtonian Scientist.*
Shapiro, A. E. (1979/80) Newton's 'Achromatic' Dispersion Law: Theoretical Background and Experimental Evidence, *Archive for History of Exact Sciences,* xxi.
—— (1980) The Evolving Structure of Newton's Theory of White Light and Color', *Isis,* **71.**
Singer, H. W. (1901) Jakob Christoffel Le Blon, *Mitt. d. Gesell. f. vervielf. Kunst.*
Spate, V. (1979) *Orphism: The Evolution of non-figurative Painting in Paris, 1910–1914.*

Taylor, B. (1719) A New Theory for Mixing of Colours taken from Sir Isaac Newton's Opticks, in *New Principles of Linear Perspective.*

Teyssèdre, B. (1957) *Roger de Piles et les Débats sur le Coloris au Siècle de Louis XIV.*

—— (1967) Peinture et Musique: La Notion d'Harmonie des Couleurs au XVIIe Siècle français, in *Stil und überlieferung in der Kunst des Abendlandes* (Akten des 21 Int. Kongresses f. Kunstgeschichte, Bonn, 1964) vol. III.

Turnbull, G. (1740) *A Treatise on Ancient Painting.*

Westfall, R. S. (1962) The Development of Newton's Theory of Colors, *Isis,* **53.**

—— (1963) Newton's Reply to Hooke and the Theory of Colors, *Isis,* **54.**

—— (1962–5) Isaac Newton's Coloured Circles twixt two Contiguous Glasses, *Archive for History of Exact Sciences,* ii.

Wildenstein, G. (1960) Jakob Christoffel Le Blon, ou le 'Secret de Peindre en Gravant', *Gazette des Beaux-Arts,* lvi.

Young, T. (1793) Observations on Vision, *Philosophical Transactions of the Royal Society,* lxxxiii.

DISCUSSION

TORMEY

I have a brief reflection on Harré's opening remarks. He discussed the problem of explaining correlations between artistic and scientific activities not only in terms of style and content but also in terms of shared metatheoretical structures. I have a methodological problem to raise: if one is sufficiently inventive it is possible to construct metatheories which are plausible enough to tie together the most disparate of artistic and scientific activities. My concern is obvious. If we do this, we end up with an apparent connection which is, of course, no less and no more substantive than the notion of *Zeitgeist* which Professor Harré, I think correctly, wanted to dismiss at the outset.

HARRÉ

I wanted to distinguish between those metatheories we might propose hundreds of years after the event and metatheories which people at the time subscribed to. What I had in mind in suggesting the concept of metatheories instead of the rather vague notion of *Zeitgeist* was that we might, on certain occasions, be able to find people explicitly subscribing to a theory of their own activity and then going about their work in terms of it. Of course there is still a 'chicken/egg' issue, but it does not pose the same sort of problem as when we ourselves provide an explanation long after the event. I wanted to concentrate on the example of Coleridge and Davy because I think we can prove that they shared an explicit metatheory. I would only regard it as legitimate to offer a metatheory to firm up the vague notion of *Zeitgeist* when we have reason to believe that the people concerned actually held the theory. If we create metatheory after the event, this has no force as an explanation of common features.

GREGORY

It is unclear to me from the *Opticks* whether Newton actually spun his disk.

GAGE

I don't think he did.

GREGORY

He doesn't say whether he did or not, but I think he probably did. This is a critical point because of the sector angles shown in the illustration of the disk (cf. Gage's Figure 1). If the disk had been spun then the angles make sense since they give an additive mixture. My guess is that later people didn't see the significance of this so they drew them at equal angles, which misses the whole point. Newton certainly understood about additive mixtures because he talked about whirling coal around and the perception of a trail of fire behind the whirling coal. So he knew about the temporal integration, in modern terms, of visual perception. Though I think he never said that he spun the disk, I believe he must have done. But if he did, then you get an additive not a subtractive mixture from the spinning disk, and that would have been of no use to painters because they are using subtractive colour. So there is a kind of tension here. There is the *scientific* validity of spinning the disk and getting additive colour, but this is of no use to *painters* because they are using subtractive colour. Thus, except in the case of pointillism, they couldn't use what he had found out.

GAGE

I agree. One of the points to emerge is that painters who claim to be using Newtonian ideas were taking a very selective and in some cases erroneous view of what those ideas were. It's exactly the same with Seurat and Maxwell in the nineteenth century. There is a very tendentious use of the data.

MERMOZ

This raises the interesting question of the co-existence of different types of discourse and the relationship between them. On the one hand we have a scientific discourse—that of Newton's *Opticks*—on the other the justificatory remarks of an artist who, in the practice of his art, finds himself in conflict with currently accepted scientific knowledge. The disparity in status between these two types of discourse (the 'scientific' and the 'artistic' or 'technological') must be taken into account if we are to make sense of the Le Blon controversy.

HARRÉ

I feel very sympathetic to the spirit of that remark. It seems to me that we ought to think in terms of discourses; we can see people not only sharing explicit metatheories, exemplified in their common practice, but also taking up aspects of each other's discourses for certain social purposes. Here we have a case where painters are borrowing from scientific discourse in order to justify some practice which they had no obvious painterly need to justify. This poses the historical problem of why they felt the need to do this, and why they drew upon that particular instance when there were many other precedents, historical precedents in their own field for example, that they might have drawn on but didn't.

MERMOZ

The valuable source material gathered by John Gage enables me to raise another issue, concerning the difference in status between the visual arts (in particular print-making) and the natural sciences (in this instance optics), and their consequences in terms of 'interdiscursive dependencies'.

Unlike John Gage I do not see Le Blon's references and tributes to Newton's colour theory as showing that, during the eighteenth century, artists and scientists 'under the dominant influence of Newton, shared several common interests, and were each prepared to draw on the experience of the others'. Quite the contrary. I see it as symptomatic of a fundamental conflict of interest between the visual arts and the natural sciences which shows in his reluctance to admit using a fourth plate. This conflict was experienced by Le Blon who, because of the much greater authority of the sciences in the general framework of eighteenth-century knowledge, could not acknowledge openly the facts of experience (the results of pigment mixing and the need for a fourth plate) in his own field (print-making).

If, therefore, the respective interests of the visual arts and the natural sciences 'were not yet considered to be antithetical', it was because the inferior status of the visual arts did not qualify arts, in the public eye, to compete with the sciences in their investigations of their common object 'Nature' (see for instance the 'Explication détaillée du système des connaissances humaines' and the diagram 'Système figuré des connaissances humaines' published in the 1759 *Encyclopédie*). Thus, a key factor in the Le Blon episode was the artist's reluctance to acknowledge his use of a fourth plate (i.e. his transgression of Newton's theory) both in public (p. 8 *Coloritto* 1723) and in private (to Antonio Conti). This interpretation is supported by the apologists of Le Blon whom, John Gage tells us, 'argued that their master never spoke of his fourth plate precisely because he used it in spite of himself, and felt that it would dishonour his system'.

In retrospect, this conflict of interest may also be interpreted in terms of the incompatibility between a theory dealing primarily with spectral colour (in which pigments were used in order to confirm a hypothesis, 'trichromacy' derived from the observation of spectral colour) and a theory developed from the handling of pigment colours. At this point, we meet with one of the factors encountered by Eric Forbes in his paper where he examines the basis of the conflict between Newton's and Goethe's colour theories.

MARWICK

Mine is a simple question that I would like to address to Newton, Blake, Goethe and the other historical personages, but I obviously can't—so I hope one or other of the speakers will give an answer. What did these people themselves think? How would they have answered our question? Were they aware of a difference between Art and Science? I suspect not. The force of my observation is to suggest that we have to look at this thing historically in another way. There is no universal question about Arts and Science, but one question related to the Arts and Science of the seventeenth and eighteenth centuries and another question related to the rather different Art and rather different Science of the twentieth century. I do think that a prior question that all speakers should ask themselves, and enlighten us on, is 'what did particular historical personages themselves think they were practising?'

FORBES

In the case of Goethe, the point that I was making was that he was very conscious of the fact that science was only a subdiscipline within the problem of understanding.

MARWICK

Did he use the word 'science'? Did he think that 'science' existed?

FORBES

He was using words like 'natural philosophy' rather than 'science' as such; and if Germans use the term 'science' it is as *Wissenschaft*, which has a wider meaning in any case. On the other question—the matter of 'holism'—I believe that we are going to witness a revival of interest in holistic interpretations of nature in the near future through the great activity that is just beginning in the field of Islamic science. The Muslims do not try to segregate out an empirical science of nature, but rather regard nature, moral conduct, religion, philosophy and other aspects of knowledge as part and parcel of one all-embracing world view.

HARRÉ

As far as the people I have instanced are concerned, I think they were all very conscious indeed of the liaisons between themselves, as painters, poets, and scientists etc. Most people at the time were very well aware that they were attempting to understand a unified universe and that there were different ways of going about it.

WOLPERT

In considering common denominators in art and science, the emphasis that has been placed on similarities in subject matter may be misleading. Perhaps it is more important to look at the process of doing art or science and to emphasise the differences. Science is part of scholarship whereas art cannot be considered in this category. Science can be viewed as an accumulation of public knowledge, and—this is crucial—it can be shown to be wrong. This is not true of art. While there are similarities in being a scientist or artist, such as being creative, this may only reflect that they are human activities. It may not be enough to point to common denominators in art and science, it may be necessary to show that they are exclusively common to art and science. It is also worth remembering that the sciences differ very much in their subject matter. There is probably much more in common between a palaeontologist and a historian than between the palaeontologist and a physicist.

HARRÉ

Perhaps by identifying what is in common we can throw into contrast what is different, if there is all that much difference. I am a bit sceptical about the thesis that these intellectual enterprises are so vastly different—but that will be for another conference!

4

THE APOCALYPTIC DENOMINATOR IN ENGLISH CULTURE OF THE EARLY NINETEENTH CENTURY

Nicholas Rupke

University Museum, Oxford

SUMMARY

A revival of apocalyptic interest occurred in England during the early nineteenth century. This interest was shared by scientists and artists alike. An appreciation of the apocalyptic element in science was apparent in the popularity of subjects like meteoritics and diluvial geology, and in the fine arts it showed in the work of men like Byron and John Martin.

The argument

This paper presents an example of a common denominator in art and science. The example dates from the late eighteenth and early nineteenth century, the heyday of Romantic culture which was uncommonly rich in instances of art-science interactions, even to the extent that individuals attempted to contribute to both fields of creativity (see especially articles by Forbes, Harré and Knight, this volume). The example of this paper focuses on the occurrence in art as well as in science of the apocalyptic element. This element was present in the study of stones which had fallen from the sky (meteoritics) and in that of granite blocks strewn across much of the northern part of Europe (diluvial geology). These two branches of science originated and became popular during the late eighteenth and early nineteenth century. At the same time the arts were enriched with some of the finest apocalyptic poetry and painting ever produced.

During the Romantic period the apocalyptic outlook experienced a revival (Schenk, 1966). It is suggested here that the apocalyptic element became a common denominator to art and science because poets, painters and naturalists shared a similar cultural environment which conditioned their interests and those of their public. This suggestion excludes such alternative explanations for the origin of the apocalyptic denominator as an inherent similarity of the creative process in art and science or a linear borrowing by art from science or *vice versa*. Borrowing of specific features did occur, but such instances only served to enhance an already present apocalyptic content.

The interest in meteoritics and in diluvial geology existed all over Europe, just like the Romantic movement was a pan-European phenomenon. This international interest may be seen as part of a reaction to the excess of *ésprit critique* of the Enlightenment or to the horrors of revolution and war coming from France. In England, however, an added reason for this interest existed, namely the apocalyptic revival. In spite of pan-European similarities, the form which reaction to Enlightenment and Revolution took tended to be different for different countries. It is doubtful that such a singular entity as *The Mind of the Romantics* ever existed. For example, the study of nature by the English Romantics stayed close to Paleyan natural theology, whereas in Germany it fostered the more secular *Naturphilosophie* (Porter, 1977 and v. Engelhardt, 1979). In England the Romantic reaction had an altogether more traditional character than that of continental Europe. Accordingly, the appreciation of apocalyptic aspects of science was largely restricted to the English Romantics. As a result, our discussion is confined to the English context, even though the description of scientific developments requires foreign excursions.

This paper is concerned only with the documentation of a common denominator and its origin, not with the origin of any art or science as such. Neither Romanticism nor its English component of apocalyptic interest are adequate explanations for the origin of geology or any of its branches, even though the Romantic fashion may elucidate their popularity. To say that the rise of Romanticism is the key to understanding the emergence of geology, as Allen (1976)—in an otherwise fine study—does, means very little indeed. After all, the very phenomenon of Romantic taste or temperament is identified by cultural predilections which include those represented by geological interests. The question of origins must be studied using factors which are not part of the identification of Romanticism itself. For example, the origin of diluvial geology in England may in part be attributed to efforts to institutionalise the subject of geology by making it academically acceptable at the old universities in the form of diluvialism (Rupke, 1983).

The apocalyptic revival

In the traditional perspective of world history the physical existence of the earth was limited to the time-span of human history. The past of the earth and that of man were not seen as separate realms, but they were believed to be intimately interwoven to produce a prospect of Judeo-Christian eschatological anticipation. Human destiny was considered expressed and given premonitions by the physical vicissitudes of the heavens and the earth, the creation of the world and its destruction by water in the deluge. On the reality of these events depended the veracity of a belief in the Second Advent of Christ, the imminence of His millenial reign, the destruction of the earth by fire and the creation of a new heaven and a new earth. Small scale phenomena such as earthquakes, comets and other signs in the sky were regarded as omens of the ultimate conflagration.

This tradition of world history had deep roots in English culture. Apocalyptic theology and especially millenarian expectations had been popular as late as the seventeenth and eighteenth centuries. But in the course of the first half of the nineteenth century a considerable amount of new enthusiasm was generated for the apocalyptic belief. The various beastly symbols in such Old Testament prophecy as *Daniel*, or New Testament apocalypse as the *Revelations of St John*, found new social and political meaning in events which ranged from the Revolution in France to the European upheavals of 1848. The rise to imperial power of Napoleon and his likeness to the apocalyptic beast almost eclipsed the evil image of the Pope as the anti-Christ, though the Catholic Relief Bill of 1829 and the 'Popery' of the Oxford Movement in subsequent decades re-established the danger of the Church of Rome as the apocalyptic harlot.

This conservative Protestant world view rested on the pillars of sacred history and the study of prophecy. These subjects remained academically viable as shown by a variety of publications. Examples are the several new Oxford University Press editions through which Stillingfleet's *Origines Sacrae* went; the *Fasti Hellenici* by Henry Clinton, the first volume of which contained a large appendix on sacred chronology; and the *Connection of Sacred and Profane History* by Michael Russell who intended his book to be a sequel to Prideaux and Shuckford. Although the authors of these and similar academic works were themselves not necessarily among the vociferous advocates of an imminent apocalypse, their contributions to sacred chronology sustained the basis on which rested the predictions of the end of the world and its precise date.

Vaticinations of this kind were earnestly preached by many worthy churchmen, both Anglican and non-conformist. In London the Scotch Presbyterian minister Edward Irving attracted large crowds to his sermons in which he expressed his belief in an imminent millennium. A ready-made platform for the voice of doom and prophecy existed in the Warburtonian Lecture at Lincoln's Inn which had been established to prove the truth of the Christian religion from the completion of prophecy in the Old and New Testament. A number of early nineteenth-century Warburtonian lecturers, like Nolan and Elliott, added their voice to the apocalyptic chorus. Elliott's later *Horae Apocalypticae* caused a considerable stir; his voluminous production contained an 'Apocalyptic Chart' which indicated that the millennium was near and that its inception was due before the end of the century, possibly as early as 1875. Elliott was a member of the so-called Clapham Sect of conservative Evangelicals. Within the Church of England, Evangelicals paid more than average attention to prophetic dates. When Conybeare (see Anonymous, 1853) wrote his famous article on church parties for the *Edinburgh Review* he commented sardonically that in Evangelical circles 'novels and fairy-tales, it is true, are forbidden luxuries: but their place is abundantly supplied by the romantic fictions daily issuing from the Prophetic Press'.

One of the most prolific apocalyptic writers of the period was William Cuninghame, initially allied to the Evangelicals and a contributor to the *Christian Observer*. The dates of his numerous publications cover the entire early half of the nineteenth century. Cuninghame combined just about all the characteristic features of the apocalyptic advocacy, namely, an interest in sacred chronology with a belief that from it the beginning and true age of the earth can be computed; a strong opinion about the relative merit of the different textual versions of the Old Testament (Hebrew *versus* Septuagint); an interest in biblical prophecy with a conviction that from it the end and true duration of the world can be calculated; an explicit anti-Papism; a desire to convert the Jews and re-settle them in Palestine; and a censorious and often vacuous rhetoric. The very long titles of his books were something of a summary of his views.[1] Cuninghame's writings were filled with millenarian anticipation; initially he dated the Second Advent of Christ for 1841, but under force of circumstances he postponed this date to 1867. Many of Cuninghame's contemporaries can be connected with the apocalyptic tradition, for example Croly and Wallace (see Rupke, 1983).

Meteoritics

The apocalyptic imagination not only fed upon socio-political upheavals, but was equally fired by unusual events 'in the heavens', dramatic and unpredictable, indications of divine intervention and of God's moral government of the physical world. In addition to the appearance of comets in the sky, the fall of meteorites had been reckoned among the most portentous celestial events. From ancient times onward meteorite showers had been recorded; an early account is believed to occur in the Old Testament, *Joshua* 10: 11 ('As they (the Amorites) were fleeing from Israel down the pass, the Lord hurled great stones at them out of the sky . . .'). Their heavenly derivation and the dramatic light and sound effects which may accompany their fall, made meteorites into objects of awe and veneration.

This association with the religious and even the miraculous led many of the Enlightenment *savants* to doubt the reality of meteor stones and their fall from the sky. Especially in France meteorites were regarded as a product of popular superstition. The *Académie royale des Sciences* appointed a commission to examine and dismiss the evidence of a particular meteorite shower. Chemists and physicists such as Lavoisier and Bertholon were among those who did not believe in the existence of meteorites and who ridiculed the common populace for its credulity when it reported a sighting. Across Europe musea discarded their meteor specimens as relics of a superstitious past. In spite of several dramatic showers, such as the one near Siena in 1794, the scientific study of meteorites remained impossible until after Enlightenment rationalism had lost its appeal.

[1] For example: '*The Fullness of the Times*: being an analysis of the chronology of the Greek text of the Seventy: showing that it rests on the basis of exact science, and comprehends various parallel streams of time, arranged in great periods of Jubilee and astronomical cycles, which connect the eras of history and prophecy with the remotest antediluvian ages, and demonstrate the divine origin of the Hebrew dispensation. Proving also that we are approaching a great crisis in the sacred chronology, which indicates the nearness of the end.' The book appeared in 1836.

The German physicist E. F. F. Chladni (1794) is credited with having founded the science of meteoritics with his booklet. He argued for the reality of meteorite falls and he linked these to the phenomenon of shooting stars. Improved chemical analyses of the stones, carried out by the English chemist E. C. Howard (1802) and by others, contributed to the growing belief in the existence of meteorites. Howard told the Royal Society: 'The concordance of a variety of facts seems to render it most indisputable, that certain stony and metalline substances have, at different periods, fallen on the earth.' Specimens from widely separate localities proved to be very similar in composition and the iron of the stones appeared to contain nickel, uncharacteristic of terrestrial rocks (see Sears, 1975).

During the first half of the nineteenth century a backwash of meteorite enthusiasm swept across Europe. Even among the *académiciens* scepticism faded after a dramatic meteorite shower in 1803 near l'Aigle. The Dutch poet and polymath Willem Bilderdijk (1813b) wrote a science fiction novel in which he used the meteorite issue to deride Enlightenment rationalism. The French geologist P. M. S. Bigot de Morogues published his classic *Mémoire historique et physique sur les chutes des pierres 1812* in which he listed some 130 instances of meteorite showers. Chladni (1819) counted more than 280 known falls, and the *Edinburgh Philosophical Journal* printed an account of his list. With reference to a middle eighteenth-century defence of the reality of meteor stones the editor commented that 'nothing can shew more strikingly the universality and obstinacy of that scepticism which discredits every thing that it cannot understand, than the circumstance that this work should have produced so little effect, and that the numerous falls of meteoric stones should have so long been ranked among the inventions of ignorant credulity'. In England an educational poster was printed with a variety of illustrations of *Meteorolites* and with a bibical quote, *Psalm* 18: 13: 'The Highest gave his thunder, Hailstones and Coals of Fire.'[1] Figure 1 shows the remarkable increase in the number of publications on meteoritics during the early nineteenth century.

Diluvial geology

Not only stones from the sky, but also rocky boulders of terrestrial origin were the subject of new scientific work during the late eighteenth and early nineteenth centuries, while at the same time they appealed to the apocalyptic interest of the period. These rocks, erratic boulders strewn across much of northern Europe, were made part of a geological theory of diluvialism. Diluvial geology no longer attributed the entire column of fossiliferous rocks to Noah's deluge, like some naturalists of the middle eighteenth century had still done, but it restricted the effect of the biblical flood to changes at the surface of the earth, like the emplacement of boulders and the excavation of valleys. These phenomena became direct evidence of the destruction of the ante-diluvial world, but also portents of the apocalyptic prophecy of the ultimate conflagration of our world.

1 The plate was printed in 1812; a copy appears in the Buckland Papers, University Museum, Oxford.

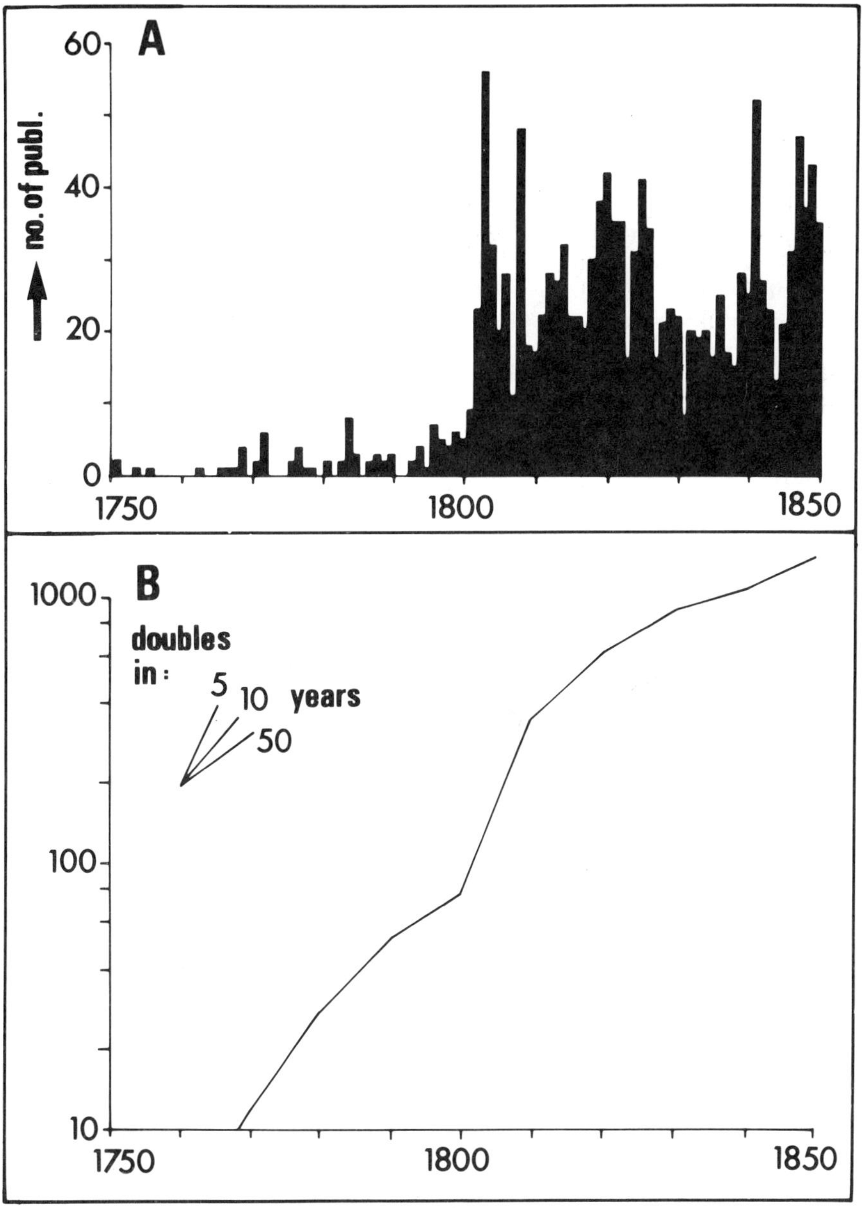

FIGURE 1 Output of literature on meteoritics (A) and its cumulative plot (B). Calculated from H. Brown (1953)

The diluvial interpretation of erratic boulders received much credibility as a result of work done by the Genevan naturalist Horace-Bénedict de Saussure. In his *Voyages dans les Alpes* (1780–96) he described the occurrence of erratics in the vicinity of the Lake of Geneva, and he attributed their origin to an aquatic *débâcle* which was widely believed to refer to the biblical deluge. Not everyone agreed; the Swiss naturalist Jean-André de Luc (1803) argued that both meteor stones and erratic boulders originated from inside the earth, ejected by volcanic eruptions. Bilderdijk (1813a) who befriended de Luc during his exile from The Netherlands, wrote a geology textbook in which he sided with his friend, but in which he also praised de Saussure and used the work of both naturalists in an attack on such Enlightenment savants as Buffon and de la Mettrie.

The diluvial theory reached its apex in England in the course of the 1810s and 1820s when the Oxford geologist William Buckland (1823) contributed a number of classic papers to the subject which he synthesised in his famous *Reliquiae Diluvianae.* Adam Sedgwick, the professor of geology at Cambridge, began his career in science with a defence of Buckland's diluvialism. Among the others who contributed as well were Henry de la Beche, John Phillips and his uncle William Smith. Much of their work consisted of the description of gravel deposits and valley morphology. Buckland (1823) wrote: 'As I shall have frequent occasion to make use of the word *diluvium*, it may be necessary to premise, that I apply it to those extensive and general deposits of superficial loam and gravel, which appear to have been produced by the last great convulsion that has affected our planet.'

However, Buckland expanded the range of diluvial phenomena by attributing the extinction of cave fauna to the biblical deluge. During a continental journey, made shortly after the end of the Napoleonic wars, Buckland acquainted himself with the cave palaeontology of J. F. Esper, J. C. Rosenmueller and other German naturalists. In 1821 a cave at Kirkdale in Yorkshire was discovered which contained a remarkable assemblage of fossil bones. Buckland examined these and found that they belonged to a non-symbiotic assemblage of animals, namely, hyena, elephant, rhinoceros, hippopotamus, horse, ox, two or three species of deer, bear, fox, water rat, and various birds. The first four belonged to species which are now extinct, and to genera which at present inhabit tropical regions. The mere description of this assemblage of vertebrate fossils put Buckland on a par with continental comparative anatomists. But he went further and developed a theory which could account for the apparently anomalous assemblage of bones. Buckland discarded the obvious possibility that diluvial waves had swept these faunal remnants together. Instead he suggested that the cave had been an ante-diluvial hyena den, and that the bone assemblage reflected the diet of hyenas. He reinforced this interpretation with such clever arguments as the occurrence of gnaw marks on the fossil bones which he showed to be identical to those produced by living hyenas on shin bones of cattle. Buckland believed that the end of the ante-diluvial period of hyena habitation had been caused by the same deluge which also had produced the gravel deposits. Both cave and gravel deposits should therefore contain identical fossils. To his delight, Buckland indeed found a hyena skull in gravels near Rugby (Rupke, 1983).

Byron's poetry

The existence of a literary and artistic apocalyptic fashion in England during the early nineteenth century is well known and will not be documented here *in extenso*. Favourite themes were the deluge, the last man, and a variety of natural disasters (Schenk, 1966). However, what is less well known is that the fine arts enhanced their apocalyptic form and content by borrowing features from science. This limited borrowing of specific elements does not add up to the origin of the genre of apocalyptic art. But this use in the fine arts of the scientific study of celestial and terrestrial phenomena does demonstrate that the apocalyptic element was recognised as a common denominator. Scientists in turn admired the use of their work in the arts and were inspired by the literary or visual imagery. One of the more remarkable examples of such scientists was the idiosyncratic Thomas Hawkins,[1] a Buckland devotee, whose books on fossil reptiles contained explicit passages on eschatological prediction combined with denunciations of Enlightenment philosophy and French politics. Two outstanding examples of men who used scientific material in their literary and artistic portrayal of apocalyptics were Lord Byron and John Martin.

Diluvialism was grafted upon Cuvier's theory of the earth which recognised a sequence of separate geological periods, each terminated by a cataclysmal inundation; the last of these was widely held to have been the biblical deluge. This view of earth history was used by Byron who worked it into his *Don Juan* (1819) and his *Cain* (1821). He attributed the notion expressly to Cuvier when he wrote in the preface to *Cain*: 'The reader will perceive that the author has partly adopted in this poem the notion of Cuvier, that the world had been destroyed several times before the creation of man. This speculation, derived from the different strata and the bones of enormous and unknown animals found in them, is not contrary to the Mosaic account, but rather confirms it; as no human bones have yet been discovered in those strata, although those of many known animals are found near the remains of the unknown' (Steffan, 1968). In *Heaven and Earth* (1823) Byron dealt in some detail with the deluge and with the effects of its cataclysmal devastation of the ante-diluvial world. Byron used such specific features of diluvial geology as the occurrence of fossils in caves and fissure pitfalls. The imminent disaster of the flood is described by a chorus of spirits, issuing forth from a cave:

> We, we shall view the deep's salt sources poured
> Until one element shall do the work
> Of all in chaos; until they,
> The creatures proud of their poor clay,
> Shall perish, and their bleached bones shall lurk
> In caves, in dens, in clefts of mountains, where
> The deep shall follow to their latest lair;
> Where even brutes, in their despair,
> Shall cease to prey on man and on each other, . . .
>
> *Part i, scene iii: 170/8*

[1] In 1834 appeared his *Memoir of the Ichthyosaurus and Plesiosaurus* and in 1840 his *Book of the Great Sea Dragons*. This latter publication contained a frontispiece engraved by John Martin.

Shelley also used geological, diluvial imagery in, for example, his *Prometheus Unbound* (1820). Ruskin, even before he had come up to Oxford where he experienced the influence of Buckland, composed verse on the diluvial theme, inspired by the erratic boulders in the Chamonix region. A number of minor poets also wrote on the deluge; as late as 1839 John Edmund Reade, to whom Byron served as a model, wrote a drama in twelve scenes on *The Deluge* which made use of contemporary geology.

Geologists were proudly aware of the literary use of their work. In the Buckland family, amusement was generated by jocular versification and imitation of, for example, Byron's *Cain*; Buckland was portrayed as engaging Lucifer in dialogue, deep inside Kirkdale Cave; to Buckland's question what is done below, Lucifer answers that he is making

> A drink to madden Byron's brain,
> To nonsense madder still than Cain,
> To fire mad Shelley's impious pride
> To final crisis, suicide.
>
> *Buckland Papers, Oxford Univ. Mus.*

Martin's art

The cause of the deluge was believed by many to have been a comet; its near passage could have produced gigantic tidal waves, engulfing the continents in powerful surges of cataclysmal punishment. Bilderdijk discussed this mechanism in some detail. Greenough (1819), the first president of the Geological Society of London, appeared to give tacit approval to the cometary hypothesis. This idea was particularly well suited to the apocalyptic vision of John Martin who portrayed it in his *Deluge*.

Martin's paintings and engravings impress by their sublime and apocalyptic spectre. Good examples are *The Fall of Babylon* (1819) and *Belshazzar's Feast* (1820); also the illustrations for Milton's *Paradise Lost* (1827). In most of these, the physical sphere is given a vast and grand expanse, at the expense of the human dimension. Individuals and their agony dwindle against the background of superhuman architecture or of the near-boundless vault of nature pregnant with apocalyptic portent. None of his paintings or mezzotints excel the Romantic grandeur of *The Deluge* with its swirling magnificence of nature's total sovereignty over man. It was painted in 1826; in 1828 Martin produced a mezzotint version, and in 1834 another oil-on-canvas which was exhibited in Paris and awarded a gold medal by Louis-Philippe (Feaver, 1975; Seznec, 1964).

Martin's contemporary appeal was formulated by Bulwer-Lytton (1833) in *England and the English.* He called Martin 'the greatest, the most lofty, the most permanent, the most original of his country, perhaps of his age'. And elaborating this he wrote: 'Look at his DELUGE—it is the most simple of his works,—it is, perhaps, also the most awful. Poussin had represented before him the dreary waste of inundation; but not the inundation of a world. With an imagination that pierces from effects to the ghastly and sublime agency, Martin gives, in the same picture, a possible solution to the phenomena he records, and in the gloomy and perturbed heaven, you see the conjunction of

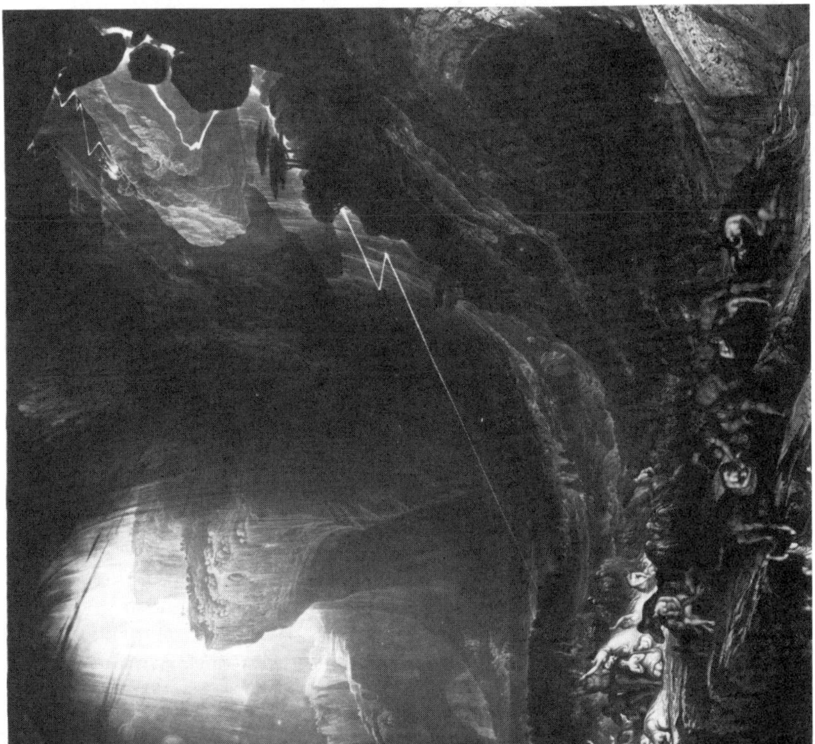

FIGURE 2 The mezzotint version of John Martin's *The Deluge,* from a print in the British Museum

the sun, the moon, and a comet! I consider this the most magnificent alliance of philosophy and art of which the history of painting can boast'.

It was indeed true that Martin used the 'philosophy' (i.e. science) of his day. He knew such geologists as Hawkins and Mantell and he illustrated ancient landscapes for their books. Cuvier visited Martin's studio in London and apparently expressed his admiration for the conception of *The Deluge* and agreed with the cometary hypothesis of the flood. In addition to the cometary mechanism, a number of additional features of *The Deluge* appear inspired by diluvial geology (Figure 2). On one side of the picture, blocks the size and shape of erratic boulders are rolling off a mountain side, while on the other side of the picture similar blocks are being transported by the tidal waves. In one corner of the mezzotint not only a large cave is depicted, but next to it occurs a den of 'ferocious animals'. Among the depicted animals are several known from cave palaeontology, like elephant or 'wolve' (hyena?). These and other features were described by Martin (1828) in a pamphlet which accompanied *The Deluge*. Even the valley morphology seems to be affected by the powerful action of the tidal waves. Martin's deluge engraving could have functioned as a contemporary illustration of diluvial geology. In fact, his idiom can still be recognised in an illustration of *The Asiatic Deluge* used in geology textbooks by Louis Figuier (1865) and by Oscar Fraas (1866).

The theme of *The Deluge* was biblical and traditional; much of its portrayal was influenced by contemporary science; but Martin found also inspiration in Byron's *Heaven and Earth* from which drama he quoted extensively in the pamphlet which described his diluvial picture. Among Martin's colleagues (and competitors) who painted similar deluge scenes were Danby and Turner.

Epilogue

This presentation is intended as a discussion paper and does not represent the product of a completed study. Among the aspects of the apocalyptic denominator not looked at here is the change which the basis of the apocalyptic obsession underwent in the course of the first half of the nineteenth century, from culturally centre stage to fringe. Also, not discussed is the fact that geology, in spite of its early apocalyptic appeal, contributed significantly to the invalidation of the Judeo-Christian eschatological perspective; even Buckland's diluvialism did so.

For stimulating discussions I am grateful to the participants in the Edinburgh conference on 'Common denominators' and in the *Romantik-Tag* in January 1982 at Heidelberg.

REFERENCES

Allen, D. E. (1976) *The Naturalist in Britain.* Lane, London.

Anonymous (1853) (by William Conybeare). Church Parties. *Edinburgh Review* (October), p. 296.

Bilderdijk, W. (1813a) *Geologie, of Verhandeling over de Vorming en Vervorming der Aarde.* Groningen.

—— (1813b). *Kort Verhaal van eene Aanmerkelijke Luchtreis en Nieuwe Planeetontdekking.* Groningen.

Brown, H. (1853), ed. *A Bibliography on Meteorites.* Univ. of Chicago Press.

Buckland, W. (1823) *Reliquiae Diluvianae.* p. 2. Oxford.

Bulwer-Lytton, E. G. (1833) *England and the English,* vol. 2. London, p. 136–7.

Chladni, E. F. F. (1794) *Über den Ursprung der von Pallas gefundenen und anderer ihr ähnlicher Eisenmassen, und über einige damit in Verbindung stehende Naturerscheinungen.* Riga.

(1819). Account of meteoric stones . . . *Edinburgh Philosophical Journal,* vol. 1, pp. 222–3.

Engelhardt, D. v., (1979) *Historisches Bewustsein in der Naturwissenschaft.* Alber, Freiburg, pp. 103–57.

Feaver, W. (1975) *The Art of John Martin.* OUP.

Figuier, L. (1865) *The World before the Deluge.* Translated from the French. London.

Fraas, O. (1866) *Vor der Sündfluth!* Stuttgart.

Greenough, G. B. (1819) *A Critical Examination of the First Principles of Geology.* London.

Howard, E. C. (1802) Experiments and observations on certain stony and metalline substances, which at different times are said to have fallen on the earth; also, on various kinds of native iron. *Philosophical Transactions,* vol. 92, p. 168.

Luc, J. A. de (1803) *Abrégé de Principes et de Faits concernant la Cosmologie et la Géologie.* Brunswick.

Martin, J. (1828) *A descriptive Catalogue of the Engraving of the Deluge.* London.

Porter, R. (1977) *The Making of Geology.* CUP, pp. 101–3.

Rupke, N. A. (1983) *The Great Chain of History.* OUP, chs. 2 and 4.

Schenk, H. G. (1966) *The Mind of the European Romantics.* Constable, London.

Sears, D. W. (1975) Sketches in the history of meteorites 1: the birth of the science. *Meteoritics,* vol. 10, pp. 215–25.

Seznec, J. (1964) *John Martin en France.* Faber, London p. 32–3.

Steffan, T. G. (1968) *Lord Byron's Cain,* p. 509. Univ. of Texas Press, Austin.

DISCUSSION

MERMOZ

I would like to return to the general notion of *discourse,* and to the problem of the relationship between the artist, the scientist and currently accepted knowledge—in this case the knowledge of the geologist and the artist's response. At the beginning of his paper, where he refers to the synchronicity of the apocalyptic element in sciences and arts, Rupke states that these should not be ascribed to the initiation by science of new theories and to an artistic imitation. However, he remarks *a propos* Martin's engraving: 'In addition to the cometary hypothesis a number of features of *The Deluge* appear inspired by geological diluvianism.' Byron's apocalyptic poetry is also given as a source of inspiration. What we are confronted with here is a situation in which two discourses—poetry and painting—are producing statements on the basis of a 'truth' produced by a third discourse (Geology). This is a crucial point already observed in two previous papers (Newton *v.* Le Blon; Goethe *v.* Newton). There seems to be a pattern emerging from these papers about the way the visual arts and poetry are related to science. Until the emergence of an aesthetic of the Imagination, with Baudelaire, the visual arts had to concern themselves with *scientific truth.* This meant that the problem of the artistic value of a work of art was directly associated with an objective *order of things* which science had the task to describe.

In his paper Rupke uses the concept of world view. I think we should examine this notion in more detail and see where we should locate the acting ground of Ideology.

RUPKE

About your first point: apocalyptic art borrowed specific scientific discoveries in order to enhance its form and content. But such instances of direct borrowing do not add up to an explanation for the existence of an apocalyptic fashion in early nineteenth-century English painting and poetry. The appreciation of the apocalyptic element which art and science shared must probably be seen in the light of a general reaction to the excesses of the Enlightenment and the French Revolution.

MERMOZ

This is a problem. But it is only a starting point. We need to focus on why scientific knowledge was used at all and how it was itself affected by the interaction between the different fields. It is above all a question of *values.* This seems to me to be one of the chief objects of an epistemological debate. Rather than examining what happened in a particular field, we should raise our debate and move out of the purely cognitive and into the epistemological.

RUPKE

About your second point: I use the term *Weltanschauung* in the double sense of a perception of the physical structure of the world and a set of values that may go hand in hand with such a world structure. For example, the apocalyptic *Weltanschauung* combined a particular belief about the origin, duration, and imminent end of the world with certain socio-political convictions.

GREGORY
I would like to go back to the water drawings and Leonardo. Gombrich, of course, wrote a very interesting essay on these, relating them, unusually for him, to the philosophy of science. His thesis goes like this: Aristotle had two natural motions, the linear and the circular, the circular obviously from looking at planets and stars. I think this idea was connected with creation not destruction for a very long period of time. If you consider Kant's very first book, which he wrote when he was about nineteen as a prize essay on cosmology, it is based on the idea of vortices producing the accretion of matter in the solar system. That was taken up by Descartes and later, mathematically, by Planck. Now when Descartes talks about it, it is mathematically simple, and I think he associated the whirlpools on the beach with primitive forms of life, cosmic dust falling from planets and stars and so on. I think that probably, as in the Gombrich cases, it is not destruction but creation that is involved. It looks like a simple natural idea—being whirled together and forming an accretion. When you have a whirlpool the bits come together and form a lump in the middle. But it turns out, of course, that the mathematics involved is unbelievably difficult, and when this gets formalised in physics it turns out to be, even now, a strictly intractable problem—although originally it looked like the natural way things could be created. This seems to be an example of a difference between science and art. When you actually code science into a mathematical form it is an absolute devil, even though intuitively it looks like a natural simple way in which nature should behave to create. I wonder if you think this happens in the history of science and art.

RUPKE
I don't quite agree. Art may depict what seems intuitively right, but the root of much scientific thought would seem to be a similar qualitative perception. I would not want to limit the definition of science to a mere imposition on ideas of a mathematical structure.

GREGORY
I agree that the roots are the same, but if you don't have a convenient mathematics, then it can drop out again in science.

RUPKE
This will depend on which branch of science one is talking about. For astronomy and physics your suggestion may apply. However, for much of nineteenth-century biology and geology, for example, it is not true. Qualitatively perceived notions were of great importance and some of these have persisted up to the present day.

WINTERBOURNE
There is a phrase Harré used in his introduction that gave me a terrible sinking feeling, because I suddenly realised how difficult it was all becoming. He talked about 'levels of correlation' rather than just 'correlation'. This means that we have to identify the level at which a correlation takes place,

between art and science. I suppose it is also true that correlations take place at different levels *within* science—so you might have a biological model used in physics or *vice versa*. Now where does the metatheory come in? Is the metatheory to link only some sort of 'top level' of correlation, which presumably the artist would know something about? Is that why artists make so many mistakes in borrowing ideas from science? i.e. they have picked up at the wrong level. And if a scientist has an explicit metatheory, he would also have, kicking around somewhere in the hierarchy, an implicit metatheory which links up the internal levels. The whole thing becomes horrendously complicated. And is it not the case that art misses the point of a whole lot of science by choosing the wrong level, and the correlations are not really plausible except on a very superficial level?

MERMOZ
It seems that you imply that art and science shouldn't seek a common truth. In fact what is meant is that there are different interests and one cannot expect them to converge entirely or to diverge. The question is not so simple.

RUPKE
The two levels of explanation I refer to are two different approaches to the history of science. The first approach, the history of ideas, tends to look at scientific theories on a fairly large scale of time and place; it traces, for example, the idea of evolution in the works of leading scientists from different centuries and different countries. The very breadth of this approach leads away from the minutiae and multiplicity of circumstances under which any particular scientist has worked. The origin of scientific ideas is therefore first and foremost sought on an abstract level of inherent logic and its improvement with time. This approach has a certain consanguinity with the philosophy of science and the history of philosophy. The second approach, practised by mainstream historians, considers scientific discovery on the level of concrete conditions under which a particular scientist worked, his social class, his political allegiances, the constraints imposed by patronage etc. This approach tends to be more restricted in the scope of its research projects. The break-up of traditional history and philosophy of science programs has something to do with the incompatibility of these two approaches.

WINTERBOURNE
Take one of the other papers—about continuity and discontinuity. Within physics this is a highly abstract and idealised theory which requires a very sophisticated logico-mathematical framework. However, you can express it discursively as being about continuity and discontinuity, and we have a certain understanding about what that means. Nobody has yet brought up the point that neither art nor science are homogeneous institutions or enterprises, nor that there is almost as much difference between some of the sciences as there is between some of the arts and sciences. Now unless you identify which particular bit is being pointed to, which 'denominator' they have in common, it seems to me that the whole thing becomes a bit fuzzy.

LLOYD JONES
I would like to turn back to some of the earlier papers, in particular one concerned with colour. The history of the influence of scientific theories on the use of colour in art is an extremely interesting one, because it is almost entirely baneful where it is not entirely irrelevant to an artist's actual decision making. This is really rather odd and I think that it must be due to the prestige of science as an institution during these particular periods when artists were interested in colour as such. Most artists who can be shown to have had some genuine acquaintance with physics or psychology are minor figures. Certainly none of the really major artists ever appear in lectures on the influence of science on art.

The colourists' problem is really quite simply stated (although not so easy to solve in practice). What the colourist needs to know is 'what colour, in what proportion, goes agreeably with another?'. This is nothing to do with the nature of light, nor with the physiology of the eye, nor even for that matter with the psycho-physics of visual perception. Look at the academic tradition of teaching colour where it has been palpably influenced by science. The structure of most books is similar. They all begin with Newton, there is a spectrum and so forth. Modern ones include a fair amount of visual perception—trichromatic theory and the like. Then at the end of the book are some colour plates of famous paintings whose colour usage is supposed to have been somehow interpreted from the previous material. Not only did the artists themselves know nothing of the science of colour but one only has to see a class of students who are faced with the very practical problem of 'how to do it?' to realise that there is not one single scrap of information in all that science that pertains to these practical problems in any way. This is equally true of people like Josef Albers who purport to go into the question of colour harmony in great detail. Today the painters seem to be the last people to hear about contemporary discussions on colour science. This is presumably because it is nowadays more directly relevant to the practical problems which face designers, for example textile designers, or graphic designers concerned with matters of different colourways or complex printing technologies.

GAGE
I think Peter Lloyd Jones puts his finger on it when he says that our papers have on the whole kept this issue at a distance. But what I was trying to say this morning was that you wouldn't have got a three colour printing technique at all if it hadn't been for the stimulus of beauty. That was what I was trying to get at. It hadn't been done before so it starts off a completely new phase of technology which goes right on to the present day.

5

COMMISSIONS, CREATIVITY AND ESTEEM: WHAT MADE HUMPHRY DAVY TICK?

David Knight

Department of Philosophy. University of Durham

SUMMARY

Davy (1778–1829) was the best-known man of science of his day, attracting large audiences to his lectures at the Royal Institution—there was even a black market in tickets when he lectured elsewhere. He was the friend of Southey, Coleridge, and Scott, to whom he seemed a man who might have made himself a reputation in literature if he had not devoted himself to chemistry. He continued to write poetry, but increasingly came to see himself as a natural philosopher with a world-view to propound. On discovering potassium, he danced about the room in ecstatic delight; but in his lectures and informal writings we find some account of his scientific creativity.

In England in the early nineteenth century, the term 'scientist' had not yet been coined, and 'artist' still generally meant the same as 'artisan'; there were still not 'two cultures', and it was possible to say that the leading man of science or 'natural philosopher' of the day could have been a great poet had his life worked out a little differently. It was not only that Davy had perhaps an artistic temperament, and was the friend of Romantic writers; his own life followed a pattern not unlike that of a painter or a poet. Science depended upon patronage, which Davy at first received and later exercised; and much of his work, including that on the safety lamp for coal-miners, was commissioned. There was no route in science to a steady income, but Davy showed that there were rewards for a man who could spellbind an audience and honours for one who could make discoveries as glittering as those of the French. His exact contemporary, Charles Gay-Lussac (Crosland, 1978; Sadoun-Goupil, 1980) can be described as a professional scientist, and his life and work seems intelligible enough; but Davy remains an enigma, despite a conference in 1978 to mark the bicentenary of his birth (Forgan, 1980).

Davy's importance cannot be gainsaid, whether in the context of science in Britain or in the internal development of chemistry. At the Royal Institution, he inaugurated a research institute supported by lectures which made science, pure and applied, fashionable; he wrote the standard work on agricultural chemistry; he alone was knighted for eminence in science; he invented the safety lamp for miners; and from 1820 to 1827 he was President of the Royal Society (Siegfried, and Fullmer, in Forgan 1980). During this time he vigorously promoted the British Museum, the London Zoo, and the growth of specialised scientific societies; and through Robert Peel, he induced the King to endow Royal Medals. Meanwhile, the boy who had written 'Davy & Newton' in his notebook had indeed succeeded in demonstrating the nature of the attractive force of chemical affinity, when in 1806 he established that it and electricity were 'manifestations of one power'. In the following year this insight led him to the isolation of potassium and sodium; and three years later his successful advocacy of the elementary nature of chlorine led to a reworking of the received theory of acidity, and thus a fundamental modification of Lavoisier's chemistry. For his work in electrochemistry, the *Edinburgh Review* had compared him to Newton, and the French had given him a prize which he went to Paris to collect despite the war.

Mr Fixit?

Morris Berman (Berman, 1978) in his study of the Royal Institution picks out the first Davy. A small dark man from the Celtic fringe, who could hold an audience and whose eyes were described as too fine to be forever peering into crucibles, he was for Berman a tool of the landed interest. Improving landowners controlled the Royal Institution, and hired this malleable orator and experimenter to assist them in social control as a 'Mr Fixit', and to improve the farming, tanning and mining industries upon which their incomes depended. Davy was indeed awarded the Copley Medal of the Royal Society in 1805 essentially for his work on tanning, and his baronetcy in 1818 for the safety lamp. He preached applied science, and practised it. These things brought him into contact with the upper strata of society, and some of his early friends worried that Davy was corrupted by social climbing.

The first biography bears out this interpretation of Davy (Paris, 1831). It was composed under the aegis of Lady Davy, the heiress, and cousin of Walter Scott, to whom Davy had been unromantically married since 1812. Paris' Davy was gauche and opportunistic, loving position and lords—who indeed might well have used him while laughing at him behind his back. Certainly the idea of his presiding at meetings of the Royal Society in the place of Sir Joseph Banks (his predecessor who had been elected a few days before Davy's birth and reigned for forty-two years), with cocked hat slightly skew and without the gravity of age and status, struck some as comical. It was enthusiasm rather than dignity that was Davy's forte: on isolating potassium he danced around the room in ecstatic delight; he took no safety precautions, and worked in brilliant spurts improvising apparatus and astonishing onlookers. Stories of his going out to dine, rushing from the laboratory and putting a clean shirt on top of his dirty one, must apply to these bursts of activity which put Davy among romantic rather than classical scientists.

This view of Davy has the disadvantage that his great achievements in chemistry are neglected or remain inexplicable. To work on fertilisers, mining safety, and the improvement of ships and gaols may strike some as evidence of being a capitalist lackey, but it seems equally natural at least to see them (with Davy) as evidence of public spirit. It is really Davy's successor, W. T. Brande, who fits Berman's picture best: his books were standard textbooks, his laboratory work was mainly analysis undertaken for a fee, and his lectures were generally covering a syllabus rather than describing current research. Davy and Faraday, while they were both in a sense professional scientists, are too big to be categorised in any simple way. It was because he felt his brother had been misrepresented that John Davy brought out his biography (Davy, 1836); and followed it in 1839–40 by a nine-volume edition of Davy's *Works,* including lectures and notebook-entries as well as published books and papers (Fullmer, 1969).

Berman's book is about the Royal Institution rather than about those who worked there, and the best recent biography of Davy (Hartley, 1966) presents the original and important chemist, working on potassium and chlorine, and making cautious theoretical advances. Davy's social role is hardly touched upon, for Hartley was writing internal history of science: yet this *genre* has its difficulties, and also fails to do justice to, or really bring to life, its heroes. Hartley told me that he could make nothing of Davy's last book, published posthumously in 1830, *Consolations in Travel*; a series of dialogues about ageing, death, and time, showing affinities to some of Davy's earlier lectures and notebooks, but intended as a kind of personal statement, or testament.

Relationships

Davy's *Consolations* is more than the senile rambling of the prematurely old man of fifty wandering lonely around Europe in search of health, and dying at Geneva; it became one of his best-selling works, and with his (Davy, 1828) other late book, *Salmonia*, it can tell us something about how his mind worked. Davy was in his youth the friend of James Watt's son, Gregory, and of Thomas Wedgwood; he was the assistant of the radical Thomas Beddoes (Levere, 1981a) who married into the Edgeworth family and was the father of a Romantic poet, and he corresponded with the aged Joseph Priestley in America who hoped that Davy's work on the oxides of nitrogen and on electricity might revive the phlogiston theory—with which Davy did indeed toy, for phlogiston can be seen as something like chemical energy rather than as a pseudo-substance. Davy thus had a good scientific pedigree and acquaintance even in his early days; and his friends also included Coleridge, Southey, and later Byron and Scott. While a young man at Bristol he recorded a pantheistic experience of nature, no doubt under Coleridge's inspiration; and Coleridge later wrote to him for advice when with Wordsworth he was proposing to set up a chemical laboratory in Grasmere (Levere, 1981b).

These were not aristocratic connections, but radical ones. While there is no doubt that Davy liked a lord, his real friends (and apparently the only people who really saw him in a relaxed frame of mind) were his fishing-companions; they were mostly medical men, with the odd country gentleman like Thomas Andrew Knight, the horticulturalist and brother of the aesthete Richard Payne Knight. Davy, himself a medical drop-out (Bynum, in Forgan, 1980), had hoped to make the practice of science fashionable; but it must have become clear to him that (with a few exceptions like Cavendish and Banks) science was going to remain a spectator-sport for the aristocracy. Davy was a very keen fisherman and a very expert one (Knight in Forgan, 1980), landing on one occasion a forty-pound salmon from the Tweed; he was also a keen shot, and the story is that he persuaded Murchison into geology by demonstrating that one need not abandon field-sports on taking up science.

In *Salmonia* we find some genuine ichthyology, and an account of a sea-eagle; and earlier Davy had written a poem about an eagle teaching its young to fly upwards into the sun. This he took as a model for himself, encouraging promising young men to fly higher. In the event he founded no school—perhaps it is difficult to see how he could have done so in Georgian London—and his relationship with Faraday became poisoned when Faraday began independent research: both, as self-made men, were edgy about priority, recognition and honour. Davy felt superior to William Hyde Wollaston who made a fortune by trading in platinum, after inventing a new process for producing it in malleable form (Kronberg, Coatsberg and Usselman, 1981). Davy had indeed entered into an unsuccessful gunpowder manufactory during the Napoleonic wars, and as President of the Royal Society rewarded his collaborator, J. G. Children, with a zoological post in the British Museum. In general he looked down on trade, refusing to patent inventions, but as a professional man accepted handsome fees for consultancy or lecturing. In applying for his first job, he had written that he hoped for a genteel maintenance, and this rather than wealth or exalted position seems to have remained his target—even though one of his last letters contains the complaint that he had not been made a Knight of the Bath and a Lord of Trade as his predecessor was!

World views and theories

Right through his life from his Bristol days to his *Consolations,* written to come to terms with the loss of youthful energy and vision, we can find a reasonably consistent world-view. He described being converted to immaterialism in his teens, as no doubt many contemporaries in England were as the French Revolution in the 1790s turned from fraternity towards terror and from defence towards aggression. What this meant for his science was that he looked from French to English (and possibly German, at second-hand from Beddoes and Coleridge) examples. He learned his chemistry in French from Lavoisier's *Elements* but his earliest research was on heat, when in melting ice by rubbing he believed that he had shown that heat was motion of particles (vindicating Newton and Locke), rather than a substance, *caloric,* as Lavoisier supposed.

In his next work, on the oxides of nitrogen, he rejected Lavoisier's term *azote* because he saw that nitrogen was not inherently poisonous; and when he demonstrated that air, nitrous oxide with its delightfully narcotic properties, and the choking brown fumes of nitrogen peroxide, were all composed of the same two elements, he came to reject Lavoisier's idea that elements were the bearers of properties at all. This he characterised as a materialistic notion (Knight, 1978). For him, in a Newtonian tradition, it was powers rather than components which characterised substances; and for him as for contemporary Germans, force was prior to matter. The final disproof for him that composition determined properties came when, after his marriage, he burnt a diamond in Florence and established that it was pure carbon, chemically identical to charcoal: a single element, whose particles were arranged differently under the power of aggregation, could display almost contradictory properties.

His researches on electricity also make sense in this context, for they were the investigation of a force which determined chemical properties. Ever since Newton, the nature of chemical affinity had perplexed theorists, because it was elective rather than universal, and therefore unlike gravitation. Davy reasoned clearly upon the basis of Volta's experiments and his own, in urging that chemical affinity was electrical. His work on chlorine, called by disciples of Lavoisier 'oxymuriatic acid' because of the dogma that oxygen was the essential component of all acids, also fits this mould. He showed that it had as much right as any other substance to count as an element. For him muriatic acid became HCl, while sulphuric acid was then thought of as SO_3: so they had no element in common, and acidity must be the outcome of forces rather than components. Davy could not therefore go on as Dulong and Laurent were to do, and evolve a hydrogen theory of acidity (Brooke, in Forgan, 1980). Similarly, his electro-chemistry remained vague and general: Faraday later remarked that a dozen incompatible theories might be derived from Davy's very general propositions, and on being challenged by John Davy he actually produced a list of published examples (Faraday, 1844). It was not Davy but Berzelius who, having arrived at similar ideas independently, worked out the detailed system called *dualism*, in which each element had its characteristic electric state and molecules had their positive and negative components.

Berzelius' theory turned out after a reign of twenty years to be inapplicable to most of organic chemistry, and unitary views like those of Gerhardt came to replace it; so one could perhaps say that Davy was wise to keep his ideas general. The same could be said of Davy's excursions into matter-theory: he did not believe that there could be over forty different kinds of fundamental particle, as Dalton's atomism seemed to require, and he appealed to the authority of Hooke, Newton and Boscovich in urging that there was ultimately only one kind of atom. Nevertheless, he was happy to argue for the elementary status of potassium, sodium and chlorine; and indeed Davy, who did not believe that elements were fundamental, was one of the most prolific discoverers of elements in the history of chemistry. It was however Prout, influenced by Davy's suggestive passages, who proposed a detailed theory of the complexity of the elements, that they were polymers of hydrogen and that the masses of their 'atoms' must be simple multiples of that of hydrogen. Like Berzelius', this theory turned out not to be true; but it was falsifiable. Davy's world view, leading to no very definite conclusions though encouraging and discouraging certain lines of thought, can hardly count as 'scientific' if we follow Popper (1959). In his determination to avoid the spirit of system which he and his compatriots saw reigning in France, Davy avoided promulgating definite and falsifiable theories; his best work began with falsifying bits of Lavoisier and Volta.

It was characteristic of Davy that rather than following a research programme steadily, guided by a testable theory and building up a series of results, he should have left an opus that could be described by Berzelius as 'brilliant fragments'. Berzelius put this down to Davy's lack of a proper scientific education; and Thomas Young noted Davy's lack of interest in those parts of chemistry where he had not himself done any work.

Given that he had a general world-view, and other people's more detailed theories to falsify, we may still ask what was the source of his scientific ideas. He referred in lectures and in *Consolations* to the imagination, that creative power made much of in the Romantic period; and to the role of analogy in science. For him, the imagination was the faculty which led to true rather than fanciful analogies: and his use of analogical reasoning can be seen most clearly in his work on iodine which he speedily saw to be the analogue of chlorine. He saw analogies too between chemical affinity and electricity, and later between electricity and magnetism; but perhaps because he lacked the faith of the Kantians that the human mind can penetrate the secret of nature because it is made on the same plan, he never saw his analogies as more than guides or hypotheses. His dread of systems, and the veneration that he and his contemporaries had for Bacon, and for the Newton who said 'hypotheses non fingo', led him to stop short of major theorising.

This then is how Davy remains enigmatic and paradoxical. He climbed from an uncarpeted cottage to the highest scientific office, where he was happiest fishing; he longed for recognition, of which one can never have enough, but found few real friends; he left neither children nor disciples; and while he was to most contemporaries the most gifted chemist of his day, his work was as much destructive as constructive, and could seem fragmentary. The lonely and prematurely-aged man writing the *Consolations* and dying abroad had been the most idolised man of science in England since Newton and, unlike Newton's, his conversation and lectures were sparkling; yet, even in a field like science given to hagiography, his reputation was ambiguous. Perhaps it is the more systematic, dogged or even plodding scientists who are safer to remember and uphold as examples: Davy's seemed too close to effortless superiority.

REFERENCES

Berman, M. (1978) *Social Change and Scientific Organization: The Royal Institution, 1799–1844.* Heinemann, London.

Crosland, M. (1978) *Gay-Lussac, scientist and bourgeois.* CUP, Cambridge.

Davy, H. (1828) *Salmonia: or days of fly-fishing.* Murray, London.

—— (1830) *Consolations in Travel, or the last days of a philosopher*. Murray, London.
—— (1839–40) *Collected Works* (ed. J. Davy), 9 vols. Smith, Elder, London.
Davy, J. (1836) *Memoirs of the Life of Sir Humphry Davy*. Longman, London.
Faraday, M. (1844) *Experimental Researches in Electricity*. vol. 2, pp. 211–17. Richard and John Edward Taylor, London.
Forgan, S. (ed.) (1980) *Science and the Sons of Genius: studies on Humphry Davy*. Science Reviews Ltd, London.
Fullmer, J. Z. (1969) *Sir Humphry Davy's Published Works*. Harvard University Press, Cambridge, Mass.
Hartley, H. (1966) *Humphry Davy*. Nelson, London.
Knight, D. M. (1978) *The Transcendental Part of Chemistry*, esp. ch. 3. Dawson, Folkestone.
Kronberg, B. I., Coatsworth, L. L. and Usselman, M. C. (1981) The Palladium and Rhodium of W. H. Wollaston, *Ambix*, **28**, 20–35.
Levere, T. H. (1981a) Thomas Beddoes at Oxford: radical politics and the Regius chair in chemistry, *Ambix*, **28**, 61–9.
—— (1981b) *Poetry realized in nature: S. T. Coleridge and early nineteenth-century science*, esp. ch. I. CUP, Cambridge.
Paris, J. A. (1831) *The Life of Sir Humphry Davy*. Colburn & Beatley, London.
Popper, K. R. (1959) *The Logic of Scientific Discovery*. Hutchison, London.
Sadoun-Goupil, M. (ed.) (1980) *Gay-Lussac*. Palaiseau.

6

DAVY AND COLERIDGE: ROMANTICISM IN SCIENCE AND THE ARTS

Rom Harré

Sub-Faculty of Philosophy, Oxford University

SUMMARY

To prove that common features of the literary, artistic and scientific works of a period are related in some more fundamental way than mere imitation it would be pleasing if an historical case could be found in which personal exchanges of views could be shown to have been instrumental in crystallising vague cultural presuppositions into definite doctrine. There does seem to have been a 'Romantic' movement in science alongside the literary and artistic revolution of the late eighteenth and early nineteenth centuries. I believe that the personal friendship between Coleridge and Davy was partly responsible for the strikingly 'Romantic' aspects of the latter's philosophy of science (Knight, 1972).

I am sure that in a sense David Knight is right in his contention (see p. 47) that Humphry Davy was a running dog, a lackey of the landowning, mining and other capitalist interests. There can be no doubt that Davy's most immediate need was patronage and that he was something of a snob. But I believe that Davy himself treated his relations with his patrons as the means by which his scientific investigations were to be supported, and, as I hope to show, those studies were inspired by something quite other than the wish to satisfy the upper-class supporters of the Royal Institution. The passion that Davy brought to his work was related neither to his social position nor to his social aspirations. Having found a support, he was unable to indulge himself to a considerable degree in satisfying his own private interests. His passions were those of a typical romantic, amplified, I am fairly sure, by the taking of various powerful drugs. His penultimate work, *Consolations in Travel* (Davy, 1830) is, to some extent, a reworking of a record of some of these experiences, though it is also within the literary conventions of the time. In short I hope to show that Davy's science was to a large extent a realisation in the practical world of a certain vision of the universe which he derived from his romantic associations and in particular from his long, though intermittent relationship with Coleridge.

I am going to try to work out my interpretation of the life and work of Davy in terms of two sets of ideas. In the first I will try to lay out the main themes of romanticism, themes which appeared in both literature and science, and which were certainly adumbrated in philosophical speculation sometime before their appearance in other forms. Then I want to try to demonstrate the extent to which Coleridge served as the focus for the transmission of these ideas to Davy in particular, and for the re-animation of English intellectual life. I am not so naive as to propose Coleridge's influence as a causal hypothesis. A detailed study of social conditions would be required to show just why this set of ideas rather than some rival spread so rapidly around the time of the French revolution and after. But I do think the relationship between Coleridge and Davy is exemplary of much that happened in that time. In the course of their twenty-year association they influenced and amplified each other's fundamental philosophical views both on metaphysics and on method.

A *Romanticism as a metatheory*

I have already suggested (p. 2) that one way in which there can be common factors in arts and science is when the practitioners of both share a metatheory. The works of the romantics, whether of science or art, make up essentially one discourse. I believe that there was one set of ideas that animated the poets, the apocalyptic artists and the scientists, all of whom were influenced by a particular world picture. David Knight has already mentioned some of these ideas (see ch. 5), but I shall set them out in a somewhat different way.

1 A METATHEORY OF CONTENT

(a) Unity and polarity: a central theme of romanticism was the belief that the world was in some sense a unity, not only through formal homologies (Goethe) but by virtue of a permanent and continuous inter-relatedness between everything in the world. In the alternative picture, the world was an assemblage of isolated atoms, any one of which could exist in the absence of all its fellows. Each atom went its independent way, 'trolleying' through empty space until, perchance, it bumped into another. This ideas was anathema to romanticism. It was seen as the metaphysical foundation of materialism (see later section on Coleridge's metaphysics). The romantic unity was a kind of balance of opposites. This implied some form of polarity, an idea that goes back through Kant to Leibniz. Polarities took various forms; for example in Kant's philosophy of science, matter existed as a balance between two fundamental force fields, one tending to attract, the other to repel (Kant, 1786).

(b) Activity: the second (and connected) theme was that of *natura naturans,* nature as productivity, a world of active beings; not *natura naturata,* nature as product, a world of passive beings, blind and immobile atoms. Active beings creatively worked in the world. Passive atoms could only transfer a pre-existing motion which had been supplied to them from elsewhere in the moment of creation. A world of active beings could, out of their own activity, as it were, engender new things.

I define the metaphysics of romanticism then in terms of two ideas, unity through polarity and universal activity.

2 A METATHEORY OF METHODOLOGY

How should one seek understanding? By passively receiving sensory stimuli and building up a representation of whatever it is one wishes to understand; or by actively employing the imagination to create a simulacrum of that which is obscure or opaque? The romantic answer to this question could be expressed in the principle of the priority of the imagination over the reason. Imagination was the instrument of higher forms of thought. It was essential to Coleridge's theory of both poetry and science. The imagination was freely creative, so it was a mental faculty appropriate to the general theme of activity. Reason, say in the form of induction from given particulars, was a secondary activity since it operated only with what was already given. It had a place in our intellectual economy but it was a dependent one, as Davy and Coleridge both emphasised.

How were these rather general and abstract notions realized in actual practice? We need to take a step back to the early eighteenth century to glance at the origins of the idea of activity in physics (Heinman and McGuire, 1971).

B *The dynamicist traditions*

During the eighteenth century two rather independent dynamicist points of view grew up, one in England the other on the Continent. Continental dynamicism has a complex origin. It was Leibniz who first began to develop a theory of the physical world in terms of paired influences or forces. Their interaction engendered a world of active things. The primary active force and primary passive force serve as the ultimate realities which engender matter as we know it. The details of this picture were not very well worked out by Leibniz (cf. Buchdahl, 1969). Gale has made a convincing case for believing that there was a consistent Leibnizean position and that certainly seems to have been the view of his Continental followers (Gale, 1970).

By the middle of the eighteenth century the Continental dynamicist tradition was well established, and it found its most influential expression in the *Theoria* of R. J. Boscovich (1763). He asks us to envisage a world of point centres of mass, each with a tendency to attract or repel other point centres of mass, varying, according to a complex law, with the distance between them. The effect of these tendencies is an architecture of matter, variously structured and relatively stable in its configurations. There can be no paradoxical interaction by contact, because everything in the universe is interacting continuously with everything else through the attractions and repulsions consequent on the law of force. The Boscovichean picture contains no 'stuff'. Though there is a computable mass attached to every body it is not to be confused with quantity of matter, since matter has no volume. The status of Boscovich's forces is clearly that which a modern philosopher would describe as dispositional. Were they to appear in the dress of modern physical theory they would be called 'potentials'.

Kant's treatment of Lockean primary qualities in his *Metaphysical Foundations of Natural Science* is very similar. In that work he treats material beings as the centres of two force laws, one of repulsion and one of attraction. A test particle will be in equilibrium according to the exact disposition of the laws of attraction and repulsion at a surface surrounding a point-centre, and that surface will appear in the world of experience as the boundary of a solid material body. Were the particle to be thrust closer to the centre of the body it would experience a force of repulsion. Were it to rise above the surface it would experience a nett attraction. By 'forces', in this context, I mean 'nett forces'. Gravity and material resistance as nett forces are secondary effects of the two fundamental force fields. Kant and Boscovich have managed to have a material world without gross matter.

The 'native' tradition: having sketched the philosophical ancestry of the dynamicist point of view with its anti-materialist conception of the physical world, I must look briefly at the criticisms of Newton's atomistic physics, criticisms which were known to Boscovich and were partly instrumental in the origins of the English native tradition of a dynamism of powers, forces and dispositions. The fundamental problem is fairly simple and can be grasped without any special physical knowledge. Imagine a collision between any two ordinary things, say two of the famous exemplary billiard balls. Though they are hard, they are still, to a degree, elastic. When they come into contact each is deformed until a certain compression is reached after which the balls separate and each returns to its original shape. Though the forces are very large they are certainly finite and though the interaction is quick it certainly takes a finite time. All that is possible because, thanks to their compressibility, the two balls have some time to decelerate and accelerate again during their contact. In Newtonian theory compression is due to a change of configuration in the many fundamental and incompressible atoms that make up the body. For example, pores between the particles allow for a change in their relations to one another. But at the surfaces which are actually in contact there must be some collisions between ultimate particles. They contain no pores and they are perfectly rigid. They cannot be compressed or distorted. What then? If their interaction is instantaneous, Newtonian physics requires that the forces between them tend to infinity. This paradoxical result was known to Boscovich, though it was first formulated clearly by Colin Maclaurin. In effect there were two possible solutions. One could abandon the idea of dynamics, a physics of forces, and settle for an ultimate system of rigid bodies. This was the route chosen by D'Alembert (see Hankin, 1970). Or following Boscovich one could try to devise a physics without matter, a thorough going dynamism in which only forces were real. Though Newton was almost certainly unaware of the paradox at the heart of a strict application of his metaphysics of rigid atoms according to his own physical laws, in his chemical writings he seems to have advocated a theory of matter as a system of physical dispositions and forces (Thackray, 1970).

There is a complicated story to be told about the relationship between Newton's chemistry, theological arguments about the relation of God to the material world and the nature of gravity (see Harré, 1980). It is clear that by and large English philosophers of physics were not matterists in the eighteenth century. The three English thinkers I pick out as exemplary of philosophy of physics in England in the sixty years prior to the rise of Romanticism are Greene, Priestly and Michell. In 1727 Greene published an enormous treatise in reply to and revision of Locke's *Essay* of 1690. It will be remembered that Locke uses the concept of 'power', referring to the active dispositions of material bodies, to explain the possibility of secondary qualities, that is qualities which appear to us in a different mode from the way they are grounded in nature. To say that a body has a certain colour, a hue, is not properly to be understood as implying that there is some quality in the body which is just that quality, but rather that a body has a power or disposition to produce just such an experience in us. Locke goes on to explain how bodies can have these powers in terms of his theory of primary qualities, which are the 'mechanical affections of matter', the bulk, figure, texture and motion of the minute corpuscles of which solid bodies are really composed. It is because a body has a certain arrangement and motion of corpuscles that it has a power to appear as having a certain colour, warmth, taste and so on. To put Locke's theory shortly: while primary qualities in our experience resemble the real qualities of bodies, this is not so of secondary qualities; a feeling of warmth does not resemble a state of motion.

But why stop at the secondary qualities? According to Greene all experienced properties should be treated as secondary, so that matter is really a system of forces or powers to produce a certain range of experiences in us. While Berkeley moved from a denial of the distinction between primary and secondary qualities to deny the existence of matter altogether in favour of God's power to create our experience, Greene interposed an active material world between man and his Maker, a world of forces. Priestley and Michell both took a more explicitly theological line. While Priestley (1788) followed the Socinean doctrine that made man through and through material, and so added to the powers and dispositions of matter, the power to think, Michell (Geikie, 1918) followed Baxter in spiritualising the material world. If, as Baxter had put it, the material bricks need an immaterial mortar (force) to make of themselves a world, what of the make-up of the bricks? Surely they too are made up of material fragments held together by the same immaterial mortar? (And this was an echo of Newton's chemical speculations). If we carry on this argument are we not in the end obliged to dispense with bricks altogether?

I believe that Davy was intimately acquainted with the English tradition of dynamism and that his own views on the nature of matter were formed by the fusion of the native theory with Continental ideas amongst which must be counted those of Boscovich and Kant.

C *Electricity and the unity of polar opposites*

At about the same time, another intellectual movement was beginning to burgeon in Germany, the movement we now know as *Naturphilosophie* (Gower 1973). It had various expositors amongst the philosophers, notably Fichte and Schelling. Though the route by which *Naturphilosophie* reached its major principles was quite different from that of the philosophers of physics, the upshot was similar in just those ways that each shared with Romanticism, Schelling (1856) in particular, appealed to those interested in electrical phenomena, since he offered a conception of a world built up on a bi-polar basis determined by a fundamental principle of the unity of all being. It seems that these philosophers had a fairly direct influence on two important electricians, Oersted and Ritter, both of whose works were well known in England. By 'direct influence' I mean that it seems likely that both scientists derived ideas from their reading of just these two philosophers. For instance, Oersted had written a treatise on *Naturphilosophie,* and though it was never translated into English from the original Danish, there was an extensive English review of a French edition, which was known to Davy (Thomson, 1819).

The philosophical writings of J. G. Fichte and F. W. J. Schelling played an important part in the development of the philosophical side of Romanticism. The way Schelling modified and developed the Kantian philosophy was particularly influential. The basic notion is that of the separation of the known world and the knowing self out of a more primal reality which Schelling believed was subjective. The physical world is identical with intelligence in some way. 'There is nothing certain except the affirmation "I am". The affirmation "There are things outside of us" will, therefore, be certain only through its identity with the affirmation "I am" ' (Schelling, 1856, pp 343–4). This leads to the general notion of polarity or opposition. 'Nature [as subject or power] exhibits duplicity [polarity] and consequently there must be opposite tendencies, even in the original productivity of nature. . . . Its original duplicity is a contest of real opposite tendencies.' Coleridge is explicit about his debt to Schelling, but as I hope to indicate (rather than to prove) Coleridge does not quite adopt the subjectivist turn that Schelling's development of the critical philosophy took. But Schelling also emphasised the other great Romantic principle, activity. Speculative physics is the general theory of the internal structures of things, but conceived as powers, not with nature as some kind of passive product, but as productivity. 'Nature as mere product [*natura-naturata*] we call "nature as object". [With this alone empiricism deals.] Nature as productivity [*natura-naturans*] we call "nature as subject", and [with this alone theory deals]' (Schelling, 1856 p. 284). Let us turn now to see how all this was worked out in the theory of electricity and in the research programmes of experimental scientists like Oersted and Ritter.

Ritter was an intimate of the circle of romantics around Novalis and

Schelling (see Gower, 1973, pp 327 ff.). It was apparently as a direct application of the *naturphilosophie* idea of polarity that he set about a research programme designed to demonstrate that all natural events were the product of essentially the same opposed forces and that these were typified by electrical actions. The fundamental powers or *Grundkräften* of the ultimate physical beings appear in various forms, electrical, chemical etc. depending on the exact arrangements among the basic potent entities.

In much the same way as Ritter had applied the neo-Kantianism of Schelling, Oersted attempted to apply Kant's metaphysics of physics directly to the development of a basic chemical theory. He had written a dissertation on Kant's *Metaphysical Foundations of Natural Science* (again see Gower, 1973, pp. 339 ff.) Chemistry was to become like physics, a theory of force. Oersted had noticed that the electro-chemical series known in fragmentary form at that period, paralleled the series of elements based upon oxidation and reduction reactions. He took this empirical evidence for the identity of electrical and chemical forces, as manifestations of the fundamental *Urkräften*, the basic polar forces of nature. His discovery of electro-magnetism was not so much of an accident as the textbooks like to make out, since like Faraday after him, he was convinced of the unity of all forces. That discovery was the serendipity of the prepared mind.

Electrochemistry was the science *par excellence* of the Romantic movement.

D *Davy and Coleridge*

In 1799 Davy was appointed as an assistant at Beddoe's Pneumatic Institute in Bristol. The Institute was primarily concerned with the study of the medical properties of gases. There, in October of that year, Davy met Coleridge. They do not seem to have met again until May of 1800. Evidently an intimacy sprang up, since by the autumn of 1800 Davy was superintending the printing of Coleridge's *Lyrical Ballads* at Bristol. From that time on, Coleridge and Davy remained in close contact. It was during the next three or four years that Coleridge began to develop his anti-matterism. He turned against Locke and Hartley as he became more interested in Kant. In 1804 both Coleridge and Davy were in London. It is worth remarking that the circle of which Davy and Coleridge were members included advocates of drug induced 'altered states'. Davy had discovered the intoxicating properties of laughing gas and had advocated the installation of a source of this enjoyment in every English village (Davy, 1800). Opium was widely taken. The description of the vision in the Coliseum, the great set piece of Davy's *Consolations in Travel* suggest that another native tradition, the chewing of certain mushrooms, was not unknown in that circle.

By the time Davy was installed in the Royal Institution he seems to have become something of a patron for Coleridge, since it was under Davy's auspices that Coleridge lectured sporadically at the Institution in the early part of 1808. Coleridge said of Davy about this time that he was 'more and more determined to mould himself upon the age in order to make the age mould itself upon him'. Their relationship continued for the next ten years. I think it likely that the tendencies which Davy would have already picked up, would have been amplified by his conversations with Coleridge, and further that it is not too fanciful to see a connection between Coleridge's anti-matterism and the conception of the world as spiritual order that grew very much upon Davy in his later years.

Coleridge's philosophy of science involved a systematic attempt to replace the concept of matter as some sort of stuff, with a more sophisticated dynamist view of nature. Coleridge was well acquainted with German philosophy and with the Kantian theories. Indeed he was the first Englishman to give lectures on Kantian philosophy. Among the foundations for the transformation that Coleridge tried to effect in metaphysics, was the distinction between a theory and a law. A theory was an account of some hypothetical, mechanical microstructure, while a law described a tendency or power of things to act. Once a law is formulated Coleridge thought that a theory becomes redundant. Materialism is just such a theory, in which the underlying mechanisms of nature are conceived of as mechanical processes just like those we experience with our ordinary sensory observation of th world.

To clinch the point there should be a theory of the acquisition of knowledge and of the construction of concepts which parallels the metaphysical distinction. According to Coleridge, 'being can transform itself into knowing . . . only on one condition: that is if it can be shown that the *vis representiva*, or the sentient, is itself a species of matter, either as a property or an attribute, or self-subsistence'. This is not to materialise mind but to dematerialise matter. And this brings us to the all important theory of the imagination.

Coleridge distinguishes between the fancy and the primary imagination (Coleridge, 1962). The fancy is the faculty with which using materials 'ready-made from the law of association' we construct conceptions of new things. 'But the fancy has no other counters to play with but fixities and definites.' According to Barfield (1972) fancy is the power to aggregate given units. At best, fancy will yield theory in Coleridge's sense. However the primary imagination is a powerful and constructive faculty. 'It dissolves, dissipates, in order to recreate. . . . It struggles to idealize and unify. It is essentially vital. . . . ' According to Barfield the primary imagination modifies the units of thought themselves. Coleridge goes on to link the power of the primary imagination with an epistemology. 'It gives birth to a system of symbols, harmonious in themselves, and consubstantial with the truths of which they are the conductors.' This explains, I think, how Coleridge thought being can transform itself into knowing.

This is a considerable development of Schelling's ideas, since I do not believe that Coleridge is offering us any kind of idealism. His epistemology (which was known to have been influenced by what he knew of Giordano Bruno's theory of knowledge) was that as mental beings we are constituted ultimately of powers and dispositions. These symbols, which come to be consubstantial with the reality they symbolise, must represent dispositions and powers. But they are themselves powers. And this coordinativeness extends the realm of the vital, the agentive and active across the Cartesian divide between mind and matter, undermining the distinction upon which traditional Lockean epistemology had been based.

Coleridge's philosophical writings are a diffuse ramble through a variety of arguments against materialism and for the priority of something essentially active. It would take me too far afield to defend with full scholarly rigour my essentially Socinean interpretation of his views, but I believe that, like Priestley, Coleridge was defending activity against an essentially passive conception of mental and corporeal being. That is not at all the same sort of enterprise as to attempt to reduce the one to the other, as they are traditionally conceived.

E *Davy's metaphysics and philosophy of science*

I propose to treat Davy's philosophy under three heads; his theory of mind, his belief in natural powers and his conception of matter.

In *Consolations in Travel* the first dialogue describes an astonishing vision that came to Davy on an early evening stroll in the Coliseum. After being permitted to watch the ascent of man from very primitive beginnings Davy is carried up past the planets on a column of light. He reaches a realm of supreme intelligences. 'Their colours', he says, 'were varied and beautiful, but principally azure and rose-coloured.' They inhabited a world in which the very clouds were works of art. Further yet removed from earth are the inhabitants of comets which are even more sophisticated in their intellectual powers. A great voice tells Davy that 'the universe is everywhere full of life, but the modes of this life are infinitely diversified'. The higher intelligences are material beings, and it is in a debate concerning their real nature that Davy offers his account of the nature of thought. Locke's famous problem, 'Whether it might not have pleased God to bestow a power of thinking on matter' is the occasion for a discussion between Eubathis and the Unknown Stranger. The Unknown is inclined to argue that thought requires some non-material basis, but Eubathis defends the Lockean possibility. One might notice that though Locke defends the possibility of thinking matter he does not seem to have actually believed that there was such a thing. In reply to Eubathis the Unknown says that these arguments 'prove that a certain perfection of the machinery of the body is essential for the exercise of the powers of the mind' but they do not prove that the machine *is* the mind. The reasoning has a somewhat modern ring. The active self is not (and perhaps could not be) included in the machine. But having denied an identity between mind and brain the Unknown is still concerned to defend a materialist theory of thought. He argues that 'though the organs of sensation . . . are destroyed by death', there is something of a more ethereal nature, 'which I have supposed may be less destructible'. He then goes on to suggest that that substance might be to electricity as electricity is to the material gases. As I read the vision in the Coliseum, I take Davy to be conceding that while the Superior Intelligences may take bodily form, the material of which they are made is more refined than anything of which we have terrestrial experience. Some puzzles still remain despite the apparently explicit defence by Davy of a 'refined material' thesis concerning mind not so advanced as Priestley's

'Socinean' view that human beings are wholly material, and that their mental attributes be understood as powers. The idea of materially grounded mental dispositions is not available to Davy since he says, quite explicitly, that mind is neither created, 'nor is it dependent on the organisation of matter'.

While Davy slips back from a power to a substance view of thought, he takes just the opposite tack in his physical theories, always eliminating fluids and the like in favour of powers and forces. So he denies all the fluid theories of action, including electrical fluids, the fluid of heat and the gravitational ether. For example, in discussing expansion in *Works II* (Davy, 1940 pp. 329 ff.) he argues that is the increased power of repulsion between the molecular components of material bodies, and that it is transferable from one substance to another. It is correlative to the power of attraction. In *Works IV* (p. 56) he says, 'Heat, or the power of repulsion, can be considered as the antagonistic power to the attraction of cohesion, the one tending to separate, the other to unite parts of bodies.' Different states of matter can be explained by differences in the relations between these forces. In solids the attractive force is dominant, in fluids and gases they are in different states of equilibrium. In ethereal substances, presumably light, heat and mind, 'the repulsive force must be considered to be predominating over and destroying the attractive force'. Here indeed is a very clear statement of the general dynamicist point of view, complete with 'polarity of opposites'.

Electrical fluids too are eliminated in favour of forces. In *Works IV*, Section 41 he says, 'Whatever view is taken, active powers must be supposed to be bestowed upon species of matter and the impulse must be supposed to be derived from the same source.' He goes on to remark, interestingly, 'In the universe, nothing can be said to be automatic, as nothing can be said to be without design.' Finally he argues (*Works II*, p. 329) 'Cohesion . . . is usually said to act only at the synthesis of bodies, or by their immediate contact. This does not seem to be the case. . . . Most of these attractions must be exerted at sensible distances . . . gravity and cohesion may be mere modifications of the same general power of attraction [weakened only because of distance].' Here is a thoroughgoing dynamical point of view.

As I have suggested, Davy knew Coleridge's philosophy of science tolerably well. That philosophy hinged upon treating the natural world as exemplifying three main features; unity, activity and polarity. Activity and polarity are realized in the theory of attractive and repulsive forces, which offer a more complete account of the material world than the theory of passive stuff. But the application of the concept of unity eludes him. At times he does play with the idea of reducing the number of independent influences, as for example in *Works V*, p. 40, he suggests that electrical attraction may be identical with chemical affinities 'and an essential property of matter'. It had to await Faraday's superb research programme before the unity of all forms of electricity was proven. It is worth remarking that the concept of a 'natural unity' is equivocal. Does it mean that there is only one kind of force or power? Or does it mean that everything is influenced by everything else, that the universe is really just one thing? Faraday thought he had demonstrated not only the first kind of unity, but also the second. In the lines of force he had found a conception which made the whole universe into one active and protean 'body'. But Davy seems to have managed no such ultimate syntheses in even the vaguest way.

Nevertheless Davy's general theory of matter was explicitly Boscovichean. The explicit ascription of the doctrine to Boscovich in the fragmentary piece that became the Seventh Dialogue in later editions of *Consolations*, tends to support the view I have been trying to demonstrate, that Davy inherited both the native English and the Continental versions of dynamism. In reply to a question about the ultimate nature of matter the Unknown replies, 'You mistake me if you suppose I have adopted a system like the *Homeoia* of Anaxagoras, and that I suppose the physical molecules endowed with the properties of the bodies we believe to be indecomposable. On the contrary, I neither suppose in them figure nor colour—both would imply a power of reflecting light: I consider them, with Boscovich, merely as points possessing weight and attractive and repulsive powers, and composing, according to the circumstances of their arrangements, either spherules or regular solids, being capable of assuming either one form or the other. All that is necessary for the doctrines of the corpuscular philosophy is to suppose that the molecules have certain attractive and repulsive powers which correspond to negative and positive electricity. This is not mere supposition, unsupported by experiments; there are various facts which give probability to the idea . . . that the elements of bodies are capable of being separated from one each other by certain electrical attractions and repulsions.'

Here we have in explicit form, the identification of the forces of attraction and repulsion with the electricities, implicit in a great deal of Davy's work. It seems that he based his programme for the decomposition of compound bodies by electrolysis upon his conviction that the ultimate polarity was realized in the opposite forms of electricity.

In my exposition of Coleridge's philosophy of science I emphasised his giving of priority to the imagination over the merely reproductive fancy in the formation of new thought. Davy too gave imagination its due weight. In Dialogue V of the *Consolations* Davy says 'With respect to the higher qualities of intellect necessary for the understanding and developing of the general laws of science . . . the imagination must be active and brilliant in seeking analogies; yet entirely under the influence of the judgement in applying them.' I suppose one might be justified in distinguishing the poetic use of the imagination from the scientific just in that last qualification.

REFERENCES

Barfield, O. (1972) *What Coleridge Thought*. London.

Boscovich, R. J. (1763) *A Theory of Natural Philosophy*, Venice; MIT Press, Cambridge, Mass, 1966.

Buchdahl, C. (1969) *Metaphysics and the Philosophy of Science*. Oxford.

Coleridge, S. T. (1962) *'Biographia Literaria'* ed. G. Watson, ch. XIII, London.

Davy, H. (1800) *Researches Chemical and Philosophical, chiefly concerning Nitrous Oxide*. London.

—— (1830) *Consolations in Travel*. London. (This edition does not contain Dialogue VII.)

—— (1840) *The Collected Works of Sir Humphry Davy* (ed. J. Davy), vols. 1–9. London.

Gale, G. (1970) The physical theory of Leibniz, *Studia Leibitiana,* **II**, **3**, 117.

Geikie, A. (1918) *Memoir of John Michell.* Cambridge.

Gower, B. S. (1973) Speculation in physics: the history and practice of *naturphilosophie, Studies in the History and Philosophy of Science,* **3**, 301–56.

Greene, R. (1727) *The Principles of the Philosophy of the Expansive and Contractive Forces.* Cambridge.

Hankin, T. (1970) *Jean d'Alembert,* Chapter 7. Oxford.

Harré, R. (1980) 'Knowledge' in G. S. Rousseau and R. Porter, *The Ferment of Knowledge,* chapter 1. Cambridge.

Heimann, P. M. and McGuire, J. E. (1971) Newtonian forces and Lockean powers: concepts of matter in eighteenth century thought, *Historical Studies in the Physical Science,* **3**, 233–306.

Kant, I. (1786) *Metaphysical Foundations of Natural Science* (translated J. Ellington, New York, 1970). Riga.

Knight, D. M. (1972) Chemistry, physiology and materialism in the romantic period *Durham University Journal,* **64**, 139–45.

Locke, J. (1690) *An Essay Concerning Human Understanding*. London.

Schelling, F. W. J. (1856–61). *Sämmlichte Werke,* III. Stuttgart, etc.

Thackray, A. (1970) *Atoms and Powers.* Cambridge, Mass.

Thomson, T. (1819) Critical and analytical account of *Recherches sur l'identité des forces Chimiques et Électriques* par M. H. C. Oersted, *Annals of Philosophy,* **13**, 369 ff.

Priestley, J. (1788) *Disquisitions relating to Mater and Spirit.* London.

For a general history of the events described in this article, see Levere, T. (1981) *Poetry Realized in Nature.* Cambridge.

DISCUSSION

FORBES

It seems to me that Harré is denying the artist one of the faculties that the scientist has. Both are creative in so far as they use their imagination to conceive new concepts. Both can use these concepts to formulate clearer concepts. However, this is where he implies that the artist's investigation stops, whereas the scientist continues by adopting the clear and distinct ideas which have thus been attained as the premises of a syllogistic argument by which he reasons backwards (or, if you prefer, downwards) into the realm of nature. It is this deductive procedure which Harré is saying that the artists are not performing. Their talent is supposed to lie only in their ability to use their imagination and apply the initial inductive procedure.

HARRÉ

Wordsworth's theory of poetic creation requires that the poet must bring his discourse down, as it were, to the language of the ordinary man, but Coleridge does not subscribe to that doctrine, so far as I know. But if one were to compare Wordsworth with Davy, one would find that Wordsworth held a view of poetry very like Davy's view of science—that is the product of imagination constrained by the judgement, i.e. by common experience. But I do not think Coleridge held that view.

FORBES

But what is the relevance of this for the relation between art and science?

HARRÉ

Well it seems to me that at different periods, people proffer different explanations of why it is scientists must go to the world for confirmation. Take the example of an ecstatic visionary—Kepler. Now Kepler believed that stellar motions, mathematics, architecture and music must all take the same form. Why then does he bother to pay any attention to observation if he knows what they *must* be like? One had to select from the multiplicity of possible forms which ones were actually exemplified. An inductivist doesn't need an account of why he goes to the world for his science because he starts from alleged data and merely generalises it. But an ecstatic scientist, say Faraday or Newton, must have an *explanation* of why he goes to the world. After all if he has a genuine ecstatic vision, then he *knows* how the world works. Someone, like Eddington perhaps, could have a total contempt for experiment, but such people are very rare. I think we find that in periods where there is a high ecstatic theory, as during the Renaissance or at the end of the eighteenth century, there is an explanation of why experimental work was thought to be required, and that perhaps because the fancy is regarded as a kind of witchcraft by the world.

WOLPERT

But isn't there perhaps a much simpler explanation and that is that if scientists don't contact the real world, they aren't taken seriously? I don't think one should take too literally what people say about why they did things. If you are a scientist and you don't go to the real world, then it simply won't be science and no one will pay the slightest attention to you—a situation which I think is quite different to art.

I am ready to follow on from what Peter Lloyd Jones was arguing earlier; I think the philosophy of science plays as little a part in determining what scientists do as the theory of colour plays in how artists actually paint.

HARRÉ

I think it varies from period to period. It's demonstrable, I think, that the philosophy of science plays a very vital role in the early formulations of quantum theory, in that people deduce physical theories from metaphysical premises—Heisenberg being a prime example of that. There are periods when science is very empirical and other periods where it depends very heavily on some prior metaphysical theory. I don't think one can generalise about it.

WINTERBOURNE

We should not neglect the influence of rationalism. If you look at Leibniz and Descartes, for example, the whole rational tradition is based upon the idea that you could get to the truth about nature just by sitting in your armchair and thinking hard. Now that may not be regarded any longer as a proper scientific method, but none the less it happened then, and in mathematics even today it is very often the case. A mathematical idea is given validity inside mathematics. Perhaps only much later is it found to have some application. So the idea that the philosophy of science or philosophy of mathematics is completely independent of, and parasitic on, science and mathematics, seems to me to be both historically and philosophically wrong. I was interested in the concept of the imagination where imagination becomes, as has been said, sovereign over reason. The idea, deriving from Kant, is that the imagination mediates between reason and sense and that art is good in so far as there is a proper balance between how much order there is in something, which would be the rational part of it, and how much imagination is given free rein. That seems to me to offer a genuine explanatory theory about a lot of good art. It is good in so far as it strikes a balance between the incoherent and the highly ordered. Something that is highly ordered is not very interesting artistically and something which is completely random is not very interesting either.

KINMONT

Surely something that is highly ordered might well be exceptionally interesting artistically. For convenience it would probably be categorised as Classical. Paradoxically, even in the Romantic period proper there are many instances of 'highly ordered art' which when considered from widely differing criteria of aesthetic judgement remain eminently acceptable. But perhaps we might take one example from Western European Art, an earlier example from the Quattrocento in which painting was considered to be a science, the work of Piero della Francesca, and in particular—as Wittkower and Carter showed in 1953—the 'Flagellation' from the Palazzo Ducale in

Urbino. Piero was an artist who was equally painter and mathematician. It was his view, as it was the view of his pupil Luca Pacioli who incorporated the whole of Piero's treatise *De Quinque Corporibus Regularibus* into his own *De Divine Proportione,* that the perfection of a work of art depended upon the use of rule and compass.

WINTERBOURNE

My point about highly ordered art is not that one. I was referring to what information theorists would think of as order; that is level redundancy. That is certainly not the case with the kind of art just referred to, which it is constantly worth going back to and we continue to perceive more in it.

But a signal which is just simply the repetition of the same sound, for example, is *highly* ordered and *highly* redundant and not very interesting. That is what I meant by order in this particular case.

CORNFORD

I wanted to ask whether in reading Coleridge's poetry one can point to the ways in which this romantic theory is applied, whether at the level of method or of content?

HARRÉ

I think that the application of his method is in the free rein allowed to a kind of continuous chain of imagery. That's something very characteristic. The theory of it is, of course, that of the primary imagination freeing itself from the constraints of the fancy. As to the issue about activities, the doctrine that the world is a kind of field of potency, I wouldn't say that that is any more exemplified by Coleridge than it is by anybody else in the period. He writes about what strikes him. His metatheory appears more in method than in content.

GAGE

Someone just now brought up the question of signals, and I think this is something worth developing. Both speakers presented a picture of Davy as someone who was fascinated by, and in tune with, a lot of contemporary thought about the nature of imagination and so on, and who aspired to art. But it's clear from your quotations and from one's reading of Davy that he was no artist. He is an appalling writer both as a poet and a prose writer. Surely we have got to get down to what it is that makes Davy a bad poet and a bad writer but Coleridge, at least from time to time, a good one. Their mental worlds appear to be incredibly close in many ways and Harré demonstrated that their attitudes towards the creative imagination have a good deal in common. This goes back I think to the question which we didn't really raise in connection with John Martin this morning. Martin, although he has come to have a certain fame in recent years, was widely despised by his contemporaries, who felt that he wasn't an artist, that he was just an illustrator. The content of his work, which we've heard was very much in tune with contemporary ideas about the Apocalypse, was not embodied in any form which had a lasting value, but was journalism or illustration of some sort. In a comparable way, quite a lot of critics of Escher in our day have argued that he is not an artist but simply an illustrator of concepts. I think this is the question—what is it that makes an artist who is lasting? I suggest that is probably the same sort of reason that makes a scientist who is lasting. Someone who does not simply throw out a few ideas which have their day and then are abandoned. I wonder if Harré can explain why Davy did not become the Poet Laureate or indeed get anywhere near it.

HARRÉ

Let me confess that I haven't the slightest idea how to answer that question, but I want to rule out one possible answer. It would be a bad answer to say that what made Davy a scientist was his devotion to the experiment and to the cult of the fact. For all sorts of people are devoted to fact and experiment and are not good scientists. I think it might be a marvellous piece of research for someone to make a comparative study of the poetry of Coleridge and Davy. It is not a very large corpus and we don't have any science from Coleridge to compare with Davy's science.

7

VITALISM AND CREATIVITY: BERGSON, DRIESCH, MARITAIN AND THE VISUAL ARTS, 1900-1914

David Kinmont
University of Bristol

SUMMARY

Henri Bergson's conception of time, perception and creativity, and his conviction that art—essentially psychological—is the revelation of an ultimate animating principle of spiritual intention are questioned by Conwy Lloyd Morgan and discussed in relation to the theory of Vitalism—a theory of the autonomy of the processes of life—as it was presented by Hans Driesch in the Gifford Lectures of 1907–8. The convergent influences on the writings of Jacques Maritain are then considered and are complemented by reference to works of the Futurists in which conspicuously Bergsonian elements occur. But arguably the paintings of Georges Rouault explore significantly deeper human insights and in them correspondences with Bergson are profoundly essayed.

If there is a single unifying preoccupation in the art of the twentieth century, a century dazzling in technological achievement and in psychological exploration, it is in the subject of Self. Like other contemporary obsessions its significance lies not so much in its novelty—for it has scarcely that—but in its increased definition.

In the late nineteenth century the Symbolist poet Gustave Kahn's propoundment of Self acted as a catalyst and hastened the flow of artistic consciousness towards psychological introversion. For Kahn, writing in *L'Événement* in 1886, 'the essential aim of our art is to objectify the subjective the externalisation of an idea instead of subjectifying the objective (nature seen through the eyes of a temperament); thus we carry the analysis of self to the extreme' (Rewald, 1956).

Already, even before the turn of the century, artists, increasingly introspective, had become painfully aware of their individual isolation and of the negativities of existence. From the mid-nineteenth century there has been a growing disbelief in objective reality, in the phenomenal world. This had a decisive effect on the development of the traditional visual arts. Increasingly for the painter the fields of topographical and documentary art lay fallow.

The first Salon exhibition of photography in Paris in 1885 was the prologue to the uncovering of a whole new visual empire. Muybridge and moving pictures became the harbingers of an ideal vehicle, especially for Expressionist energies, the cinema. And—though slightly outside our period—in 1919 Robert Wiene's extraordinary film, *The Cabinet of Dr Caligary*, remarkably essayed a disordered and imbalanced universe. The surface structures of reality, those categories which constitute ordinary experience seemed disrupted and invalidated largely by an explosive increase in scientific knowledge. With the French philosopher Henri Bergson, 1859–1941, reality was identified as dynamic. Matter was substance no more, but energy.

In Science the emphatic movement away from Euclidean geometry and Newtonian physics was decisively marked in 1900 by Planck's Quantum Theory, in 1902 by Rutherford's work on radioactivity, and in 1905 by the appearance of Einstein's *photons*; Specific Theory of Relativity. But significantly, for example, Einstein's ideas could have had neither general currency nor identifiable influence on any of the visual arts of the period until his General Theory of Relativity was published in 1916, by which time Cubism was moribund. It is true that there had been an appeal to mathematical theory, reflecting Riemann's work, in the important 'La Section d'Or' Exhibition in the Galerie de la Boétie in October 1912, and that Apollinaire had made reference—though vague—to the fourth dimension in 1911 and that was published in 1914 as part three of Les Peintures Cubistes. But if there were here links between art and science it is likely that they will appear clearer and more fundamentally within the Cubist method itself. That method implied both the relativity of knowledge and the supposition that the intellect is superior to the senses as the instrument for understanding the world (Bird, 1975, pp. 124–43).

At the very commencement of this paper there is, therefore, a cautionary suspicion that the anomalies and complexities implicit in the intuitive nature(s) of practice in art and science may cause precise influences, parallels, or quantifiable denominators to remain fugitive. But at least Bergson provides a beginning.

In attempting to escape the ensnarements and the deceits of language, and the associated illusions of conceptual thinking Bergson became aware of the inadequacies of the mechanism and determinism of nineteenth century 'scientisme', especially as they were expressed in Spencer's *First Principles* (Alexander, 1957, p. 8). What seemed to him as the reconstruction of evolution with fragments of the evolved, was unacceptable, not least because it avoided confronting the crucial question of time. The notion of the mysterious fourth dimension had been popularised by H. G. Wells when his *Time Machine* was published in 1895. But Time with its many distinctions, had surprised Bergson (Bergson, 1946, p. 10). He realised that the time of consciousness, existing on multiple levels, was a fusion of heterogeneous instants, a duration; it was a qualitative internal relation and as such was demonstrably dissimilar to the purely quantitative numerical relation of time as described by the physicist or by the clock face. Thus duration was not to be confused with extension (Bergson, 1923, p. 55); essentially it was a perpetually simultaneous yet everchanging multiplicity of interlocking and penetrating mental states. Most importantly to Bergson duration meant memory. Consciousness was memory and none of its states could be adequately represented spatially. This concept, or dream (Langer, 1953, p. 113) is central to all Bergson's theories, and he therefore rejected the assertion of the relativity of knowledge and the notion that time was a homogeneous medium assimilable in space. He considered the empirical psychology of Taine to be inadequate with its suggested explanation of the mental life and of external perception laying in terms of the association of sensations and of brain images. Equally, Kantian idealism accounting for knowledge and perception as the product of formal construction on the part of the mind was incomplete. For Bergson the discovery of duration gave him the certainty that the mind can attain knowledge of the Absolute by intuition (Bergson, 1946, p. 190). But intuition as Bergson conceived it is so close to mystical experience that it really eludes philosophical analysis (Langer, 1953, p. 375). For him, however, the faculty of intuition bears only upon phenomena which exist in that time, which he describes as real, 'La durée'; it would not engage in questions concerned with the purely material, atomistic world.

In 1896, concerned with the problem of expression, Bergson published *Matière et Mémoire.* He argues for an organic philosophy and like the phenomenologists conceives the mind and consciousness as being intentional in structure. Perception is syncretically informed by memory.

Fundamentally there are two forms of memory, the memory of acquired habit, and the true memory 'La mémoire par excellence' which enables the past to be recollected and to appear spontaneously. For although memories can exist independently of the brain it is the brain which actualises them, gives them images.

The universe presents itself through a multiplicity of images which perception, a process of concentrated selection by the memory, interprets in terms of action rather than of knowledge. The question raised is one of 'what is to be done about it?' rather than 'what is it?' (Pilkington, 1976, p. 13). It is a psychological process in which reality is simplified for expedience. Significantly the artist's vision is essentially detached from the need to act, his vision of reality is immediate and non-utilitarian.

Perception is essentially selection, mastering space 'in the exact measure in which action is the master of time'. Aesthetic perception, a refinement of normal perception, is able through its heightened sensitivity of mind and memory to increase precision. It is able to clarify and intensify as it subtly discriminates and crystallises essences.

Art does not imitate the perceived world. It reinterprets our experiences of it, transcending time, and provides new insights to feed new perceptions which in turn condition the way in which the world successively appears. The aesthetic experience, like the art object, is not an end in itself but the amalgam of a whole process; a complicated equation displacing practical categories. Art, for Bergson, is revelation. It is the creation of a uniquely original pattern. Yet although Bergson's regard for art is not confined to the brief account in 'Le Rire' (Bergson, 1906, pp. 153–167) he does not make frequent explicit references to art, and perhaps surprisingly in the light of a view that he is 'the artist's philosopher par excellence' (Langer, 1953, pp. 114–15) his work contains no fully developed aesthetics. This despite his stated aim for philosophy as being to make 'explicit the implicit' (Bergson, 1932, p. 131). Distinctively the demand 'Bergson makes on philosophy—to set forth the dynamic forms of subjective experience—only art can fulfil' (Langer, 1953, p. 114).

It is, in his view, that beyond the veil of appearances there lies a spiritual intention developing in time that Bergson may appear at his most intellectually illusive, at his most metaphysical. The task of the metaphysician is seen by Bergson as the articulation of the real, as the revelation of essences, metaphysics is the 'science which claims to dispense with symbols' (Bergson, 1946, p. 191).

As Art is preoccupied with the power of suggestion it cannot dispense with symbols. The role of suggestion is the cradle for Bergson's thinking on art (Bergson, 1906, p. 164). In *Le Rire* he was to follow Mallarmé (Mallarmé, 1966, p. 368) in focusing on the poet's ambition to circumvent the 'mot banal et social' in order to convey something of the 'état d'âme individuel'. Like Baudelaire and Valéry he claims that art procures vision and knowledge of the absolute. It is a vision which is mediated by symbols, indeed artistic meaning consists of the formulation or representation of the emotions by means of a spatial, symbolic projection. Artistic invention is a sense-giving activity. It is concerned with entering into immediate communion with things and the artist in 'making a rapid sketch, substitutes for the real and internal organisation of the thing an external and schematic reconstruction (Bergson, 1946, pp. 201, 208). He creates a symbol.

Symbols suggest the unquantifiable and mysterious aspects of existence. They are neither, simply, signs nor are they allegories. An allegory seeks to teach rather than to inspire. A symbol, unlike a sign, does not stand for something else, it is what it stands for. Like Yeats' 'Far off most secret and inviolate rose'—for him the symbol of eternal love—it participates in that otherness which it intrinsically images without losing its own identity. Often it is close to myth for it grows out of correspondences and affinities.

But although an image, the visual form taken by a symbol, cannot replace the intuition of duration, it can, as Bergson asserts, be more than purely decorative. It can be used in a dialectic of images as a means of communication. 'The image has at least the advantage of keeping us in the concrete.' Many different images will be able 'through the convergence of their action to direct the consciousness to the precise point where there is a certain intuition to seize on' (Bergson, 1946, p. 195).

The sharpest direct influence of Bergson's thinking on the visual arts is in Futurism. 'Évolution Créatrice' had been published in Paris in 1906 and despite Marinetti's efforts to aquit himself of the charge of being under the influence of Bergson, he would, along with Boccioni, Carra and Severini, have been familiar with the philosopher's theories (Carrieri, 1963, p. 80). In 1913 (Marlborough, 1913) to define his concept of 'plastic perception'—a synthesis of external and internal visions—Severini extended Bergson's axiom 'To perceive . . . is nothing more than the opportunity to remember', adding 'perception being a recollection of aspects and symbols.' Although

Worringer's 'Abstraktion und Einfühlung' was published in 1908, it is especially Bergson's concept of empathy which would have been known to the Futurists, probably through his 'Essai sur les données immédiates de la conscience' (Martin, 1968). Consider, for example, two 1912 works by Boccioni: 'States of Mind' and 'Bottle in Space.' Within the principle of dynamism for Boccioni, process, intuition and synthesis interpret the manifold experiences of sense and memory. Reverberations of this view are found in Cubism, Constructivism and Vorticism, and in Dada and Surrealism.

In passing from psychology by successive intuitions to metaphysics, in the manner initiated by Maine de Biran, the mind perceives psychically its response to its biological and cosmic environment and finds in Divine creativity the inspiration for its being and action. *L'Évolution Créatrice* is based on Bergson's conception of *élan vital*, and in it, despite the many ambiguities, he strives to clarify his idea of creation. He emphasises that creation should not be regarded in terms of a creator and a thing created. The vital impulse, the life force, before which and outside which there was nothing, is a conception of pure creative activity, an ultimate animating principle. But God in *Les Deux Sources*—a work which Bergson considered provided the natural resolution of his earlier work—is conceived as existing independently of the world. He is the Creator and the world is the embodiment of His intention. Creative energy is love and 'l'Absolu se révèle très près de nous et, dans un certaine mesure, en nous. Il est d'essence psychologique' (Bergson, 1959, p. 298).

In his work of 1912 *Instinct and Experience* Conwy Lloyd Morgan—Professor of Zoology and Geology and from 1900, the first Vice Chancellor of the University of Bristol joins issue with Bergson, gently questioning the validity of his philosophical synthesis. Lloyd Morgan's parallel theory was one of Emergent Evolution and he argues that at certain levels of complexity in the evolutionary process new properties suddenly emerge. Bergson conceives life as a spiritual force whose object it is to insert the utmost amount of indetermination into matter; but Morgan, complaining that Bergson assumes his conclusions in his premises, questions the security of a notion which imagines the possibility of a 'force which shall be immaterial' (Kitchen, 1914, pp. 287, 296). Morgan's view would have been representative of a large body of contemporary scientific opinion (Kitchen, 1914, p. 286).

In an earlier related article on Vitalism, published in the Monist of 1899, Lloyd Morgan had become equally uneasy with the concept of a Vital Force. In response to Professor Japp's 1898 address on Vitalism to the Bristol meeting of the British Association, Morgan concluded, 'that if by Vitalism we give expression to the fact that living matter has certain distinctive properties, it may be freely accepted; but that, if by it we imply that these properties neither are nor can be the outcome of evolution it should be politely rejected' (Morgan, 1899, p. 196).

In the early years of the twentieth century Vitalism's most articulate advocate was Hans Driesch. Driesch felt strongly the need for a new and immediate denomination of philosophical concepts—a 'characteristica universalis' in the sense of Leibniz (Driesch, 1908, vol. 2, p. vi). In 1907 and 1908 before the University of Aberdeen he delivered the twenty Gifford

Lectures—the 1922 Gifford lecturer at the University of St Andrews was Lloyd Morgan. Driesch's lectures were concerned with 'The Science and Philosophy of the Organism'. He took the view that natural sciences only acquire demonstrable significance when they are coupled to philosophy (Driesch, 1908, vol. 1, p. 3). Biology he argues, is an elemental science concerned with the analytical and experimental study of the living organism (vol. 1, p. 20). It is from this analysis of the living individual, its morphogenesis and its inheritance that the elemental principles of biology have been gained. This has yielded the concept of entelechy whose characteristics are extensive and intensive manifoldness (vol. 1, p. 329). His conviction that Biology is not simply an empirical science, a kind of applied mechanics, led him to confirm links with epistemology and ontology. He claimed that Vitalism enabled life to be seen not as a mere field of chance, an indifferent and mechanistic biological roulette, but as a harmonious, equipotential, homogeneous and regenerative system. Driesch illustrates his theme by examining cellular structures of the same morphogenetic potencies—the maturation and fertilisation of an egg, for example—which can be transformed into a heterogeneous distribution of realities when specific parts of cells acquire specific functions. A discussion of Adaptation and Inheritance—and in Part 11 the weaknesses in Darwinism and Lamarckism—aims at demonstrating the anatomy of life.

For Driesch (1914, p. 19) this theory of life and its autonomy began with Aristotle. Complementarily Jacques Maritain would take a similar view (Maritain, 1966, p. 5) noting that all that Aristotle called physics included the ensemble of science of the phenomena of nature which is now called Science. With Aristotle, importantly, Driesch distinguishes between a work of art and a work of nature, 'art is the source and form of what is becoming, working on the something outside itself; whereas the movement of nature takes place in the thing itself' (Driesch, 1914, p. 16). All development resembles the production of works of art; all development is creative. And with Descartes, Eduard von Hartmann, and Bergson—whom he considered the 'last great metaphysician'—Driesch defends the Aristotelian hypothesis that 'the non-mechanical agent', the 'soul' may alter the direction of material particles. From purely mechanical grounds he argues (Driesch, 1908, vol. 1, pp. 218–25) that whenever individualising causality is at work we have systems embracing potential and kinetic energy.

But Vitalism is more than energy, it is for Driesch the theory of the autonomy of the processes of life which even as the organism develops and changes, it simultaneously conserves energy. This he sees as a 'deductive' Vitalism creating a real union of logic and biology (Driesch, 1914, p. 188). He asserts that there is in life an essentially teleological or purposive unity which is determined by the central irreducible concept of wholeness. Such a unity is implicit and participates in the process of becoming. Additionally, there is within this stream of consciousness and change a part of becoming itself. It is the substantial element of 'enduring' by which he means 'identity petrified'. Thus Driesch develops his argument to include the polarities of 'identity' and 'consequence', of 'this' and 'because', to illustrate the degrees of manifoldness. Real action is an individual answer to an individual stimulus—

founded on an historical basis. It forms the basis, he states, for example, of what the theory of immunity calls antibodies.

Unlike crystals, living bodies are not simple geometric forms, they are typically combined forms, genetic forms, processing from the 'egg'. The egg forms a microcosm of the universe. Constantly changing and adapting, the universe is an expanding system but it is essentially one organism. This is a postulate of monism of order not dissimilar to that advanced by Henri Bergson whom he had studied and admired (Driesch, 1908, vol. 2). Indeed he even sees his 'individuality' as the equivalent of Bergson's *élan vital* (Driesch, 1908, vol. 1, p. 313).

At the Sorbonne Bergson had influenced equally his student Jacques Maritain, opening the young man's eyes to the fallacies which lie at the heart of rationalism. Maritain developed Bergsonian ideas and became convinced that coherence and meaning necessarily implied the postulation of a more accessible Absolute. He was to see his teacher as inadequately realist, seeking within physico-mathematical science for a metaphysical stuff unknown to science, and which is only discovered by the 'intuition of pure change' (Maritain, 1940, p. 48). Maritain considered Bergson's primary objective to be more concerned with the philosophy of nature than with metaphysics. His trenchant critical work 'La Philosophie Bergsonienne' appeared in 1913. This followed his study of 'Darwinism and Neo-Vitalism' which had been published in 1910 and in which Maritain had been able to draw to the notice of French intellectuals the theory of Vitalism of Hans Driesch, under whom in 1907 and 1908 in Heidelberg he had studied Biology.

Maritain was increasingly aware that biologists were beginning to turn to philosophy in their search for a deeper understanding of the living organism, and wrote 'I need only to mention the works of Hans Driesch, which have done so much towards a new orientation of biology . . .' (Maritain, 1940, p. 64). Where, as Driesch noted (Driesch, 1908, vol. 2, p. 330), Bergson had made the concept of *durée*—not *le temps*—the centre of all epistemology and biology, Maritain gave his philosophy a Christian, specifically Aquinian, definition. In this the influence of his close friend and sponsor in baptism Léon Bloy was all important.

Maritain's first series of articles dealing with problems of modern thought in the light of the philosophy of St Thomas Aquinas—were eventually published under the title of 'Anti-moderne', two years after the appearance of 'Art and Scholasticism'. But his influence on modern painting can be most conveniently located in Versailles in 1911 when he and his wife Raissa became close friends of Georges and Martha Rouault.

Rouault's art, its perceptions and instincts are founded in the Romanesque churches and Gothic Cathedrals of France, in the glories of French medieval glass. 'I create,' he said, 'the way the wind blows and the fire burns.' And out of glazed harmonious colours applied with simple dynamic brush strokes Rouault forged his own mysterious ideograms; his paintings were to become like icons. Rouault was preoccupied with the human predicament, its spiritual problems and psychological states and his work illustrates an altogether different degree of human experience to that explored by the Futurists for example, to which reference has already been made.

Towards the end of April 1901 Rouault withdrew from what he considered to be the unwholesome conflicts of secular life in Paris, and with his studio companion, Antoine Bourbon, sought refuge in the Benedictine Abbey retreat of St Martin at Ligugé, near Poitiers. There he met Joris-Karl Huysmans, newly converted to Catholicism.

In what was arguably a twilight Romanticism, Huysmans pursued an elusive ideal. Like his own hero des Essientes in his notorious novel *À Rebours* of 1884, a novel dedicated to his friend Léon Bloy, in 'hatred of the present century' (Bollery, 1949), Huysmans unsuccessfully attempted to escape the intrinsic dissatisfactions of the modern world.

At this time Rouault became familiar with the writings of Ernest Hello and Léon Bloy. To Hello, Art and Religion were synonymous; art was the natural vehicle for religious truth; it was the agent of goodness and in aspiring to beauty it conquered the quintessence of evil, ugliness.

Bloy was a Catholic philosopher of medievalism and a proponent of salvation through suffering. Rouault's friendship lasted until the writer's death in 1905. Bloy identified art as a bearer of healing and atonement to a derelict and orphaned humanity. He argued that in suffering lay the perfect penitence. According to Maritain (Maritain, 1966, p. 87) it is a view which is not dissimilar in kind to that expressed by Bergson, 'I have suffered enough from my friend to know him', illustrating the love of creature for creature as a most evident natural analogue. Like St John of the Cross and like St Teresa of Avila, Bloy reflects an aspect of the medieval concept of love, of blessures d'amour (Maritain, 1966, p. 36). Rouault found in Bloy a sense of suffering and religious contemplation akin to his own. It was the intellectual certitude he needed.

Two of Bloy's novels, *Le Désesperé*, and later, *La Femme Pauvre*, were of seminal importance in Rouault's development. Many of the ferocious images which inaugurated the painter's personal style reflect the writer's consuming preoccupation with sin and redemption, with the extremities of human suffering and with the polarities of good and evil. Yet two years after having seen Rouault's three works in the Salon d'Autome of 1905; 'How was it possible', Bloy wrote, 'for an obedient soul to paint such horrible canvases.' Like Kandinsky, Rouault painted from 'inner necessity'. 'Tenderness, pity and a longing for harmony, calm and serenity are', as Jacques Maritain was to write, 'at the true heart of Rouault' (Maritain, 1973, p. 6).

Maritain considered that in the process of transforming nature the artist directed everything to the poetic sense (Maritain, 1966, pp. 35, 36) 'to the pure, free and immediate passage into the work of the creative intuition born in the depths of the soul.' This is an extension of the Baudelairean importance and primacy of the imagination, the queen of the faculties. Maritain includes in his list of exemplars Rouault and Chagall (Chagall, 1948, pp. 126–7, 46–9, 83, 94, 98).

In Cézanne's 'little sensation' and 'vision', in Rouault's 'inner promptings', and in the language of artists, Maritain claims that the word 'vision' is probably for them a 'very close equivalent of what in a philosophical perspective we call poetic intuition' (Maritain, 1966, p. 266).

REFERENCES

Alexander, I. W. (1957) *Bergson*. Bowes, London.
Bergson, Henri (1906) *Le Rire* (4th ed.) Alcan, Paris,
—— (1923) *Durée et Simultanéité* (2nd ed.) Alcan, Paris.
—— (1932) *Les Deux Sources de la Morale et de la Religion.* Alcan, Paris.
—— (1946) *The Creative Mind.* Marbelle L. Anderson, New York.
—— (1959) *L'Évolution Creatrice* (86th ed.) Alcan, Paris.
Bird, Elizabeth (1975) *Cubism and the End of Individualism* (unpublished Doctoral thesis), pp. 124-43. University of Sussex.
Bollery, Joseph (1949) *Léon Bloy: Ses Débuts Littéraires.* Albin Michel, Paris.
Carrieri, Raffaele (1963) *Futurism,* Edizione del Milione, Milano.
Chagall, Marc (1948) *L'Orage Enchanté,* Editions des Trois Collines, Geneva—Paris.
Driesch, Hans (1908) *The Science and Philosophy of the Organism.* Black, London.
—— (1914) *The History and Theory of Vitalism.* Macmillan, London.
Kitchen, Darcy B. (1914) *Bergson for Beginners* (2nd ed.) Allen, London. Lloyd Morgan's own annotated copy in University Library, Bristol.
Langer, Susanne K. (1953) *Feeling and Form.* Routledge, London.
Mallarmé, S. (1966) *Oeuvres Complètes.* Bibliothèque de la Pleiade, Paris.
Maritain, Jacques (1940) *Science and Wisdom.* Charles Scribner's Sons, New York.
—— (1966) *Challenges and Renewals.* University of Nôtre Dame, Indiana.
—— (1973) *Georges Rouault.* Henry N. Abrams, New York.
Marlborough Gallery (1913) Preface to *The Futurist Painter Severini Exhibits His Latest Works.* London.
Martin, Marianne W. (1968) *Futurist Art and Theory, 1909-1915,* pp. 89-94. Clarendon Press, Oxford.
Morgan, C. Lloyd (1899) *The Monist.* The Open Court Publishing Co., Chicago.
—— (1912) *Instinct and Experience.* Methuen and Co., London.
Pilkington, A. E. (1976) *Bergson and His Influence.* Cambridge University Press, Cambridge.
Rewald, John (1956) *Post-Impressionism From Van Gogh to Gauguin.* See esp. p. 148. Museum of Modern Art, New York.

DISCUSSION

GREGORY

Can I take David Kinmont up on his definition of symbol? He uses the term 'intrinsic' and I would like to hear him defend that as I wish to attack it. I think he said, very neatly, that a symbol is a 'rubbing off', that it's one thing representing another (that other thing being abstract probably), but he used the word *intrinsic* in his definition. Now to me that word means that it is a symbol irrespective of the understanding of the observer. I don't believe that for a minute. I don't believe that you can have one thing representing another, apart from the appreciation, the understanding that an observer brings to bear on it. If you—say—look at an arrow, you have to have a convention that this is pointing to the Gents or something. You have to have the knowledge base to read it as pointing to something else.

KINMONT

Yes, of course cultural background must condition interpretation, but firstly I think we need to distinguish between a sign and a symbol. Unlike a sign, a symbol—which is more than an emblem—does not simply stand for something else but it is what it stands for, while at the same time it retains its own identity. For example, if in the course of travelling, say, to Edinburgh we notice a marker naming that city and pointing in its direction then we are looking at a sign rather than a symbol. It doesn't intrinsically embody what perhaps you will permit me to describe as the essence of 'Edinburghness'. In other words it is not a symbol of Edinburgh. Obviously signs can become symbols. In my paper, in providing an illustration of a symbol I chose Yeats' 'Far-off, most secret and inviolate rose'. He used the image of a rose not solely on account of its physical properties and attributes, though in them must reside part of any acceptable explanation, but he chose it because, for him, it intrinsically recreated an image of eternal love. I use the word intrinsic because I can find no other adequate alternative, and I use it essentially, signifying an intangibility, a correspondence, to which I am able only to allude.

HARRÉ

Can I just chip in with a thought. In a recent book on hair,[1] there is a distinction made between hair as a sign and hair as a symbol that might help us with the exegesis of 'intrinsic.' The author points out that when at the time of the French Revolution, people wished to show they were radicals they cut their hair short (i.e. they were seen as people whose hair was formerly long). In the 1968 uprising people wishing to show they were radical grew their hair long (i.e. formerly short). Hair functioning as a *sign* of radicalism is a contrastive rather than an absolute indicator. However, Cooper argues that throughout the known history of hair as a *symbol*, older men with long, flowing, grey hair are regarded as wise and God-like. She

[1] W. Cooper, 1971 *Hair, Sex, Symbol, Society.* Alden Press, London.

argues that this has something of the character of symbol. That is that there is something intrinsic to that kind of hair which makes it always, whatever culture it appears in, the symbol of wisdom, dignity, knowledge, etc.

LLOYD JONES

I suggest that our discussion of symbols is not likely to get very far because it is too atomistic. It seems to me one really ought to be talking about sentences at least—validated ways of 'doing business' with the language rather than a single notion, encapsulated in a sound or an ikon of some sort. We have been considering the metaphor, 'My Love is a Rose'; what kind of structure do we have here? I personally believe that it is much more than a kind of compressed simile. I go along with the notion that 'My Love is a Rose' only works because it actually violates deep rules for the use of English—the rules for marking human versus non-human qualities. You produce a non-standard English sentence, which yet could only be understood by those who know standard English—a very peculiar kind of beast. It forces us into a quite unique and special effort to understand in a way that is creative, because in a sense it unhinges a categorical apparatus of understanding the world which is embedded in the language's deep structure. When it happens, not only does one's notion of Love and Roses change, but the whole pack of cards of which these things are merely elements also moves around a little bit. The sense of every other word of the language and of every other valid way of using it also shifts.

If you take another metaphor—'light waves', let us say—this has the same kind of conceptual shock because one's understanding of waves and particles is embedded in continuous sequences of ordinary language apart from this very specific one. I suppose I am groping for some kind of concrete notion of how ordinary natural, spoken language which is one way of understanding the world and capturing it, is shared between artists and scientists: how this creative aspect of metaphor-making is involved in specific concepts which drift backwards and forwards. But I think that trying to capture a word like 'power' or 'energy' or 'information' isn't enough, you need to take a whole complex of ideas and the relations between them and see how they actually move when the conversation shifts from one group to another.

KINMONT

Well, there are many questions which are raised by that observation. It seems to me that symbols have neither indestructible nor absolute existences. They have particular, temporal relevances. Their significance is as much to groups as it is to individuals, as much to generations as to nations. In considering the structure of the metaphor 'My love is a rose', and in attempting to decide whether or not it violates deep rules of the English language—I suspect that it doesn't—we are directly faced with a larger and more unmanageable question concerning the nature of art—arguably and unfashionably—the nature of excellence. Art implies value-judgements and at best works of art—intensely complicated equations—embody equilibriums created from the intermingling of reason, imagination and passion. Is it possible, I wonder, for us to recall for a moment a work with which we are doubtlessly all familiar, say, the Tate Gallery's 'Chair of Vincent', of 1888/9? In order to portray a convincing figurative image of a chair, ideally Van Gogh needed, in addition to a mastery of the medium of oil paint, a knowledge of the chair—understood, so to speak, as a 'piece of structural engineering'. That informing of reason simultaneously provided a springboard for the imagination, and the painter made an imaginative interpretation of the subject by deploying colour not programmatically but symbolically. What might have remained diagrammatic and quantifiable was transformed by the infusion of feeling, of involvement, of passion. In Art, in the sense in which I use the term, there is always an expression of personality.

WOLPERT

For me this discussion highlights the difference between art and science. I don't think you could discuss vitalism and science in the sort of language which we have been using here. I would like to refer to Hans Driesch, whom you mention in your paper, because it illustrates the point quite nicely. Driesch was a very distinguished embryologist and made some of the most fundamental discoveries of embryology, and it is quite interesting why he became a vitalist. He became a vitalist because he really thought the problem was too difficult. He had arrived at an experimental situation where he was driven to try to imagine that a coordinate system could, as it were, always be recreated no matter how much the system was destroyed. He found that intolerable; he therefore felt that there had to be a vital force—guiding development—the entelechy—and he got involved in Vitalism. Now there are two interesting points there. First of all he was simply wrong—he just didn't know there are ways of solving those problems. Secondly he had absolutely no further influence in embryology. You could not have a discussion like this of the influence of vitalism on embryology in the twentieth century or the late nineteenth century—it had none, nobody paid the slightest attention to it, and the reason is it was totally irrelevant. I think this tells us something terribly important about the difference between art and science.

8

SUBJECTIVISM AND INTERACTIONISM IN ARTS AND SCIENCE

Philip Gell

Dunn School of Pathology, University of Cambridge

I want to talk about two tendencies which I think are developing in modern science, of which we have learnt a certain amount already, in David Kinmont's paper; one is subjectivity, that is the recognition of the central role of the observer in science, the other is interactionism which is the recognition of the many-sided nature of causation in the real world. Abstractionism, which has been the standard methodology of science hitherto, now raises doubts as to whether it is in fact the major or the only possible methodology. Both these tendencies, I think, are relevant to the world of the creative arts. Subjectivity in science is most obtrusive of course in physics and relativity theory but it is also evident in the life sciences, in which I am myself most interested. We begin to realise that truth is tripartite, that it is a product of the interaction of a natural phenomenon with the observer, and also with the ultimate audience, since the scientist can only speak intelligibly in terms of a shared paradigm, a paradigm shared with the audience in the Kuhnian sense.

In the literary arts subjectivity was well analysed fifty years ago by Edmond Wilson in *Axel's Castle*, where he discussed the methods and also the aims of symbolist writers like Eliot and Joyce and Valéry. Its philosophical aspects have been elaborated by writers like Roger Poole (1971) and Roszak (1970) and others and can no doubt be paralleled in the evolution of modern semi-abstract painting—Braque, Picasso—in which reality is altered, filtered through the will of the painter. Edmond Wilson had already identified the start of a swing *against* subjectivity which has now I think taken the form of committed, ideological art, of which the most important aspect is pop-art. In science, lagging as usual behind the evolution of the arts, the possibility of the observer being a necessary and inevitable component of scientific truth has only comparatively recently begun to worry scientists in general, though of course relativity theory was just about contemporary with the symbolist writers. (Incidentally none of the symbolists as far as I know took any particular creative interest in modern physics; much the most scientifically minded of those considered by Wilson was Valéry, who was mainly interested in thought processes and in particular analogical thinking in science and poetry.) All the same, the naive concept of the natural mechanism as being existent platonically, independent of the mind of an analytical observer who is merely comprehending it, is unfortunately still accepted teaching in the life sciences. However I want rather to draw attention to the other theme in science which I mentioned, which can be called interactionism and to suggest that scientific thinking on these lines has a close parallel in the psychology of artistic creativity. I hope I will be forgiven an excursion into amateur aesthetics at this point.

Interactionism entails a re-analysis of the naive concept of causation as being a chain type of reaction, a concept for which rightly or wrongly I think Descartes generally takes the blame. In the real world of the living, the causation of most biological phenomena is not normally of this form, but is reticulate, that is to say many elements interact with one another to produce also interacting partial causes for any final effect.

A good example is the genetic mechanism, and a particularly apt one of course in this place where I know the seminal influence of Professor Waddington still persists.

In the phenotype, the organism as it functions in the world little or nothing is decided by single genes, but rather a large number of genes—in the ultimate analysis the whole of the genome—cooperate with past and present environmental causes to produce the given reaction of the individual. It is only in the artificial stripped-down world of analytical Galilean science that one can seem to identify a single cause, and the stripping down process throws out with the bath water a number of very promising babies.

The metaphor which this sort of causation generates is a network and indeed in my own particular branch of science, which is immunology, network theories are all the rage. One of the characteristics of a network is that one can move from one point to another, in a causation nexus from one partial cause towards a final phenotypic event, along a variety of different routes passing through what one can call nodes; these are points where elements, say *a* and *b*, have interacted to generate *c*, though you could maybe get from *a* to *c* by way of the whole of the rest of the alphabet. Now the point which may be relevant to this meeting is that network causation would seem absolutely characteristic of artistic creativity and communication. The process of production of a work of art—forgive me if I state a whole string of truisms now which I hope will be accepted as being at least true—the production of a work of art entails a set of conditioned choices which have to be coherent, that is to say have to satisfy some sort of probability function. This probability is not in a sense of something rational but of something which is determined by its relata, a probable consequence of its environment. However as far as a work of art is concerned, no line can enclose its causes, you can't say that *anything* is irrelevant.

These partial causes constitute the nodes and are activated, or traversed, when the artist makes the particular choice and in many though not all pictures there will be a large number of choices. (I'm developing this metaphor in terms of painting, one can also do it perfectly well in terms of poetry.) Some of these nodes may be inevitably private to the artist but many will be shared with the viewer in so far as the viewer shares the cultural and visual background of the painter and has a sympathy with the kind of thing that the painter is trying to do.

If analogous nodes in the mind of the viewer are activated as were activated in the mind of the artist while making the picture, successful communication takes place. Nodes in the viewer's mind, background experience that is, and routes through the network from sensibilia to enjoyment, may be activated which are quite different in the viewer from any traversed by the painter. If however there are enough shared nodes, these additions by the viewer will legitimately augment the aesthetic experience, though this obviously has its dangers. Clearly in apprehending art of a totally foreign culture, like reading poetry in translation, much impoverishment of the network inevitably takes place, which has to be supplied from the viewer's own background, legitimately or no. But in general the more nodes involved the greater the spread of the network and the richer will be the aesthetic experience.

As I said before, I am aware that this formulation may be no more than a string of truisms but I feel that the concept of a coincidence of networks gives a useful clarifying metaphor in discussing artistic creation and communication. It gives an explanation of cultural restrictions of communication, the different ways in which different people appreciate a work of art; and also provides some sort of a definition of bad art (which I think is very important), as art where there has been a failure to traverse a sufficiently extensive network either in creation or in appreciation.

Now just as subjectivity in science can be correlated with symbolism, we can perhaps correlate the interactionists' reaction against abstractionism, against Galileo, with the modern tendency to blur the distinctions between an art object and its environment. If one believes that this sort of activity is properly art, (which many people don't), perhaps that is the analogous tendency.

The use of metaphor and analogical thinking is crucial to theory building in biology, in fact possibly theory building in biology is no more than the development of useful metaphors—which is much more crucial than measurement. The shared use of metaphors in art and in science seems to me possibly the cement that keeps the two together.

REFERENCES

Bateson, G. (1973) *Steps to an Ecology of Mind.* Paladin.*

v. Bertalanffy, L. (1971) *General Systems Theory.* Penguin University Books.*

Polyani, M. (1959) *Personal Knowledge.* Chicago U.P.*

Poole, R. (1971) *Towards Deep Subjectivity.* Lane.

Roszak, T. (1970) *The Makings of a Counter Culture.* Faber.

* Of general relevance. Not specifically cited in text.

DISCUSSION

LLOYD JONES

I think it would be very interesting to ask what kind of science there would be if it were contrived by people that were interacting physically with the world around them but didn't speak; i.e. if they had no language. Can one imagine some sort of cinematic activity amongst living agents of some kind that didn't ever happen to develop language first? What would that actually be like? Where would they get model building from? Going on from that it seems to me that one still has to insist upon, not just isolated metaphors but structures of metaphors, which all go together.

I would like to pick up Kinmont's example of Van Gogh and his use of colour symbolism when painting Gaugin's chair and his own chair. An even better example is his two café paintings. He has one called 'A Night Café' which is an interior scene of a café with a billiard table, and he writes somewhere of wanting to represent the terrible passions of mankind in red and green. There indeed is his picture in red and green. Immediately afterwards he did a companion to it called 'A Pavement Café at Night', where you see this café from the outside. Everything is lit up and all is painted in blue and orange. He talks about the café as being a haven of peace and song and so forth. Much of what Van Gogh does when he is talking about expressive symbolism is not in anyway meant to endorse a kind of bucket theory of symbols; he is a thorough going structuralist in this sense. This is no accident either; I think it is the influence of the French academic teaching tradition, the 'Grammaire des Arts'. This system built upon a linguistic model which was much discussed at that time.

HARRÉ

I think we are being offered two contradictory theories and I would just like to ask to have a little separation of these. If it is a structuralist theory of colour symbolism, then it works by one colour excluding the other in pairs or triads. So then we would have blue and yellow excluding green and red. But there is also an atomistic theory of symbols where, for instance, red is the colour of one type of emotion; green is the colour of another. This is a non-structuralist account. Could we have a resolution of this?

MERMOZ

We must be very careful when we describe colour as a convention in the visual arts. We must, in particular, take into account the context in which colour symbolism comes into play. The difference in colour between the two chairs painted by Van Gogh was concurrently determined by aesthetic considerations and by the affect Vag Gogh projected onto the two chairs, before and when he painted them. Thus, Van Gogh's statement, 'I use colour more arbitrarily, in order to express myself forcibly' (Arles, August 1888) may be related to the aesthetic of 'suggestive colour' he had derived from Monticelli, Delacroix and Japanese prints. When Van Gogh wrote about his painting of Gaugin's chair, in two letters to Theo, he described it as a 'strange' study in which 'I searched for a light éffect with clear colours'. However, his psychological motives for associating certain colours with specific moods (and therefore with affect) remained for him largely unconscious.

GELL

Let us agree that the colour as such has no impact, it is the gestalt which has the impact in both these pictures. Exactly the same colour can occur in a calm picture by Poussin or a stormy sea or in a Chinese miniature or anything else you like—an identical tint that doesn't have any particular symbolical meaning. I feel further that a symbol is something which as used can have a whole set of different meanings. Therefore it is much easier to consider symbols verbally, say in terms of Yeats' 'Secret and inviolate rose' which has already been cited; this is not simply a poem about God, the phrase can mean many different other things which are to a certain extent arbitrary to the person who is reading it. It is not a thin poem, it is not a poem which is simply about God, it is one in which Yeats has inserted a great possibility of choice by the reader. It is much more subtle than meaning just one thing; what means just one thing is a simile or allegory. But colours do not have the same particularity of reference as words, they only offer a crude sort of symbolism.

MERMOZ

Right! What matters is that colour, at a certain point, becomes associated, in the artist's mind, with specific kinds of affect. Colours can represent (i.e. be signs of) affect in actual experience as well as in works of art, and can do it at the level of conscious (aesthetic) choice and unconscious motivation. This provides two complementary directions for our research on the structure of meaning: a stimulating challenge for the interactionist hypothesis!

GELL

I use 'choice' meaning the subconscious choice equally, that is to say there are possibilities and one possibility comes out, so to speak. It is chosen to the extent that the artist has to put the pigment on with his brush.

CORNFORD

I should like to give a brief summary of my views on the general theme of this conference that goes beyond what Philip Gell has been saying. I have a candidate for the post, if it is still vacant, of metatheory, assuming that I correctly understand what is meant by the term. Also for its counterpart or anti-metatheory; and they do not preside solely over Western European culture in the nineteenth century: they have other sources, they start earlier and they are not finished yet. Let me explain. There is a way of looking at the history of the last 300 years or so which brings out, not the commonalty between art and science (though this is undoubtedly present and very important) but rather their neutral opposition on different sides of the huge and still unresolved disagreement between the ecological world view (a sense of the dynamic 'interconnectedness of everything', combined with a cherishing attitude towards the natural world) on the one hand; and all mechanistic, reductionist, hyper-specialised, tunnel-visioned, exploitative, technocratic world-views on the other.

Primitive animism, whatever its limitations, is ecological in the sense that invests natural forces and creatures with spirits that are to be respected and propitiated. But this already comes under attack as idolatrous in the ancient Hebrew tradition: Adam not only *names* the beasts, he *has dominion* over them, and the fruits of the earth are there for *his* benefit. Conformably, Western man has ever since maintained and intensified an attitude of aggression, domination and acquisitiveness towards the physical environment and is currently exhausting its resources; polluting its land, air and waters; destroying its species and their habitats and rendering this globe progressively less habitable by all living creatures including himself. And today the diabolically ingenious products of nuclear technology threaten to make short work of us even more quickly than we can make short work of the planet.

> The white man, through his insensitivity to the way of Nature, has desecrated the face of Mother Earth. The white man's advanced technological capacity has occurred as a result of his lack of regard for the spiritual path and for the way of all living things. The white man's desire for material possessions has blinded him to the pain he has caused Mother Earth by his quest for what he calls natural resources. And the path of the Great Spirit has become difficult to see by almost all white men, even by many Indians who have chosen instead to follow the path of the white man.

These words were written by members of the Hopi tribe in a letter to President Nixon in 1970, protesting against the strip-mining of their sacred lands for coal. Their indictment cannot be gainsaid: my contention here is that it is the scientific attitude—not all of it, certainly, but that overwhelmingly common aberration of it that regards nature with cold, detached inquisitiveness and nothing else—which has been and still is the chief ideological accessory to the species-genocidal and species-suicidal course we are still following. It is scientists, after all, as well as technologists, who man Aldermaston and Lawrence Livermore, or who systematically torture baby monkeys by putting them on the far side of glass panels from their frantic mothers in order to 'measure' how much distressed either party becomes (I have seen these experiments transmitted *without adverse comment* on British television). It is not the artists who do these things, venal and stupid though many of them are (ironically, the monkey-torturer or weapons designer probably goes home to a ranch-style house and listens to Brahms on hi-fi).

How, historically speaking, did this exponentially-rising curve of insensibility and schizophrenic destructiveness come about? What prior philosophical sanctioning prepared the public mind for it, caused us to think it normal or even enjoined? I have already pointed a finger at the Hebrew tradition, which had its prolongation in Christianity. A long and learned study would be needed to tell the subsequent story in all its complex unfolding. But let me name one great man—not, admittedly, a scientist—who appears to have played the single most important role: Descartes. His dualism, it seems to me, was what gave full philosophical articulation and status to a tendency already endemic in Western thought; and by doing so, by turning the physical universe into a soulless mechanical 'out there', finally wrenched us away from any residual empathy with what the Hopi letter calls The Great Spirit. A gate was thereby opened through which Western man could perhaps have taken more than one path: but the one we have in fact taken has brought us within sight of self-extermination. Therefore the negation or repeal of this dualism (which I hereby nominate as the big meta-theory) appears as the prime intellectual and psychic enterprise of the centuries following Descartes, and of our own times. A gigantic anti-Cartesian revision, an epochal process of cultural therapy and reintegration had to be entered upon as soon as the impact of the dualism became manifest to perceptive spirits and continues to this day.

Among its greatest forerunners or protagonists I would name Blake, Wordsworth, Coleridge, Geothe, Tolstoy, Ruskin, Morris, Kropotkin, Einstein, Gandhi, D. H. Lawrence, Aldous Huxley and Heidegger, along with such recent apostles of ecology as Rachel Carson, Schumacher, Illich, Commoner and Bookchin. They do not of course mutually agree on all issues, but taken together, it is their general drift of sensibility that I would nominate as the big anti-metatheory to mechanistic or Cartesian kinds of thinking. Now it is noteworthy that in my hagiology above I have listed persons famed for poetry, novel-writing, criticism of the arts and philosophy—in some cases two or more of these activities—but only four scientists: Kropotkin, Einstein, Commoner and Carson.

If one were to draw up the corresponding and antithetical list, the 'demonology'—which I do not feel competent to do—it would certainly have to include figures from the humanities side: Francis Bacon, Descartes and Locke, to name but three, along with plenty of beefy nineteenth-century publicists for commercial and imperial 'greatness'. But we would be hard put to it to find a poet or novelist or dramatist or painter of quality to put amongst them. That is why I say that, *in a sense and to a degree*, there is warfare as well as commonalty between the two cultures.

But that is not my last word. If there is any validity in the scheme I have sketched out, it would seem to be one of the rare instances in which the arts people may have influenced the scientists in the long run—there being plenty of instances of flow in the reverse direction. For not only does the reaction against mechanistic and reductionist science seem to begin as early as Goethe and Coleridge; it seems still to be gaining ground, as for example in what Philip Gell called 'subjectivism' and 'interactionism' in science (does not Heisenberg's Uncertainty Principle also point towards subjectivision of a sort?) How far such developments are coincidental rather than causally related probably no-one could ever say: but the upshot is likely to be a drawing-together of scientists with artists on ground from which the Hopi Indians have never shifted.

GELL

I would like to think that is true. Thinking wholistically in this sense is perhaps essentially liberalising and the villains of the piece are Galileo especially, and Descartes. At least I put that to the historians to ask if that is so. (Wholism or holism? a logico-scientific method (Duhem, Quine, cf. Popper): an epistemiology (cf. Piaget): an aesthetic (cf. Roszak): a cosmology (cf. J. C. Smuts): all rather different; which do we mean?)

LLOYD JONES

It seems to me that there is nothing about wholism which is either essentially liberalising or unliberalising. Each concept animates certain people to some conclusions and after all it is not many years since Popper delivered an enormous blast against the notion of wholism because for him it underpinned anti-liberal tendencies everywhere he saw it. I am not too sure about organicism as being essentially more sympathetic and genial, more likely to foster brotherly love than an atomistic view of things. Popper provocatively said that all the humanists when you actually lined them up are in the other camp: no doubt he over-simplified his position.

I would like to ask two questions related to today's proceedings. Rom Harré started with a forthright assertion that there were undoubted correlations between art and science; they were so obvious that we needn't go into details. Then he passed on to a number of features which any explanation of these correlations would have to fulfil. I would like to ask question one. What's left standing of that initial assumption after the day's proceedings? Question two is 'And so what?' If we actually could discover that there were some correlations, why would we be expected to be excited by it, what else would we have expected and can we really point to something that we could really see would have been dramatically different if Snooks hadn't met Bloggs.

MERMOZ

Some of the difficulties we have encountered might have come from the fact that the problem of the correlation between art and science has been discussed largely in terms of influences (for or against). The interactionist hypothesis was more useful as it focused our attention on the way each discipline produces meaning. It is important, therefore, that we should distinguish between discourses which use language—such as we are now using for communication—discourses which use mathematics to construct models of reality and, finally, discourses which linguists have termed 'a-systematic', i.e. discourses which do not present the characteristics of a system. Here are three major distinctions in the language of art and science which we ought to take into account in our assessment of their respective epistemological status. Having encountered Language (artistic and scientific languages) we have to acknowledge the fact that in any situation of contact or interaction between discourses we are dealing with relative representations involving conscious and unconscious processes. Before we can further our understanding of the correlations between art and science we need to outline a theoretical framework in which the arts and the sciences will be considered as semiological activities (i.e. as activities concerned with the production of meaning). As long as we persist in viewing these correlations from the standpoint of art or from that of science, the common denominators we set out to discover will remain opaque and elude our quest.

WOLPERT

I wish to put in a word against interactionism, which I regard as wholism in disguise and I think you can go an awfully long way without network theory. Maybe immunology will gain something terrific by it but as yet it hasn't really proved its worth. I'm an atomist; I really believe in causation, with single events causing something. If you change a gene, you change the protein, and you actually get an abnormality of the haemoglobin which leads to sickle cell anaemia: that is a linear causal event. I also think that a great deal of what we are saying about art and science is really coming back to Peter Lloyd-Jones' question. What else would you expect? We are all creative; we are creative in tennis, creative in golf, creative in business, it is just the human condition. I think a great deal of the apparent commonality that we see between art and science is frankly trivial.

HARRÉ
I think we have had two different network theories offered to us which we need to separate. The network theory we were offered originally was an open bounded net which never will become wholistic. It is a quite different theory to say that the network is bounded, by which is meant *intrinsically* bounded. So only a very small sub-species of network theories are wholistic and I think that is a point worth making. I agree that wholistic theories do have nasty fascist associations which I feel uneasy about. But I don't feel the same with open network theories. I think that is a distinction well worth making. Secondly, as to the viability of interactionism, well it may not be viable in biology, I don't know, but without it physics would be totally and completely lost. There isn't a single physical parameter that is definable in terms of a single particle. They are all definable in terms of the structure into which the entities enter, such as electric charge, mass, etc. There is no such thing as a physical atom any more in physics; it is essentially a network theory and we just have to live with that.

9

SOME REMARKS ON THE RELATIONSHIPS BETWEEN ART AND MATHEMATICS

(By way of introduction to two films shown at the Conference, the first on M. C. Escher, the second on the Moebius band as interpreted by Max Bill)

Michele Emmer

Istituto Matematico 'G. Castelnuovo', Università di Roma

M. C. Escher (1971) said himself: 'By keenly confronting the enigmas that surround us, and by considering and analyzing the observations that I had made, I ended up in the domain of mathematics. Although I am absolutely without training or knowledge in the exact sciences I often seem to have more in common with mathematicians than my fellow artists.'

In the last fifteen years the prints of Escher have regularly appeared in books, articles and newspapers, not only to illustrate mathematical problems. As Coxeter (1971) said: 'Many examples illustrate the compatibility of Escher's work with the world of mathematics'; similarly Bruno Ernst (1976): 'Le tournant curieux dans l'oeuvre d'Escher se situe entre 1934 et 1937. . . . Il ne puise plus son inspiration dans la vision extérieure, mais dans des processus de pensée qui peuvent être interprétés mathématiquement. . . . N'eût-ce été déjà une disposition de son caractère. Ne cherchons cependant pas cette predisposition dans un intérêt pour les mathématiques. . . . Il ne travaillait pas comme un mathématicien, mais beaucoup plus comme un excellent menuisier qui, avec la seule aide d'un mètre souple et d'un compas, finit par produire un objet concret.'

The mathematical properties of the Escher's prints have been investigated by H. S. M. Coxeter (1971), a well known mathematician, and B. Ernst (1976). A famous essay on the symmetric drawings of the Dutch graphic artist was written with his direct help by the Dutch crystallographer C. MacGillavry (1976). Of course many other scientists have written on different aspects of Escher's work.

Coxeter has directly cooperated with Escher who was attracted by a figure in a book by the mathematician. This figure was a model of hyperbolic geometry due to the mathematician Poincaré (Coxeter, 1961). Escher made four prints of the series 'Circle Limit' to illustrate the model, following the suggestion of Coxeter. Coxeter (1979) himself wrote an article to explain how the prints were made.

In his article Coxeter demonstrated how 'Circle Limit III', 'based on his (Escher's) intuition is perfect, even though his poetic description of it was only approximate'.

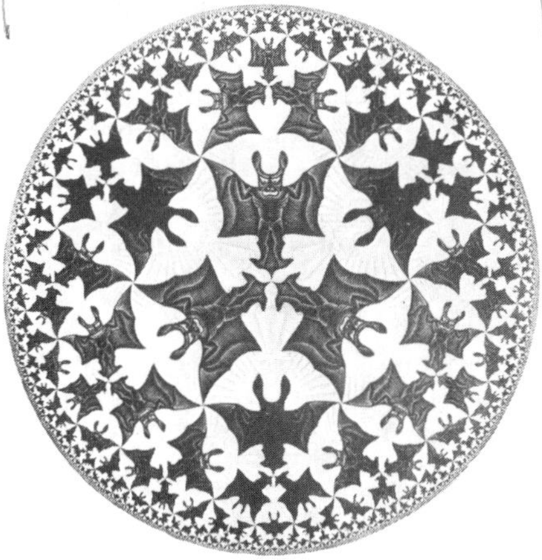

FIGURE 1 M. C. Escher, 'Circle Limit IV' (Heaven and Hell), woodcut, 1960, diameter 42 cm. Collections of Gemeentemuseum, The Hague

Coxeter (1971) considered 'from an artistic point of view' that 'this woodcut (Circle Limit III) would have been still more beautiful without the white arcs which artificially divide each fish into two unequal parts'. His favourite was 'Circle Limit IV' (Figure 1): 'Perhaps it is the absence of such backbones that makes Circle Limit IV so particularly appealing.'

The interest of Escher in the so-called impossible objects devised by L. S. and R. Penrose (1958) is also well known. As I have written elsewhere (Emmer, 1980b), Roger Penrose told me in 1979 that Escher made his print 'Belvedere' in 1958 before he received the Penroses' article on impossible objects. Thus the way to depict the object of the type of an impossible triangle was independently devised by Escher and R. Penrose.

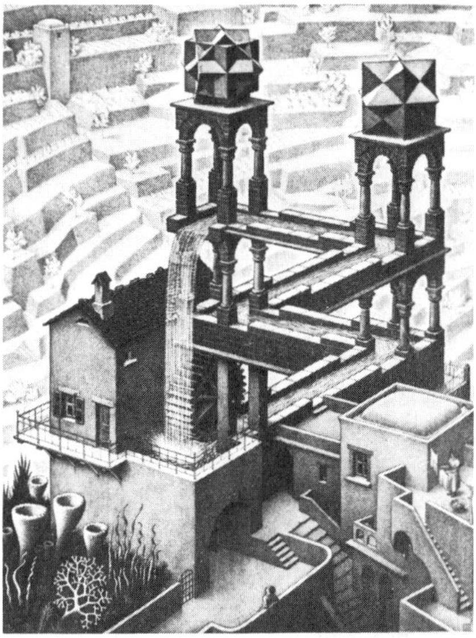

FIGURE 2 M. C. Escher, 'Waterfall' Lithograph, 1961, 38×30 cm. Collections of Gemeentemuseum, The Hague

Escher (1971) used the impossible objects of the Penroses in two other prints: 'The endless stairs which are the main motif of this picture (ascending and descending) were taken from an article by L. S. and R. Penrose while in the 'Waterfall' (Figure 2) appears a copy of the impossible triangle.

So in examining the relationships between Art and Mathematics the work of Escher is particularly interesting. Escher was not a mathematician but he was attracted by mathematics and he was able to construct 'perfect' models of mathematical objects.

Furthermore, as Coxeter (1971) pointed out,

> In 1951 and subsequent years A. V. Shubnikov, N. V. Belov and others extended the theory of crystallographic groups by combining the systematic repetition of shapes with a systematic repetition of colours. The Russians were almost certainly unaware of the fact that Escher, using his artistic intuition without any mathematics, had anticipated many of their results.

Escher not only used mathematical models to construct his prints but was able to construct his own models and sometimes to anticipate mathematical results: an artist who was able to construct mathematical theories using his intuition and an empirical approach.

Of course the aim of Escher was 'beauty' but the mathematician G. H. Hardy (1940) said:

> A mathematician like a painter or a poet is a maker of patterns. The mathematician's patterns, like the painter's or the poet's, must be beautiful; ideas like the colours or the words must fit together in a harmonious way. Beauty is the first test: there is no permanent place in the world for ugly mathematics.

A similar idea is formulated by the French mathematician F. Le Lionnais (1962):

> La beauté se déploie en mathématiques comme dans les autres sciences, comme dans les arts, comme dans la vie et comme dans la nature. Parfois comparables à celles de la musique pure, de la grande peinture ou de la poésie, les émotions qu'elle éveille sont le plus souvant d'une nature différente qui ne peut guère se comprendre lorsq'en n'en a pas ressenti en soi-même l'illumination.

Many mathematicians and artists have been attracted also in recent times to formulating a mathematical theory or a mathematical approach to art.

In the 1930s an outstanding mathematician G. D. Birkhoff (1932) formulated a theory for 'A Mathematical approach to Aesthetics':

> The typical aesthetic experience can be regarded as compounded of three successive phases: (1) a preliminary effort of attention, which is necessary for the act of perception and which increases in proportion to what we shall call the complexity (*C*) of the object; (2) the feeling of value or aesthetic measure (*M*) which rewards this effort; and finally (3) a realization that the object is characterized by a certain harmony, symmetry, or order (*O*), more or less concealed, which seems to be necessary for the aesthetic effort.
>
> This analysis of the aesthetic experience suggests that aesthetic feelings arise primarily because of an unusual degree of harmonious interrelationship within the object. More definitely, if we regard *M*, *O*, and *C* as measurable variables, we are led to write
>
> $$M = \frac{O}{C}$$
>
> and thus to embody in a formula (which was first presented in 1928) the conjecture that the aesthetic measure may be regarded as determined by the density of order relations in the aesthetic object.
>
> If we admit the validity of such a formula, the following mathematical formulation of the fundamental aesthetic problems may be made: within each class of aesthetic objects, to define the order *O* and the complexity *C* so that their ratio $M = O/C$ yields the aesthetic measure of the different objects of the class.

For the meaning of order the reader should refer to 'Statements on the relationships between the natural sciences and the visual arts and, in particular, on the meaning of order', a collection of invited papers in *Leonardo* (1981).

As A. Hill (1979) pointed out in his introduction to *Visual Art, Mathematics & Computers*: 'Birkhoff's approach was not looked upon with much favour by those predisposed to the development of a science of aesthetics. Nevertheless, more than an echo of Birkhoff's work is found in the ideas proposed by other writers such as N. Rashevsky, H. J. Eysenk, A. Moles, M. Bense, H. W. Franke and F. Nake.'

Birkhoff's effort was not isolated. As A. Hill (1979) noted:

> Concerning a broader approach to art and mathematics, I have found no piece of writing in our century that is comparable to a chapter in Oswald Spengler's two volumes *Decline of the West*. Entitled 'The Meaning of Numbers' it appears in the first volume that is subtitled 'Form and Actuality'. It is a historical review of nearly 40 pages on the relationship between the arts and mathematics.

Another interesting example is the book by J. Schillinger (1948) *The Mathematical Basis of the Arts.*

It is well known that many artists have a particular interest in the 'Golden Section'. Matila Ghyka (1927; 1931) was particularly interested in this theory of proportion which is also important in nature (Thompson, 1942). It is worthwhile remembering the famous book by Luca Pacioli (1509) and Leonardo da Vinci's *De Divina Proportione* which contains 60 plates of regular solids, in particular the Platonic solids (Emmer, in press).

Not only mathematicians have been attracted by the possibility of formulating a mathematical theory of the arts but of course also artists, like Max Bill. In his *A Mathematical Approach in Contemporary Art* Bill (1973) wrote:

> I am convinced it is possible to evolve a new form of art in which the artist's works could be founded to quite a substantial degree on a mathematical line of approach to his content. . . . Just as mathematics provides us with a primary method of cognition, . . . so too, some of its basic elements will furnish us with laws to appraise the interactions of separate objects . . . since it is mathematics which lends significance to those relationships, it is only a natural step from having perceived them to desiring to portrait them. . . . It must not be supposed that an art based on the principles of mathematics, such as I have just adumbrated, is in any sense the same thing as a plastic or pictorial interpretation of the latter.
>
> Indeed, it employs virtually none of the resources implicit in the term 'pure mathematics'. The art in question can, perhaps, best be defined as the building up of significant patterns from the everchanging relations, rhythms and proportions of abstract forms, having their own causality, and is tantamount to a law unto itself. As such, it presents some analogy to mathematics itself where every fresh advance had its immaculate conception in the brain of one or other of the pioneers.

As I pointed out (Emmer, 1980a) it is also interesting that when in 1935 Max Bill made his sculpture 'Endless Ribbon' (Figure 3) he thought he was the first to discover the so-called Moebius band, already described by the German mathematician Augusts Ferdinand Moebius in 1858. In my film on the 'Moebius band' Bill is recorded as saying in 1979: 'I made the first

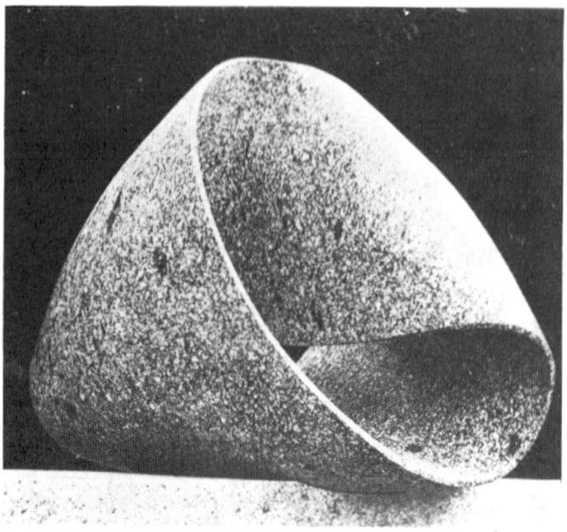

FIGURE 3 M. Bill, 'Endless Ribbon', granite, 159×100×120 cm, 1935 (A second 'Endless Ribbon' was made in 1953) Centre Nationale d'Art et de Culture Georges Pompidou, Paris

Moebius band in 1935 without being aware of the work of the mathematician Moebius.'

Several articles by mathematicians appeared in the review of the Neo-plasticism movement 'De Stijl'. Mondrian (1919; 1920) wrote 'The Neo-plasticism can be called an abstract-real painting because the abstract (as in mathematics) can be expressed by a plastic reality. . . . I saw the reality as a unity: all its different aspects show an unique element, the immutability. We try to express in a plastic way this immutability, the plastic expression of unchangeable connections: this is why we use orthogonal straight lines and the primary colours (Figure 4).

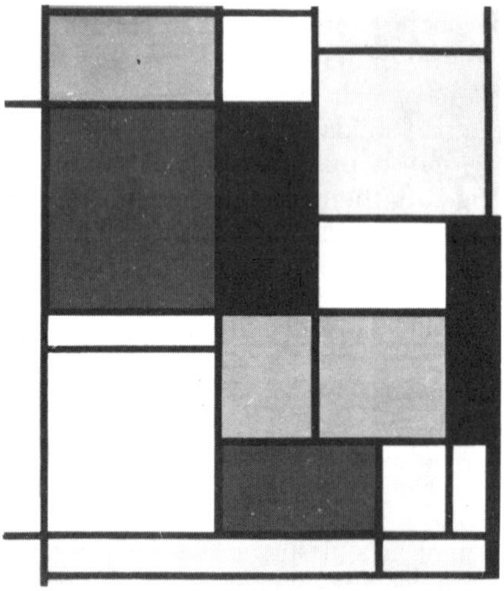

FIGURE 4 P. Mondrian, 'Painting II', 1921–5, Oil on canvas, 75.5×65 cm. Private collection

As the physicist Careri (1981) said: 'Abstraction is generally viewed as a cognitive process which consists in the removal of features that characterize only the individual or a particular phenomenon. This process coincides with the recognition of permanent relations in a class of data.'

Looking for this 'Characteristica Universalis' (Leibnitz, 1667) or 'Invariant' is one of the fields of research of modern abstraction in art as well as in different fields of modern mathematics.

These are only a few examples of the recent connections between art and mathematics. Another interesting problem is the influence of the so-called new geometry, the non-euclidean geometry, on the artistic movements at the beginning of the century (Compton, 1980; Henderson, 1975).

Relationships are not only between art and mathematics, but more generally, between art, mathematics and natural sciences.

My intention in making the films of the series 'Art and Mathematics' was to provide visual stimuli capable of exciting the imagination of people with the most varied interests, providing what should be an interdisciplinary point of view, but of course concentrating on visual effects, never forgetting that we were making a film, using the language of the camera and not editing a book.

So the films are the result of my personal ideas on the connections between art and mathematics, both in modern and ancient times, but also the result of a stimulating cooperation with artists and scientists of different disciplines.

In the various films it is sometimes a fascination with mathematics that prevails while at other times it is the artistic aspect, and at yet others, the biological.

REFERENCES

Bill, M. (1978) The Mathematical Approach in Contemporary Art, reprinted in E. Huttinger, *Max Bill,* p. 112. ABC Edit., Zurich.

Birkhoff, G. (1931) A Mathematical Approach to Aesthetics, *Scientia* (Sept.), pp. 133–46; 'A Mathematial Theory of Aesthetics, *The Rice Inst. Pamphlet,* (July, 1932), v. 19, pp. 189–342.

Careri, G. (1981) The Idea of Order in the Natural Sciences and in the Visual Arts, *Leonardo* vol. 14, p. 146.

Compton, L. Adelman-M. (1980) Mathematics in early Abstract Art, in *Towards a New Art* p. 64. The Tate Gallery, London.

Coxeter, H. S. M. (1961) *Introduction to Geometry,* p. 285. J. Wiley and Sons, New York.

—— (1971) The Mathematical Implications of Escher's Prints, in *The World of M. C. Escher* ed. J. L. Locher, p. 49. H. Abrams Publ., New York.

—— (1979) The non-Euclidean Symmetry of Escher's Picture 'Circle Limit III', *Leonardo,* vol. 12, p. 19–25.

Emmer, M. (1980a) Visual Art and Mathematics: the Moebius Band, *Leonardo,* vol. 13 p. 108–11.

—— (1980b) Comments on the Note by Jean C. Rush on the Appeal of M. C. Escher's Pictures, *Leonardo,* vol. 13, pp. 209–10.

—— Art and Mathematics: the Platonic Solids, *Leonardo,* vol. 15, pp. 277–82.

Ernst, B. (1976) *Le Miroir magique de M. C. Escher,* pp. 27–8. Chêne edit., Paris.

Escher, M. C. (1971) *The Graphic Work,* pp. 8 and 16. MacDonald, London.

Ghyka, M. C. (1927) *Esthétique des Proportions dans la Nature et dans les Arts.* Gallimard, Paris.

—— (1931) *Le Nombre d'Or.* Gallimard, Paris.

Hardy, G. H. (1940) *A Mathematician's Apology,* p. 25. Cambridge University Press, London.

Henderson, L. D. (1975) *The Artist, the Fourth Dimension and Non-Euclidean Geometry, 1900–1930,* a Romance of Many Dimensions, Doctoral Dissertation, Yale University.

Hill, A. (1979) Introduction to *Visual Art, Mathematics and Computers; Selections from the Journal Leonardo* (ed. F. J. Malina). Pergamon Press, Oxford.

Leibnitz, G. W. (1667) Towards a Universal Characteristic, reprinted in *Leibnitz, Selections,* pp. 17–20 (ed. P. P. Weiner). C. Scribner's Sons Edit., New York.

Le Lionnais, F. (1962) 'La Beauté en mathématiques' in *Les Grands Courants de la Pensée mathématique,* pp. 457–8 (ed. F. Le Lionnais). Librairie Scient. et Technique Edit., Paris.

Leonardo (1981) vol. 14, pp. 144–49, 230–37 and 311–22.

MacGillavry, C. (1976) *Fantasy and Symmetry: the periodic drawings of M. C. Escher.* H. N. Abrams Edit. New York.

Mondrian, P. (1919) Dialog over de Nieuwe Boelding, *De Stijl*, n. 5, p. 50.

—— (1920) Le Neoplasticisme Principe général de l'équivalence plastique, *Editions de l'Effort Moderne,* Paris; reprinted in *Piet Mondrian: tutti gli scritti,* Feltrinelli Edit., p. 148. Milano.

Pacioli, L. (1509) De Divina Proportione, *Fontes Ambrosiani in luce editi cura et studio Bibliothecae Ambrosianae* XXXI, Milano (1956), based on the original codex edited in Venice (1509).

Penrose, L. S. and R. (1958) Impossible Objects: A Special type of visual Illusion, *Brit. J. Psychol.,* **49,** 31.

Schillinger, J. (1948) *The Mathematical Basis of the Arts*. Edit. Philosophy Library, New York.

Thompson, D'Arcy W. (1942) *On Growth and Form*. Cambridge University Press, Cambridge.

10

CONTINUITY AND DISCONTINUITY IN EARLY TWENTIETH-CENTURY PHYSICS AND EARLY TWENTIETH-CENTURY PAINTING

Alex Keller

Department of History of Science, University of Leicester

SUMMARY

G. P. Thomson has summarised the changes in early twentieth-century physics as a move from continuity to discontinuity. This aspect of the revolution in physics which followed the theory of the electron, the quantum and relativity was already being discussed at the beginning of the century: Oliver Lodge called attention to it in his presidential address to the B.A.A.S. in 1913; other attempts to deal with the philosophical issues arising were made by Poynting, Langevin and S. McLaren. Was this swing away from continuity of radiation and energy, and the irrevocable solidity of the atom, purely a response to experimental problems, which only radicals could solve? Or were other changes in intellectual approach pushing these radicals toward discontinuity? Lodge, McLaren and others saw the changes in physics as symptoms of a wider revolution. Can we find a comparable crisis in the artistic movements of the time—for instance in neo-impressionism, fauvism or cubism?

A dozen years ago, Sir George Thomson, himself one of the leading physicists of his time, and son of another more revolutionary physicist, J. J. Thomson, summed up the characteristic feature of sixty years of physics as 'first, a great increase in the importance of the idea of atomicity, namely that the fundamental things in the universe, and many of the less fundamental, are mass-produced as vast numbers of identical units (G. P. Thomson, 1969). Now, it was hardly a discovery of the twentieth century to propose that the immense variety of natural objects conceals a true simplicity, in that all are composed of great numbers of homogeneous monads of a very few types differing only in mass (and in the earlier versions, also shape). Not only does the concept 'atom' go back to the Greeks, but atomism has proved an essential foundation for any scientific physics and chemistry in the manner that they have developed since the days of Newton and Boyle. What then did

G. P. Thomson mean? I suspect, judging by the remainder of the article on 'Matter and Radiation', from which the above passage is quoted, that he had in mind the breakdown of the atom itself into sub-atomic and more homogeneous units; and the encroachment of atomistic concepts of a discontinuous radiation into regions where a continuum had been held to prevail—the transmission of energy and radiation.

The atom of Dalton and nineteenth century physicists and chemists, like the atom of Newton, was indivisible, a continuous body floating within the ether, which had replaced the ancient atomists' void—for the ether was substance, albeit imperceptible, imponderable and unlike matter in that it was not divisible into independent but identical least units at all. The revolution in physics which Thomson describes broke down the atom into sub-atoms. The apparent variety of atoms, classified by late nineteenth-century chemists into nearly a hundred elements, could henceforth be translated into different arrangements and quantities of universal electrons, all of identical mass. Indeed, for some years an electric theory of matter suggested, in its most popular and exciting formulation, that all atoms were wholly constructed of these electrons, evidently in vast crowds, given the disparity of mass—nearly two thousand to one in the case of the lightest element, hydrogen—between atom and electron. Inasmuch as all electrons are negative in charge, the theory like most new theories had its difficulties but it could be supposed that electrons were embedded in spheres of positive electricity, and probably this positive charge would prove to be fundamentally divided into positive electrons in the end. The symmetry of the world so demanded it. Faraday had put forward the hypothesis that electricity is not a continuous fluid but particulate, so that electric current is the motion of the particles which are the least units of electric charge, and this idea, unpopular at first, was in the 1880s revived by Helmholtz and Stoney. The hypothesis that the cathode ray is likewise a stream of particles, not a wave of ether, also appeared dubious when first advanced. However, J. J. Thomson in 1897 was able to deflect the cathode ray in magnetic and electric fields and obtain thereby a mass/charge ratio of its components which enabled him to argue that these were not only particles possessed of mass, but moreover of mass much smaller than that of atoms. Given the wide variety of sources of cathode particles, all with the same mass, they could plausibly be presented as the universal constituents of matter. I say, 'plausibly', because this proposition was by no means obvious, and other researchers who were attempting to find the same ratio did not all agree that if these were indeed particles they were the building blocks of which all atoms are built—indeed not all agreed that they were particles anyway. For these particles, Thomson revived the old name of corpuscle once used by Newton and Boyle: a term which stresses the atomicity of his conception of their role. What proved the making of his theory was its association with parallel theories of electricity as the interaction of ether and matter, which led to the adoption of the name 'electron'.

A distinctly dualist view was popular in the latter part of the century. As J. J. Thomson explained in his Presidential Address to the British Association for the Advancement of Science in 1909, matter forms 'but minute islands in the great ocean of the ether, the substance with which the whole universe is filled'. In more recent times, when the ether hypothesis has been abandoned as useless, more postivist scientists have been inclined to dismiss it out of hand. If now outworn, they appear to feel, it was always fanciful, indeed dubious, and serious scientists can never have taken it quite seriously. Not so: as Thomson continues, 'The ether is not a fantastic creation of the speculative philosopher: it is as essential to us as the air we breathe.' That being so, the study of its properties will be 'probably the most fascinating and important duty of the physicist' (J. J. Thomson, 1910). But these properties *were* baffling. The ether, an imperceptible, imponderable, indivisible and all-pervading active medium for the flux of energy and the wave motion of all forms of radiation, was therefore opposed to inert, massy, passive, atomic matter. Ether acted upon matter—but how? Could the ether itself be particulate? Or was matter but temporary connections, bonds, fibres, or vortices in ether? That would rescue our model of the world substance from the dualism, which many found so unsatisfactory. This issue is tackled by John Poynting (1900), president of the Mathematics and Physics section of the British Association at their Dover meeting of 1899 (where Thomson first expounded his conclusions to a general public). Can we, Poynting asked, simply observe what we observe as a sequence of events, one following another? If we did, we should regard energy as multifold in diverse types, thermal, electrical, chemical—and yet we do feel energy, however protean, is one. 'We are not content with such discontinuous descriptions. We dislike the discontinuity and think of an underlying continuity.' And, he remarks later, we feel unhappy with the rigorous dualism of the contemporary distinction between matter and ether. We are eager to reduce matter to ether, because apparent discontinuity would then be dissolved in an underlying continuity. Poynting remarks that historically the most ancient form of atomism was presumably devised 'to explain the phenomena of expansion and contraction, evaporation and solution', which would have to be taken for granted if matter be continuous, but if it be 'a crowd of separate particles with interspaces', these phenomena can easily be explained in terms of their relations and movements in respect of one another. So, 'the most evident properties of matter are then similar to what may be observed in any public meeting (Poynting, 1900).

To this dualism, Thomson's results and his theory could be opposed, when subsumed into 'the electric theory of matter', in which mass—or at least inertia—ceased to be a fundamental property of matter but was a product of charge, which *is* fundamental, moving in ether, the effect of mass being related to the velocities of these moving charges. Over the next few years, some forms of matter at least were revealed to have the property of spontaneous disintegration. The atoms of radioactive elements break down, unaffected by external impulse and emit radiation as they do so, emit electrons and even heavier bodies which, it was soon suggested, could well be atoms of one of the lightest elements, helium. Hence the solidity and permanence of matter was an appearance only; atomic continuity concealed an inner discontinuity. If the disintegration of radioactive atoms and the view that all atoms are entirely composed of electrons disclose a discontinuity within the atom, yet the atom as a concept had always functioned as a discontinuous principle in the system of physical science: it was the ether that was taken to represent continuity. Hence the attraction of any model which reduced the atoms to ether, and hence too those 'energeticists' who denied the very existence of atoms, in their opinion a convenience for our minds but no more. The only thing we can observe and measure is the exchange and transmission of energy, and we should posit no more than we can perceive, without supposing any imaginary bodies which serve only to let us feel the world is coarser grained than it truly is.

However, in 1900, the year after Poynting's speech, energy itself began to develop discontinuities; that year Planck's celebrated constant made its appearance. In earlier versions of Planck's model of energy quanta, energy could only be transmitted or absorbed in multiples of this constant, although, eager not to challenge the accepted fundamental ideas of physics more than he had to, Planck still regarded energy as one, and radiation continuous as it undulated across the ether. Only in interaction with resonating atoms or electrons would it be received or emitted in bites of this constant. Actually, a few years later, J. J. Thomson did toy with the idea that electromagnetic radiation may travel not as a continuous wave-front but as discontinuous points localised along the front. However, the real snapping of the old axiom came with Albert Einstein. In 1905, in one of the papers of his *annus mirabilis*, he proposed that radiation did travel in discontinuous 'darts of light' (later called photons). This he derived as a conclusion from Planck's earlier exposition of his quantum theory, but was able to support by showing his model made sense of a number of electronic phenomena difficult to reconcile with existing views of the interaction of radiation and atomic matter. The historical course of the quantum debate is traced in the 'Black-Body Theory and the Quantum Discontinuity 1894–1912' of Kuhn (1978). By the latter date it had become clear that the quantum theory was here to stay, even if Einstein's view of light sounded still too much like the old particle theory of light to win acceptance for some years. It had also become clear that Einstein's Special Theory of Relativity, also put forward in 1905, would have to be reckoned with in any serious attempt to reconstruct physics. Photon (to use the word a little anachronistically) and Relativity suggested the ether could be dispensed with altogether. Einstein did not need it to explain the movement of light, therefore why suppose it exists at all? Where only a few years before, some of the greatest minds in physics were trying to reduce atoms to ether or energy—now ether was reduced to Space-Time occupied only by discontinuous particles.

In an attempt to save the old electromagnetics from what he saw as the unfortunate consequences of these innovations, S. McLaren, a young lecturer at Birmingham university, published in January 1913 in the *Philosophical Magazine*, 'The Theory of Radiation'. He opens with the comment that 'the unrest of our time has invaded even the world of Physics, where scarcely one of the principles long accepted as fundamental passes unchallenged by all' (McLaren, 1913). It is not only he adds, 'that Einstein's idea of the Quantum is destructive of the continuous medium and all that was built upon it in the nineteenth century', for he claims that Einstein's hypotheses shatter the very foundation of mechanical philosophy—that all change may be reduced to motion. With Einstein, 'the changes of which he speaks are not motions, they need no longer be even continuous'. McLaren therefore urges his theory of radiation precisely in order to save the concept of it as 'a continuous wave motion'. Later that year he produced a Theory of Gravitation, with similar intention. A few months before he wrote his Radiation paper he had made friends with Niels Bohr, when Bohr came to England as a research student; Bohr regarded McLaren as one of the few there who understood his own objectives in physics. This I mention because the world of science has largely forgotten McLaren, whose ideas proved to be tied to the old physics that was dying, not—like Bohr's—the new phoenix rising from the ashes. However, had McLaren not been killed on the Somme in 1916, it is likely enough that he would have moved on, and we should have heard more of him. He was certainly no old fogey desperately defending the redoubts of a besieged and crumbling stronghold.

Perhaps it would be possible to cast the accusation of elderly conservatism at Sir Oliver Lodge, who made Continuity the theme of his presidential address to the British Association in September 1913 (Lodge, 1914). When Lodge announced this title, he was asked by journalists whether he intended to speak of the continuity of human existence—that is to say, of the immortality of the human soul. The question may have arisen because many years before, Balfour Stewart and P. G. Tait (1875), two physicists then very well known, had collaborated on a book on *The Unseen Universe*, which did argue for immortality on the grounds that it follows from the general principle of continuity. Lodge insisted that this was not his purpose, although he does end his address to the B.A.A.S. putting the case that there are many things which science can not investigate but nevertheless are there, and clearly he means immaterial, immortal souls to be among them. However, he opens the Summary of the Argument of his address with the words: 'A marked feature of the present scientific era is the discovery of, and interest in, various forms of Atomism; so that Continuity seems in danger of being lost sight of.' In the course of the address he remarks how the rapid progress of recent years had been accompanied by scepticism about the basic assumptions of previous generations, leading to passionate controversies in every field of action. Atomism had taken over; mathematics and chemistry are perhaps necessarily discontinuous in their approach but now the same approach had spread to biology—first in the cell theory and now with the success of Mendelism. Above all, in physics, debate turns on 'the ultimate victory in the fight between Continuity and Discontinuity'. For him it was 'the theory of the Quantum or least indivisible unit or atom of energy' which had so radically promoted this fight. The implications of this concept are made manifest, he suggests, in a passage quoted from Poincaré: 'a physical system is susceptible of a finite number only of distinct conditions; it jumps from one of these conditions to another without passing through a continuous series of intermediate conditions'. But this is barely the half of it; Lodge goes on: 'for if the Principle of Relativity were to be accepted . . . it seems as if even Time would become discontinuous and be supplied in atoms', and our life 'turn out to be no more really continuous than the events on a kinematograph screen'. That was evidently almost as dreadful a consequence as the dissolution of the Ether of Space. Lodge made no bones about his unhappiness at this trend of thought. Like McLaren he proclaimed himself eager 'to retain the old and yet embrace the new': to accept the evidence for the quantum and relativity without abandoning the continuity of energy and the ether. 'The apparent discontinuous emission of radiation is, I believe, due to features in the real discontinuity of matter'—that is, to the discontinuous structure of atoms and the enormous velocities of their components. Much of the rest of the address is devoted to Lodge's attempt to defend the ether and save continuity by taking refuge in the electrical theory of matter—a theory which had indeed seemed 'discontinuous' and destructive of received ideas itself only ten years before.

Among the eminent foreign visitors at the 1913 meeting of the British Association was Paul Langevin, who within a few weeks of his return to Paris, delivered to the Société Française de Physique on November 27 1913 a paper on 'La Physique du Discontinu' (Langevin, 1923). Like Planck and Poincaré, and unlike Lodge, he was an enthusiast for the quantum and his talk rather assumes the quantum theory in its current state than seeks to defend it. He begins: 'The profound change which has recently been produced in Physics is characterised above all by the penetration into all the domains of our science of the fundamental notion of discontinuity.' Not only is this concept embodied in 'molecules, atoms and electrons, and probably magnetons' (the supposed elementary units of magnetism) but it has now become clear that 'matter can only emit electromagnetic radiation in a discontinuous manner, by quanta of energy proportionate to the frequency'. This will require a new mathematics, in as much as the calculus was 'created in order to translate analytically the notion of continuity'. We will need a new statistics of discontinuity which will link the phenomena of the discrete units, the 'grains' of things, to 'the phenomena of their aggregates', a statistics which will allow for fluctuations and variations. The physics of the discontinuous will be a physics that rests therefore on the statistical calculation of probability. It will need to investigate the most probable distribution or configuration of a particular assemblage of units under certain given circumstances—equilibrium states relating to radiation theory or thermodynamics, for example. Or it will treat of spontaneous fluctuations of the system around that distribution or configuration which is the most probable but not the only one possible, and is observed only as a mean. Thus the 'universal shuddering around the rigid configurations' predicted by thermodynamics might be intimately linked to the discontinuity of structure. He then proceeds to apply these discontinuous probability theorems to a range of problems of statistical mechanics and radiation, and concludes by returning to the essential importance of Planck's constant. This, introduced as 'measuring the extent of the elementary domain of probability in the problem of the resonator', in fact probably determines the elementary domain in all questions of statistical mechanics 'as already demonstrated in the emission of Roentgen radiation, of secondary cathode rays, of photoelectric phenomena, even the laws of chemical mechanics . . .'. It will be seen that although like Lodge he sees the quantum as the source of the contemporary victory of discontinuity, his approach is very different. That is not only because he was talking to a different audience, or simply because he was enthusiastic for those developments which repelled Lodge, but also because it is through an appropriate mathematics that he hoped to reach his goal. However, it is certainly not a mathematics which identifies the new school. McLaren's emotional response was more like that of Lodge, yet his treatment was mathematically as sophisticated as Langevin's.

Enough has been said, I hope, to give some meaning and a little detail to the assertion that the revolution in physics in the early years of the twentieth century was regarded by many observers at the time, and since, as a move from continuity to discontinuity. As a matter of convenience, addresses to such bodies as the British Association provide a useful source wherein general views about nature and the progress of science could be articulated in language intended both for the knowledgeable colleague and for a wider public, less knowledgeable but no less thoughtful. The evidence of Langevin suggests moreover that this antithesis was by no means confined to Britain. I have dealt only with physics, although Lodge at least extends his analysis to biology and beyond. Yet if basic physics is only a part of science, it has always been regarded as a highly important part, the guide wheel on which the rest may roll forward, or even change direction. Of course, the theories of Planck and Einstein, no less than those of strict 'experimentalists' like Lodge and Thomson, were constructed in order to answer questions which had arisen in the process of experimental research; these questions the accepted models had been unable to resolve. Yet, as is plain from the passages quoted, some saw these new answers as part of a wider revolution against all received beliefs. Certainly, few historians and philosophers of science would now maintain that scientific theories are dictated to us by naked facts, as the results of objective observation and experiment, which the genius simply *sees first*, so that once he has seen the answer only the stupid and obscurantist fail to agree with his interpretation. The subjective appeal of any one model to interpret the evidence must have some bearing on the welcome given to one exposition, the rejection of another. That does not mean, however, that we must have recourse to external pressures, class or group relationships, least of all glib allusions to mysterious zeitgeists of the sort popular at the time these great physicists were working. Frankly, I do not have a satisfactory explanation at all. It is hard to be a positivist any more but by no means easy to decide what can be put in the place of positivism, so that we might account for this kind of change in the thinking-cap, in Herbert Butterfield's metaphor.

Was there any similarity in the contemporary revolutions in art? Many people have commented on the temporal coincidence of these great shifts in thought and feeling. It is tempting to look for parallels. A fairly obvious place to look would be in the school of 'neo-impressionism' of the 1880s and 1890s. I am neither an artist nor a critic of art nor a historian of art—merely a looker at pictures. No more could be claimed for the remarks which follow than that they are the immediate reaction of a looker—an innocent eye (what a claim!). Everything that appears in these closing paragraphs should be provided with question marks and should be understood as so many hesitant and bashful queries—was it, perhaps, maybe, if it pleases you—rather like that? And if the reply comes back—No!—then if that retort is made good, I am quite satisfied. If I do nevertheless begin by citing a contemporary commentator, even that is with some hesitation, since many doubts could be expressed as to the value of manifestoes or expositions which purport to tell us what a school of artists intends—as much when they try to link the school to supposed progenitors as when they reject the past altogether. Outstanding artists seldom draw up such declarations of faith, although occasionally they can be talked into attaching their signatures afterwards. Cubism especially has called up a busy swarm of publicists and interpreters, who have often talked of the Fourth Dimension, non-Euclidean algebra, Relativity. But I do wonder whether Appollinaire and the others really knew so much about the scientific and mathematical developments, with which they drew such enthusiastic parallels (Rosenblum, 1961; Fry, 1966; Adler, 1974).[1] All the same . . . Paul Signac was a reasonably good artist as well as a reasonably good theoretician and his 'D'Eugène Delacroix au Neo-Impressionisme' of 1899 is a reasonable justification of the techniques which his friend Seurat had used in his great paintings of the late 1880s (Signac, 1899).

Signac explains that the objective of the neo-impressionist school was to obtain 'the benefits of luminosity colouring and harmony' by a process of

1. the optical mixture of pure pigments only
2. the separation of diverse elements
3. the equilibrium of these elements and their proportion
4. the choice of a brushstroke (?=*touche divisée*) proportionate to the dimensions of the picture.

By the first of these clauses, I understand him to mean that diverse colour effects would not be obtained by the mixture of pigments on the palette, but by setting colours next to one another according to supposedly scientific principles, so as to form an opticalo combination at the viewer's eye—which will thus turn the 'grains' (in Langevin's antithesis) into the right aggregates. Now we need not take too literally the enthusiasm of the neo-impressionists for the explanations of colour of Chevreul, still less of Henry, whom several of them so much admired. But yet this insistence that the new style is a 'divisionism' is striking—it does appear to its own practitioners to depend on the division of a surface into its pure components—those units of divided strokes which will form the aggregate when looked at properly. For the painting of this group, the name pointillisme has stuck. But Signac repudiates it. He would have nothing to do with a nickname which implied that all Seurat and his friends were doing was to paint in dots—or spatter their canvasses with confetti, as unkind critics said. It is *division* which is the essence—the 'touche divisée', not the use of dots or points. 'The divided

[1] Such parallels are drawn by many of the writers cited in E. F. Fry (1966), a collection of documents. But all seem to me vague and rhetorical—as Picasso is supposed to have commented—'pure literature, not to say, nonsense'—as Einstein also said (although less succinctly) about parallels between Cubism and Relativity. Unfortunately, I have not been able to consult P. Laporte, Cubism and Science, *Journal of Aesthetics and Art Criticism*, vii (1949).

stroke is changing, is living, is "light"; it is not at all the same as the point, which is uniform, is dead, is "matter"'. Signac's contrast between 'matter' and 'light' echoes the physical dualism described earlier. This divisionism then is the expression of a discontinuity of substance which adds up to the apparent visible continuity. The artist divides in order to reach back to this underlying discontinuity.

But is there not more? Links between painting and science have been found in Neo-Impressionism and in Cubism, the most blatantly revolutionary of all movements in art. Could we look to a bridge between them, a bridge partly concealed by artistic rebels' taste for denouncing the tameness of their predecessors? A surface or body can be shown to reveal, first, discontinuity within continuity. We may break down an area of paint which represents such a surface into its 'grains' through the 'touche divisée', and so clarify the visual construction—to attain a truer light and a truer colour, and truer relations between them. But there might then be a further stage, a discontinuity which bursts the barriers of the surfaces of bodies altogether, a discontinuity in which particular regions of colour cease to correspond to the outlines of objects. For some while Matisse held to a neo-impressionist divisionism fairly close to the description of Signac—indeed, one of his last paintings in this manner, 'Luxe, Calme et Volupté' (1904) recalls Signac, even to its theme—one might compare Signac's 'Au Temps de la Harmonie' (although that is even so, less bold). This painting of Matisse certainly displays the 'touche divisée', but also retains the boundaries of bodies, human, plant or hill. Contrast this with a remarkable landscape he brought back from his summer in Collioure in 1905. The shapes and boundaries of trees and hills have gone; space is discontinuous, broken by white void. The like fragmentation is vividly revealed by some landscapes painted by Georges Braque, a younger 'Fauve', in the following year, also at Collioure.

The 'touche divisée' seems to me to have enjoyed further progression later in that decade, in the first Cubist paintings of Braque and Picasso. Inasmuch as Braque began in 1906 almost where Matisse left off, his own development shows this progression most fully—more perhaps than Picasso, who entered the French school from the outside and did not wholly share their aesthetic history. In these works the discontinuous facets of the surfaces are disassembled quite, so that a body can be viewed from several angles of vision simultaneously and a new aggregate be composed of these atomised units. To suggest that in the mosaic of fragments, if not identical, at least resembling one another much more than the whole of which they once formed part, which come together to become Braque's 'Woman Reading' of 1911, or Picasso's 'Man with a Mandoline' of the same year—to suggest these fragments correspond to quanta, say . . . is not a suggestion that can be demonstrated. Is there a succession in divisionism, Seurat-Matisse-Braque? Is it in any way comparable to the successive advances of the physics of discontinuity? In 1899 a leading physicist regards the search for underlying continuity as natural to the human mind. Fourteen years later, other physicists agree that this search is *not* natural: they may welcome the shift or resist it but they do agree that science is now looking for underlying discontinuity. The avant-garde of art in 1899 looks to the atomising of surface to recover truer continuity. A dozen years later, the procedure of division and fragmentation leaves a mere suggestion of the original surface—perhaps only the convenience of a title. But are these apparent similarities and even convergences merely accidental? Are both tendencies the result of forces working on both physics and the plastic arts, acting quite accidentally to drive them in similar directions? Or does this similarity imply some deeper bond, which leads both series of innovation upon similar paths?

REFERENCES

Adler, J. (1974) Patterns of Art and Scientific Thought (University of Manchester MSc thesis).

Fry, E. F. (1966) *Cubism* Thames and Hudson, London.

Kuhn, T. S. (1978) *Black Body Theory and the Quantum Discontinuity, 1894–1912.* Clarendon Press, Oxford.

Langevin, P. (1923) La Physique du Discontinu, published as chap. iv, pp. 189–264, in his *La Physique depuis Vingt Ans.* Librairie Octave Doin, Paris.

Lodge, O. J. (1914) 'Continuity', President's Address, pp. 3–42 in Report of the Eighty-Third Meeting of the British Association for the Advancement of Science, Birmingham 1913. John Murray, London.

McLaren, S. B. (1913) The Theory of Radiation, *Philosophical Magazine,* ser. 6, xxv, pp. 43–56.

Poynting, J. (1900) Report of the Sixty-Ninth Meeting of the British Association for the Advancement of Science, Dover 1899, pp. 615–24. John Murray, London.

Rosenblum, R. (1961) *Cubism and Twentieth Century Thought* Thames and Hudson, London.

Signac, P. (1964) *D'Eugène Delacroix au Neo-Impressionisme* originally published in 1899, but I have used an edition presented by F. Cachin, Hermann, Paris.

Stewart, B. and Tait, R. G. (1875) *The Unseen Universe.* (later editions publ. by Macmillan, London.)

Thomson, G. P. (1969) Matter and Radiation, ch. 3, pp. 43–105, in *Scientific Thought 1900–1960* (edited by R. Harré). Clarendon Press, Oxford.

Thomson, J. J. (1910) President's Address, pp. 3–29, in Report of the Seventy-Ninth Meeting of the British Association for the Advancement of Science, Winnipeg 1909. John Murray, London.

11

FROM DARWIN'S INHERITANCE TO THE EVOLUTION OF ART

Ivor Davies

Coleg Addysg Uwch, Gwent

SUMMARY

The general concept of evolution is ancient: history progressing from Primitive through Classical to Modern civilisation. Between 1860 and 1880 Biology became real science, the doctrine of evolution of species causing vitalism and mysticism to recede temporarily. Concurrently Semper saw art as decoration evolved from functional marks, a by-product of craft emerging from technics.

Even more mechanistic, twentieth-century Behaviourist psychology, coinciding with mass-production, inspired standardisation, clear-cut forms and mechanical precision in the arts. Futurists replaced archaic conventions; Corbusier's architecture introduced natural and mechanical laws and post-revolutionary Russian arts studied economy, bio-morphism and Taylorist mass-production gestures in theatre. Art shed aesthetic decoration which hid function. Utopianism and mechanical evolution revived.

Mechanical evolution

Showing ways in which the ideas of Evolution, Behaviourism and Relativity in art during the 1920s now appear as historic events, this paper is concerned neither with the truth of these theories which have been superseded in art and science, nor with the search for a *Zeitgeist*. The general concept of evolution is ancient: history progressing from Primitive through Classical to Modern civilisation. The idea of the Primitive and Golden Age had been visualised by Plato and an analogy between the physical and intellectual growth and development of the human being and of mankind was made by Saint Augustine and, in 1827, by Victor Hugo.

The philosophy of Positivism was influenced by nineteenth-century science and it influenced many disciplines including the writing of history (Marvin, 1918). Auguste Comte (1798–1857) founder of the method believed it possible to discover 'determined laws' that governed human society in the same way that nature has physical laws (Comte, 1830–42). Economic and social history also owe their origins to this period (Mill, 1843; 1844). The materialist conception of history, formulated by Karl Marx, introduced the

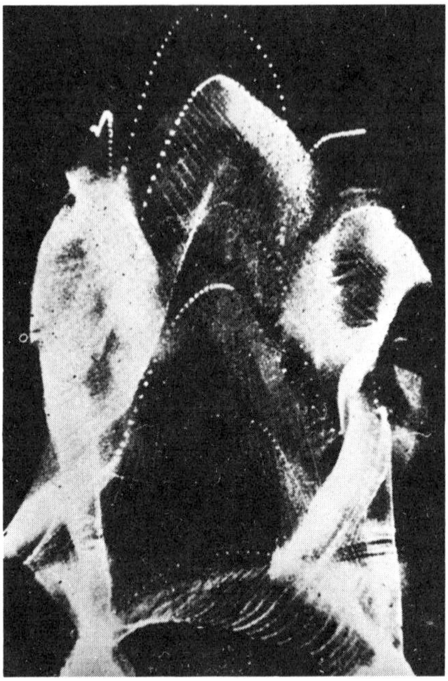

FIGURE 1 Jules-Étienne Marey. Multiple photographic exposure of a high jump. 1885.

theory that the evolution of society is conditioned mainly by the economist structure of its existence (Marx, 1848).

Darwin began to accumulate observations in 1837 that appeared in his famous book, *On the Origin of Species by Means of Natural Selection, or the Preservation of Favoured Races in the Struggle for Life* published in 1859.

Darwin's theory was applied to a great number of other subjects. The idea of social progress became popular and was systematised through the unparalleled progress of the mechanical arts. As machines began to supersede one another through the ingenuity of invention in engineering, technology and the mechanical arts, the theory of evolution seemed to extend from the means of natural selection in man and animals to mechanical innovations.

In 1860 Gottfried Semper's *Der Stil in den Technischen und tektonischen Kuensten* was published. It argued that art emerged from the spirit of technics as a by-product of craft and was related to the particular quality of the material, its treatment and function. Aloïs Riegl, who opposed this view, described it as an application of Darwinism to cultural history. Riegl (1901) stressed the naturalistic imitative origin of art and the deliberately conscious struggle against material conditions. To describe this artistic intent he used the word *Kunstwollen*. Arnold Hauser (1893) has pointed out that this opposition of the mental and the material, of the content and the means of expression is of basic significance for the whole theory of art and had formed a fundamental division in archaeological theorising.

The German Industrial Revolution became evident in the 1820s (Armytage, 1976). The speeding up of production as a result of new inventions and technological advances was described by Kurd Lasswitz (1848–1910) with optimism:

> What distinguishes the consciousness and indubitable cultural advance of modern humanity from the ancient and medieval is not so much the ethical and religious ideas; they were, in the main, already present in past ages. It is rather the conception of the power of man over nature, the conviction of the possibility of theoretically understanding and technically controlling nature. Modern man has attained maturity with the growth of the natural sciences (see Armytage, 1976, pp. 192/3).

William Morris's political influence also took root in Germany as one of the varieties of revisionism founded by Eduard Bernstein in the 1890s, emphasising political and artistic evolution rather than revolution (Egbert, 1970). At the turn of the century many people had no confidence that utility and aesthetic values might go together. The machine was seen as an instrument of human debasement. Art for art's sake, an independence from social responsibility, the isolation of artists, the academy or a bohemian attitude were the only choices for artists. However as early as 1882 the designer Lewis F. Day said:

> Whether we like it or not machinery and steam power, and electricity for all we know, will have something to say concerning the ornament of the future (see Armytage, 1976).

In the late nineteenth century there was a conscious attempt to create a new style in Germany, associated with Morris's arts and crafts movement. Opposed to what seemed to have degenerated into a charming fantasy, in Vienna, Adolf Loos (1870–1933), developed a severe architecture, elimating unnecessary detail, combined with a consciousness of modern requirements and spatial planning.

Also, in Munich, in 1907, the *Deutscher Werkbund* was founded, emphasising the concern to bring art and industry together in building and design. Its most prominent figure was the founder Herman Muthesius (1861–1927) who, in contrast to the general tendencies of Art Nouveau sought a new *Maschinestil* and a pure utility (Benham, 1970).

In Germany the generation of electricity during the nineteenth century affected many industries (Armytage, 1976). Important companies in and around Berlin such as the *AEG, Allgemeine Electrizitäts Gesellschaft*, and those of *Siemenstadt* came to commission radically new designs from Peter Behrens (1868–1940) and from Walter Gropius (1883–1969) respectively. Behrens joined the AEG in 1907.

German industries had been becoming interested in better and more efficient design: the *Stahlwerksverband* employed Bruno Taut; the Deutsche *Werkstatten* had begun to develop furniture for mass-production in 1906 and it became associated with the *Werkbund* from the start. Economic considerations prompted these plans. Muthesius introduced the idea that standardisation was a virtue and abstract form the basis of the aesthetic of product design, in a speech at the *Werkbund* Congress in 1911 (see Benham, 1970, p. 70). The audience included Mies van der Rohe, Walter Gropius, Bruno Taut, young Germans who were to revolutionise design, as well as Charles Edouard Jeanneret, later called 'Le Corbusier' who had come to study German progress in design. Like artists, architects and designers in other countries he was calling for a radical reorganisation of thought with regard to form and a rejection of superficial application of text-book styles.

Beauty in economy

Related to nineteenth-century Positivism, a second phase of the materialist, scientific and even more mechanistic approach to life appeared,

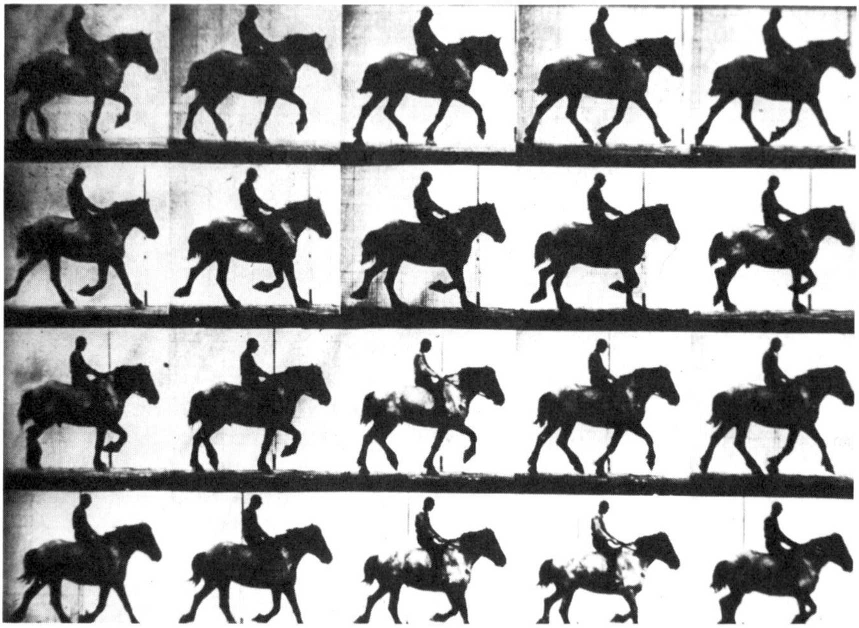

FIGURE 2 Eadweard Muybridge. High-speed photograph of a horse trotting.

Behaviourism, first developed by the American psychologist John Broadus Watson in 1913. He emphasised the objectively observable actions of organisms. Living organisms were observed as responding to conditions dependent on the outer environment and on inner biological functioning. This aspired to being a science of consciousness, experience and mind handled in terms of stimulus and response rather than an introspective study. Psychology was in this respect seen as a purely objective experimental branch of natural science.

During the 1920s the Behaviourist method was paramount in American psychology, and in Russia behaviour therapy was applied, primarily based on the experiments of Ivan Pavlov who published his work in the 1920s and 30s on the application of conditioning techniques and theories to abnormal behaviour. Unlike traditions of psychiatry these aimed to change the personality through conscious processes. Consequently, discussions on changing human nature became popular.

This occurred after the development of mass production at the beginning of the century. There followed a desire for perfection, precision, clean-cut forms. The standardisation of occupations such as factory work led to a standardisation of other activities and amusements, and with mass-production quantities of standardised commodities were manufactured. Manufacturing concentrated on the principle of power, accuracy and economy. System, continuity, speed and repetition were developed and interpreted through studies of operation and machine development. The aim

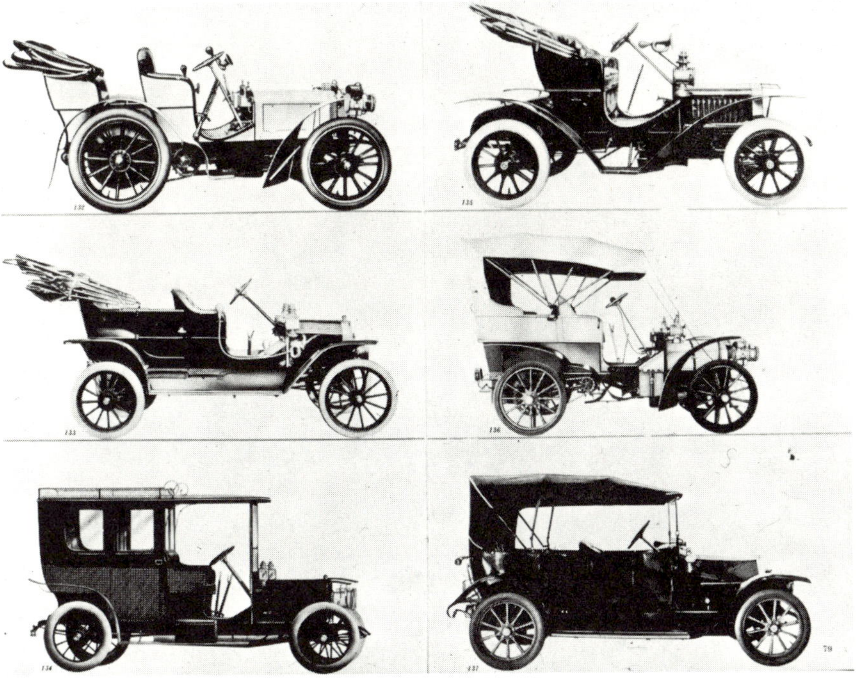

FIGURE 3 Miscellaneous car designs of the 1920s.

was to produce standardised products in continuous quantities—useful commodities of standard material and design at minimum cost. It was necessary to predict the conditions able to absorb a large production. Selling, propaganda and advertising techniques were therefore developed, and concerned with efficient financial organisation, management became scientific.

The general conception of the division of labour, machine-assisted manufacture and assembly of standardised parts had already been established by the middle of the nineteenth century. In 1881 Frederick W. Taylor had begun studies in the organisation of manufacturing by making stop-watch measurements of the time required to perform each step (see Figures 1 and 2).

At the same time Frank B. Gilbreth and his wife, American industrial engineers, began to study human movements required to carry out tasks. Applying new methods of motion pictures they analysed motion patterns and work areas to achieve maximum economy of effort. These 'time and motion' studies were important in planning mass-production lines. In 1913 Henry Ford's Motor Company set up a moving belt conveyor in which carefully synchronised simultaneous operations were planned for speed and efficiency and these mass production principles were set up in Europe soon after.

In relation to this, the new movements conceived of Art and Design to be in

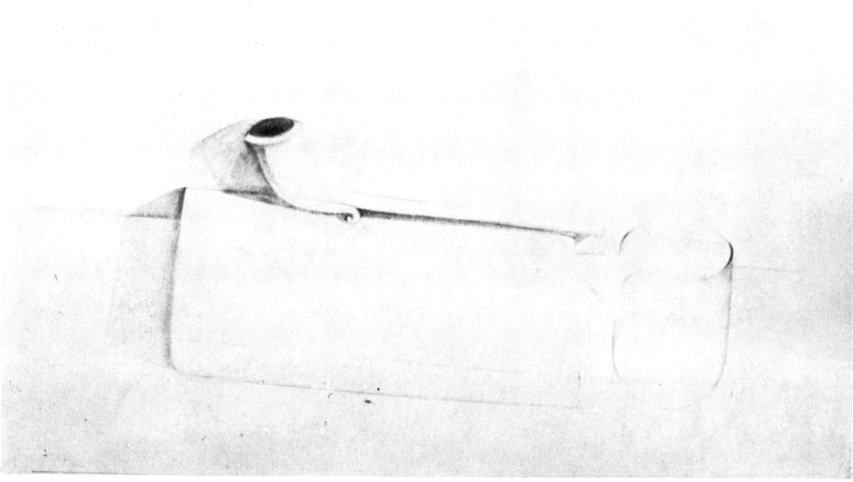

FIGURE 4 Amédée Ozenfant. *Still Life with pipe* (Pencil on Paper). Pushkin Museum, Moscow.

some ways pre-determined, not aesthetic, because response to natural laws seemed more efficient. Aesthetic decoration only hid the function, and art and design could be mass-produced.

Le Corbusier stated that industry on a grand scale should concern itself with building and establish the elements of the house on a mass-production basis. At the beginning of his book *Towards a New Architecture* Le Corbusier (1927; p. 1) summarised his ideas of the inter-dependence that architecture and 'the Engineer's Aesthetic' must have:

> The Engineer, inspired by the law of Economy and governed by mathematical calculation, puts us in accord with universal law. He achieves harmony.
>
> The Architect by his arrangement of forms, realizes an order which is a pure creation of his spirit; by forms and shapes he affects our senses to an acute degree and provokes plastic emotions; by the relationships which he creates he wakes profound echoes in us.

He considered the simplest forms to be the most beautiful and believed that engineers arrived at these geometric forms by calculation because they had to work according to strict needs of exactly determined conditions. He saw styles to be false and considered that 'our epoch is determining, day by day, its own style' (See Figure 3).

The concept of necessity evolving the principles of economy he applied to architecture in relation to the aeroplane, steam-ship and motor car:

> The airplane is the product of close selection. The lesson of the airplane lies in the logic which governed the statement of the problem and its realization. The problem of the house has not yet been stated. Nevertheless there do exist standards for the dwelling houses. Machinery contains in itself the factor of economy, which makes for selection. The house is a machine for living in (Le Corbusier, 1923, p. 10).

In this connection he made reference also to the efficiency of sleeping cars in comparison to the poor design of domestic architecture generally.

But Le Corbusier asserted that architecture is, like the other arts, an expression of ideas peculiar and appropriate to a particular time. The social need for large numbers of cheap dwellings in Russia inspired the avant-garde architects with the same spirit and their idea that human nature could be changed by propaganda is similar to Le Corbusier's complaint that 'The right state of mind does not exist' for producing mass-production houses (Le Corbusier, 1923, p. 211). With Amadée Ozenfant (1886–1966) (see Figure 4) Le Corbusier also developed a phase of paintings inspired by the machine, stripped of unnecessary detail under the name 'Purism' and related to the works of Juan Gris in 1914.

Ozenfant (1931), in his book *The Foundations of Modern Art,* defined 'machines' as 'relays' created by man:

> The honey-bee is a relay that nature uses; mankind, too, is a relay like the bee; machines are relays created by man, and the collaboration of men and machines creates natural objects which artificially we call artificial.
>
> * * *
>
> Mechanical evolution is comparable with natural evolution, the law of mechanical selection is comparable with the law of natural selection. I went into these questions in *L'Esprit Nouveau* and formulated this principle under the name of 'mechanised selection' (p. 151).

He envisaged the role of aesthetics as superfluous and put forward an argument similar to that of Malevich's idea of 'economy':

> Aesthetics introduced into the sphere of mechanics, is always an indication of inadequacy somewhere. Old fashioned telescopes are aesthetic, but up-to-date ones whose capacity is infinitely vaster are in no wise so. . . .
>
> * * *
>
> When the time comes there will be no place for aesthetic invention, which serves to hide the absence of knowledge (p. 152) (see Figure 5).

But his utopianism was also counterbalanced with pessimism:

> The working day will diminish even more. Mankind will soon be better served by its slave machines than was any overlord of feudal ages by his serfs. A few chosen engineers will suffice to work out such new mechanisms as 'progress' makes necessary, and machines will put them together under the supervision of a few mechanics. What will the rest of humanity do? Have holidays: immense periods of leisure in which to think? But thinking means inevitably seeing Death face to face.
>
> * * *
>
> The aim of both science and art is to create fantasies which solace us for reality (p. 183).

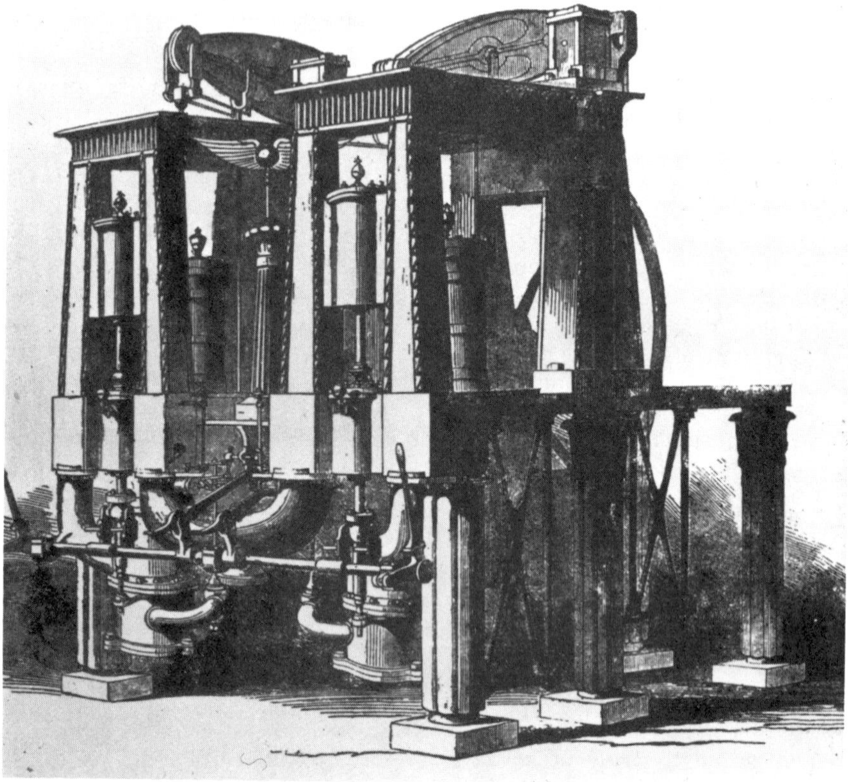

FIGURE 5 Mid-nineteenth-century engine in the Egyptian taste (B. Hick & Son of Bolton). Envelope machines closely followed several actual movements of the human form divine (*Illustrated London News*).

He observed that precision of timing ruled modern efficiency. This had led to mass production; to the desire for perfection and to habits of speed in daily life.

To differentiate between 'the surface ornamentation' of 'decorative art' and forms that function as organs, Ozenfant (1931) pointed out that what to us often resembles decoration may really have been functional to begin with:

> In the days when men lived in caves says the prehistorian Breuil, our ancestors perceived that in order to prevent the implement from sliding out of the hand and to make sure of a good grip it was necessary to modify the too smooth handle and introduce irregularity into it; whence the incisions of the edges or the more or less deep striations on the plane or curved surfaces. But these incisions are not made irregularly: man has observed the pleasure to be drawn from the regularity of markings and so he has been careful to make the incisions at regular intervals and

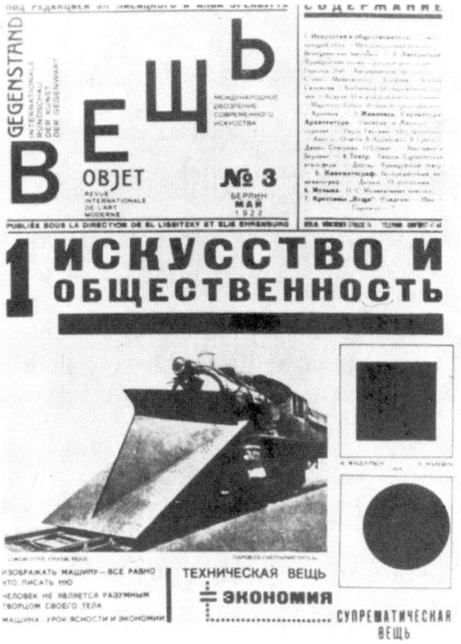

FIGURE 6 *Gegenstand, Veshch, Objet,* the third number (May 1922) of the trilingual magazine of modern art published under the direction of El Lissitzky and Elie Ehrenburg.

> parallel to each other, at times uniting them in recurring groups, the rhythmical arrangement of which he took pleasure in seeing. Here very well described you have the oldest aesthetic manifestations known to us (p. 235).

He believed that a universality exists in great art because common factors among all men produce and respond to certain lines of designs with a similar psychological impact.

> When a particular kind of feeling is dominant in certain epochs, the general distribution of certain 'modes' creates what is known later as its 'style'.
>
> * * *
>
> Modes depend on manners of thinking and feeling and not on technic: fashions of building, painting, writing are determined by modes of feeling and thinking (p. 265).

He also affirmed that mathematics is present in the greatest works.

> Pure art is not what is achieved: purity, as I understand it, is a maximum efficiency, intensity and quality issuing from an utmost economy of means. Our brains are so made that we inevitably respond to the restrained eloquence that is able to express itself economically and finally.
>
> That same tendency determines primary forms, as, for instance, the egg, or the rocket's flight (p. 300).

Mass production, time and motion in Russian art

In Russia after the 1917 Revolution the administration of education and the arts was reorganised (Fitzpatrick, 1970). El Lissitzky, (1890–1947), was influenced by Behrens, Gropius and others whose aesthetic expressed expediency and who renounced ornament (see Figure 6). The basic principle of his life's work was to be 'Architecture—that is art in its highest sense, mathematical order' (Lissitzky-Küppers, 1968).

Mies van der Rohe and Hans Richter published a periodical called *G* (short for *Gestaltung*—Form), for which Lissitzky wrote an article 'Wheel—Propellor and what follows' for the second number. He described the evolution of new inventions and systems of motion, from walking to flying:

> While buildings rise up and new energies are exploited, the speed of the rolling wheel increases and a new shape originates—MOVABLE ARCHITECTURE—the Pullman car, dining-car, ocean liner. The train—a rolling, collective dwelling.
>
> * * *

The new design must supersede the old machine, which is only an imitation of the human hand. Only inventions will move us forward. Only inventions will determine design. Even for revolutions new forms must be invented (see Lissitzky-Küppers, 1968, p. 345).

Lissitzky summed up the aims of the new phase in Russia:

(a) Repudiation of art as a mere emotional, individual, romantically isolated matter.
(b) 'Material' creation in the silent hope that later the resulting product will eventually be regarded as a work of art after all.
(c) Conscious fixity of purpose is creating an architecture based on previously worked out, objective, scientific principles, which presents a coherent artistic impression (From 'Ideological Superstructure' (1929) in *Neues Bauen in der Welt: I Russland*. See Lissitzky-Küppers, 1968, p. 372/3).

Many painters gave up making easel pictures altogether as it seemed to be a luxury product hardly connected with the reality of the post-revolutionary days and the period of reconstruction. Constructivism was concerned with 'real' materials either aimed at a purely artistic construction which employed these materials according to qualities peculiar to them, similar to the idea of truth to material; or it had a utilitarian application in mind, sometimes called 'Objectism' and developed at INKHUK (Institute of Artistic Culture). An effort to adapt design to an industrial scale in Russia and to plan for mass production was assumed, and applied—art production was given over to artists to design.

INKHUK aimed at formulating an ideological and theoretical approach to the arts based on scientific research and analysis. This inspired the development of 'laboratory art'. Members of the institute included Alexander Rodchenko (1891–1956) who, also as head of '*Vkhutemas*' (Higher Technical Art Studios) reorganised the Department of Metalwork according to his principles of industrial art and mass-production (see Figure 7).

Arvatov (1922) attacked the notion of an art in production as being a fundamental contradiction. He considered that human nature could not be transformed in two or three years and he accused machine aesthetics of being merely another fetish.

Tatlin's scope was very wide and his design of real material objects such as his utilitarian stove and worker's clothes (see Figure 8) separated him from any specific group:

Constructivism did not take into account the organic relation between the material and the tensile capacity, its working character. Essentially it is only as an outcome of the dynamic force resulting from these mutual relations that a vitally inevitable form is born (see Gray, 1971).

Professional architects were to regard early works by Tatlin as innovatory though formalistic or 'symbolic' (Lissitzky, 1930). In 1929 he began planning a form of glider, applying ideas from two articles written by a pioneer of rocket research, K. E. Tsiolkovsky. From observations of birds and insects he arrived at an exact calculation of air resistance, wing surface and the amount of energy required to propel a flying machine (Tsiolkovsky, 1912).

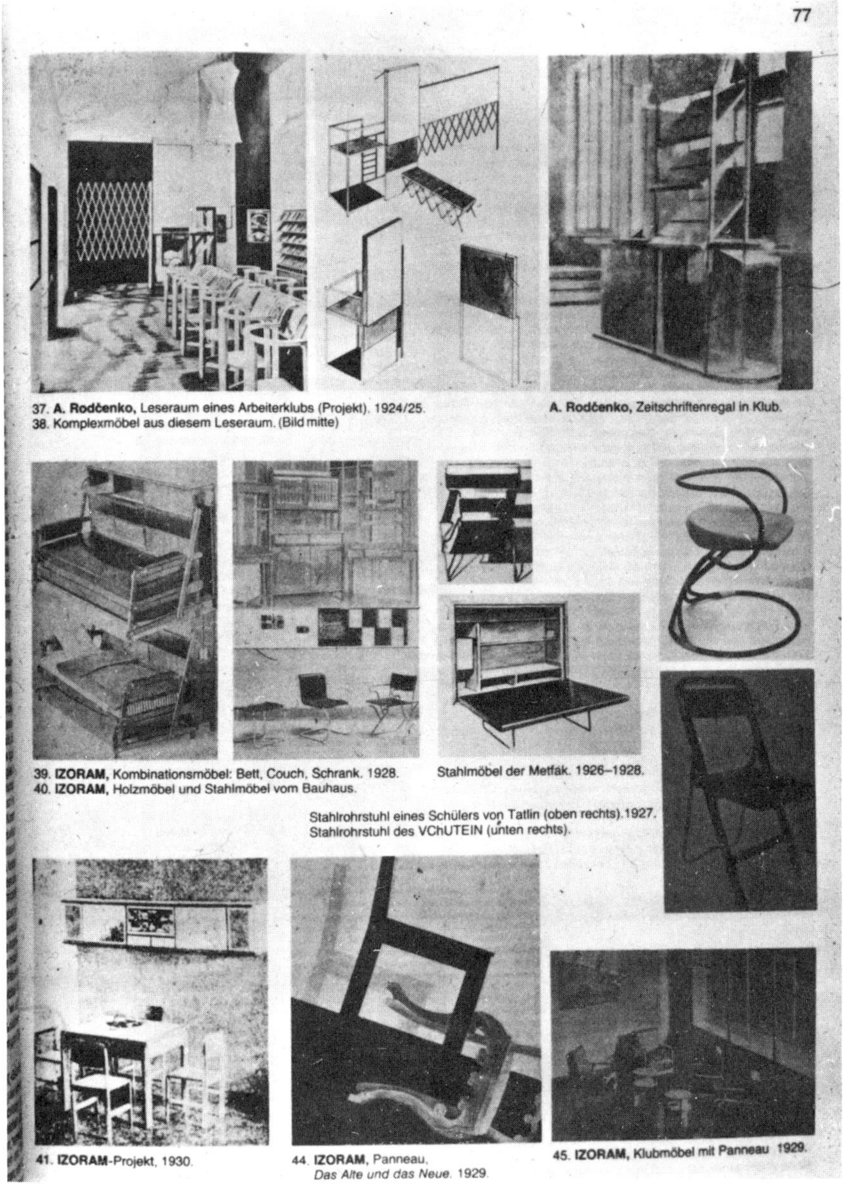

FIGURE 7 Utilitarian Projects carried out in Russia in the 1920s: 37 A. Rodchenko. Reading-room of a workers' club, 1924/5. 38 Adaptable furniture for the same reading-room. 40 Wooden and steel furniture from the Bauhaus. 41–45 Izoram Projects.

Tarabukin's lectures and publications defined the aims and ideas of Productivism:

> In the future when the interest in 'pure art' will be weakened under the influence of the growing 'Americanisation' of life, instead of being artists, people of talent will be practical men (Tarabukin, 1972).

Tarabukin noticed that Spengler, in his book *The Decline of the West*, though starting at a different position, arrived at similar conclusions to the Productivists. After discussing the degeneration of art, Spengler had said:

> The people who are concerned with practical, industrial, organisational and other affairs, write better, more truthfully and more profoundly than the majority of *litterati* who have made style a sport.
>
> For highly intellectual forms of striking purity, for a fast steamship, a steelworks, machines, I would be prepared to exchange all the stylistic nonsense of contemporary literary industry, with a bonus of painting and sculpture thrown in (Tarabukin, 1972).

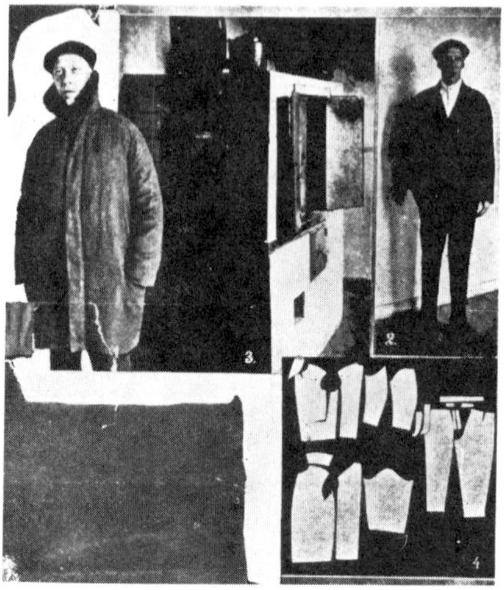

FIGURE 8 A newspaper cutting headed 'Tatlin's New Way of Life'. The artist, Vladimir Tatlin, is shown modelling the workers' clothes he designed and a stove to consume the minimum of fuel while giving maximum heat.

The idea of completely mechanised theatre was also developed by the 1920s (Fuerst and Hume, 1928; Carter, 1929; see Figure 9). Mayakovsky was the most prominent theatrical writer to introduce the mechanical element as a symbol, especially in his *Revolt of Objects*, his first theatrical presentation in which he compared rigid characters to machines. The view was expressed that Russia's hope lay in the mastery and use of machines that would enable her to become a mechanical civilisation.

In 1920 Meyerhold introduced his system of 'bio-mechanics' to the theatre. With this the actor learned to be conscious of himself and of his movements as if he were a machine (see Figure 10). Meyerhold and Eisenstein visualised the greatest economy of effort, the application of 'Taylorism' on the stage; and courses at Meyerhold's school seemed like acrobatic training (see Figure 11). In order to manage to climb among the inclined planes, steep stairs, vertical ladders and high platforms of the Constructivist stage, courses entitled 'The Technology of the Human Body' were also included and actors learned to run, climb, and even jump from a train (Fuerst and Hume, 1928, p. 62; see Figure 12). Psychological drama was condemned but the theatre aimed mainly at Communist propaganda. On this stage little settings came and went at different points with film-like rapidity. Eisenstein's debt to

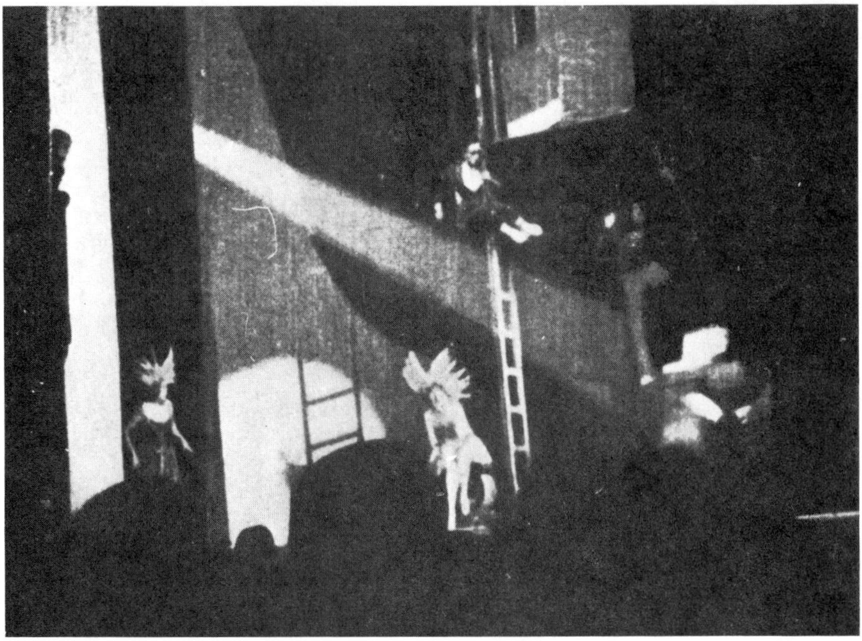

FIGURE 9 Operetta by Lecocq: *Le jour et La nuit*. Photo by Dr Gregor taken during the performance.

Meyerhold extended to paying particular attention to the movements of cats and tigers, which in Meyerhold's view exemplified the secret of bodily plasticity (Wollen, 1969).

Gabo's constructions

Utopian optimism in engineering associated with art and design evolved from the Saint-Simonists of the French Revolution. Mass-production, Taylorism and the study of behaviour in association resulted from the Industrial Revolution. Modern science also appeared to have taken the attention of Modern artists in various ways.

After Gabo and Pevsner published their *Realist Manifesto* during August 1920, being principally an attack on mass in sculpture and a recommendation of structured forms inspired by engineering, it was countered by the *Productivist Manifesto*, issued by Rodchenko and Stepanova in Moscow.

Naum Gabo was born in Russia in 1890. In 1911 he gave up medicine to study natural science and in 1912 began studying under the German art historian Wölfflin. In 1910 he met Kandinsky who had just begun abstract improvisations and in 1915 he began to make constructions. Some of his works resemble scientific models. The vibrating rod of 1920 (see Figure 13) which creates a form in space by means of its rapid vibrations, and in a similar way constructions strung like a harp, creating forms through the

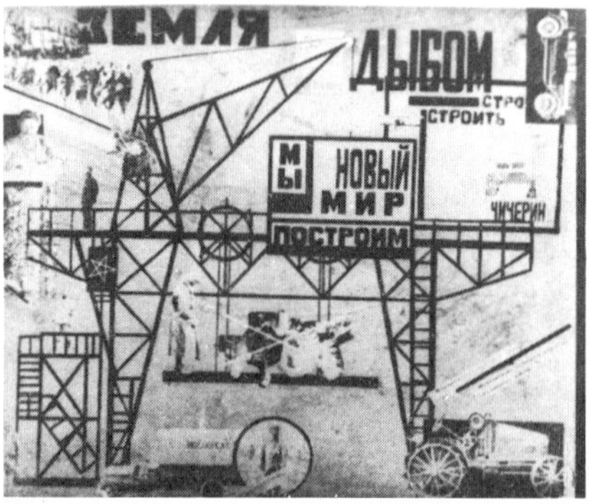

FIGURE 10 Liubov Popova. Design for Meyehold's production of *The Earth in Turmoil* (Moscow, 1923). An adaptation by Sergei Tretyakov of Martinet's *La Nuit*.

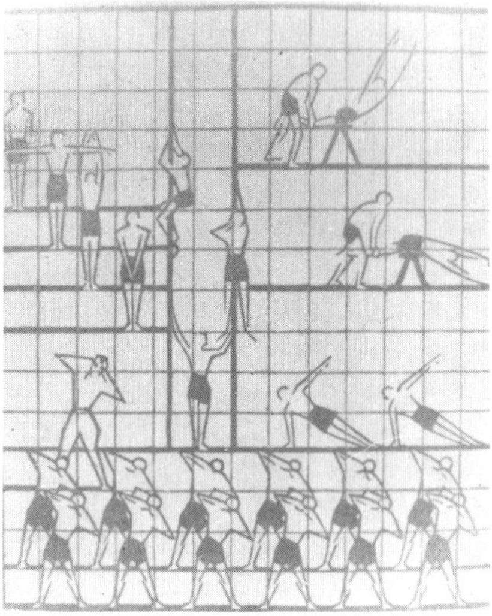

FIGURE 11 Diagram of movements for a course in physical education which was adapted by Eisenstein in his bio-mechanics.

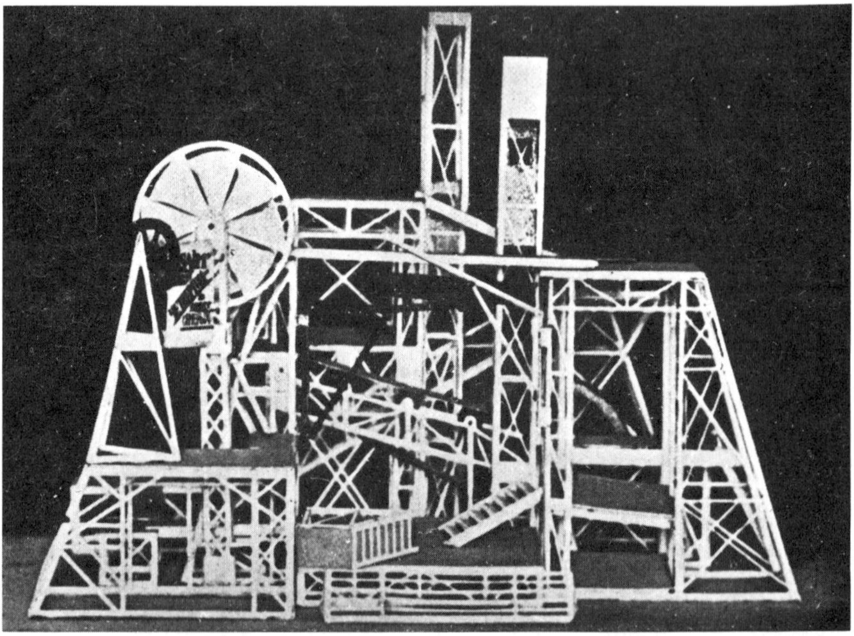

FIGURE 12 Alexander Vesnin. Constructivist setting for *The Man who was Thursday* produced in the Moscow Kameny Theatre by Meyerhold in 1923.

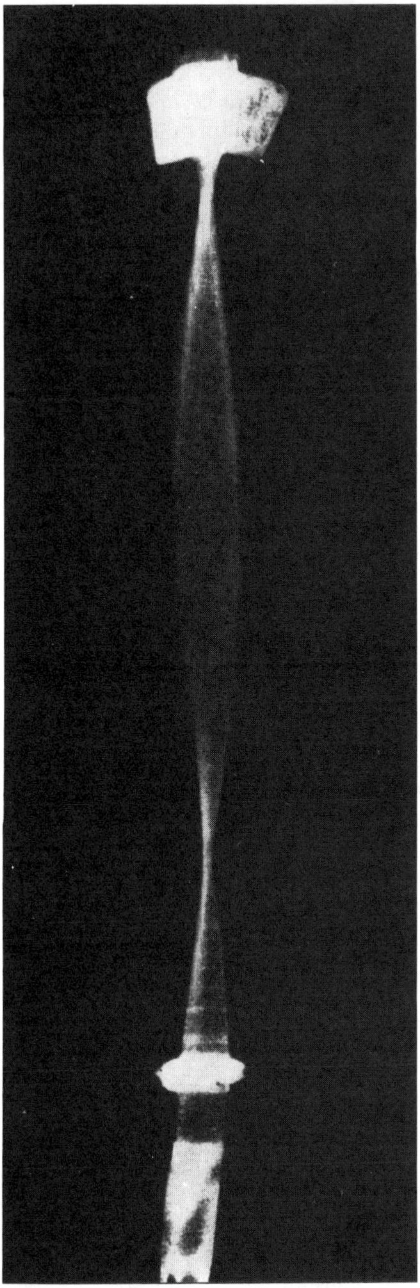

FIGURE 13 Naum Gabo. *Kinetic construction,* 1920. Metal rod vibrating by means of a motor.

multiplicity of lines in space, as well as certain later works of Pevsner, are strongly suggestive of Einstein's imagery of constructions with rods and curvilinear motion which he uses to make inferences from his general theory of relativity where time is considered on a spherical surface instead of an Euclidean plane:

> Are these beings able to regard the geometry of their universe as being plane geometry and their rods withal as the realisation of 'distance'? They cannot do this. For if they attempt to realise a straight line they obtain a curve which we 'three-dimensional beings' designate as a great circle (Einstein, 1920, p. 109).

Discussion of the spherical universe in two and three dimensions led Einstein to describe a concrete model of the type that both Gabo and Pevsner introduced from mathematical structure into art:

> Suppose we draw lines or stretch strings in all directions from a point, and mark off from each of these the distance *r* with a measuring-rod. All the free end-points of these lengths lie on a spherical surface. We can specially measure up the area (*F*) of this surface by means of a square made up of measuring rods.
>
> * * *
>
> At first the straight lines which radiate from the starting point diverge farther and farther from one another, but later they approach each other, and finally they run together again at a 'counter point' at the starting point. Under such conditions they have traversed the whole spherical space. It is easily seen that the three-dimensional spherical space is quite analogous to the two-dimensional spherical surface. It is infinite (i.e. of infinite volume), and has no bounds (Einstein, 1920, p. 112).

The idea of 'elasticity' of bodies which was begun in art by the Futurists especially Boccioni in his sculpture and which was continued by the Constructivists in various forms and probably derived from statements by Bergson corresponds to Einstein's physical theories (see Davies, 1975).

Einstein's 'Relativity' was first published in a popular form in 1920. There are a number of similarities between Gabo's remarks about the measurement of space published in his 'Realist Manifesto' of 1920 and Einstein's theory published the same year.

Einstein was dissatisfied with the inadequate Newtonian definitions of motion and space and Gabo expressed a dissatisfaction with the scientific explanation of the phenomena of weight and speed because they are nothing to do with the experience of the events or ideas. Gabo (1959, p. 55) denounced scientific laws of nature and its symbols as merely laws of physics or chemistry:

> I realised that in my scientific journey I had been under the power of a magic spell of a work of art whose reality was just as true as the verity of the image in an artist's vision (Gabo, 1959, p. 21).
>
> * * *
>
> I accept the image of the world which science is constructing, not because that image is the only true reality of Nature and life, but because it is a beautiful work of art, perfectly performed (Gabo, 1959, p. 58)

Conclusion

Similar fundamental assumptions may be observed in various systems of thought, art and science at a certain time, systems which the epoch unconsciously presupposes. Such assumptions appear so obvious, because no other way of putting things has occurred. Correlations of style or of content may be drawn out through various historical accounts, or theoretical features may take a Positivist or Metaphysical view; a deeper utopian structure may be observed or even some pre-structure, a profounder underlying element linking art and science. On the other hand the action may be seen to take place on the surface; it is possible to discern that certain ideas have been dispersed abroad, applied to new fields and their original function almost forgotten.

As if interpreting a foreign language, scientists and technologists have been inspired by the prophecies of art, and artists have looked to science for justification. The mutual relationship has taken distinctively different forms during each century, and as the division between art and science deepened each understood the other less well. This division takes its form in the specialising institutions which foster art and science. In academies and universities, the sciences have taken a different direction from art and from one another. For artists, the academy, design or applied art and bohemianism have provided conflicting alternatives and systems of support. During the age of the avant-garde 'Modern Art' has appeared to be more and more esoteric and autonomous to the uninitiated. But as if in need of justification, artists have looked to Science and Philosophy, relying on the popular publications which explained science: Helmholtz in the 1860s, Bergson before 1914 and Einstein in 1920.

The influence of philosophy and science on artists of the twentieth century has been considerable but the changing attitudes that science takes, appear to be inspired by the same events as those which also inspire art. J. D. Bernal (1954) in his introduction to *Science in History* affirmed that the laws, hypotheses and the theories of science have a wider bearing than the objective facts they claim to explain.

> Most of them necessarily reflect in large part the general non-scientific intellectual atmosphere of the time by which the individual scientist is inevitably conditioned. The result is that the phenomena of Nature and of the manual arts are interpreted in social, political or religious terms. Thus Newton's theory of inertia came from the prevailing rational interpretation of religion [his solutions stopped short of any fundamental questioning of the existence of a divine plan], and Darwin's natural selection from the current conception of the natural justice of free competition.

Artists seem to have at times arrived independently at similar conclusions as scientists, and philosophers arrive at the same conclusions as poets. If their background or environment was similar, it may be only the medium into which each individual translates his observations of what he considers to be significant reality that differs.

REFERENCES

Armytage, W. H. G. (1976) *A Social History of Engineering* (fourth edn.), 1976, p. 194.

Arvatov, B. (1922) Criticism of Vesch, in *Pechat i Revolutsiya*, no. 7, quoted in Vieri Quilici, *L'architectura del construttivismo*, (Editori Laterza), Bari, 1969, p. 27.

Benham, R. (1960) *Theory and Design in the First Machine Age* (fourth impression, 1970), pp. 68–78.

Bernal, J. D. (1954) *Science in History*. p. 28.

Carter, H. (1929) *The New Spirit in the Russian Theatre, 1917–1928*, and a sketch of the Russian Cinema and Radio. Brentano's, New York; Shaylor, London.

Comte, A. (1830–42) *Cours de Philosophie Positive*.

Corbusier, Le (1923) *Towards a New Architecture*. Translated from the French by F. Etchells. Editions Cres, Paris. (under title *Vers une Architecture*). First published in English in 1927.

Davies, I. (1975) Western European Art Forms influenced by Nietsche and Bergson before 1914, particularly Italian Futurism and French Orphism. *Art International*, vol. 19 (March), pp. 49–55.

Egbert, D. D. (1970) *Social Radicalism and the Arts, Western Europe: a cultural history from the French Revolution to 1968*, p. 587.

Einstein, A. (1920) *Relativity: The special and general theory. A popular exposition*, p. 109. Translation first published by Methuen.

Fitzpatrick, A. (1970) *The Commissariat of Enlightenment. Soviet organization and the arts under Lunacharsky, October 1917–1921*. C.U.P.

Fuerst, W. R., and Hume, S. (1928) *XXth Century Stage Decoration*, vol. I, pp. 60–2. A. A. Knopf, London.

Gabo, N. (1971) *Of Divers Arts*. The A. W. Mellon Lectures in the fine arts delivered at the National Gallery of Art, Washington, D.C. 1959. *Bollingen*, series xxxxv, 8, p. 55. Princeton Univ. Press, 1971.

Gray, C. (1971) *The Russian Experiment in Art 1863–1922*. p. 260 Quotation from a statement by Tatlin in his exhibition catalogue: *Vuistavka rabot zasluzhennovo deyatelya iskusstv* V. E. Tatlina. Katalog. Moscow, 1932.

Hauser, A. (1893) *The Social History of Art*, ch. I ('Prehistoric Times').

Lissitzky, S. (1930) *Neues Bauen in der Welt, Russland*, p. 11.

Lissitzky-Küppers, S. (1968) *El Lissitzky, Life, Letters, Texts*, p. 19. Thames and Hudson.

Marvin, E. S. (1918) *Science and History*.

Marx, K. (1848) *Manifesto of the Communist Party*.

Mill, J. S. (1843) *System of Logic*.

—— (1844) *Essays on some Unsettled Questions of Political Economy*.

Ozenfant, A. (1931) *Foundations of Modern Art*, p. 151. Translated by J. Rodker. (The first French edition appeared in 1928.)

Riegl, A. (1901) *Spatromische Kunstindustrie*. Vienna.

Tarabukin, N. (1972) *The Last Painting* (Le Dernier Tableau), p. 57. Editions du Champ Libre, Paris. French translation by A. B. Nakov.

Tsiolkovsky, K. E. (1912) Ustroytsvo Letatel'nogo Apparata Nasekomykh i ptits i Sposoby ikh polota (1880) printed in *Tekhnika Vosdukhoplavania*, no. 3.

—— (1894) Aeroplan ili Ptitsepodobnaya (Aviatsionnaya) Letatel'naya Machina, *Nauka i Zhizn*, nos. 43–6. Moscow. Published in book form 1895.

(Both articles quoted from Tsiolkovsky's *Collected Works*, vol. I, pp. 37, 34, 41 Moscow 1951, and quoted in Troels Anderson: *Vladimir Tatlin*, catalogue of the exhibition the Moderna Museet, Stockholm, July–Sept. 1968, pp. 9–10.

Wollen, P. (1969) *Signs and Meanings in the Cinema*.

DISCUSSION

CLAIRE MORRIS

I am glad that Ivor Davies has brought the engineer into the discussion, because the engineer has to be admitted into the company of scientists nowadays. I would like briefly to refer to the micro-electronics engineer and technologist, and to bring the discussion up to the present, particularly with regard to the new technology.

David Knight suggested earlier that the divergence of science and art (I would prefer 'science and the humanities') started during or after the lifetime of Humphry Davy, and that up to that period the term 'science' was used to cover any body of knowledge, whilst an 'artist' was a technician. As another participant said, the history and causes of this divergence should perhaps be the subject of another conference: that it exists now is undeniable, particularly in the field of microelectronics. This is not the case where design is concerned, certainly, but I regard design as to do with surface structure, not deep structure.

I have lived amongst engineers for many years and have observed their education and their approach to their work with alarm. Part of the problem with their education is that the subject of electronics is so difficult, so dense, and is progressing so rapidly under pressure from governments and industry, that there is no time to give the students a broader education in history and philosophy and the humanities in general, with the result that the graduate engineer can emerge with a narrow attitude to his work. As far as I can see, the engineer is not trained to examine or judge the implications of what he is doing, and he is even encouraged to regard himself as detached from any use that is made of his devices.

As I understand it, when an engineer is presented with a problem, he will approach it as one dealing simply with engineering. He will design circuitry for weapons systems and tele-communications and at the same time instruments for advancing medicine or solving the problems of drought or of the world food shortage, without drawing any moral distinction between these exercises. It is my contention that this stance of moral detachment is dangerous and wrong and that no body of scientists should be given such power without being *educated* to recognise and take some responsibility for it. This is not to suggest that engineers as individuals are without conscience, that would be nonsense, only that their education is deficient.

I would like participants at this conference, as educators and people with some influence in our universities, to consider whether greater effort—and I realise that some efforts *are* already being made—should be put into restoring the balance of what I see as the engineer's dangerously unbalanced education.

POLLOCK

Referring to Keller's paper, there are also, surely, many examples of discontinuity in modern trends of interpretation in biology. Quite apart from obvious examples such as genes and other subcellular entities of various kinds, there is a contemporary tendency to analyse a whole series of adaptive phenomena—the specific reactions of an organism to its environment—in terms of selective switching on or off of a wide range of pre-existing (i.e. genetically determined) elements by specific stimuli. This applies, for instance, to the process of recording a visual pattern through the retina by receptor stimulation in the visual cortex of the brain and to the mechanism of de-repression of enzymes and enzyme-forming systems in many forms of adjustment of an organism to its environment. The process seems to work like a computer of the digital, rather than of the analogue, type: that is, through pattern formation by discontinuous operation of a series of on/off switches rather than by smooth copying of a particular shape.

MERMOZ

If we are to adopt the two notions of continuity and discontinuity for comparing artistic and scientific ideas and practices during the period 1880–1910, it must not be on the ground of external analogies (atomic particles/the 'touche divisée' of the Neo-Impressionists), but indeed on a much firmer basis upon which the hypothesis of a structural correlation may be examined and tested.

The cursory characterisation of Neo-Impressionism presented here does not provide such a basis, for it does not take into account *how* the alleged 'discontinuity' (located in the 'touche divisée' of Seurat and Signac and the fragmented planes of the cubists) fits within the system of their paintings. If the principle of discontinuity is to be found operating simultaneously in physics and in painting at the turn of this century (or, for that matter, during any period), it must be at a structural level, otherwise we are as justified in linking 'stipple engraving' in the eighteenth century with the Atomism of Leibniz.

In art as in science a structure may be broadly defined as a set of elements/units which stand in functional relations to each other, thereby constituting a more complex whole. For Signac, the structure of a painting consisted in the sum of its formal relations envisaged from the standpoint of its optical properties. Thus, structure could be envisaged simultaneously as a set of abstract (internal) relations forming a 'system' (the system constitutive of a given picture as opposed to a system—or set of rules—pre-existing the works) and as a tangible form representation (the picture as 'signifier'). In the former sense, structure expressed for Signac the order of natural phenomena as it had been 'scientifically' studied by Chevreul and Charles Henry and empirically investigated by Delacroix and the Impressionists as regards light and colour. In its latter sense, it subjectified the natural order of things into psychological values ('harmony').

Considering the importance of Henry as a colour theorist and his contribution to the theoretical debate of Neo-Impressionism and Symbolism (his lectures were attended and his books were read by Signac, Seurat, Feneon, G. Kahn, Valéry, Mallarmé, etc.) we cannot simply dismiss his work as of little relevance to this discussion. For it was Henry himself who devised a system capable of unifying mind and matter on the basis of the interaction between the two principles of 'continuity' and 'discontinuity'.

Having noted a structural correlation between physical phenomena and their representations in the mind (a correlation that could be expressed in mathematical terms) Henry studied the complementary roles of 'continuity' and 'discontinuity' in the economy of psychic functions. Thus, in *Le Cercle Chromatique* (Paris 1888) Henry notes:

> Visual sensation is projected in space; the representation of space as being continuous is projected on a cycle oriented within from left to right. But sensation is an arrest, thus the visual is projected on a cycle oriented from right to left; it is discontinuous (p. 57)

and further

> we can define pleasure: the continuity of psychic functions; pain is the discontinuity of these functions. But we can only represent—and thus study scientifically—ourselves as movements: we must make precise what relation exists between psychic functions and movements.

Summing up his work in the *Conclusion* Henry writes:

> The psychic functions are virtual movements, either continuous or discontinuous; I have studied the conditions of continuity and discontinuity, which are nothing other than the conditions of dynamogeny and inhibition of physiological functions, and I have mathematically made precise the forms of perception imposed by these conditions. The essential result is that our representations are necessarily cyclical in form, either continuous or discontinuous. As dynamogeny is only an emission of electricity, and inhibition an emission of heat or a raising of temperature, I have been able to make precise the intimate and evident liaisons within the living being in psychic phenomena such as pleasure and pain; in mechanical phenomena such as continuity and arrest; and in physical phenomena such as electricity and heat.

VANDA COOK

When we witness in a particular epoch, as we have in the last hundred years, convulsive changes in all fields of culture, we are led to wonder if there is not some overall psychic change taking place in the deep recesses of the mind. The synchronicity of these seemingly unrelated shifts is not so difficult to understand if we remember that all men have common inherited patterns of emotional and mental behaviour. Can we locate the source of these changes? No-one can answer this but all creative persons know that the intellect deals with such problems only secondarily. Writers, artists and musicians are less able to pin-point such evolutions in their work. They are more likely to talk of searching or of finding. But there are many scientific discoveries whose origin have been variously described as 'the grace of God', and a 'flash', or seen in a dream; or because of a deeply held conviction of the ultimate rightness of some basic form or number. During a period of great change in scientific understanding the process seems to be not a gradual building of knowledge, but a sequence of forward leaps. The continuous chain is not broken but the links differ. With hindsight we see it is the same in all cultural fields. Schools or styles of painting will persist in a comparable form until suddenly there comes a complete shift, caused by social upheaval or a thorough change in the grounds of being. Darwin's theories, and research into nuclear physics in the nineteenth century caused such a revolutionary change in the concept of reality: a new reality took over from the 'natural world' which is ruled by the laws of classical physics. At the same time new relativities and paradoxes were discovered in the realms of the psyche.

Painters are prisoners in the cell of time and as they have always been the mirror for society and the spokesmen for the age, they will all unconsciously invent new forms and new techniques to express changing phenomena. Painters have always understood this. To quote Kandinsky: 'Every epoch is given its own measure of artistic freedom and even the most creative genius may not leap over that boundary of freedom.' Or Bazaine: 'Nobody paints as he likes. All a painter can do is to will with all his might the painting his age is capable of.' Or Marc: 'The great artists do not seek their forms in the midst of the past, but take the deepest soundings they can of the genuine, profoundest centre of gravity of their age.' Or Matisse: 'We are born with the sensibilities of an epoch. We don't choose what we paint—it is forced upon us'. When we consider the poetry and painting of that period, we witness, as Kurt Badt has said, 'an authentic case of spiritual synchronization, which enables us to recognise the interrelationship of different manifestations of the spiritual life of a people in a particular epoch. There is no question of any derivation or influence; we are dealing with the homogeneity of the spiritual life of the nation being manifested in various fields simultaneously and in particular in the deepest stratum of aims and realization, far deeper than differences between material and medium and between the ways in which different individuals are attuned to life.'

Perhaps here we have the common denominator in Art and Science, but it would be an error to try and give an intellectually formulated interpretation. The connections are infinitely subtle and differentiated. Thus it would be folly to think of Pointillism as a preoccupation with atoms, or Matisse's 'espace spirituel' expressed by fragmented colours as an expression of scientific principle or suppose cubism to be a formal description of a space/time continuum. Each change in technique or style is a logical, wholly artistic question.

Nevertheless, as we see the picture surface change from an illusion of space to concrete pictorial space, we see it reflecting twentieth-century man's concept of reality, and whatever plastic form then appears on that surface, it becomes a counter image to our ground of being. As painting reflects man's dark fears as well as his longings and aspirations, perhaps the most hopeful pictorial image that has appeared in this century is comprised in the late paintings by Cézanne, the father, or as he has been called, the destiny of modern painting. The close knit ordered depths of his painting and the stability of his composition, where all things stand together and all is one, reflect the will to order of the human psyche. It may prevail. However, in the ensuing three-quarters of a century events have been mirrored in art expressing fear, despair, aggression and mockery. These evocative paintings show us how modern man lives in the world today. We note the banality of Lichstenstein and the 'Hiroshima style' of Marini. Yet more recently we have encountered three trends that move away from such abdication of individual responsibility and from such utter despair. We note paintings based on the perfection of numbers, paintings of extreme formal order and paintings based on the autonomous figuration of colour which become screens of meditation. Such paintings indicate that the individual consciousness is not wholly submerged in darkness. We must also remember that we can no longer speak of European art but of global art, just as science is global. Whether the constructive or destructive tendencies in mankind and in science prevail, painting will reflect them because they all stem from the same source.

GAGE

I think that one of the elements in Neo-Impressionism which has been overlooked is the source of Seurat's technique, and his is a technique which is paramount in this sort of painting. The propaganda for Neo-Impressionism in Seurat's day and later by Signac related it to methods of perception. Its justification was seen to be in the behaviour of the eye, particularly regarding optical mixtures. It is curious that exactly at the time Signac was writing his apology he had himself abandoned the view that the function of painting is to reflect the real or observed world in any way and we know from other writings and from his style—a style which leads on to the Fauves—that it is very far from being based upon theories of perception and there is no attempt to reconstitute tones by optical mixtures. So by the time Signac was writing, the chief preoccupations of French painters seem to have been with the autonomy of painting: that the only function of the painter is to produce paintings and not to reflect the outside world by technique. Although Signac was claiming that the reason for the development of the style was precisely a method of analysing the real world, the phase of French aesthetics at that time was quite different and was, I think, looking forward to the creation of objects and displayed a pro-constructivist attitude to painting.

KELLER

In my paper I was very much concerned to show what I thought were two parallel developments which were quite independent of one another; that in fact it was not a question of artists being influenced by scientific developments of the time. I suspect they were completely ignorant of these and that the scientists were just as ignorant of artistic activities at the time, certainly those of which I spoke. It appears that there was this curious parallel without any suggestion of an interaction or an influence or anything. I used Signac because he does try and describe in his famous treatise what he thought he and Seurat were doing and his words do reflect some of the observations on continuity and discontinuity in physics at the time.

MARWICK

I want to try to relate the two very interesting papers of Keller and Davies to Rom Harré's idea of metatheories. It seems to me Harré's idea took a bit of a dent because both speakers were talking roughly about the same period, the early twentieth-century, and yet they seemed to present almost opposite metatheories for the same period. Keller stressed discontinuity whereas Davies was talking about the continuity of tradition from Darwin. There is a great danger, when scientists and philosophers get together of wanting to find a simple formulation like discontinuity and make that somehow explain things. I am in sympathy with what Martin Pollock said because, oddly enough, with historical discourse, historians are more and more looking for the discontinuities in the study of the past. But that is pretty recent and Keller and Davies were talking about pre 1914, and we have to remember that ideas don't exist for twenty-five years and then get replaced by a totally different set of ideas. So when trying to establish these relationships, we have got to be clear what period we are talking about. I don't think it is metatheories which are the prime movers, it is much more cultural and economic factors, and at the turn of the century period we are talking about, for many people (not all, because different people have different ideas) the optimism of the great economic expansion of the nineteenth century is beginning to fade, and there is an uneasiness for those who have eyes to see. One can then see that there is a shared uneasiness that assumptions of the mid-nineteenth century, which were broadly optimistic ones, can no longer be held, and I think Ivor Davies put his finger on it: in any historical period one should look to the assumptions about what is possible and what is permissible. I think it is in that realm that we will find the link between what scientists are doing and what artists are doing. But really the warning I want to give is not to think in terms of there being one meta-theory in any particular period of time which links everything together.

HARRÉ
I would like to take a muted defence of metatheories just a little bit further. I was suggesting that one of the possible mechanisms that we might look for to explain correlations, would be a shared metatheory. Now I did not mean to suggest that each epoch has one and only one metatheory and that thereby everything is systematically constrained. But I think it is worth pointing out that the example of the Bauhaus and the group around Gropius is a very elegant example of the formulation of a metatheory, not of grand scope but of very great interest. After all, what these people did, I presume, was to extract from the socio-economic conditions of the day a theory about man and his relation to the built environment and then to exploit that theory deliberately. Le Corbusier and others constructed furniture, buildings and so forth, in accordance with the theory. I think one can even find the same theory reverberating in art and music (in the relationship between Gropius and Berg etc., for instance). There is a good case here, but it is narrow, and I don't wish to claim that it was a universal metatheory.

WINTERBOURNE
I think it is a bit unfair for Marwick to suggest that it is the philosophers who bring out slogans like 'continuity versus discontinuity' in the first place. The point is a very important one; the idea of discontinuity in modern physics does not have to do with breaking up individual objects in this way: it is about the *behaviour* of particles rather than the discontinuity of particles. Now if you think about atomism as involving a distinction between bits, and things which aren't bits, why didn't we have (if there is any power in this at all to influence art) this kind of art much earlier when atomism was the prevalent scientific theory. I would suggest that it is because in art it wasn't

historically possible; it just wasn't possible to paint like that when those theories were around. I think there is a great danger of picking out the wrong bit of the science to be influenced by. There has been, for example, a sort of cottage industry in philosophy fairly recently in trying to show, from Gödel's incompleteness theorem, that freewill must exist in the phenomenal world for human beings. The arguments I think are egregious. Generally speaking they have a surface plausibility but you can't easily go from the behaviour of sub-elementary particles to the behaviour of the phenomenal world: there is a huge jump involved there. Because there is discontinuity in the sub-atomic level it doesn't follow that the phenomenal world is not continuous; and so the idea of a parallel development is a very important one. It is the art-historical possibility which interests me, and in this particular case I think it is a good example of parallelism without any cause or connection whatsoever.

MARTIN ROBERTSON
Mosaic, which is perhaps the most 'atomistic' of all craft-techniques, began to be developed by the Greeks as an art-form in the late fifth and fourth centuries BC. This is just the time when Leucippus and his more famous follower Democritus were developing their atomic theory of matter. I think it most improbable that there was any conscious connection between the two phenomena, and this may serve as a warning against too easy an assumption of such links in later times; but this is not of course to assert that there might not be a deeper level at which both do reflect some common tendency of the time.

LLOYD JONES
Surely, one of the salient differences between science and art relates to their different ranges of reference. If you say that in a certain period in history scientists were working on certain characteristic problems you imply that any scientist anywhere would, if properly acquainted with these issues, naturally wish to pursue them. In art this is by no means the case. 'Divisionism' in science, if this is a relevant concept at all, is presumably relevant everywhere. Division in art was really the concern of a few dozen artists mostly in Paris. It is quite false to assume that they were somehow, unbeknown to themselves, speaking suddenly for the rest of humanity. True, with hindsight, their achievements can sometimes seem global in range. The staggering prices of Impressionist paintings on the international art market might serve to suggest their universal significance. In more recent times however quite different and hitherto unregarded styles, that were contemporary with Impressionism are being revalued often quite drastically (the Pre-Raphaelites for example).

One idea of Kuhn's that I do recognise as familiar within the experience of my own two very different educations is his characterisation of the anti-historical nature of the teaching of elementary science. His contrast between the student of science with his text books (constantly updated and rewritten from within the framework of the current paradigms) and the student of humanities with his original texts (fixed in time at the moment of their creation) strikes me as accurate and important. The practice of art is, to a much greater extent than that of science, local in space and time, the preoccupations of small groups at certain moments within specific cultural traditions.

EMMER

It is obvious to me why we are interested in the artistic movement in Paris at the beginning of this century. We are looking for the influences of this movement on the art and culture of our world. I speak only of the world of Western culture because that is the world I know something about.

In passing I would like to comment on order. This provides one important point of view for looking at art and science. One of the last things Frank Malina did, with the co-operation of the scientist G. Careri, was to make a collection of papers in the international review of art and science *Leonardo* on the nature of the meaning of order in art and science.

On the question of continuity and discontinuity and analogies between art and science, I do not really believe in these analogies, but there was a strict relationship between art and the new geometries at the end of the last century. In the 'manifesto' on Cubism by Metzinger and Gleizes[1] and in Apollinaire there are clear references to 'four dimensional geometry'. I do not think that non-euclidean geometry had any direct influence on Cubism, but it is very interesting to see the translation of the new ideas of four-dimensional geometry into the science fiction of the end of the last century. A four dimensional object first appeared in the book *Flatland* by E. A. Abbott in 1884.[2] There were then the books by Hinton,[3] Wells,[4] Ouspensky,[5] Pawloswki[6] and many others, where there is a sort of philosophy or theology of four-dimensions.

These 'translations' of new geometrical ideas provided a link with the Avant-Garde in France. The first book on four-dimensional geometry with drawings appeared in 1903 by E. Jouffret in Paris.[7] He used the only possible technique to display a four-dimensional object—i.e. by means of three dimensional projections. As the famous French mathematician H. Poincaré said, our world is neither euclidean nor non-euclidean; these are just conventions.[8] With the idea that geometry is a convention, it is the relativity of space, not the Theory of Relativity, and the fact that there is a way to produce part of the meaning of a four-dimensional space which gives Cubism one of the techniques for making more interesting images of objects and people—i.e. by using several different projections simultaneously.

[1] A Gleizes and J. Metzinger (1912) *Du Cubism*. Paris.

[2] E. A. Abbott (1884) *Flatland*. London.

[3] C. H. Hinton (1884) *What is the fourth dimension?* London.

[4] H. G. Wells (1895) *The time machine: an invention*. London.

[5] P. D. Ouspensky (1910) *The fourth dimension: an experiment in the examination of the realm of the immeasurable* (in Russian). St Petersburg.

[6] G. de Pawlowski (1912) *Voyage au pays de la quatrième dimension*. Paris.

[7] E. Jouffret (1903) *Traité élémentaire de géométrie à quatre dimensions*. Paris.

[8] H. Poincaré (1902) *La science et l'hypothèse*. Paris.

LLOYD

Relativity supports continuity, not discontinuity, which was supported by the quantum theory of which Einstein was in favour, though he was unwilling to accept the implications of the uncertainty principle.

BRISKMAN

I would like to come in on the point made by Lloyd. As far as I can see Keller's paper claims that there was a parallel between a certain development in physics in the early years of this century—the breakdown of continuity in favour of discontinuity—and certain developments in art. The trouble with this view is that in physics the early years of this century were actually characterised by two movements. The development of relativity theory was in effect the triumph or high point of continuity physics (field theory). On the other hand problems for the continuum theory of energy—such as black-body radiation and the photo-electric effect—led to the development of the quantum theory. In contemporary physics we still can't say that we live either in a world characterised by continuity or by discontinuity. What we live in is a mess at the foundations of theoretical physics, because on the one hand we have a gravitational theory (General Relativity) which is a field theory and therefore a continuum theory, and on the other hand we have theories of the atomic and sub-atomic realms which are quantum theories and thus theories of the discrete and discontinuous. The basic problem of physics is how to marry these two together, and this problem hasn't been solved. So I think it highly misleading to say that what happened in physics in the early part of this century was the breakdown of continuity. Quite the contrary, what we had was the triumph of continuity and its breakdown, and we are still living with both its triumph and its breakdown without being able to quite solve the problem.

12

ON THE SYNCHRONISM BETWEEN ARTISTIC AND SCIENTIFIC IDEAS AND PRACTICES: AN EXPLORATION OF HYPOTHESES, 1900–1930s

Gérard Mermoz

City of Liverpool College of Higher Education

SUMMARY

The *coincidence* of an artistic with a scientific event (e.g. Cubism and the Theory of Relativity) could either be interpreted in terms of 'influence' or 'derivation' or in terms of a simultaneous response, by artists and scientists, to a common stimulus. The latter approach, suggested by Gabo, is particularly fruitful for it invites us to examine the hypothesis of a connection between artistic and scientific practice at a deeper ('archaeological', in the sense defined by Foucault) level. In this perspective both arts and sciences will be treated as 'semiotics of the real'.

1 *Art History and the search for 'influences'*

The relationship between the visual arts and the sciences in the period which saw the rise of Planck's Quantum Theory, Freud's *Interpretation of Dreams*, Minkowski's four-dimensional space-time continuum, Einstein's Special and General Theory of Relativity, Fauvism, Cubism and Abstraction has been the subject of a long-standing debate involving initially artists and critics (Fry, 1966) and, more recently, art historians (Laporte, 1948; 1949; 1966).

The published evidence of this debate may be classified into two groups: one supporting the view of a direct connection between art and science, the other opposing it. The former view (expressed in terms of formal or structural analogies, teleological similarities or differences, interplay of influences, etc.) has been argued in the main by art critics and historians while the latter is to be found in the writings of artists, scientists and historians of art and science.

In support of the latter view scholars have sometimes suggested that decisive influence came not from science but from philosophy. Thus, in turn,

Bergson, Husserl's phenomenology (Fry, 1966; Klein, 1970), the works of Russell, Hilbert and Brouwer in the field of logic (Richardson, 1969), Nietsche's philosophy (Nash, 1980) have been presented as possible sources of Cubism or as relevant interpretative tools.

Concurrently, Henderson (1971) has argued that 'the mistake of art historians anxious to explain references to the fourth dimension and non-Euclidean geometry has been to read back into cubist writings of 1911 and 1912 a breakthrough in physics which was not published until 1916' and, further, that in their book *Du Cubisme* (Herbert, 1964) Gleizes and Metzinger had borrowed some of their ideas on space from *La Science et l'Hypothèse* Poincaré (1902). At that point art historians agreed that a tangible proof of the influence of science—in this instance geometry—upon art had been established, on the concrete basis of textual criticism. However, Henderson made no attempt to show *what effect* Poincaré's ideas on space had on artistic practice, nor did Nash (1980) who, in a recent article, has argued that *Du Cubisme* 'throws light on the history of Cubism'.

During the seventies, scholars have begun to consider the fourth dimension from the wider perspective of art, geometry and philosophy combined. Compton (1974) and Williams (1977) have outlined some possible connections between Malevich's Suprematism and the fourth dimension as theorised by Jouffret (1903), Hinton (1888; 1904), Ouspensky (1931; 1981), Bragdon (1913; 1916) and others. Still, many difficulties remain, for, on the one hand, such disparate material is not easy to correlate and, on the other, too little attention has been paid to the ways an idea borrowed from science or philosophy can actually affect the works of an artist who is familiar with it. Picasso's remarks (Ashton, 1972): 'When I read a book on Einstein's physics of which I understand nothing, it does not matter: that will make me understand something else' gives us a measure of some of the difficulties involved.

It seems reasonable to posit that, in order to affect artistic practice, an idea or a concept borrowed from another discipline must operate directly on the constituent processes of the creative act. Thus, if we are to further our understanding of the epistemological status of the arts and the sciences in a general theory of discourse, the search for influences—as it now stands in art historical writings—must be replaced by a study of structural correlations.

2 *A strategy of denial*

> Mathematics, trigonometry, chemistry, psychoanalysis, music and whatnot have been related to cubism to give it an easier interpretation. All this has been pure literature, not to say nonsense, which brought bad results, blinding people with theories. Cubism has kept itself within the limits and limitations of painting, never pretending to go beyond it, *Picasso* (Ashton, 1972).

Picasso's denial—reiterated by a large number of artists in a conscious effort to oppose the reductionist interpretations of art critics and historians—seems to find confirmation in the more recent statements of scientists and art historians. Thus, we may agree with Heisenberg (1958) when he writes: 'There is little reason for thinking that modern science has had a direct influence on; say, the artist's discourse with nature' or with Kubler (1969) when he states: 'There are few signs that the basic theoretical ideas of science affect artists very much, or that scientists take many fundamental suggestions from artists. Their domains are separate, being anchored in vague perception among artists and in measured nature among scientists. Artists do not make science, nor scientists art.'

In the light of what we know about the creative process (Ghiselin, 1952; Koestler, 1964; Vernon, 1970) which in art as in science appears deeply rooted in subconscious layers of the psyche, manifesting itself in a complex interplay of thought processes and metaphors (Ortony, 1979), Picasso's denial reads as an exhortation not to try to 'understand' Cubism, but to experience it in the same terms it was experienced by the artist in the creative act. By doing so Picasso outlined a fundamental conflict of interests between artistic practice and art criticism (and any other form of rationalisation of artistic practice). Schoenberg was alluding to a similar kind of problem when he wrote, in his preface to Webern's *Six Bagatelles for String Quartet*: 'These pieces (as indeed, Webern's music in general) will only be understood by those who believe that through sound something that can only be expressed in sound can be said' (Bradshaw, 1978).

Taken in its deeper implications, Picasso's denial of external influences expresses the artist's belief in the sovereignty of the creative process and proclaims the irrelevance/irreverence of the search for influences.

3 *Synchronism and the 'Spirit of the Age'*

In the *Constructive Idea in Art* (Herbert, 1964), first published in 1937, Gabo presented the 'coincidence' between artistic and scientific 'revolution' as an expression of the logic of the 'creative human genius': 'The creative processes in the domain of Art—he argued—are as sovereign as the creative processes in Science . . ., the same spiritual state propels artistic and scientific activity at the same time and in the same direction.' As to the 'forms' in which this genius manifested itself simultaneously in art and science, Gabo claimed they were 'analogous'.

In both areas Gabo recognised the same manifestation of a 'spirit of fearless analysis' and of a 'sharpened and cultivated capacity for analytic thought to undertake the task of revaluation of old values'. However, when it came to the question of the possible interaction between art and science Gabo stressed their differences in a set of contrasting metaphors:

> Art and Science are two different streams which rise from the same creative source and flow into the same ocean of the common culture, but the currents of these two streams flow in different beds. Science teaches, Art asserts; Science explores and apprehends, informs and proves. . . . Art is not concerned with the meditation about what is and how it came to be. That is the task for knowledge. Knowledge is born of the desire to know, Art derives from the necessity to communicate and to announce. The stimulus of Science is the deficiency of our knowledge. The stimulus of Art is the abundance of our emotion and our latent desires. Science is the vehicle of facts—it is indifferent, or at best tolerant, to the ideas which lie behind facts. Art is the vehicle of ideas and its attitude to facts is strictly partial.

Whether this text is, as its modern editor (Herbert, 1964) claims, 'one of the most sensible statements of the relationship between modern abstract art and science' is open to debate. Personally, I read it as an unconditional assertion of the autonomy of art from all other disciplines. Even in his treatment of the rapports between art and philosophy, Gabo felt obliged to reject all claims of external influences for, he argued, 'Art has no need of philosophical arguments, it does not follow the sign-posts of philosophical systems; Art, like life, dictates systems to philosophy.' A similar view was expressed more recently by Paul Laporte (1966), who remarked: 'Artists and scientists started from common roots and were compelled to move in the same direction by an inner logic in the situation.'

4 *Remarks*

To pose the problem of the rapports between art and science at a given period in terms of 'influences' or a 'Spirit of the Age' dangerously limits the scope of our analyses. The adoption of a mechanistic model (cause-effect) in the search for 'influences' and the reference to a metaphysical order of things beyond the reach of analysis in the search for a 'Spirit of the Age' both constitute an insuperable obstacle to a true epistemological debate.

The fact that artists and scientists justify their views in cognitive terms—and, doing so, often make contradictory statements—combined with our incapacity to 'produce definitive versions of scientists' actions and beliefs' (Mulkay, 1981) confront us with a series of methodological problems culminating in the question: 'Is further research possible?' My answer to it is 'yes', provided that we re-define the direction of our study on the basis of the methodological tools available and capable of accounting for our object in its constituent forms or 'structure'. Thus, descriptions of 'what really happened' in art and science during any given period 'must be replaced by attempts to describe the recurrent forms of discourse whereby participants construct their versions of (the facts)'. 'One focuses, not on action as such, but on the methods scientists themselves use to account for, and make sense of, their own and other's actions' (Mulkay, 1981). This methodological shift presents the notable advantage of introducing a more critical attitude towards quotation data.

Another way of approaching the problem was outlined by Kuhn (1970b), when he remarked apropos of scientific progress, 'the explanation must, in the final analysis, be psychological or sociological'; it must take the form of a 'description of a value system, an ideology, together with an analysis of the institution through which that system is transmitted and enforced'.

The realisation of these aims stands well beyond the scope of the present paper. What I would like to suggest, at this preliminary stage, is a theoretical framework within which the problem of the rapports between art and science may be seen in terms of 'structural correlations' (Foucault, 1978).

Foucault's definition of 'discourse' as 'un ensemble à la fois cohérent et transformable de modèles théoriques et d'instruments conceptuels' (Foucault, 1971) allows us to envisage a theoretical space in which the arts and the sciences may be apprehended in their *constituent forms, relationships and successive transformations.* Such theoretical space is of considerable methodological value, for it enables us to study the 'play of dependencies' (Foucault, 1978) *within* and *between* discourses of seemingly different functions.

One dimension of this theoretical framework may be represented in the form of the following diagram where different discourses—chosen for their relevance to our discussion—feature according to their *traditionally assumed dominant roles* (cognitive/aesthetic) as well as to a *common epistemological function* (production of a symbolic 'order'):

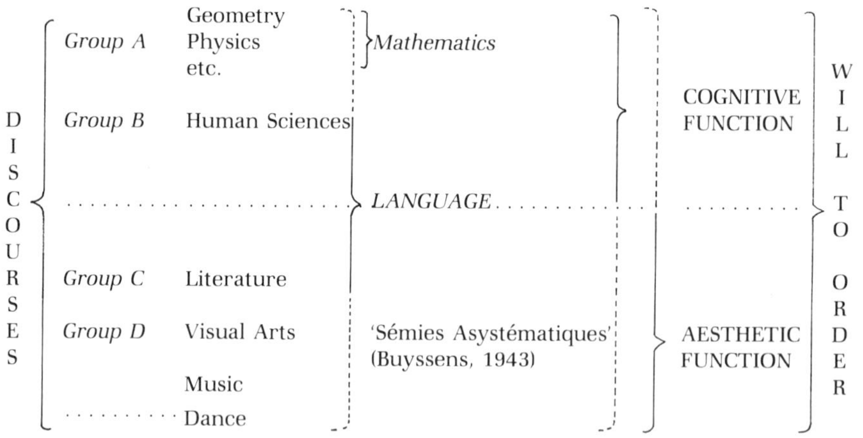

Let us note that, in addition to its specific character and mode of functioning each discourse shares with its counterparts the fundamental assumption that a rapport of structural equivalence may be found between the physical world (in science) or an existential experience (in art) and their representation (be it a scientific theory or a work of art). In so far as the arts and the sciences have defined themselves as a representation (of natural laws, feelings, ideas, experience) important features of both need to be interpreted by means of semiological analyses. Thus, a discussion of the synchronism between artistic and scientific events must, at some stage, take the form of a comparative study of their semiological functions within the wider framework of a theory of discourse.

One of the direct consequences of this methodological switch will be the re-definition of the 'aesthetic' and the 'cognitive' functions of art and science as 'semiological' functions, and the description of their semiological functions in terms of an interaction between different semiological layers. What this diagram does not show, however, is the deeper structural correlations which exist between the various semiological functions of each discourse (Jakobson, 1960) and 'extradiscursive' formations (Foucault, 1978). This blank defines a project still awaiting consideration by art historians indifferent, in the main, to the progress of the human sciences.

5 *The arts and the sciences as 'semioses' of the real*

> For the painter, the poet, and artists in general, each work becomes a new universe with its own laws. (This is what differentiates artists from other men, especially from scientists). *Apollinaire* (Breunig, 1972).
> The (truly exact) work of art is a metaphor of the universe obtained with artistic means. *Van Doesburg* (1969).
> Our experience up to date justifies us in feeling sure that in Nature is actualized the ideal of mathematical simplicity. . . . In a certain sense, therefore, I hold it to be true that pure thought is competent to comprehend the real, as the ancients dreamed. *Einstein* (1933).

If we examine the ways painters and physicists have represented nature in the first decade of this century, we note a number of significant differences in their conceptual frameworks, working processes and strategies.

The task of modern science, Gabo wrote in 1937, consists in the 'construction of a new stable model of the universe' (Herbert, 1964). In their attempts to produce such a model physicists had to avail themselves of adequate (i.e. 'logically true' and 'factually true' in the terminology of Carnap (Carnap, 1939)) mathematical calculi. This was made quite clear by Einstein (1933) in his Herbert Spencer lecture *On the Methods of Theoretical Physics*, delivered in Oxford on 10 June 1933: 'It is my conviction that pure mathematical construction enables us to discover the concepts and the laws connecting them which give the key to the understanding of the phenomena of nature.' But whereas some physicists, like Niels Bohr, were 'convinced that a complete physical explanation should absolutely precede the mathematical formulation', others, with Heisenberg, were seeking a 'mathematics which in a certain sense worked automatically, independently of all physical models' (Rozental, 1967). Whatever their approach, their representations of the objects of experience culminated in a mathematical formulation.

In their elaboration of theoretical models atomic physicists did not claim to produce a 'picture of nature', but indeed a 'picture of our relationships with nature' (Heisenberg, 1958). Thus, concludes Heisenberg, 'the atomic physicist has had to resign himself to the fact that his science is but a link in the infinite chain of man's argument with nature, and that it can not simply speak of nature "in itself"'.

The artist, in so far as his concern was to produce with each piece of work a 'new universe with its own laws', had constantly to reinvent his means of expression. To the physicist's recourse to an underlying 'mathesis', artists opposed an unconditional faith in deep subjectivity: 'There is nothing real outside ourselves—write Gleizes and Metzinger (Herbert, 1964)—except the coincidence of a sensation and an individual mental direction. We seek the essential, but we seek it in our personalities, and not in a sort of eternity, laboriously fitted out by mathematicians and philosophers.' Outbidding them, Gabo, in *The Constructive Idea in Art* (Herbert, 1964), proclaimed: 'There is and there can be only one reality—existence.'

Dismissing scientific and philosophical absolutes (the 'essences' of Kantian philosophy) as well as the optical conventions of official art and other modernist trends, the Cubists invented a new pictorial language in which the 'referential', 'denotative' or cognitive functions of painting were subordinated to its 'emotive', 'poetic' and 'conative' functions (Jakobson, 1960). To a greater extent than in any other contemporary trend this shift of emphasis was marked by the production of *undecipherable* works (Fry, 1966). However, the striving for formal coherence and for expressiveness may be paralleled with the scientific requirements for a physical theorem to be logically true and factually true.

The semiological transformations the object underwent in this new mode of representation was described by Picasso in 1935, during a private conversation with Christian Zervos: 'Do you think it concerns me that a particular picture of mine represents two people? Though these two people once existed for me, they exist no longer. The 'vision' of them gave me a preliminary emotion; then little by little their actual presence became blurred, they developed into a fiction and then disappeared altogether, or rather they were transformed into all kinds of problems. They are no longer two people, you see, but forms and colors: forms and colors that have taken on, meanwhile, the idea of two people and preserve the vibration of their life' (Ashton, 1972). From object to fiction and idea—transformed by the emotional response of the artist and by his formal preoccupations—the physical world ['One cannot go against nature' said Picasso (Ashton, 1972)] assumed a parallel existence as 'representation'. The metaphors of art as 'structure' or 'architecture' of forms, 'composition', 'construction' and autonomous object ('tableau-objet') spread in artistic literature, concurrently with the notion of *precursor*.

For avant-garde artists of the cubist era, the notion of *precursor* replaced the classical notion of *model*. Both played, though in different ways, the function of 'exemplars' [Kuhn (1977) defines 'exemplars' as the 'concrete problem solutions accepted by the group as paradigmatic']; however, whereas the models of classical aesthetics were presented as the embodiment of formal properties to be imitated or emulated (with a low probability of ever being surpassed), the *precursors* of Modernism were regarded as the fore-runners of the new art. Thus, the notion of precursor implied a dynamism in the history of art (if not a progress) which oriented the works of artists towards the full realisation of ideas and principles first formulated by the predecessors, but not taken to their logical limits: 'The modern concept—wrote Léger in 1913—is not a reaction against the ideas of the impressionists but is, on the contrary, a further development of their ideas and a widening of their aims by the use of means which they neglected' (Fry, 1966).

The consensus which placed Cézanne as the precursor of Modernism among the Nabis, the Cubists, the Suprematists, etc. would remain an unresolved paradox if we expected his 'lesson' (today we would say his relevance) to have been that of a model in the classical sense. Cézanne's contribution to Modernism consisted in a 'lesson' (Cézanne's proverbial 'lesson') which *changed with the preoccupations of those who studied his works.* Thus, between the summers of 1907 and 1909, his paintings were regarded by Picasso and Braque as guides to the way of applying paint on canvas as well as to the mode of constructing a picture. By 1910 the 'actuality' of Cézanne had changed radically as a result of Braque's and Picasso's recent experiments [Picasso: *Portrait of Clovis Sagot* (Daix 270), *Portrait of Manuel Pallares* (Daix 274): spring 1909; *Portrait of Albroise Vollard* (Daix 337), *Portrait of Wilhelm Uhde* (Daix 338): spring 1910; *Portrait of D.-H. Kahnweiler* (Daix 368): autumn 1910] and Metzinger could write in autumn 1910: 'Cézanne showed us forms living in the reality of light, Picasso brings us a material account of their real life in the mind' (Fry, 1966). Other works produced by Picasso at Cadaquès during the summer of 1910 [*The Dressing Table* (Daix 356), *The Rower* (Daix 360), *Woman with Mandolin* (Daix 361), *Nude Woman* (Daix 363)] illustrate this conceptual tendency which was to culminate in the hermetic works of 1911–12 (Daix 415, 424, 425, 428, etc.). In 1935, looking back on the events, Picasso summed up the significance of Cézanne by saying: 'What forces our interest is Cézanne's anxiety—that's Cézanne's lesson' (Ashton, 1972).

At that time atomic physics was evolving models of reality independent from empirical observation and anthropomorphic representation (Miller, in Wechsler, 1981). Thus, in the mathematical formulation of the Special Theory of Relativity, 'the time co-ordinate plays exactly the same role as the three space co-ordinates' (Einstein, 1920) and, in the General Theory of Relativity Einstein provided a model of the space-time continuum by means of Gauss coordinates which did away with the 'fictitious rigid body of reference' of Euclidean properties (Einstein, 1920).

Minkowski's paper *Space and Time* of 1908 (Einstein, Minkowski and Others, 1923) provides a further point for comparison. Working from an electro-magnetic model of the world ('discovered' by Lorentz and 'further revealed' by Einstein) Minkowski was able to formulate his hypothesis of the world as a four-dimensional space-time continuum. In this instance, Lorentz and Einstein played for Minkowski the role of precursors, for they provided him with a *theoretical framework* within which he was able to formulate his hypothesis. However, Minkowski's contribution was only a *link* in the chain of scientific work, later to be fitted by Einstein in the General Theory of Relativity (Einstein, 1920, 1954). Thus, in 1920 Einstein assessed the significance of Minkowski by saying: 'The discovery of Minkowski, which was of importance for the formal development of the theory of relativity, does not lie here (i.e. in his 'four-dimensional mode of consideration of the world'). It is to be found rather in the fact of his recognition that the four-dimensional space-time continuum of the theory of relativity, in its most essential formal properties, shows a pronounced relationship to the three-dimensional continuum of Euclidean geometrical space' (Einstein, 1920, chapter XVII).

I would not dare to suggest that Minkowski played in the history of Relativity the same role as Cézanne did in the history of Cubism (by their very nature their respective achievements are 'incommensurable'); however, what a comparison between innovation in art and science *does* reveal is the existence of a similar play of dependencies between concepts, operations, and theoretical options *within* each discipline. This guaranteed for both a degree of continuity which, in art, cannot be fully reconciled with Kuhn's view of history as a 'succession of tradition-bound periods punctuated by non-cumulative breaks' (Kuhn, 1970a). Our inability to apply the axiomatic method to the study of artistic 'development' does not justify us into defining the so-called 'breaks with tradition' which punctuate the history of art as 'non-cumulative'. Given the state of art historical knowledge, new works of art (new artistic 'exemplars') only appear as 'non-cumulative' as we are unable to follow *without break* the invisible processes which underlie their emergence. Thus, the mysterious 'leap forward' which characterises the creative process in art and science need not be interpreted in terms of *discontinuity* with the past, but rather in terms of a *problematic* (i.e. still unresolved) *continuity*. Einstein's and Minkowski's references to the works of other physicists seem to agree with Picasso's statement: 'Toute oeuvre procède toujours plus ou moins d'une autre' (Cabanne, 1975, vol. II).

In science, innovation usually follows the resolution of a 'crisis' brought about by the emergence of discrepancies between the data of experience and current theories. This resolution takes place when a new theory is found to accommodate all the known facts of experience. In this respect Einstein's Theory of Relativity was a 'revolution' (in Kuhn's sense of the term), for it could 'do justice to the entire range of the data of experience in a manner even more complete and satisfactory than was possible with Newton's principles' (Einstein, 1933).

Unlike scientific models, works of art aspire to live in an eternal present: 'To me', wrote Picasso in 1923, 'there is no past or future in art. If a work of art cannot live always in the present it must not be considered at all. The art of the Greeks, of the Egyptians, of the great painters who lived in other times, is not an art of the past; perhaps it is more alive today than it ever was' (Ashton, 1972). But this may be more an expression of wishful thinking (a 'désir d'éternité'); in reality, both art and science are exposed to the erosion of time and to ideological manipulations. As a new scientific paradigm transforms the discipline in which it appears, a new paradigm in art redefines artistic practice (at the level of its concepts, techniques, materials, etc.) modifying the relationships between the artist and the works of the past. In science new paradigms replace old ones by making them obsolete.

In conclusion, it may be argued that, at the level of their working processes, Cubism and early-twentieth-century Physics stand more as responses to existing paradigms (works of art, scientific concepts or theories) than as direct responses to nature. As Einstein (1933) remarked: 'The axiomatic basis of theoretical physics cannot be inferred from experience, but must be free invention'. Still, the 'free invention' of the scientist had to be verified by the facts of experience; 'Reason gives the structure of the system; the data of experience and their mutual relations are to correspond exactly to consequences in the theory. On the possibility alone of such a correspondence rest the values and the justification of the whole system, and especially of its fundamental concepts and basic laws' (Einstein, 1933). In art, the equivalent part is played by social recognition. Thus, if a theory may be said to 'work' when it accounts for all the data of experience known in a given field and when it seems *acceptable* to the scientific community, a painting 'works' when it elicits a positive response from other individuals who share—to a certain degree—the same *competence* and similar *interests* with the artist. As we know from *Le Chef d'Oeuvre Inconnu* a work of art cannot survive (nor, for that matter, can the artist) without some degree of communication (and acceptance) taking place between the artist and other individuals (artists, dealers, collectors, etc.) or institutions (private and/or public).

REFERENCES

Ashton, D (1972) *Picasso On Art.* London.
Bohr, N. (1958) *Atomic Physics and Human Knowledge.* New York.*
Bradshaw, S. (1978) The Works of A. Webern, in: *Webern-Boulez.* C.B.S. Records.
Bragdon, C. (1913) *A Primer of Higher Space.* New York.
—— (1916) *Four-dimensional Vistas.* New York.
Breunig, L. C. (1972) (ed.) *Apollinaire On Art.* London.
Buyssens, E. (1943) *Les Langages et le Discourse.* Brussels.
Cabanne, P. (1975) *Le Siècle de Picasso.* 3 vols. Paris.
Carnap, R. (1939) *Foundations of Logic and Mathematics.* Chicago.
Compton, S. (1974) *Malevich and the Fourth Dimension,* in: *Studio* (April), pp. 190–5.
Einstein, A. (1920) *Relativity: The Special and the General Theory.* London.
—— (1933) *On the Methods of Theoretical Physics.* Oxford.
—— (1954) *The Meaning of Relativity.* London.
Einstein, A., Minkowski, H. *et al.* (1923) *The Principle of Relativity.* London.
Foucault, M. (1971) *L'Ordre du Discours.* Paris.
—— (1978) *Politics and the Study of Discourse* (1968 1st edn.), English translation in: *Ideology and Consciousness,* no. 3 (Spring), pp. 7–26.
Fry, E. (1966) *Cubism.* London.
Ghiselin, B. (ed.) (1952) *The Creative Process.* Berkeley.
Heisenberg, W. (1958) *The Physicist's Conception of Nature.* London.*
(1959) *Physics and Philosophy.* London.*
Henderson, L. D. (1971) *A New Facet of Cubism: 'The Fourth Dimension' and 'Non-Euclidean Geometry' Reinterpreted,* in: *Art Quarterly,* vol. 34, IV. pp. 410–33.
Herbert, R. L. (ed.) (1964) *Modern Artists On Art.* Prenctice-Hall, Englewood Cliffs, New Jersey.
Hinton, C. H. (1888) *A New Era of Thought.* London.
(1904) *The Fourth Dimension.* London.
Jakobson, R. (1960) Linguistics and Poetics, in T. Sebeok (ed.), *Style in Language.* New York.
Jouffret, E. (1903) *Traité Elémentaire de Géométre à Quatre Dimensions.* Paris.
Klein, R. (1970) *La Forme et L'Intelligible.* Paris.
Koestler, A. (1964) *The Act of Creation.* London.
Kubler, G. (1969) *Comment* (on the Relations of Science and Art), in: *Comparative Studies in Society and History,* vol. II, no. 4 (Oct.), pp. 398–402. Cambridge.
Kuhn, T. S. (1969) *Comment* (on the Relations of Science and Art), in: *Comparative Studies in Society and History,* vol. II, no. 4 (Oct.), pp. 403–12. Cambridge.*
—— (1970a) *The Structure of Scientific Revolutions.* Chicago. (rev. edn.).
—— (1970b) Logic of Discovery or Psychology of Research? in: I. Lakatos and A. Musgrave (eds.), *Criticism and the Growth of Knowledge,* pp. 1–23. Cambridge.
—— (1977) *The Essential Tension.* Chicago.
—— (1979) *Metaphor in Science,* in A. Ortony (1979), pp. 404–19.*

* Of general relevance. Not specifically cited in text.

Laporte, P. (1948) The Space-Time Concept in the Work of Picasso, *The Magazine of Art,* vol. 41, part 1, pp. 26–32.
—— (1949) Cubism and Science, *The Journal of Aesthetics and Art Criticism,* vol. 7, part III, pp. 243–56.
—— (1966) Cubism and Relativity, *Art Journal,* vol. 25, part III, pp. 246–8.
Minkowski, H. (1923) *Space and Time* (1908 1st edn.), English translation in: A. Einstein, H. Minkowski *et al., The Principle of Relativity.* London.
Mulkay, M. (1981) *Action and Belief or Scientific Discourse? A Possible Way of Ending Intellectual Vassalage in Social Studies of Science, in: Philosophy of the Social Sciences,* vol. II, pp. 163–71.
Nash, J. M. (1980) The Nature of Cubism: a study of conflicting explanations, in: *Art History,* vol. III, no. 4 (Dec.), pp. 435–47.
Ortony, A. (ed.) (1979) *Metaphor and Thought.* Cambridge.
Ouspensky, P. D. (1931) *A New Model of the Universe.* London.
—— (1981) *Tertium Organum* (1912 1st edn.). London.
Poincaré, J. H. (1902) *La Science et l'Hypothèse.* London.
Richardson, J. A. (1969) Un Mythe de la Critique Moderne: le Cubisme et la Quatrième Dimension, in: *Diogène,* 65, 103–15.
Rozenthal, S. (ed.) (1967) *Niels Bohr, his life and work as seen by his friends and colleagues.* Amsterdam.
Van Doesburg, Th. (1969) *Principles of Neo-Plastic Art* (1925 1st edn.), English translation. London.
Vernon, M. D. (ed.) (1970) *Creativity.* London.
Wechsler, J. (ed.) (1981) *On Aesthetics in Science.* Cambridge, Mass. (1st ed. 1978).
Williams, R. C. (1977) *Artists in Revolution.* London.

Note All the works by Picasso referred to in the text are reproduced in the catalogue of the exhibition held at the Museum of Modern Art, New York, 1980.

DISCUSSION

TORMEY

Influence is a notoriously opaque concept and, contrary to some of the remarks made earlier, it seems to me that what is of the utmost importance in understanding the impact of science on art is not so much an accurate description of the scientific theories involved as of the interpretations or misinterpretations that artists have placed upon them.

MERMOZ

I agree with you about the irrelevance of the search for influences but I don't think that we will get very far in trying to document cases of artists misinterpreting scientific ideas. Both perspectives fail to embrace art and science in terms of common denominators (be it structures, processes, values, external/internal determining factors, etc.).

GELL

One of the problems is that although the aims of art are unchanging, the aims of science are constantly shifting. This is not meant to be a paradox, but science is changing, as far as ethos, all the time. Almost every statement which Gabo made about science in your quotation was either wrong or it was open to question. Not perhaps wrong at the time but certainly wrong now and so it does seem to me important that art historians, artists and so on should look at science in a real way, rather than at the popularisation of it. Now it seems to me that the question we have to approach is, 'Is anything exchanged between sciences and art or do they proceed in parallel streams both being influenced by the spirit of the age? If anything is exchanged, what is it? Models? Schemata? Metatheory? is there any genuine dialectic interaction? I feel that these latter questions need more precise answers than any we have been able to give so far.

MERMOZ

First let me say that I do not know many artists who would agree that the aims of art are unchanging. To be precise we should indicate what sort of aims we have in mind; conscious or unconscious, etc.

Gabo's rhetorical piece as well as Picasso's denial of influences should not be described in terms of a 'lack' but as the expression of a 'difference', otherwise we are falling back into the old argument about the 'two cultures'. This difference depends, to a large extent, on the language each discipline uses to construct its model of reality (be it a painting or a theory). It is, therefore, important that we should examine how each discipline depends upon its own language in what it can say about the world. Underlying the practice of art and science, however, we find a common need to assert: reality $= x$, y or z. In this act of simultaneous assertion the arts and the sciences have mapped out reality in terms of their own language. This is indicated by the structure of the diagram on page 138 where the arts and the sciences feature according (a) to the language they adopt in their construction of reality and (b) to their currently assumed dominant functions (cognitive for the sciences and aesthetic for the arts).

GELL
I would like to take that up. I think your use of that scheme is language-oriented. My theory is that what is exchanged is sometimes in language but sometimes is just a structural symbol or metaphor.

MERMOZ
This diagram is not intended to be a complete model, but a working scheme to initiate some kind of discussion about the forms in which the arts and the sciences represent reality. The central position of language on this diagram is to be explained by the status of language in the production of knowledge. As a property of language and thought, metaphor could not feature separately beside language, for it is encompassed by language. Finally, I agree that metaphor could constitute a link between the arts and the sciences but more in terms of their working processes than in those of something that would be exchanged between the two.

GELL
I take your point, but I think we have to be aware of confining our exchanges to language because that does tend to cut off the visual arts from the scientific process. The science process is not a linguistic process entirely.

MERMOZ
When I say language, I don't mean it simply in a linguistic sense. However, in a linguistic sense language constitutes a platform upon which artists, scientists and historians of art and science may talk about activities carried out through different symbolic systems. What the diagram is saying is that art and science produce models or representations of reality, through specific systems of signs, and that their products fit within the general system of knowledge according to their dominant function (cognitive or aesthetic).

HARRÉ
I would have thought that only *one* of the ways of characterising music is as a form of mathematical abstraction from the sonic world. There is a very puzzling relationship between its phenomenology and its mathematics; e.g. the equal-tempered scale is a mathematically imperfect compromise. But there is an essential mathematical element in music as we currently understand it in the West. To those who are familiar with the Laban notation and the modern development of dance, the same thing goes for dance. So mathematics, I would argue, forms an essential part of how dance and music are constituted for us. It follows that there is a semiological hypothesis in your diagram which I want to question, namely the implication that there is a parallelism between mathematics and cognitive function. It seems to me that there is at least as good a relationship between mathematics and aesthetic function that has been demonstrated in the way we currently understand dance and music. If the column headed mathematics is a semiology, a sort of condensed semiological theory, then I think the theory must be modified to take account of this.

MERMOZ
The association on my diagram between mathematics and cognitive function

is only representing, as I pointed out earlier, the currently assumed dominant function of mathematics. This is represented by a continuous line. If you look at the diagram you will see that a dotted line links mathematics with aesthetic function. I have used a dotted line to indicate the problematic nature of the association between discourses and functions and I am glad you have taken up the problem at this level. As to the classification of dance and music with respect to mathematics I do not share the same conviction. As systems of notation, dance and music may share some properties with mathematics but what about performances? A good dance or a good piece of music will convey a sense of order, but will I say of them, as I would of a mathematical demonstration, that they are 'logically true'? What I shall not be able to state, for certain, is whether or not they are 'factually true'.

HARRÉ
If mathematics is related to both the aesthetic and the cognitive functions then, I would feel much better.

GREGORY
Surely there is an ambiguity over 'mathematics' here. Do you mean mathematics as a language?

MERMOZ
Yes, mathematical language.

GREGORY
Well, may be you are okay but I think it should be in language.

MERMOZ
Language in the middle of the diagram stands for linguistic language.

GREGORY
Why do you think mathematical language is not a linguistic language?

MERMOZ
I would not deny an intimate connection between language and mathematics at a deeper level, and would welcome any comment going in that direction.

HARRÉ
To follow up Gregory's point, isn't there something else working here, namely a syntax versus semantics distinction? When we peel off mathematics in this formal sense, we are peeling off syntax. One might say that all mathematical *calculi* are purely syntactical. We need an interpretation to provide them with semantics. Music, painting and verbal language are such that their semantics and syntax interact with one another. We can make only an analytical distinction. Every thing that is semiological must have a syntax but only some semiological systems have a semantics and those are the ones that we can actually use.

I didn't mean Mermoz to put mathematics under music, I meant that the form in which music is represented by us, for instance in a score, is a mathematical notation with strict tautological rules of use. Physics is represented by us in a mathematical notation with a strict system of tautological rules. It is the semiology I want to talk about, not the subject-matter.

GELL

Mathematics as such is a technique and a tool, and it seems to me not relevant to dance and music, except in so far as they are exemplifications of order.

LLOYD

I would like to suggest that the relation between art and science is similar to that between rhetoric and logic. The stimulating diagram we have just been discussing could be amplified by adding engineering, the production of artefacts to meet human need, and by emphasising the traffic between Arts and Sciences via Education. The whole diagram might be best drawn on a Moebius strip!

13

THE DEATH OF ABSTRACTION: SCIENTIFIC METAPHORS IN TWENTIETH-CENTURY ART AND DESIGN

Peter Lloyd Jones

School of Three-Dimensional Design, Kingston Polytechnic

SUMMARY

The theory of design during the twentieth century has been dominated by a complex of ideas known as 'functionalism'. How an artefact looks is supposed to be decisively influenced, if not determined, by its purpose and use. In fact, functionalist theory is an aesthetic theory of a rather special kind which serves to justify and legitimise a limited range of appearances in man-made goods that is usually called abstract.

From its inception, abstract art, and with it design, was influenced by metaphors drawn from contemporary science. These formed part of an influential body of theoretical writings which overlapped both abstract art and functional design. Scientific metaphors served to answer awkward theoretical problems of communication between 'abstract' creators and their would-be audiences, but abstract art has never really communicated with a wide audience. Ironically, it was renewed metaphorical borrowings from more recent sciences (information theory, linguistics, and social anthropology) which finally provided the ammunition to destroy its theoretical foundations.

Abstract art and the influence of Gestalt psychology

Abstraction, it must be assumed, is truly democratic. A purely 'abstract' art or design, precisely because it is culture-free, must be able to speak to everyone, not just to those who know the conventions and symbols on which earlier styles were based. Now, neither magnetism, nor resonance nor a supposedly shared access to a hidden geometric or organic substrate of reality (all variously adduced as metaphors for the processes of 'abstract' artistic communication) are particularly convincing explanations of how this is supposed to occur. For this reason there has been, right from the beginning of abstract art and design, an abiding interest in a truly scientific psychology, particularly in those areas which promised to support existing aesthetic commitments to inherently expressive forms. None has proved more congenial to apologists for abstraction than Gestalt Psychology. Now as everyone knows 'Gestalt' means 'form' and Gestalt Psychology speaks of the processes of perceptual form-making.

Psychologists such as Köhler, Koffka and Wertheimer pointed out that there were many areas—and visual perception was an important one—where *complex* structures of behaviour were the primary ones. Three dots together read as a triangle directly and automatically. We do not have to learn to associate them together into the triangular form. Many perceptual regularities were observed in which elements were apparently linked together as complex units or *gestalten*.

A simple explanation was offered in terms of supposed electrical patterns in the brain which corresponded point for point spatially to the spatial pattern in the stimulus (the doctrine of *iso-morphism*). These brain fields were supposed to exhibit a tendency—like electric fields in the physical world—to collapse spontaneously towards regularity and symmetry under the universal tendency to minimum energy. This simple picture borrowed from physics indicated in a general way how it was that groups of elements became fused into 'wholes' where the 'whole was greater than the sum of the parts'. There is no doubt that, while the oversimple metaphor of brain fields has had to be abandoned in the face of new evidence, the experimental findings of gestalt psychology endure. To stress that the eye and the brain deal with complex organisations *ab initio* is still a valuable correction to over ambitious attempts to reduce perception to the additive activity of the associationist. But why was all this of such interest to artists? What excited them was the 'proof' that geometric figures had, as it were, a life of their own. Moreover, the *gestalt* processes were universal and innate, rooted in biology, more fundamental than culture. They offered the promise of a universal keyboard of the senses on which a sensitive artist could play a universal democratic harmony. In this, Gestalt Psychology appeared to offer a contemporary scientific endorsement of the ancient Neo-Platonic vision of a single geometry at the heart of creation and of the soul. Ettlinger (1961) has written interestingly of borrowings from Gestalt Psychology and their mingling with latter day Neo-platonistic mysticism in the theory and works of Kandinsky. Later on, when Bauhaus pedagogy had taken a somewhat more rational turn under the direction of Hannes Meyer, a number of distinguished scientists were invited to lecture there, including a number of psychologists (Wingler, 1969).

Rudolf Arnheim has been the leading propagandist for the incorporation of the ideas of Gestalt Psychology into the theory and practice of art. His book *Art and Visual Perception* (Arnheim, 1967) first published in 1956 is still widely read in art schools and has influenced a generation of designers' notions of the origin of visual form. Now what Gestalt Psychology has done is to give to artists a possible mechanism for communicating abstractly. But what exactly is it that is communicated? What exactly are the messages that pass between the artist and the recipient of a geometrical *gestalt*, some complex of visual elements seen 'as a whole'?

Abstraction and empathy . . . and alienation

The answer to this question was given in a prophetic early essay by Wilhelm Worringer (1963) first published in 1908 called 'Abstraction and Empathy'. This was really a radical (and somewhat mystical) restatement of the idea of resonance with natural forces somehow embodied in abstract forms. Worringer argued that the naturalism of classic art which expresses most perfectly man's empathy with the natural world is only one limited way of seeing that world. Other cultures, and other periods within our own culture have seen the world differently. In the art of Northern cultures (he held) there is a persistent tendency to oblate naturalistic detail and flatten the roundness of three-dimensional objects in space. An urge to *abstraction* contradicts the urge to empathy. The two are in increasing disputation during the fluctuating evolution of historical style. But there are occasionally those periods where

> the outer world begins to live and receives all its life from man who now anthropomorphises all its inner essence, all its inner forces. The sensation of oneself-in-things naturally sharpens the feeling for the inexpressibly beautiful content of organic forms, and paths revealed to artistic volition, the paths of an artistic naturalism for which the natural model merely serves as a substratum to the will-to-form which is guided by its feelings for the organic. Now the artist learns to apprehend every random form as a theatre within which to experience the joy of moving hither and thither in the company of nameless force . . . the need for empathy abandons the sphere of the organic . . . and takes possession of abstract forms (Worringer, 1963).

This premonitory vision of the emotional possibilities of abstraction, written as a doctoral thesis by an unknown German art historian became immediately famous, arriving as it did at the dawning of a stylistic revolution in painting and sculpture. Its rapturous tone anticipates a thousand later essays (and effusions) on what we call 'abstract expression'. A favourite scientific metaphor for the intuitive perceptions of such abstract vibrations was the seismograph. The artist is supposed to register, like the most sensitive seismograph, the preliminary shock-waves which anticipate a coming earthquake. And not only artists. For Herbert Read, prophet of the 'Meaning of (abstract) Art' and friendly with abstract sculptors like Gabo, Henry Moore and Arp, the abstract forms of modern design were also charged with meaning through empathetic projection. Read was the most influential design propagandist of his generation and when he juxtaposed an illustration of an 'organic' abstraction by Jean Helion with that of an electric shaver by Ken Grange he had a ready audience. Some have gone further. The logical extreme in the union of abstraction and empathy is the empty rectilinear Cartesian grid, the total geometric megastructure envisaged by latterday constructivists like Vasarely. He argued that since we all possess the crucial perceptual mechanisms to respond to primary abstract forms we could not but move through an abstract three-dimensional polychrome grid with joy. Simple combinatorial games with primary coloured rectilinear panels would never weary or bore (Joray, 1965). Fortunately no such vision has ever been built although some modern architecture comes near it.

Now the public reaction has *not* been one of unmixed joy, unlimited empathy. Rather the contrary. Countless complaints about the results of an unrelenting functional abstraction suggests that it leads instead to alienation and *anomie*. Far from the precious symbols of a joyful future, primary geometry and functional forms have lead to an arid desert. Some artists, sensitive to the increasingly hostile feelings generated by the reality of functional abstraction, especially in urban architecture and interiors, turned Platonic geometry against itself. Robert Smithson (1966), one of the leaders of the Minimal Sculpture movement, indicated the ironic and critical role of his anonymous geometric repetitions in what he called 'Impure Purism'. The hallowed symbols of modernism were further assaulted by painting them in 'lurid and gorgeous colour' such as 'Hi-Fi' from the Harley-Davidson motorcycle company. Many films of the 1960s dwelt upon the alienating effect of the Purist world, expensively stripped of all human content. At the level of everyday artefacts, physiognomic projection became impossible as the 'physical' metaphors—the mechanics of crank and piston, rotation and oscillation—gradually disappeared from appliances. It became more and more difficult to 'see the works' since growing diminution in size entailed increased protection, usually by the complete shrouding of motors and moving parts. Finally, with the electronic revolution, mechanics vanished altogether. Invisible circuits are now encased in anonymous rectangular boxes that give no hint of their 'function'. A toaster becomes indistinguishable visually from a radio set. The world of functional goods gradually becomes visually meaningless in the sense that the projection of body imagery onto imagined functions is impossible.

As the geometric dream became a bore, Robert Venturi's study of undesigned commercial vernacular in *Learning from Las Vegas* focused attention on areas of the ordinary environment which had previously been regarded as mere blight (Venturi, 1972). This interest can now be seen as another part of the 'Pop' revolution which, by using imagery from 'low' life as its raw material threw out previous 'formalist' canons of purity and integrity in art. At the same time as this upheaval in professionally approved imagery there occurred several important conceptual developments in various fields of science which provided new metaphors for structure and new models of artistic communication. These finally undermined the theoretical basis of abstraction which still rested ultimately on the psychology of the 1920s.

Apologists for abstraction and formalist design had long been accustomed to speak of the 'grammar' of forms or the 'language of vision' sometimes in quasi-scientific tones. In reality these were merely fanciful metaphors—a fact which became clear once real sciences such as information theory developed clear and logically-precise notions of pattern or 'form', and linguistics made unprecedented advances towards an algebraic description of language. Behind both these developments was the rise of the computer and of the logical soft-ware to go with it.

Not energy but information

There was already plenty of evidence accumulating from within the field of experimental psychology that vision was much more complex, and, at the same time, more active than earlier models had allowed. During the late 1950s and early 1960s computer software provided the exciting analogies for the conceptualisation of visual activity. Instead of 'brain-fields' and verbal generalities about 'wholes', models of perception now were based on information processing sequences using 'coded' input from the eye. Physiological structures were now seen as 'black-boxes', sampling, storing, comparing, retrieving and passing-on a flow, not of electricity, but of *information*. Complex shapes were still seen as a 'whole' but this was now conceived merely as the output of a long chain of operations in which 'parts' were recognised by quite specific groups of neural 'feature-detectors' and then passed-on for further analysis and final 'assembly'. If no less miraculous in their ingenuity, visual processes thus described became demystified.

The man who was responsible for introducing these new insights into the study of art was the historian E. H. Gombrich. His scholarly range was enormous and his understanding of psychology was thorough and painstaking. Books like *Art and Illusion* (Gombrich, 1960) and his collection of essays *Meditations on a Hobby-Horse* (Gombrich, 1963) have changed the course of art history and criticism permanently. Most of his attention has been reserved for the innumerable and subtle problems of artistic representation of the real world and he had little time for abstract art and its debates. He did not like abstract art however and in several penetrating essays used his mastery of (then) recent psychological theory to destroy its pretensions to being, in any serious sense, scientific, caricaturing for his purpose an earlier metaphor drawn from science—the artist as a wireless transmitter that had been proposed by Roger Fry (Gombrich, 1963, p. 60). Using the analogy of the coded transmission of information as described in the mathematical theory of communication he tried to show that *no* forms, abstract or otherwise, were inherently meaningful or expressive. They carried meaning by virtue of their ability to select from an ensemble of alternatives common to sender and receiver. Even physiognomic or 'undifferentiated' perception could be described as partial or incomplete processing, a read-out from an intermediate step on the way towards the complete categorisation of ordinary 'analytic' vision. Gombrich's work made a profound impact from the moment of its publication, comparable perhaps with that of Worringer. His argument insisted that the ensembles from which alternatives are selected were in large part learned. So that we could only come to understand what a particular painting from, say, the Renaissance, expressed by the painstaking reconstruction of these possibilities which might realistically have been adopted by the artist but in fact were not. It was a matter for the historian to reconstruct this set of possibilities for us since in the art of the past, the passage of time prevents us from knowing the 'logic of the artist's situation' directly. Gombrich did not deny the reality of physiognomic perception or 'natural expressiveness' and its role in art. Indeed, his theory needs it, at any rate, in a weak sense. For as Wollheim (1968) showed, it is only if the ordered set of alternatives is anchored in some determinate way to specific inner-states that are 'natural' and not conventional, that we can see immediately that a movement within the series of alternatives towards one end or another has a particular expressive significance. Be that as it may, what Gombrich did demonstrate was that abstract forms too create their meaning by selecting from an ensemble and this was more culture-bound than apologists for abstract art cared to admit. After all, despite the fact that abstract forms were supposed to elicit 'wired-in' responses in everyone, the fact that most people who were not familiar with abstract art, found it meaningless could not be denied.

Interpretative systems—the metaphor of language

Wollheim considered some further difficulties which arose from Gombrich's idea of an ensemble of alternatives or what he called a 'repertoire'. Which alternatives were relevant for comparison purposes? Clearly one didn't need to know, one *couldn't* know *all* the possible moves an artist might have made. Yet in order to decide which ones were relevant one had *already* in a sense 'understood' his meaning. Reconciliation of these paradoxes was found in the adoption of the analogy not of visual communication as a *code* with its code book fixed for both sender and receiver, but as a language. This development was stimulated by the rise of modern linguistics, particularly the work of Noam Chomsky. Chomsky developed a detailed description of languages as two-level structures expressable in 'algebraic' form. In his 'generative grammar', sentences were constructed by the transformation of so called 'deep structure' forms. At this 'deep' level similarities were found in many languages and Chomsky thought that these might correspond to innate mental processes. (At the 'surface-structure' level there is of course great variety and diversity.) Any competent speaker learns these structures and the so-called transformation rules in early infancy. Once this has been achieved there is no limit to the infinite variety of new sentences that he subsequently can create.

For the reasons already described, Wollheim argued that the notion of a code book needed to be replaced by the more flexible concept of an interpretative system. It was here that the new models of language acquisition came in. The problems with the early Gombrich model of a code is that it does not explain how the processes of reading codes could ever get started since in effect, one needs to know the code in order to read the code book. According to Wollheim, our interpretative system can be built-up gradually, starting with a few key or canonical instances ('great works' or 'characteristic pieces') and then developing a set of transformational rules which would generate other works of art for which there are indeed historical instances. In this sense expression is seen as rooted in an act of interpretation both 'structured' and 'generative', the products of this generative interpretation being then tested against historical fact and emotional credibility. Of course there are several limits to the usefulness of the metaphor from generative grammar. For a start there are in works of art no easily segmented or natural units, no obvious sentences within which determinate structures can be imposed or extracted. 'Parseing' a building is a crude exercise indeed and the many references to Saussure or Chomsky that occur in architectural criticism are rarely more than ritual genuflections. Then again, for artistic forms there are no obvious definitions of grammaticality even approaching the limited ones available to linguistics *via* operational definitions from a community of competent speakers. Art is, compared with natural language, ambiguous, even vague by its very nature. Yet, despite these obvious limitations, the linguistic metaphor was persuasive because it highlighted once again the possibilities for a universal appreciation or expressive understanding of works of art. The thrust of the metaphor is that *all* utterance is structured creation whether the linguistic metaphor is couched in the strong terms of Chomsky's 'rewrite rules' or in some more cautious and open-ended model of analogising. Art and language are *not* categorically different. And, to the extent that the analogy with language holds, art may be seen as a democratic and universal carrier of expressiveness. In a way then, the metaphor from language comes to play much the same role in explaining artistic communication that gestalt psychology had done much earlier. This time the emphasis is on learning—however mysterious the processes which lead to the acquisition of structured interpretative systems may be in practice.

Now Chomsky's ideas are still widely controversial in linguistic theory and he himself has always cautioned against the extrapolation of linguistic models beyond their original area of application. The same reservations must be made about other borrowings from linguistic theories by Barthes and Levi-Strauss and their later recycling by theoreticians of art and design. Binomial taxonomies based on a metaphorical analogy with the phonetic system of Jakobson undoubtedly oversimplify the flexible taxonomies of real-life interpretative systems.

In the last ten years, the theory of art and of design (in particular architecture) has been totally transformed by all these borrowings from science. It has to be said that the main impetus for this revived criticism involving metaphors from science has come from the 'practical' and not the 'fine' arts. To be sure, abstract art no longer holds the sway it once did, but its current artistic rivals owe little to critical speculation on the linguistic model. (For a short while there was indeed an 'Art-Language' movement of almost impenetrable obscurity). There is certainly nothing to compare with the stirrings in recent critical theory relating to architecture and design—nor with the momentous possibilities for the man-made world which are beginning to be manifest as a result.

Science and the Zeitgeist in the 1960s

It is worth sketching in a few dates for these events—minor eddies in the history of ideas maybe—but events which have redirected the focus of attention in the teaching of architecture and design. Gombrich's important arguments came out in 1960 (*Art and Illusion*) and 1963 (the papers later published in *Meditations on a Hobby-Horse*). Both owed much to then recent texts on communication such as Colin Cherry's important popularising book

On Human Communication (Cherry, 1957). Other sources that were easily available to theoreticians who had a mind to seek them out (they were mentioned by Gombrich) were *The Application of Information theory to Psychology* by Atteneave (1959) and *The Measurement of Meaning* by Osgood (1957). The latter was important in giving to the visually inclined a pictorial way of imagining interpretative systems as structured arrays of points in a three-dimensional 'semantic-space'. Wollheim's suggestive allusions to Chomsky's work come in *Art and its Objects* published first in 1968. Such was the prestige of science at the time, that magazines such as *Scientific American* which carried trailers for these ideas, were widely taken up in colleges of Art and Design. Early application of these scientific ideas began to be discussed around 1967–8. *Meaning in Architecture* (Jencks and Baird, 1969) for example was a seminal text for the new linguistic criticism which is still used widely by students. Many of the key concepts have been further exploited by Charles Jencks, one of its editors. First appearances in critical journals (*Architectural Design, Arena* and *The A.A. Quarterly*) to begin with (magazines for designers were later in the field) also date from the late 1960s and early 1970s (Jencks, 1969).

We have already noted that theories from academics are only influential at certain times when the practice of design is already in an unstable state. A small stone will trigger an avalanche only if the mountain is already about to slip. Whether the 'scientific' speculations I have described were indeed that small pebble or whether they were on the contrary merely part of the debris thrown up by an upheaval already in motion are questions that demand a close scrutiny of the *minutiae* of the period—meetings, friendships, the gossip of the studio or workshop as well as identifiable 'first appearances' in published form. Only when this has been done will we be really sure what precisely was the role of science as a source of metaphor in one of the crucial polarising issues of our time. A piece of personal gossip may suggest some clues about one tiny aspect of the problem.

The notions of a polarising issue—a salient metaphor which for a time focuses debate and delineates the axes of polemic was introduced by E. H. Gombrich (1974) in his celebrated paper 'The Logic of Vanity Fair' (an essay on the theory of fashion which was written for a volume of essays in honour of Karl Popper). In it he mentions a young painter friend who felt that he was forced against his own inclinations almost to join the abstract camp. He succumbed because he felt the need 'to be where the fighting was'. I was that young painter and I can indeed testify to the ideological pressures of that time. My eventual reconversion to a position based on figurative imagery, culturally validated symbols and conventional meanings, dates (ironically) from a lecture that I was invited to give at the Royal Academy as part of the opening celebrations for the fiftieth anniversary exhibition of the Bauhaus in 1968. I had been asked to make a critical appraisal of the claims of the Bauhaus idiologues to some kind of scientific status for their aesthetic theories. Such claims seemed hollow indeed and I said so. My modest counter-proposal to what I felt to be misunderstood gestalt psychology was a theory of design based on the metaphor of language. Somewhat provocatively, given the occasion, I suggested that 'Palladianism' had much to recommend it as a robust, easily understood yet flexible and potentially profound language! At that time all this was regarded as academic knockabout—suitable as a *pièce d'occasion* but nothing more. (As a newcomer to the field I knew nothing of Venturi's recent work in America.) Among the audience was a young American also unknown to me who was, even then, working on that collection of essays I mentioned earlier, Charles Jencks. Also on that, for me, fateful occasion I bumped into Joseph Ryckwert and I discovered that Ryckwert had been writing about the theory of classical architecture for years. And through him I . . . and so on and so on.

For me they seemed to be mere chance meetings, lucky encounters with particular persons and happy collisions with new ideas. But were they? Clearly my early training as a scientist gave me something of a start in understanding these new ideas—perhaps even pre-disposed me to take them seriously. 'Knowing the lingo', so to speak, I could join in the debate on what I have now learned to call Structuralism. But how did it get going so quickly and moreover—as subsequent reading revealed—do so apparently spontaneously in different countries? Were we all straws in the same wind? If so, how did the winds of change start blowing?

I have already betrayed in my fragment of memorabilia, my personal inclination towards explanations of cultural diffusion in terms of the contingent interaction of persons through specific institutions of communication: books, articles, academic lectures and seminars, art galleries and magazines. What could be made however of the opposite approach? Suppose we were compelled to look at the interaction of art and science from a remote distance—the proverbial Martian's aspect—or, perhaps more realistically, as remote in time—rather like, say, the shifts of sense and structure that marked the confluence of the Saxon and Latin tongues after the Norman Conquest. Ignorant of persons long dead and unable to trace their meetings and conversations we should perforce have to focus instead on a study of the *language* of the time. We should quickly detect the use of specialised languages by different social groups such as artists and scientists. By comparing internal regularities and structural features and by using our knowledge of similar systems in our own time, we could gain a great deal of insight into the significance of particular usages for those unknown interlocutors. We should quickly notice the ebb and flow of certain forms between these groups and equally quickly perceive that at certain times some forms, or, more usually, groups of forms, suddenly spread everywhere with an apparently irresistible force. Clearly they were not only serviceable, but also very exciting. Enthusiasts adopt new usages almost instinctively, for pleasure, long before they have exhausted or even understood their implications. Examples of forms which could be shown to have flowed between science and art in recent times would be: 'force', 'tension', 'energy', '*Gestalt*', 'software', 'information', 'code' and 'language'. All are examples of hyper-metaphors, metaphors that spread rapidly since they both lit-up their users and also transformed their new universe of discourse.

With the coining of a successful metaphor the set of paradigmatic relations—that is, relationships which a particular symbol or form may have *within* a particular structure—is changed. If, as we are now led to believe, 'love' is a 'rose' then clearly the relationships of 'love' to the rest of the human world and 'rose' to the rest of the vegetable kingdom are not quite what we thought.

But, more than that. The syntagmatic relationships may change as well. Things human may be things non-human. This violation of the deep-structure rules for 'normal' thoughts prises open our existing category system for understanding the world. In turn this demands of us a creative restructuring of the way we think and the way our thoughts relate to the facts of the world. 'Waves are particles' is just such a metaphor. 'Visual Form is redundancy' is another, 'Architecture is a language' is a third. Pregnant, way beyond the confines of any particular subject-fields or 'normal' divisions of creative enquiry, such metaphors are surely more than mere paradigms in Kuhn's sense of the word. I shall coin a name (not entirely in jest) for these hyper-metaphors. Just for this meeting I shall, on the analogy with *para*digms call them '*hyper*phors'. I shall now suggest that useful business for workshops in art and science is not to look for common denominators (whatever *those* metaphorical beasts might be) but to get on the trail of hyperphors.

Abstraction in art and design was a hyperphor of great and often devastating power. Those future enquirers with structuralist leanings would surely want to put on to their agenda an investigation of those particular hyperphors which united a particular group of artists in a vital if transient community of metaphor with scientists during the first half of the twentieth century. This community of metaphor not only furnished certain artists with an apparently technical endorsement of the possibilities of 'abstract' communication. The emotional charge of a new way of seeing the world through a restructured category-system gave them the consolation and enthusiasm that they needed to press on with abstraction against manifest public incomprehension.

I do not know enough about linguistics even to guess at the results of such an enterprise. My own money would be (as I said) on historical sleuthing: 'who said what to whom' (what has been called the 'linear' method). From where we stand now it is surely possible (and long overdue) to do for these recent hyperphors what Basil Willey did for 'Nature' or Lovejoy for the 'plenitude'. However time *will* pass and *that* particular enterprise get more difficult as the detail is lost. It would certainly be nice to think that there *was* some alternative and really productive level of enquiry in between Hegel and Sherlock Holmes.

REFERENCES

Arnheim, R. (1956) *Art and Visual Perception.* Faber. London.

—— (1967) *Visual Thinking,* University of California Press, Berkeley. London.

Atteneave, F. (1959) *The Application of Information Theory to Psychology.* Holt, Reinhard & Winston.

Cherry, C. (1961) *On Human Communication,* Science Editions, New York (1st edn. 1957).

Ettlinger, L. (1961) *Kandinsky's 'At Rest',* Charlton Lectures on Art, Oxford University Press, London.

Gombrich, E. H. (1960) *Art and Illusion.* Phaidon Press, London.
—— (1963) *Meditations on a Hobby Horse and other essays.* Phaidon Press, London.
—— (1974) The Logic of Vanity Fair, in *The Philosophy of Karl Popper,* P. A. Schilpp (ed.), p. 925. Open Court, La Salle, Illinois.
Jencks, C. (1969) *A.A.Q.*, Architecture Association, London, pp. 45, 56. [In his article on 'Pop/Non Pop' Jencks quotes recent works on Psycholinguistics such as that by Osgood and Sebeok.]
Jencks C. and Baird, G. (eds) (1969) *Meaning in Architecture,* pp. 11, 245. Barrie and Rockliffe, The Cresset Press, London.
Joray, M. (1965) *Victor Vasarely,* vol. 1. Editions du Griffon, Neuchatel.
Osgood, C., Suci, G. and Tannenbaum, P. H. (1957) *The Measurement of Meaning.* University of Illinois Press, Urbana, Illinois.
Smithson, R. (1966) Entropy and the New Monuments, *Art Forum,* 4, 26.
Venturi, R., Scott-Brown, Denise and Izenour, S. (1972) *Learning from Las Vegas.* MIT Press, Cambridge Mass.
Wingler, H. M. (1969) *Bauhaus,* p. 164. MIT Press, Cambridge Mass. London.
Wollheim, R. (1968) *Art and Its Objects,* p. 49 ff. Harper and Row, New York, Evanston and London.
Worringer, W. (1963) *Abstraction and Empathy,* trans. Michael Bullock, p. 48. Routledge and Kegan Paul, London.

DISCUSSION

POLLOCK

If I am correct in my interpretation, Peter Lloyd Jones implies that abstract geometric forms are, from an artistic point of view, sterile, meaningless and without information or interest. Yet the Platonic purity of sphere, cone, cylinder, regular polyhedra etc., has certain aesthetic attractions that are difficult to dissociate from the beauty of their many counterparts in nature. I wonder if the feeling of unrealistic sterility that they often engender is due to the absence of the imperfections which characterise their counterparts in 'real life'—whether artifactual or natural— and that is the presence of certain small irregularities and asymmetries—blemishes, one might say—which generate a sense of reality and thus create a work of art out of what would otherwise be a relatively dull geometric design.

LLOYD JONES

I certainly tried to indicate that the forms of abstract geometric art are not in themselves *meaningful.* There is no doubt that abstract painters and theoreticians thought that they were—not only meaningful in a generally suggestive way, allusive to everyday 'real-life' meanings, but more strongly meaningful in the sense of being carriers of profound, even transcendental messages about the order of Nature. What I tried to show was that their attempts to locate the ultimate geometric substrate of the world in the perceptual process disclosed by contemporary Gestalt psychology were mistaken. If I am right, it took later successive influences from science (information-theory and linguistics) to make clear to all that meaning is not inherent in *any* forms, abstract or otherwise. (This is what Gombrich derided as the 'bucket' theory of meaning.) Now this is not to say that abstract forms and in particular the geometry of the Platonic solids and Pythagorean proportions are visually uninteresting or unpleasing. Quite the contrary. They often form an essential part of the 'hidden order' of great art—especially architecture, where the scale of the embracing geometry is so great in relation to the viewer that it cannot be perceived as a whole but informs our feelings at the margins of perception.

Your point about the visual interest of individual forms in 'real-life' being located precisely in their deviations from geometric purity or, as it used to be said, in their 'inperfections', harks back to much earlier artistic theory. It was of particular interest to Renaissance artists who were faced with the problem of negotiating a Platonic theory of beauty pointing towards ideal types with the realities of individual often highly idiosyncratic sitters not to mention their own complex personalities. As an issue it lingered on in the dispute between the Poussinists and the Rubenists and we can still see it in the ambiguity between token and type in twentieth-century portraits—especially those who are influenced by Cézanne's latterday Platonism. The whole issue is very complex and is probably best handled by Gombrich's model of 'schemata and correction'. Those who are for the 'imperfections' of everyday life—'warts and all' in the Rembrandt mould—make the point that if an artist starts with an over-simple schema (the routine geometry of the conventional academy which teaches students how to work-up a head from an ellipse) run the risk of woodenness and dullness. However much you subsequently refine and complicate the schema, the original 'egg-head' remains giving a kind of 'Paolo Uccello' toy-town quality to a likeness. If your aim is vividness, this is a trouble. But the artists I referred to were surely aiming at something more radical. What they were out to do was to tap the Springs of Nature direct. Those they located not merely in the geometrical regularities of ideal types, i.e. generic forms or universals abstracted from diverse and imperfect individuals, but in geometry itself. It was this I was concerned to attack.

MERMOZ

In Lloyd Jones' paper it is not always clear whether he is arguing against the theory and practice of 'abstraction' or against its ideological appropriation by the exponents of 'functionalist' design. The two issues are sufficiently complex and specific to deserve not to be confused. Furthermore, the objections raised against 'abstraction' on the basis of information theory might not hold if we examined the ideological assumptions which underlie the cybernetic model. Clearly, if 'abstraction' is to be defined (or dismissed) as a language it must be from the psycho-sociological stand-point of a general theory of signs (Semiotics). One of the key issues in this debate (an issue on which art historians have mysteriously kept silent) is that of the distribution of functions within the act and the processes of representation (Jakobson, 1960).[1] Next in importance is the definition of the structural relations constituent of the pictorial sign. In our search for meaning (the meaning of an abstract painting for instance) we should remember that meaning is to be located not in the physical support of the sign but in the activity of the viewer.

LLOYD JONES

Point taken. It is certainly necessary to separate the theory and practice of abstraction from its ideological appropriation by exponents of functionalism. The conflation is however not mine. It is a matter of historical fact that the two movements were very closely linked. I have tried to show (over many years) that the issues are in fact unrelated; 'functional' artefacts could perfectly well look otherwise than misplaced constructivist sculpture. It is also true that, as Mermoz says, the meaning of a sign is located in the activity of a viewer. With hindsight we can only feel astonished that anyone ever thought otherwise. My suggestion is that such a view was supported by borrowings from contemporary branches of science which were then currently particularly prestigious—especially Gestalt psychology.

GELL

Is there not indeed a danger for psychologists such as Gombrich who have dealt with art appreciation to undervalue the complexity of the process

[1] Jakobson, R. (1960) Linguistics and Poetics, in T. Sebeok (ed.) *Style in Language*. New York.

between the unit in the picture and the individual response? Seeing is a process which has to be learned in ontogeny and this learning process influences everything subsequently seen: what is seen is not necessarily identical among individuals.

HARRÉ

I believe that in the period Lloyd Jones is describing the language analogy was (or perhaps one should say 'could have been') drawn in two somewhat different, perhaps even antithetical, ways. In using the Chomskyian theory of language forms as an analogy, one is directed to start with a given deep structure and transform it according to rule. One is always looking, as it were, at what is positively on offer from the semantic objects that form the sentence, for a grasp of its meaning. But there was another notion abroad at much the same time, a notion that was always much used by anthropologists, and is finding increasing favour in other fields. It is Saussure's idea of language as a system of exclusions. When one hears a word its meaning is a product of *valeur* and *signifie,* the former being defined by relations of exclusion, the latter by positive coordination of world and concept. The Saussurean idea is that a word is a nexus in a system of exclusions, so part of my understanding of what *is* said is by virtue of what is *not* said.

It seems to me that if one analyses artistic creation in the Gombrichian spirit one should be thinking of a system of exclusions. The repertoire of schemata which Gombrich describes as the foundation of a style in art is used to provide a framework for the writing off of alternatives, so to speak. When a late medieval artist is drawing a whale or a city, to take two of Gombrich's most vivid examples, he refines the schema to eliminate certain alternatives. It seems to me to follow from Gombrich's hypothesis that we and the artists we can understand share a repertoire of schemata, that we read a work of art not only in its positive display of features, but also as an opportunity to see that certain things have not been expressed.

I would have thought that Lloyd Jones' line in his presented paper should have been to emphasise analogies with linguistic theory based on the principle of exclusion. If we are going to judge that something was missing from abstract art, it could be argued to have been a clear exposition in the art object of what has been excluded, which requires that artist and public share a *determinate* schema. But from an abstract work of art nothing is excluded, if anything whatever could be put in consistent with the features of the art object. No clear negative reading is possible. If the Gombrichian theory is right, the ultimate Gombrichian refutation of abstractionism should be to say that since abstract art can exclude nothing it lacks a crucial dimension of meaning. But the true work of art excludes all sorts of things, so it works in our mental life like a word. I would very much like to see Lloyd Jones emphasising the Saussurean line rather than drawing an analogy with Chomsky's theory of the genesis of linguistic forms.

LLOYD JONES

As I recall, little or none of the detailed argumentation over Chomsky's ideas from *within* the field of linguistics flowed over into the theory of art. Certainly I am not endorsing Chomsky's particular brand of generative theory for I have no competence to pronounce upon the matter. Nor I think was Wollheim when he used the generative grammar analogy in *Art and its Objects*. What transformational grammar in the Chomsky mode did provide was a new sharpness to old ideas, ideas of art as a visual language, of 'reading' a painting, of a grammar of form. The whole notion of 'deep-structure'—which Rom Harré used so suggestively in his opening paper and which in another sense has been familiar since Freud—was given a sharper formulation by its expression as a function in a species of algebraic linguistics. Some at least of these new overtones carry over into contemporary art-theory.

Whatever may be the rival merits of Chomsky and Saussure, there is no doubt that it was Chomsky's work which fed one important stream of thought in the revision of the theory of art along structuralist lines. Saussure came on the agenda here only after Continental theoreticians such as Roland Barthes became widely available in translation. I have, of course, grossly simplified an incredibly complex set of influences and extrapolations. What I suggest is that one of the reasons for the immediate, almost impulsive acceptance of a generalised structuralism by artists was because the idea of linguistic 'universals' (however described) seemed to re-establish the universal brotherhood of man, including the artist and his audience, but this time locating them not in abstract geometry but in specific cultures. Whether or not Chomsky's work can bear the weight put upon it, is another matter. I was merely trying to describe his historical influence.

As to Harré's support for an exclusion theory of the meaning of works of art, I am not sure that his account is really antagonistic to Gombrich's ideas. Gombrich often used the analogy of the successive partitioning of an infinite set in the progressive exclusions of the 'Twenty Questions' game to make this point. What is surely crucial for any account of the meaning of works of art is that, unlike 'Twenty Questions', the game doesn't, mustn't, end. There is never one unique concept, for that would be an exit from the work altogether. The guessing game of unravelling the complex orders of a work of art—abstract or otherwise—can never come to an end, for the orders of art fold back on themselves, interlocking and recursive. Of course they must at once *appear* to be meaningful in a literal 'Twenty Questions' sense. If they are not they would not elicit our initial engagement and hold it long enough to stimulate and direct the flow of attention in the effort after meaning. We would simply look away. Yet they must also remain ultimately indecipherable or we would soon exhaust their interest. 'Poetry must resist the intelligence almost successfully' as Wallace Stevens put it in one of his most pregnant 'Adagia'.[1] In this sense, 'alternatives' are not merely logical necessities in a theory of communication, they are like shades, transiently co-present possibilities, which we never quite lose sight of in the mind's endless inquisition of artistic structures.

[1] Stevens, W. (1957) *Opus Postumus*, p. 171. A. Knopf, New York.

14

REPRESENTATION AND ILLUSIONS OF PERCEPTION

Richard L. Gregory

Brain and Perception Laboratory, Department of Anatomy, Bristol University

SUMMARY

Illusions of the senses have traditionally been seen as errors or mistakes: and so, far removed from data suggesting knowledge or truth. It is a turn-about to accept illusions as crucial data, for scientific understanding of the nature of science and understanding. On the other hand, illusions of many kinds are the hallmark and stock-in-trade of the artist. Possibly science's dismissal of illusions, as at the best trivial and the worst misleading, has generated distrust of Art. This would apply especially to the visual arts, and less to music, which is not propositional and so is either not flawed by illusions—or is too far from physical observation and description to be judged in terms where 'illusion' can apply.

By examining phenomena and origins of illusions—which are now extensively studied—we may relate at least observational science to the activity and intention of the visual arts.

If art is evocative while science is expositive—as well as being explanatory—then illusions are bound to be very different in art and in science. An illusion in art would be a failure to evoke or provoke; while an illusion in science would be some kind of departure from the truth: perhaps ultimately a discrepancy between subjective and objective. Illusions of perception, including scientific observation, are discrepancies between perceptions and what is being observed. This at once implies that perceptions are not selections, or samples, of what is observed—and so they are not within the reality of the physical world—but are related in some way that needs to be described to the world of science if we are to understand perception. That perception is not direct knowledge of the world, but is highly indirect, with illusions as discrepancies between how things seem and how they are, is a relatively new idea. For the Greeks, and with but a few exceptions until the middle of the last century, perception was supposed to be direct and certain knowledge: or it was supposed not to be knowledge at all. There was considerable confusion over these extremes. Illusions were seldom discussed by the

Greeks, and were not investigated in any detail, though some are mentioned (not always accurately) by Aristotle.

The broad sweep of development of theories of perception imply corresponding theories of illusion, though this connection was not until recently made explicitly. Just because theories of illusions are (or should be) closely related to theories of perception, illusory phenomena are extremely important for suggesting and testing theoretical accounts of perception as well as for practical reasons, including techniques of art. The theoretical interest in illusions does not however apply to Direct Realism, which is the 'common sense' account, and prevailed in ancient and most modern philosophy. It is held even by some distinguished living, and only recently dead, experimental psychologists. Direct Realists, who deny that there is a relation other than identity between perceptions and objects, have to ignore or dismiss illusions. Conversely, illusions are indeed knock-out evidence against Direct Realist accounts of perception—they demand acceptance of some indirect relation, such as *representing*.

Representations can fail in many kinds of ways, if only because there are many kinds and uses of representations. To start with the earliest representational pictures, Sir Ernst Gombrich (1950) says in *The Story of Art* of palaeolithic cave painting of around 30,000 BC, that they were functional—presumably for jacking up the fecundity of Mammoths and Mothers to ensure the proliferation of useful mammals, including bison and babies. On this account 'photographic' accuracy of the paintings would be less important than their magical powers: and these powers might best be conferred by distorted, highly exaggerated, shapes especially of women as found in palaeolithic statuettes. To judge these early representations we need to know the magical or other functional significance (including showing ownership of objects and places) of these paintings and statues, and the 'abstract' marks dating from long before recorded history. More generally, all drawings are distorted in some ways, for no drawings correspond in form exactly to what they represent; but whether we call one 'illusory' depends upon whether it misleads in ways that handicap its use or function. Thus, a perspective drawing may be appropriate and useful for some purposes, and an isometric or some other projection, (including the various map projections) may be more useful for other purposes. Which of them is a 'true likeness' depends upon what kind of use is to be made of it—and they may be 'true' without being in conventional, or in usual terms 'like' what they represent. So there is a kind of pragmatism in illusion, as well as in knowledge and truth.

Not only use, but also a different reference frame, or a different set of scale functions or projection grid, will make things appear different: change perhaps from 'like' and 'true', to 'unlike', 'wrong' or 'illusory'. Much of the same seems to hold for scientific descriptions and explanations. Scientific observations and generalisations may be significant when seen from (and related to) some conceptual schemes or frames but meaningless or wrong from some other references. This is part of what Thomas Kuhn (1962) attributes to his 'Paradigms' of normal science.

The implication here is that what is illusion depends on the scale, and conceptual schemes and scale functions, for measurement of representations and descriptions. So, what is illusion is relative and can perhaps never be determined objectively—apart from the manner of description and the adopted scale functions.

To consider particular examples of conceptual scale functions, lengths are usually measured on linear scales in which it is assumed that a standard length is additive throughout space. On the other hand Information, for example, is measured on a logarithmic base to make it simply additive, as information is technically defined (Shannon and Weaver, 1949). Now it is conceivable that space is non-linear—and indeed Minkowsky and Einstein said just this—in which case our linear scale measures look wrong: they make space look distorted. In this extremely general case of a measure universally applied, the measuring scale adopted can make reality appear distorted, and so in some ways illusory. Much more commonly (because there are few such extremely general measures or scales) it is the observation, or measurement, that appears distorted and in need of correction to be true for accepted reality to be preserved.

Considering map projections, such as Mercator's flat projection of features on a sphere, the situation is subtly different. Although the shapes and relative areas are not congruent, there is an explicit transformation relation that can be applied to 'read' one from the other. The same is indeed so for any scale map or drawing, for though different in size they are not distortions, because the size of the objects or features depicted can be read correctly when the explicitly given scale correction is made. They are not illusory because they are not misleading. Here the scale correction is part of the description; and scaling (down or up) is often useful: it would be more than inconvenient to have a map of France the size of France!

Are perceptions themselves like maps? The best known psychological theory of perception as maps, (or internal pictures) is the Gestalt theory of the 1920s and 30s. The Gestalt perceptual theorists supposed that objects are represented by isomorphic brain traces; so a viewed circle would be represented by a circular trace, and presumably a sphere by a spherical trace. They attributed visual distortions to inherent tendencies of brain traces to change to other shapes—generally towards forms of lower potential energy. Thus, an elliptical trace would tend towards a more nearly circular form; corners would be rounded, and gaps would tend to be filled in—because of physical properties of the map-like electrical traces in the brain (Köhler, 1920).

Gestalt writers pointed out rules of perceptual organisation, and these remain important in the very different current accounts of perception, which emphasise heuristic processes rather than analogue isomorphic representations on which the Gestalt writers based their account of perception and illusion. Wertheimer (1923), in an important paper, gave seven organising rules by which perceptual features are linked and which, when inappropriate, may produce scale distortions of various kinds. Wertheimer's organising rules are:

1 Proximity: Points close to in space, or tones close to in time, are linked and experienced as pairs.

2 Similarity: Similar features are linked, and treated as 'belonging' or as parts of the same object.
3 Common fate: Features moving together, or moving in clearly related ways, are seen as belonging, and as parts of the same object.
4 Continuity: Points lying on straight lines, or simple curves, are taken as belonging, and as outlining the same object.
5 Closure ('Pregnance'): Points or dots tend to be grouped—and selected from other dots—on the basis of a preference for closed figures.
6 Symmetry: Symmetrical forms are favoured over asymmetries; and there may be distortions towards symmetry—by rejection of dots falling outside the symmetrical chosen form, or by shifts in perceptual space or time.
7 Hysteresis: Organisations tend to persist through small changes of patterns.

Further, although Gestalt writers generally emphasised innateness of the organising rules, Wertheimer conceded that individual past experience could affect and perhaps even generate new rules. This concession of effects of learning from past experience on organising and grouping did not however fit easily into the Gestalt isomorphic brain theory, because these organising principles (and they were seen as sources of illusory distortions) were supposed to be due to the physical characteristics of the traces. How were physical properties of brain traces, such as tendency to adopt low potential energy forms, supposed to be affected by experience? This was never answered; and I am not sure that the question was ever asked. There are plenty of other objections to the internal pictures theory of the Gestalt school. They never got around to saying that the brain should change *colour* when objects of different *colours* are seen; but to be consistent, or at least sufficiently general in their account, they should have said that when we see a traffic light turn from red to green, part of the observer's brain trace turns green. Presumably they could not imagine this true for the physiology of the brain so picture properties such as colour were ignored, though they were needed. We now believe that there is no physiological possibility for their isomorphic brain traces, even though many retinotopic brain maps have been discovered which represent various visual characteristics including form and colour. These maps do not however explain perception, because a map must be read—and if the 'reader' requires an 'eye' feeding into another map, we have an endless regress of eyes and maps. The brain, it now seems, analyses shapes with tuned feature filters to extract from its maps what is useful for describing the scene. Here the Gestalt rules of perceptual organisation take on a new significance. They are also important in the very different context of Artificial Intelligence accounts of scene analysis by computer or brain. The new twist is to see such rules as based on restraints in the shapes of objects, which hold for most if not all objects. The new notion is that processing procedures—especially for reducing the inherent ambiguity of retinal images—are geared to reflect and make use of the limited variety of shapes of objects, especially for reducing the essential ambiguity of sensory patterns, including retinal images.

A key paper is by David Waltz (1975), 'Understanding Line Drawings of Scenes with Shadows'. The general notion is that, for example, corners are generally rightangular; that converging lines probably represent depth by perspective, because most nearly parallel lines are in fact parallel (at least in Western environments of railways, roads, rooms in square houses and so on) and that, as lighting usually is from above, shadows from overhanging or sticking out features give information of the third dimension in a two dimensional retinal image or picture. It is interesting that these restraint-cues, as we may call them, can overpower competing stereo depth signals from the two eyes, though stereo signals are not ambiguous and do not depend upon assumptions of the shapes of objects. So knowledge and assumptions can win out over the most direct signals of the senses.

That restraint-cues are important for vision is not strictly new, since Helmholtz; but recently scene analysis computer programs have made them more explicit, and more widely known and appreciated. The related notion that when restraint-cues are inappropriate they can generate illusions, especially distortion illusions, is at least implicit in Helmholtz's writings on perception and techniques of drawing and painting.

Distortions may be due to procedures being inappropriate to the situation—to not matching the usual restraints. The various Ames demonstrations are very clear examples of this. For example, the famous 'Ames Window' is treated as though it is a rectangle having parallel sides, though in fact they converge. It is historically interesting that Helmholtz exactly describes (though he may not have made) the equally famous 'Ames Room' nearly a century before Adelbert Ames built his (Helmholtz, 1862).

The notion that perceptions are descriptions—descriptions based on common features of objects and scenes—leads at once to comparing perception's rules and strategies, based on the limited variety of shapes and relations found in the world, with linguistic description. This, in turn, suggests that perceptual illusions may be classified much as we classify linguistic or logical errors. Thus we have in language and logic: *Ambiguities; Distortions; Paradoxes; Omissions; Fictional Commissions.* It is highly suggestive that these are also a useful classification of illusory perceptual phenomena.

An interesting implication of the notion of distortions generated by inappropriate restraint-cues in unusual situations, when read as though they are typical—and of course without this, paintings and drawings could not be seen as the quite other realities they depict—is that these illusions are not contingent upon brains, but must also occur in any future object-recognising Robot even though its 'brain' be ever so different from ours (Gregory, 1967). The point is that cue based illusions are bound to occur in environments in which the usual restraints mislead. If the operating rules were rich enough to cover all possible cases, they could not simplify the problem and so would be of no use. Or one might say that if they were rich enough the system would fail through indigestion with possibilities; but since unlikely possibilities must occur (conditions cannot always be typical) there must be cue-based errors, which may be sufficiently systematic and misleading to be classed as illusions. So illusions are logically necessary—they are bound to occur in some situations.

A visual process which has been appreciated since Descartes, is correction of scale distortions of received patterns, especially retinal images, to preserve 'objective' scale. These corrections are seldom if ever complete, but they do serve to correct for the shrinking of retinal image size with increased object distance fairly completely over the behaviourally important distance range. Robert Thouless (1931) who did many experiments on this, called it 'Regression to the Real Object', but this term has since been dropped and it is now generally known as 'Size and Shape Constancy'. This is clearly given by active neural scaling, set by restraint-based cues—such as perspective convergence given the parallel lines assumption (Ponzo illusion), and the right-angularity of corners, from the retinal pattern of flat 'arrow heads' (Muller-Lyer illusion). It has been suggested (Gregory, 1963) that these distortions occur when the flat patterns of pictures of typical three-dimensional form set Constancy Scaling appropriately for the three dimensional objects represented—which is necessarily inappropriate to the flat (perspective) pattern of the picture. The depicted *distant* parts are *expanded* in the illusion figures, as the theory predicts.

It is still often suggested, however, that these distortions are not cognitive (knowledge based) but are due to signal distortions of the visual channel, especially associated with low band pass spatial filtering (Ginsberg, 1971). It seems, however, important to point out here that:

(a) these distortions still occur fully when the figures are accepted by binocular fusion of pairs of random dot patterns—so that neither retina receives the figure, but only random dots which are cross-correlated to provide the information centrally, after fusion by the two eyes. The neural origin of the distortion must therefore be not retinal, or in the early stages of processing, but after fusion of the signals from the eyes (Julesz, 1971) and so cannot be due to retinal or peripheral band pass filtering in the early stages of the visual channel.
(b) These illusion distortions (though not some others) are essentially unaffected by luminance contrast or received energy; indeed, contrast of the line figures may be reversed—or their background/line energy difference reduced to zero, with isoluminance colour contrast—and the distortions remain essentially unchanged (Gregory, 1977).
(c) The illusions occur equally with 'illusory contours' (Farné, 1968).
(d) They do not occur with three dimensional objects or models seen normally in depth—though the models provide the same lines and angles to the eyes as the (perspective) illusion-producing figures (Gregory and Harris, 1975). This last seems to rule out any kind of signal channel distortion anywhere in the nervous system as significant, as there is strictly no distortion when the perspective is correct for the viewing distance and the objects or models are seen in their true depth. When, however, they are not seen in correct depth there is distortion—though with the same retinal image. Also ambiguous three dimensional objects (such as wire cubes) change shape with each perceptual reversal, though the retinal image remains unchanged (Gregory, 1970). This shows that Constancy Scaling occurs both 'upwards' from stimulus patterns, and

> also 'downwards' from the prevailing 'hypothesis' of depth. It is essential to note that both the 'upwards' cue-set scaling and the 'downwards' depth-hypothesis scaling must be *appropriate* to the situation for distortion to be *absent*. In practice this is not usually possible for perspective drawings, though it can be achieved with stereo projected pictures.

So much for distortion illusions occurring in perspective pictures. Returning to the classification of illusions based on linguistic and logical errors of description, we are left with *Ambiguity*—which may be reversals of depth (the Necker cube, the Schroeder staircase), and may be changes of object perception (Jastrow's duck-rabbit; Boring's wife-mistress figure). These may be thought of as alternative hypotheses entertained on object-ambiguous data, between a few (usually two) likely candidates.

We are left also with *Paradoxes*. These may occur when accepted restraint-cues are misleading to generate perceptual hypotheses from false assumptions, (the Penrose impossible triangle, the Escher engravings). We are left also with *Omissions*, which have no simple explanation but may be due to attentional filtering, among other things; and *Commissions of Fiction*. These include the fascinating Illusory Contours (or rather bounded surfaces) which have been made famous by Gaetano Kanizsa's beautiful examples (Kanizsa 1955, 1979). These may be attributed to perceptual postulation of masking or eclipsing surfaces, to account for the gaps in these figures—the illusion-inducing gaps always being unlikely and the shapes they form always likely object shapes. They are thus, on this view, postulated on a Beyesian-like strategy. This notion is extremely different from the filling-in processes described by the Gestalt school's isomorphic brain traces. It is however entirely in accord with, and is indeed based on, the notion of restraint-cues. The 'restraints' here give the improbability of the gaps; and so provide evidence for a nearer eclipsing object, though this is not sensed. It is indeed only possible in normal conditions to see that an object is complete, when parts are hidden by nearer objects, from the unlikelyhood of the missing regions of retinal images being due to gaps in the object rather than to being hidden by some nearer object, which may not itself be sensed. Fictions are thus generated by our ability to see by the surprising absence of signals from the world; but not all fictions are illusory.

Conclusion

Theories of illusions always reflect theories of perception. As perception is seen more and more to be knowledge-based, to operate from generalisations of how things usually are, many (though by no means all) illusions are seen as due to misapplied knowledge. It is misapplied especially in atypical situations which have typical surface features. Pictures are atypical in just this way.

That the flat shapes of perspective drawings are read essentially as though they are other (depicted) objects, is necessary for a picture to be accepted and seen as a picture, and not merely as the bunch of marks or scratches on rock or paper, that indeed it is. The fact that at the same time we see it as something else, and as marks on rock or paper is truly remarkable. We are illuded, though not deluded, by the allusions of pictures. This is the perceptual basis of representational art.

REFERENCES

Farné, M. (1968) Alcune osservazioni con linee virtuali e margini quasi percettivi, *Bollettino della Societa Italiana di Biologia Sperimentale,* **44,** (19), 1613–16.

Ginsburg, A. P. (1971) Psychological correlates of a model of the human visual system, *Proc. IEEE NAECON,* Dayton, Ohio, 283–90.

Gombrich, E. H. (1950) *The Story of Art.* Phaidon.

Gregory, R. L. (1963) Distortion of visual space as inappropriate constancy scaling, *Nature* (London), **199,** 678–80.

—— (1967) Will seeing machines have illusions? *Machine Intelligence I* (N. L. Collins and D. Michie, eds.). University of Edinburgh Press.

—— (1970) *The Intelligent Eye.* Weidenfeld.

—— (1977) Vision with Isoluminant Colour Contrast: 1. A projection technique and observations, *Perception,* **9,** 113–19.

—— and Harris, P. J. (1975) Illusion-destruction by appropriate scaling, *Perception,* **4,** 203–20.

Helmholtz, H. von (1862) *Treatise on physiological optics* (J. P. C. Southall ed.), vol. 3, section 26.

Julesz, B. (1971) *Foundations of Cyclopean Perception.* Chicago University Press.

Kanizsa, G. (1955) Margini quasi-percettivi in campi con stimolazione omogenea, *Rivista di Psicologia,* **49,** 7–30.

—— (1979) *Organisation of Vision: Essays on Gestalt Perception.* New York.

Köhler, W. (1920) Die physischen Gestalten in Ruhe und im stationären Zustand, *Eine naturphilosophische Untersuchung.* Erlangen. Trans. Physical Gestalten in *A Source Book of Gestalt Psychology* (W. D. Ellis, ed.), pp. 17–54. Routledge and Kegan Paul (1938).

Kuhn, T. (1962) *The structure of scientific revolutions.* Chicago University Press.

Shannon, C. E. and Weaver, W. (1949) *The mathematical theory of communication.* Illinois.

Thouless, R. H. (1931) Phenomenal Regression to the Real Object, 1, *Brit. J. Psychol.,* **21,** 339.

Waltz, D. L. (1975) Understanding Line Drawings of Scenes with Shadows, in *The Psychology of Computer Vision,* 19–92, (P. H. Winston, ed.). McGraw-Hill.

Wertheimer, M. (1923) Untersuchungen zur Lehre von der Gestalt, II, *Psychol. Forsch.,* **4,** 301–50. Trans. Laws of organisation in perceptual forms, in *A Source Book of Gestalt Psychology,* pp. 71–88 (W. E. Ellis, ed.). Routledge and Kegan Paul (1938).

DISCUSSION

POLLOCK

I was struck by a point in Richard Gregory's paper (which I do not think he mentioned in his talk), namely the question of cue-restraints in visual perception. These I have understood to act rather like short-cuts, or gross approximations and over-simplifications, arising from limitations of types of shape in the store of those available as reference (for interpretation of information from the retina) which at times can be very misleading and so responsible for many of the illusions he has referred to.

I am wondering whether something analogous may be occurring in our *thinking processes*, on the hypothesis that these often depend upon the exploitation of visual models. May not similar mechanisms thus be responsible for the tricks played and impasses reached in our brains (e.g. the ideas of function and purpose—i.e. the constant tendency to anthropomorphise), the strange difficulties with which we may be faced in trying to grasp certain types of problem (e.g. probabilities, indeterminism etc.), the limitations we suffer in approaching concepts (action at a distance, fields of force, incompatible properties of single entities such as the electron etc.) and the dependence we feel on the acceptance of what are almost mystical principles such as that of cause and effect.

If there is anything in this idea, it would bring the processes operating in visual artistry very close to those involved in scientific thinking—in the particular sense that research into the mechanism of visual perception could have a bearing on the understanding of the development of scientific concepts and scientific explanation in general.

DAVIES

Being concerned with illusion in art, Richard Gregory has appropriately placed much emphasis on the work of Escher. But I would say that, as an artist, Escher is of poor quality. Perhaps at some future date people will look at Escher and say he was of some importance in the twentieth century, but I doubt that as an artist he will be seen as anything more than one of those minor Flemish painters of the sixteenth century whose illusions and tricks were more skilful and amusing. Ideas of illusion have perhaps stimulated art over a short period rather than really had any parallels with it and probably Gregory's observations have influenced kinetic artists as much as he received ideas from them.

GREGORY

Yes, well I want to try and push the idea that he uses object-restraints, which can, when accepted for perception, be powerful tools for evoking perceptual paradoxes, as well as distortions and so on, as phenomenal experiences. There are, clearly, close connections between perceptual research and this kind of art—as both are concerned with and stimulated by phenomena of these kinds. Some have been discovered or invented through visual research, and others by artists, including Escher though he was largely inspired by the Penroses' Impossible drawings (which perhaps rather unfortunately they called 'Impossible Objects').

LLOYD

I should like to describe an example of an illusion (or delusion) which is, perhaps, rather different from the types mentioned by Richard Gregory but may be relevant to the subjective interpretation of pictorial images in general.

My wife and I have male monozygotic twins, B and O, who have always been slightly different in appearance. At the age of about four, when shown a photograph of the two of them side-by-side looking at the camera, each child was convinced that the picture of B showed O's face and the picture of O showed B's. They could not be shaken from this conviction. The explanation seems to be that O and B knew they were identical, and because each saw his brother much more often than he saw his own face in the mirror, he accepted his brother's face as representing his own so that it displaced his mirror-image in his mind's eye. Both faces were symmetrical.

There are four images, O, O reversed, B, and B reversed. For O the descending order of frequency of seeing the images is B, O reversed, B reversed, O, and apparently the possessive claim on the most familiar image as being his own outweighs the difficulty of reconciling the unfamiliar O with his well-known brother B. This implies that attachment to one's self-image overcomes logic, as it certainly did when we tried to convince them that they were wrong.

MONTGOMERY

I should like to know what Richard Gregory thinks about Bridget Riley's paintings as possible contributions to the understanding of the mechanism of perception and various visual illusions.

GREGORY

Well, as one would expect, basic theories of perception come from the laboratory rather than from the artist's studio; but we have learned a great deal about perception from artists. Perhaps, though, only a few artists really want to explain perceptual phenomena, and I believe that Bridget Riley very much dislikes explanations, as they seem to take away something of the mystery. I remember she told me once that when an illusion is explained she can no longer use it.

MONTGOMERY

I was under the impression that she acknowledged there was some science in her work, some underlying mathematics.

GREGORY

Yes, they are often drawn according to rules, and painted in colours that have curious contrast effects; but what she doesn't like is the idea that repeated lines and so on, let's say, upset movement detectors of the retina or further up in the brain. Is it the case that once phenomena are attributed to *physical* causes they tend to be rejected as *mentally* significant? If so, I think this is a pity—why shouldn't phenomena be significant when understood in this kind of way? Is this a deep difference between the ways artists and scientists think and what they try to do?

RUPKE

What about examples of so-called 'anamorphic' art? This is a form of illusion that has been going on for quite a long time.

GREGORY

Yes, but I didn't want to include those, as at all the same sort of illusion. Frankly, they are much less interesting! What they do is to change the way in which the retinal image is given. That is really all. Anamorphs are not essentially different from any pictures and they do not upset perception. If the perceptual system could recognise and compensate for the cylindrical mirror of an anamorph—or indeed for an ordinary plane mirror—this would be interesting, but it doesn't!

In anamorphs, you have got a highly distorted picture (and all pictures are more or less distorted from what they represent), which is undistorted by a cylindrical or other curved mirror like the distorting mirror used to make the anamorph picture. As it is optically distorted and then undistorted it looks not particularly distorted. In the illusions I am talking about the perception is distorted from what the retinal image would normally give—which is totally different.

15

PERCEPTION AND REPRESENTATION

Alan Tormey

Department of Philosophy, University of Maryland, Baltimore County, USA

Pictures, together with visual illusions in nature, constitute the primal epistemic shock for naive realism. In a world devoid of both, the rift between appearance and reality would remain forever unnoticed. Pictures, then, are both perceptual puzzles and epistemic tools.

Since space is limited, I shall aim my remarks more at provocation than at persuasion. The supportive arguments may be found elsewhere (Tormey and Tormey, 1979; Tormey, 1980).

In his paper on illusions of perception, Professor Gregory (see this volume p.165) remarks that:

> . . . all drawings are distorted in some ways, for no drawings correspond in form exactly to what they represent: but whether we call one 'illusory' depends upon whether it misleads in ways that handicap its use or function. Thus, a perspective drawing may be appropriate and useful for some purposes and an isometric, or some other projection . . . may be more useful for other purposes. *Which of them is 'true likeness' depends upon what kind of use is to be made of it—and they may be 'true' without being in conventional or usual terms 'like' what they represent* [italics added].

Although these remarks are illuminating, they require interpretation, for as they stand they are apt to mislead. I cannot, for example, simply confer upon a picture the relational property 'true likeness' by establishing its use as that of, say, a blueprint or a symbolic emblem. Surely, the *success* of a picture is in part a function of its intended use, but being a 'true likeness' is not the *hallmark* of success but rather one among various standards against which pictorial success is measured. So, there is indeed a kind of pragmatism here, as Gregory notes, but a pragmatism that counsels admission of a variety of pictorial purposes, not one that encourages unrestrained relativism in speaking of pictorial truth or pictorial likeness.

Secondly, as epistemic tools pictures are often thought to be virtual windows into the perception of other persons and other periods, their stylistic diversity transparently reflecting both different ways of seeing the world and differing conventions for representing the way it is seen. Witness, for example, James Gibson who has said, 'It is true that the varieties of painting at different times in history and among different peoples, prove the existence of different ways of seeing, in some sense of the term' (Gibson, 1960). Or Rudolph Arnheim who argues that:

> As a rule in a given cultural context the familiar style of pictorial representation is not perceived at all—the image looks simply like a faithful reproduction of the object itself. . . . The Picassos, the Braques, or the Klees look exactly like the things they represent. . . . As far as the artists themselves are concerned, there seems to be little doubt that they see in their works nothing but the exact equivalent of the object (Arnheim, 1964, pp. 117–19).

Or Nelson Goodman who asserts that:

> Each different way of painting represents a different way of seeing; . . . And we need only look hard at the pictures by any such artist [Dürer, Manet, Cézanne or Picasso] to come to see the world in somewhat the same way (Goodman, 1960, p. 52).

Assertions of this sort are closely allied with the thesis of *conventionalism*, that is with the view that pictorial systems are themselves conventions analogous to linguistic systems. Further, we are asked to believe that each different way of painting represents a different way of seeing and that the varieties of painting at different times in history and among different people proves the existence of different ways of seeing. And there is a powerful motivation for asserting this latter proposition, for, if it *were* true, it would provide us with direct, unmediated models of the perceptual content of minds other than our own. Ironically, however, if conventionalism were true, the evidence offered by different styles of picturing would be *irrelevant* to the question of different ways of seeing. One cannot conclude both that different ways of depicting are conventional on the one hand and that they are *necessarily* linked to different ways of seeing the world on the other. One can only argue that differing ways of depicting are *evidence* for differing ways of seeing if one accepts the premise that the way the world is seen is immediately and causally related to the way it is depicted. If Picasso had painted the world 'as he saw it' he would deserve not credit for his inventive genius but rather compassionate curiosity for his peculiarly anomalous perceptions. More generally, the diversity of styles of systems of pictorial representation no more proves that there are radically different ways of seeing the world than the diversity of natural languages proves that there are radically divergent criteria of meaning or truth. What then is the alternative?

Perception and representation are correlative possibilities. (The correlations are so striking that they led to the development of a comprehensive representational theory of perception in the seventeenth century—a theory that conflates correlation and causation and holds that internal impressions stand in a representational relation to whatever causes them.) The great Renaissance artist-theoreticians, Brunelleschi, Alberti, Piero della Francesca, and Leonardo all thought of the practice of painting and design as a virtual mirror image of the scientific study of visual perception. Much of Renaissance theorising about the visual arts is derived directly or indirectly from medieval optics. Geometrical laws governing visual perception were described, inverted, and transformed into rules for the production of faithful images of natural scenes and the concept of art-as-imitation-of-nature was given new vitality and renewed plausibility through the construction of a systematic mathematical basis for pictorial representation.

Studying the geometry of visual perception and veridically depicting the seen world were, for Leonardo and his contemporaries, complementary means of investigating and expressing their knowledge of fundamental physical laws and of nature itself. It is not surprising that in this atmosphere the concept of pictorial fidelity was enshrined as the dominant artistic paradigm. Given the subsequent success of this paradigm and its constituent theory of linear perspective one is tempted to conclude that fidelity is to pictures what truth is to propositions. The opponents of this view, the conventionalists, in particular, have a final recourse. Their position, schematically, is this: both seeing and picturing involve selection. Perception and representation are equally subject to the filters of habit, history, interest, attention, and abrogation. The naive eye is blind, the uninterpreted image nonexistent, the perfect picture a chimera. The artist does not, cannot, xerox what he sees, nor do we perceive the world as an image etched on the tissues of the retina. Habits of expectation and acculturation, genetic and psychological determinants, affect the ways we perceive and the ways we depict the world. What, finally, we 'see' is a construct issuing from the process of selection subjectively guided by habits and motives remote from the rigid laws of Euclidean optics; and the pictured world is a product of preferred systems of representation, artistic temperament, historical styles and the limitations of material and technique.

Well, what is left, then, of the ideal of pictorial fidelity? I would argue that even if all these deeply problematic contentions were acceptable, the answer is, surprisingly, everything. Pictures, however peculiar, are part of the real world. The influence of selecton and subjectivity is operative on both and does nothing, as conventionalists seem to believe, to obviate the identity-of-optical-array standard of fidelity. What is selectively organised by the perceiver from natural stimuli will be comparably organised from artefactual stimuli. In the *limiting* case, the eye (or mind) which is uninformed of the causal origins of its input, will perform the same transformations for pictures as for objects. Thus, even if our 'habits of seeing' *were* varied and relative, the matching optical array standard of fidelity would remain intact, such habits being, necessarily, unable to reach beyond the image to discriminate between object and picture.

There is, of course, no such thing as a 'perfect likeness'. No picture can exactly replicate the optical array from a natural scene except under severely restrictive and perhaps aesthetically uninteresing conditions. But, there is nothing absurd or inapt in the concept of a standard of fidelity that is unrealised in practice. What is not realised can still be approached, and that is as much as we have a right to expect.

There is an illuminating parallel to this story in the behavioural sciences. The cultural anthropologist, Paul Ekman, has recently demonstrated that Darwin's theory of the universality of emotional expression is both sound *and* compatible with cultural variation in expressive behaviour (Ekman, 1973). The truth is that cultural variation is a gloss on biologically deter-

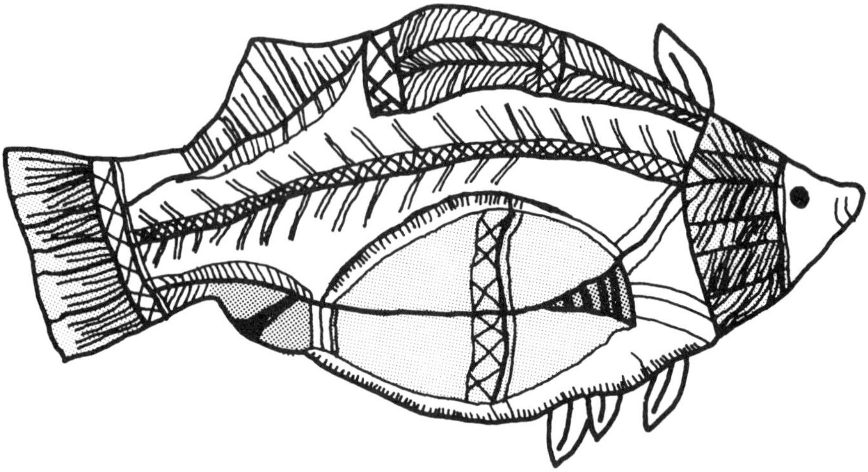

FIGURE 1 'X-Ray' Fish (after an aboriginal cave painting, North-Western Australia).

minate patterns of emotional expression and not an originating force. Just as Darwin's once maligned theory of the universality of behavioural expression has now been largely vindicated with the aid of more rigorous arguments and the accretion of sophisticated cross-cultural and perceptual studies, so, with similar assistance has the Renaissance paradigm of pictorial fidelity been reinstated, salvaging both the possibility of truth in representation *and* the importance of artistic departures from fidelity in the pursuit of expressive freedom, neither of which the conventionalist can explain.

It seems evident that there may be differing pictorial systems with which we may associate differing pictorial purposes, and distinct forms of realism as well, if it is granted that realism is relative to pictorial purposes as well as to representational systems. For example, we might speak of *cognitive* realism where objects are portrayed as they are believed to *be* rather than as they (merely) appear. Cognitive realism is the result of the attempt to depict objects in such a way that their most important, defining or essential characteristics are clearly represented. One of the most striking instances of this form of realism is found in aboriginal art, as shown in the accompanying figure.

Much primitive as well as a good deal of children's art is of this sort, and we may justify calling it 'cognitive' as opposed to 'optical' realism since the artists depict as coexistent—somewhat in the manner of cubism—aspects and features that would not, or could not, constitute a single visually perceptible pattern, but which are known or believed to be 'true' of the object.

Hard-core relativism is on the run in several quarters and it should be of more than passing interest to take a stereoscopic look at future developments in theories of the arts and the behavioural sciences. I strongly suspect that the images will be highly coherent.

REFERENCES

Arnheim, R. (1954) *Art and Visual Perception: A Psychology of the Creative Eye*. University of California Press, Berkeley.
Ekman, P. (1973) *Darwin and Facial Expression: A Century of Research in Review* (ed. P. Ekman). Academic Press, New York.
Gibson, J. J. (1960) Pictures, Perspective and Perception, *Daedalus*, **89**, 216–27.
Goodman, N. (1960) The Way the World Is, *Review of Metaphysics*, **14**, 48–56.
Tormey, A. (1980) Seeing Things: Pictures, Paradox, and Perspective, in *Perceiving Artworks* (ed. John Fisher). Temple University Press, Philadelphia.
Tormey, A. and Tormey, J. (1979) Seeing, Believing, and Picturing, in *Perception and Pictorial Representation* (eds Calvin F. Nodine and Dennis F. Fisher). Praeger, New York.

DISCUSSION

DAVIES

The idea of realism and photographic representation in the way Tormey describes it is of course recent and the fish drawn by an Australian aboriginal which shows its internal anatomy in a diagrammatic way has been the commonest method of representation and has also been used by sophisticated artists. Of course visual perception is opposed to the conceptual method employed by numerous so-called primitive representations and 'X-ray' images all over the world, but even during the period of realism, which was mostly in the middle of the nineteenth century, an alternative tradition was representing the world in this way: for example, Cézanne began to distort so as to allow the inside and the outside of things to be seen at the same time. Also, throughout the whole of the eighteenth and nineteenth centuries topographical illustrators who were asked to depict the country houses owned by their patrons represented as much as they could in order to give as much information as possible about the architecture.

TORMEY

Yes, there are a tremendous number of variations on this theme of pictorial purposes and my point was simply to illustrate one among many possibilities as an alternative to the rather naive, but nevertheless deeply entrenched, recent view that we can utilise differing styles of pictorial representation as direct epistemological evidence of differing ways of seeing the world.

GELL

I should like to repeat a little parable by Borges about realism which seems to me relevant to our discussion of realism in art. There was once an emperor of China who wanted a better map of the Empire, showing every town. This was done, but he was unsatisfied: he wanted one necessarily on a larger scale showing every village, every house. But even this was insufficient for him. He realised that the only thing which would satisfy him was to represent every stone, every grain of dust, a map in fact co-terminous with the Empire. Unfortunately he died before this project could be completed.

16

A PROPOSAL FOR SOFTENING THE BOUNDARIES OF SCIENCE

José Reissig

Department of Biology, Long Island University, NY, USA

I would like to focus this discussion on the present and future, rather than on history. Common denominators or not, it appears to me indisputable that today art and science inhabit different 'worlds'. I mean 'worlds' in the sense of what William James calls 'sub-universes' of reality, or what Alfred Schutz (1971) calls 'finite provinces of meaning', i.e. segments of our conceptual universe characterised by an internal cognitive consistency. I believe that the multiplicity of sub-universes into which we subdivide our reality constitutes a cognitive asset and I do not expect that anyone would today suggest that we try to combine the world of art and the world of science to make a hodgepodge of the two. The problem is, rather, one of how to interconnect the various sub-universes, how to get them to engage in discourse, so that they will become integrated into the network of our reality. Since, by definition, no algorithms exist to translate the reality of one sub-universe into that of the other, interconnection requires the use of boundary-transgression techniques like the 'leaps' of Alfred Schutz and/or the 'bi-sociations' of Arthur Koestler (1949).

A difficulty arises, however, in the case of science because it has barricaded itself against acts of boundary transgression. Open borders, yes, on the technological front; but on the conceptual front the boundaries are to remain closed as science cultivates the myth of historical and philosophical self-sufficiency. A closed border requires surveillance, and this is accomplished largely by the requirements of the specialised language and publications of science. Other languages are used, it is true, in connection with science, as when talking down to the public at large or in fictional or historical accounts; but then these languages are not part of the making of science, and are clearly out of the bounds of its province of meaning. In contrast, the contemporary art world has chosen to function within conspicuously soft borders, and has developed a battery of techniques to facilitate transgressive leaps across them.

How, then, can we soften the boundaries of science? How can we 'de-groove' our scientists, to use the expression of Martin Pollock and Tom

Barrett (1981)? On the basis of the preceding considerations, I propose that this can be best accomplished by the import into science of the transgressive techniques and languages of the art world. The proposal, in concrete terms, consists in organising art-like exhibitions by scientists, wherein the participating scientists would have an opportunity to express their concepts in the media most suitable for their work, including drawing, painting, sculpture, earthworks, or the languages developed by conceptual, video or computer art. The task is not likely to be easy. A major difficulty will be the near illiteracy of most scientists in the languages of art. However, because change can often result from the work of one or a few trail-blazers, I do not think that the proposal is hopeless.

In order to clarify my meaning let me differentiate my proposal explicitly from other initiatives which are superficially similar, but fundamentally different from it. I do not plan to create yet another science exhibit or museum for enlightening the general public on the accomplishments of 'normal' science (Kuhn, 1970) nor do I propose a re-run of the Arts & Technology movement of the sixties (Tuchman, 1971) in which technologically oriented scientists provided the artists with means for their artistic explorations. No: the suggested exhibition is meant to promote the creation of 'works of science', equivalent in their significance to the works of art of the art world.

REFERENCES

Koestler, A. (1949) *Insight and Outlook. An Inquiry into the Common Foundations of Art, Science and Social Ethics.* MacMillan, New York.

Kuhn, T. S. (1970) *The Structure of Scientific Revolutions,* 2nd edn. Univ. of Chicago Press.

Pollock, M. R. and Barrett, T. (1981) Common Denominators in art and science, *Interdisciplinary Science Reviews,* 6, 214.

Schultz, A. (1971) *Collected Papers,* M. Nijhoff, The Hague; vol. 1, part 3; vol. 2, pp. 135–58.

Tuchman, M. (1971) *Art and Technology.* Viking Press.

DISCUSSION

DAVIES

The idea of a scientist regarding his works as being worthy of aesthetic contemplation is valuable. Perhaps artists would benefit from a similar exchange by entering the world of science and carrying out experiments in a scientific way. What does José Reissig feel about that?

REISSIG

I find that suggestion fascinating. Indeed, I would like to see what happens if some artists are introduced to the methods and ideas of one or another limited area of biology and let loose in it; I mean, given the opportunity to contribute to that area. This may sound preposterous to the purist, and yet the recent revolution in biology, the one that led to the birth of molecular biology, was primed by a comparable if less radical approach. I am referring to the introduction of cadres of physicists to narrow areas of biology—like bacteriophage genetics—in the forties and fifties, often through courses taught at Cold Spring Harbor. They revolutionised biology in spite of—or maybe because of—the incompleteness of their indoctrination.

GELL

I think Reissig's point is that he wants scientists to use the language of art—which of course needs to be defined. The scientist needs to be instructed or inspired to use forms of expression for scientific concepts with which he may be already moderately familiar in other contexts. He must use them not just to make superior science fiction or competent or pretty scientific illustration but to deploy imaginatively the language of original creative art. It is very difficult to define what this language is going to be and how it is to be used. Scientists and artists will have to work together on it. This implies that the artist will have to empathise with the processes of creative scientific thinking as well as the other way round.

REISSIG

Indeed. It is not a question of making scientific presentations pretty, but of using the art-like languages creatively. In some instances this could be facilitated by collaboration with artists; but in other cases the scientist may already know enough of an art language, even if (s)he has not yet explored its potential as a tool for conceptual transgression. For instance, many scientists are already literate in computer and video language.

CLAIRE MORRIS

I couldn't make out whether Reissig is proposing to demystify science by finding a common language accessible to everybody or whether he is going to mystify further by expecting scientists to express themselves in an alien medium.

REISSIG

I presume that by mystification Claire Morris means the creation of myth. Science in my opinion is as much involved in the construction of a mythical system as everyone else is, but what is special about science is that it pretends not to be. By helping science develop an openly symbolic system I hope to provide a better alternative to this surreptitious mythology.

JUDITH RICHARDS

I am very puzzled about the prospect of discovering some common language which might allow scientists and artists to speak to each other and at some stage allow scientists to create art or artists to create science. To my mind it is not enough to share a language or even to share whatever is the wind of change, as Peter Lloyd Jones called it: a kind of common social fabric we may all move in. It seems to be that there is a very fundamental relationship of the artist to his work and of the scientist to his, which are so distinct and so different as to be impossible to unite. In that I mean the scientist would never wish to make so personal a creation that no other scientist could reproduce it. An essential part of a scientific discovery is that anyone who goes through the same steps can come to the same conclusion. In that sense the 'person' should not ever appear in the creation, whereas the artist works in a totally opposite way. It should never be the case that his painting could be recreated by anyone who went through the same procedure.

REISSIG

That is a very coherent point. You suggest that the scientist is there merely to make reality transparent. To me, that is not the whole story. I see the scientist as a creator when (s)he selects one out of many possible theoretical constructs as the relevant one. There is also room in science for the creative selection of what systems to make observations on, as in the often unique systems studied by ecologists. Surely there are, and there will continue to be, stylistic differences between art and science. My point is that science could benefit from some infusion of the artistic, contextual, outlook: that a dose of insight, over and above transparency, would be beneficial.

GENERAL DISCUSSION

POLLOCK

Before inviting contributions to a more general discussion, I would like to steal a moment, as Chairman's privilege, to offer a challenge, on the central issue of this conference, to Lewis Wolpert's rather negative attitude to the idea of 'Common Denominators etc. . . .' My own belief is that at least in one—overwhelming—sense there is indeed a true sharing between artists and scientists. This is in their common need, which is to a large extent exclusive, to express—albeit in very different ways—their own particular sense of *reality* in the world around them. I hope there may be an opportunity to discuss this later on.

LLOYD

I was rather worried when José Reissig talked about inviting scientists to be 'transgressive'. One of the basics of science is that we abhor elegant variation, and it is an excellent convention that when expressing science we don't use rhetoric. Now I think that this is also true for the best art, and have a nasty feeling that we might, by going for this mish-mash of an exhibition, be indulging in rhetoric and stepping away from the highest standards both of art and of science.

REISSIG

I should say these high standards require exploration of different possibilities and we only know what is wrong when we try it.

GAGE

It seems to me that one area we have left totally out of consideration which is rather crucial to the whole operation, is the background institutions, and the way they operate in very different ways among scientists and among artists. One element of this would be something suggested by what someone else said: that the artistic community has quite a different sort of shape from the scientific community. Scientists, as I see it, develop their thoughts by talking almost exclusively to each other, because only their fellows actually know the problems that they are facing. The artistic community is a very much wider one; it depends not simply on artists talking to each other, but also on the consumer, who, in the long term, is certainly on a par with the producer. Pluralism, which has been invoked as an artistic virtue, is not something that artists feel; it is something which the consumer, in his liberal and slightly less attached way, may feel because he recognises that there is a range of objects and activities which he is pleased to call art, whereas I suspect that the artist like the scientist is very narrow-minded at the time he is producing. What makes him concentrated enough to produce is precisely the feeling that only what he is doing is the right thing at that time, and not what he has done or what other people are doing. He once thought that art was about coloured squares, but now he thinks it is not—for him. Other artists still do, and the consumer may be saying they are right. So the whole area of a breakthrough seems to me to be quite different, and it is only at a time in the 1920s, when, as Ivor Davies was saying this morning, artists felt especially that they had the fate of the whole of society at their fingertips, that they saw themselves as engineers, controlling the fate of human nature.

BARD

There is another intersection of arts and sciences that appears not to have been mentioned yet and that is the aesthetic pleasure that both give. Outsiders tend to think of science as a highly intellectual, cerebral activity. This it is, but it is not completely so either in its creation or in its appreciation. There is a rightness and a properness about the best of scientific work that transcends academic correctness. I suppose that the sharpest examples that come to mind are Einstein's theory of relativity and Maxwell's equations of electromagnetism. The former altered the framework of most of classical physics; the notable exception was the latter, it was already correct, even though it had been published more than thirty years earlier.

As a student, I remember being overwhelmed by Maxwell's equations: the large amounts of data on electricity and on magnetism was seen to cohere into four simple equations from which sprang the whole of electromagnetic wave theory with all its ramifications. I was given far more than an insight into the physical world, I was shown how beautiful was its architecture. And not only in physics; in every branch of science there are gems both great and small that give as much pleasure as they impart knowledge. All this may seem odd to someone who has chosen to avoid the scientific world. Perhaps I can summarise by saying that, although the formalisms of the arts and the sciences are very different, they reach the same parts and excite the same responses.

KNIGHT

It seems a pity that a conference like this has so far not mentioned botanical and zoological illustration, as a region where art and science have long coalesced. The artist can be taught what to see by the scientist, as happened when Ferdinand Bauer worked for Robert Brown or Matthew Flinders' voyage round Australia and produced some of the finest botanical illustrations. His work is also subject to constraints imposed by the techniques used in printing illustrations, and by theory—he may be doing systematic or ecological plates, he may have to show the life-cycle of a species, and he will have the problems of depicting a species from perhaps a single individual, often long-dead. In this field, artists' intentions and objectives are easier to judge against the background of the science of the day; and a Bauer, a Lear or a Wolff can produce masterpieces of art and science.

GELL

Three words before we come to the summing up. First, can I say something about letting the moral of this meeting seep into our approach to our own subject and our teaching of it? I believe this can be done. Second point, everybody I talked to thinks it would probably be a good idea to have a similar meeting, perhaps in a year's time: there are a number of possibilities, but at any rate a repeat of this *kind* of thing. I feel myself that it would be nicer to give a bit more emphasis to the literary arts, but this is a personal bias. Thirdly, though I don't want to propose a formal vote of thanks, I feel we should informally thank all the organisers of this meeting which has been so well managed and has gone so completely smoothly, for all the work they have done to make it a success.

17

SOME CONCLUSIONS: WHAT HAVE WE DONE AND WHY HAVE WE TRIED TO DO IT?

Arthur Marwick

Department of History, Open University

In one of my local pubs in Hampstead there is a notice on the wall which says: 'We have an agreement with our Bank, we do not cash cheques and they have undertaken not to sell beer.' I feel in somewhat the same position; I am an historian and my summing up will be very much through the eyes of an historian. I am simply going to try to answer two questions. The first is the 'why': why have we been doing what we have been doing?—a question that Peter Lloyd Jones raised yesterday afternoon, and one to which Claire Morris returned this morning. To this first question I shall give three answers. I shall then move on rapidly to the 'what'. In answering what we have been doing, I am going to make six points. And that is how I shall fill the fifteen minutes the Chairman has allotted me.

First of all, then: Why? At once I have to say that I think Rom Harré may have got us off slightly on a wrong footing when he said he took it for granted that there were correlations between art and science. Lewis Wolpert was right to resist our taking this assumption too readily for granted. I think that what we have to face up to is that in the early nineteenth century, the period Harré studies, there was no real distinction between the artist and the scientist; but what has happened is that since then the two have grown very far apart and what we have to deal with is the situation we are in now, where, like it or not, there are enormous chasms between artist and scientist. It may be possible to bring them together: indeed the first good that can come out of this sort of exploration is that artists can understand a little more of how scientists actually work and vice versa.

There is a dangerous ignorance: on the one hand, people have been saying that there are no similarities, that artists and scientists inhabit different worlds; while on the other hand, there are those who, in a rather vague and 'liberal' way, were saying: 'No, artists and scientists are essentially engaged in the same activity.' Now, while the truth is no doubt somewhere in between, the immediate problem is that scientists are dangerously ignorant about what arts people really do and arts people are dangerously ignorant about the realities of science. I have promised Gérard Mermoz, whose work I admire very much, that I am not going to say anything specifically critical of him. Yet I have to point out that often, in what are called the human sciences or the social sciences, there is a kind of false science, a pseudo-science, which is also rather dangerous. In aspiring to be 'scientific', social scientists misunderstand the nature of science. It is revealing that this very conference has been structured around a couple of mathematical metaphors ('common denominators' and 'correlation'). Social scientists, too, are prone to reach for mathematical metaphors in their pursuit of a false precision: I prefer Mermoz's word *rapport*. So the first of my 'why' points is that this conference has encouraged the exploration of real differences, as well as making easy (and sometimes dubious) 'correlations'.

My second point is that this whole question of the relationship between art and science is a fundamental historical problem. Some years ago I was commissioned to write a book for Penguin, *British Society since 1945*, and one of the questions I have had to deal with, however inadequately, is the continuing impressive record of big science in this country, including the large number of Nobel prizewinners; I have also had to deal with the question of the efflorescence of art in the sixties which Peter Lloyd Jones was talking about. Whether or not there are 'common denominators' or 'correlations', that is certainly an issue which, as an historian, one cannot afford to shirk.

Thirdly, it is most valuable to get insights from the different cultures and the different disciplines. History, as a discipline, has much to contribute. One insight that history brings is that one should always try to use the language of the people one is studying. I part company with David Kinmont when he says he does not really see the difference between art and science. People today use the word 'art' and they use the word 'science' and they know what they mean. Another point that the historians would bring out is that we are dealing with a time of very rapid change; science has changed, art has changed and, most important of all, science has changed the world. Thus, although we may try to extrapolate conclusions from the early nineteenth century or from the activities of Christopher Wren, we have to recognise that the conditions of the seventeenth century or of the early nineteenth century just do not apply to the twentieth century. Nicholas Rupke made a valuable contribution when he stressed the importance of institutions. I would like to emphasise the importance of the cultures and the sub-cultures in which the scientists and artists grow up. And there is an extremely important historical development that we have not stressed enough, the growth of professionalism and the growth of specialisation. It is part of the way in which society has developed that we have become more professionalised. Artists are trained, scientists have their own institutions; and in that way the different worlds—the world of art, the world of science—that José Reissig was talking about, have come into being. In part, these different worlds spring out of the increasing specialisation of subject matter; in part they arise in the culturally determined institutions that scientists occupy and that arts people occupy. However, all is not lost in this country! Though I am not, myself, the most enthusiastic supporter of the two traditional English Universities that we have heard about, I recognise that someone like Professor Jack Plumb who is the general Editor for the Penguin Social History series in which my volume features, really does feel that he belongs to a Cambridge culture, in which arts and science are one: he criticised my book for not saying enough about science and technology and he truly feels that, in his upper-class higher education world at least, there is a common discourse between artists and scientists. In response to Claire Morris's plea, we perhaps need to re-emphasise that kind of communication which still takes place in what is unfortunately a very privileged world. It would be good if it could take place in less privileged places as well.

My third point, then, is that by bringing different disciplines together, as at this conference, we are able to study our major problem in a more subtle and refined manner.

I now turn to the 'What', and I am suggesting six conclusions. Lewis Wolpert remarked, rather scathingly, that of course we all know that artists are creative and scientists are creative, but having said that, there's nothing more to be said. But what is worth saying is that we are all engaged in the attack on the unknown, an attempt to achieve control and freedom over the world in which we live through advancing knowledge, developing insights. Philip Gell proposed the idea of subjectivity and interactionism as something that scientists and artists have in common. There were many, many interesting points along these lines, but obviously my job is not just to repeat all the good points that people have already made. But I would still like, under this first heading of the commonality of pursuits, to look at the much humbler level. David Knight brought out, very strikingly, that Humphry Davy's motivation was simply that of an ordinary person who had to make a living. I remember being very impressed when I read *The Double Helix* and realised that these scientists were just fallible, vainglorious human beings like myself and other arts people. So, at the highest and at the lowest levels, the activities of artists and scientists *are* similar, and this is a serious and documented point which has emerged from this conference.

In making my second point I do not wish to undervalue Rom Harré's very interesting leading comments. Indeed, I want to stress what I believe lay behind his contribution: in the early nineteenth century, there was one discourse or metatheory which could involve both those we would now call scientists and those we would now call artists; if that could be true in the early nineteenth century why can it not be true in the twentieth? That basic point of Harré's leads into a more complex third point: can we, as Harré puts it, identify the metatheories that group people together? I suggested earlier in this session that what we have to look at is shared values and shared assumptions, that in any society in any period certain things are possible, certain assumptions are accepted, people hold to certain 'truths' and ways of looking at things. I would not go beyond that: to try to structure that into a metatheory would be to go too far. But it is through shared values that I think we get the commonality of the problem that scientists at a particular time address themselves to, the problem that artists address themselves to. Peter Lloyd Jones spoke of 'winds of change' and asked where they come from. But in a way this is a false question: non-historians expect historians to come up with slick answers like those of great meta-historical formulations such as Marxism. If I were asked certain things about the state of Britain today, I suspect that in a book of 400 pages I could provide some kind of explanation. But to look for universal explanations of 'winds of change' is asking historians to do something that they would prefer not to do. However, the point I want to reiterate is that if we wish to find the 'common denominators', we should seek them in the shared assumptions and shared values of a particular society.

My fourth point is something I picked out of Gerard Mermoz's paper; he did not refer to this in introducing his contribution and I rather gather, in discussions with him later on, that I misunderstood his meaning. But sometimes people are wiser in what they write than they realise. . . . What he actually wrote was, '. . . . A theory may be said to work when it accounts for all the data of experience in a given field' and then goes on to add that 'a painting works when it elicits a positive response from other individuals'. I think that is a profound insight. I often have arguments with the Dean of Technology at the Open University where he maintains that the difference between arts and science subjects is that if science does not work there is a disaster—the bridge falls down—whereas in arts, mistakes can go on being made and nobody will notice. This is the sort of simple thought which is actually worth very serious consideration. A painting has got to *work*: if the relationships between Mondrian's blocks of colour were ever so slighlty different, then I do not think we would accept Mondrian as an outstanding painter. His paintings must 'work' in the same way that science has got to 'work'. Here, perhaps, is the most important common denominator and I wish I had time to explore it more fully.

My fifth point I take from Brian Lloyd who spoke of the 'bridges' provided by technology and by education. Againt I notice the metaphor, an engineering metaphor instead of a mathematical metaphor; I suppose one cannot escape from metaphors. A further response to Claire Morris's point would be that if these bridges could be strengthened, this might be a way of bringing arts and science back together.

My final point is that this very conference has been a demonstration that there can be dialogue and that therefore there must be common denominators. We could not have had Richard Gregory's marvellous presentation (just to take one example) were it not being given by someone who has a standing both in science and in the arts. The same could be said of Peter Lloyd Jones's talk which, for me, provided a fascinating primary source for the period of my own recent studies, the 1960s. Michele Emmer's films were the product of art *and* science. Without scientific knowledge, David Knight could not have given us these insights into the life of Humphry Davy; similarly with Alex Keller's discussion of 'discontinuity' at the beginning of this century. Obviously here we had actual exemplification of the fact that there are areas in which people are both scientists and artists.

One final reflection I must add to that. While we talk about Einstein, or about Christopher Wren, we should remember that most scientists are busy making a new kind of detergent or a brighter television picture; we should remember that the world of science is not basically that of the people making big discoveries. Similarly with the arts: most artists are illustrating books for children or designing advertisements in newspapers or drafting posters to put up in pubs. So if critics wish to comment that the scientific knowledge of historians of science—the true 'bridging' subject in my view—is rather modest, let us not forget that much scientific activity is in fact at a fairly mundane level.

Personally, I have got a great deal out of this conference. It has, indeed, shown that there are 'common denominators' or, as I should prefer to phrase it, there is common ground between arts and sciences.